United States
Military Aircraft

since 1909

The North American F-86 Sabre was one of the most significant fighters in the history of the USAF – the first in service with wing sweepback, the first capable of supersonic speed (in a dive) and the first to engage in jet-to-jet combat (over Korea against the MiG-15). In this photo, three F-86As are accompanied by (foreground) an F-86E, all from Nellis-based training school.

United States Military Aircraft

since 1909

Gordon Swanborough
Peter M. Bowers

Smithsonian Institution Press
Washington D.C.

CONTENTS

Foreword	vi
Preface	vii
Introductory Note	ix
History of U.S. Air Force	1
Aircraft Procurement And Disposal	6
Aircraft Designation Systems	10
Aircraft Colouring and Markings	32
Aircraft Descriptions	45
Appendix A—Pre-1917 Aircraft	597
Appendix B—Lesser Types, 1917 to date	611
Appendix C—Foreign-Built Aircraft	677
Appendix D—Balloons and Airships	712
Designation Index	731
General Index	756

FOREWORD
to the first edition

By General Curtis E. LeMay
Former Chief of Staff
United States Air Force

The development of United States Military Aircraft, from the first purchase of a Wright Flyer to the forthcoming XB-70, has closely paralleled one of the most dramatic periods in American history. It has been a period of rapid technological development without precedent in the annals of man's scientific endeavours.

The book effectively highlights the chronology of aviation as seen through the development of heavier-than-air machines. The evolution of these aircraft, from the flimsy vehicle held together by baling wire and glue to the sleek, supersonic weapon systems of today, is carefully traced, documented and illustrated in this Encyclopedia of Airpower Vehicles.

General, USAF (Retd)

PREFACE

The history of military flying in the United States now extends over more than three-quarters of a century. In that period, an enormous variety of aircraft types has entered service with the U.S. Air Force and its antecedent organizations, the Signal Corps, the Army Air Corps and the Army Air Force.

These military aircraft range from lighter-than-air craft and examples of the Wright Brothers' biplane—closely related to the machine in which Orville Wright made the world's first successful powered, controlled, sustained flight—to the supersonic, missile-armed, jet-powered swept-wing fighters and bombers of the present day. The intervening years have seen the U.S. air forces en- gaged in four major conflicts—World War I of 1914–1918, World War II of 1939–1945, the Korean War of 1950–1953 and the war in Vietnam which had no clear beginning but escalated throughout the 'sixties and did not end until 1975. Each of these wars has had a lasting impact on the equipment of the air forces, both in the large-scale production of aircraft required at short notice and in the long-term development of newer types to meet ever-changing concepts of the tactical and strategic value of air power.

An attempt to chronicle, between the covers of a single volume, the history of all these many types of aircraft might at first seem doomed to fail. Nevertheless, this seemed to the authors to be a worthwhile project, since it would represent a unique record, obtainable in no other single source, of the technological achievements of seventy-odd years, and the operational successes which they made possible.

To provide this record, it has proved necessary to describe and illustrate over 350 different types of aircraft, many of which existed in a multitude of variants. This total is made up only of those aircraft which have been operational with the U.S. army and air forces. Purely experimental types and prototypes have been excluded from the present survey. This somewhat arbitrary division was essential to keep the size of the volume down to manageable proportions—but every effort has been made to include, rather than exclude, the marginal types, such as those evaluated in sizeable quantities but not subsequently put into production. Also included are a few prototypes—such as the XB-43 and XC-35—because they represented significant engineering "firsts".

Four appendices illustrate, respectively, the aircraft procured prior to 1917 (when the U.S. entered World War I), the less-important U.S.-built types procured from 1917 to date, types of foreign manufacture which have gone into service with the air forces, and balloons and airships.

To help readers of this work to obtain maximum value from the infor- mation it contains, there is a chapter on the designation systems used for

Army and Air Force aircraft to date. Another chapter deals with aircraft markings, knowledge of which enhances the interest in the more than 850 illustrations in this volume. A brief history of military aviation in the U.S. is also included.

Since 1920, the aircraft procured by the USAF and its predecessors, and more recently by the U.S. Army for its air units, have been designated according to consistent schemes. This makes it possible to list, with little chance of omission, every design which has ever been adopted, including prototypes and, in a few cases, unbuilt projects. Advantage of this fact has been taken to provide another unique feature, the Designation Index. By referring to this index, the reader can find vital facts on every aeroplane which has been designated since 1920, plus a reference, where appropriate, to the pages where it is more fully described in this book.

This work is the result of the collaborative efforts of many individuals and of the generous help extended by them, over many years, to the authors. Without that help, and their willingness to share the results of research and photography undertaken in many parts of the world, this book would lack many of its most interesting items. Every effort has been made to include, beneath each illustration, the name of the photographer, and the authors here extend their grateful thanks to all the individuals thus credited, as well as to the public relations staff of most of the U.S. aircraft manufacturers, whose contributions have also been most useful.

When so many have contributed, over so long a period, to the accumulation of data and photographs on which the authors have been able to draw, it may be invidious to single out individuals for further mention. Nevertheless, a special "thank-you" must go to the late Gordon S. Williams and to Howard Levy, for the many unique illustrations they so willingly supplied for the first edition; to Dave Menard, for contributions that make this third edition more complete and more accurate than it otherwise would have been, and to Donald C. Woodward and James R. Shock for their contribution to Appendix D, Balloons and Airships.

The late L. E. Bradford made his own unique contribution to the first and second editions by providing the three-view drawings that so enhance the value of this work. The drawings added to this edition are by John A. Sizer.

December 1988   F. G. S.
                                                                 P. M. B.

HOW TO USE THIS BOOK

Maximum value will be obtained from this volume if readers have a clear idea of its scope and the arrangement of the material in it. It is concerned with the aircraft types which have served with the U.S. Army Signal Corps, the U.S. Army Air Corps, the U.S. Army Air Force, the U.S. Air Force and Army Aviation. It is not concerned with the experimental types and prototypes which have been designated by these services, nor with the aircraft of the U.S. Navy, U.S. Marines and U.S. Coast Guard, which form the subject of a companion volume.

Arrangement of Material. Aircraft are described in one of five sections of the book. In each of these sections, the descriptions are arranged alphabetically by manufacturer. In those cases where a type has been built by more than one company, it is listed according to the designing firm or the maker with which it is most usually associated.

The main section provides photographs, descriptive text, three-view drawings and technical data of the most important service types. The first appendix is concerned with pre-1917 aircraft. The second appendix illustrates and describes the less important service types from 1917 to date. Foreign types procured for service with the U.S. forces are illustrated and described in the third appendix. Balloons and airships form the subject of the fourth appendix.

Technical Data. Wherever possible, the data is derived from official reports or "Airplane Characteristics" charts, rather than manufacturers' claims. "Gross weight" is the highest weight at which operations were permitted.

Serial Numbers. The serial numbers listed for each aircraft type are derived primarily from unclassified Air Force documents supplemented by other published sources. Additional information comes from daily aircraft reporting forms which record the modification state of the aircraft in service. Most of the serials for the World War I aircraft come from an inventory of U.S. Army aircraft printed in the Congressional Record in 1919.

Unit Information. No attempt has been made to compile complete listings of U.S. units operating each aircraft type. Information is given in most cases on the first user units, and others are referred to in relation to major operational achievements.

Photo Credits. The source of each photograph is given, with the negative number where known. In the case of private collectors, the name of the individual who took the photograph has been given where known, rather than the name of the supplier of the print.

U.S. MILITARY AVIATION—
A BRIEF HISTORY

RESPONSIBILITY for military aviation activities in America rested with the Army until 1947, when the U.S. Air Force was created as an independent service. As early as 1898, the Army invested in the development of a man-carrying aeroplane by making $50,000 available to Samuel P. Langley. A quarter-scale model was successfully flown in 1901, but the full-size "Aerodrome", as Langley's machine was known, failed in its two attempts to fly from the Potomac river in October and December 1903. Although never accepted by the Army, the "Aerodrome" was the first aeroplane paid for by public funds, and its failure brought criticisms from the public and Congress.

This episode delayed Army recognition for the Wright brothers, who achieved their historic break-through to sustained, controlled, powered flight at the very moment of Langley's failure. More than four years elapsed before the Army again invested in an aeroplane—and then only after the personal intervention of President Theodore Roosevelt. On February 10, 1908, the Army accepted a tender from the Wrights to build for $25,000 a military biplane capable of carrying two persons at 40 m.p.h.

On August 1, 1907, an Aeronautical Division was established in the Office of the Chief Signal Officer of the U.S. Army, as the first formal military unit concerned with heavier-than-air flying. Its first chief was Captain Charles de Forrest Chandler, with a staff of two enlisted men. Two years after its formation, on August 2, 1909, the Aeronautical Division accepted the Wright Model A at Fort Myer, just outside Washington, D.C. This aircraft remained the sole strength of the Division for two years, in the course of which the first Army flying field was established at College Park, Maryland, and the Army's first aviators soloed on the Wright A.

Additional expenditure authorized by Congress in Fiscal Year 1912 allowed the Army to buy additional aeroplanes and in March 1913 the 1st Aero Squadron was formed at Texas City to become the nucleus of the first U.S. air combat unit. Equipped with Curtiss R-2 biplanes, this unit saw action across the Mexican border in March 1916, in support of General Pershing's punitive expedition. By this time, U.S. military flying was the responsibility of the Aviation Section of the Signal Corps. Created on July 18, 1914, the Aviation Section had a strength of 60 officers (who had to be unmarried lieutenants) and 260 enlisted men.

By early 1917, the Aviation Section had been expanded to have seven squadrons—the 1st, 3rd, 4th and 5th in the U.S., the 2nd in the Philippines and the 6th and 7th in Panama. Further expansion was being planned

1

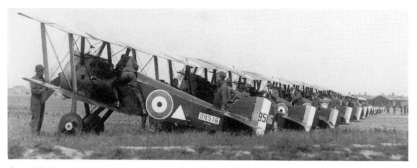

Sopwith Camels (in British colours and markings) were flown by the 148th American Aero Squadron in France – one of 45 squadrons that reached the front in Europe by November 1918 (*Signal Corps/National Archives 78846*).

when America entered World War I on April 6, 1917, and by the time of the Armistice in November 1918, 45 squadrons had reached the front in Europe, with many others in various stages of formation and training.

Aviation was divorced from Army authority briefly in 1918, when the Overman Act of May 20 set up two air departments—the Division of Military Aeronautics to look after operations and the Bureau of Aircraft Production responsible for aircraft procurement, supply and training. These two departments together became known as the Air Service.

In Europe, the operational units became the Air Service, A.E.F. (American Expeditionary Force), subdivided by November 1918 into First, Second and Third Army components. The first unit to reach Europe was the 1st Aero Squadron, on September 3, 1917. On April 3, 1918, the 94th Pursuit Squadron, with its "Hat-in-Ring" insignia, became the first American-trained pursuit squadron in action at the front.

The independence of the Air Service was short lived and the Army Re-Organization Act of June 4, 1920, made it a component of the Army once again. The name was changed to U.S. Army Air Corps by the Air Corps Act of July 2, 1926. From a wartime peak of 200,000 personnel, the strength of the Air Service dropped to fewer than 10,000 by June 1920 and stayed at this level until 1926. The Air Corps Act then put into motion a re-equipment programme with a target Corps strength of 1,650 officers and 15,000 men.

Progress with this programme was made only slowly and was held back by rivalry between the Army and the Navy and uncertainty about the role of air power in both offence and defence. An important development was the formation on March 1, 1935, of the G.H.Q. (General Headquarters) Air Force, which was relieved of responsibility for providing primary support for Army ground forces. By the time World War II began in Europe, a large proportion of all U.S. military aircraft was attached to G.H.Q. Air Force for deployment in the defence of the North American continent and overseas territories.

On June 20, 1941, Army Regulation 95-5 created the Army Air Forces, with the Air Corps and the G.H.Q. Air Force (renamed Air Force Combat Command) as its principal components until they were discontinued on March 9, 1942. This laid the foundation on which the independent Air Force was eventually built.

Rapid growth of the USAAF led to the formation of numbered Air Forces as subdivisions of the Service. The first four of these were originally known as Northeast, Northwest, Southeast and Southwest air districts, later becoming the First, Second, Third and Fourth Air Forces. Others were formed as the strength of the USAAF was built up following Japan's attacks of December 7 and 8, 1941, on Pearl Harbor in Hawaii and on installations in the Philippines. While the first four Air Forces remained permanently based in the U.S., the Fifth, Seventh, Tenth, Thirteenth, Fourteenth and Twentieth served in the Asiatic-Pacific Theater; the Eighth, Ninth, Twelfth and Fifteenth in the European-African area (with the Eighth re-deployed to the Pacific in 1945); the Sixth in the Panama Canal Zone and the Eleventh in Alaska.

Further organizational and operational subdivisions were made with the creation of such specialized units as Technical Training Command and Flying Training Command (later merged into a single Training Command); Air Corps Maintenance Command, Air Corps Ferrying Command (eventually Air Transport Command), and others. At its wartime peak, reached in March 1944, the USAAF had 2,411,294 men under arms, and the number of aircraft in the inventory reached 78,757. By April 1945, the Air Force had 243 active groups of which 224 were overseas and combat ready.

The run-down in both manpower and equipment after the end of the

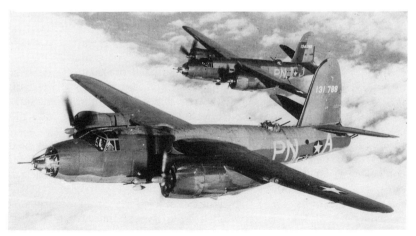

Martin Marauders – a B-26B in the foreground and a B-26C beyond – in the markings of the 322nd Bomb Group, one of four Marauder groups operating with the Eighth Air Force from bases in the U.K. in mid-1943.

war was rapid, and in May 1947 the personnel totalled only 303,614. On September 18, 1947, the National Security Act created the U.S. Air Force as one of three independent military departments in its own right, and a gradual build-up of strength began again. Prior to this, on March 21, 1946, USAAF had formed its combat squadrons and wings into three commands—Strategic Air Command, Tactical Air Command and Air Defense Command. U.S. Strategic Air Forces in Europe, set up in January 1944, continued under the title of U.S. Air Forces Europe (USAFE) and had its counterpart in the Pacific in the Far East Air Force (later, Pacific Air Forces).

Since 1945, the strength of the USAF has fluctuated widely, reflecting the temperature of international relations and America's involvement in the Korean War (1950–1953) and the Vietnam War (1961–1975). The latter conflict made severe demands upon the USAF and led to the evolution of many new weapons and tactics to fight the Viet Cong forces.

With the changing requirements of national defence, the Air Force's role in the deterrent force and its growing concern with activities in space, significant changes were made in the organization and structure of the major commands. In 1988, these totalled 13, of which those principally concerned with operating manned aircraft were Strategic Air Command, Tactical Air Command, U.S. Air Forces Europe, Pacific Air Forces, Military Airlift Command, Alaskan Air Command and Air Training Command. The Air University also has Command status, and the total is made up by the Space, Communications, Electronic Security, Logistics and Systems Commands.

The operating roles of the principal aircraft-operating Commands in 1988 were:

Strategic Air Command (SAC). The major USAF deterrent force. SAC controls two-thirds of the US nuclear triad and has a personnel strength of more than 119,000. It operates more than 300 bombers, nearly 700 tankers and about 100 reconnaissance aircraft and also controls 1,000 ICBMs. Its major components are the 8th and 15th Air Forces, plus the 1st Strategic Aerospace Division.

Tactical Air Command (TAC). This Command maintains tactical air power on a highly mobile basis. It has a force of tactical transport aircraft that can fly, at short notice, to anywhere in the world, all the necessary elements to support TAC fighter squadrons in the field. It also has responsibility for the air defence of the continental United States, previously the task of Aerospace Defense Command. With a personnel strength of more than 113,000 (plus Reserve and Air National Guard forces attached), TAC controls over 4,000 aircraft, through its 1st, 9th, and 12th Air Forces, 28th Air Division and other direct-reporting units.

U.S. Air Forces Europe (USAFE). Responsible for the geographical area extending from Britain eastwards through Europe to the borders of Pakistan, USAFE forms a vital United States contribution to NATO. Providing a tactical force, logistic support and rescue service, USAFE employs 63,000 military personnel and 11,000 civilians and controls the 3rd, 16th and 17th

4

Air Forces with their HQs respectively in Britain, Spain and West Germany.

Pacific Air Forces (PACAF). With its HQ in Hawaii, this Command has similar duties in the Pacific area to those of the USAFE in Europe. Employing some 38,000 personnel, it controls the 5th, 7th and 13th Air Forces in Japan, Korea and the Philippines respectively, to operate more than 300 aircraft.

Military Airlift Command (MAC). The primary MAC role is to provide world-wide logistic airlift support for all three American armed services, for which it uses some 92,000 military and civilian personnel, operating over 1,000 aircraft. Reserve and Air National Guard attachments provide an additional 70,000 personnel and some 400 aircraft. Its major organizations are the 21st, 22nd and 23rd Air Forces.

Alaskan Air Command (AAC). Providing "Top Cover for America" (its motto), AAC is served by some 7,500 military and 1,500 civilian personnel at five bases in Alaska and maintains two Tactical Fighter Wings in addition to other units.

Air Training Command (ATC). The flying training of all categories of air crew is among the many responsibilities of this Command, which employs nearly 88,000 personnel. Principal aircraft-operating organisations are Flying Training Wings and Combat Crew Training Wings.

Air Force Reserve (AFRES). Constituted as a separate operating agency in August 1968 to succeed Continental Air Command, AFRES has a permanent staff of 305 regular Air Force personnel, but 12,500 civilian members, serving on a committed part-time basis. AFRES provides a major portion of United States airlift resources through the 4th and 14th Air Forces, with their squadrons supporting MAC. The 10th Air Force embraces fighter and ground support squadrons dedicated to TAC and tanker squadrons serving SAC.

Air National Guard (ANG). Organizationally a part of AFRES (see above), the ANG provides a reserve of trained manpower, ready for operations at a moment's notice. Its 159 units in 1987 were equipped with a variety of the aircraft types used by SAC (tankers), TAC (tactical fighters, air defence and forward air control), MAC (transports and rescue/recovery helicopters) and PAF (tactical fighters).

After the Air Force had become a separate military service, the Army again established its own air arm in 1948 as the U.S. Army Air Forces. Its function was limited to short tactical operations and supply duties. The interpretation of "tactical operations" led to considerable friction between the USAF and the Army, which eventually relinquished fixed wing combat aircraft but retained armed helicopters in its inventory, in addition to light transports, observation and surveillance aircraft and other types.

Although the Air Force or the Navy remained responsible for procurement of Army aircraft, they are maintained and flown by Army personnel and, from 1958 to 1962, they carried distinctive Army designations which were independent of the Air Force system. In 1960, the Army obtained authority to procure certain of its aircraft directly from the makers.

5

PROCUREMENT AND DISPOSAL
OF U.S. ARMY AND AIR FORCE
AIRCRAFT

PROCUREMENT of Army Air Force aircraft is normally by direct purchase from the manufacturer. Just before and during World War I, a number were obtained as gifts from private individuals or organizations. In cases where civilian aircraft were "drafted" into military service, suitable compensation was given to the owners.

Foreign designs sent to the U.S. during World War I for evaluation were usually on loan from various European governments and did not become Army property. These were generally flown in their original markings and serial numbers. A few were donated by foreign governments after the Armistice. Captured enemy types tested during World War II were Army property but did not receive either Army designations or serial numbers.

Several hundred World War I German aeroplanes were obtained in 1919/20 as war reparations, but only Fokker D-VIIs became active in the Air Service. Since they were not purchased through normal channels, they were not given regular serial numbers. For the most part, they flew with the original German serial numbers. One two-seat Fokker C.1, several D.VIIs and two D-VIII monoplanes, all built in Germany during the war but smuggled into Holland by Fokker, were purchased from the Dutch Fokker firm in 1920 with experimental funds and were given standard serial numbers in the 64,000 range and in the special 94,000 block.

In the early post-war years, a few aircraft were obtained from the Navy, but instead of being simple transfers they were outright purchases, sometimes at a token price of $1.00. An example was the Curtiss R2C-1 racer which became the Army R-8 model after such a deal. During World War II, and later, Naval aircraft were obtained on direct transfer. Usually there was a favourable balance, for the Navy used more Army designs than the Army used Naval types.

During World War I and the early 1920s, the designers of a prototype aeroplane did not retain proprietary rights to it after its sale to the government. If production articles were desired, the government could and did put the order up for industry-wide bidding. The original designers were sometimes underbid by other firms and in some cases actually went out of business as a result. This situation was soon corrected by legislation.

Shortly before World War II, the American need to rearm was partially met by requisitioning aeroplanes which were under construction in U.S. factories for the British government. As described in the chapter on Designations, these aircraft were recognized as non-standard procurements and were not given standard Air Corps serial numbers. In 1941, on the other hand, when European aircraft needs were supplied by Lend-Lease, the aeroplanes, even though equipped to foreign specifications, were given standard U.S. type designations and serial numbers because they were purchased with U.S. Army Air Corps funds. When aircraft on these orders were requisitioned to fill Air Corps needs there was no need to make compensation to Britain since the machines were already U.S. property.

Another source of Army aircraft in 1941 and 1942 was civil aviation. Many transports were drafted from the airlines, some with civilian crews provided by the airlines on a contract basis. Most new transports in the factories were diverted to the military and such new designs as the Douglas DC-4 (C-54), scheduled for delivery early in 1942, and the Lockheed Constellation (C-69), due in 1943, did not reach the airlines until 1946. Lighter transport and liaison types and a few training gliders were obtained by direct purchases from private owners. A small number of fighters and bombers was received as gifts, which were usually paid for by subscription from members of a trade union, industrial plant or fraternal or social organization.

"Reverse Lend-Lease" was also effective, and many British designs were transferred to U.S. jurisdiction in England. Again, these were non-standard types and did not carry standard U.S. designations or serials. A single de Havilland Moth Minor was probably unique in being assigned a regular serial (42-94128) but had no standard designation. A few captured German Fieseler Storch liaison aircraft and a few liberated Italian transports and trainers were pressed into use as non-standard types in U.S. markings but had no designation.

U.S. funds were used during World War II to finance some manufacture in foreign factories, with the result that the aeroplanes carried Army serial numbers. Examples were Canadian Harvard IIs, which were licence-built North American AT-6s known as AT-16s, and 200 Canadian-built de Havilland Tiger Moths known as PT-24s. Of these, only a few AT-16s were used by the Army, and they were obtained overseas through Reverse Lend-Lease.

Disposal of Army and Air Force aeroplanes has been handled in a

Republic P-47D presented to the USAAF by the bankers of Rockville Centre, N.Y., showing typical presentation lettering on the fuselage (*Republic photo*).

This civil Douglas DC-2-112 airliner was drafted from TWA and designated C-32A. The 22 C-32As were the only examples of drafted civil aircraft being given the same model number as an existing USAAC model, instead of receiving a new model number (*Peter M. Bowers*).

variety of ways. At the end of World War I, thousands of surplus aeroplanes and engines were dumped on the market at almost giveaway prices. This dealt the budding civil aircraft industry in America a crippling blow from which it took nearly seven years to recover. Surplus aeroplanes and material in the United States were sold to the public on an "as-is-where-is" basis, either on military airfields or surplus parks or in the original crates still in warehouses. U.S.-built aircraft overseas were mostly stacked and burned but many items such as foreign-built engines and armament were sold back to the same governments or for scrap.

Few, if any, surplus Army aircraft of the between-war years fell into civil hands. Air Service (Air Corps from 1926) funds were meagre, and the fullest possible use was obtained from existing airframes. Many ended their days in Air Corps mechanics' schools. Complete aircraft used for such purposes were identified as "Class 26" material, and were placarded "not to be flown". Other obsolete planes not given to Air Corps or civilian schools were scrapped or set out as air-to-ground gunnery targets. Those given to civil schools went under highly restrictive conditions. Not only could they not be flown; they could not even be disposed of as identifiable aircraft, but only scrapped or returned to the Army.

In 1941 and during World War II, a new use was found for obsolete types. Some were converted to radio-controlled aerial targets, a practice that continues to this day even with such high-performance service types as the F-4 and F-102. A limited number of war-weary bombers was expended against German ground targets in 1945 as radio-controlled bombs (BQ series).

As many as possible of the requisitioned airliners were returned to the airlines after the war ended or, in some cases, shortly before. As the airlines didn't always get their original machines back, odd situations developed, such as an airline using Douglas DC-3s with Pratt & Whitney engines receiving Wright Cyclone-powered models while other lines with air terminal procedures based on left-side entry doors received DC-3s with doors on the right.

The end of World War II again saw enormous surplus sales, but this time on a more controlled basis. Those types having direct commercial application, such as trainers, liaison models and transports, were made available for direct sale to the public through the War Assets Administration. These were evaluated by the Civil Aviation Agency, which determined the modifications necessary to qualify them for approval type certificates.

Such surplus military aircraft could be used as any standard commercial model. More specialized types, such as bombers and attack planes, were eligible only for "limited" licences. They could be used for crop spraying, photography, etc., but could not be used to carry fare-paying passengers. A company could convert a bomber to a transport and carry its own employees, however.

Fighters were eligible only for "restricted" special purpose licences and were used for cloud seeding, photography and air racing. Surplus equipment of all kinds was again given to civilian schools, again with the restrictive contracts governing its use, and many examples of the more famous types, especially the B-17, were given to cities as war memorials.

Surplus World War II aircraft unsuited to any normal civil use were sold as scrap metal at prices way below "aircraft" prices, usually in great quantities to large salvage firms, with the strict stipulation that they be melted down for scrap and that none of their components be usable for their original purpose.

Since the World War II surplus parks were cleaned out by the late 1940s, further sales of surplus Army/Air Force aircraft continue to be made as they become available. If other governmental agencies have no claim on them, types suitable for civil use are offered to the public for competitive bidding. Jet fighters can be given to schools, but most are scrapped.

Bell P-39 "Cobra I" was typical of many World War II fighters sold as surplus after the war ended and used for air racing. Bell test-pilot Jack Woolam was killed when "Cobra I" crashed on a test flight prior to the Thompson Trophy race in 1948; many others have enjoyed greater success and heavily-modified P-51s and other types still compete at the annual Reno Air Race event in the late 'eighties (*H. G. Martin*).

U.S. MILITARY AIRCRAFT
DESIGNATIONS

THE reader will have a better understanding of this book if he first under-
stands the various systems used over the years to identify the aircraft as
to designated type, model, series and special purpose.

For their first 12 years, U.S. military aeroplanes had no official designations. They were procured and operated under the manufacturer's names
and model numbers, which fortunately resulted in only one duplication,
involving the Thomas-Morse MB-2 and Martin MB-2. Late in 1919, the
Army Air Service decided to identify its aircraft according to the designated mission and adopted a letter-and-number system based on that used
by the German Army during World War I, when the letter designated the
aeroplane as to basic type. This system has undergone considerable
revision and expansion since it became effective in 1920, and in its final
form appears as follows. Numbers in parentheses indicate sequence of
adoption of various parts of the designation and identify the explanations
in following paragraphs.

$$K \quad C \; - 135 \quad A \; - \; 80 \; - \; BN$$
$$(4) \quad (1) \qquad (2) \quad (3) \quad (5) \qquad (6)$$

1 Type symbol	4 Status or special-purpose prefix
2 Model number	5 Block number
3 Series letter	6 Manufacturer identification

1. Type Symbol. This letter is used to identify the aeroplane as to type,
whether Bomber, Observation, Trainer, etc. When first adopted, the
system sometimes used additional letters to further qualify specialized
functions within the basic type, as NBS for Night Bomber, Short Distance,
or specific aircraft characteristic, as PW for Pursuit, Watercooled (engine).

Under the 1919 system, Army aircraft were divided into fifteen basic
types, with a few odd designations appended to the list. Aircraft already
in service at the time the system went into effect retained their original
designations except in cases where subsequent modification justified the
assignment of a new type number. An exception was the Martin MB-2,
which was in test status before the system was adopted but was ordered
into production as NBS-1 afterward. For the de Havilland DH-4, most
numerous service model of the post-war years, the original British manufacturer's designation was treated as a standard service designation and
modified to indicate the status of a particular aeroplane as indicated

under section (3) below. The fifteen original type designations were as follows:

Type	Designation	Symbol
I	Pursuit, Watercooled	PW
II	Pursuit, Night	PN
III	Pursuit, Aircooled	PA
IV	Pursuit, Ground Attack	PG
V	Two-seat Pursuit	TP
VI	Ground Attack	GA
VII	Infantry Liaison	IL
VIII	Night Observation	NO
IX	Artillery Observation	AO
X	Corps Observation	CO
XI	Day Bombardment	DB
XII	Night Bombardment, Short Distance	NBS
XIII	Night Bombardment, Long Distance	NBL
XIV	Training, Aircooled	TA
XV	Training, Watercooled	TW

Miscellaneous

Alert Pursuit (Special)	PS
Ambulance	A
Glider	G
Messenger	M*
Racer	R
Seaplane	S
Transport	T

*Messengers converted to radio-controlled Aerial Torpedoes were MAT.

In May 1924 the original letter-and-number system was revised and simplified and additional letters were provided to give greater flexibility. Aircraft in service under the old designations retained them, but all subsequent production was under the new system. An exception was made for the Boeing PW-9, in production at the time of the change, and the PW designation was retained for this one model until production ended in 1928.

The 1924 system, with various additions and deletions, remained in use until 1948, at which time further revisions and some reassignment of letters was made. Further revisions were made in 1962 when the Department of Defense ordered the use of a uniform designating system for all aircraft used by the USAF, USN and Army Aviation. All major types in service in mid-1962 were assigned designations in this unified system, so that USN and Army types were redesignated, but as the tri-service system was basically the same as that already used by the USAF, comparatively few USAF designations were changed.

In the following list, all type symbols used since 1924 are shown. Those included up to 1987 in the tri-service system introduced in 1962 are in bold type. The letters "G", "H", "V" and "Z" are "vehicle type" designators in the post–1962 system, to be used only together with a mission designator prefix.

Type Symbol	Designation	Remarks
A	Aerial Target	1940/41. Radio Controlled*
A	Amphibian	1948/1962. Formerly OA
A	Attack	1924/1947. Became B†
A	**Attack**	**1962-to date**
AG	Assault Glider	1942/1944
AT	Advanced Trainer	1925/1947. Became T
B	**Bomber**	**1925-to date**
BC	Basic Combat	1936/1940. Became AT
BG	Bomb Glider	1942/1944
BLR	Bomber, Long Range	1935/1936. Became B
BT	Basic Trainer	1930/1947. Became T‡
BQ	Bomb, Controllable	1942/1945
C	**Cargo (Transport)**	**1925-to date**
CG	Cargo Glider	1941/1947. Became G
CQ	Target Control	1942/1947. Became D-Prefix
E	**Special Electronic Installation**	**1962-to date**
F	**Fighter**	**1948-to date. Formerly P**
F	Photographic	1930/1947. Became R-Prefix
FG	Fuel Glider	1944/1947
FM	Fighter, Multiplace	1936/1941
G	**Glider**	**1948-to date**
G	Gyroplane	1935/1939. Became O, R
GB	Glide Bomb	1942/1947
GT	Glide Torpedo	1942/1947
H	**Helicopter**	**1948-to date. Formerly R**
HB	Heavy Bomber	1925/1927. Became B
JB	Jet-Propelled Bomb	1943/1947
L	Liaison	1942/1962. Formerly O
LB	Light Bomber	1924/1932. Became B
O	Observation	1924/1942. Became L
O	**Observation**	**1962-to date. Formerly L**
OA	Observation Amphibian	1925/1947. Became A
OQ	Aerial Target (Model Aeroplane)	1942/1947. Became Q
P	Pursuit	1925/1947. Became F
P	**Patrol**	**1962-to date**
PB	Pursuit, Biplace	1935/1941
PG	Powered Glider	1943/1947
PQ	Aerial Target	1942/1947. Formerly A; to Q
PT	Primary Trainer	1925/1947. Became T‡
Q	Aerial Target	1948/1962. Formerly OQ, PQ
R	**Reconnaissance**	**1948-to date. §Formerly F**
R	Rotary Wing	1941/1947. Became H
S	Supersonic/Special test	1946/1947. Became X
S	**Anti-submarine**	**1962-to date**
T	**Trainer**	**1948-to date. Formerly AT, BT, PT‡**
TG	Training Glider	1941/1947
U	**Utility**	**1952-to date**
V	**VTOL or STOL**	**1954-to date**
X	**Special Research**	**1948-to date. Formerly XS**
Z	**Airship**	**1962-to date**

* Some were model aeroplanes, some full-size.

†Douglas A-26 became B-26 without conflict with Martin B-26, then out of service. Douglas A-24 became F-24 to avoid conflict with remaining Consolidated B-24s.

‡BT-13 and PT-13 designations retained for a while after change to distinguish between remaining examples of each model still in service.

§TR and SR have come into use to indicate tactical reconnaissance and strategic reconnaissance; note that the T and S are not, in this case, modified mission symbols as described on page 17.

Under an interim designating system of the Army Air Forces (as distinct from the separate U.S. Air Force), aircraft were identified by a dual-letter system combining basic aircraft form and function, followed by the model number.

AC   Airplane, Cargo
AO   Airplane, Observation
AU   Airplane, Utility
HC   Helicopter, Cargo
HO   Helicopter, Observation
HU   Helicopter, Utility
VZ   VTOL research

2. Model Number. Under the German system, the number following the type symbol identified the aeroplane model as to the number of separate models of that type procured from a particular manufacturer. The Fokker D-VII was the seventh D-model (fighter) procured from Fokker. The U.S. system differed in that the number indicated the number of different models that had been ordered under each type designation, regardless of the manufacturer involved. The B-17, for example, was identified only as the seventeenth bomber design, in spite of having been built by Douglas and Lockheed-Vega as well as by Boeing.

Once the system was established, the actual model numbers within each type division were assigned by the Contract Branch of the Materiel Section at McCook Field, Dayton, Ohio, and later at Wright Field. These numbers were supposedly assigned strictly in sequence of contracts for the aeroplanes, but often the designation was established during early pre-contract negotiations. Model numbers were not reassigned in cases of contract cancellation.

This system appears to be inconsistent when it is noted that many aeroplanes with a "high" number have been flown before those with a lower number in the same series. The system has in fact functioned perfectly in these cases, and the inconsistency lies in the time at which the system was applied to the particular aircraft.

In many cases, an aeroplane would be tested while still the property of the manufacturer. Not being Army property, no Army model designation was applied. This was common practice when a manufacturer had developed a new model at his own expense in the absence of an official requirement, and the Army was testing it under a "Bailment Contract" where the machine was returned to the manufacturer at the end of the testing. In some cases, these aeroplanes were tested under an "experimental plane" number (see Non-Standard Designations, page 22).

In cases where the Army decided to buy the particular aeroplane after such tests, the proper type and model numbers were assigned by the Contract Branch at the time of purchase even though the machine might be several years old at the time. In only a few cases were standard designa-

13

tions assigned to tested aircraft that were not purchased. Examples are Boeing Model 202 (XP-15), Fokker F-11 (C-16), and Fokker F-32 (C-20).

The opposite situation resulted when a new and yet undesignated model was contracted for with a manufacturer. Since the new design was to be Army property from its origin and paid for from Army funds, the appropriate designation was applied at the time the contract was signed. Because of the time required to design and build a prototype and tool up for production, several years might elapse before that particular design entered service.

A combination of these two examples can be found in the Bell P-63 and the North American P-64. The "P-for-Pursuit" series had reached P-62 late in 1940, when the Army was negotiating with Bell for an improved version of the P-39, which was just then entering service. This received the designation of XP-63. In the meantime, six export North American NA-68 (ex-NA-50A) fighters ordered by the government of Thailand (Siam) were undeliverable because of the prevailing American arms embargo and were drafted into the USAAC right off the dock. These were not first-line fighters even by pre-war U.S. standards, and were, therefore, relegated to training duties. They were given the "P-for-Pursuit" designation because it was the most suitable, and acquired the next available number, P-64. The XP-63 did not fly until December 7, 1942.

Different model numbers are assigned to separate designs, of course, but extensive modification of an existing model that seriously affects interchangeability of parts is ample justification for a new number, as in the case of the change from the water-cooled Liberty engine of the Douglas O-2K to the air-cooled Wright R-1750 radial of the O-29. Up to World War II, any change of power-plant usually resulted in assignment of a separate model number. More recently, however, even radical changes generally result only in a change of series letter, as in the Allison to Packard-Merlin engine changes of Curtiss P-40E/F and North American P-51A/B. In these cases the change was to a very similar and thoroughly proven liquid cooled engine and did not result in any serious alteration of operating technique or equipment installation.

In the 1962 tri-service system, numbers are still allocated in strict sequence, but now apply to aircraft of any of the three services. Thus, in the new "F for fighter" category then introduced, numbers from F-1 to F-11 were allocated, but only the F-4 and F-5 were Air Force designations, the remainder being Navy aircraft.

3. Series Letter. A letter was applied after the model number to indicate modifications of the original model, a practice that had been widely used throughout the world as far back as the beginning of World War I. In U.S. Army practice under the 1919 and 1924 systems, the basic model was without a letter and the first significant change resulted in the A-variant, to be followed by B, etc. By the end of World War II, however, this practice was altered so that only prototypes went without a suffix and the

14

A, or even a subsequent letter, applied to the first *production* model.

An example is the North American P-86 (later F-86) series. The prototypes were XP-86 and the production version was P-86A. This applied even when there was no similarly designated experimental prototype, as in the case of the Boeing B-50. The actual prototype was the XB-44, a converted B-29, and the production version was to have been B-29D. At Army request, this was changed to a new model, B-50, but the first one, a production article, was B-50A.

The alphabetical sequence of the series letter does not necessarily indicate the sequence of aircraft manufacture. For example, most Curtiss P-6s and P-6As were converted to P-6D before the P-6E was put in production, while the XP-6B was itself a converted P-1C. In other cases, additional series letters were reserved by the Army for its own experimental work with what were originally standard models. Sometimes those reserved letters were never used.

Assignment of a new series letter did not always result in that letter being used permanently to identify a new feature. The designation of XP-47K was applied to an early P-47D-5 that was used to test the suitability of a bubble canopy on the P-47 design. When the feature was adopted for production, it was incorporated on late P-47Ds, then on the production lines, without changing the series letter. The modification was marked by a new block number (see item 5 below).

There were a few exceptions to the use of series letters to indicate development sequence. While the de Havilland 4 had originally conformed, with DH-4B being applied to indicate an improvement of the original Americanized "Liberty Plane" (DH-4A had already been used in England), then DH-4C, etc., other letters with specialized meanings came into use, such as DH-4M for "modernized", DH-4M-2K for dual control target tug, etc.

Curtiss JN-4s of World War I followed the straight alphabetical

The Republic XP-47K was a P-47D-5 given an experimental new series letter when used to test a bubble canopy configuration. The new feature was put into production on the P-47D-25 (*Wright Field photo 125651*).

sequence, but the Army jumped from JN-4D to JN-4H for "Hisso" to indicate models powered with the 150 h.p. Wright–Hispano engine in place of the 90 h.p. Curtiss OX-5. Under the 1919 system, modified JN-4s and 6s became JNS for "standardized", and used additional letters and numbers to indicate power plant, as in JNS-E when powered with the Wright–Hispano E engine. The suffix E was also applied to World War I aircraft modified in the early 1920s by Eberhardt, as in S.E.5E and Spad 13E. The letter "R" was used briefly in 1940/41 to indicate radio-controlled, as on the Douglas BT-2BR, also known as the A-4 aerial target.

In the alphabetical assignment of series letters, it was specified that the letters "I" and "O" would not be used because they could be mistaken for numbers. The Army violated its own regulation, but produced no problem, when Douglas BT-2Bs were converted to instrument trainers as BT-2BI. The same conversion of North American BC-1s to produce BC-1I, however, illustrates the very situation the original regulation sought to avoid.

4. Status Prefix. In May 1924, when the designating system was revised, the prefix "X" was added to the standard designation to indicate experimental status of an aeroplane, usually a prototype. Aviation writers and data collectors have applied this procedure retroactively to give entirely unofficial X-designations to earlier prototypes.

Official use of the X-prefix was not limited strictly to prototypes. It was frequently desirable to conduct test work on a standard type, which would be withdrawn from squadron service or diverted at the time of delivery and be given the X-prefix for the duration of the test period. Sometimes the aeroplane was sufficiently modified to be truly an "X-job", as it was generally called, but sometimes the change (even to a new model number) was accomplished to protect the test programme from time lost through grounding of the aeroplane in order to comply with routine maintenance bulletins issued against the standard service models.

In 1928, the prefix "Y" was added to the type and model designation to indicate the service test status of a new design. It was the custom around the 1930s first to order a single X-model of a new design and then a service test quantity, usually thirteen. The X-model went to Wright Field for evaluation of the aeroplane itself and its suitability as a type, after which the service test models were distributed among using organizations for pilot familiarization, development of maintenance procedures, etc.

Sometimes the Y-prefix was followed by a number "1" during 1931/1936 to indicate that the aircraft had been purchased with "F-1" funds rather than from the regular Army Air Corps appropriation. This additional symbol was purely budgetary and of no technical significance, although there might be differences between a Douglas YO-31C and a Y1O-31C, for example, because of changes made to the basic design between the two purchases. While the X, particularly when assigned to prototypes, was usually permanent, the Y and Y1-prefixes were removed at the end of the service test. The Y1C-37 of 1937 became plain C-37 after a year, then

UC-37 in 1943, as an example of this procedure being followed.

The letter "Z" was adopted at the same time as the Y to indicate an aeroplane that was obsolescent although still in service. In some cases the Z-prefix was added to the X or Y, as on the Curtiss ZXA-8. The X and Y, on the other hand, take precedence when used in connection with other special-purpose prefixes, as, for example, the Boeing YDB-47B.

In January 1943, additional prefixes were adopted. Aircraft that were no longer considered suitable for their primary military mission, but still useful for other purposes, were given the prefix "R" to indicate "Restricted" status. At the time of adoption, this restriction applied to almost every U.S. Army combat model built prior to Pearl Harbor and to several late models. At the same time, the prefix "U" was applied to "C" transport/cargo models with a capacity of less than eight persons or 1,400 pounds of cargo.

Toward the end of World War II, other prefixes were adopted to designate special purpose use of standard models. In the change of 1948, models that had undergone a complete change of type and model designation because of change of purpose reverted to their original basic designations and were given prefixes to indicate the change. Examples are redesignation of the Boeing F-13, a photographic B-29, to RB-29, the "R" in this case indicating "Reconnaissance", the earlier R-for-Restricted having been dropped at the time of the change.

The idea was further developed in the 1962 tri-service system, with a "modified mission symbol" added as a prefix to the basic mission symbol and type number in many cases. At the same time the use of a status prefix symbol was confirmed, in combination with the basic mission symbol alone or with both a basic and a modified mission symbol. The letters now in use as status prefixes are G, J, N, X, Y and Z, as listed below.

An alphabetical listing of all prefix letters from 1924 to date appears below with appropriate remarks to indicate dates and changes. These letters are used only as status prefixes in combination with the type symbols listed on p.12 and current after 1948. Those specified as "modified mission symbols" in the 1962 system are shown in bold type.

Prefix	Status	Remarks
A	**Attack**	**To date**
C	**Transport**	1943-to date
D	**Director (Drone Controller)**	1948-to date
E	Exempt (Bailment to USAF Contractor)*	1946/1955
E	**Special Electronic Installation**	1948-to date
F	Photographic	1945/47
F	**Fighter**	1962-to date
G	Carrier (of parasite aeroplane)	1948
G	Permanently Grounded	To date
H	**Search and Rescue**	To date
J	Special Test Status (temporary)	1956-to date
K	Ferret	1944/47
K	**Tanker**	1949-to date

Prefix	Status	Remarks
L	**Cold Weather**	To date
M	Medical	1951/1962
M	**Multi-mission**	To date
N	Special Test Status (permanent)	1956-to date
O	**Observation**	1962-to date
P	Passenger Transport Only	1948/1963
P	**Patrol**	1963-to date
Q	**Radio Controlled Drone**	1948-to date
R	Restricted	1943/1947
R	Reconnaissance (Photographic)	1948-to date
S	Search and Rescue	1948/1962
S	**Anti-submarine**	To date
T	**Trainer**	1943-to date
U	**Utility**	1951-to date
V	**Staff (V.I.P. Transport)**	1945-to date
W	**Weather**	1948-to date
X	Experimental	1925-to date
Y	Service Test	1928-to date
Z	Obsolete	1928-to date

*Aircraft bailed (leased) to manufacturers or equipment companies for special test or development programmes and exempt from compliance with routine technical directives.

Application of the standardized system since 1962 has produced some apparent anomalies. Designation of the Lockheed SR-71 (the SR indicating strategic reconnaissance and the 71 continuing the previous bomber series) did not conform to the principles laid down by Air Force Regulation No 66-11, which set out the new designation system. When the Strategic Air Command adopted an F-111 variant as a bomber, the designating system should have required that this be called the BF-111 (with the "B" serving as the modified mission symbol), but instead it became the FB-111. Another more glaring deviation from the system came with the use of AV-8A for the Hawker Siddeley Harriers acquired by the USMC. The 1962 system specified that when "G", "H", "V" or "Z" are used as the basic type symbol, a second letter should also be used to indicate the mission. However, "AV-8" was numerically in the Attack series (A-8) whereas the system properly applied would have designated the Harrier as the V-12 in the VTOL series (or perhaps V-6, as this had already been used for the Hawker P.1127 prototypes tested by the USAF) and would have used the "A for Attack" prefix with this number. Correct use of the "V" and "H" symbols was shown with such types as the OV-10 and the AH-56.

5. Block Numbers. By 1941, the increasing complexity of aircraft made it desirable to establish a new system whereby the many minor differences between otherwise similar models could be indicated without changing the series letter. Since those changes were usually accomplished on a number of consecutive aeroplanes in a particular production lot, or "block", the new designations were called "Block Numbers".

The first block was identified by the figure "-1", as on the Curtiss P-40F-1, the first model to use it. The P-40F was well into production before the system was adopted, so it was not applied until the 97th production

After Curtiss Kittyhawk production was financed by the U.S. Army, it was designated P-40E-1. This use of a dash number suffix to the aeroplane model designation was made a year before the adoption of the present "Block Number" system (*Curtiss-Wright photo 329*).

article. Following block numbers were assigned on the production line at intervals of -5, -10, -15, etc. The gaps permitted the designation of further changes made to the aircraft at modification centres. This system is still in use.

An apparent earlier application of the block number system was on the Curtiss P-40E-1 of 1941, where the "-1" actually served an entirely different purpose. When Lend-Lease was adopted in March, 1941, aircraft supplied to the Allies were subsequently delivered with standard USAAC designations and serial numbers. While the Curtiss Kittyhawk then in production was virtually identical with the USAAC P-40E, it had essential differences that prevented it from being regarded as a standard P-40E. The "-1" suffix was added to the P-40E designation to distinguish the British version from the American. No USAAC P-40Es were delivered with block numbers, but some P-40E-ls were drafted (requisitioned) from British orders for USAAC use.

Usually, block numbers started over at -1 with each new series: P-40F-1, P-40K-1, etc. In some cases, though, the block numbers continued through several series, as KC-97F ending at -85 and KC-97G starting at -90. Oddly, KC-97Es ended with -50 and KC-97Fs started with -50.

6. Manufacturer Identification. The huge aircraft building programme of 1941/42, under which several manufacturers built aircraft of the same model, made it desirable to identify these models as to actual source. This was accomplished by adding two letters after the block number or after the series letter when no block was used. Waco, the primary source of CG-4A gliders, was identified by CG-4A-WO, while the 15 other builders were identified by CG-4A-CE for Cessna, CG-4A-FO for Ford, etc.

As various manufacturers expanded their own facilities to include separate plants, new letter combinations were devised to identify them, as -DO for Douglas Santa Monica, -DE for Douglas El Segundo (formerly Northrop), -DL for Douglas Long Beach, and -DT for Douglas Tulsa.

19

A complete listing of manufacturers' identification letters follows:

Code	Manufacturer	Address
AD	Aero Design & Engineering Co.	Bethany, Okla.
AE	Aeronca Aircraft Corp.	Middletown, Ohio
AG	Air Glider Inc.	Akron, Ohio
AH	American Helicopter Co., Inc.	Manhattan Beach, Calif.
AV	Avro Canada	Montreal, Canada
BA	Bell Aircraft Corp.	Atlanta, Ga.
BB	Babcock Aircraft	Deland, Fla.
BC	Bell Aerosystems Co.	Buffalo, N.Y.
BE	Bell Aircraft Corp.	Buffalo, N.Y.
BF	Bell Aircraft Corp.	Fort Worth, Tex.
BH	Beech Aircraft Corp.	Wichita, Kans.
BL	Bellanca Aircraft	New Castle, Del.
BN	Boeing Airplane Co.	Renton, Wash.
BO	Boeing Airplane Co.	Seattle, Wash.
BR	Briegleb Sailplane	Beverley Hills, Calif.
BS	Bowlus Sailplane	San Francisco, Calif.
BU	Budd Manufacturing	Philadelphia, Pa.
BV	Boeing Co., Vertol Division	Morton, Pa.
BW	Boeing Airplane Co.	Wichita, Kans.
CA	Chase Aircraft Co., Inc.	West Trenton, N.J.
CC	Canadian Commercial Corp.	Toronto, Canada
CE	Cessna Aircraft Co.	Wichita, Kans.
CF	Convair (Consolidated-Vultee Aircraft Corp.)	Fort Worth, Tex.
CH	Christopher Aircraft	St. Louis, Mo.
CK	Curtiss-Wright Corp.	Louisville, Ky.
CL	Culver Aircraft	Wichita, Kans.
CM	Commonwealth Aircraft	Kansas City, Mo.
CN	Chase Aircraft Company, Inc.	Willow Run, Mich.
CO	Convair (Consolidated-Vultee Aircraft Corp.)	San Diego, Calif.
CR	Cornelius Aircraft	Dayton, Ohio
CS	Curtiss-Wright Corp.	St. Louis, Mo.
CU	Curtiss-Wright Corp.	Buffalo, N.Y.
CV	Chance Vought, Vought.	Dallas, Tex.
DA	Doak Aircraft Company Inc.	Torrance, Calif.
DC	Douglas Aircraft Co.	Chicago, Ill.
DE	Douglas Aircraft Co.	El Segundo, Calif.
DH	De Havilland Aircraft	Toronto, Canada
DJ	SNCA Sud-Ouest	Marignane, France
DK	Douglas Aircraft Co.	Oklahoma City, Okla.
DL	Douglas Aircraft Co.	Long Beach, Calif.
DM	Doman Helicopter, Inc.	Danbury, Conn.
DO	Douglas Aircraft Co.	Santa Monica, Calif.
DT	Douglas Aircraft Co.	Tulsa, Okla.
FA	Fairchild Aircraft Division	Hagerstown, Md.
FB	Fairchild Aircraft Division	Burlington, N.C.
FE	Fleet Aviation Ltd.	Fort Erie, Ontario, Canada
FL	Fleetwings, Inc.	Bristol, Pa.
FO	Ford Motor Co.	Willow Run, Mich.
FR	Frankfort Sailplane	Joliet, Ill.
FS	Firestone	Los Angeles, Calif.

20

Code	Manufacturer	Address
FT	Fletcher Aviation Corp.	Pasadena, Calif.
GA	G & A Aircraft Co.	Willow Grove, Pa.
GC	General Motors (Fisher)	Cleveland, Ohio
GE	General Aircraft	Astoria, Long Island, N.Y.
GF	Globe Aircraft	Fort Worth, Tex.
GK	General Motors	Kansas City, Kans.
GM	General Motors (Fisher)	Detroit, Mich.
GN	Gibson Refrigerator	Greenville, Mich.
GO	Goodyear Aircraft Co.	Akron, Ohio
GR	Grumman Aircraft Corp.	Bethpage, Long Island, N.Y.
GT	Grand Central Aircraft Eng. Co.	Tucson, Arizona
GY	Gyrodyne Co., of America Inc.	St. James, Long Island, N.Y.
HE	Helio Aircraft Corp.	Norwood, Mass.
HI	Higgins Aircraft, Inc.	New Orleans, La.
HI	Hiller Helicopter Corp.	Palo Alto, Calif.
HO	Howard Aircraft Corp.	Chicago, Ill.
HP	Handey Page Aircraft Ltd.	Radlett, Herts, U.K.
HS	Hawker Siddeley Aviation	Kingston, Surrey, U.K.
HU	Hughes Aircraft Co.	Culver City and San Diego Calif.
IN	Interstate A. & Eng.	El Segundo, Calif.
KA	Kaman Helicopter Corp.	Windsor Locks, Conn.
KE	Kellet Autogyro Corp.	Philadelphia, Pa.
KM	Kaiser Manufacturing Corp.	Willow Run, Mich.
LK	Laister-Kauffman Aircraft Co.	St. Louis, Mo.
LM	Lockheed Aircraft Corp.	Marietta, Ga.
LO	Lockheed Aircraft Corp.	Burbank, Calif.
MA	Martin Co., The Glenn L.	Baltimore, Md.
MC	McDonnell Aircraft Corp.	St. Louis, Mo.
MD	Martin Co.	Baltimore, Md.
MF	Martin Co.	Orlando, Fla.
MH	McCulloch Motors Corp.	Los Angeles, Calif.
MM	McDonnell Aircraft Corp.	Memphis, Tenn.
MO	Martin Co., The Glenn L.	Omaha, Nebr.
NA	North American Aviation, Inc.	Inglewood, Calif.
NC	North American Aviation, Inc.	Kansas City, Kans.
ND	Noorduyn Aviation Co., Limited	Montreal, Canada
NF	North American Aviation, Inc.	Fresno, Calif.
NH	North American Aviation, Inc.	Columbus, Ohio
NI	North American Aviation, Inc.	Downey, Calif.
NK	Nash-Kelvinator Corp.	Detroit, Mich.
NO	Northrop Aircraft, Inc.	Hawthorne, Calif.
NT	North American Aviation, Inc.	Dallas, Tex.
NW	Northwestern Aeronautical Corp.	St. Paul, Minn.
OM	Ou Mark Engineering Co.	Van Nuys, Calif.
PA	Piper Aircraft Corp.	Lock Haven, Pa.
PH	Piasecki Helicopter Corp.	Morton, Pa.
PI	Piper Aircraft Corp.	Lockhaven, Pa.
PI	Piasecki Aircraft Corp.	Philadelphia, Pa.
PL	Platt-LePage Aircraft Co.	Eddystone, Pa.
PR	Pratt, Read & Co.	Deep River, Conn.
RA	Republic Aviation	Evansville, Ind.

Code	Manufacturer	Address
RD	Read-York, Inc.	Kenosha, Wisc.
RE	Republic Aviation Corp.	Farmingdale, Long Island, N.Y.
RI	Ridgefield Mfg. Co.	Ridgeville, N.J.
RO	Robertson Aircraft	St. Louis, Mo.
RP	The Radioplane Co.	Van Nuys, Calif.
RY	Ryan Aeronautical Co.	San Diego, Calif.
SA	Stroukoff Aircraft Corp.	West Trenton, N.J.
SE	Seibel Helicopter Co.	Wichita, Kans.
SI	Sikorsky Aircraft Division	Stratford, Conn.
SL	St. Louis Aircraft	St. Louis, Mo.
SP	Spartan Aircraft	Tulsa, Okla.
SW	Schweizer Aircraft	Elmira, N.Y.
TA	Taylorcraft Aviation	Alliance, Ohio
TE	Temco Aircraft Corp.	Dallas, Tex.
TG	Texas Engineering & Manufacturing Co.	Greenville, Tex.
TI	Timm Aircraft	Van Nuys, Calif.
TP	Texas Engineering & Manufacturing Co.	Grand Prairie, Tex.
UH	United Helicopter Corp.	Palto Alto, Calif.
UN	Universal Molded Products	Bristol, Va.
VE	Vega Aircraft Corp.	Burbank, Calif.
VI	Canadian Vickers, Limited	Montreal, Canada
VL	Vertol Aircraft Corp.	Morton, Pa.
VN	Vultee Aircraft Corp.	Nashvillee, Tenn.
VO	Chance Vought Aircraft	Dallas, Tex.
VU	Vultee Aircraft Corp.	Downey, Calif.
VW	Vultree Aircraft Corp.	Wayne, Mich.
WA	Ward Furniture Co.	Fort Smith, Ark.
WI	Wichita Engineering	Wichita Falls, Tex.
WO	Waco Aircraft Co.	Troy, Ohio

NON-STANDARD AIRCRAFT DESIGNATIONS

At various times, the U.S. Army has procured and operated aircraft without applying the standard designations to them. In some cases, the aircraft were obtained by direct purchase and given regular serial numbers but no designations, as in the case of the commercial Driggs Dart (26–205) and the Waco 9 (26–206). Similarly, some aeroplanes procured for the use of U.S. Air Attachés in Europe before World War II were flown with their manufacturer's designations, as Morane-Saulnier MS-322 (32–419).

Others were leased from foreign governments and not even given serial numbers, as the Italian Romeo-Fokker C-VE, flown with U.S. military markings but with the original Italian Air Force serial number. An exception was the assignment of XC-44 (39-718) to a Messerschmitt Me-108B used by the U.S. air attaché in Berlin. This machine was absorbed into the Luftwaffe after the U.S. entered World War II.

American rearmament shortly before its entry into World War II resulted in shortages of certain aircraft types being filled by requisition of equivalent types then being built in American factories on British Government contracts. In cases where there was no directly-equivalent design in use by or under development for the Army, it was possible to treat the

22

requisitioned Britisher as any "new" model and assign it a standard designation. This was done in the case of the Lockheed Hudson, which became A-28 for the Pratt & Whitney-powered model and A-29 for the Wright-powered model.

Where equivalent models were in production for both countries, the designation problem was complicated by the great differences in details of equipment and military installation. The Bell Airacobras ordered by Britain were structurally similar to the U.S. Army P-39s, but were otherwise so different they could not be integrated into the Air Corps maintenance and supply systems as P-39s. Consequently, the requisitioned examples were identified by the manufacturer's model number of 400 preceeded by the letter "P" to identify them as pursuit types. Further deviation from normal procedure was reflected by the fact that all aircraft requisitioned from British direct-purchase contracts were flown with their original British serial numbers and were not given regular Army Air Corps serials. The major American-built aircraft models procured and operated in this way were:

British Model	Equivalent U.S. Model	Non-Standard U.S. Designation
Airacobra	P-39	P-400
Lightning	P-38	P-322
Boston	A-20	DB-7
Liberator	B-24	LB-30
Ventura	B-34	Model 37
Vengeance	A-31	V-72
Buffalo	F2A-2 (Navy)	B-399

This particular designation problem disappeared with the production of Lend-Lease aircraft after that programme was initiated, but the aircraft requisitioned from the earlier direct-purchase contracts retained their non-standard designations and British serial numbers. Under Lend-Lease, the aircraft were paid for with American funds, even when no equivalent model was being developed for the U.S.

Lend-Lease aircraft destined for the R.A.F., as distinguished from those for the Fleet Air Arm, were ordered through Army Air Corps procurement channels and had to be given standard Air Corps designations and serial numbers. However, the Lend-Lease types similar to U.S. models were still fitted in some cases with British-specified equipment. Later, Douglas and Boeing-built DB-7 Bostons became A-20Cs to distinguish them from the considerably different A-20As built for the Army. When these were diverted to U.S. service they retained the British colouring and often the British serial numbers and fin flash. They had U.S. stars painted over the roundels, sometimes on both wings in opposition to standard U.S. practice of only one star on upper and one on lower wings, and used the U.S. serial numbers for identification while still carrying the British numbers.

As mentioned under item (2) above, aircraft were frequently tested by the Army under an "Experimental Plane" number. This system had its origin at McCook Field in 1917 when aeroplanes used in test work were given the letter "P" followd by a sequential number for individual aeroplane identification. This came to mean "Plane (P) number —". Sometimes experimental status was indicated by adding an X-prefix to the P after the 1924 change. These P-numbers were also applied to non-army aeroplanes tested at McCook Field and later at Wright Field.

This system ended in April, 1930, at P-599. A new system was then set up in 1931 for aeroplanes owned by their manufacturers but tested by the Army on Bailment Contracts, either in civil or military markings. Two or three prefix letters were used: X-for-Experimental, B-for-Bomber, PT-for-Primary Trainer, etc. The series started at XP-900 for the Detroit-Lockheed adaptation of the civil "Altair" design that became the YP-24 and ended with the Vought V-143 designated XP-948 in 1936. In between were such designs as the Ford trimotor bomber XB-906, the Boeing XP-936 that became the P-26, and the XPT-943 that was not purchased by the Army but which led to the PT-13.

During World War II and early post-war years, the Project numbers were replaced by MX-prefixes and new numbers. Usually the aeroplanes that resulted from those studies were given standard designations, but in some cases "Flying Mock-up" aircraft used the MX numbers, as in the case of the Northrop MX-324 that led to the turbine-powered XP-79B ramming interceptor. These in turn were replaced by "weapon system" numbers which were now used for most combat aircraft developed for the USAF, or by "support system" numbers for other types including trainers and transports.

POPULAR DESIGNATIONS

While Army and USAF aircraft have been officially designated by letters and numbers since 1920, popular names have been applied either officially or unofficially to certain general series for almost the same length of time. Early examples are the Sperry M-1 Messenger of 1922 and the internationally famous Curtiss Hawk and Falcon series that began in 1925. The Curtiss names resulted from the manufacturer's promotion of the designs separate from their military designations while the Messenger was merely the spelling-out of the M-for-Messenger designation which became so widely used in official circles that a directive had to be issued in 1924 to have the aeroplane called by the proper numerical designation.

Other manufacturers adopted names for some of their designs and used them in their advertising but they did not catch the public fancy. Examples are the Huff-Daland/Keystone Cyclops and Panther bombers. Curtiss was successful again in 1932 with the XP-31 Swift and the A-8/A-12 Shrike and Boeing's B-17 Flying Fortress of 1935 was the only other name of the 1930s to win popular favour.

Aircraft built in the U.S. for Britain from 1938 on became widely known by their official British name-type designations, especially when equivalent

models were not in service with the U.S. Army under standard designations. Shortly before U.S. entry into the war, the government encouraged the use of type names rather than numbers as a security measure. It was felt that such generalizations as Lightning for all Lockheed P-38s would do for general public information and discussion and screen the current production and developmental stages of the design from those who had no need to know it.

In cases where the manufacturer did not choose a name of his own, one was supplied by the Army. Wherever possible, the established British names for American-built aeroplanes were applied retroactively to the corresponding U.S. Army and Navy models. This scheme was accepted oniy half-heartedly by the cognizant portion of the public and the aviation press and was almost useless in the services and industry where exact definitions were essential. As a result, official press releases used the correct designations more and more toward the end of the War.

The dual use of standard designations and "popular" given names continued after World War II to the present with official sanction but by no means the original emphasis. Application is usually limited to such generalized non-technical areas as newspaper accounts involving aeroplanes of the particular model or to air-show commentaries.

MISSILE DESIGNATING SYSTEMS

While this book is not concerned with missiles, it is necessary to record that some of the earlier operational missiles on the Air Force inventory were originally given standard aircraft designations and therefore appear in any complete listing of Army/Air Force aeroplanes by designation.

The initial "aeroplane-type" missiles fitted into the aeroplane designating system according to their functions. The Northrop Snark and Bell Rascal, launched from the air against ground targets, were given the bomber designations of B-62 and B-63. The Martin Matador, also directed toward ground targets but launched from the ground, was given the bomber designation of B-61. The Bomarc (the name is a composite derived from Boeing and Michigan Aeronautical Research Center), an anti-aircraft ground-launched interceptor missile, was given the fighter designation F-99. The air-launched Hughes Falcon interceptor missile was likewise designated as a fighter, the F-98. All of these missiles were subsequently withdrawn from the standard aircraft designating system but retained the original numbers, which were not replaced. The prefixes were revised to reflect more accurately the true characteristics of the missile as follows:

Missile	Original Designation	Revised Designation	Function
Bomarc	F-99	IM-99	Interceptor missile
Matador, Mace	B-61, 67	TM-61, 67	Tactical missile
Snark	B-62	SM-62	Strategic missile
Rascal	B-63	GAM-63	Guided airborne missile
Falcon	F-98	GAR-1	Guided air rocket

25

Confusion continued, however, because newer missiles in the TM, SM and GAM series took numbers from the original bomber series. A list of these will be found in the designation index at the end of this book.

A completely new system of missile designation was introduced in 1963, the weapons of all services being integrated in this common series of numbers. The new system comprised three basic letters indicating, in order, the launch environment, the mission and the vehicle type. This letter group was followed by a number, starting from 1 and continuing in sequence for each of the three vehicle types. A suffix letter could be applied to the designation indicating special status, and two-letter groups were assigned to all missile manufacturers, to be applied after the designation.

In the standard missile designating system, as applied in 1987, the launch environment symbols were:

A	Air-launched	L	Silo Launched
B	Multiple	M	Mobile
C	Coffin	P	Soft Pad
F	Individual	R	Ship
G	Runway	U	Underwater Attack
H	Silo Stored		

The mission symbols were:

D	Decoy	Q	Drone
E	Special Electronic	T	Training
G	Surface Attack	U	Underwater Attack
I	Intercept-Aerial	W	Weather

Vehicle type symbols were:

M	Guided missile/Drone	R	Rocket
N	Probe		

The status prefix letters used for missiles were:

C	Captive	X	Experimental
D	Dummy	Y	Prototype
J	Special test, temporary	Z	Planning
M	Maintenance		
N	Special test, permanent		

Manufacturers' code letters adopted for use on missiles were:

Symbol	Manufacturer	Address
AB	Army Ballistic Missile Agency	Redstone Arsenal, Ala.
AJ	Aerojet	Sacramento, Calif.
AL	Atlantic Research Corp.	Alexandria, Va.
BC	Bell Aerosystems Co.	Buffalo, N.Y.
BD	Bridgeport Brass	Riverside, Calif.
BH	Beech Aircraft Corp.	Wichita, Kans.
BO	Boeing Co.	Seattle, Wash.
BP	Bureau of Naval Weapons	Washington, D.C.
BX	Bendix Corp.	Detroit, Mich.
BY	Bendix Corp.	Michawaha, Ind.
CM	Chrysler Missile Div.	Detroit, Mich.

Symbol	Manufacturer	Address
CN	Chrysler Space Div.	New Orleans, La.
CO	General Dynamics/Convair	San Diego, Calif.
CP	General Dynamics/Pomona	Pomona, Calif.
CV	Chance Vought Corp.	Dallas, Tex.
DO	Douglas Aircraft Co., Inc.	Santa Monica, Calif.
FA	Fairchild Stratos Corp.	Hagerstown, Md.
FN	Ford Motor Co. Aeronutronic Div.	Newport Beach, Calif.
FS	Firestone Tire & Rubber Co.	Los Angeles, Calif.
GO	Goodyear Aircraft	Akron, Ohio.
GP	General Electric	Philadelphia, Penn.
GT	Grand Central Aircraft Co.	Tucson, Ariz.
HA	Hughes Aircraft Co.	Culver City, Calif.
HU	Hughes Tool Co.	Culver City, Calif.
KA	Kaman Aircraft Corp.	Bloomfield, Conn.
LD	Lockheed Missiles & Space Co.	Sunnyvale, Calif.
MA	Martin Co.	Baltimore, Md.
MC	McDonnell Aircraft Corp.	St. Louis, Mo.
MD	Martin Co.	Denver, Col.
MF	Martin Co.	Orlando, Fla.
MG	Martin Co.	Marietta, Ga.
MP	Honeywell	Hopkins, Minn.
MS	Motorola	Scottsdale, Ariz.
MX	Maxson Electronics Corp.	Great River, L.I., N.Y.
NA	North American Aviation, Inc.	Inglewood, Calif.
NH	North American Aviation, Inc.	Columbus, Ohio.
NL	Norris Thermador	Los Angeles, Calif.
NV	Northrop Ventura	Van Nuys, Calif.
PP	Philco	Philadelphia, Penn.
RL	Raytheon	Lexington, Mass.
RW	Raytheon	Waltham, Mass.
RY	Ryan Aeronautical Co.	San Diego, Calif.
ST	Space Technology Lab.	Redondo Beach, Calif.
SU	Sperry Utah Engineering Laboratories	Salt Lake City, Utah
TH	Thiokol Chemical Corp.	Bristol, Penn.
TX	Texas Instruments, Inc.	Dallas, Tex.
WE	Western Electric Co.	New York, N.Y.

EXTERNAL STORES DESIGNATING SYSTEM

In addition to guided missiles, which have their own designating system as set out above, the modern military aircraft is able to carry a wide variety of other stores externally or in weapons bays. The Department of Defense has developed a series of unit designations for these stores, made up of a two-letter indicator preceding a "U" (for unit) and followed by a sequence number, as in aircraft and missile designations. Several of these unit designations are in common use and are to be found in the text of this volume, in descriptions of the post-World War II aircraft types; others will probably be encountered only in official handbooks or close encounters with full-size aircraft at air displays, etc., but the full list of item identifiers is given here for the sake of completeness:

BB	Explosive Items	LK	Ammunition Links
BD	Simulated Bombs	LM	Ground-Based Launchers
BL	Bombs & Mines	LU	Illumination Units
BR	Bomb Racks & Shackles	MA	Miscellaneous Armament Items
BS	Munition Stabilizing & Retarding Devices	MD	Miscellaneous Simulated Munitions
CB	End Item Cluster Bombs	MH	Munitions Handling Equipment
CC	Actuator Cartridges	MJ	Munitions Countermeasures
CD	Clustered Munitions (not End Items)	ML	Miscellaneous Munitions
		MT	Mounts
CN	Miscellaneous Containers	PA	Munition Dispensing Devices, External
DS	Target Detecting Devices		
FM	Munitions Fuzes	PD	Leaflet Dispensers
FS	Munitions Fuze Safety-Arming Devices	PG	Ammunition
		PW	Internal Dispensers
FZ	Fuze-Related Items	RD	Dummy Rockets
GA	Aircraft Guns	RL	Rockets
GB	Guided Bombs	SA	Gun-Bomb-Rocket Sights
GF	Gun Related Items	SU	Stores Suspension & Release Items
GP	Podded Guns		
GU	Miscellaneous Guns	TM	Miscellaneous Tanks
KA	Munitions Clustering Hardware	TT	Test Items
KM	Kits	WD	Warheads
LA	Aircraft Installed Launches	WT	Training Warheads

A separate series of designations for "iron" bombs uses simple mark numbers, usually rendered as "MK" and followed by a series number—e.g., MK-84, for a 2,000 lb. bomb, MK-117 for a 750 lb. bomb. These same bombs can figure in external stores unit designations. For example, a MK-84 fitted with a KMU-353 acquires an electro-optical guidance capability and is then designated GBU-8 as a homing bomb. The same iron bomb with a KMU-351 becomes a laser-guided bomb (LGB) designated the GBU-10.

Yet another series of designations applies to external and internal electronics equipment, some of which in the form of pods becomes a prominent feature on contemporary military aircraft. This equipment carries an AN/ALQ (often rendered simply as ALQ) series number.

SERIAL NUMBERS

From 1909 onwards, U.S. Army aeroplanes were assigned serial numbers (s/ns) in sequence of purchase until the end of U.S. Fiscal Year 1921 (June 30, 1921). The highest number reached was 68592, plus a special block of 1919-1921 experimental procurements in the 94022/94112 range.

In 1918 and into the early 1920s, U.S. Army aeropanes usually, but not always, carried prefix letters to the serial numbers on their fuselages and/or rudders: S.C. for Signal Corps, A.S. for Air Service, and after 1926 and into 1941, A.C. for Air Corps. In a few cases, 1918 and 1919 aeroplanes were seen with S.C. prefixes on the rudder and A.S. prefixes on the fuselage. By 1925, when the size of the fuselage s/n was standardized at 4 inches, the use of the appropriate prefixes was consistent.

Starting in July, 1921 (the beginning of the U.S. Fiscal Year 1922), a new system was adopted based on procurement within each Fiscal Year. Aeroplane 22-1 was the first procured in that year; for the first aeroplane procured in FY 1923, the number was 23-1, and so on. This system is still in use. The highest number ever assigned in one year was 42-110188, to a Convair B-24J-140.

It should be emphasized that the s/n reflected the Fiscal Year in which the order for the aeroplane was placed, not the year in which it was completed. For example, the XB-19 was ordered in FY 1938 but did not fly until June of Calendar Year 1941, the very end of FY 1941. Conversely, the North American NA-68s drafted by the Army in November, 1940, as P-64s, were given FY 1941 s/ns.

Through the 1920s, the size of the s/n printed on the side of the aeroplane became smaller and was gradually combined with the words U.S. ARMY and the make and model designation of the aeroplane. This block of data was standardized in a spot on the left side of the fuselage near the cockpit in 1932 and has remained there to this day.

In January 1942, the s/n was again applied in large figures, this time to each side of the vertical tail with a minimum height of 8 inches. There were minor variations and some relocations to the fuselage on small-tail aeroplanes and those uncamouflaged types that retained rudder stripes to May 15, 1942. For the tail application, which came to be called the "tail number", the first digit of the Fiscal Year was removed and the dash deleted so that, for example, s/n 41-1234 appeared as 11234. No conflict with a later aeroplane 51-1234 was anticipated; military aeroplanes were not expected to last 10 years at that time. When this problem did arise in the 1950s, it was taken care of by adding an "O" prefix to the tail number of those aeroplanes over 10 years old, e.g. O-11234. This was chosen to indicate "over ten", not "obsolete" as frequently suggested in subsequent references. Some T-33s, the oldest aeroplanes in the inventory in 1988, had nearly completed four full

The first aeroplane to carry a serial number incorporating an indication of the Fiscal Year of procurement was this Engineering Division/Sperry Messenger converted to radio-controlled MAT (Messenger Aerial torpedo). Marking on the fuselage is the insignia of the 11th Bomb Group (*McCook Field photo*).

Army serial number (s/n) applications from January 1942. Left, the full s/n with service name and model designation on left side of nose. Right, shortened form with the "4" of "41" (the Fiscal Year indication) and dash deleted for "Tail Number".

decades of service, but no changes had been made to the tail number since the first decade. Upgrade programmes would put some KC-135s into a sixth decade of service, past the year 2000.

U.S. Army (later U.S. Air Force) aeroplanes used the last four digits of the s/n or tail number as a radio call sign, so those with short s/ns had them built up to a minimum of four digits, on the tail only, by adding zeros. The tail number of XB-29 s/n 41-2 thus became 1002. The minimum was increased to five digits in 1958, so B-52H s/n 60-8 was given the tail number 00008. Since the Vietnam conflict, the tail number has been reduced to the last five digits of the s/n, so the full aeroplane s/n cannot always be determined from the tail number. On camouflaged USAF aeroplanes it became customary to use the last three digits of the five-digit tail number as an individual identification number, with these three digits appearing in large figures. These were used in conjunction with a two-letter unit identification. The preceding two digits of the s/n and the prefix letters AF appeared in smaller figures—usually black.

The s/n is no longer an accurate indicator of the total number of aeroplanes procured or even ordered in any fiscal year. From 1958 to 1967, various Air Force missiles, including both emplaced types like the LGM-30 Minuteman and the airborne types like the AIM-9 Sidewinder and the AGM-28 Hound Dog, were procured with aeroplane serial numbers. Also, in FY 1971, the Army began a new serial series, which started at 20000 and has continued consecutively since then, without reference to the Fiscal Year of purchase. For the Fiscal Years 1967 to 1970, the Army had used the system of a digit prefix for the year, but began its serials at 15000 each year; frequently, however, the year prefix was omitted from the presentation of the serial on the tail or rear fuselage of the aircraft, leading to apparent duplication of serials on different aircraft.

In recent years, the assignment of USAF serial numbers has not always been in strict or complete sequence. The s/ns 62-6000 and 72-7000 for the two "Air Force One" VC-137Cs would indicate that they were ordered 10 years apart, when actually the difference was only seven years. Similarly, two Presidential VC-25As ordered simultaneously in FY 1986 were assigned s/ns 86-8800 and 86-8900 and then, to allow better distinction of the radio call signs, had these numbers changed to 82-8000 and 92-9000!

Since FY 1987, assured funding for certain long-range production programmes has made it possible to assign s/ns for several years ahead, as for example the allocation in FY 1987 for F-16A, B, C and D procurements with FY s/ns for all years from 1987 through 1993.

When some existing civil aircraft have been acquired by USAF, either by purchase or confiscation, s/ns have frequently been assigned out of sequence. In some cases, the numbers have deliberately matched the former civil registration numbers, as for the C-22B 83-4610 having been civil Boeing 727-35 N4610 purchased from National Air Lines.

In this book, a range of serial numbers such as 42-43518 through 42-43617 inclusive, is presented as 42-43518/43617. Zeros have also been added, where appropriate, so that the form in which the s/n appeared on aircraft tails can more easily be appreciated.

NATIONAL GUARD AND AIR NATIONAL GUARD

In Fiscal Year 1926 the National Guard, an auxiliary of the U.S. Army, adopted a separate serialization system similar to the Army's but prefixed by the letters N.G. This system was abandoned after reaching only N.G.26-14. Since National Guard aeroplanes were procured through Army channels, the s/ns for aeroplanes destined for the Guard were assigned in sequence with regular Army procurements but were prefixed with N.G. instead of A.C. However, instead of the letters U.S. ARMY on the lower wing surfaces, National Guard aeroplanes carried the letters N.G. beneath the left wing and the abbreviation of the particular state to which the Guard unit belonged beneath the right wing. This practice continued until the United States entered World War II.

After the war, National Guard air units were reactivated as such, many with their prewar squadron numbers and insignia. Identification was rather inconsistent, some deleting the established "Buzz Numbers" on the fuselage in favour of the abbreviation of the state plus the letters N.G. Others used the letters NG as prefixes to the last three digits of the s/n, as used in the "Buzz Number".

In some cases where the fuselage numbers were not used, the last three digits of the s/n, plus the prefix NG, were applied to the upper right and lower left wing. When the Air National Guard took over the former National Guard air units in 1947, the letters ANG were used in place of NG. The use of the ANG prefix and the last three digits of the s/n continued into the 'sixties. To the time this book was prepared, some ANG aeroplanes carry a mix of USAF and ANG lettering on their fuselages.

AIRCRAFT COLOURING
AND MARKINGS

THROUGHOUT the last fifty years, the colouring and markings applied to U.S. military aircraft have changed with such frequency that an informed observer can estimate the date of an old aeroplane photograph quite closely by studying the way the machine is painted. Since this book is concerned primarily with the technical development of the aeroplanes themselves, the markings, which in all their detail form a separate sub-category of aviation history, are described here only in their fundamental applications so that the reader can derive more than mere technical detail from the photographs.

The usefulness of photographs as a guide to colouring will be increased if certain photographic characteristics are first understood. Well into the late 1920s, most photographs were taken on orthochromatic film. The colour sensitivity of this type was such that the prints showed red in a dark shade, yellow fairly dark, and blue as quite light. When panchromatic film came into use in the 1930s, these renderings were reversed—the blue showed up dark, red was lightened, and sometimes the yellow appeared almost white, especially if a yellow filter were used. A check of the known colour arrangement of the national marking makes it possible to determine the type of film used for any photograph being studied.

STANDARD COLOURING

At first, there was no standard colouring for military aircraft of the U.S. or any other nation. All aeroplanes were "aeroplane colour", usually white

Boeing P-12B in typical colours of the 1927–31 period, with type designation and serial number in white, squadron marking and machine number on fuselage. Taken on ortho-chromatic film, this picture shows the vertical blue rudder stripe lighter than the horizontal red stripes (*Paul Laudan*).

32

Vultee BT-13As in 1940 trainer finish with blue fuselage and yellow wings. The "M" in yellow on the fuselage indicates Moffett Field (*Peter M. Bowers*).

fabric shaded to a light buff by several coats of varnish. World War I brought about the application of protective colouring to the warplanes of 1916, but this did not concern the U.S. Army until 1918, when the upper surfaces of otherwise clear-doped machines were painted in khaki brown or O.D. (olive drab). The first American-built DH-4s were delivered to France with this scheme. By late 1918, the colouring had changed to all-over olive drab, even for trainers, and this was retained to 1927. Combat aircraft obtained from the Allies in 1918 were painted in the standard camouflage patterns of those countries, khaki brown for Britain, patches of green and brown for France and Italy, and all with clear-doped under-surfaces. Most trainers obtained from France were clear-doped.

A major change took place in 1927, when wing and tail surfaces were painted chrome yellow for high visibility, the rest remaining O.D. In 1928, some trainers and reserve observation planes had the fuselage painted a light blue. By 1936, this blue had replaced the O.D. on all painted machines. The introduction of the all-metal Ford trimotor to Army service in 1929 resulted in a new colour scheme, natural metal finish. Most other all-metal models continued to use the two-colour paint for several years. Douglas transports and such combat types as Seversky P-35, Curtiss P-36 and Northrop A-17A appeared in natural metal in 1937.

By 1939, natural metal or silver-doped fabric was officially established as the standard colour for tactical aeroplanes. For subsequent production, only light transports, amphibians, and primary and basic trainers were to be painted blue and yellow. However, some existing blue-and-yellow tactical models retained their original colouring into World War II.

The repainting of some older blue-and-yellow aeroplanes with silver in 1940 and 1941 led to the belief that the change of colour was to distinguish them as obsolete. In spite of their obvious obsolescence, such models as the O-38B and P-12E of 1932, then serving in National Guard units and Army flying schools, were still considered tactical aeroplanes and were therefore repainted to conform to tactical aeroplane standards.

After the start of World War II, U.S. Army aircraft reverted to camou-flage, O.D. for top and side surfaces and grey undersurfaces, first applied to the Curtiss P-40 in 1940. Another 1940 change was the application of all-over silver paint to obsolescent types still in service. For all-metal types, it was far easier to spray on silver paint then to strip off the original blue and yellow. All new trainers were delivered in silver from the end of 1941, and many older ones were repainted.

The O.D. and grey remained the standard U.S. Army "warpaint" to 1944, when it was abandoned for all but a few liaison types. Commanders then had the option of stripping the warpaint from their machines when it became shabby or restoring it, whichever was easier. Natural metal has now been superceded as the favoured finish for aircraft in virtually all categories.

Vietnam operations prompted the re-adoption of camouflage for most operational types. The standard scheme, which became known as SEA (South-East Asia) camouflage, consisted of two shades of green and one of tan for the top and side surfaces, and light grey undersides. Special applications used white or black undersurfaces and sometimes black on each side of the fin, and there were many variations adopted in the field for special purposes.

After the end of the Vietnam war, the SEA scheme remained in use for most USAF combat aircraft, but the light grey undersurfaces gave way to a "wrap-round" camouflage with the tan and greens continued right round the aircraft. Subsequently, a dark grey was introduced in place of the tan, producing the "European One" camouflage, often known as "lizard". This also was applied as a wrap-around, and was applied to most combat types and to transports—the bombers having black undersides. By the mid 'eighties, European One had given way, on the fighter force, to various interpretations of a two-tone grey scheme known as "Egyptian One," and several other finishes were adopted for various categories of aircraft, as for example the overall black of the U-2R, TR-1 and SR-71, and charcoal grey for the upper surfaces and sides of the KC-10 and KC-135 tankers.

SPECIAL COLOURING SCHEMES

Specialized uses of aircraft have resulted in special colouring. The first of these to appear was the application of French World War I type camouflage in varied water colours to machines engaged in the various "War Games" of the 1930s. When the games were over, the camouflage was washed off if rain hadn't already done the job.

Conversion of obsolete machines to target drones just before World War II produced aeroplanes with red fuselages and tails and silver wings, soon changed to all-red, and is retained today for built-for-the-purpose target drones and for such converted service types as QF-80F. In 1944, the Bell P-63s used as manned targets for frangible machine gun bullets were painted all orange, and international orange over-all was standard colouring for drones in 1971.

The introduction of the P-70 night fighter and other night intruder types resulted in an overall matt black finish, changed to glossy black for

The fuselage of this Douglas C-124A is painted silver instead of being left in natural metal, with white top only over crew compartment. The diagonal blue band with white stars was used on aircraft of Strategic Air Command. Insignia-red "Arctic" markings are applied to outer wing panels and tail, but the original all-red marking was compromised by a subsequent directive that fabric-covered surfaces be left silver (*USAF photo*).

the P-70s and P-61s of 1944. This was retained by the night flying F-82s in Korea and Martin B-57B Canberras of the 1950s. Silver B-29s used for night bombing had only their undersurfaces painted glossy black.

For desert operations, some camouflaged machines used a sand-colouring of light buff (no longer used) and all white was adopted as Arctic camouflage (used to a limited extent on liaison types to date). All-white finish was also used on ambulance aeroplanes from World War I to 1936. Overall yellow has been used on some rescue helicopters since the end of World War II and a few special test or research machines are painted overall with orange or fluorescent "day-glo" paint for easy identification.

Smaller areas of colour are often used to designate special use of an otherwise standard machine. The first of these, adopted just before World War II and still in use, is the "Arctic operations" colouring, in which the wings from the inboard end of the ailerons to the tips and the entire empennage are painted insignia red for visibility against the snow. This is sometimes done on machines otherwise painted all-white in Arctic camouflage! A variation of this from 1958 has been "conspicuity colouring" as a protection against mid-air collision on those occasions when the pilots can see other traffic. This consists of flourescent "day-glo" red-orange paint on nose, wingtips and as a wide band around the rear fuselage that usually includes the forward portion of the fixed vertical tail surfaces of all but combat types. The standard for application of Arctic and conspicuity markings in 1971 was the first 72 inches of the nose, the first 72 inches inboard from each wingtip, and the entire surface of the vertical fin and the horizontal stabilizer.

Instrument trainers, starting in World War II, were painted with insignia red cowlings and vertical tails and had wide 45-degree red stripes on the wings in the form of a chevron to warn nearby aircraft that the pilot was "under the hood" and couldn't see where he was going. From the end of World War II,

This 1970 picture shows Vought A-7s in tan and two-green camouflage, with light grey undersides. The fin markings comprise a two-letter indicator of the unit, the "last three" of the serial number in white, and "AF" and the first two digits of the serial number in black. Unit crests and checkerboard markings are also carried.

air-sea rescue craft had yellow wing-tips and a wide yellow band around the aft fuselage, set off by black outlines. This was often used in conjunction with Arctic or conspicuity colouring.

From 1946 to its dissolution, the all-weather flying centre used a variation of the instrument colouring by adding a horizontal yellow chevron to the red tail, adding red to wingtips, and outlining the red tips and nose with yellow stripe.

During World War II, target tugs had moveable control surfaces, nose and engine cowls painted chrome yellow. The present target tug colouring is orange for the vertical tail and the top half of the fuselage. White has been used in two different applications since the early 1950s—on the top of the fuselage of passenger-carrying "C" types to reflect sunlight and reduce cabin temperatures and on the entire undersurfaces of "B" types carrying thermonuclear weapons as a protection against blast radiation; in the latter case, no national markings were applied over the white finish.

A special and highly conspicuous marking used by the Allies during the Normandy invasion in June 1944, was called "Invasion Stripes". Three broad bands of white and two of black were painted entirely around the rear fuselage and chordwise around the wings. For other airborne assaults after these D-Day landings in France, the striping was removed from the top of the wing and fuselage or was painted over. Some aeroplanes and gliders retained their lower-half striping into 1945.

Since the end of World War II, some aeroplane types have been distinguished by special over-all solid colouring applied to that model or to related types alone, such as the early production Lockheed P-80s and the Republic XP-84 and North American XP-86 prototypes. This was a special aerodynamic sealer, not a distinguishing colour as such, but was so difficult to retain on the leading edges of high-speed fighters that it was soon deleted.

Over-all light grey was adopted as standard colouring for the Convair F-102 and F-106 models when they appeared.

Since the late 1950s, over-all light grey has been used as a corrosion-prevention measure on all types of aeroplane and was used as camouflage for such models as the Cessna O-1 and O-2 and the North American OV-10 during the Vietnam war. The over-all white formerly used for ambulance planes became standard colouring for Northrop T-38s and the Boeing E-3 and E-4 series. KC-10 and KC-135 tankers, originally in a combination of white tops and corrosion-prevention grey, gradually adopted a drab charcoal for their upper surfaces and white undersides, while the B-1B bombers were near-black overall. Yet further special schemes were to be seen on the EF-111A Ravens, in shades of pale blue and grey, copied on the EC-130H Hercules.

NATIONAL MARKINGS

The first form of a national insignia applied to U.S. Army aircraft was a red five-pointed star adopted during the Mexican Border incidents of 1916. This was not standardized, and while usually applied to the rudder, was sometimes used on the fuselage or under the wings. The first "official" marking was adopted for both services on May 17, 1917, and consisted of a white five-pointed star against a circular blue field with a red centre circle tangent to the inner projection of the points of the star. In World War I and to the mid-1920s, this blue was a fairly light shade. The present "insignia blue" that came into gradual use in the 1920s is so dark as to be almost black.

The original insignia application was to the full chord of the wing and inboard of the ailerons. It was not used on the fuselage. The rudder was striped in the British/French manner with the red at the trailing edge, then white, and blue at the leading edge. When the star marking began to appear on American trainers in France late in 1917, the Allies noted that the white star resembled a white-bordered German cross at a distance. As a result, the U.S. was requested to adopt a tricolour circle marking (also called "Cocarde" and "Roundel") similar to the other Allies, and responded by taking the former Imperial Russian circle with red on the

A Waco CG-4A glider with hastily-applied "Invasion Stripes", after landing in a Normandy pasture, June 6, 1944 (*Crown copyright*).

A B-17G-15-BO of the 8th Air Force, thoroughly representative of the bombers and fighters operating from England in 1944. In O.D. and grey camouflage, it has the individual aeroplane name "Chow Hound", an appropriate cartoon of a Disney-type dog, and nine bombing mission symbols on the nose. The triangle-A on the fin identifies the 91st Bomb Group and the red fin, rudder and horizontal stabilizer identify the 1st Combat Wing. The British-style letters LG on the fuselage identify the 322nd Bomb Squadron and the letter R on the fuselage and fin identify the individual aeroplane within the group (*USAAF photo*).

outside, blue and a white centre. (This virtually amounted to an exchange, as the Bolshevik Russians adopted the old U.S. Red Star.) The tail striping was reversed to put the blue at the trailing edge.

This marking remained official to August 1919, when the star and the original tail stripes were restored, but was not completely replaced until the early 1920s. On early deliveries of French aircraft to the A.E.F., the manufacturers assumed that the U.S. tailstripes should match the colour sequence of the circles, and painted the rudders in the order of red at the rear, then blue and then white, but this arrangement was short-lived. In the U.S., many 1917-built aircraft retained the stars throughout 1918 while others were painted over. It was not unusual to see both markings on a machine that had been fitted with a replacement wing.

In November 1926 the Army adopted a new form of tail striping proposed by Chief Engineer C. N. Montieth of the Boeing Airplane Company. This retained the original vertical blue but substituted the 13 alternating red and white horizontal stripes of the American Flag for the other vertical stripes. This was used by all Army planes until February 1941, when it was deleted from camouflaged types, and for all others until May 15, 1942, when it was abolished completely.

The star marking underwent changes of location in March 1941. For camouflaged types, one was deleted from the upper right and lower left wings while one was added to each side of the fuselage. Non-camouflaged types retained stars on both wings only until one wing star and fuselage stars were standardized for all types in 1943.

The star markings underwent basic changes as a result of World War II. On May 15, 1942, the red centre was removed because of resemblance to the Japanese insignia. In July 1943, the basic marking was modified by the addition of a white rectangle on each side of the blue field, with the whole surrounded by a red border. This use of red again brought the possibility of confusion with Japanese colours, so the red border was replaced by blue in September 1943. The last change to the national marking took place in January 1947, when red was again added in the form of a red stripe down the centre of the long dimension of the white rectangles.

Some camouflaged aircraft operating in Vietnam, and subsequently all camouflaged USAF aircraft, used national markings reduced to a basic diameter of 15 inches. On some camouflaged aircraft, the surrounding blue border was deleted. Since Vietnam, some U.S. Army aircraft have operated with no national markings at all.

The modification of national insignia to reduce its visibility began in World War I when white was removed from British night fighter markings. Late in 1942, the USAAF reduced the visibility of national markings on aircraft operating in the European Theatre by overpainting the white star (and the bars when adopted in 1943) with grey. This practice died out early in 1944, soon after the deletion of camouflage on most combat types.

Reduced visibility of national insignia was again practiced by the USAF in the Vietnam era, with a considerable reduction in the size of the standard marking or, in some cases, its deletion altogether. Starting in the early 'eighties, numerous "low visibility" variations of the standard "Stars and Bars" insignia were applied to camouflaged aircraft. In most cases, the red and white were deleted and the outline only of the insignia was applied solely in black or light grey, depending on the camouflage background, and in some cases using "broken" lines to give a stencil effect, as shown in accompanying photographs.

The Boeing YP-12K displaying the "Wright Field Arrow" used from 1932 to 1941. Taken on panchromatic film – compare with P-12B on page 32 (*Peter M. Bowers*).

The Waco 9, tested in commercial colours, with McCook Field number XP447 and Army serial A.C.26-206. *(McCook Field photo)*

SPECIAL MARKINGS

This fascinating subject could fill an entire book, but can be dealt with only briefly here. The first marking of any kind applied to U.S. Army aircraft was the Signal Corps emblem, applied to the outer sides of the twin rudders of the first Army aeroplane. When it became necessary to distinguish between individual aircraft by 1914, the serial number of the machine was painted on the rudder. By 1915, it was applied in large block figures to each side of the fuselage.

During World War I, the large serial number on the fuselage was generally used for identification of most training planes, but some fields reduced the size of the serial and applied larger "field numbers" of their own. Combat types in France deleted the fuselage serials and were numbered sequentially within the squadrons by large numbers on wing and fuselage. Post-World War I training aeroplanes followed this practice through to World War II, and combat types carried it into the middle 1920s.

The expanded training programme of World War II brought a change in trainer numbering. The particular training base was identified by a letter on the fuselage which was followed by the number of the aircraft at that base. In the late 1920s, tactical types began to be numbered within their respective groups, each made up of several squadrons, by a number on the vertical fin. This was changed to two letter-and-number systems, the first used in 1937/39 and a revised one from 1940 to the end of 1941.

For the first system, the group type and number were combined with the aeroplane number in the group on the vertical fin, on the upper left wing, and the lower left wing ahead of or behind the word ARMY. The first letter identified the type of group, as B-for-Bomber, P-for-Pursuit, etc., while the second letter identified the specific group. Determining the group number in the field took a little counting at times, since the number corresponded to the

40

position of the letter in the alphabet. The 20th Pursuit Group was identified by the letters PT, the T being the 20th letter of the alphabet. In 1940, the system was revised to identify the group by its actual number, as 56P for the 56th Pursuit Group. During World War II, this specific group marking was eliminated.

Aircraft in the European theatre of operations used the British system of two letters on the fuselage for the group and a single following letter to identify the individual machine. This was supplemented by a great array of individual group colours and devices on vertical tails through World War II to the present.

At the end of World War II, a new system was adopted for Fighter, Bomber, Transport, Trainer and Liaison types, called "Buzz numbers". These consisted of the last three digits of the serial number preceded by two letters that identified, respectively, the type and model of aircraft—CS-593 for the YC-97A 55-59593, for example. When the last three digits were matched by another machine of the same model, a suffix letter A was added. This system gradually fell into disuse for all types but fighters and some trainers, and was abandoned in the 'sixties.

The "type" letters used for these buzz numbers comprised: A, Attack; B, Bomber; C, Cargo; F, Photographic (until 1948); F, Fighter (after 1948); G, Glider; L, Liaison; O, Observation; P, fighter (until 1948); Q, Drone; and T, Trainer. For a short time after buzz numbers were first introduced, BT and PT were used as the type designators for the BT-13 and PT-13 trainers, respectively. Within each of these types, the letters indicating specific models were re-allocated to new types as the older types were withdrawn from service.

Of course, there were occasional misapplications, as for example TF instead of FT on a P-80C, TC instead of CD on a C-66D, and VC on a VC-47B. There were also unofficial "Buzz Letters" used, as XB on the Martin

Two Curtiss P-36As illustrate the group identification systems used from 1937 through 1941. At left, the letter T, 20th letter in the alphabet, identifies the 20th Pursuit (P) Group (*Gordon S. Williams*). At right, the revised system of 1940 identifies the group by its actual number (*Peter M. Bowers*).

XB-51, and the YF used by North American on the YF-86D, YF-93A, and YF-100A, plus NF on some Lockheed NF-104As.

Prefixes other than B and P were used for some special-purpose aeroplanes as follows:

D	Drone directors
E	Exempt from normal Technical Order compliance
L	Liaison, exclusively for LT-6s in Korea
T	Tactical types used for training
Q	Radio-controlled drones

The type and model combinations used since 1945 were as follows:

AA	A-24 (FA later)		CU	C-117
AB	A-25		CV	C-118
AC	A-26 (BC later)		CW	C-121
AD	A-31		CY	C-122
AE	XA-41		CZ	C-123
BA	B-17; B-57 later		FA	F-2
BB	XB-19; B-66 later		FB	F-5
BC	B-24, B-26 (Douglas) later		FC	F-6 (FF and RF later)
BD	B-25		FD	F-7
BE	B-26 (Martin), B-45 later (became		FE	F-9 (BA later)
	BH)		FF	F-10 (BD later)
BF	B-29		FG	F-13 (BF later)
BG	B-32; B-35 later		FH	F-15 (FK later)
BH	B-37; B-45 later (replaced BE)		FT	F-14; RF-80 later
BJ	XB-39		FA	P-38; F-24 later; F-94 later; F-5A
BK	XB-42; B-50 later			later
BL	XB-44		FB	P-39; F-101 later
BM	B-36		FC	P-40; F-102 and F-106 later
BX	B-70		FD	P-42; F-103 later
			FE	P-47; F-106 later
CA	CQ-3; C-124 later		FF	P-51
CB	C-43		FG	XP-55; F-104 later
CC	C-45		FH	XP-58; F-105 later
CD	C-46		FJ	P-59; F-84 later (became FS);
CE	C-47			F-110/F-4 later
CF	C-48		FK	P-61
CG	C-49		FL	P-63
CH	C-53		FM	P-75
CJ	C-54		FN	P-80 (FT later)
CK	C-60		FP	XP-81
CL	C-64		FQ	P-82
CM	C-69		FR	XP-83; F-107 later
CN	C-74		FS	F-84
CP	C-78; C-131 later		FT	F-80 (replaced FN)
CQ	C-82; C-119		FU	F-86
CR	C-87		FV	F-89
CS	C-97		FW	F-100
CT	XC-99		FX	YF-12A

Left, the original standard presentation of a "Buzz Number" on a B-45: B-for-Bomber, E for B-45 (later changed to H). Note the inclusion of zeroes in the tail to make a five-digit number from the Fiscal Year serial (48-7), as explained on page 30. Right, a P-80 with NG for National Guard substituted for the PN "Buzz Number" that normally identified P-80s (*Peter M. Bowers*).

GA	PG-2
GB	XPG-3
GC	CG-4
GD	XCG-10
GE	CG-13
GF	XCG-14
GG	CG-15
GH	XCG-18
GJ	XG-20
JT	YAT-37D (also YT)
LA	L-2; L-4 later
LB	L-3; L-5 later
LC	L-4 (became LA); L-16 later
LD	L-5 (became LB); L-17 later
LE	L-6; L-15 later; L-18 later
LF	L-14; L-19 later
LG	L-13; L-20 later (became UG)
LH	L-16; L-21 later (became VH)
LJ	L-17 (became LD); L-23 later
LK	L-26 (became UK)
LM	L-28
LTA	LT-6
OA	OA-9
OB	OA-10
OC	O-47
OD	YO-60
OE	PB2B-1

PA to PS: see FA to FS	
QF	H-21
QK	PQ-14
RF	RF-51
TA	T-6
TB	T-7
TC	T-11 (also MiG-15); TF-102 later
TD	T-21; T-34 later
(B)TE	BT-13; T37 later
(P)TF	PT-13; TP-51D later; T-38 later
TG	T-17; TF-104G; T-39 later
TH	T-19
TJ	PQ-8/Q-8; T-29 later
TK	PQ-14 (QK later)
TL	T-28
TP	T-29
TQ	T-31
TR	T-33
UG	L-20/U-6
UH	L-21/U-7
UK	L-26/U-9
YT	YAT-37D

When the U.S. Air Force was formed as a separate service in 1947, the U.S. Army retained a fleet of liaison and light transport types for its own air arm. Army aeroplanes were procured by USAF, however, and

43

The two Boeing VC-137Cs and others used as the Presidential aircraft from 1962 on were distinguished by the special finish shown here. Note the change of fuselage lettering from US Air Force, also accomplished on USAF aircraft assigned to overseas diplomatic missions, etc. (*Boeing photo*).

carried standard AF colouring, model designations and serial numbers. The only distinction was the application of the word ARMY in large contrasting letters to the fuselage or fin and sometimes the wing of Army-owned aircraft.

Individual squadron insignia were adopted for combat types during World War I, and are still in use for fighters, applied to each side of the fuselage. Squadrons had insignia during World War II, but they were seldom applied to the aircraft in combat zones. Squadron and flight leaders were identified starting after World War I by two vertical stripes in the squadron colour around the fuselage for the squadron leader, a forward-sloping single 45-degree stripe for "B Flight" leader and a rear-sloping stripe for "C Flight" leader. These were deleted in combat zones during World War II. In between-wars and post-World War II years, the group leader frequently used three vertical stripes, one in each squadron colour of a normal three-squadron group.

Each squadron within the group had an identifying colour, usually painted around the forward portion of the engine cowling. The post-World War II combinations of squadron, group, leader and other special markings are too involved to describe here but numerous examples will be found in the photographs. Mention should be made, however, of two uses of red fuselage striping. On multi-engine propeller types, a stripe is painted on the fuselage in the plane of the adjacent propellers as a warning to personnel on the ground. On turbojet types, a stripe is painted around the fuselage or nacelle in the plane of the turbine wheel as a warning to personnel not to stand in line with it because of the hazard of the turbine throwing blades.

After 1968, the use of unit and individual aeroplane markings was revived for camouflaged aircraft. Two letters, applied to the vertical fin in white, were used to identify the unit. The last three digits of the tail number, in white and half the height of the letters, identified the individual aeroplane. Growing use of low visibility finishes in the 'eighties, however, led to some variations in these standards.

44

Aeronca L-3B (*William T. Larkins*).

Aeronca L-3, TG-5, L-16 Grasshopper

The use of light aircraft for observation and liaison duties by the U.S. Army was a new departure in 1941. In that year, the Army obtained four examples each of the contemporary Aeronca, Piper and Taylorcraft commercial high-wing lightplanes, and ordered larger quantities of each for field evaluation in the 1941 manoeuvres.

The first Aeronca aircraft obtained by the Army in 1941 were four examples of the Model 65TC Defender, a light training monoplane in production for club and private use, with tandem seating and dual controls. They were designated YO-58 in the Air Corps observation category, and were powered by 65 h.p. Continental YO-170-3 engines. Substantially the same were the fifty O-58s. The twenty O-58As had a four-inch wider fuselage and the design was then fully modified for Army duties, with increased window area in the cabin for improved visibility. This version was designated O-58B, with a gross weight of 1,850 lb. compared with the 1,200 lb. of the original Defender.

After 335 O-58Bs had been delivered, the aircraft was re-classified (in common with the Piper and Taylorcraft types) in the Liaison category. The YO-58 and O-58 became the L-3; the twenty O-58As became L-3A and the O-58B became the L-3B, under which designation production continued until a total of 875 of this model had been built. They were followed by 490 L-3Cs in which the radio was revised and the gross weight reduced to 1,800 lb. This concluded production of the L-3 for the Army.

In common with many other commercial aircraft, a number of privately-owned Aeroncas were commandeered for military use in 1942 after the U.S. entered the War. These were designated in the L-3 series as follows:

L-3D. Eleven Aeronca 65-TF with Franklin AC-167 engines.

L-3E. Twelve Aeronca 65-TC with Continental A-65-8 engines.

L-3F. Nineteen Aeronca 65-CA Super Chief (42-78044) with side-by-side seating and Continental A-65-8 engines.

L-3G. Four Super Chiefs, as L-3F with Lycoming O-145-B1 engines.

L-3H. One Aeronca 65-TL Defender with Lycoming O-145-B1 engine.

L-3J. One Aeronca 65-TC Defender with Continental A-65-7 engine.

TG-5. A useful contribution to glider pilot training was made by Aeronca with the TG-5. This development, like that of the O-58 and L-3, exactly paralleled similar work by Piper and Taylorcraft. The TG-5 was a three-seat training glider comprising the L-3 wings, tail unit and rear fuselage with a new front fuselage. All three seats had basic flying controls and instruments, the instructor being in the new front seat and pupils in the tandem seat positions of the original L-3. A single production batch

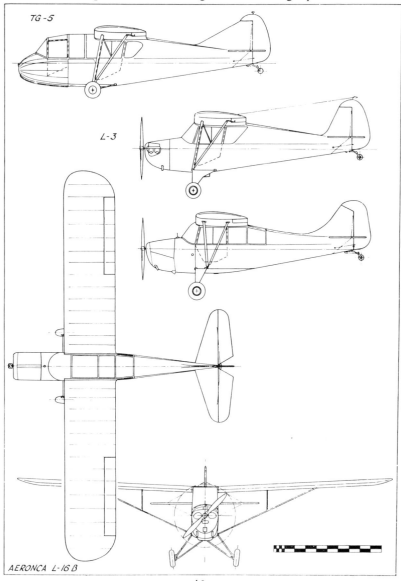

TG-5

L-3

AERONCA L-16B

Aeronca L-16A for the U.S. Army (*Peter M. Bowers*).

of 250 TG-5s was built, and three more were procured later for evaluation by the Navy.

L-16. Another series of Aeronca lightplanes was purchased by the Army in 1947/48. These were the post-War Model 7BC Champions, with few changes from the basic L-3 design. The L-16s were allocated to the Civil Air Patrol in the mid-1950s. There were 509 L-16As with 85 h.p. Continental O-190-1 engines, of which 376 were produced originally for the National Guard. The heavier L-16Bs, of which 100 were delivered, had 90 h.p. Continental O-205-1 engines and dorsal fins.

TECHNICAL DATA (L-3)

MANUFACTURER: The Aeronca Aircraft Corporation, Middletown, Ohio.
TYPE: Light liaison.
ACCOMMODATION: Pilot and observer in tandem in enclosed cabin.
POWER PLANT: One 65 h.p. Continental O-170-3 piston.
DIMENSIONS: Span, 35 ft. 0 in. Length, 21 ft. 0 in. Height, 7 ft. 8 in. Wing area, 158 sq. ft.
WEIGHTS: Empty, 865 lb. Gross, 1,300 lb.
PERFORMANCE: Max. speed, 87 m.p.h. at sea level. Initial climb, 400 ft./min. Service ceiling, 7,750 ft. Range, 190 st. miles.
ARMAMENT: None.
SERIAL NUMBERS:
L-3: 42-456/459; 43-2809/2858.   L-3A: 42-7793/7812.
L-3B: 42-14713/14797; 42-36075/36324;   L-3C: 43-1471/1960.
    42-38458/38497; 43-26754/27253.   TG-5: 42-57229/57478; 43-12493/12495.

TECHNICAL DATA (L-16B)

As L-3 except as follows:
POWER PLANT: One 90 h.p. Continental O-205-1.
DIMENSIONS: Span, 35 ft. 0 in. Length, 21 ft. 6 in. Height, 7 ft. 0 in. Wing area 170 sq. ft.
WEIGHTS: Empty, 890 lb. Gross, 1,450 lb.
PERFORMANCE: Max. speed, 110 m.p.h. Cruising speed, 100 m.p.h. Initial climb, 800 ft./min. Service ceiling, 14,500 ft. Range, 350 st. miles.
SERIAL NUMBERS:
L-16A: 47-788/1296.   L-16B: 48-424/523.

Beech YC-43, serial 39–139, for the U.S. Embassy, London (*Beech photo*).

Beech C-43 Traveler

One of the most distinctive aeroplanes in appearance used by the Army in World War II was the Beech Model 17, a light transport biplane with backward staggered wings. The Model 17 was the first product of the Beech Aircraft Corporation after its foundation in 1932, and its enclosed cabin and retractable undercarriage were among the features which quickly recommended it to private and business owners in the U.S.

When the Air Corps needed a small communications aeroplane in 1939, the Beech 17 was selected for evaluation and three examples of the commercial model D-17S were purchased with the designation YC-43 (39-139/141), one being allocated to the U.S. Air Attaché in London. These had Pratt & Whitney R-985-17 radial engines and with civil-type interiors weighed 4,700 lb. The top speed was 200 m.p.h.

Production orders did not follow immediately, but with the expansion of the Air Force in 1941/42, the need for a swift communications aircraft which could be allocated for use by executive officers became imperative. An initial contract for 27 production model UC-43s (42-38665/38691) was placed, these being similar to the service test aircraft apart from having the R-985-AN-1 engine and some equipment and furnishing changes which put the gross weight up to 4,800 lb. Further contracts brought the total procurement of UC-43s to 207.

Immediately after the entry of the U.S. into World War II, considerable numbers of Beech 17s were impressed for military service with UC-43 designations. These, with their equivalent Beech Model numbers, were: UC-43A(D-17R); UC-43B(D-17S); UC-43C(F-17D); UC-43D(E-17B); UC-43E(C-17R); UC-43F(D-17A); UC-43G(C-17B); UC-43H(B-17R); UC-43J(C-17L); UC-43K(D-17W).

TECHNICAL DATA (UC-43)

MANUFACTURER: Beech Aircraft Corporation, Wichita, Kansas.
TYPE: Utility transport and communications.
ACCOMMODATION: Pilot and three passengers.

48

POWER PLANT: One 450 h.p. Pratt & Whitney R-985-AN-1.
DIMENSIONS: Span, 32 ft. 0 in. Length, 26 ft. 2 in. Height, 10 ft. 3 in. Wing area, 296 sq. ft.
WEIGHTS: Empty, 3,085 lb. Gross, 4,700 lb.
PERFORMANCE: Max. speed, 198 m.p.h. Initial climb, 1,500 ft./min. Service ceiling, 20,000 ft. Range, 500 st. miles.
SERIAL NUMBERS:

YC-43: 39-139/141.

UC-43: 42-38665/38691; 43-10818/10892; 44-67700/67804; 44-76029/76091 (USN).

UC-43A: 42-38226/38231; 42-38245; 42-38282; 42-38357/38358; 42-47383; 42-52999; 42-68339.

UC-43B: 42-38232/38236; 42-38281; 42-38359; 42-46905; 42-47384; 42-53002; 42-56085; 42-61097; 42-68340.

UC-43D: 42-43845; 42-46636; 42-46909/46910; 42-46915; 42-47442/47448; 42-49070; 42-53000/53001; 42-53005; 42-53007/53008; 42-53013; 42-53021; 42-53508/53509; 42-53511; 42-53516/53517; 42-56087; 42-61092/61093; 42-68359/68360; 42-94124.

UC-43C: 42-22246; 42-36825; 42-38237/38241; 42-38243/38244; 42-38246/38248; 42-38283/38284; 42-38361/38363; 42-43517; 42-46635; 42-46906/46908; 42-46914; 42-47385/47388; 42-47449/47450; 42-68337; 42-88636; 42-97048/97050; 42-97411; 42-107411; 42-107414.

UC-43E: 42-47389; 42-70839; 42-97417; 42-97424; 42-97431.

UC-43F: 42-49071.

UC-43G: 42-53006; 42-68855; 42-88620; 42-88628/88629; 42-88634; 42-97415; 42-97426/97428.

UC-43H: 42-68856; 42-78019; 42-94137.

UC-43J: 42-94133; 42-97413; 42-97420.

UC-43K: 42-107277.

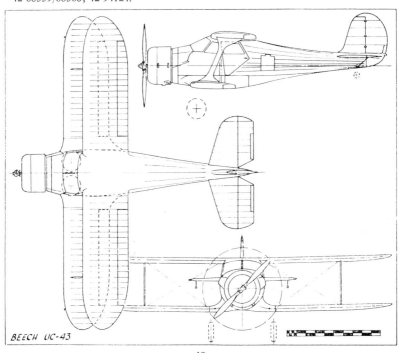

BEECH UC-43

49

Beech C-45 in yellow and blue colour scheme, 1941 (*Peter M. Bowers*).

Beech C-45, AT-7, AT-11, F-2

Two modest 1940 contracts were awarded to Beech Aircraft Corporation by the Army Air Force for variants of the Model B-18S commercial light transport, preceding the more than 4,000 examples which were built for the military in the ensuing five years. The first purchase was of eleven C-45s furnished as six-seaters for use as staff transports They were similar in all respects to the commercial model, with 450 h.p. R-985-17 engines.

A second batch ordered in 1941 had eight-seat interiors, D/F loops on the rear fuselage, 420 h.p. R-985-AN-1 engines and an inevitable performance penalty as a result of a 650 lb. increase in gross weight. Twenty were bought, as C-45As. Further revisions to the interior arrangements increased the weight of the C-45B still further, to 8,727 lb., and the speed dropped again. Orders, however, increased in step with the expansion of the Air Force in 1942, and totalled 223, followed by contracts for 1,137 of the standardized C-45F, with seven seats and a slightly lengthened nose. The designation of all variants was amended to the "UC" category after its introduction in January 1943, and the name of Expeditor was applied.

Other models in the UC-45 series were two commercial B-18S transports impressed for war service as UC-45C; two aircraft from an AT-7 contract completed for communications use as UC-45D, and six others similarly completed from an AT-7B contract as UC-45E.

AT-7. The AT-7 had first been ordered in 1941 as a version of the C-45 specially equipped as a navigation trainer (the Army's first) with individual chart tables and instruments for three students. A rotatable astrodome on the fuselage just behind the cockpit was an external distinguishing feature. After an initial purchase of 67 AT-7s, orders steadily multiplied to a total of 577 of this model, with 450 h.p. R-985-25 engines and gross weight of 7,835 lb. Another nine, basically similar, were winterized and designated AT-7B. The six AT-7As with R-985-AN-1s were floatplanes, with a large

Beech AT-11 (*William T. Larkins*).

ventral fin added to compensate for the added side area of the Edo floats; provision was made for alternative installation of skis.

The final production run of Navigators, as this variant was officially named, comprised 549 AT-7Cs, with R-985-AN-3 engines and gross weight increased to 8,060 lb.

AT-11. From the AT-7 was evolved in 1941 the AT-11 Kansan, for bombing and gunnery training. The special navigation equipment was removed, and a bomb-bay provided in the fuselage in its place. The nose was remodelled with a bomb-aiming position, and nose and dorsal guns were fitted. With R-985-AN-1 engines, the AT-11 grossed 8,195 lb. Production totalled 1,582, of which 36 were modified as AT-11As for navigation training. The Army also re-possessed for use in the U.S., 24 AT-11s which had been ordered by the Netherlands.

F-2. The fourth wartime variant of the Beech Model 18 used by the Army was the F-2, the first specialized photographic reconnaissance type used operationally. Fourteen modified commercial B-18s were ordered in 1940 as F-2s, with two multiple-lens mapping cameras mounted in tandem in the cabin, and a piped oxygen system for the crew. During 1942/43, thirteen UC-45As and UC-45Bs were modified to F-2As with four fuselage cameras and R-985-AN-1 or -3 engines.

The final photographic version, the F-2B, was a variant of the UC-45F with a trimetrogen camera system, and camera ports in each side of the fuselage as well as the floor. Forty-two of these were produced.

Beech C-45G of First Air Force (*Howard Levy*).

51

CQ-3. In the late stages of the War, a small number of UC-45Fs was used in the role of "director" for radio-controlled targets, under the designation CQ-3.

T-7, T-11. Many of the Beechcraft twins, of all varieties, survived the War and were still on hand in June 1948 when the designations of many Air Force aircraft were changed. Under the new system then introduced, the AT-7, AT-7C and AT-11 became, respectively, the T-7, T-7C and T-11; the few F-2As and F-2Bs became RC-45As; and the CQ-3s became DC-45Fs. The remaining UC-45A thru D models were out of service by 1951, but the continuing value of the Beechcraft as a light personnel transport led in that same year to a large programme of "rejuvenation" for most surviving C-45Fs, T-7s and T-11s, and RC-45As.

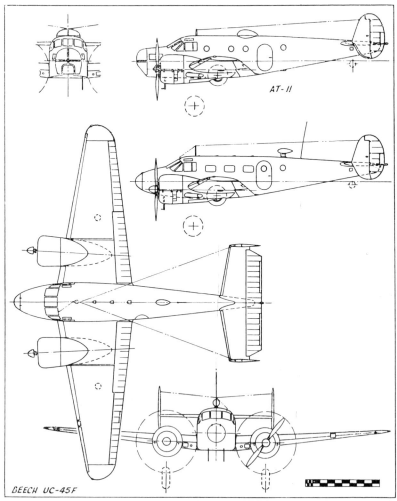

AT-11

BEECH UC-45F

After re-manufacture by Beech, these aircraft, with new serial numbers, were designated C-45G, with 450 h.p. R-985-AN-3 engines and a Jack and Heintz A-3A auto-pilot, or C-45H with R-985-AN-14B engines and no auto-pilot. All were six-seaters and production totalled 468 C-45G and 432 C-45H; subsequently, 96 C-45Gs were modified as TC-45Gs for use as navigation trainers carrying three students.

TECHNICAL DATA (C-45/AT-7)

MANUFACTURER: Beech Aircraft Corporation, Wichita, Kansas.
TYPE: C-45, light transport and communications.
          AT-7/AT-11, navigation and bombardier trainer.
          F-2, photographic reconnaissance.
ACCOMMODATION: C-45, six seats.

	C-45	AT-7	AT-11	F-2
Power Plant:	2 × 450 h.p. R-985-AN-1, -3	2 × 450 h.p. R-985-AN-1, -3	2 × 450 h.p. R-985-AN-1, -3	2 × 450 h.p. R-985-19
Dimensions:				
Span, ft., in.	47 8	47 8	47 8	47 8
Length, ft., in.	34 3	34 3	34 2	34 3
Height, ft., in.	9 8	10 0	9 8	9 4
Wing area, sq. ft.	349	349	349	349
Weights:				
Empty, lb.	5,890	5,935	6,175	5,208
Gross, lb.	7,850	7,850	8,727	7,200
Performance:				
Max. speed, m.p.h.	215	224	215	225
Time to 10,000 ft., min.	8·6	9·6	10·1	6·9
Service ceiling, ft.	20,000	18,400	20,000	26,200
Range, miles	700	585	850	930

ARMAMENT: Nil (AT-11 only, two 0·30-inch guns, ten 100 lb. bombs).
SERIAL NUMBERS:
C-45: 40-180/190.
C-45A: 41-1861/1880.
C-45B: 42-56852; 43-35446/35667.
UC-45C: 42-22247; 42-53510.
UC-45D: 42-56785; 43-33281.
UC-45E: 42-43484; 42-43486; 43-33282/33285.
C-45F*: 43-35668/35945; 44-47049/47748; 44-86898/87441.
C-45G: 51-11444/11503; 51-11600/11911.
TC-45G: 51-11504/11599.
C-45H: 52-10539/10970.
F-2: 40-682/695.

AT-7: 41-1143/1209; 41-21042/21155; 42-2415/2513; 42-43461/43477; 42-43488/43510; 42-56703/56784; 42-56786/56851; 43-33265/33280; 43-33286/33378.
AT-7A: 41-21156/21161; 42-53522.
AT-7B: 42-2414; 42-43485; 42-43487; 42-43478/43483.
AT-7C: 43-33379/33664; 43-49963/50223; 43-52226/52227.
AT-11: 41-9437/9586; 41-27332/27681; 42-36826/37713; 43-10318/10489; 44-72005/72026.

* These serial batches include 42 aircraft completed as F-2B, 343 assigned to the US Navy (20 JRB-3 and 323 JRB-4), and 1,137 delivered to USAAF as C-45F.

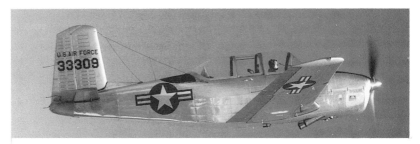

A production Beech T-34A in original natural metal finish (*Beech photo 11409*).

Beech T-34 Mentor

Early in 1950, the USAF initiated an evaluation programme to select a new primary trainer. This action followed several years of uncertainty over pilot training programmes best suited to the needs of a jet force. No new primary trainers had been procured by the USAF since 1944 and the possibility of selecting a jet trainer for primary instruction was carefully considered before the decision was made to buy another low-powered primary.

Among the types evaluated in 1950 were three Beechcraft Model 45s, designated YT-34 by USAF. Beech had first flown a Model 45 on December 2, 1948 (with the civil registration N8591A) as a primary trainer derivative of the Bonanza. It differed from the latter in having a conventional rather than "V" tail unit, and a new cockpit with tandem seating for pupil and instructor; power was supplied by a 205 h.p. Continental E-185-8 engine. A second prototype had the same engine and a third was built with a 225 h.p. Continental E-225-8 engine. Civil certification of the type was obtained on July 17, 1950.

The first YT-34 flew in May 1950, followed by the others in June and July. Extensive testing followed, with pupils being trained on these aircraft and on others involved in the competition. On March 4, 1953, the Beech 45 was announced winner and went into production as the T-34A Mentor. A little over a year later, on June 17, 1954, the U.S. Navy also adopted the Mentor for primary training, and designated it the T-34B. The YT-34 and T-34A versions were powered by the 225 h.p. Continental O-470-13 engine. USAF procurement of the T-34A totalled 350 from Beech and 100 from Canadian Car and Foundry in Montreal.

Deliveries of the T-34A to Air Training Command began in 1954, and the type progressively equipped the primary training schools at such bases as Moore A.F.B., Texas; Bainbridge A.F.B. and Spence A.F.B., Georgia; Graham A.F.B. and Bartow A.F.B., Florida and Malden A.F.B., Mo. The T-34s replaced T-6s and other types for primary training and, after the introduction of the more powerful North American T-28, were used to give 30 hours of flying procedure familiarization to all trainees before they progressed to the T-28 and the jet-powered T-37. The T-34s became redundant in 1960 with the introduction of all-through jet training.

In July 1951, the first YT-34 (50-735) was used for an Army evaluation of armed trainers suitable for light ground support duties. For these trials it carried two 0·30-inch machine guns in the wings and six rockets or two 150-lb. bombs under the wings.

TECHNICAL DATA (T-34A)

MANUFACTURER: Beech Aircraft Corporation, Wichita, Kansas, and Canadian Car and Foundry Co., Ltd., Montreal, Canada.
TYPE: Primary trainer.
ACCOMMODATION: Pupil and instructor in tandem.
POWER PLANT: One 225 h.p. Continental O-470-13 flat-six.
DIMENSIONS: Span, 32 ft. 10 in. Length, 25 ft. 10 in. Height, 9 ft. 7 in. Wing area, 177·6 sq. ft.
WEIGHTS: Empty, 2,055 lb. Gross, 2,900 lb.
PERFORMANCE: Max. speed, 189 m.p.h. at sea level. Cruising speed, 173 m.p.h. at 10,000 ft. Service ceiling, 20,000 ft. Range, 975 st. miles.
ARMAMENT: None.
SERIAL NUMBERS:
YT-34: 50-735/737.   T-34A (BH): 52-7626/7685;
T-34A(CCF): 52-8253/8286;   53-3306/3395; 53-4157/4206;
  53-4091/4156.   55-140/289.

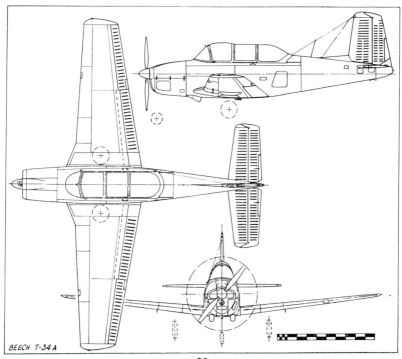

BEECH T-34 A

Beech U-8F (formerly L-23F) in U.S. Army olive drab with white top and vertical tail surfaces (*Beech photo BL14639J*).

Beech L-23, U-8 Seminole, U-21 Ute, C-6

To provide an aeroplane suitable for communications, transport and liaison work around the world, the U.S. Army adopted the Beech Twin Bonanza. Four examples were purchased "off-the-shelf" for evaluation and designated YL-23, the first reaching Fort Sill, Oklahoma, on January 30, 1952. Purchase of a production quantity of L-23As which followed gave the Army its largest twin engined aircraft at the time, with a gross weight of 6,000 lb.

Powered by 260 h.p. Lycoming O-435-17 engines, the L-23As were six-seaters and by the end of 1953 were serving throughout the U.S. and at Army installations in Europe and the Far East. The 55 L-23As purchased were followed by 40 L-23Bs, which were similar but had metal rather than wooden propellers. In January 1955, development of the L-23D began, based on the commercial E50 model with 340 h.p. O-480-1 supercharged engines. The L-23D first flew in October 1955 and was first delivered in November 1956. In addition to 85 new aircraft purchased between 1956 and 1958, 93 surviving L-23As and L-23Bs were re-manufactured as L-23Ds, and allocated new serial numbers. Also in 1956 the Army purchased six L-23Es, equivalent to the commercial D50 model with 295

Beech L-23A, olive drab overall (*A. U. Schmidt*).

56

h.p. Lycoming GO-480-G2D6 engines. One XL-23C was purchased for USAF evaluation—and eventually became an Army U-8G.

In January 1959, Beech flew the first of three L-23Fs ordered for evaluation. These were equivalent to the Beech Model 65 Queen Air with its much deeper fuselage, and after successful trials at Fort Rucker, starting in March 1959, the Army placed further orders to bring total procurement to 82.

In 1958 the Army began a programme to develop the L-23 for radar observation and radar photography using side-looking airborne radar (SLAR). Based on the L-23D, these aircraft were given the designation RL-23D. Two were fitted with Motorola APS-85 in 1959, and during 1960 four more RL-23Ds were converted to have Texas Instruments' APQ-86 SLAR in a similar installation. Another trials aircraft was fitted with Texas

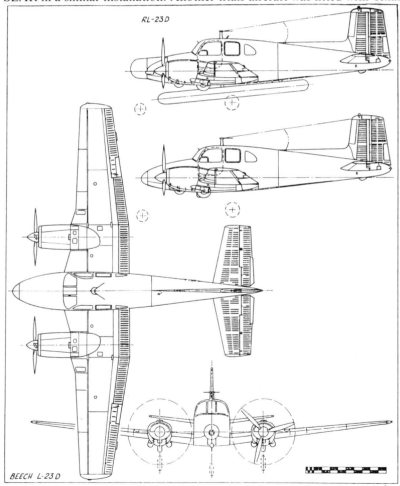

RL-23D

BEECH L-23D

57

Beech RL-23D with Motorola SLAR (*Beech photo 14012B*).

Instruments' AN/UPD-1 battlefield surveillance radar in a large ventral blister, while another was flown with RCA AVQ-50 weather radar. In all, 20 RL-23Ds were purchased as such, but another 10 to 12 U-8Ds were later converted.

In 1962, current versions of the L-23 were re-designated as follows: L-23D to U-8D; RL-23D to RU-8D; L-23E to U-8E and L-23F to U-8F. Some 20 RU-8D, U-8E and U-8F aircraft were later modified to U-8Gs with improved cabin accommodation for two pilots and four passengers, and GO-480-CSC6 engines. In 1981/83, the Army purchased an additional quantity of used commercial Queen Air 65s for use by Army National Guard units, these also being designated U-8Fs.

In May 1963, Beech made the first flight of a converted Queen Air with 500 h.p. Pratt & Whitney PT6A-6 turboprop engines, as Model 65-90T. Delivered to the U.S. Army on March 17, 1964, for tests at Fort Rucker as the NU-8F, this prototype was a stepping stone in the development of the Beech 65-90 King Air, the first true example of which flew on January 20, 1964. In October 1966, the US Army adopted an unpressurized variant of the King Air as a utility aircraft designated the U-21A (Beech Model 65-A90-1C). Powered by 550 s.h.p. PT6A-20 engines, the U-21A could carry 10 combat troops, six command personnel, three stretchers and three

Beech U-21A for Vietnam in over-all brown finish with no national insignia (*Beech photo 29714U*).

58

Beech VC-6A operated by 89th Military Airlift Wing, Special Missions, for VIP transport duties (*Beech photo BL 18947*).

seated patients or up to 3,000 lb. of cargo.

The initial Army order was for 48 U-21As, the first of these flying in March 1967; deliveries began on May 16, 1967 and the total procured eventually increased to 166. Production for the Army ended with five U-21Fs, versions of the larger King Air A100, able to carry 13 passengers with a crew of two and powered by 680 s.h.p. PT6A-28 engines. Several U-21Fs were updated to U-21G standard, with T74-CP-700 engines (military variants of the PT6A).

For special electronic reconnaissance (ELINT) duties, principally in Vietnam, as many as 50 of the U-21As were specially equipped, with designations ranging from RU-21A to RU-21E according to equipment and airframe standard. The RU-21A was the basic U-21A fitted with Army Security Agency EW equipment, and the RU-21B (Beech Model 65A-90-2) was improved with 620 s.h.p. PT6A-29s. The similar RU-21Cs (Model 65A-90-3) had different aerial arrays and the RU-21Ds were improved RU-21Bs. The RU-21Es were RU-21Ds with 620 s.h.p. T74-CP-700 military

Beech U-21F, in Army olive drab and white scheme, as first delivered in August 1971 (*Beech photo 37852-11*).

59

versions of the PT6A-29 and equipped for surveillance missions in combat zones, and many were upgraded to RU-21Hs with new wing tips and landing gear, for higher weights and different electronic equipment. The RU-21J was the larger, T-tailed Beech Super King Air 200, three examples of which were acquired by the Army in 1974 to serve as test-beds for EW equipment in the Cefly Lancer programme. They later were converted to serve as U-21J VIP transports and then became C-12Ls. The C-12 designation was applied to subsequent purchases of the Super King Air 200, as described separately.

A single example of the King Air operated with the USAF as the VC-6A. Procured in FY 1966, this aircraft had a VIP interior and operated since February 1966 with the 1254th SAM Squadron, 89th MAW, at Andrews AFB, Washington.

TECHNICAL DATA (L-23, U-8, U-21)

MANUFACTURER: Beech Aircraft Corporation, Wichita, Kansas.
TYPE: Army staff transport and all-weather battlefield surveillance.

	L-23D	U-8F	U-21A
Accommodation:	6 seats	6 seats	Up to 12 seats
Power Plant:	2 × 340 h.p.	2 × 340 h.p.	2 × 550 s.h.p.
	Lycoming	Lycoming	Pratt & Whitney
	O-480-1	IGSO-480-A1A6	PT6A-20
Dimensions:			
Span, ft., in.	45 3½	45 10½	45 10½
Length, ft., in.	31 6½	33 4	35 6
Height, ft., in.	11 4	14 2	14 2
Wing area, sq. ft.	277	277	280
Weights:			
Empty, lb.	4,974	4,996	5,235
Gross, lb.	7,000	7,700	9,650
Performance:			
Max. speed, m.p.h.	233	240	—
Cruising speed, m.p.h.	203	200	248
Initial climb, ft./min.	1,560	1,300	1,950
Service ceiling, ft.	26,300	27,000	26,100
Range, st. miles	1,355	1,370	960

SERIAL NUMBERS:
YL-23: 52-1800/1803.
L-23A: 52-6162/6216.
L-23B: 53-6153/6192.
XL-23C: 55-3465.
L-23D: 56-3695/3718; 57-3084/3101;
  57-6077/6094; 58-1329/1353;
  57-6029/6076*; 58-3048/3092.*
RL-23D: 58-1357/1364; 59-2535/2543;
  59-4990/4992.
L-23E: 56-4039/4044.

U-8F: 58-1354/1356; 60-3453/3470;
  60-5386/5389; 61-2426/2430;
  62-3832/3875; 63-7975; 63-12902;
  63-13636/13637; 66-15360/15361;
  66-15365; 81-23658/23659; 82-24054;
  83-23840/23841; 83-23844; 83-23847;
  83-23850; 83-23857; 83-23872.
VC-6A: 66-7943.
U-21A: 66-18000/18048; 67-18049/18128;
  70-15875/15907.
U-21F: 70-15908/15912.
RU-21J: 72-21058/21060.

* re-manufactured.

Beech C-12F of 1403rd MAS, Det 1, (foreground) in MAC all-white finish and C-12A in U.S. Army grey, at Clark A.F.B., Philippines, in 1988 (*Robbie Shaw*).

Beech C-12 Huron

After Beech Aircraft had developed the Super King Air 200 as an enlarged derivative of the original King Air 100, the U.S. Army acquired the first three production examples under the RU-21J designation as test-beds for EW and ELINT-gathering equipment (see other RU-21 variants described). They were delivered in 1974 and in the same year the Army, USAF, USN and USMC began off-the-shelf acquisition of standard Super King Air 200s for use as staff transports throughout the world, in eight-passenger, two-pilot configuration. The designation U-25A was briefly applied to the initial Army purchase of these aircraft but C-12 was later adopted as the common basic designation for all four service versions.

Service use of the C-12A began in July 1975 with the U.S. Army at Fort

Beech RC-12D, showing wing-tip radomes and fuselage antennas, serving with 1 MIB in Europe, 1985. Note absence of national insignias (*MAP photo*).

61

Monroe, Virginia, and 60 were delivered. The USAF received 30 identical C-12As, all having 750 s.h.p. Pratt & Whitney PT6A-38 turboprops. The Army later adopted PT6A-41 engines in its C-12As and bought 14 additional C-12Cs with these engines. Upgraded USAF C-12As with PT6A-42 engines were redesignated C-12Es. Further production for the U.S. Army was in the C-12D version (Beech Model A200CT), with PT6A-41s, fuselage-side cargo door, high flotation landing gear and provision for wing-tip fuel tanks. By mid-1986, the Army had ordered 55 C-12Ds, of which five were for FMS and 13 were converted RC-12Ds for ELINT duties, as noted below. Generally similar to the Army C-12Ds were six UC-12Ds for the Army National Guard and six for the USAF.

When the USAF selected the Super King Air 200 to meet its specification for an operational support aircraft (OSA), the C-12F designation was adopted, these being Model B200Cs with side cargo doors. Forty were ordered and deliveries began in May 1984 to Scott A.F.B., Illinois, for use by MAC.

The Army chose the C-12 to supplement its RU-21H "Guardrail V" battlefield reconnaissance and ELINT aircraft serving in Europe and South Korea. Carrying AN/USD-9 communications intercept and DF systems, an airborne relay facility and radio data link, plus ECM in wing-tip pods, the RC-12D was first delivered in the summer of 1983; 13 C-12Ds were modified and the Army bought six more under a May 1983 contract. Three *Cefly Lancer* RU-21Js (see page 60) were later redesignated as C-12Ls. Production then continued with the RC-12K, of which nine were ordered in October 1985, featuring a large cargo door and oversized wheels.

The UC-12B designation applied to the Navy/Marine Corps variant of the C-12A and the C-12J was the larger Beech Model 1900C, five examples of which were acquired for operation by the Air National Guard starting in September 1987.

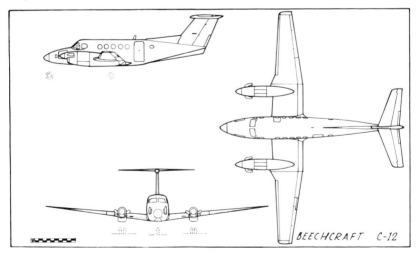

BEECHCRAFT C-12

In pale grey and white finish as a staff transport, Beech C-12J was one of five operated by the Air National Guard (*Beech photo 870744-37*).

TECHNICAL DATA (C-12F)

MANUFACTURER: Beech Aircraft Corporation subsidiary of Raytheon Company, Wichita, Kansas.
TYPE: Operational support aircraft; light general-purpose transport.
ACCOMMODATION: Two pilots and six passengers.
POWER PLANT: Two 850 s.h.p. Pratt & Whitney Canada PT6A-42 turboprops.
DIMENSIONS: Span, 54 ft. 6in. Length, 43 ft. 9 in. Height, 15 ft. 0 in. Wing area, 303 sq. ft.
WEIGHTS: Empty, 7,538 lb. Gross, 12,500 lb.
PERFORMANCE: Max. speed, 339 mph. at 25,000 ft. Cruising speed, 325 m.p.h. at 25,000 ft. Initial climb, 2,450 ft./min. Service ceiling, 35,000 ft. Range, 1,682 miles at 25,000 ft.
ARMAMENT: None.
SERIAL NUMBERS:

RU-21J (C-12L):	72-21058/21060
C-12A (USAF):	73-1205/1218;
	76-158/173; 76-3239; 83-0494/0498
C-12A (Army):	73-22250/22269; 76-22545/22564;
	77-22931/22950
C-12C:	78-23126/23139
C-12D:	81-23543/23546; 82-23780/23785;
	83-0494/0499; 83-24145/24150; 84-24375/24380
RC-12D:	78-23140/23145*; 80-23371/23380;
	81-23541/23542; 82-23638/23642
C-12F:	84-0143/0182; 84-0484/0489; 85-1261/1272
C-12J:	86-0078/0082
RC-12K	85-147/155
	*conversions from C-12D

(Plus later contracts)

Bell P-39D in 1941 fighter finish (*Bell photo 10913A*).

Bell P-39 Airacobra

Among Army fighters used in World War II, the P-39 was unique for its engine arrangement, having an Allison V-1710 buried in the fuselage behind the cockpit. Bell designers led by Bob Wood had found that this arrangement facilitated the nose-mounting of the American Armament Corporation's 37-mm. T-9 cannon, around which the whole design was drawn. This gun had been demonstrated in May 1935 and its potential intrigued the Bell company executives who witnessed the tests. The decision to locate the gun on the aircraft centre line in the nose—for optimum effect—dictated the engine position. Some early drawings had the cockpit virtually in the base of the fin behind the engine, but by the time the project was first submitted to the Air Corps in May 1937, it had been moved forward to obtain an adequate view for the pilot.

With the engine on the centre of gravity, the Bell fighter could hardly fail to have a tricycle undercarriage, there being ample stowage space for the nosewheel under the cannon. It was the first tricycle single-engined fighter ordered by the Air Corps, which contracted for a single XP-39 prototype on October 7, 1937. The armament was to comprise two 0·50-inch guns in the nose in addition to the cannon (either the 37-mm. T-9 or a 25-mm. weapon), and Bell estimated a top performance of 400 m.p.h. at 20,000 ft. for a gross weight of 5,550 lb. on the 1,150 take-off h.p. of a V-1710-17 engine. The latter, with a five-foot extension shaft to drive the propeller reduction gear, had a B-5 turbo-supercharger; radiators were on each side of the fuselage just aft the cockpit.

The XP-39 (38-326) was first flown at Dayton by James Taylor in April 1938, and in the same month a year later, the Army ordered a service test batch of 12 YP-39s and one YP-39A, the latter to have no turbo-supercharger. While work on these aircraft progressed, the XP-39 was subjected to close examination by NACA, which recommended a number of design changes. These included a change from lateral radiators to a wing-root

Bell P-39F (*USAF photo 28112AC*).

type with leading-edge intakes; main-wheels doors, a lower cockpit canopy, a carburettor air scoop on the centre fuselage and deletion of the turbo-supercharger. With these changes made, the prototype was re-designated XP-39B and first flew on November 25, 1939.

Improved performance was obtained, and all these changes were applied to the trials aircraft then being built. In January 1940, the Army decided to abandon the turbo-supercharger—thus jeopardising the aircraft's future success at high altitudes—and all 13 trials aircraft were completed as YP-39s (Bell Model 12) with 1,090 h.p. V-1710-37 engines. The armament was increased by the addition of two 0.30-inch guns in the nose and the top weight went up to 7,235 lb.

On August 10, 1939, the Bell fighter was ordered into full production, with an Army order for 80 examples of the P-45; this designation was, however, soon abandoned in favour of P-39 and the first 20 aircraft, delivered from January 1941 onwards, were P-39C (Bell Model 13). They were similar to the YP-39s, but the fully militarized P-39D (Bell Model 15) had leak-proof fuel tanks, and four 0.30-inch wing guns replacing the two of this calibre in the nose, where the two 0.50-inch and single 37-mm. guns remained. Provision was made for a 500 lb. bomb or 75 gallon drop tank under the fuselage.

Bell P-39K with British camouflage and U.S. markings (*Peter M. Bowers*).

65

Bell P-39L of 93rd Fighter Group, Tunisia, 1943 (*Howard Levy*).

The first order for P-39Ds was placed in September 1940 (for 369 aircraft) but 60 of the 1939 production contract also appeared to this standard. Deliveries of the P-39D began in April 1941, and about the same time the first export Airacobra appeared. This was one of several hundred ordered as Bell Model 14 by Britain on April 13, 1940, and was similar to the P-39D apart from the use of a 20-mm. gun rather than the 37-mm. cannon. The British Purchasing Commission had planned to buy 675 of these aircraft, but in fact only one squadron ever became operational with the R.A.F. Over 250 British Airacobras were made over to the Soviet Air Force as part of British aid to Russia, nearly 200 were re-acquired by the USAAF in Britain at the end of 1942 and about 200 were repossessed in the USA by the Army Air Force in December 1941 after Japan attacked the U.S.

The repossessed British Airacobras were designated P-400 in U.S. service and retained R.A.F. serial numbers. They were used principally for training and for the emergency re-inforcement of airfields in the South Pacific, a typical example being their use by the 347th Fighter Group at Guadalcanal in 1943.

The P-39s already in service with the AAF at the time of the Pearl Harbor attack were deployed at home bases but were quickly moved

Bell P-39Q-20 (*Peter M. Bowers*).

Bell P-39Q-5 with second cockpit added (*Peter M. Bowers*).

forward to overseas bases in Alaska, Hawaii, Panama and New Guinea. From Port Moresby, the P-39Ds first went into action, in April 1942, and for the next 18 months this type, together with the Curtiss P-40, was the principal front-line equipment of Air Force fighter units in the Pacific and European theatres. Among the first P-39 Fighter Groups to go to Europe were the 31st and 52nd, but because of the P-39s poor performance, these Groups left their aircraft in the US and re-equipped on Spitfires upon arrival in England.

Late in 1942, P-39s and P-400s were assigned to support Operation "Torch" landings in North Africa, where three groups (Nos 68, 81 and 350) eventually operated with success in the ground attack role, achieving the lowest loss rate per sortie of any AAF fighter used in the European theatre. The Airacobra was at its peak in AAF service by early 1944, with 2,150 in the inventory, but after this date the rundown was rapid as P-47s, P-51s and P-38s reached the battle areas.

Development and production of the P-39 continued, none-the-less, at high pressure, not only to meet Army requirements but also for Lend-Lease supply, to Russia (which received 4,773 of the 9,558 built). The first Lend-Lease order was for 494 Bell Model 14As and was placed in June 1941. These were delivered, starting in 1942, as P-39D-1s (336) and P-39D-2s (158); the latter had V-1710-63 engines and all had 20-mm. guns like the British version.

The P-39D was followed by 229 P-39Fs which were similar apart from an Aeroproducts propeller replacing the Curtiss type, and 25 P-39Js, similar to the F with a V-1710-59 engine. Like the D, these were Bell Model 15s.

In August 1941, the Army placed a contract with Bell for 1,080 P-39s of a new series (Bell Model 26) with various detail refinements. None of these was delivered as a P-39G, under which designation they had been ordered, further changes in power plant and equipment leading to new designations during production. Delivered in 1942, the 210 P-39Ks and 250 P-39Ls had the V-1710-63 engine and were identical apart from the propellers—respectively Aeroproducts and Curtiss. A change to the

V-1710-83 engine then led to the P-39M, of which 240 were built.

Final production versions, also the most-produced, were the P-39N and P-39Q, the principal Lend-Lease variants for Russia. The P-39N had a V-1710-85 engine, a larger diameter Aeroproducts propeller, and reduced fuel capacity and armour to improve the climb and speed performance. Production totalled 2,095. The P-39Q was distinguished by the small underwing fairings for two 0·50-inch guns, replacing the four 0·30-inch guns in the wings. The engine was the V-1710-85 and several sub-types existed, differing in amounts of fuel and armour; some batches had a four-bladed propeller but most had the bigger Aeroproducts three-blader. Production of the P-39Q totalled 4,905.

Neither the P-39H nor the P-39P designation was used. The XP-39E was an experimental version ordered in April 1941 to investigate the use of a laminar flow wing. This had square tips and the tail unit also was re-designed, varying on each of the three examples built (41-16501/2 and 42-71464). The XP-39E was to have had a Continental IV-1430-1, but an Allison V-1710-47 was fitted for the flight trials, which began in February 1942. An order for 4,000 production models of this type, placed with the Bell Marietta factory in the same month, was cancelled three months later;

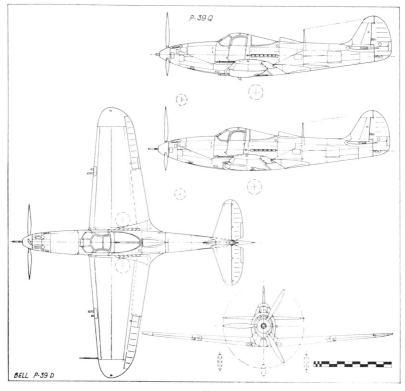

P-39 Q

BELL P-39 D

these would have been designated P-76s. Work on the XP-39E was utilized, however, in the design of the P-63 Kingcobra (see pp. 70-72).

One P-39 was converted by Bell into a two-seat trainer, with armament deleted and a second cockpit forward of the first under a lengthened canopy. Additional fin area was provided above and below the fuselage, and kits were made available for field conversion of P-39s to this standard. The first conversion was re-designated TP-39F, and a few other two-seaters were known as RP-39Qs. During 1941, a radio-controlled target version of the P-39 was proposed and the designation A-7 was allocated. This project did not materialize.

TECHNICAL DATA (P-39)

MANUFACTURER: Bell Aircraft Corporation, Buffalo, New York.
TYPE: Single-seat pursuit and advanced trainer.
ACCOMMODATION: Pilot in enclosed cockpit.

	P-39D/F/J	P-39K/L	P-39M	P-39N	P-39Q
Power Plant:	1,150 h.p. V-1710-35	1,325 h.p. V-1710-63	1,200 h.p. V-1710-83	1,200 h.p. V-1710-85	1,200 h.p. V-1710-85
Dimensions:					
Span, ft., in.	34 0	34 0	34 0	34 0	34 0
Length, ft., in.	30 2	30 2	30 2	30 2	30 2
Height, ft., in.	11 10	11 10	11 10	12 5	12 5
Wing area, sq. ft.	213	213	213	213	213
Weights:					
Empty, lb.	5,462	5,658	5,610	5,657	5,645
Gross, lb.	8,200	8,400	8,400	8,200	8,300
Performance:					
Max. speed, m.p.h. at ft.	368/13,800	368/13,800	386/9,500	399/9,700	385/11,000
Cruising speed, m.p.h.	213	213	200	—	—
Climb, min. to ft.	5·7/15,000	5·7/15,000	4·4/15,000	3·8/15,000	4·5/15,000
Service ceiling, ft.	32,100	32,000	36,000	38,500	35,000
Range, st. miles	800	800	650	750	650
Armament:	1 × 37 mm. 2 × 0·50 in. 4 × 0·30 in. 1 × 500 lb.	1 × 37 mm. 2 × 0·50 in. 4 × 0·30 in. 1 × 500 lb.	1 × 37 mm. 2 × 0·50 in. 4 × 0·30 in. 1 × 500 lb.	1 × 37 mm. 2 × 0·50 in. 4 × 0·30 in. 1 × 500 lb.	1 × 37 mm. 4 × 0·50 in. 1 × 500 lb.

SERIAL NUMBERS:

XP-39: 38-326.
YP-39: 40-027/039.
P-39C: 40-2971/2990.
P-39D: 40-2991/3050; 41-6722/7052;
  41-7057/7058; 41-7080/7115;
  41-28257/28406; 41-38220/38563.
XP-39E: 41-19501/19502; 42-71464.
P-39F: 41-7116/7344.

P-39J: 41-7053/7056; 41-7059/7079.
P-39K: 42-4244/4453.
P-39L: 42-4454/4703.
P-39M: 42-4704/4943.
P-39N: 42-4944/5043; 42-8727/9726;
  42-18246/19240.
P-39Q: 42-19446/21250; 44-2001/4000;
  44-32167/32666; 44-70905/71504.

Bell P-63A-6 (*Bell photo 42043*).

Bell P-63 Kingcobra

Of the several fighter designs which reached the preliminary flight stage after the U.S. entered World War II, only the P-63 went into large-scale production and operational service before the end of the conflict. That this rapid development was possible is attributable to the fact that the P-63 was not a new design, but evolved from the P-39. As noted on page 57, three XP-39Es were built during 1941, using P-39D fuselages with new laminar-flow wings, angular tail units and Allison V-1710-47 engines. In June 1941, before the first XP-39E had flown, the Army Air Corps ordered two prototypes of the Bell Model 33 having this same wing and power plant, with further refinements of the P-39 design. Designated XP-63, the first of these prototypes (41-19511) flew on December 7, 1942 and the second (41-19512) on February 5, 1943.

Both prototypes were lost at an early stage in their trials, but a third aircraft, designated XP-63A, flew on April 26, 1943. This prototype had provision for external bombs and was powered by a 1,325 h.p. V-1710-93 engine. A proposal to fit a Packard-Merlin V-1650-5 engine in this same aircraft to produce the XP-63B was cancelled.

Production of the P-63, to succeed the P-39, had been ordered in September 1942 and deliveries of the P-63A began 13 months later. Bell built 1,725 of this model, but only a few reached USAAF units, the great majority going to Russia on Lend–Lease. Several distinct sub-series of the

Bell P-63E-1 (*Bell photo*).

70

"A" appeared, differing principally in armament and operational equipment. The basic armament comprised one 37 mm. cannon in the nose and one 0·50-inch gun in each wing; blocks A-1 and A-5 could carry a 75- or 175-gallon tank or 522-lb. bomb under the centre section but on A-6 wing racks were added for another two 522 lb. bombs or additional tankage, and the A-10 could carry three rocket projectiles under each wing. The weight of armour increased from 87·7 lb. on the P-63A-1 to 236·3 lb. on the P-63A-10. The sub-types up to A-8 carried only 30 rounds for the nose cannon, but this was increased to 58 on the A-9 and A-10.

The P-63C, supplied principally to Russia and France (which received 300) differed from the A model in having a V-1710-117 engine and a ventral fin; production totalled 1,227, with deliveries starting in December 1944. The single P-63D had a V-1710-109 engine, modified wings and bubble canopy but the latter was abandoned on the otherwise similar P-63E, ordered into large scale production in 1945. The first P-63E (Bell Model 41) with the 10-inch greater wing-span, was ready for testing in May 1945, but only 13 in all had been built by the War's end and contracts for 2,930 were cancelled. Two P-63Fs tested in 1945 were similar to the E but had a V-1710-135 engine and a taller fin and rudder with a small dorsal extension.

During 1943, a special version of the P-63 was developed for use as a manned target aircraft which could actually be shot at—so far as is known, a unique idea. Based on the P-63A-9 the first five examples were identified as RP-63A-11s and had all armament and armour removed. In its place, a toughened skin, weighing 1,488 lb., was used on wings, tail, fuselage and rear canopy, to withstand the impact of frangible bullets. To indicate hits, a red light blinked at the wing-tip like a pinball machine. All but one of the first five targets had the dorsal air intake replaced by a clam-shell intake, and the latter feature was retained on the 95 RP-63A-12s, with increased internal tankage (126 gallons). Another 200 targets were built as RP-63Cs, with the V-1710-117 engine, and Kingcobra production ended in 1946 with 32 RP-63Gs with the V-1710-135 engine; 420 of the latter version were cancelled. The designation of these targets was later changed to QF-63A, QF-63C and QF-63G respectively, although they were never flown as pilotless drones.

Bell RP-63G "Pinball" target painted orange overall (*Bell photo*).

One P-63 was modified to flight test a V-tail arrangement, two others were flown with swept-back wings for U.S. Navy tests and Bell modified about two dozen to have a second cockpit in the rear fuselage for use as instrument and equipment test beds.

TECHNICAL DATA (P-63A)

MANUFACTURER: Bell Aircraft Corporation, Buffalo, New York.
TYPE: Fighter and fighter bomber; (RP-63) target aircraft.
ACCOMMODATION: Pilot in enclosed cockpit.
POWER PLANT: One 1,325 h.p. Allison V-1710-93 piston Vee-in-ine.
DIMENSIONS: Span, 38 ft. 4 in. Length, 32 ft. 8 in. Height, 12 ft. 7 in. Wing area, 248 sq. ft.
WEIGHTS: Empty, 6,375 lb. Gross, 10,500 lb.
PERFORMANCE: Max. speed, 408 m.p.h. at 24,450 ft. Cruising speed, 378 m.p.h. Initial climb, 7·3 min. to 25,000 ft. Service ceiling, 43,000 ft. Range 450 st. miles.
ARMAMENT: (P-63A-10) One 37-mm. and two 0·50-in. fixed forward firing guns in nose and one 0·50-in. beneath each wing; three 500 lb. bombs externally.
SERIAL NUMBERS:

XP-63: 41-19511/19512.
XP-63A: 42-78015.
P-63A: 42-68861/69879 (inc. five RP-63A); 42-69975/70685.
P-63C: 42-70686/70860; 43-10893/10932; 43-11133/11717; 44-4001/4427.
P-63D: 43-11718.

P-63E: 43-11720/21; 43-11725/35.
P-63F: 43-11719; 43-11722.
RP-63A: 42-69647; 42-69654; 42-69769; 42-69771; 42-69801; 42-69880/69974.
RP-63C: 43-10933/11132.
RP-63G: 43-11723/11724; 45-57283/57312.

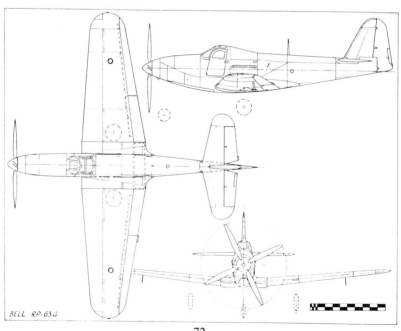

BELL RP-63G

72

Bell P-59A (*Bell photo 78869*).

Bell P-59 Airacomet

To take advantage of early British work on gas turbine power plants for aircraft, the USAAF requested Bell Aircraft Corporation on September 5, 1941, to undertake development of a jet fighter design. Preliminary drawings of such an aircraft, the Bell Model 27, were submitted before the end of that month and were approved. At this time, Bell was also working on a new radial-engined twin-boom pusher fighter design for the USAAF, the XP-59, and to preserve secrecy the jet propelled project was designated XP-59A. The XP-59 was later cancelled.

The XP-59A, actual construction of which began in the spring of 1942, was a mid-wing monoplane with a slender fuselage of conventional construction. The turbojets were carried on each side of the fuselage under the wings, and the main undercarriage units were further out on the wings, folding inwards to retract. Three XP-59A and a service trials batch of 13 YP-59A were ordered and the first XP-59A was moved to Muroc (later Edwards AFB) for flight tests in September 1942. This aircraft had two General Electric Type I-A turbojets, developed from the Whittle-type General Electric Type I engine which had first been bench tested on March 18, 1942. With these engines, the XP-59A first taxied on September 30, and was flown on October 1 by Robert M. Stanley, Bell's chief test pilot.

The YP-59As were delivered during 1944 after the first had flown in August, 1943, and were used for flight development of the engines. These were the rather more powerful General Electric I-16s, giving a nominal 1,600 lb s.t. each and in due course designated J-31.

Production models of the Airacomet were ordered primarily to be used as trainers, although they were single-seaters and carried nose armament of one 37-mm. cannon and three 0·50-inch machine guns, and bomb-racks under the outer wings. The first 20 production aircraft were designated P-59A and were similar to the YP-59A but slightly longer and with a shorter fin and rudder. The engines were 2,000 lb. s.t. J31-GE-3s, but in November 1944 one P-59A flew with the 1,800 lb. General Electric I-18s for the first time.

Small changes and J31-GE-5 engines distinguished the P-59B, only 30 of which had been delivered when the contract was cancelled on October 30, 1944. Fifty more were then on order and a further 250 planned, but successful development of the P-80 made further work on the P-59 unnecessary. The P-59s were issued to the 412th Fighter Group, a specially-formed trials unit in 4th Air Force, for operational evaluation and were also used for a wide variety of test work. Some were eventually modified as drone directors, with an open front cockpit ahead of the pilot. This modification was first made on the original XP-59A, which first flew with an observer on October 30, 1942.

TECHNICAL DATA (P-59B)

MANUFACTURER: Bell Aircraft Corporation, Buffalo, New York.
TYPE: Jet fighter familiarization trainer.
ACCOMMODATION: Pilot in enclosed cabin.
POWER PLANT: Two 2,000 lb. s.t. General Electric J-31-GE-5 turbojets.
DIMENSIONS: Span, 45 ft. 6 in. Length, 38 ft. 10 in. Height, 12 ft. 4 in. Wing area, 385 sq. ft.
WEIGHTS: Empty, 8,165 lb. Gross, 13,700 lb.
PERFORMANCE: Max. speed, 413 m.p.h. at 30,000 ft. Cruising speed, 375 m.p.h. Initial climb, 3·2 min. to 10,000 ft. Service ceiling, 46,200 ft. Range, 525 st. miles.
ARMAMENT: One 37-mm. and three 0·50-in. fixed forward firing guns in nose.
SERIAL NUMBERS:

XP-59A: 42-108784/108786.	P-59A: 44-22609/22628.
YP-59A: 42-108771/108783.	P-59B: 44-22629/22658.

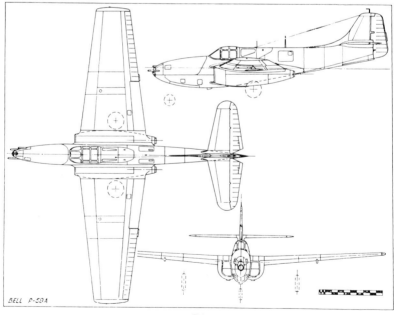

BELL P-59A

74

Bell OH-13S, U.S. Army (*Bell photo*).

Bell H-13 Sioux

More Bell helicopters have been purchased by the U.S. military than those of any other manufacturer. The first of the Bell types, in service since 1946, was the H-13, used for casualty evacuation, training, reconnaissance, observation and general utility duties, principally by the U.S. Army. It gave distinguished service in Korea, and it has been posted to all regions of the World.

A batch of 28 Bell Model 47As was delivered to the Air Force in 1947 with the designation YR-13, ten of these being transferred to the Navy and the others being used for extensive evaluation tests in a wide range of conditions. Three of this batch (46-228/230) were winterized for cold-weather trials in Alaska and became YR-13As. All were powered by the 175 h.p. Franklin O-335-1 engine.

In 1948, the first quantity production order for the type was placed, with a contract for 65 H-13Bs, equivalent to the Model 47D with 200 h.p. O-335-3 engine, convertible bubble canopy with removable top, and detailed refinements. One aircraft was stripped in 1950 for special tests and, with a skid in place of wheel undercarriage, was designated YH-13C. Fifteen more were converted in 1952 to H-13Cs, with the rear fuselage covering removed and external stretcher carriers fitted.

The next major production versions were the H-13D and H-13E (Model 47D-1) of which Bell built 87 and 490 respectively. These had O-335-5 engines, skid undercarriage, stripped rear fuselage and side stretcher carriers. The two-seat D had single control and the three-seat E, dual; gross weights were 2,400 lb. and 2,500 lb. respectively. One H-13 was fitted with a Continental XT51-T-3 Artouste turbine and tested early in 1955 as the XH-13F (Bell Model 201).

Production by Bell of the improved Model 47G in 1953 led to the H-13G, of which the Army eventually purchased 265. This model introduced a small elevator, with endplate fins, geared to operate in conjunction with the rotor tilt to improve the CG range and stability. The engine remained unchanged in the H-13G, but the H-13H (Bell Model 47G-2) first ordered in June 1955, introduced the 250 h.p. Lycoming O-435, all-metal rotor blades and an overload gross weight of 2,700 lb. Deliveries of the H-13H began in December 1956 and production eventually totalled 470, including some for USAF use and a small quantity for MAP. Late in 1960, two H-13Hs were converted to Model 47G-3 standard with 225 Franklin 6VS-335 engines for high altitude performance and bigger diameter rotors; these went to Fort Rucker for evaluation as H-13Ks.

In 1957, the USAF purchased two Bell Model 47J Rangers with special

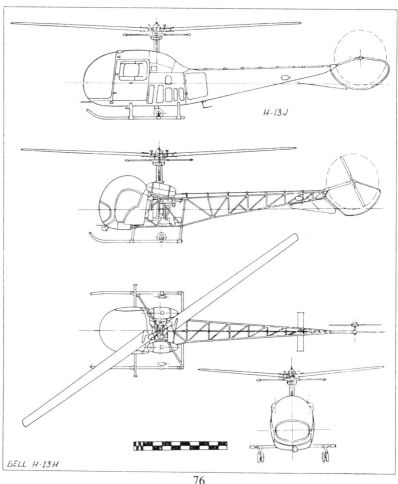

H-13J

BELL H-13H

Bell H-13J, one of the two acquired for use by President Eisenhower in 1957 (*Associated Press photo*).

interiors for Presidential use. With 240 h.p. Lycoming O-435 engines, these two helicopters were designated H-13J.

In 1962, the Army H-13D, H-13E, H-13G, H-13H and H-13K became OH-13D, OH-13E, OH-13G, OH-13H and OH-13K respectively, as observation helicopters. Air Force models became UH-13H and UH-13J and Navy versions went up to UH-13R.

Starting in 1963, the Army began procurement of two new variants similar to the commercial Model 47G-3B and differing from earlier models in having a turbosupercharged Lycoming engine. The OH-13S was a three-seat observation type to succeed the OH-13H, of which 265 were built. The TH-13T was a two-seat basic instrument trainer for helicopter pilots, and a total of 411 was delivered. The OH-13S engine was the 260 h.p. TVO-435-25, while the TH-13T had the 270 h.p. TVO-435-D1B.

TECHNICAL DATA (H-13H)

MANUFACTURER: Bell Aircraft Corporation, Niagara Falls, New York, and Bell Helicopter Company, Fort Worth, Texas.
TYPE: Army utility helicopter.
ACCOMMODATION: Pilot and two passengers.
POWER PLANT: One 200 h.p. Lycoming VO-435 piston engine.
DIMENSIONS: Rotor diameter, 35 ft. 1 in. Fuselage length, 27 ft. 4 in. Height, 9 ft. 6 in.
WEIGHTS: Empty, 1,564 lb. Gross, 2,450 lb.
PERFORMANCE: Max. speed, 100 m.p.h. at sea level. Cruising speed, 85 m.p.h. Initial climb, 770 ft./min. Service ceiling, 13,200 ft. Range, 238 st. miles.
SERIAL NUMBERS:

YR-13: 46-227/254.
H-13B: 48-796/860.
H-13D: 51-2446/2531; 51-16642.
H-13E: 51-13742/14231.
H-13G: 51-14232/14241; 52-7790/7993; 53-3654/3674; 53-3785/3814.
H-13H: 55-3355/3356; 55-4613/4633; 56-2161/2244; 57-1792/1875; 57-6203/6244; 58-1497/1552;

58-5304/5395; 58-6984/6998;
59-4911/4972; 60-6035/6046.
H-13J: 57-2728/2729.
OH-13S: 63-9072/9221; 64-15318/15432.
TH-13T: 64-17845/17903; 65-8038/8080; 66-4273/4298; 66-8040/8130; 67-15912/15965; 67-17003/17144; 67-17882/17885.

Bell HU-1B, U.S Army (*Bell photo 234642*).

Bell HU-1, H-1 Iroquois, HueyCobra

With its Model 204 design, Bell was successful in a June 1955 competition to select a new utility helicopter for the U.S. Army. Its mission was defined as front-line evacuation of casualties, general utility, and instrument flying training, and it was assigned the designation H-40 in the Air Force helicopter category. Development of the design was made under the weapon system designation SS443-L. The Lycoming T53 free turbine engine chosen to power the Model 204 made it the first turbine-powered aircraft, either fixed wing or rotary, ordered by the Army. Versions of the basic design have subsequently been adopted by the USAF, USN and USMC and have been produced in greater quantity than any other helicopter.

Three prototype XH-40s were ordered, and the first of these was flown by Floyd Carlson at Fort Worth on October 22, 1956, less than 16 months after design work began. Before the first flight, a service test batch of six YH-40s had been ordered, and these were delivered by August 1958. One remained with the makers, together with the XH-40s; one went to Eglin A.F.B. for climatic and cold weather testing, one to Edwards A.F.B. for Air Force testing and three to Fort Rucker for Army trials. Numerous small changes were made in the YH-40s, including a 12-inch lengthening of the fuselage to increase cabin capacity to four stretchers, an increase of ground clearance by four inches, wider crew door and changes in the controls.

When the H-40 was ordered into production, it was redesignated HU-1A in the Army category for utility helicopters and named the Iroquois. The HU designation gave rise to the "Huey" nickname for the type, which is unofficial but more frequently used than the official Iroquois. Delivery of the first of nine pre-production HU-1As was made on June 30, 1959, by which time further production contracts had been placed. These aircraft were generally similar to the YH-40s, with 700 h.p. Lycoming T53-L-1A engines, but 14 HU-1As were delivered to the Army Aviation

Bell HU-1A in U.S. Army Arctic colours (*Bell photo 234671*).

School as TH-1A instrument trainers with dual controls and provision for blind flying instrumentation.

Deliveries of the HU-1A were completed in March 1961. In addition to their use in the U.S. with Aviation and Medical Ambulance Companies, HU-1As were overseas as early as the spring of 1960, when two from the 82nd Airborne Division exercised in the Panama Canal Zone. Early in 1961 the first HU-1As arrived in Korea for the 55th Aviation Company and others were deployed to Europe and Alaska, the latter in customary red, white and yellow finish. HU-1As were among the first Army helicopters deployed to Vietnam, modified to carry 16 × 2·75-in. air-to-ground rockets and two 0·30-in. machine guns. Others served primarily in the medical evacuation role. Production of the HU-1A totalled 173.

Development of an improved model of the Iroquois began in June 1959 when the Army ordered four prototypes of the YHU-1B. This model was powered by the 960 s.h.p. Lycoming T53-L-5 engine, or the 1,100 s.h.p. T53-L-9 or T53-L-11 in later batches, and had an enlarged cabin to accommodate eight passengers (or three stretchers). Increased-chord rotor

Bell UH-1D with side armament, in Vietnam, showing over-all brown finish with no military markings except service name and serial number (*USAF photo*).

79

Bell UH-1F in USAF camouflage and tail codes of 4408th CCTS (*Duane A. Kasulka*).

blades of honeycomb construction were fitted. First flight was made in 1960 and deliveries began in March 1961.

Deployed to Vietnam in large numbers, the HU-1Bs served principally in utility and armed escort roles. For the latter, a variety of alternative armament installations was developed, the most favoured being the M6 flexible quadruple machine gun fixture, with two guns on each side of the fuselage, or the XM3 kit comprising a total of 48 × 2·75-in. rockets in two packs on the fuselage sides. Production continued from 1961 to 1965, with 1,014 built, plus one NUH-1B for test purposes.

In 1962, the Iroquois became the H-1 in the new tri-service designation system, with the HU-1A and HU-1B becoming UH-1A and UH-1B respectively. Also affected by this redesignation was the UH-1D, the proto-type of which had made its first flight on August 16, 1961, as the YHU-1D. This variant was based on the Bell Model 205 design, with a 1,100 s.h.p. Lycoming T53-L-9 or -11 turboshaft, a larger rotor diameter and redesigned cabin which would accommodate up to 12 troops in addition to the pilot.

Bell UH-1H in Army finish, with no national markings, serving with Puerto Rico National Guard in 1981 (*Austin J. Brown*).

Deliveries to the U.S. Army began on August 9, 1963, and production totalled 2,008, primarily for service as troop carriers in Vietnam.

The UH-1B and UH-1D were succeeded, as standard Army variants, by the UH-1C and UH-1H respectively. The UH-1C, deliveries of which began in September 1965, differed from the "B" in having an improved rotor with better performance, and increased fuel capacity. The T53-L-11 engine was standard and the same armament was carried as on the UH-1B. Production totalled 767. In the UH-1H, which followed the "D" onto the production line in September 1967, a 1,400 s.h.p. Lycoming T53-L-13 engine was fitted. Orders were spread from 1966 to 1976, for a total of 5,435, making this the most produced of any "Huey" variant and for many years the standard Army transport helicopter. Many UH-1Ds were also upgraded to UH-1H standard, and in 1968 a number of UH-1Ds was modified as HH-1Ds for crash rescue duty, carrying water tanks and spray booms.

A small number of UH-1Cs was modified to UH-1M configuration for the Army in Vietnam. These aircraft had the Hughes Aircraft INFANT (Iroquois Night Fighter and Night Tracker) system which used low-light-level TV and searchlights to help aim the side-mounted XM-21 gun installation. The first three UH-1Ms, with T53-L-13 engines, were operational in Vietnam at the end of 1969.

In 1976 development began of a version of the UH-1H as a Special Electronic Mission Aircraft (SEMA), with the code-name Quick Fix. Testing of the first three modified UH-1Hs, redesignated as EH-1Hs, by the 313th Military Intelligence Battalion of the 82nd Airborne Division, began in 1982, these aircraft having extensive jamming and monitoring gear. A further development was designated EH-1U, but the programme was cut back to 10 aircraft in favour of a Quick Fix version of the Sikorsky Blackhawk. The final Army variant was the UH-1V, a modification of the UH-1H for medevac duty. About 220 were converted, the first entering service with the 397th Aeromedical Detachment, New Hampshire ANG.

Introduction of the Huey into USAF service followed a design competition in 1963 when the Bell Model 204 was selected for missile site support

Bell UH-1N in South-East Asia finish, with no national markings, serving with 67th ARRS in 1983.

Bell EH-1H "Quick Fix" variant, showing IR suppression modification of engine exhaust pipe.

duties. Designated XH-48A in prototype form, this differed from Army models in being powered by the 1,000 s.h.p. General Electric T58-GE-3 engine, with provision to handle cargo loads of up to 4,000 lb. Up to 10 passengers could be carried. The first flight was made on February 20, 1964, with the designation changed to UH-1F, and deliveries began in September the same year. Production totalled 120, and some were deployed to Vietnam where 20 were modified as gunships to serve with the 20th Special Operations Squadron. Another 26 were built as TH-1Fs for instrument and hoist training.

In May 1968, the USAF announced a contract for 79 UH-1Ns. These helicopters were Bell Model 212, differing from earlier models in having twin-engined reliability provided through a Pratt & Whitney (UAC) T400-CP-400 engine which comprised two PT6T turboshafts driving a single rotor shaft through a combining gear box. Similar in most other respects to the UH-1H, the UH-1N could carry up to 14 passengers. First deliveries to the USAF were made on October 2, 1970.

Most of the UH-1Ns were later converted to HH-1N configuration, and 30 more ordered in 1970 were built as HH-1Ns, equipped for crash rescue duties. Most of these served with AF Reserve units but 10 were assigned to the 20th Special Operations Squadron for COIN and anti-terrorist missions. Some of

Bell UH-1M showing side-mounted XM-22 wire-guided missile installations (*MAP photo*).

82

the Air Force UH-1Ns also were converted to VH-1N staff transports, serving with the 1st Helicopter Squadron at Andrews AFB. Also for service in the crash rescue role, the Air Force bought 30 HH-1H versions of the Army's UH-1H, equipped with roof-mounted hoists and delivered between 1971 and 1973.

The E, J, K, L, T and W sub-variants were Navy or Marine versions. The Army AH HueyCobra versions, with G, Q, R and S designations, are described separately on following pages.

TECHNICAL DATA (UH-1)

MANUFACTURER: Bell Helicopter Company, Fort Worth, Texas.
TYPE: Utility, troop transport and armed reconnaissance helicopter.

	UH-1B	UH-1H	UH-1F	UH-1N
Accommodation:	9 seats	13 seats	11 seats	15 seats
Power Plant:	960 s.h.p.	1,400 s.h.p.	1,325 s.h.p.	1,250 s.h.p.
	Lycoming	Lycoming	GE.	P & W
	T53-L-5	T53-L-13	T58-GE-3	T400-CP
Dimensions:				
Rotor diameter, ft., in.	44 0	48 0	48 0	48 2½
Fuselage length, ft., in.	39 7½	41 10¾	41 5	42 10¾
Height, ft., in.	14 7	14 6	12 6	14 4¾
Disc area, sq. ft.	1,520	1,809	1,809	—
Weights:				
Empty, lb.	4,369	4,973	4,430	6,169
Gross, lb.	8,500	9,500	9,000	10,000
Performance:				
Max. speed, m.p.h.	147	127	138	121
Cruising speed, m.p.h.	126	127	123	—
Initial climb, ft./min.	2,660	1,600	2,123	1,460
Service ceiling, ft.	16,900	12,600	22,000	11,500
Range, st. miles	260	318	347	296

ARMAMENT: Basically unarmed, but numerous armament installations developed for use in Vietnam, especially on UH-1B and UH-1C. Principal armament systems were XM-3, comprising 48 × 2·75-in. FFAR (folding-fin aerial rockets); XM-5, comprising 40-mm. M-75 grenade launchers; XM-6 with four 7·62-in. M60C machine guns and 6,000 rounds; XM-16 combining XM-6 with rocket pods (on UH-1D and UH-1H); XM-21 as XM-16 but with two M-134 six-barrel mini-guns; XM-22 with six AGM-22B (Nord SS-11) wire-guided missiles; XM-23 comprising a pair of 7·26-in. M60D guns door-mounted; XM-26 with six TOW missiles in two pods; XM-30 with two side-mounted 20-mm. cannon; XM-31 with two 20-mm. M24 side-mounted gun pods; XM-39 with a 20-mm. cannon through each door of the UH-1B; XM-59, similar to XM-23 with 0·50-in. gun; XM-93 with hand-operated 7·62-mm. GAU-28/A six-barrel mini-guns in each door; XM-94, similar to XM-93 with two 40-mm. grenade launchers; XM-157/XM-158 with seven-round rocket pods added to SM-16 or SM-21 syb-systems; and XM-159/XM-200 with 19-round rocket pods.

SERIAL NUMBERS:

XH-40: 55-4459/4461.
YH-40: 56-6723/6728.
HU-1A: 57-6095/6103; 58-2078/2093;
  58-3017/3047; 59-1607/1716;
  60-3530/3545; 61-7170.
YHU-1B: 60-3546/3549.
HU-1B: 60-3550/3619; 61-686/803;
  62-1872/2105; 62-4566/4613*;
  62-12515/12555; 63-8500/8738;
  63-12903/12955*; 63-13086/13089*;
  63-13586/13593*; 64-13902/14100;
  64-14192/14201; 64-18261.
UH-1C: 64-14101/14191; 64-17621/17623*;
  65-9416/9564; 65-12738/12744;
  65-12759/12764; 65-12772*; 65-12846*;
  65-12853/12856*; 66-491/745; 66-14420*;
  66-15000/15245; 66-15358; 66-15360/15361;
YUH-1D: 60-6028/6034.
UH-1D: 62-2106/2113; 62-12351/12372;
  63-8739/8859; 63-12956/13002;
  64-13492/13901; 65-9565/10135;
  65-12773/12776; 65-12847/12852;
  65-12857/12895; 66-746/1210;
  66-8574/8577; 66-16000/16306;
  70-4507/4510*.

UH-1F: 63-13141/13165; 64-15476/15501;
  65-7911/7965; 66-1211/1224.
TH-1F: 66-1225/1250.
UH-1H: 66-16307/17859; 67-18411/18413;
  67-18558/18577; 67-19475/19537;
  68-15214/15794; 68-16050/16628;
  69-15000/15959; 69-16650/16679;
  69-16692/16732; 70-15700/15874;
  70-15913/15932; 70-16200/16518;
  71-20000/20339; 72-21465/21647;
  73-21661/21860; 73-22066/22135*;
  74-22295/22544; 76-22651/22690.
HH-1H: 70-2457/2486.
UH-1N: 68-10772/10776; 69-6600/6670;
  69-7536/7538.

*Includes some or all for MAP

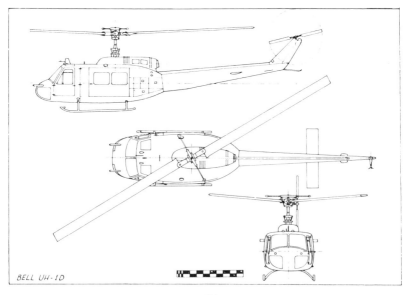

BELL UH-1D

84

Bell AH-1G, showing original TAT 102A nose turret and rocket pods on stub wings.

Bell AH-1 Cobra

During 1965, Bell undertook a radical redesign of the Model 204 (UH-1A Iroquois) to provide the Army with an interim advanced aerial fire support system (AAFSS), for which the Lockheed AH-56A Cheyenne was under long-term development. As a private venture, Bell built a prototype of this Model 209, making its first flight on September 7, 1965. Although its new, slender, fuselage, with seats for a gunner and pilot in tandem, gave it a very different appearance, the Model 209 made use of the rotor, transmission and power plant of the UH-1, with which it actually had some 85 per cent commonality of basic components. Using a derated Lycoming T53-L-13 engine and UH-1C dynamics, the Model 209 had a nose turret mounting a single 7·62-mm. Mini gun, and stub wings with two strong points each side, primarily intended to carry rocket pods.

The Army announced adoption of the Bell Model 209 as its interim AAFSS on March 11, 1966, assigning the designation AH-1G to two pre-production examples ordered on April 4. The first production order followed that same month, and subsequent contracts brought total procurement to 1,118 (inclusive of two pre-production aircraft and 38 diverted to USMC). The name Cobra was officially approved, but the type more often became known as the HueyCobra, stressing its relationship to the UH-1 Huey series. The Emerson Electric TAT-102A nose turret at first mounted the single Minigun in the XM-134 (GAU-28/A) system, but the XM-28 system later adopted featured two of the 7·62-mm. Miniguns or two XM-129 40-mm. grenade launchers or one of each. As alternatives to the XM-159 19-tube rocket pods, the stub wings could carry XM-18 or XM-35 pods with, respectively, 7·62-mm. or 20-mm. multi-barrel guns and their ammunition boxes.

Deliveries of the AH-1G Cobra began in mid-1967 and deployment to South-East Asia began at once, with the New Equipment Training Team at Vung Tan given the task of training Army personnel in the field. Starting on

September 1, 1967, NETT converted pilots, gunners and ground crews of the 334th Assault Helicopter Company at Bien Hoa, and this unit was ready to use its Cobras in the TET offensive of February 1968. Thereafter the AH-1G force in Vietnam built up steadily and the Cobra became an effective and deadly weapon in the hands of the Assault Helicopter Companies and the Air Cavalry. To assist with the conversion training, some Cobras were fitted with instructor flight controls and instrument panels, and were designated TH-1Gs.

With the ending of the war in Vietnam, the Army switched a substantial portion of its Cobra fleet to Europe, where the nature of potential armoured targets, including tanks, called for increased fire power. An interim solution to this problem was to adapt the helicopter to carry the Hughes BGM-71 TOW wire-guided anti-tank missiles. With the ability to carry a four-TOW pack on each outboard wing hardpoint and the necessary equipment changes, including a Sperry Rand Univac helmet sight for the gunner, 290 AH-1Gs were converted to AH-1Qs from 1973 onwards. A single YAH-1R was an AH-1G fitted with a 1,825 s.h.p. Lycoming T53-L-703 engine and served primarily as a prototype.

Features of the Q and R models were then combined in the AH-1S, which emerged in the early 'eighties as the major U.S. Army anti-armour helicopter, pending full service introduction of the AH-64A Apache. The designation actually covered four distinct groups of aircraft, comprising 755 modified AH-1Gs (including those previously converted to AH-1Qs); 100 new production "Step 1" AH-1S helicopters, 98 "Step 2" or "Up-gun" Cobras and 149 "Step 3" or Modernised AH-1S (of which 50 for the ANG). The T53-L-703 engine and TOW missile installations were common to all groups of AH-1S, but other features were introduced progressively. Among these features were the Kaman-developed composite main rotor blades, improved communications, a flat-plate canopy and revised instrument panel. The Step

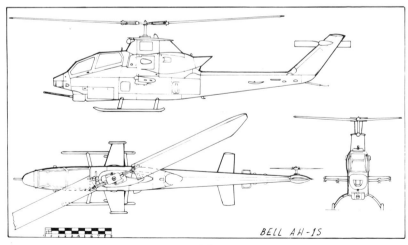

BELL AH-1S

2 Up-gun introduced a General Electric universal nose turret able to accommodate the XM-197 multi-barrel 20-mm. cannon or a 30-mm. gun, and a Baldwin Electronics XM-138 stores management sub-system.

After delivery of the Up-gun AH-1S helicopters, from September 1978 to October 1979, the Modernised AH-1S appeared, with many new features. Especially, there was a fully modernised fire control system, an infrared suppressor on the engine exhaust and various new avionics items including ECM. Fifteen of the Mod AH-1S or Step 1 aircraft were modified to TH-1S, with FLIR and integrated helmet and display sighting systems (IHADSS), to serve as trainers for AH-64A Apache gunners. In 1987, the Modernised AH-1S was redesignated AH-1F; at the same time, the Step 1 and Step 2 aircraft became AH-1P and AH-1E respectively. Of 378 modified AH-1Gs that eventually became AH-1Fs, 41 were TAH-1F trainers; the 377 earlier AH-1G conversions retained the AH-1S and TH-1S designations.

TECHNICAL DATA (AH-1S)

MANUFACTURER: Bell Helicopter Textron Inc. (a subsidiary of Textron Inc.), Fort Worth, Texas.
TYPE: Anti-armour attack helicopter.
ACCOMMODATION: Gunner and pilot in tandem.
POWER PLANT: One 1,800 s.h.p. Avco Lycoming T53-L-703 turboshaft engine.
DIMENSIONS: Main rotor diameter, 44 ft. 0 in. Length overall (rotors turning), 53 ft. 1 in. Height, 13 ft. 5 in. Rotor disc area, 1,520·5 sq. ft.
WEIGHTS: Empty, 6,598 lb. Gross, 10,000 lb.
PERFORMANCE: Max. speed, 141 m.p.h. Initial climb, 1,620 ft./min. Service ceiling, 12,200 ft. Range, 315 miles.
ARMAMENT: General Electric universal turret in nose houses one XM-197 three-barrelled 20-mm. cannon, with 750 rounds. Four weapons points on stub wings, normally carry eight BGM-71 TOW missiles and two pods with 7-19 FFARs each.
SERIAL NUMBERS:

AH-1G: 66-15246/15357;
  67-15450/15869; 68-15000/15213;
  68-17020/17113; 69-16410/16447;
  70-15936/16105; 71-20983/21052.

AH-1S: 76-22567/22610; 76-22692/22713;
  77-22729/22810; 78-23043/23125;
  79-23187/23252; 80-23510/23521;
  81-23526/23540; 83-24065/24076;
  83-24189/24199.

Bell Modernised AH-1S, later redesignated AH-1F, showing universal nose turret and TOW missile installation (*MAP photo*).

Bell OH-58C in standard Army finish, devoid of national insignia, and clearly showing the flat windscreen distinguishing this variant (*Bell photo 017872*).

Bell H-58 Kiowa

The Bell Model 206 was one of the three finalists in a US Army design competition launched in 1960 for a new Light Observation Helicopter (LOH). Twelve manufacturers submitted designs; in addition to Bell, they were Boeing-Vertol, Cessna, Gyrodyne, Hiller, Hughes, Kaiser, Kaman, Lockheed, McDonnell, Republic and Sikorsky. The finalists, announced on May 19, 1961, were Bell and Hiller, with the Hughes design added later, and five prototypes of each were ordered, respectively, as the Bell HO-4, Hiller HO-5 and Hughes HO-6. In the 1962 designation changes, these helicopters became the H-4, H-5 and H-6.

The Bell design, identified as D-250 at the project stage, was powered by an Allison T63-A-5 turboshaft engine and in compliance with the specification was a four-seater with a 400 lb. payload and a cruising speed of 110 knots. The first of the five prototype OH-4As made its first flight on December 8, 1962, at Fort Worth.

In April 1965, Bell began development of a civil derivative of the original OH-4A as the Model 206A Jet Ranger, and a prototype of this model flew on January 10, 1966. The powerplant, transmission and rotor were similar to those of the OH-4A, but the fuselage was redesigned to seat five. During 1967, the Army re-opened its LOH Competition, naming Bell the winner of this contest with the Model 206A on March 8, 1968.

Production models of the Model 206A were designated OH-58A rather than continuing the H-4 series previously used. Procurement plans for a total of 2,200 were announced, to be spread over five years with the first increment placed with Bell at the time the Model 206A was selected. Deliveries to the U.S. Army began on May 23, 1969.

Deployment of the OH-58A to Vietnam began in the late summer of 1969, and the type was widely used throughout the combat and thereafter. In 1976,

Bell began work, under U.S. Army contract, to improve the Kiowa through a series of modifications that included installation of an uprated version of the 317 s.h.p. T63-A-700 used in the OH-58A, together with "Black Hole" exhaust stacks and hot metal shroud for IR suppresion. A flat glass canopy was adopted, to reduce glint, and a number of internal improvements made. Three OH-58As were modified to this new OH-58C standard for testing, after which the Army contracted with Bell for a total of 435 Kiowas to be brought up to OH-58C configuration, this task being completed by March 1985. The OH-58B designation applied to a batch of 12 helicopters similar to the OH-58A exported to Austria.

A further modification of the OH-58 was selected by the Army in September 1981 for its Army Helicopter Improvement Program (AHIP) to provide a near-term scout helicopter (NTSH) pending the introduction of a wholly new design. Designated OH-58D, the AHIP Kiowa was the Bell Model 406, indicating that it had the new Bell four-bladed soft-in-plane main rotor in place of the two-bladed rotor of the original Model 206. The engine was a 650 s.h.p. variant of the Allison 250 designated T703-AD-700, and an extensively revised avionics fit was adopted. A feature of the OH-58D was its mast-mounted sight (MMS) above the main rotor, giving it a close combat aerial reconnaisance capability, with the added provision to carry an armament of four Hellfire or eight Stinger AAMs, two 7·62-mm gun pods, two Hydra-70 rocket pods or any combination of these on the sides of the fuselage. The MMS gave the OH-58D a day and night long-range vision capability and allowed the aircraft to designate targets using its laser range finder.

The first of five OH-58D prototypes flew on October 6, 1983, and after successful completion of trials in February 1985 the Army began a programme to convert 585 OH-58As and Cs to the AHIP configuration from 1985 to 1991. Deliveries of the modified (unarmed) aircraft began in December 1985 and deployment to Europe started in mid-1987. Early in 1988, 15 of the OH-58Ds with full armament provisions were delivered for evaluation by the 18th Airborne Corps Aviation Brigade at Fort Bragg, North Carolina. Unofficially, these were called AH-58D Warriors.

Bell OH-58D, showing mast-mounted sight above rotor (*Bell photo 027440*).

TECHNICAL DATA (OH-58C)

MANUFACTURER: Bell Helicopter Textron, Inc., Fort Worth, Texas.

TYPE: Light observation helicopter.

ACCOMMODATION: Pilot and co-pilot/observer plus provision for two passengers in cabin.

POWER PLANT: One 420 s.h.p. Allison T63-A-720 turboshaft.

DIMENSIONS: Rotor diameter, 35 ft. 4 in. Fuselage length, 32 ft. 7 in. Height, 9 ft. 6½ in. Rotor disc area, 979 sq. ft.

WEIGHTS: Empty, 1,818 lb. Gross, 3,200 lb.

PERFORMANCE: Max. speed, 138 m.p.h. at sea level. Cruising speed, 117 m.p.h. Initial climb, 1,800 ft./min. Service ceiling, 18,500 ft. Range, 300 miles.

ARMAMENT: None. (OH-58D carries two or four GD AIM-92A Stinger missiles for self-defence and two 7.62-mm. gun pods or rocket pods.)

SERIAL NUMBERS:

YOH-4A: 62-4202/4206.

OH-58A: 66-16687/16986; 69-16080/16379; 70-15050/15649; 71-20390/20865; 72-21061/21460; 73-21861/21934.

OH-58D: 85-24693/24716; 86-8901/8939.

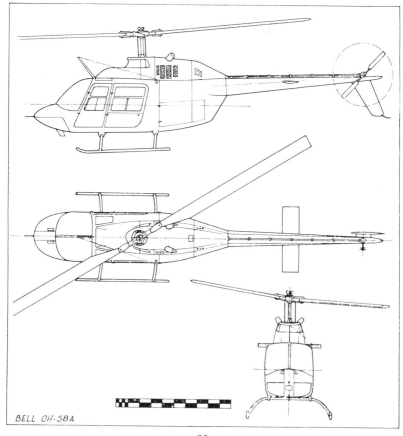

BELL OH-58A

90

Boeing PW-9 of 1925, with the then standard vertical tail stripes (*Boeing photo 122259*).

Boeing PW-9

Boeing's connection with U.S. Army fighters began in 1921, when the company successfully bid for a contract to build 200 MB-3As of Thomas Morse design (see pp. 503–505). While these were being built, work began on a new fighter prototype, the Boeing Model 15, as a private venture. First flown by Frank Tyndall on April 29, 1923, the Model 15 was tested by the Army later that year at McCook Field. Although the private-venture Curtiss XPW-8 had already been tested and ordered into production, the Boeing design was sufficiently promising for the Army to purchase the prototype and order two more examples in September 1923 which were then designated XPW-9 in the water-cooled pursuit category.

Powered by a 435 h.p. Curtiss D-12 engine, the XPW-9 had a steel tube fuselage structure and wooden wings, all fabric covered. All three had straight axle landing gear, but a split axle type was later tested on 23-1216, and was then used on production models. Following further comparative tests with the XPW-9s, a production order was placed on September 19, 1924, for 12 Boeing PW-9s, this order being increased to 30 on December 16. These aircraft were similar to the prototype, but the final 18 were strengthened to the same standard as the Navy's FB-1 version. One PW-9 was fitted with all-metal wings by Thomas Morse, with corrugated dural top skin and fabric undersurfaces.

Further orders for the PW-9 followed. In October 1925, a batch of 25 was ordered, these being PW-9As (Boeing Model 15A) with duplicated flying and landing wires to increase the safety factor. Another 15 were ordered in June 1926 as PW-9B but were converted to PW-9C before completion, and a second batch of 25 PW-9Cs (Boeing Model 15C) was ordered in August 1926. Changes again were small, including cockpit and landing gear details and larger wheels. The final contract was placed in

Boeing XPW-9, the first Boeing Model 15 (*USAF photo*).

August 1927 for 16 PW-9D after the last 9C had been converted to the prototype 9D (Boeing Model 15D). Differences in the D model included a new radiator, revised cowling lines and rudder balance area (which was added retroactively to earlier models). The weight of the PW-9D increased to 3,533 lb. compared with 3,039 lb. of the PW-9A. All models from A to D were powered by the 440 h.p. Curtiss D-12 (V-1150) engine.

No PW-9s were built after 1928, but several were converted to other models. The last PW-9 (25-324) became the XP-4 when fitted with a turbo-supercharged 500 h.p. Packard 1A-1500 and longer span bottom wings. Performance was poor and only five hours' flying was done. The final PW-9D (28-41) became the XP-7 with a 600 h.p. Curtiss V-1570-1 and deep chin radiator. It was later reconverted to PW-9D and a contract for four service test P-7s was cancelled. The 24th PW-9A (26-374) was

Boeing PW-9C in overall olive drab finish. The combination of vertical and horizontal stripes in the tail marking was developed by Boeing and adopted by the Army in 1926, but note here how early film has shown the vertical blue stripe as a light shade. Compare with P-12E picture on page 94 (*U.S. Army photo*).

modified into the single-seat AT-3 advanced trainer, with a 180 h.p. Wright V-720 (Model E) engine.

TECHNICAL DATA (PW-9D)

MANUFACTURER: Boeing Airplane Co., Seattle, Washington.

TYPE: Single seat interceptor.

ACCOMMODATION: Pilot in open cockpit.

POWER PLANT: One 435 h.p. Curtiss D-12D piston Vee-in-line.

DIMENSIONS: Span, 32 ft. 0 in. Length, 24 ft. 2 in. Height, 8 ft. 8 in. Wing area, 241 sq. ft.

WEIGHTS: Empty, 2,328 lb. Gross, 3,234 lb.

PERFORMANCE: Max. speed, 155 m.p.h. at sea level. Cruising speed, 124 m.p.h. Initial climb, 4 min. to 5,000 ft. Service ceiling, 18,230 ft. Endurance, 2·87 hr.

ARMAMENT: Two fixed forward firing 0·30-in. guns.

SERIAL NUMBERS:

XPW-9: 23-1216/1218.   PW-9C: 26-443/457; 27-178/202.

PW-9: 25-295/324.   PW-9D: 28-026/041.

PW-9A: 26-351/375.

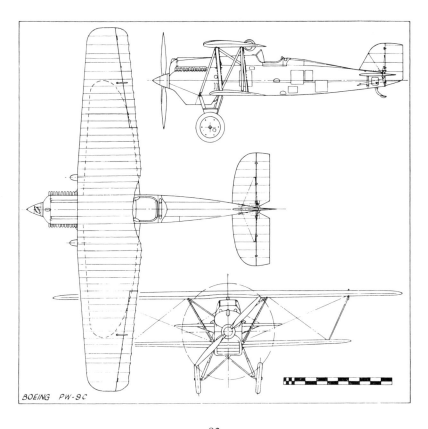

BOEING PW-9C

Boeing P-12Es from Selfridge Field. Here, the tail markings appear in their correct shades. Compare with PW-9C picture on p. 76 (*Boeing photo 5759*).

Boeing P-12

One of the best known Air Corps fighters of the inter-war period, the P-12 series originated in the private venture Boeing Models 83 and 89, built in 1928 and eventually purchased by the U.S. Navy as the XF4B-1s. These two aircraft first flew on June 25 and July 8, 1928, respectively, and were purchased by the Navy on June 19, 1929, after thorough testing. On the basis of the Navy test results, an Army examining board took the unusual step of ordering an equivalent version for the Air Corps without first acquiring and testing a prototype. On November 7, 1928, the Boeing company received a contract for ten aircraft of slightly modified design. The first nine were to be production type P-12s (Boeing Model 101).

The first P-12 flew at Seattle on April 11, 1929, and was identical with the Navy F4B-1 apart from deletion of the arrester hook and Naval equipment. In general, the design followed that of the earlier PW-9 series, but the use of a radial engine—the 450 h.p. Pratt & Whitney R-1340-7—was a break with Army precedent, all previous production fighters except a few Curtiss P-3As having had water-cooled in-lines. An unusual feature of the fuselage construction was the use of square-section bolted aluminium tubing, rather than conventional welded steel tube. The wings were fabric-covered wooden structures and the tail surfaces and ailerons had corrugated dural stressed skin. No cowling was fitted round the engine but streamlined "hats" were positioned behind each cylinder.

Modifications incorporated in the XP-12A included a long-chord NACA cowling round the 525 h.p. R-1340-9 engine, Frise balanced ailerons, a shorter undercarriage and a castoring tail skid in place of the fixed skid on the P-12s. First flown on May 10, 1929, the XP-12A was delivered to the Army next day but was destroyed on May 18 in a mid-air collision with another P-12.

The first major service version of the P-12 was the P-12B, 90 examples of which were ordered in June 1929—the largest single Army order for fighters since 1921. This version was identified as the Boeing Model 102B. Differences from the P-12 were small, and comprised the removal of the cylinder streamliners and use of Frise balanced ailerons as fitted on the XP-12A. In service, a ring cowl, first introduced on the P-12C, was fitted retroactively. The weight of the P-12B increased a little and performance, compared with that of the P-12, suffered accordingly. The Pratt & Whitney R-1340-9 was fitted.

Deliveries of the P-12B to pursuit squadrons were made in the first half of 1930. In 1932, the first "B" (29-329) was used as an engine test-bed with the designation XP-12G, flying with a turbo-supercharged R-1340-15 and other experimental versions of the R-1340 before reverting to P-12B standard.

Production continued with the P-12C, ordered in June 1930. This version, Boeing Model 222, introduced the engine ring cowl as a production item, a revised landing gear based on that designed for the experimental XP-9, and wing-tip navigation lights for night flying. The R-1340-9 was retained and the weight again increased. Of the contract for 136 aircraft, 96 were completed as P-12C and these went to pursuit squadrons in 1931.

They were followed by 35 P-12Ds (Boeing 227) in which the 525 h.p. R-1340-17 engine was introduced, with improvement in performance. Later, many P-12Cs and P-12Ds were fitted retroactively with the less angular vertical tail of the P-12E. In 1932, one P-12D (32-273) was fitted with a Pratt & Whitney XGRS-1340-E commercial geared engine and the P-12E tail, and was re-designated XP-12H. It later reverted to standard.

On September 29, 1930, Boeing flew a private venture development of the P-12 design, known as the Model 218, and tested by the Army as the

Boeing P-12B showing Frise-type ailerons (*U.S. Army photo*).

95

XP-925A, bearing the civil registration X66W. It introduced a number of new features, including a completely redesigned fuselage of monocoque design, modelled on that of the XP-9 and XP-15. A pilot's headrest was provided behind the cockpit. The fin and rudder, originally the same as

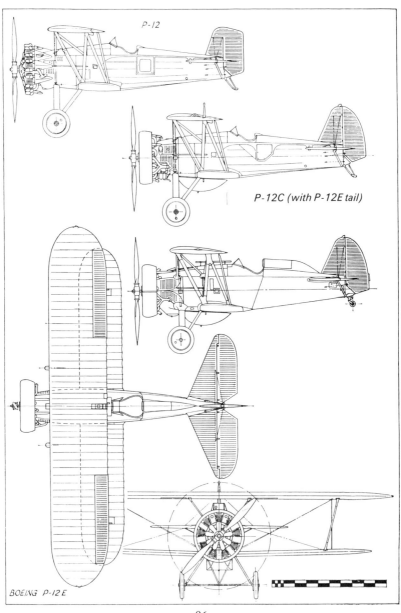

P-12

P-12C (with P-12E tail)

BOEING P-12E

A Boeing P-12D of the 35th Pursuit Squadron (*Peter M. Bowers*).

on the P-12B, were soon enlarged to a more rounded form. The 525 h.p. R-1340-17 engine, as fitted in the P-12D, was used. Following successful testing of X66W, the Army ordered 135 of the improved model P-12 in March 1931. Designated P-12E, the first 110 of this order were similar to the Boeing Model 218 prototype and were built as Model 234s. This was the most widely used of all the P-12 variants, remaining in service with front-line pursuit squadrons until replaced by Boeing P-26As in 1934 and 1935. Deliveries were complete by mid-March 1932.

The final 25 aircraft of the March 1931 order were powered by 600 h.p. R-1340-19 engines, rated for maximum performance at 10,000 ft., 3,000 ft. higher than the -17 in the P-12E. As this significantly altered the performance characteristics, these aircraft were designated P-12F (Boeing

Boeing YP-12K, one of seven modified from P-12Es (*Gordon S. Williams*).

97

Model 251). The last aircraft of the batch was fitted experimentally with an enclosed cockpit and sliding canopy.

One P-12E (32-43) was flown temporarily with a 575 h.p. R-1340-23 engine, which improved the service ceiling but gave few other advantages. While so re-engined it was known as the P-12J. Seven other P-12Es (31-553, 32-33, -36, -40, -42, -46 and -49) were re-designated YP-12Ks when Q-2 fuel injection systems were fitted to their R-1340-17 engines. The effect of this modification was to increase the gross weight to 2,769 lb. and the speed to 192 m.p.h. at 4,000 ft. One YP-12K was flown with a combination of ski-wheel chassis. One of the YP-12Ks was further modified to the single XP-12L when an F-7 turbo-supercharger was fitted, and the remaining six then became known as P-12Ks before reverting eventually to P-12Es.

In 1940, the designation A-5 (in the Power Driven Aerial Target category) was reserved for a converted P-12, but this project was discontinued by the Army. However, 23 P-12s were converted for use as radio-controlled targets and transferred to the US Navy as F4B-4As.

TECHNICAL DATA (P-12)

MANUFACTURER: Boeing Airplane Co., Seattle, Washington.
TYPE. Single seat pursuit.
ACCOMMODATION. Pilot in open cockpit.

	P-12	P-12B	P-12C	P-12E
Power Plant:	450 h.p. R-1340-7	450 h.p. R-1340-7	450 h.p. R-1340-9	500 h.p. R-1340-17
Dimensions:				
Span, ft., in.	30 0	30 0	30 0	30 0
Length, ft., in.	20 1	20 3	20 1	20 3
Height, ft., in.	9 7	8 10	8 8	9 0
Wing area, sq. ft.	227·5	227·5	227·5	227·5
Weights:				
Empty, lb.	1,758	1,945	1,938	1,999
Gross, lb.	2,536	2,638	2,630	2,690
Performance:				
Max. speed, m.p.h./ft.	171 5,000	166 5,000	178 8,000	189 7,000
Cruising speed, m.p.h.	135	135	141	160
Initial climb, ft./min.	2,080	2,040	1,410	—
Service ceiling, ft.	28,200	27,450	26,200	26,300
Range, miles	—	540	580	—

ARMAMENT. Two fixed forward firing 0·30-inch guns.
SERIAL NUMBERS:
P-12: 29-353/361.
XP-12A: 29-362.
P-12B: 29-329/341; 29-433/450; 30-029/087.
P-12C: 31-147/242.
P-12D: 31-243/277.
P-12E: 31-553/586; 32-001/076.
P-12F: 32-077/101.

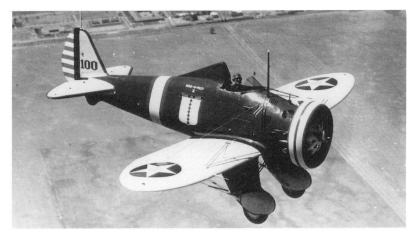

Boeing P-26A flown by leader of the 20th Pursuit Group, at March Field in 1934 (*USAF photo*).

Boeing P-26

Often known as "Peashooter" to its pilots, the P-26 was the first monoplane fighter produced for the U.S. Army Air Corps as well as being the first all-metal production fighter. The design was evolved during 1931, as Boeing Model 248, jointly by Boeing and the AAC, and a contract was signed in December 1931 for construction of three company-financed prototypes for which the Army would supply engines and equipment. Designated XP-936, the first of these flew on March 20, 1932, by which time the second airframe had already been delivered to Wright Field for static trials. The third XP-936 went to Selfridge Field for squadron trials while the first was evaluated at Wright Field.

Upon the successful conclusion of these trials, the three prototypes were purchased by the AAC and were successively designated XP-26, Y1P-26 and P-26 but were never issued as front-line equipment. In November 1932, a new specification was drawn up for a production development of the Boeing 248 and on January 11, 1933, the Air Corps signed a contract for 111 of the revised Boeing 266 type, designated P-26A. This contract was later increased to 136, the largest single contract placed since 1921.

Deliveries of P-26As began on December 16, 1933. From 1934 until replaced by Seversky P-35s and Curtiss P-36As in 1938–1940, the P-26s were front-line equipment in Air Corps pursuit squadrons at home and in Hawaii and the Panama Canal Zone. They operated with the 1st, 16th, 17th, 18th, 20th, 32nd and 37th Pursuit Groups.

Of the final batch of 25 aircraft, the first two had R-1340-33 engines with fuel injection and were designated P-26B. The first flew on January

10, 1935. The remaining 23 aircraft were completed with the original R-1340-27 engine without fuel injection and were designated P-26C, differing only in minor control changes from the P-26A. The P-26Cs, delivery of which began in February 1936, were all later converted to P-26B standard with installation of the fuel injection engines and revised fuel system.

TECHNICAL DATA (P-26A)

MANUFACTURER: Boeing Airplane Co., Seattle, Washington.
TYPE: Single-seat pursuit.
ACCOMMODATION: Pilot only in open cockpit.
POWER PLANT: One 500 h.p. Pratt & Whitney R-1340-27 piston radial.
DIMENSIONS: Span, 27 ft. 11½ in. Length, 23 ft. 7¼ in. Height, 10 ft. 0½ in. Wing area, 149·5 sq. ft.
WEIGHTS: Empty, 2,197 lb. Gross, 2,955 lb.
PERFORMANCE: Max. speed, 234 m.p.h. at 7,500 ft. Cruising speed, 199 m.p.h. Initial climb, 2,360 ft./min. Service ceiling, 27,400 ft. Range, 360 st. miles.
ARMAMENT: Two fixed forward firing 0·50-inch guns, or one 0·50-inch and one 0·30-inch. Up to 200 lb. bombs external.
SERIAL NUMBERS:

Y1P-26: 32-412/414.	P-26B: 33-179/180.
P-26A: 33-028/138.	P-26C: 33-181/203.

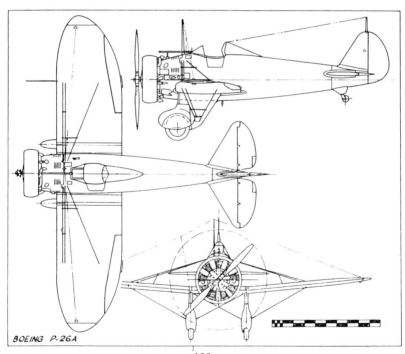

BOEING P-26A

Boeing Y1B-9A in War Games camouflage, May 1933 (*USAF. photo G956-876F-14*).

Boeing B-9

More bombers have been built by the Boeing company for the U.S. Air Forces than by any other single manufacturer. Nevertheless, the first Boeing bomber was designed and constructed as a private venture and only seven examples were built.

When Boeing engineers began project work on Models 214 and 215 in 1930 the Air Corps bomber squadrons were equipped with assorted biplanes of limited performance. Prototypes had been ordered of bomber variants of the Fokker XO-27 and Douglas XO-35 monoplanes, but neither of these designs took full advantage of all-metal construction. Boeing had meanwhile gone ahead with the Model 200 Monomail, an all-metal low-wing monoplane with a monocoque fuselage, an internally-braced cantilever wing and a retractable undercarriage. In 1930, Boeing proposed a twin-engined bomber of similar construction.

The Boeing bomber, given the experimental designation XB-901 by the Army, retained the same general layout as the Monomail, apart from having two 575 h.p. Pratt & Whitney R-1860-13 Hornet engines in nacelles ahead of the wing. The first flight was made by Les Tower on April 13, 1931, and in June the XB-901 was delivered to Wright Field for official evaluation; an average speed of 158 m.p.h. was achieved on the long flight across the continent, with only two refuelling stops. In the evaluation which followed, the design was well received, and the Army purchased the completed prototype as well as a second uncompleted machine powered with V-1570 engines, and a service test batch of five on an August 1931 contract, for a little over $100,000 apiece.

As the YB-9 (Boeing Model 215) the prototype was re-engined with supercharged R-1860-11 engines, boosting the top speed to 188 m.p.h. at 6,000 ft. The same engines were used in the five service test aircraft, which were designated Y1B-9A (Boeing Model 246) and delivered in 1932/33. The second prototype, first flown at Seattle on November 5, 1931, was delivered as the Y1B-9 (Boeing Model 214), with 600 h.p. Curtiss V-1570-29 Conqueror in-line engines, but had "inferior" performance according

101

to Army test reports, and the engines were replaced by Hornets. Although the Boeing B-9s amply vindicated the use of revolutionary structural and aerodynamic features, hoped-for production orders went instead to a still newer design, the Martin B-10 (page 432).

TECHNICAL DATA (Y1B-9A)

MANUFACTURER: The Boeing Airplane Co., Seattle, Washington.
TYPE: Light bomber.
ACCOMMODATION: Pilot, navigator/bombardier, radio operator, two gunners.
POWER PLANT: Two 600 h.p. Pratt & Whitney R-1860-11 piston radials.
DIMENSIONS: Span, 76 ft. 10 in. Length, 51 ft. 9 in. Height, 12 ft. 0 in. Wing area, 954 sq. ft.
WEIGHTS: Empty, 8,941 lb. Gross, 14,320 lb.
PERFORMANCE: Max. speed, 188 m.p.h. at 6,000 ft. Cruising speed, 165 m.p.h. Initial climb, 900 ft./min. Service ceiling, 20,750 ft. Range, 540 st. miles.
ARMAMENT: One 0·30-in. machine gun each in front and rear cockpits; 2,260 lb. bombs.
SERIAL NUMBERS:
YB-9: 32-301.   Y1B-9A: 32-303/307.
Y1B-9: 32-302.

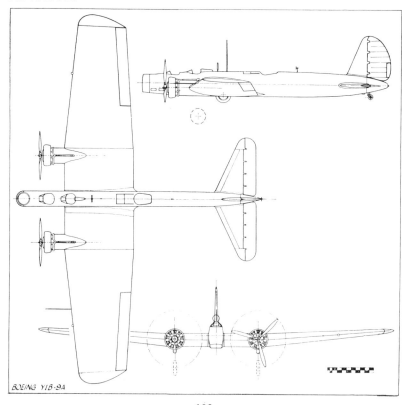

BOEING Y1B-9A

102

Boeing B-17G from the A.A.F. Tactical Center, Orlando (*USAF photo 28363AC*).

Boeing B-17 Flying Fortress

On June 18, 1934, Boeing engineers initiated design work on a four-engined aircraft to represent the company in an official design competition announced during May for a new multi-engined bomber. The Army specification, written at Wright Field, specified a bomb load of 2,000 lb. to be carried for not less than 1,020 miles and if possible 2,200 miles, at a speed of at least 200 m.p.h. and if possible 250 m.p.h. A flying prototype had to be available for Army trials by August 1935. Construction of a prototype was started by Boeing just one year earlier.

The Boeing design to meet this requirement was the Model 299, which had been sketched in outline earlier in the year together with a similar four-engined transport, the Model 300. Boeing was also already working on the design of the Model 294 bomber, ordered in 1935 to be built as the prototype XB-15 (see page 618). The 299 was smaller than the XB-15 but had similar lines; in construction it followed the techniques adopted by Boeing in their Model 247, the first twin-engined low-wing high-performance commercial transport. Flying Fortress was registered as a trade mark for the Model 299 before its first flight, to emphasize its defensive armament concentrated in five fuselage stations. From the outset, production of the design was a gamble, with no official backing likely until the prototype had been flown and tested, but the promise of large-scale orders for the winner of the competition. Eventually, 12,731 examples of the Model 299 were built by Boeing, Lockheed and Douglas.

103

Built in the Boeing factory in Seattle, the prototype 299 was assembled at Boeing Field early in July 1935, and was ready for its first flight on July 28. Boeing test pilot Les R. Tower was at the controls. Of metal construction throughout, the Model 299 had a circular fuselage section, with the wing low-mounted but having a root section of thickness equalling half the fuselgae diameter. Large plain flaps on the wing helped to reduce take-off and landing speeds at the comparatively heavy weight planned for the aircraft. Armament comprised a single machine gun in the nose and in each of four blisters on the fuselage aft the wing. A 4,800 lb. bomb load could be carried in the fuselage bomb bay. The engines were 750 h.p. Pratt & Whitney R-1690-E Hornet single-row radials, and as the prototype was privately financed it bore the civil registration X13372 and military markings but no military designation.

On August 20, 1935, the prototype was flown to Wright Field for its official tests, making a remarkable 2,100-mile non-stop flight in nine hours in the process. Preliminary trials were promising but on October 30 the aircraft was destroyed when a take-off was inadvertently attempted with the controls locked. A service test quantity of the Boeing bombers was ordered by the Army on January 17, 1936, and the designation YB-17 (later Y1B-17) was allocated, but the aircraft was not fully integrated into Air Corps procurement plans for another three years.

The first Y1B-17 (36-149) flew on December 2, 1936, and differed from the prototype (which had become known, inaccurately, as the XB-17) in having 930 h.p. Wright GR-1820-39 radials, crew increased from eight to nine, and other small changes. Twelve of the 13 Y1B-17s (Boeing Model 299B) were delivered between January and August 5, 1937, to equip the 2nd Bombardment Group at Langley Field, while the remaining aircraft went to Wright Field for trials. While the 2nd Bombardment Group flew their B-17s on many record-breaking flights, eventually totalling 9,293 hours without a serious accident, another aircraft, originally ordered for static testing, was completed as the Y1B-17A (37-369, Boeing Model 299F) with Moss/General Electric turbosuperchargers on GR-1820-51 engines. The planned static testing of the B-17 was considered unnecessary after a Y1B-17 had flown through a severe storm without damage. The Y1B-17A flew on April 29, 1938, was delivered to the Air Corps on

Boeing B-17 from 38th Reconnaissance Squadron, July 1941 (*Peter M. Bowers*).

Boeing B-17D in 1941 colours (*Peter M. Bowers*).

January 31, 1939, and increased performance of the B-17 to a maximum speed of 311 m.p.h. and service ceiling of more than 30,000 ft. Turbosuperchargers were a feature of all subsequent B-17s.

Experience with the B-17s in service with the 2nd Bombardment Group (the Y1B-17 designation was dropped when the service test period ended) strengthened the Air Corps' belief in this type of aircraft but also strengthened the opposition from the U.S. Navy, which claimed the right to defend America's shores from attack. In consequence, plans to purchase B-17s had to be scaled down, the first contract for a fully developed operational variant being placed in 1938 and covering 39 aircraft to be designated B-17B. The first of these (38-211) flew for the first time at Seattle on June 27, 1939, and was distinguished by a larger rudder, larger flaps and modified nose shape with the bomb-aimers' optically-flat panel further forward. The B-17B was originally designated Model 299E by Boeing, this being later changed to Model 299M. Delivery of the whole batch was completed by the end of March 1940.

Production continued with the B-17C (Boeing Model 299H), 38 of which were ordered in 1939. The first B-17C (40-2042) flew on July 21, 1940. The gross weight increased to 49,650 lb. from 47,920 lb. and R-1820-65 engines were fitted Externally obvious changes were the deletion of the fuselage-side gun blisters, changed shape of the ventral blisters and the use of two guns in place of one in the nose. Only slightly different from the B-17C was the B-17D, of which 42 were ordered in 1940 and delivered in 1941 after the first had flown on February 3. The changes

Boeing B-17F of 322nd Bomb Squadron, 91st BG, showing white areas of national insignia overpainted with grey (*Boeing photo*).

included introduction of self-sealing fuel tanks, provision for a tenth crew member, and deletion of external bomb racks. Twenty B-17Cs were supplied to the R.A.F. in 1941; those remaining in USAAF service were later modified to B-17D standard.

These Flying Fortresses were issued to the 19th Bombardment Group, which in May 1941 flew 21 of its B-17Ds to Hickam Field, Hawaii. This Group's 14th Bombardment Squadron moved to Clark and Del Monte Fields in the Philippines on September 5 and another 26 aircraft followed in October from California. All but two or three of the 19 B-17s at Clark Field were destroyed in the Japanese attack on December 8, 1941, while

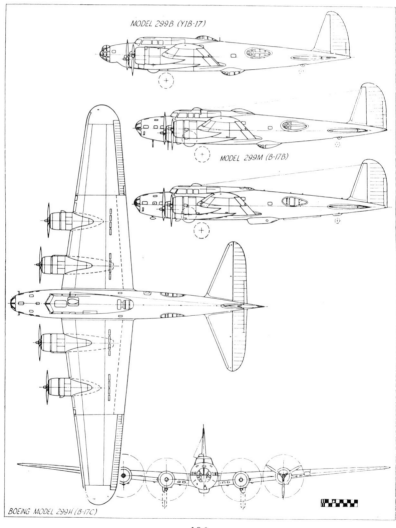

MODEL 299B (YIB-17)

MODEL 299M (B-17B)

BOEING MODEL 299H (B-17C)

Boeing B-17H of the Air Rescue Service (*Gordon S. Williams*).

many others were destroyed at Hickam Field in the Pearl Harbor attack of December 7. The survivors, including 16 which had been at Del Monte on the 8th, became the first U.S. aircraft in offensive action in World War II, starting on December 10. On that day, three B-17s attacked Japanese shipping, but before the end of the year the 19th Bombardment Group was withdrawn to Australia. In January, it moved into the attack again from bases in Java, and in the same month began to be re-equipped with B-17Es, the first model of the Flying Fortress to incorporate modifications dictated by operational experience—obtained in Europe by the R.A.F. flying 20 B-17Cs in 1941.

Changes made in the B-17E (Boeing Model 299-O) included a new, much enlarged tail unit to improve stability, especially at high altitudes, and a completely revised defensive armament. A manually-operated tail turret was introduced, together with power-operated turrets behind the cockpit and below and behind the wing. All these positions, and the radio compartment, carried two 0·50-inch machine guns. A single 0·50-inch was mounted at each waist station and two 0·30s were retained in the nose. The gross weight increased to 54,000 lb. Production of this model on two contracts at Seattle totalled 512, commencing with 41-2393 first flown on September 5, 1941, and deliveries were made to the 7th Bombardment Group which joined the 19th in the Pacific in December 1941, and to units of the Eighth Air Force in Europe.

The first B-17E in Europe arrived in the United Kingdom on July 1, 1942, and, together with succeeding aircraft, it went to the 97th Bombardment Group. This unit made the first B-17 sortie in the European Theatre of Operations on August 17, taking 12 B-17Es on a daylight raid against Rouen. Attacks at comparatively short range across the channel continued into 1943, but much of the Eighth Air Force's B-17 force was diverted to North Africa in the autumn of 1942.

Early operational experience with the B-17Ds in the Pacific Theatre led to a further series of design improvements, worked out in the early part of 1942 and introduced on the B-17F (Boeing Model 299P), the first of which (41-24340) flew on May 30, 1942. The most obvious external change was to the nose, which became a one-piece moulding. R-1820-97 engines were installed and a strengthened undercarriage allowed the gross weight to increase to 65,000 lb. and, eventually, 72,000 lb. Boeing built 2,300 B-17Fs at Seattle, and additional sources were provided by Lockheed Vega at Burbank (building 500) and by Douglas at Long Beach (building 605). Further modifications were introduced on later B-17Fs, either on the production line or, more usually, at modification centres to which new aircraft went before delivery to the USAAF. These changes, largely dictated by experience with the B-17E in Europe, were mostly concerned with armament, armour and fuel capacity, which was increased by additional tanks in the wings; external bomb racks also allowed an increase in bomb-load to a maximum of 20,800 lb. at the expense of operational radius.

In North Africa, the 16 squadrons of B-17Es which made up the 2nd, 97th, 99th and 301st Bomb Groups were in action from the beginning of 1943 as the strategic component of the Anglo-American Northwest African Air Forces, eventually becoming part of the 15th Air Force. The B-17Fs meanwhile went into action with the 8th Air Force in Europe, and were used for the first American attack of the War against the German homeland on January 27, 1943, in a raid on Wilhelmshaven. On the first anniversary of the first European operation by B-17s, August 17, 1943, B-17Fs from the 94th, 95th, 100th, 385th, 388th and 390th Bomb Groups struck at German factories at Schweinfurt, Wiener Neustadt and Regensburg in a spectacular daylight mission which cost 60 of the 376 bombers despatched. On October 14, in a second raid on Schweinfurt, 60 of 291 B-17s were lost.

Losses of this magnitude could not be accepted, and it was the experience of the 8th Air Force on these and other raids in the latter part of 1943 which led to development of the most-produced of all Flying Fortress variants, the B-17G (Boeing Model 299). The most important change made in the B-17G was the introduction of a "chin" turret below the nose, mounting two 0·50-inch machine guns. Other armament changes were made on B-17G sub-variants to meet local requirements, and on later aircraft improved turbo-superchargers were fitted to the R-1820-97 engines to increase the service ceiling to 35,000 ft. The B-17G, like the F, was built at three factories, production totalling 4,035 by Boeing at Seattle, 2,395 by Douglas at Long Beach and 2,250 by Lockheed Vega at Burbank.

Boeing QB-17 at Cape Canaveral, January 1956 (*USAF photo 158901AC*).

This variant was used almost exclusively in Europe, from the end of 1943 onwards, and was used for the first USAAF attack on Berlin, on March 4, 1944.

Meanwhile, B-17 strength in the Pacific area was gradually built up, from the beginning of 1942, with the establishment of the 10th Air Force in the China–Burma–India area.

Although the USAAF accepted a total of 12,677 B-17s during the War, the great majority of these were either written off before the end of hostilities in 1945, or taken out of service soon after. Thus, when Strategic Air Command was formed in 1946, it took on strength only a few hundred B-17Gs, and these were quickly phased out. The Fortress did continue, however, to serve in several specialized roles for a number of years. The first of these, adopted in the closing stages of the War, was as an air-sea rescue aircraft, with provision for a lifeboat to be carried under the fuselage, search radar replacing the chin turret and other armament deleted. Plans were made for about 130 to be converted as B-17H and TB-17H (trainers) but only a dozen B-17Hs were delivered; they later became SB-17Gs.

Some B-17s were fitted out as staff transports and flew as CB-17Gs and VB-17Gs, and others took the TB-17G designation for special training duties. The last variants to serve with the USAF were radio-controlled drones for air-to-air and ground-to-air target use, with the designation QB-17L and QB-17N. This variant was based on some wartime experiments in the use of a pilotless, stripped bomber with a massive bomb-load, from which the crews bailed out soon after take-off. (See BQ-7 below.) The post-war QB-17 drones were controlled from the ground or from specially-equipped DB-17P directors, by the 3235th Drone Squadron and similar units. All these variants were B-17G conversions.

XB-38. One B-17E (41-2401) was converted by Lockheed Vega in 1943 to have 1,425 h.p. Allison V-1710-89 engines and redesignated XB-38. First flight was made on May 19, 1943.

B-40. This designation applied to a bomber escort variant of the B-17 design, produced in an attempt to provide better defences for B-17 formations attacking Germany. The XB-40 (41-24341) was produced by conversion by Lockheed Vega from a B-17F, and incorporated an additional powered dorsal turret with two 0·5-in. machine guns, a chin

Boeing XB-40 conversion from B-17F, serial 41–24341 (*Boeing photo 95584*).

turret (as adopted later on the B-17G), twin instead of single guns in the waist positions, and armament storage in the bomb bays. Twenty more B-17Fs were converted to YB-40s at Tulsa, plus four TB-40 trainers, and a variety of different armament arrangements was used on these, including in some cases powered four-gun nose and tail turrets. Guns of up to 40-mm. calibre were fitted, and at least 30 machine guns and cannon were carried by some of the YB-40s.

The effect of the increased drag of the turrets plus the weight of the extra guns and ammunition was to reduce the operational speed of the YB-40 to the point where it was unable to keep formation with the B-17. Consequently, it proved an operational failure, although it flew nine combat missions, starting May 29, 1943, against St. Nazaire.

BQ-7. Under this little known designation, converted B-17s were operated against German targets from British bases as pilotless flying bombs. Stripped of armament and most equipment, they were packed

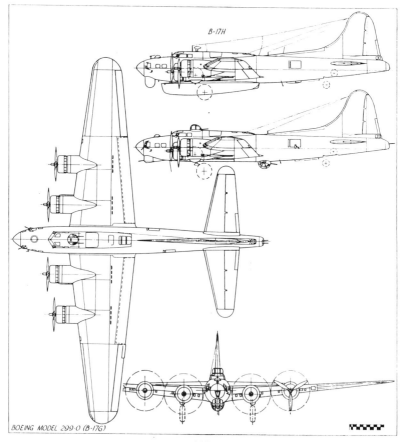

B-17H

BOEING MODEL 299-0 (B-17G)

Boeing XC-108A cargo conversion of B-17E (*USAF photo*).

with a powerful explosive, and were set on course by a pilot and radio operator, who then bailed out, leaving the BQ-7 to be radio-controlled from an accompanying B-17. Both B-17Es and B-17Fs were converted, about 25 being available to the 3rd Air Division in 1944; eleven operational flights were made against Germany, but unreliability of the control equipment detracted from the results, and the project, code-named Castor, was abandoned.

C-108. As noted above, a number of B-17s served as transports post-War, being designated CB-17. The C-108 designation had previously been adopted for four wartime conversions. These included a single XC-108 (41-2593) which retained nose and tail armament, but had all other guns deleted, and accommodated 38 persons. With extra fuselage windows, and a specially-equipped interior it was used by General Douglas MacArthur. Like the XC-108, the XC-108A was a 1943 conversion of a B-17E (41-2595). It was intended to serve as a heavy cargo freighter, having a large loading door in the port fuselage side. The YC-108 was a B-17F conversion (42-6036) with a V.I.P. interior, and the single XC-108B (42-30190), also a B-17F, was fitted as a fuel tanker to investigate the possibility of air-ferrying fuel over the "Hump" between Burma and China.

F-9. To serve as long-range photographic reconnaissance aircraft, a number of B-17s were converted to F-9s between 1942 and 1944. The first F-9s were B-17Fs with tri-metrogon cameras in the nose, and other cameras in the bomb-bay and rear fuselage. Different camera arrangements distinguished the 25 F-9A and F-9B, while the 10 F-9C were conversions of the B-17G. Those that remained post-war were eventually re-designated RB-17G. Some other camera-equipped Fortresses also operated as FB-17s. The RB-17 designation had also been used previously for all models prior to the B-17E declared obsolete on October 22, 1942.

TECHNICAL DATA (B-17)

MANUFACTURERS: Boeing Aircraft Co., Seattle, Washington (all variants); Douglas Aircraft Co., Long Beach, California (B-17F and G); Lockheed (Vega) Aircraft Corp., Burbank, California (B-17F and G).
TYPE: Medium bomber and reconnaissance aircraft.
ACCOMMODATION: Two pilots, bombardier, radio-operator, five gunners.

111

	YB-17	B-17C	B-17E	B-17G
Power Plant:	4 × 930 h.p. R-1820-39	4 × 1,200 h.p. R-1820-65	4 × 1,200 h.p. R-1820-65	4 × 1,200 h.p. R-1820-97
Dimensions:				
Span, ft., in.	103 9	103 9	103 9	103 9
Length, ft., in.	68 4	67 11	73 10	74 4
Height, ft., in.	18 4	15 5	19 2	19 1
Wing area, sq. ft.	1,420	1,420	1,420	1,420
Weights:				
Empty, lb.	24,458	27,650	32,250	36,135
Gross, lb.	42,600	46,650	53,000	65,500
Performance:				
Max. speed, m.p.h./ft.	256/14,000	291/25,000	317/25,000	287/25,000
Cruising speed, m.p.h.	217	231	210	182
Climb, min. to ft.	6·5/10,000	7·1/10,000	7·0/5,000	37·0/20,000
Service ceiling, ft.	30,600	36,000	36,600	35,600
Range, mi. with bombs, lb.	1,377/10,496	2,400/4,000	2,000/4,000	2,000/6,000
Armament:	5 × 0·30-in. 10,496 lb.	6 × 0·50 in., 1 × 0·30-in. 10,496 lb.	12 × 0·50-in. 1 × 0·30-in. 17,600 lb.	13 × 0·50-in. 17,600 lb.

SERIAL NUMBERS:

Y1B-17: 36-149/161.
Y1B-17A: 37-369.
B-17B: 38-211/223; 38-258/270; 38-583/584; 38-610; 39-1/10.
B-17C: 40-2042/2079.
B-17D: 40-3059/3100.
B-17E: 41-2393/2669; 41-9011/9245.
B-17F-BO: 41-24340/24639; 42-5050/5484; 42-29467/31031.
B-17F-DL: 42-2964/3482.
B-17F-VE: 42-5705/6204.
B-17G-BO: 42-31032/32116; 42-97058/97407; 42-102379/102978; 43-37509/39508.

B-17G-DL: 42-3483/3563; 42-37714/38213; 42-106984/107233; 44-6001/7000; 44-83236/83885.
B-17G-VE: 42-39758/40057; 42-97436/98035; 44-8001/9000; 44-85492/85841.
XB-40: 41-24341.
YB-40: 42-5732/5744; 42-5871; 42-5920; 42-5921; 42-5923/5925; 42-5927.
TB-40: 42-5833; 42-5834; 42-5872; 42-5926.

Eighth Air Force B-17G in post-March 1944 natural metal finish, with tail marking identifying 379th Bomb Group and number "1" at apex of triangle for the 524th Squadron (*USAF photo*).

Early Boeing B-29-1-BW, in olive drab finish with grey undersides. Most B-29s were delivered in natural metal finish (*USAF photo*).

Boeing B-29 Superfortress

Development of the B-29 Superfortress can be traced back to the XB-15 (Boeing Model 294—see page 540) which was built to an official requirement for a bomber able to carry a 2,000 lb. bomb-load for 5,000 miles. The idea that an isolationist America needed a strategic bomber of this kind of performance did not gain widespread support until 1939, but Boeing engineers made a series of private design studies for a so-called superbomber based on the XB-15 and the contemporary B-17. By 1939, these designs had evolved through Models 316, 322, 333 and 334 to the 341, able to carry a one-ton bomb load for 7,000 miles at an estimated top speed of 405 m.p.h.

On February 5, 1940, Boeing received the official requirement for a "Hemisphere Defense Weapon"; a bomber to carry 2,000 lb. of bombs for 5,333 miles, with a speed of 400 m.p.h. A heavy defensive armament was wanted, plus self-sealing fuel tanks, armour protection, and a maximum bomb-load of 16,000 lb. To meet this specification, the Model 341 was further developed into the Model 345, which met all the requirements, on paper, except the speed, which was down to 382 m.p.h. In competition with the designs by Consolidated, Lockheed and Douglas, the Boeing 345 was adjudged best, and on August 24, two prototypes were ordered, to be designated XB-29. The Consolidated design was continued also as the XB-32, but the Douglas XB-31 and Lockheed XB-30 did not proceed beyond the design stage. A third XB-29 was ordered in December 1940 together with a static test specimen.

Following Air Force inspection of the mock-up XB-29, in April 1941, drawings were issued and construction of the prototypes began at Boeing's Seattle factory. With the war in Europe spreading and the likelihood that America would become involved growing daily, the B-29 suddenly became top priority in 1941, and the subject of unprecedentedly large orders for an unproven type. A service test batch of 14 YB-29s was ordered, followed by a production contract for 250 in September 1941, another 250 in January 1942, and orders for more than 1,000 more by September 1942.

113

Boeing B-29-BA in post-war markings, with APQ-7 radar (*Crown Copyright*).

The first XB-29 (41-2) was flown at Seattle by Edward Allen on September 21, 1942, and the second (41-3) on December 28, 1942.

The Model 345 design featured a high-aspect ratio wing mid-mounted on the circular-section fuselage; Boeing's traditional bridge-type truss structure was abandoned in favour of web construction in the wings. Large Fowler flaps on the wings allowed a high wing loading without unduly high landing speeds. Special attention was paid to the nacelle designs to reduce drag; each nacelle housed two turbo-superchargers and the inners also had to accept the main units of the undercarriage when retracted. Wright R-3350 engines (-13 model in the prototype) had been adopted and a unique feature of the design was the use of two separate pressurized sections in the fuselage, connected by a small-diameter tunnel above the bomb-bay.

To meet the requirement for a heavy defensive armament the XB-29 was designed with Sperry remotely-controlled gun turrets, sighted periscopically, and originally intended to be retractable. This armament was fitted in the second XB-29, but was replaced in the third XB-29 (41-18335) by a General Electric system of turrets sighted from adjacent astrodomes, which became the production standard. The first flight of the third XB-29 was made in June 1943, closely followed on June 26 by the first YB-29 (41-36954). The 14 YB-29s and most production Superfortresses built by Boeing were produced at Wichita, where Boeing had acquired the Stearman factory. In addition, a new factory at Renton, originally built for Navy PBB-1 production, was given over to build B-29s, and further production lines were laid down by Bell at Marietta, Ga., and by Martin at Omaha.

On June 1, 1943, the first Superfortress unit—the 58th Very Heavy Bombardment Wing—was activated, in advance of deliveries of the YB-29s; seven of the latter had been delivered by July and apart from having R-3350-21 engines were similar to the third XB-29. At the end of 1943, a policy decision was taken not to use the B-29 against targets in Europe but to concentrate its use in the newly-formed 20th Bomber Command against Japanese targets from Indian and Chinese bases.

Deliveries of the B-29-BW from Wichita began in the autumn of 1943 and were followed in 1944 by Bell B-29-BAs and Martin B-29-MOs. These B-29s had R-3350-23, -23A or -41 engines and a normal gross weight of 133,500 lb. with a permissible maximum of 138,000 lb., compared with the prototype's 120,000 lb. The armament comprised two 0·50 in. guns in each of four fuselage turrets with 1,000 r.p.g., and two more in the tail together (in early aircraft) with a 20-mm. M-2 Type B cannon. Production of the B-29 totalled 1,634 at Wichita, 357 by Bell and 536 by Martin. The new plant at Renton built only the B-29A-BN which had a new centre section which increased the span by 12 inches, R-3350-57 or -59 engines, a small reduction in fuel capacity, and a four-gun top front turret, which had been introduced on later B-29s. Production of this version continued until May 1946, and 1,119 were built.

Four Groups—Nos. 40, 444, 462 and 468—of the 58th Bombardment Wing moved to India in the spring of 1944. A short period of training followed, the first B-29 operation taking place on June 5, 1944, against Bangkok, using landing fields in China as staging posts to refuel and rearm. Japan's mainland was hit on the second B-29 sortie, on June 15. In the summer of 1944, five B-29 bases, each large enough for a 180-aircraft Wing, were built on the Mariana Islands, and from these Tokyo was first attacked, on November 24. In these and other attacks, the B-29s made high level daylight raids with limited success; on March 9, 1945, a switch was made to low-level night operations using incendiary bombs, and 334 B-29s attacked Tokyo with devastating effect. Fire raids against Japanese cities with their close-packed wooden dwellings continued at high pressure from then until the end of the War, and the almost complete absence of Japanese air opposition led to field modifications to strip all but the tail armament, in favour of increased bomb load. Bell also completed 311 Superfortresses similarly stripped, with the designation B-29B.

For attacks on Japanese oil refineries, some B-29s were stripped of all armament and sighting blisters except the tail turret, and equipped with APQ-7 radar bomb sight, the aerial for which was carried in a 14-ft. "wing" under the fuselage. Based on Guam, these B-29s were used by the 315th Bomb Wing.

To cover B-29 operations photographically, 118 bombers were converted to F-13 and F-13A reconnaissance versions (re-designated RB-29A in 1948) carrying K-17, K-18 and K-22 cameras, with long-range tanks in the bomb-

Boeing F-13A reconnaissance version of B-29A (*Peter M. Bowers*).

Boeing ETB-29A with EF-84Bs attached at each wing tip for "Tip-Tow" experiments in 1950-53 (*USAF photo*).

bay. These became operational with the 311th Photo-Reconnaissance Wing's 1st Squadron in the Pacific Theatre in December 1944. Other wartime variants were the single XB-39 (41-36954) which was the first YB-29 re-engined with Allison V-3420-11 units, and the XB-44, which had Pratt & Whitney R-4360-33 engines and was the prototype of the B-50 series (see pp. 104–8).

Earlier in 1944, a special unit was formed to undertake atomic bombing missions; this was the 393rd Bombardment Squadron (VH), part of the 509th Composite Group. It was equipped with 15 specially modified B-29s, which were used for dropping trials with dummy weapons early in 1945 and then went to Tinian, in the Marianas, for operational training and simulated atomic missions against Japanese targets. On August 6, 1945, seven B-29s were used for the first atomic raid, comprising the B-29-45-MO *Enola Gay* carrying the 9,700 lb. "Little Boy"; a reserve aircraft; three weather reconnaissance B-29s, and two more carrying observers and recording equipment. Piloted by Colonel Paul W. Tibbets, the squadron commander, the *Enola Gay* reached the primary target of Hiroshima without incident and the bomb was dropped from 31,600 ft. The destruction was on an unprecedented scale, but the number of killed was actually fewer than in the first great B-29 fire raid against Tokyo, when 80,000 died.

The second atom bomb, "Fat Boy", was dropped on Nagasaki three days later, by the B-29 *Bock's Car*, and Japan surrendered five days after the second attack, on August 14. Over 2,000 B-29s had then been delivered to the USAAF and the production total eventually reached 3,960 before the Renton line was closed in May 1946. Over 5,000 B-29s on order in September 1945 were cancelled, including the B-29C variant which was to have had improved engines. The B-29D, on which work was also proceeding at Renton, was re-designated B-50 in 1946 and was built in some quantity for Strategic Air Command.

Numerous other B-29 variants appeared between 1946 and 1953 as conversions of the wartime bombers. The single XB-29E was a 1946

116

conversion for fire control tests and the XB-29H was used for armament tests in 1947; the six B-29Fs were winterized B-29s for Alaskan trials, and the XB-29G (44-84043) was a jet engine test-bed with a retractable J35, J47 or J73 in the bomb-bay.

About six B-29s became YB-29Js when fitted with R-3350-CA-2 fuel injection engines and revised nacelles with oil cooler intakes moved aft. Some were used for photo-rconnaissance as FB-29Js (later RB-29Js) and remaining F-13As became RB-29As before becoming obsolete. During the operations against Japan, specially equipped B-29s known as Super-dumbos had accompanied the bombers with rescue and survival gear. This version was developed post-war into the SB-29, carrying an A-3 lifeboat under the fuselage; 16 such conversions went into service. Others modified for weather reconnaissance were designated WB-29, remaining in service until 1957.

One aircraft was stripped for cargo use in 1949 and became the CB-29K. B-29s were also used as carriers for the Bell X-1 series and (in U.S.N. service as P2B-1s) the Douglas D-558-II, while the EB-29B (44-84111) was used to launch the McDonnell XF-85 parasite fighter during trials in August 1948. EB-29 designations were used on several Superforts for equipment testing.

In November 1947 a significant new role for the B-29 was first considered, when the USAF asked Boeing to develop methods of air-to-air refuelling, primarily for SAC bomber operations. On March 28, 1948, two B-29s demonstrated the feasibility of the project, using trailing hoses and grappling hooks to make contact. Only water was passed on this test, but full fuel-flow trials were made in May 1948, and the Air Force ordered conversion of 92 B-29s to serve as tankers using this British-developed system. They were designated KB-29Ms, and equipped the newly-formed Air Refueling Squadrons. Another 74 B-29s were modified to receive fuel from KB-29Ms; the designation B-29L reserved for this version was not

The Boeing YKB-29J (right) refuels a B-50D through Boeing-developed flying-boom system (*Boeing photo P-9983*).

117

used and they were known instead as B-29-MRs. In addition to Boeing's own development of the hose type refuelling, several B-29s were modified and tested by Flight Refuelling Ltd. in England, including the sole YKB-29T (45-21734) which was the first triple-point tanker for Tactical Air Command. Hoses for the probe-and-drogue refuelling method were trailed from the rear fuselage and from each wingtip.

In May 1948, Boeing suggested an alternative refuelling method, chiefly to increase refuelling rates, in which an aerodynamically-controlled telescopic pipe or boom was lowered from the tanker to connect with a socket in the receiver. Two YB-29Js were converted to YKB-29J tankers to test this idea, and in May 1949, the USAF ordered 40 B-29 conversions with this equipment, designated KB-29P. A total of 116 was eventually

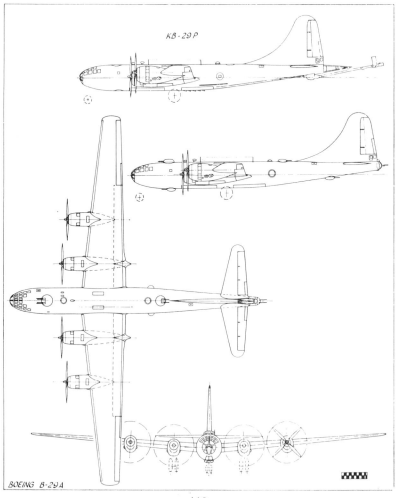

KB-29P

BOEING B-29A

modified, the first being delivered to SAC in March 1950.

Several SAC units were still using the B-29 in 1950 and the 19th, 22nd, 92nd, 98th and 307th Bomb Groups were in action in the Korean War, first operating from the Japanese mainland on June 18, 1950. The 19th BG used in Korea the 1,000 lb. Razon radio-controlled bomb and a few of its B-29s also carried the 12,000 lb. Tarzon. Operations by B-29s and RB-29s in Korea ended in July 1953. Other uses for Superforts included radar evaluation and target towing by TB-29s (until June 1960), VIP transport by VB-29s, and clandestine operations in 1952/53 by three Air Resupply and Communications squadrons.

TECHNICAL DATA (B-29)

MANUFACTURER: Boeing Airplane Co., Seattle and Renton, Washington; Wichita, Kansas. Bell Aircraft Corporation, Atlanta, Georgia. Glenn L. Martin Co., Baltimore, Maryland.
TYPE: Medium strategic bomber and reconnaissance aircraft; flight re-fuelling tanker.
ACCOMMODATION: Normal crew of ten.
POWER PLANT: Four 2,200 h.p. Wright R-3350-23, -51, -57, -79 or -81 piston radials.

	B-29	B-29A	B-29B	KB-29P
Dimensions:				
Span, ft., in.	141 3	141 3	141 3	141 3
Length, ft., in.	99 0	99 0	99 0	120 1
Height, ft., in.	29 7	29 7	29 7	29 7
Wing area, sq. ft.	1,736	1,736	1,736	1,736
Weights:				
Empty, lb.	70,140	71,360	69,000	69,011
Gross, lb	124,000	141,100	137,500	138,500
Performance:				
Max. speed, m.p.h./ft.	358/25,000	358/25,000	364/25,000	400/30,000
Cruising speed, m.p.h.	230	230	228	315
Climb, min. to ft.	38/20,000	38/20,000	38/20,000	500 ft./min.
Service ceiling, ft.	31,850	31,850	32,000	38,000
Range, st. miles	3,250	4,100	4,200	2,300

ARMAMENT: Two 0·50-in. guns in each of four remotely-controlled turrets plus two 0·50-in. and one 20-mm. or three 0.50-in. guns in tail turret. Up to 20,000 lb. bomb load.

SERIAL NUMBERS:
XB-29: 41-002/003; 41-18335.
YB-29: 41-36954/36967.
B-29-BW: 42-6205/6454*;
   42-24420/24919; 44-69655/70154;
   44-87584/87783; 45-21693/21872.

B-29-MO: 42-65202/65313;
   42-65315/65401; 44-27259/27358;
   44-86242/86473.
B-29-BA: 42-63352/63751†;
   44-83890/84156‡.
B-29A: 42-93824/94123; 44-61510/62328.

   *Ten numbers assigned to Bell and Martin for first five B-29s respectively from Atlanta and Omaha.   †Includes 168 completed as B-29B.
   ‡Includes 143 completed as B-29B, and four numbers cancelled before completion

119

Boeing B-50A from USAFE (*Planet News photo 188519*).

Boeing B-50 Superfortress

In 1944, Pratt & Whitney converted a B-29A Superfortress (42-93845) to have R-4360 Wasp Major engines, and this conversion was re-designated XB-44. With the same power plant and other production changes, a new Superfortress variant was put into production at Renton in 1945 as the B-29D. This designation was changed to B-50 before deliveries began. Changes, apart from the more powerful engines in redesigned nacelles, included a taller fin and rudder; a wing structure which used 75ST instead of 24ST alloy and was 650 lb. lighter but 16 per cent stronger than that of the B-29; a new undercarriage for higher operating weights; hydraulic rudder boost; hydraulic nose-wheel steering and other improvements.

An order for 60 B-50s (Boeing Model 345-2-1) had been placed before the War ended and work on these continued at a slow rate through the difficult period immediately after the War's end when the production rate at Renton was cut from 155 to 20 a month almost overnight. The first B-50A (46-002) did not fly until June 25, 1947. The B-50 became the first new bomber type delivered to Strategic Air Command, which had come into existence in 1946 with about 250 B-17s and B-29s, and it remained in front-line operational service alongside the B-36 for several years.

In all, 79 B-50As were built before being followed in production by the B-50B, in which structural changes were made to permit an increase in gross weight from 140,000 lb. to 170,000 lb. All but one of the 45 B-50Bs, as well as 57 B-50As, were adapted for in-flight refuelling by the early hose method from KB-29 tankers. Delivery of 45 of the B-50B model began in 1949, the first flight having been made on January 14, 1949. In the same year, the B-50D appeared. First flown on May 23, 1949, this was the most-produced B-50, distinguished by its two 700 U.S. gallon external fuel tanks, revised internal equipment, one-piece Plexiglas nose moulding, and new top forward turret. This was also the first variant produced with single-point refuelling and provision for use of the Boeing flying-boom

120

Boeing RB-50B reconnaissance version of B-50A (*Boeing photo BW45008*).

for aerial refuelling. Production of the B-50 was stepped up as the Cold War deepened in the period immediately preceding the Korean War, a total of 222 B-50Ds having been ordered by 1950 to equip SAC medium bombardment squadrons.

In 1947, all but one of the 45 B-50Bs were converted to RB-50Bs for service with strategic reconnaissance squadrons. The conversion included installation of four camera stations with nine cameras, weather reconnaissance instruments, and fittings for 700 U.S. gallon underwing tanks. In 1951, 43 of the 44 RB-50Bs were again modified: 14 became RB-50E; 14 became RB-50F with SHORAN, and 15 became RB-50G with changed radar equipment (distinguished by five small radomes), a B-50D-type nose, 16-man crew and increased armament. One B-50B (47-118) was flown experimentally with a track-type nose and main landing gear and was designated EB-50B while operated by Boeing on bailment from the USAF. A DB-50D was used for preliminary dropping trials of the Bell GAM-63 Rascal stand-off bomb.

Boeing B-50D (*Gordon S. Williams*).

121

Boeing TB-50D unarmed trainer (*Boeing photo P11028*).

As the B-50Ds reached the end of their front-line service, many were converted for supporting duties. These included crew trainers for Convair B-36 crews, using 11 TB-50A and 11 TB-50D conversions. The final Super-fortress production contract was for 24 TB-50H crew trainers, delivered in 1952 after the first had flown on April 29. This variant had no in-flight refuelling provision and no armament. Some later were converted for weather reconnaissance, as well as the TB-50Ds, as WB-50H and WB-50D respectively, before becoming KB-50Ks.

After successful trials in Britain with the single YKB-29T triple-hose refuelling tanker, similar conversions were made of B-50Ds as they became surplus to SAC requirements. The conversion to KB-50 standard

Boeing B-50D converted to KB-50J, with hose refuelling pods at wingtips and J57 turbojet pods on the auxiliary fuel tank pylons (*Peter M. Bowers*).

involved the deletion of armament and operational equipment, addition of fuel tanks in the bomb-bay and installation of A-12B-1 refuelling drums in the rear fuselage and in pods under each wing tip. Refuelling operator's control stations were added on each side of the fuselage, aft of the pressure shell, with observation blisters. The underwing fuel tanks were retained on the KB-50, which went into service with Tactical Air Command in 1957. The increasing performance of operational TAC fighters and bombers subsequently made it necessary to boost the speed of the tankers, and this was done by adding a J47 jet pod under each wing in place of the fuel tanks.

A total of 136 jet-boosted tankers was produced in this way by Hayes Aircraft Corporation, taking the designation KB-50J and KB-50K. The KB-50J designation applied to the 11 TB-50Ds and 101 B-50Ds after modification, many having been KB-50s in the interim. The 24 TB-50Hs, when modified, became KB-50Ks. The full modification comprised

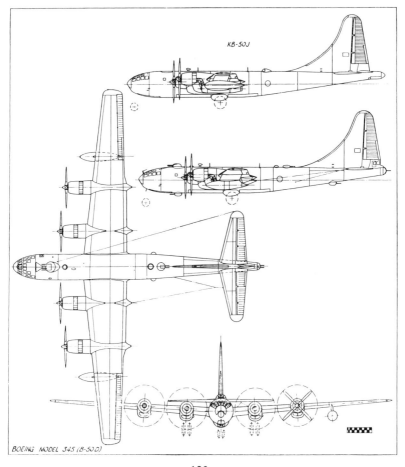

BOEING MODEL 345 (B-50D)

123

strengthened wing structure, additional crew stations, revised airframe systems, an additional rear fuselage tank and lengthened fuselage tail cone. The KB-50J first flew in December 1957 and deliveries began in January 1958. The KB-50J and KB-50K served as front-line equipment with TAC until 1964 and a few were still available to be pressed into service in Vietnam in 1965 to undertake emergency refuellings of fighters over hostile territory.

When the B-50 was first ordered, a further design stage was evolved, to take the gross weight to 207,000 lb. with a longer fuselage, larger wing and R-4360-51 turbo-compound engines. One prototype of this model was laid down as the YB-50C, actually being the last of the first production batch of 60 B-50As ordered, but it was not completed. Production orders had been placed for this version, comprising 14 bombers re-designated B-54A and 29 reconnaissance bombers designated RB-54A, but these were cancelled on April 7, 1949.

TECHNICAL DATA (B-50)

MANUFACTURER: Boeing Airplane Co., Renton, Washington.
TYPE: Medium strategic bomber and reconnaissance aircraft; flight-refuelling tanker.
ACCOMMODATION: (KB): Two pilots, engineer, radar-navigator and two refuelling operators.
POWER PLANT: Four 3,500 h.p. Pratt & Whitney R-4360-35, -35A or -51 piston radials plus (KB-50J and K only) two General Electric J47-GE-23 turbojets.

	B-50A	B-50D	KB-50J/K	TB-50H
Dimensions:				
Span, ft., in.	141 3	141 3	141 3	141 3
Length, ft., in.	99 0	99 0	105 1	105 1
Height, ft., in.	32 8	32 8	33 7	33 7
Wing area, sq. ft.	1,720	1,720	1,720	1,720
Weights:				
Empty, lb.	81,050	80,609	93,200	78,970
Gross, lb.	168,408	173,000	179,500	120,000
Performance:				
Max. speed, m.p.h./ft.	385/25,000	380/25,000	444/17,000	418/31,000
Cruising speed, m.p.h.	235	277	367	410/35,000
Climb, ft./min.	2,225	2,165	3,260	2,270
Service ceiling, ft.	37,000	36,700	39,700	35,000
Range, st. miles	4,650	4,900	2,300	5,000

ARMAMENT: Two 0·50-in. guns in each of three remotely-controlled turrets plus four in front upper turret and two more 0·50-in. and one 20 mm. in tail turret. Up to 20,000 lb. bomb load (KB variants unarmed).
SERIAL NUMBERS:
B-50A: 46-002/060; 47-098/117.   B-50D: 47-163/170; 48-046/127;
B-50B: 47-118/162.   49-260/391.
                                                         TB-50H: 51-447/470.

Boeing C-97A in MATS markings. Note full-length application of white paint to top of fuselage (*USAF photo*).

Boeing C-97 Stratofreighter

Design work on a transport variant of the B-29 Superfortress was begun by Boeing in 1942, with a preliminary engineering summary completed by June 20 in that year. The proposal was accepted by the USAAF and a contract for three prototypes designated XC-97 (Boeing Model 367) was awarded on January 23, 1943. The first of these prototypes (43-27470) flew on November 15, 1944, and had much in common with the B-29 as then in production, including the whole wing and tail structure and the R-3350-23 engines; the fuselage was of double-bubble section, the lower section being basic B-29 structure.

On July 6, 1945, the Air Force ordered ten more C-97s, the first six of which were completed as YC-97 cargo transports with R-3350-57 engines; first flight was on March 11, 1947, and these aircraft went into service with Air Transport Command on October 11 of the same year, flying a scheduled freight service between Hawaii and California. Features of the B-50, including the taller fin and R-4360 engines, were introduced on all Stratofreighters subsequent to these six aircraft. The three YC-97As had these features and were built as troop carriers; the first flew on January 28, 1948 and one of these aircraft (45-59595) flown by SAC crews, carried more than 1 million lb. of freight into Berlin in 27 flights in May 1949 during the Berlin Air-Lift. The tenth of the service test aeroplanes was designated YC-97B with 80 airline-type seats and was delivered to

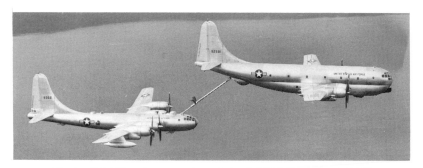

A Boeing KC-97A tanker conversion refuels a B-50D (*Boeing photo P10488*).

MATS on January 31, 1949, for service with the Pacific Division between California and Hawaii, later operating as the C-97B.

The first production contract was for 27 C-97As (on March 24, 1947) with R-4360-27 engines, capable of carrying a 53,000 lb. payload or 134 equipped troops. The quantity was increased to 50 in December 1948 and the first of these flew on June 16, 1949 and was delivered on October 15, 1949. These aircraft served with MATS, seeing service during the Korean War, and with SAC units to support B-50 operations. The three YC-97As were later converted to C-97A standard and redesignated. One of these, plus the C-97B and five C-97As, were converted to C-97Ds with cargo provisions deleted and special fittings for passengers. Three of these conversions operated for a time as VC-97D flying command posts.

The second production contract for Stratofreighters was for 14 C-97C aircraft, with R-4360-35A engines, strengthened fuselage, detail changes and equipment for use in casualty evacuation. In this role, they were sometimes known as MC-97Cs; the first was delivered in February 1951 and they were widely used in the medical capacity in the Korean War, carrying casualties back to the U.S. West Coast from Japan.

All subsequent Stratofreighter production was concerned with the tanker-transport KC models but two KC-97Gs were converted in 1955 at

Boeing C-97K conversion from KC-97G in SAC service, as shown by star-spangled blue fuselage band (*Boeing photo P39215*).

126

Jet-assisted Boeing KC-97L of Texas ANG, with F-4D (*USAF photo*).

Renton to test-fly Pratt & Whitney YT34-P-5 turboprops. Originally designated YC-137, these two aircraft (52-2693 and 52-2762) were restyled YC-97J before delivery. First flight of the YC-97J was made on April 19, 1955; the first was delivered to Edwards AFB on August 11, 1955, for testing and both were flown later by MATS 1700th Air Transport Group's Service Test Squadron.

Following development of the Flying Boom flight refuelling technique in 1948 and 1949, Boeing applied this system to the C-97A Stratofreighter in 1950. In December of that year the existence of the KC-97A conversion was first revealed; three such aircraft were modified at Renton, and served as prototypes for the KC-97E, 60 of which were built at Renton in 1951

Boeing KC-97G, serial 53-3816, the last of 888 C-97s built (*Boeing photo P17597*).

127

and 1952; the first delivery was made on July 14, 1951. Both the KC-97E and later models were convertible tanker/transports. Without refuelling equipment, the full transportation capability of the original model was retained; with the addition of the refuelling boom, the boom operator's position and extra tankage, partial transport capability was still available.

The KC-97E was followed in production by the KC-97F, of which 159 examples were built at Renton. It differed only in having 3,800 h.p. R-4360-59B engines in place of the 3,500 h.p. R-4360-35Cs. With delivery of the Es and Fs to SAC (the latter commencing on April 23, 1952), full refuelling capability of the Command began to be built up, with 20 tankers attached to each 45-aircraft wing of B-47s.

Further development produced the KC-97G, announced in July 1953 and the most-produced variant. By re-locating the tanks used to carry the fuel for delivery through the boom, it was made possible for the KC-97G

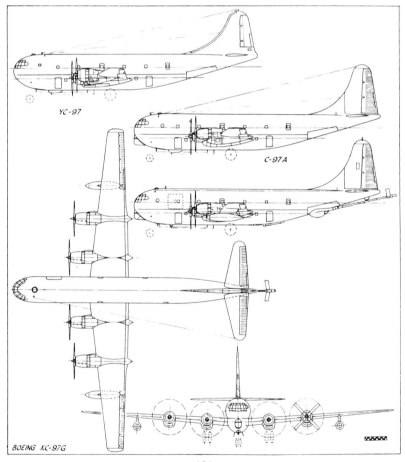

YC-97

C-97A

BOEING KC-97G

128

to serve as a transport or as a tanker without modification. The most notable modification was the addition of large permanent fuel tanks under the wings. Modifications were also made to the boom; the engines were unchanged from the KC-97F. The first "G" was delivered to the Air Force on May 29, 1953, and production of this model had totalled 592 by the time the last Stratofreighter was delivered. This aircraft (53-3816) was the 888th C-97 built; it was rolled out at Renton on July 18, 1956, and was delivered to the 98th Air Refueling Squadron on November 16, 1956.

The designation YC-97H was originally reserved for the two YT34 test-beds but during the period that these aircraft were tentatively known as YC-137s, the "H" designation was reassigned and in 1953 appeared as the single KC-97H. This was a KC-97J modified as a hose tanker using the probe and drogue method.

From 1957 onwards, KC-97Gs were gradually replaced by KC-135A jet tankers and many were modified for continued use in other roles. A total of 135 had their refuelling equipment removed by Garrett AiResearch and continued in service as C-97Gs and 27 became C-97Ks for SAC mission support duties, with all tanker features deleted, cargo doors sealed and passenger seats permanently installed. In 1964, when C-97Gs were assigned to Air National Guard units, 82 were modified by Hayes to KC-97Ls by the addition of J47-GE-25A jet pods removed from surplus KB-50s, and 28 others were converted to HC-97G air-sea rescue aircraft for interim use by the Air Rescue Service pending delivery of Lockheed HC-130H Hercules. The HC-97Gs were transferred to the AF Reserve in 1970, equipping two squadrons. Some KC-97Es and KC-97Fs were converted, respectively, to C-97E and C-97F, with aerial refuelling equipment removed and special provision for cargo carrying.

TECHNICAL DATA (KC-97G)

MANUFACTURER: The Boeing Airplane Co., Renton, Washington.
TYPE: Flight refuelling tanker and transport.
ACCOMMODATION: Crew of five—two pilots, flight engineer, navigator-radio operator, boom operator. (As a transport) 96 combat troops or 69 litters.
POWER PLANT: Four 3,500 h.p. Pratt & Whitney R-4360-59 piston radials.
DIMENSIONS: Span, 141 ft. 3 in. Length, 110 ft. 4 in. Height, 38 ft. 3 in. Wing area, 1,720 sq. ft.
WEIGHTS: Empty, 82,500 lb. Gross, 175,000 lb.
PERFORMANCE: Max. speed, 375 m.p.h. Cruising speed, 300 m.p.h. Service ceiling, 35,000 ft. Range, 4,300 st. miles.
ARMAMENT: None.
SERIAL NUMBERS:

XC-97: 43-27470/27472.	KC-97E: 51-183/242.
YC-97: 45-59587/59592.	KC-97F: 51-243/397; 51-7256/7259.
YC-97A: 45-59593/59595.	KC-97G: 51-7260/7271; 52-826/938;
YC-97B: 45-59596.	52-2602/2806; 53-106/365;
C-97A: 48-397/423; 49-2589/2611.	53-3815/3816.
C-97C: 50-690/703.	

Boeing B-47B-II in anti-radiation finish, with no national markings (*Boeing photo P15771*).

Boeing B-47 Stratojet

As the first swept-wing jet bomber built in quantity for any air force, the B-47 occupies an important place in USAF history. Although not flown until the end of 1947, its design began in the autumn of 1943, when the Air Force outlined its first tentative requirement for a jet bomber. In the early months of 1944, Boeing designers studied four possible layouts and submitted one of these, the Model 424, in March. It had a straight wing, a fuselage and tail unit like that of the B-29, and engines paired in nacelles on each wing. In December 1944, a new project, Model 432, had four engines grouped in the centre fuselage, with intakes alongside the cockpit and tailpipes on top of the rear fuselage. The wing was still unswept, but this project obtained a Phase I contract, covering design study including mock-up and wind tunnel models, but not construction.

While this Phase I study continued, Boeing designers had a chance to visit German research establishments immediately after the end of the European War, and as a result of this visit, the significance of wing sweep-back in relation to the jet bomber was first realized. By September 1945, a new design, Model 448, had been proposed, with four engines in the forward fuselage exhausting over the top of the wing, two more engines in the rear fuselage exhausting under the tail, and a swept-back wing. One month later, the design changed again, to Model 450, with a two-engine pod under each wing, and additional engine nacelles at each wing tip.

Construction of a mock-up of the bomber had been authorized in June 1945, and the Air Force team inspected this mock-up, representing the

Boeing RB-47H for electronic reconnaissance (*Boeing photo BW1155514*).

Model 450, in April 1946. As a result, further changes were made, to extend the span from 100 ft. to 116 ft., put the outer engines in pods like the inners, and to use a bicycle undercarriage with wing-tip outriggers and main wheels retracting into the fuselage. In this modified form, and at an estimated gross weight of 125,000 lb., two prototypes of the Boeing jet bomber were ordered by the Air Force in May 1946 and the designation XB-47 was applied. Metal was first cut for the prototypes in June 1946.

Construction proceeded rapidly, and the first XB-47 (46-065) was ready to fly in December 1947. The first flight—from Boeing Field in Seattle to nearby Moses Lake A.F.B.—was made on December 17 (the 40th anniversary of the Wright Brothers' first flight) by Bob Robbins and Scott Osler.

The thin, laminar-flow wing was swept back 35 degrees and mounted high on the fuselage; the flexibility of the structure allowed the wing to have anhedral when at rest, but not when under load in flight. The oval section fuselage was given over almost completely to fuel and bomb stowage, with the three-man crew seated in tandem in a pressurized, fighter-like cockpit in the nose. To boost the take-off performance, provision was made for 18 solid rockets to be mounted in the rear fuselage. Six Allison J35-2 turbojets of 3,750 lb.s.t. each powered the prototypes, which both flew at the original design weight of 125,000 lb.

The second XB-47 (46-066) flew in July 1948 and was similar to the first, but like all subsequent B-47s had the more powerful General Electric J47 engines. With 5,000 lb. J47-GE-3s installed, the first XB-47 (46-065) flew for the first time on October 7, 1949. The two prototypes were accepted by the Air Force in November and December, 1948, respectively, and the first contract for production aeroplanes was placed on September 3, 1948. The weapon system concept had not at that time been adopted by the USAF, but when it was, the B-47 became the first aeroplane to receive a Weapon System designation, the bomber and photo-reconnaissance versions being WS-100A and WS-100L respectively.

The first contract, valued at $30 million, was for only ten aeroplanes, production replicas of the XB-47s but with 5,200 lb.s.t. J47-GE-11 engines

131

and built in the Government-owned, Boeing-operated factory at Wichita, Kan. Designated B-47A, these ten aeroplanes were built to a gross weight of 160,000 lb. and the first flew on June 25, 1950. New equipment in the production model included the K-24 and, subsequently, K-4A radar bombing/navigation system and the A-2 armament system, comprising two 12·7-mm. machine guns in a remotely-controlled tail position. Delivery of the A models to the Air Force began in December 1950.

The first major production version of the Stratojet was the B-47B, first flown at Wichita on April 26, 1951. This model had structural modifications to allow the weight to go up to 200,000 lb., provision for two 1,500 U.S.-gallon fuel tanks under the wings and fittings for in-flight refuelling by the Boeing-developed flying boom method. In November 1948, 87 B-47Bs were ordered, to follow the As, and these were powered by the J47-GE-11 engines. The outbreak of war in Korea in 1950 brought greatly increased demands for Stratojets, however, and the contracts for the B increased eventually to 399, including ten built by Douglas at Tulsa and eight by Lockheed at Marietta to get second and third source production lines going. All these aircraft subsequent to the first 87 had 5,800 lb.s.t. J47-GE-23 engines.

Deliveries of the B-47B to the Air Force began in mid-1951, the first unit equipped being the 306th (Medium) Bomb Wing (comprising the 367th, 368th and 369th Bomb Squadrons of 15 aircraft each). By 1953, most of the Bs were in service, and Strategic Air Command was providing training and maintaining mobility by rotating the B-47 Wings through overseas stations in the Pacific, North Africa and the United Kingdom, each Wing remaining overseas for 90 days at a time. The first B-47 visit to the U.K. under this scheme was made in April 1953.

A total of 24 of the B models were converted in 1953 and 1954 to RB-47B and YRB-47B reconnaissance types, carrying eight cameras and associated equipment in a special package in the bomb bay. These were used mostly as crew trainers for the operational RB-47E. Another 66 were

Boeing B-47E in rocket-assisted take-off (*Boeing photo P16859*).

Boeing RB-47E. "O" prefix on tail serial number indicates aircraft is more than 10 years old.

modified for general crew training in 1953 and 1954, taking the designation TB-47B. Most of the Bs remaining in service as bombers were converted to B-47B-II under a modification programme which brought them up to B-47E standard. The changes included deletion of the fixed JATO installation in favour of a jettisonable 19- or 33-rocket assisted take-off pack; addition of a 16-foot drag parachute for landings; installation of ejection seats (two upward, one downward); substitution of 6,000 lb.s.t. J47-GE-25 turbojets with water injection and installation of General Electric radar-directed rear turrets mounting two 20-mm. guns.

All these features were standard on the B-47E, which followed the B into production at Wichita, Tulsa and Marietta. The first flew on January 30, 1953, and this version was the major production type. In addition to 1,241 B-47Es built at Wichita, Tulsa and Marietta, S.A.C. received 240 Wichita-built RB-47Es, with cameras in the bomb-bay and with a slightly lengthened nose (first flight, July 3, 1953). The gross weight of the E increased to 230,000 lb. Production of the B-47E continued until February 15, 1957, and S.A.C. reached its peak utilization of the Stratojet in the same year, with about 1,800 in service.

By 1960, the total was down to about 1,400, and a new system, known as Reflex, had been adopted to maintain the efficiency of the B-47 Wings. Under this system, all B-47 Wings were based in the U.S., but were rotated to bases in North Africa, Spain, the U.K., Alaska and Guam, for a 21-day "alert" period. In 1959, B-47 squadrons also began training in low-level "under-the-radar" penetration flights, involving operations known by the code name "Oil Burner" at less than 2,000 ft. altitude by day and night in all types of weather. On November 30, 1959, a SAC B-47 completed the longest-ever jet flight of 80 hours 36 minutes, covering a distance of 39,200 miles. Most B-47Es later were modified to B-47E-II standard.

In addition to the RB-47E, the Air Force used 15 RB-47Ks, which were E conversions with equipment for photo or weather reconnaissance at high or low level. The RB-47H was an electronic reconnaissance version with radomes in the nose, on each wing and under the rear fuselage,

133

and a special compartment in place of the bomb-bay containing receivers, recorders and three specialist operators. In all, 35 of the H model were built at Wichita, including three converted B-47Es designated ERB-47H for special missions with a crew of five.

Some B-47Es were converted to ETB-47E crew trainers, and in December 1958 Lockheed Georgia Division began work to convert the Stratojet as a pilotless drone, primarily to be used in testing the effectiveness of North America's missile defences. A trials aircraft was tested in May 1959 and full operational capability was attained in July 1960. Lockheed converted 14 RB-47Es to QB-47E configuration for use by the 3205th Drone Group at Eglin A.F.B., major changes including an arrester hook behind the rear wheels in addition to the necessary electronic gear. Four DB-47B conversions served as control aircraft.

In 1958, one Stratojet designated YDB-47B (51-2186) was used to carry a Bell GAM-63 Rascal stand-off bomb (weapon system WS112A) for its initial Stratojet dropping trials, and on October 13, 1959, another B-47

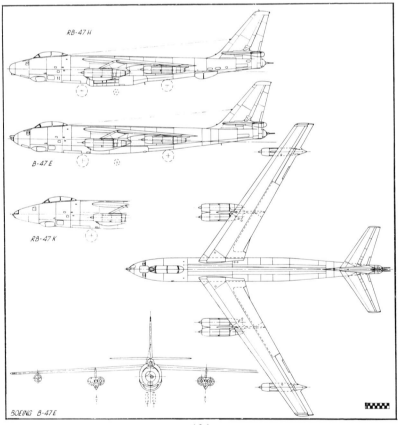

RB-47 H

B-47 E

RB-47 K

BOEING B-47 E

launched a Bold Orion experimental ballistic missile (weapon system WS199B) in an anti-satellite test against the Explorer VI. Two YDB-47Es and two DB-47Es were similar conversions from B-47Es for service tests with the Rascal.

One B-47B airframe (50-082) was set aside for conversion to the XB-56, later YB-47C, with four Allison YJ71-A-5 engines. This programme, and the proposed RB-56A, was cancelled before completion. Two other B-47Bs became XB-47Ds when converted to test-beds for the Wright YT49-W-1 turboprops; one of these engines replaced each inboard pod.

In 1953, two B-47Bs were converted for trials with the British-developed probe and drogue refuelling system. The receiver (50-009) became the YB-47F and the tanker (50-040), the KB-47G. The single YB-47J was a test-bed for a new radar bombing-navigation system.

During 1963, 35 B-47Es were modified to EB-47Ls as communication relay stations, and 24 WB-47Es went into service with MAC Air Weather Service, replacing some WB-47Bs used earlier. SAC retired its last B-47E on February 11, 1966, and the last operational Stratojets, WB-47Es, were phased out of service in 1969.

TECHNICAL DATA (B-47E-II)

MANUFACTURER: Boeing Airplane Co., Seattle, Washington, and Wichita, Kansas; Douglas Aircraft, Co., Tulsa; Lockheed Aircraft Corp., Marietta.

TYPE: Strategic medium bomber; photo, electronic and weather reconnaissance.

ACCOMMODATION: Two pilots and navigator, plus three electronic engineers in RB-47H only.

POWER PLANT: Six 6,000-lb.s.t. General Electric J47-GE-25 or 25A turbojets.

DIMENSIONS: Span, 116 ft. 0 in. Length, 109 ft. 10 in. Height, 27 ft. 11 in. Wing area, 1,428 sq. ft.

WEIGHTS: Empty, 80,756 lb. Gross, 206,700 lb.

PERFORMANCE: Max. speed, 606 m.p.h. at 16,300 ft. Combat speed, 557 m.p.h. at 38,550 ft. Initial climb, 4,660 ft./min. Service ceiling, 40,500 ft. Range, 4,000 st. miles.

ARMAMENT: Two 20-mm. M24A1 guns in remotely-controlled tail turret, 350 r.p.g. Up to 20,000 lb. bombs internally.

SERIAL NUMBERS:

XB-47: 46-065/066.

B-47A: 49-1900/1909.

B-47B: 49-2642/2646; 50-001/082; 51-2045/2356*.

B-47E-BW: 51-2357/2445; 51-5214/5257; 51-7019/7083; 51-17368/17386; 52-394/620; 53-2261/2417; 53-4207/4244; 53-6193/6244.

B-47E-LM: 51-15804/15812; 52-202/393; 52-3343/3373; 53-1819/1972.

B-47E-DT: 52-019/120; 52-146/201; 52-1406/1417; 53-2028/2040; 53-2090/2170.

RB-47E-BW: 51-5258/5276; 51-15821/15853; 52-685/825; 52-3374/3400; 53-4245/4264.

RB-47H-BW; 53-4280/4309; 53-6245/6249†.

RB-47K-BW: 53-4265/4279.

* Includes eight completed by Lockheed and ten completed by Douglas, and one not built (51-2145).

† Includes three B-47E converted to ERB-47H.

Boeing B-52H carrying four dummy GAM-87 Skybolts (*Boeing photo BW119399*).

Boeing B-52 Stratofortress

After going into service with Strategic Air Command in 1955, the B-52 assumed growing significance, until by 1958 it represented the most important component of the World's most powerful military force. With the ability to carry nuclear weapons to any target in the World, the B-52 was the deterrent upon which American foreign policy was based; the addition of Hound Dog stand-off bombs served to extend the useful life of the B-52 for several years after SAC's surface-to-surface ballistic missile force of Atlas, Titan and Minuteman variants had assumed primary responsibility for the deterrent.

The history of the B-52 goes back to April 1945, when the USAF first indicated to Boeing its interest in a turbine-powered long-range bomber. This was visualized with turboprop engines, and Boeing was asked to begin a design study, concurrently with Phase 1 development of the XB-47. In June 1946, a design competition was held by the Air Force for this category of aeroplane, and Boeing won a contract for further development. Although the gross weight was already 350,000 lb., this project did not meet the range requirement; by January 1948, the weight had gone to 480,000 lb., and flight refuelling became an integral part of the project, to keep the weight down and provide the necessary range.

In July 1948, Boeing received a contract for two prototype long-range bombers to be designated XB-52, powered by turboprop engines and with 20 degrees of wing sweep-back. Before the end of 1948, however, the design had been scrapped in favour of a new one (Model 464) with eight jet engines and 35 degrees wing sweep—a big brother of the B-47. In this form the two prototypes took shape at Seattle, designated XB-52 (49-230) and YB-52 (49-231). The XB-52 was rolled out for ground tests on November 29, 1951, but was later returned to the factory for installation of extra equipment and did not fly until October 2, 1952; the YB-52 was

Boeing XB-52 (*left*) and YB-52. The fuselage markings are photo-theodolite targets for test programmes (*Boeing photo P13414*).

rolled out on March 15, 1952, and was first flown on April 15, 1952, by A. M. "Tex" Johnson.

Like the B-47, the B-52 was a high-wing monoplane of all-metal stressed skin construction, the thin flexible wing having natural anhedral when the aircraft was at rest but taking on dihedral when loaded in flight. The main wheels were carried in the fuselage, and comprised four separate twin-wheel units, in two staggered pairs, fore and aft. Small outrigger wheels, retracting into the wings, provided for lateral balance. The comparatively small size of the bomb-bay, between the forward and aft main wheels, was indicative of the nuclear warfare which the B-52 was designed to wage. This bomb-bay was, nevertheless, able to accommodate McDonnell ADM-20 Quail (WS122A) decoy missiles in addition to a hydrogen bomb.

A production order for 13 B-52s was placed by the Air Force in February 1951, and the Stratofortress was assigned the designation WS101A in the new category of strategic weapon systems. Large scale production was not initiated until later, as the Air Force was still regarding the B-52 as competitive with the Convair B-60 which had yet to fly. By the time the first production B-52A flew on August 5, 1954, however, production was assured and a second line had been established at Wichita, Kansas. Only three B-52As were built (52-001 to 003). They differed from the prototypes in having a new cockpit seating the two pilots side-by-side rather than in tandem as in the B-47; a cross-wind landing gear; J57-P-9W engines in place of the 8,700 lb.s.t. -1 models; provision for flight refuelling and 1,000-U.S. gallon tanks under the outer wings. They were used for experimental programmes and the first was not delivered to SAC until November 27, 1957. One of the B-52As was modified to NB-52A in 1959 as a carrier for the North American X-15, making the first flight with an X-15 on June 8, 1959. The first B-52A (52-001), after flying from Edwards AFB at weights up to 415,000 lb., was retired in 1960.

Following the B-52A on the Seattle production line was the RB-52B,

137

27 of which were built, and the B-52B, 23 of which were built. Powered by J57-P-19W, -29W or -29WA turbojets, the "B" model was distinguished primarily in being equipped to operational standards and for a multi-mission role. The RB-52B (which had been designated XR-16 briefly) was the first Stratofortress able to carry in its bomb-bay a pod with four camera positions or electronic reconnaissance equipment as well as a two-man crew. The first RB-52B flew at Seattle on January 25, 1955, and deliveries to Strategic Air Command began on June 29, 1955, the first unit to receive these aircraft being the 93rd Heavy Bombardment Wing at Castle A.F.B., California.

In November 1956, eight B-52Bs of the 93rd H.B. Wing completed a 32-hour, 17,000-mile flight around North America and over the North Pole, as a preliminary to a round-the-world non-stop flight made between January 16 and 18, 1957, by three aircraft in 45 hours 19 minutes, refuelling three times en route from KC-97s. On May 21, 1956, a B-52B dropped the first known airborne hydrogen bomb, from 50,000 ft. over Bikini Atoll. One RB-52B was converted to a carrier for the X-15 as the NB-52B.

On March 9, 1956, the first B-52C flew. Powered by J57-P-29W engines, it had the same multi-mission capability as the B-52B, but the gross weight was increased from 420,000 lb. to 450,000 lb. and larger underwing tanks were carried. Delivery of 35 to SAC began on June 14, 1956. A similar version equipped exclusively for long-range bombing operations was built both at Seattle and Wichita, and was designated B-52D. The first B-52D (55-049) was rolled out at Wichita in December 1955 and was flown for the first time on June 4, 1956, followed on September 28 by the first from Seattle. Deliveries began on December 1, 1956, and production totalled 170.

The "D" was followed in production at both factories by the B-52E, first flown from Wichita on October 31, 1957, and from Seattle on October 3, 1957, with general improvements to the bombing, navigation and

Boeing RB-52B with wing tanks (*USAF photo 153353AC*).

Boeing B-52E carrying AGM-28 Hound Dog missiles (*Peter M. Bowers*).

electronics system. Delivery of 100 began on July 1, 1957. The 13,750 lb.s.t. J57-P-43W engine was introduced in the B-52F, the first of which flew from Seattle on May 6, and from Wichita on May 14, 1958. The last B-52F was completed at Seattle in November 1958 and was the last Superfortress built at that factory. Deliveries of the B-52F began on June 18, 1958, and totalled 89.

Following the B-52F in production at Wichita, the B-52G introduced major changes, including integral fuel tanks in the wing (the so-called "wet wing") to increase capacity and range; fixed, 700 U.S. gallon tanks under the wings; a shorter fin of greater chord, and a remotely-controlled rear turret. The rear gunner was moved forward to a rearward-facing seat alongside the electronic countermeasures operator to make up the defence team in the crew; forward facing behind and below the two pilots were the bombardier and radar navigator making up the offence team. The first B-52G flew at Wichita on October 26, 1958, and deliveries began on February 13, 1959. An indication of the great inherent range of the B-52G was given in December 1960 when an aircraft of this type from the 5th Bombardment Wing flew 10,000 miles in 19 hours 45 minutes, exceeding by over 3,500 miles the longest recorded flight by a B-52D.

The deterrent effectiveness of the B-52G was increased by its ability to carry two North American AGM-28 Hound Dog (WS131B) air-to-surface missiles, one under each wing inboard of the inner engines. Deliveries of the production model AGM-28 to the USAF began on December 21, 1959, by which time training and test rounds had already been dropped from a B-52. In February 1960, a B-52G from the 4135th Strategic Bomb Wing at Eglin A.F.B.—the first to be equipped with Hound Dogs—successfully launched two missiles on a single flight, and in April the same crew flew a 22-hour, 10,800-mile mission from Eglin to the North Pole and back, firing an AGM-28 near the end of the flight. Production of the B-52G totalled 193.

Still higher weights and greater ranges were achieved with the B-52H, which succeeded the B-52G in production at Wichita and from which it was distinguished primarily in having 17,000 lb.s.t. Pratt & Whitney TF33-P-3 turbofan engines. Other changes included a dual-radar gun-

A camouflaged Boeing B-52D, with blank undersides, over Vietnam dropping 750lb. bombs from the bomb bay and wing pylons (*USAF photo*).

firing control system and an ASG-21 Gatling gun for rear defence improved cabin arrangements for low-level penetration flights and provision to carry two Douglas GAM-87 Skybolts (Weapon System RS638A) under each wing. Pods containing penetration-aid rockets were provided under the wings between the nacelles of the inner and outer pairs of engines.

A B-52G (57-6471) was fitted with TF33 engines for flight tests and flew in July 1960; another made the first flight carrying four dummy GAM-87s on January 12, 1961. The first of 102 B-52Hs (60-0008) flew at Wichita on March 6, 1961, and the first aircraft of this model was delivered to SAC on May 9, 1961, at Wurtsmith A.F.B., where the 379th Wing became the first equipped with this Superfortress model.

The last B-52H off the production line was delivered to SAC on October 26, 1963. Eighteen months later, the Superfortress entered combat in South-East Asia, with deployment of the 2nd and 320th Bombardment Wings, both flying B-52Fs. The first mission was flown on June 18, 1965, with only moderate success and the loss of two of the 27 aircraft launched, in mid-air collision. Able to carry only a limited load of conventional weapons (27,000 lb. in 1,000 lb. bombs), the B-52Fs went through a modification programme in 1966, adding wing racks for up to 24 more 750 lb. bombs, after which B-52Ds were given the so-called "Big Belly" modification that allowed them to carry 84 of the 500 lb. bombs. The B-52D became operational in Vietnam in March 1966 with the 28th/484th Bomb Wing (Provisional), by which time the B-52B had been phased out of SAC service. While the B-52C and most B-52Fs also were phased out by the early 'seventies, the B-52Gs were used to supplement the B-52Ds in Vietnam, where operations by the Superfortress continued until August 15, 1973.

140

The B-52D, G and H remained in the SAC inventory throughout the 'seventies, and the 'D' models went through a "Pacer Plank" modification programme to extend their service lives, with structural strengthening and updated avionics. Starting in 1971, 281 B-52G and H models were modified to carry 20 Boeing SRAM (short-range attack missiles) each, the first of these entering service on August 4, 1972. All of these aircraft were also equipped with AN/ASQ-151 EVS (electro-optical viewing system) shown by two small chin "turrets", side by side under the nose. Other update programmes added so-called Phase VI avionics and an OAS (offensive avionics system), with 168 "G" and 96 "H" models modified by 1989.

In 1978, work began to equip 99 B-52Gs and 96 B-52Hs to carry 12 Boeing AGM-86 ALCM (air-launched cruise missiles) each on underwing pylons, deliveries of the modified aircraft starting in August 1981 for use by the 416th BW. A later programme provided the CSRL (common strategic rotary launcher) in the bomb-bay, allowing carriage of SRAMs, ALCMs or free-fall nuclear weapons.

By 1987, with all B-52Ds out of service, two squadrons of B-52Gs from the 42nd and 43rd BWs were operating in a conventional maritime support role, having been modified to carry AGM-84 Harpoon anti-ship missiles. The AGM-86-carrying B-52Gs were fully deployed by December 1984, serving with the 2nd, 92nd, 97th, 379th and 416th Bomb Wings. Deployment of the B-52Hs with this weapon then proceeded as the Rockwell B-1B took over the primary nuclear deterrent role. Two wings of B-52Hs (the 5th and 7th) were assigned to support conventional ground warfare, using their ability to strike at short notice over very long range.

Boeing B-52G in three-tone camouflage with light grey undersides, photographed in 1977 (*USAF photo*).

TECHNICAL DATA (B-52G)

MANUFACTURER: Boeing Airplane Co., Seattle, Washington, and Wichita, Kansas.
TYPE: Strategic heavy bomber.
ACCOMMODATION: Two pilots side-by-side; navigator, radar-navigator, E.C.M. operator and gunner.
POWER PLANT: Eight 13,750 lb.s.t. Pratt & Whitney J57-P-43WB turbojets.
DIMENSIONS: Span, 185 ft. 0 in. Length, 160 ft. 11 in. Height, 40 ft. 8 in. Wing area, 4,000 sq. ft.
WEIGHT: Gross, 488,000 lb.
PERFORMANCE (approx.): Max. speed, 600 m.p.h. at high altitude. Cruising speed, 510 m.p.h. at high altitude. Service ceiling, 55,000 ft. Range, 7,500 st. miles.
ARMAMENT: Four 0·50-in. guns in Bosch Arma MD-9 remotely-controlled rear turret. Up to 20 Boeing AGM-69 SRAM (eight internal, six on each inner wing pylon; or 12 Boeing AGM-86 (six on each wing), plus nuclear free-fall bombs.
SERIAL NUMBERS:

XB-52: 49-230.
YB-52: 49-231.
B-52A: 52-001/003.
B-52B: 53-373/376; 53-380/398.
RB-52B: 52-004/013; 52-8710/8716; 53-366/372; 53-377/379.
B-52C: 53-399/408; 54-2664/2688.
B-52D-BW: 55-049/067; 55-673/680; 56-657/698.

B-52D-BO: 55-068/117; 56-580/630.
B-52E-BW: 56-699/712; 57-095/138.
B-52E-BO: 56-631/656; 57-014/029.
B-52F-BW: 57-139/183.
B-52F-BO: 57-030/073.
B-52G: 57-6468/6520; 58-158/258; 59-2564/2602.
B-52H: 60-001/062; 61-001/040.

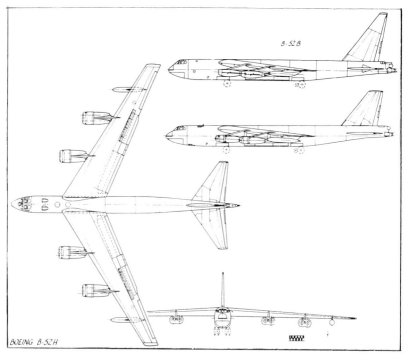

BOEING B-52H

142

Boeing KC-135A tanker (*Boeing photo P25840*).

Boeing C-135 Stratotanker, C-137

Delivery of the first KC-135A to the USAF on June 18, 1957, ushered in a new era for air refuelling, transport and numerous special-duty units which had previously had no chance to operate jet aircraft. During the 'sixties, the KC-135A became the standard USAF tanker and by 1970 was serving in many other roles. A total of 820 was built and these aircraft operated under at least 20 different designations in the C-135 series. In addition four similar but larger transports were acquired by the USAF as C-137s and the same basic design was the basis of the new E-3 AWACS aircraft selected for development by the USAF in 1970.

The C-135 family was developed from Boeing's jet transport prototype which was launched on May 20, 1952, and made its first flight on July 15, 1954. The design studies leading to this new aircraft originated as improved versions of the Model 367 Stratofreighter (C-97). As such, they had Model 367 numbers, the design chosen for construction being the 80th configuration studied, Model 367-80. The civil derivations of this prototype, which became known as the Dash 80, entered production as the Boeing 707, while the military C-135 family were Model 717 and Model 735. Following demonstrations with the Dash 80 fitted with the Boeing-developed flying-boom system, the USAF placed an initial order for 29 of the KC-135A tanker/transport version on October 5, 1954, subsequent contracts increasing the total to 732 KC-135As and 88 other versions. Following its adoption by the USAF, development continued under the WS-119L strategic weapon system designation.

The first KC-135A (55-3118) flew on August 31, 1956, at Renton, and was accepted by the USAF on January 31, 1957. The Stratotanker became

Boeing EC-135C flying command post (*Boeing photo P36016*).

operational with the 93rd Air Refueling Squadron on June 18, 1957. Its flying-boom refuelling system provided for a maximum transfer rate of nearly 1,000 U.S. gallons per minute, and its entire fuel capacity of 31,200 U.S. gallons was available either for transfer or for use by the KC-135A itself. In addition to its tanker role, the KC-135A could be used as a cargo or personnel transport, with an 83,000 lb. payload or carrying up to 160 troops.

In addition to the 732 KC-135As, the USAF procured 12 C-135Fs for sale to France, and 76 examples of the basic airframe configured for other-than-tanker duties, as described below. The C-135Fs were similar to the KC-135As but were adapted to use probe and drogue refuelling combined with the flying-boom.

Uniquely among USAF aircraft, the Lockheed SR-71, entering service in 1966, was unable to refuel from standard KC-135A tankers, because it used special JP-7 fuel. To suport the SR-71s, therefore, 56 KC-135As were converted to KC-135Qs, with suitably-modified fuel systems and specialized avionics for rendezvous with the SR-71As. They were operated by the 100th Air Refueling Wing out of Beale A.F.B., California.

In 1982, Boeing began delivery of a total of 128 converted KC-135As in which the original turbojet engines were replaced by JT3D-3B turbofans, designated TF33-PW-102 in USAF service. The engines came from ex-airline Boeing 707s (and their spares support packages) purchased by USAF, most

A Boeing KC-135R of the 19th ARW in 1987, showing the SAC sash, fin-tip Wing marking and large nacelles for F108 turbofans (*MAP photo*).

144

One of the two Boeing RC-135S special reconnaissance aircraft converted from C-135Bs, with nose radome and fuselage-mounted sensors.

of the airframes being used as a source of spares and equipment supplies (but some becoming E-8A and C-18, mentioned later). The re-engined tankers were designated KC-135E, 104 being for ANG units and 24 for Air Force Reserve; the first was delivered on July 26, 1982, to the 161st Air Refueling Group, Arizona ANG, at Phoenix. Similar conversions were made on 23 of the special-duty C-135s, as noted later.

A programme to re-engine the regular Air Force's C-135As—which had meanwhile had structural improvements to prolong their service lives to year 2020—began in 1980. The CFM International CFM56-2B-1 engine was chosen, with the designation F108-CF-100, and a prototype KC-135R conversion of a KC-135A first flew on August 4, 1982. A programme to modify some 630 KC-135As to this standard then began, the first operational KC-135R being delivered to the 384th Air Refueling Wing at McConnell AFB in July 1985. Eleven French Air Force C-135Fs were converted to C-135FR standard with the same engines, the first of these flying on August 3, 1985. The KC-135R had extensively updated systems, carried a greater fuel load and took off at the increased gross weight of 322,500 lb. Before the CFM56 programme got under way, at least four turbojet KC-135As had carried the KC-135R designation (between 1963 and 1971), when fitted with special reconnaissance equipment.

The non-tanker variants built by Boeing comprised 17 KC-135Bs, four RC-135As, 10 RC-135Bs, 15 C-135As and 30 C-135Bs. The KC-135Bs were

Boeing RC-135U conversion, lacking enlarged nose radome of other RC variants (*MAP photo*).

equipped to serve as airborne command posts (ABNCPs) primarily fulfilling the SAC commitment (under Project Looking Glass, commencing on February 3, 1961) to have an ABNCP airborne at all times, night and day throughout the year, carrying a battle staff headed by a general officer to maintain a command communications structure in case of war. The KC-135Bs had TF33-P-9 turbofans, in-flight refuelling receptacles, and flying-boom equipment. Immediately upon delivery, 14 were redesignated EC-135C and the other three became EC-135J equipped to serve in the Pacific area; one EC-135C was also later converted to EC-135J.

Numerous other "EC" versions appeared subsequently, some of these to serve in the ABNCP role in various parts of the world, others in more specialised roles calling for non-standard electronic installations. Other than the EC-135C and EC-135J already mentioned, these were all conversions from KC-135A or C-135A airframes, and therefore, in the first instance, powered by J57-P-59W turbojets. The ABNCP aircraft comprised five EC-135H used in the NATO area; three EC-135K for TAC and five EC-135P for various Commands. These were all KC-135A conversions with different equipment suites. One EC-135K and one EC-135P were lost, and two EC-135P reverted to KC-135A; the remainder—five "H", two "K" and two

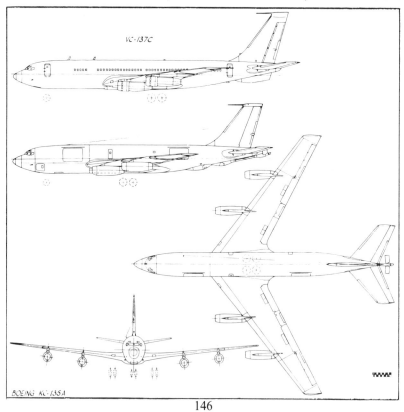

VC-137C

BOEING KC-135A

146

NKC-135A equipped for special research flights and used by 4952nd Test Squadron at Wright Patterson A.F.B. (*Norman Taylor collection*).

"P"—received TF33-PW-102 turbofans (ex-commercial JT3D-3Bs) in a programme begun in 1981. Serving as radio link aircraft in support of the SAC Post-Attack Command Control System were six EC-135A, four EC-135G and five EC-135L conversions from KC-135As, retaining the turbojets.

In 1967, eight C-135As (of 15 built—see later) were converted by Douglas to EC-135Ns to serve as spacecraft-tracking aircraft in the Apollo and Saturn programmes. They had 10 ft. long nose radomes to contain 7 ft. diameter dish antenna, and retained J57-P-59W engines. After their mission had been completed, they became C-135Ns with the tracking radar removed but nose radomes retained, for general test support duties, two being fitted with TF33-PW-102s in 1981. The designation EC-135B applied to two modified C-135Bs (turbofan engines) used as Advanced Range Instrumented Aircraft (ARIA) with similar nose radomes to, and some of the equipment from, retired EC-135Ns. The EC-135Y was a redesignation of NKC-135A (permanent test aircraft with Air Force Systems Command) when reconfigured for command/control/communications use in support of NATO commitments. The EC-135E was one of the last of the EC variants designated, being a modification of the C-135A with TF33-PW-102 engines for special USAF missions.

The first of the aircraft in the C-135 series to carry reconnaissance designations were the four RC-135As and 10 RC-135Bs built as such. The four RC-135As were actually the last of the entire family delivered to the USAF, in 1965/66. They were equipped to serve with MATS in the 1370th Photo Mapping Wing for photomapping and geodetic surveying, for which purpose they carried cameras in place of the usual forward fuselage fuel tank. In 1980 they were converted to serve as tankers, with the designation KC-135D. Whereas the RC-135As had standard J57 turbojets, the RC-135Bs were built with TF33-P-9 engines and were fitted, by the Martin company, with special reconnaissance equipment before entering service with the USAF in 1964/65. Two years later, all 10 became RC-135Cs with large side-looking radar (SLAR) cheek fairings along each side of the forward fuselage. Eventually, with further equipment modifications, three

147

Boeing C-135B for MATS. Apparently white markings on nose and rear fuselage are actually "Day-glo" red photographed through a filter (*Boeing photo P29004*).

became RC-135U and seven became RC-135V.

As with the EC series, several RC variants were produced by modifying KC-135As or C-135Bs to have special equipment for electronic/information gathering (ELINT) missions that were for the most part flown close to the borders of the Soviet Union and Communist bloc nations. These conversions included four RC-135Ds from KC-135As; a single RC-135E from a C-135B, supplemented later by at least one KC-135A conversion with TF33-PW-102s; six RC-135Ms from C-135Bs; two RC-135Ss from C-135Bs; one RC-135T from a KC-135A; three RC-135Ws from RC-135Ms and one RC-135X from EC-135B. Another EC-135B became the TC-135S to train crews for the RC-135S.

Another role for the C-135 was that of weather reconnaissance, for which 10 C-135Bs were converted in 1965 to WC-135Bs, serving principally with the 55th Weather Reconnaissance Squadron. They had TF33-P-5 engines and, like most of the EC and RC variants, lacked the refuelling boom.

Reference has already been made to the C-135A and C-135B that were among the variants built as such by Boeing. This resulted from the decision in 1961 to procure 45 Boeing transports based on the KC-135A airframes as a stop-gap measure to strengthen Military Air Transport System (MATS, later MAC). Able to carry up to 126 troops or 89,000 lb. of cargo, the C-135s had the refuelling boom and associated equipment deleted (although the boom

Boeing VC-137A VIP transport (*USAF photo*).

148

VC-137C s/n 62-6000 was first of two Presidential transport versions of Boeing 707-320B (*Boeing photo P30490*).

operator's station was retained). The tall fin and powered rudder, introduced on later KC-135As and made a retrospective modification on those in service, was standard on the C-135, but three early short-fin KC-135As were modified to interim C-135A standard pending completion of the first of 15 C-135As. The first flight of one of these interim aircraft was made on May 19, 1961. With TF33-P-5 engines replacing J57-P-59Ws, the first of 30 C-135Bs flew on February 15, 1962.

The C-135A and B transports served with various MATS wings until 1965, when Lockheed C-141As replaced them. Many were then modified for other missions, including EC and RC variants as already described. Others assigned to a permanent test configuration became NC-135As. Five VC-135Bs were conversions for use by the 89th MAW at Andrews A.F.B. as high-level government transports. Three WC-135Bs (conversions of C-135Bs) later became C-135Cs when used for transport and test duties, and the C-135E designation distinguished one or more C-135A conversions with the ex-commercial TF33-PW-102 turbofans.

Three examples of the Boeing 707-120 jet transport were ordered "off-the-shelf" by the USAF in May 1958, for transportation of personnel or high-priority cargo. Although generally resembling the KC-135A in layout, the 707 differed greatly in detail, and also had a greater fuselage cross section. Consequently the new aircraft were designated VC-137A rather than being

Boeing EC-18B ARIA replacement for similarly-equipped EC-135N (*USAF photo, via Dave Menard*).

149

numbered in the C-135 series. All three were subsequently modified to commercial 707-120B standard with TF33 turbofans and were redesignated VC-137B. They were joined in 1962 by a single VC-137C which was equivalent to the larger commercial 707-320B and was purchased to serve as the Presidential transport. A second VC-137C was acquired later.

Operated by the 89th Military Airlift Wing, Special Missions, based at Andrews A.F.B., Maryland, the VC-137C became known as the "Flying White House" or Air Force One—the official nomenclature for any aircraft in which the US President flies. One VC-137B was outfitted as a back-up for the VC-137C until the second VC-137C was acquired, this then becoming the primary Air Force One. The V prefix was eventually dropped from the C-137B and C-137C designations.

The designation C-18A was adopted for eight ex-American Airlines Boeing 707-320Cs, acquired by the USAF in 1981. Four became EC-18Bs as replacements for EC-135N Advanced Range Instrumentation Aircraft (ARIA) operated by the 4950th Test Wing. Two other similar 707s became EC-18Cs, subsequently redesignated E-8As, as prototypes, equipped by Grumman, to carry J/STARS, the USAF/Army Joint Surveillance Target Attack Radar System. In 1988 the USAF announced that it would use the EC-8B designation for 21 aircraft with CFM F108 engines, similar to the Navy's E-6As, to be used for the J/STARS mission, and one E-6A airframe was acquired as an additional, E-8B, prototype. Two EC-18Ds were equipped as cruise missile mission control aircraft.

TECHNICAL DATA (KC-135A)

MANUFACTURER: The Boeing Company, Renton, Washington.
TYPE: Tanker and transport.
ACCOMMODATION: Two or three pilots, radio-navigator, boom operator.
POWER PLANT: Four 11,200 lb. (13,750 lb. with w.i.) s.t. Pratt & Whitney J57-P-59W turbojets.
DIMENSIONS: Span, 130 ft. 10 in. Length, 136 ft. 3 in. Height, 38 ft. 4 in. Wing area, 2,433 sq. ft.
WEIGHTS: Empty, 98,466 lb. Gross, 297,000 lb.
PERFORMANCE: Max. speed, 585 m.p.h. at 30,000 ft. Cruising speed, 530 m.p.h. Initial climb, 2,000 ft./min. Service ceiling, 50,000 ft. Range 1,150 st. miles with 120,000 lb. of transfer fuel; 9,200 st. miles ferry mission.
ARMAMENT: None.
SERIAL NUMBERS:

KC-135A: 55-3118/3146; 56-3591/3658; 57-1418/1514; 57-2589/2609; 58-001/130; 59-1443/1523; 60-313/368; 61-261/325; 62-3497/3580; 63-7976/8045; 63-8871/8888; 64-14828/14840.
RC-135A: 63-8058/8061.
C-135A: 60-369/378; 61-326/330.
RC-135B: 63-9792; 64-14841/14849.

KC-135B: 62-3581/3585; 63-8046/8052; 63-8053/8057.
C-135B: 61-331/332; 61-2662/2674; 62-4125/4139.
C-135F: 63-8470/8475; 63-12735/12740.
VC-137A: 58-6970/6972.
VC-137C: 62-6000; 72-7000.
C-18/EC-18: 81-891/898.
E-8A: 86-0416/0417.

Boeing E-3A Airborne Warning and Control Systems aircraft (*Boeing photo*).

Boeing E-3 Sentry

In the early 'sixties, to provide a replacement for the Lockheed EC-121s serving in the airborne early warning role, the USAF drew up a requirement for a new Airborne Warning and Control System (AWACS). On July 10, 1970, the USAF accepted the proposal made by Boeing to use the commercial Model 707-320B as the air vehicle to carry a sophisticated radar system that would provide for all-altitude surveillance of airborne targets over land and water. Two prototypes were ordered, one each to fly competing radars proposed by Hughes and Westinghouse.

The prototypes were designated EC-137D (see Boeing C-135 entry for other C-137 variants) and were little-modified commercial airframes. The radar system required a large disc-like radome, of 30 ft. diameter, to be carried on struts above the rear fuselage and able to rotate. Both EC-137Ds flew in February 1972 (the first on the 9th) and after extensive testing, the Westinghouse AN/APY-1 radar was chosen on September 5, 1972, followed by the initiation of full-scale development of AWACS on January 26, 1973. The designation E-3 and the name Sentry were adopted for the production aircraft, which were to be powered by TF33-P-7 turbofans, more powerful than the JT3Ds retained in the prototype.

Two E-3As were ordered, and both EC-137Ds modified, for the FSD programme. Subsequent orders brought total procurement of the E-3A to 34 airframes (including the modified prototypes), of which one was retained by Boeing until 1987 as a test system, and the remainder delivered to the USAF. The first flight of an E-3A with full mission avionics was made at Seattle on May 25, 1976, and the first aircraft was delivered to the 552nd AWAC Wing (later, Division) at Tinker A.F.B., Oklahoma, on March 23, 1977. The 552nd was the sole user of the Sentry, including the 963rd and 964th AWAC Squadrons at Tinker and the 960th and 961st AWAC Support Squadrons based respectively at N.A.S. Keflavik, Iceland, and Kadena A.B., Okinawa, Japan.

The first 24 aircraft delivered to the USAF were in Core E-3A standard and the final 10 to US/NATO Standard. In a programme begun in July 1981, the Core E-3As were upgraded to E-3Bs with a number of improvements to their avionics systems, including ECM-resistant voice communications and *Have Quick* anti-jamming improvements. The first E-3B was re-delivered to the USAF on July 18, 1984. In 1984, work began to modify the 10 other E-3As to E-3C standard, with *Have Quick* and additional computing and communications capability, as in the E-3B. All Sentry aircraft in the USAF were fitted eventually with Joint Tactical Information Distribution Systems (JTIDS) for anti-jam communications.

TECHNICAL DATA (E-3A)

MANUFACTURER: Boeing Aerospace Company, Kent, Washington
TYPE: Airborne Early Warning and command post aircraft.
ACCOMMODATION: Flight crew of four, and 13 to 16 AWACS specialists.
POWER PLANT: Four 21,000 lb.s.t. Pratt & Whitney TF33-PW-100A turbofans.
DIMENSIONS: Span, 145 ft. 9 in. Length, 152 ft. 11 in. Height, 41 ft. 9 in. Wing area, 3,050 sq. ft.
WEIGHTS: Gross, 325,000 lb.
PERFORMANCE: Max. speed, 530 m.p.h. Service ceiling, over 29,000 ft. Endurance, 6 hours at a distance of 1,000 miles from base.
ARMAMENT: None
SERIAL NUMBERS:
EC-137D: 71-1407/1408
E-3A: 73-1674/1675; 75-556/560;
  76-1604/1607; 77-351/356;

78-576/578; 79-001/003;
80-137/139; 81-004/005;
82-006/007; 83-008/009

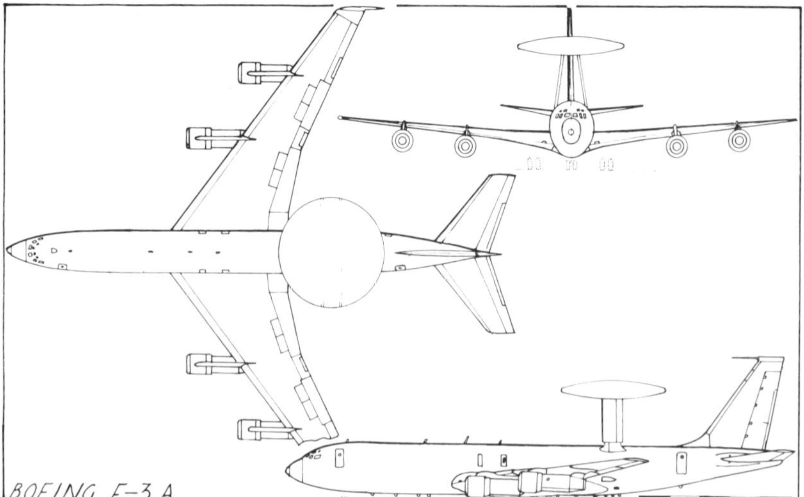

BOEING E-3 A

Boeing E-4B Advanced Airborne Command Post (*MAP photo*).

Boeing E-4, C-25

The Boeing 747 was selected in 1973 in an "off-the-shelf" buy to provide the airframe for the SS-481B Support System, an Advanced Airborne Command Post (AABNCP). Designed and equipped to provide a communications link at all times between the U.S. National Command Authority and the retaliatory forces maintained by the USAF, USN and U.S. Army, the AABNCP system is one of the most significant items in the armoury. The initial order for two aircraft, to be designated E-4A, was followed in July 1973 by a contract for a third, and a fourth was ordered in December 1973, to be equipped to a later standard and designated E-4B.

The first E-4A was flown on June 13, 1973, and, with an interim standard of equipment, was delivered to the USAF in December 1974, followed by the second in May 1975. These two aircraft originally had Pratt & Whitney F105-PW-100 (JT9D) engines; the third, delivered in September 1975, and fourth, delivered in August 1975, had General Electric F103-GE-100 (CF6-50E) engines and the first two were fitted with these engines also in 1976. The three E-4As were also progressively modified, from mid-1983 to early 1985, to the E-4B standard of the fourth aircraft.

Flight testing of a fully-equipped E-4B began on June 10, 1978, the equipment including a 1,200 kVA electrical system (with two 150 kVA generators on each engine), 13 external communication systems embracing VLF, LF, HF, MF, VHF, UHF and SHF wavebands, and provision for in-flight refuelling. No fewer than 46 antennae were fitted, one of these being the tracking aerial for the VLF communications system, with a length of 5 miles when trailed.

Operational testing of the E-4B began in the second half of 1978, but full service status was not achieved until January 1980, the aircraft being operated out of Offutt A.F.B., Nebraska, by the 55th SRW, SAC. An operational crew numbered up to 94, including a battle staff of 30 responsible for handling incoming and outgoing communications. The four-aircraft fleet was sufficient to ensure that one fully operational E-4B was airborne at all times, with a senior officer on board capable of assuming command of U.S. forces in extreme emergency. With an unrefuelled endurance of more than 12 hours the E-4Bs were cleared and crewed to fly missions lasting up to 72 hours.

During 1986 the USAF also selected the Boeing 747 as the new Presidential transport ("Air Force One") and two aircraft were ordered to replace the long-serving Boeing VC-137Cs. Based on the commercial 747-200B, the Presidential aircraft were designated VC-25A and were powered by 56,750 lb. s.t. F103-GE-102 engines, more powerful than the CF6s used in the E-4Bs. They also were equipped to an advanced standard in terms of cabin amenities, communications and survivability. With accommodation for 80 passengers, the VC-25As were operated, by the 89th MAW at Andrews AFB, by a 23-man crew. Delivery was scheduled for November 1988 and May 1989.

The designation C-19A was reserved for ex-commercial Boeing 747s for operation by the ANG.

TECHNICAL DATA (E-4B)

MANUFACTURER: The Boeing Company, Seattle, Washington (BCAC Everett Division and Boeing Aerospace Co., Kent, Washington).
TYPE: Airborne Command Post.
ACCOMMODATION: Up to 94 crew members, including flight crew and 30-strong battle staff.
POWER PLANT: Four 52,500 lb. s.t. General Electric F103-GE-100 turbofans.
DIMENSIONS: Span, 195 ft. 8 in. Length, 231 ft. 4 in. Height, 63 ft. 5 in. Wing area, 5,500 sq. ft.
WEIGHTS: Max. take-off, 800,000 lb.
PERFORMANCE: Max. level speed, more than 600 m.p.h. at 30,000 ft. Cruising ceiling, over 45,000 ft. Endurance (internal fuel), more than 12 hours.
SERIAL NUMBERS:
E-4A: 73-1676/1677;   E-4B: 75-125
    74-787   VC-25A: 82-8000; 92-9000.

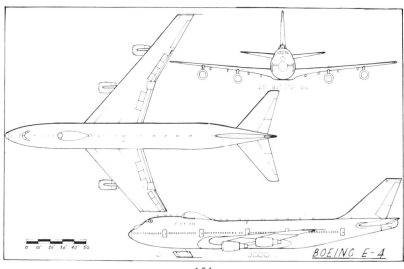

BOEING E-4

154

Boeing-Vertol CH-47B in Army all-brown finish.

Boeing-Vertol H-47 Chinook

The Chinook was selected by the Army Air Corps as its first standard VTOL transport in March 1959 after a design competition for Weapon System SS471L. An outgrowth of the Boeing Vertol 107 tandem-rotor, turbine-engined helicopter family, the Model 114 Chinook was designed to carry a maximum of 40 troops with full equipment and the fuselage—with rear loading provision—was large enough to contain all the components of the Pershing missile system (although not in a single load).

Five YHC-1B service test Chinooks were ordered in June 1959 and the first of these (59-4982) was rolled out for ground resonance testing in the spring of 1961. The second aircraft of the test batch (59-4983) was the first to fly, completing an initial 15-minute hover test in the hands of Leonard La Vassar at Philadelphia Airport on September 21, 1961.

Procurement of the Chinook began in 1960 with an initial contract for five HC-1As; the designation was changed to CH-47A in 1962. Deliveries of production aircraft to the US Army began on August 16, 1962, and in October 1963 the Chinook was designated as the Army's standard medium transport helicopter. Funds for additional Chinooks were provided in each Fiscal Year appropriation up to FY 1971, by which time over 600 had been procured.

Initial production CH-47As were powered by 2,200 s.h.p. Lycoming T55-L-5 turboshaft engines and later aircraft had 2,650 s.h.p. T55-L-7s. In October 1966, one of the YCH-47As made the first flight with 2,850 s.h.p. T55-L-7C engines, revised rotor blades and some drag reduction improvements to the rotor pylon and rear fuselage. This variant entered production as the CH-47B, with deliveries starting on May 10, 1967. It was followed in production by the CH-47C, first flown on October 14, 1967. This model had 3,750 s.h.p. T55-L-11 engines and more fuel.

An updated Chinook was developed by Boeing Vertol in the late 'seventies as the CH-47D, featuring T55-L-712 turboshafts with an emergency rating of 4,500 s.h.p. each, composite rotor blades, an APU, a triple cargo hook installation, extensively modernised systems, avionics and flight deck and a higher gross weight. Prototype YCH-47Ds were produced by modifying one each of the A, B and C models, first flight being made on May 11, 1979. The U.S. Army then contracted between 1980 and 1985 for 328 earlier Chinooks to be modified to CH-47Ds, whilst planning to contract for up to another 144 subsequently. The first production conversion flew on February 26, 1982, and initial operational capability of the CH-47D was achieved on February 28, 1984, in the 101st Airborne Division. Unusually, new serial numbers (commencing with FY81) were issued for the airframes rebuilt as CH-47Ds.

In 1987, the U.S. Army contracted for the development of the MH-47E, a version of the Chinook for use by the Special Operations Forces, which had a requirement for up to 50 of these helicopters. Its features included 4,000 s.h.p. T55-L-714 engines with FADEC, enlarged fuel capacity, air-to-air refuelling capability, FLIR and multi-mode radar, enhanced communications and navigation capabilities, a rescue hoist and armanent of two

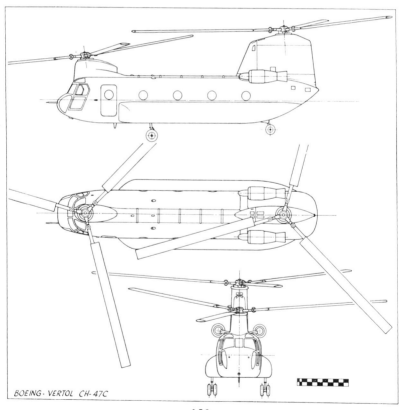

BOEING · VERTOL CH-47C

156

Boeing CH-47C Chinook in Army finish (*Boeing photo*).

12.7-mm. machine guns to fire through the rear cabin windows, one each side. Some of these features, including the avionics improvements and increased fuel capacity, were to apply to the CH-47E, which the U.S. Army was considering for its modification programme beyond the 328 CH-47Ds committed by 1988.

TECHNICAL DATA (CH-47D)

MANUFACTURER: Boeing Helicopter Company, Philadelphia, Penn.
TYPE: Army logistics and assault transport helicopter.
ACCOMMODATION: Crew of three and 44 troops or 24 litters.
POWER PLANT: Two 4,500 s.h.p. (emergency rating) Lycoming T55-L-712 turbo shafts.
DIMENSIONS: Rotor diameter, 60 ft. each. Length of fuselage, 51 ft. 0 in. Height, 18 ft. 6½ in. Disc area, 2,827·5 sq. ft. each.
WEIGHTS: Empty, 23,149 lb. Gross, 44,000 lb. Max permissible, 50,000 lb.
PERFORMANCE: Max. speed, 183 m.p.h. at sea level. Cruising speed, 150 m.p.h. Initial climb, 1,333 ft./min. Hovering ceiling, 5,600 ft. Range, 70 st. miles.
ARMAMENT: None.
SERIAL NUMBERS:

YHC-1B: 59-4982/86
CH-47A: 60-3448/3452; 61-2408/2425;
    62-2114/2137; 63-7900/7923;
    64-13106/13165;
    65-7966/8025; 66-066/125;
    66-19000/19097.
CH-47B: 66-19098/19143;
    67-18432/18493.

CH-47C: 67-18494/18551;
    68-15810/15869; 68-15990/16022;
    69-17100/17126; 70-15000/15043;
    71-20944/20959; 74-22275/22294;
    76-22673/22684; 79-23394/23400.
CH-47D: 81-23381/23383;
    82-23762/23799; 83-24101/24124;
    84-24156/24179; 85-24322/24359;
    85-24735/24742; 86-0084/0089;
    86-0390/0401; 86-1635/1682;
    87-0069/0116; 88-0062/0109.

Cessna UC-78 in O.D. finish (*Cessna photo*).

Cessna AT-8, AT-17, UC-78 Bobcat

Late in 1940 the Army ordered a small batch of twin-engined Cessna Model T-50s for evaluation as advanced transition trainers for pilots going on to fly multi-engined operational types. The T-50 was originally produced in 1939 as a commercial five-seat light transport, and was adopted in 1940 for use as a conversion trainer for the Commonwealth Joint Air Training Plan in Canada—where the type was known as the Crane.

The 33 AT-8s of 1940 had 295 h.p. Lycoming R-680-9 radial engines and a gross weight of 5,100 lb. With the rapid expansion of Air Corps training programmes in 1941, further contracts for the Cessna trainer were placed, but the power plants were changed to 245 h.p. Jacobs R-775-9s. This change was accompanied by a change of designation to AT-17. This model had wooden propellers and a gross weight of 5,300 lb.; 450 were built. The 223 AT-17As were similar but had metal propellers and the

Cessna AT-17 in early 1942 trainer colours (*Peter M. Bowers*).

Cessna AT-8 in 1940 (*Cessna photo*).

weight held down to 5,100 lb. Equipment changes distinguished the AT-17B (466 built) and the AT-17C (60), the latter having a radio change. Of the total built, 550 went to Canada as Crane 1As under Lend–Lease.

In 1942, the Cessna T-50 was adopted by the Air Force as a light personnel transport, designated the C-78 (later UC-78) and named the Bobcat. Similar to the AT-17, the UC-78 had a permissible gross weight of 5,700 lb. Cessna delivered 1,287, and 17 commercial model T-50s were commandeered for Air Force use as UC-78As.

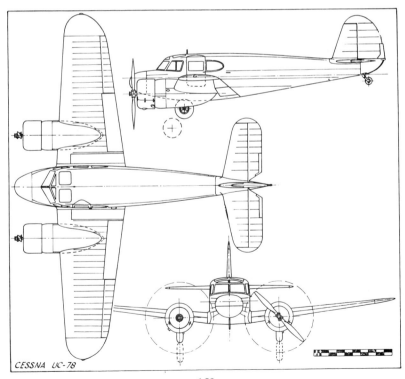

CESSNA UC-78

As USAAF training requirements slackened after the initial build up in 1941/42, some outstanding contracts for AT-17Bs and AT-17Ds were changed, with effect from January 1, 1943, to provide for delivery of these aircraft as UC-78B and UC-78C respectively. Both these models differed from the UC-78 in having two-blade fixed-pitch wooden airscrews, differing from each other only in respect of minor equipment variations. Production of the 5,700-lb. UC-78B totalled 1,806 and Cessna built 327 of the UC-78C model, which had a gross weight of only 5,300 lb. All models of the Bobcat had been declared surplus by 1949.

TECHNICAL DATA (UC-78)

MANUFACTURER: Cessna Aircraft Co., Wichita, Kansas.
TYPE: Light personnel transport.
ACCOMMODATION: Pilot and four passengers.
POWER PLANT: Two 245 h.p. Jacobs R-755-9 piston radials.
DIMENSIONS: Span, 41 ft. 11 in. Length, 32 ft. 9 in. Height, 9 ft. 11 in. Wing area, 295 sq. ft.
WEIGHTS: Empty, 3,500 lb. Gross, 5,700 lb.
PERFORMANCE: Max. speed, 195 m.p.h. at sea level. Cruising speed, 175 m.p.h. at sea level. Initial climb, 1,325 ft./min. Service ceiling, 22,000 ft. Range, 750 st. miles.
ARMAMENT: None.
SERIAL NUMBERS:

AT-8: 41-005/037.
AT-17: 42-002/451.
AT-17A: 42-13617/13806; 42-13867/13899.
AT-17B: 42-38692/39157.
AT-17C: 42-13807/13866.
AT-17D: 42-13900/14030.
UC-78: 42-58110/42-58540; 43-7281/7853; 43-31763/32112.

UC-78A: 42-38276/38278; 42-38374/38375; 42-97033/97039; 42-38377; 42-38379; 42-43844; 44-52998; 44-53001.
UC-78B: 42-39158/39346; 42-71465/72104; 43-7854/8180; 43-32113/32762.
UC-78C: 42-14031/14166; 42-72105/72164.

Cessna UC-78B with fixed-pitch wooden propellers, photographed in 1946 (*Peter M. Bowers*).

Cessna L-19As for National Guard and Army. The overall olive drab finish became standard on all Army aircraft in 1951 (*Peter M. Bowers*).

Cessna L-19, O-1 Bird Dog

Cessna won a 1950 competition to select a new two-seat liaison and observation monoplane with its Model 305A, a development of the commercial Model 170 with similar wings, tail unit and landing gear. Under the designation L-19A, the Model 305A was ordered in June 1950, the initial contract being for 418 aircraft. Deliveries began in December 1950 and further contracts followed quickly; by October 1954 Cessna had delivered 2,486 Bird Dogs (as the L-19 was named in September 1951) of which 60 were diverted to the U.S. Marine Corps as OE-1s and six were for MAP use.

To serve as instrument trainers, 66 L-19A-ITs delivered in 1953 had rear instrument panels, adjustable rear seats and blind flight curtains. These were followed in 1956 by the first of 310 TL-19Ds (Cessna Model 305B) which were similar apart from having constant speed propellers, O-470-15 engine and 2,400 lb. gross weight instead of 2,100 lb. Production of a new series of liaison Bird Dogs began in 1957 when the Army ordered the first L-19Es (Cessna 305C) incorporating new equipment and increased gross weight of 2,400 lb. Delivery of this batch of L-19Es was completed during 1958 and Bird Dog production ended temporarily in January 1959, with a total of over 3,000 built including foreign contracts. Additional contracts for the L-19E from the Army put the type back into production in 1961 and the final total built was 3,431.

The L-19 was the subject of a number of interesting experiments conducted both by the Army and other contractors. On November 5, 1952, the XL-19B (52-1804) made its first flight powered by a 210 e.h.p. Boeing XT50-BO-1 turboprop, and a year later this aircraft set a lightplane altitude record of 37,063 ft. A similar installation of the Continental XT51-T-1 Artouste turboprop produced the two XL-19Cs in 1954.

Grey-painted Cessna O-1F for the USAF in Vietnam, with "O-for-Over-10" prefix to tail number, reduced from full serial 57-2859.

After evaluation of an L-19A (51-12304) on Edo 339 2250 amphibious floats, the Army purchased four amphibious L-19s for Continental Army Command, and all late production Bird Dogs had provision for float gear to replace the wheels.

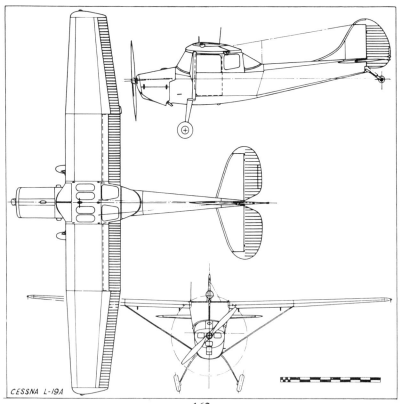

162

The Bird Dog was re-designated O-1 in the revived observation category in mid-1962. At that time, the L-19A, TL-19D and L-19E became O-1A TO-1D and O-1E respectively. Some O-1As were converted to trainers as TO-1As. Operating in Vietnam, Bird Dogs became the standard mount for Forward Air Controllers who played a vital role by providing visual spotting of enemy targets for attacking aircraft. For this role, many O-1s were transferred to the USAF and modified to new variants. Former TO-1Ds became O-1D, or O-1F (Cessna 305E) with gross weight increased to 2,800 lb., while O-1As became O-1G (Cessna 305D) with gross weight of 2,400 lb. The O-1B and O-1C designations referred to Marine Corps versions.

TECHNICAL DATA (L-19E)

MANUFACTURER: Cessna Aircraft Company, Wichita, Kansas.
TYPE: Army liaison and observation monoplane.
ACCOMMODATION: Pilot and observer/passenger in tandem.
POWER PLANT: One 213 h.p. Continental O-470-11 piston flat-four.
DIMENSIONS: Span, 36 ft. 0 in. Length, 25 ft. 9½ in. Height, 7 ft. 3½ in. Wing area, 174 sq. ft.
WEIGHTS: Empty, 1,614 lb. Gross, 2,400 lb.
PERFORMANCE: Max. speed, 151 m.p.h. at sea level. Cruising speed, 104 m.p.h. at 5,000 ft. Initial climb, 1,150 ft./min. Service ceiling, 18,500 ft. Range, 530 st. miles.
ARMAMENT: None
SERIAL NUMBERS:

L-19A: 50-1327/1744; 51-4534/5109;
  51-7286/7481; 51-11912/12911;
  51-16428/16462; 51-16864/16973;
  53-508/532; 53-2873/2878*;
  53-7698/7717; 53-7968/8067*.
XL-19B: 52-1804.

XL-19C: 52-6311/6312.
TL-19D: 55-4649/4748; 57-2772/2981.
L-19E: 56-2467/2696; 56-4034/4038*;
  56-4161/4235; 57-1606/1609*;
  57-5983/6028; 57-6268/6277;
  59-5928/5929; 61-2955/3024;
  62-12280/12288*; 63-12741/12758.

*These batches for supply to other nations.

Cessna TL-19D instrument trainer as first in Army service, in overall bright orange finish for high visibility (*Peter M. Bowers*).

Cessna T-37B with red conspicuity markings appearing as white because of camera filter (*Cessna photo*).

Cessna T-37, A-37

After much hesitation, the USAF decided to develop a jet trainer for primary flying instruction in April 1952. In the ensuing design competition, Cessna Aircraft Company was successful with its Model 318 design, named winner of the competition early in 1953 and designated T-37. The design was for a simple, low-mid wing all-metal monoplane, having two Continental-built Turboméca Marboré turbojet engines in the thickened wing centre section. Side-by-side seating was adopted for the first time in a USAF primary trainer since the TW-3, the instructor and pupil being provided with ejection seats beneath a one-piece moulded canopy and one-piece windscreen. To be clear of the jet exhaust, the tailplane was mounted part-way up the fin.

Two XT-37 prototypes were ordered by USAF and the first of these (54-716) was first flown on October 12, 1954, by Bob Hogan at Wichita Municipal Airport. It was powered by prototype engines, designated YJ69-T-9 rated at 920 lb. s.t. each. An initial production batch of 11 T-37As was ordered during 1954, and the first of these flew on September 27, 1955.

Service use of the T-37A did not begin until early 1957, after changes had been made to the cockpit and other modifications had been introduced. Initially, the T-37 was used as a basic trainer, for pilots who had received primary training on the Beechcraft T-34. With effect from April 1961, the USAF switched to all-through jet training, but the high cost of producing initial training on T-37s for pupils who were eventually turned down led to reintroduction of a 30-hr. primary phase on Cessna T-41As (page 543) in 1965, followed by 90 hours on the T-37.

During 1959, production switched to the T-37B, with 1,025 lb. s.t. J69-T-25 engines and new Omni and UHF equipment. The first T-37B was accepted by the USAF on November 6, 1959, and all T-37As were cycled through a modification programme to convert them to "B" standard with the more powerful engine.

Three T-37As (56-3464/66) were loaned to the U.S. Army in 1957 for

164

evaluation of their suitability for ground support missions. They were tested at Fort Rucker for a year, and subsequently at Salinas.

Procurement of the T-37B included several batches for delivery to foreign nations through the Mutual Aid Programme. A further version, the T-37C, was produced only for MAP use, differing from the US trainer in having underwing armament and wing-tip fuel tank provision.

During 1962, two T-37Bs (62-5950/5951) were evaluated at the USAF Special Air Warfare Center in an armed role, after 62-5951 had first served as the T-37C prototype. The two aircraft were first tested with their original engines but with increased gross weight of 8,700 lb. Subsequently, they were converted to YAT-37Ds with 2,400 lb. s.t. General Electric J85-GE-5 turbojets and the gross weight increased, in increments, to 14,000 lb. The first flight as a YAT-37D was made on October 22, 1963, and the designation was subsequently changed to YA-37A.

The needs of the Vietnam war led to a sudden new interest in the armed T-37 in 1966, and the USAF requested Cessna to complete 39 T-37Bs then in production as A-37As for close air support, armed reconnaissance and similar duties. Based on the YAT-37Ds, they had eight underwing hardpoints, a 7·62-mm. GAU-28/A Minigun in the forward fuselage, wing-tip tanks and derated J85-GE-17A engines. A squadron of A-37As was evaluated in Vietnam in the second half of 1967, while Cessna was test-flying the prototype A-37B, which was the productionized version with full-rated 2,850 lb. s.t. engines, provision for in-flight refuelling, 6g airframe stressing, increased maximum fuel capacity and other changes. Delivery of 577 began in May 1968, and, during 1970, the USAF assigned the A-37As to the South Vietnamese Air Force and began transferring A-37B Dragonflies to the Air National Guard, the first such unit to fly the type being the 175th Group of

Cessna A-37B from the first production batch, in natural metal finish (*Cessna photo*).

165

Cessna A-37B in South-East Asia camouflage, serving with "The Boys from Syracuse" (inscribed on wing-tip tanks), the New York ANG unit (*Howard Levy*).

Baltimore, Maryland. One of the first overseas deployments of the A-37 was late in 1969, to the 24th Special Operations Wing in the Panama Canal Zone. Air Force Reserve units also later flew the A-37B.

To replace the Cessna O-2A in the forward air control role, modified A-37Bs were issued to three ANG Tactical Air Support Groups, adopting the designation OA-37B in this guise. At least 130 aircraft were modified to serve in this role, the OA-37B also being used to replace OV-10s in the Pacific Air Forces 5th Tactical Control Group in South Korea, the 24th Composite Wing in the Panama Canal Zone and with relevant home-based training units. The OA-37B was serving with these units until 1989/90.

Cessna OA-37B in Europe One colours and toned-down national insignia, serving with the USAF Southern Air Division in Panama (*Robert S. Hopkins, III*).

166

TECHNICAL DATA (T-37B)

MANUFACTURER: Cessna Aircraft Company, Wichita, Kansas.
TYPE: Primary and intermediate flight trainer.
ACCOMMODATION: Pupil and instructor side-by-side.
POWER PLANT: Two, 1,025 lb. s.t. Continental J69-T-25 turbojets.
DIMENSIONS: Span, 33 ft. 9 in. Length, 29 ft. 3 in. Height, 9 ft. 2 in. Wing area
184 sq. ft.
WEIGHTS: Empty, 3,870 lb. Gross, 6,574 lb.
PERFORMANCE: Max. speed, 425 m.p.h. at 20,000 ft. Cruising speed, 360 m.p.h. at
35,000 ft. Initial climb, 3,370 ft./min. Service ceiling, 39,200 ft. Range, 870 st. mile.
SERIAL NUMBERS:

XT-37: 54-716/718.

T-37A: 54-2729/2739; 55-2972;
55-4302/4321; 56-3464/3590;
57-2230/2352; 58-1861/1977;
59-241/285.

T-37B: 59-286/390; 60-071/200;
61-459/473; 61-2494/2508; 61-2915/2919;
62-5950/5956; 64-13409/13466;
65-10823/10826; 66-7960/8006;
67-14730/14768; 67-22240/22262.
68-7981/8084.

A-37A: 67-14503/14541.

A-37B: 67-14776/14823;
67-22483/22491; 68-7911/7980;
68-10777/10827; 69-6334/6446;
70-1277/1312; 71-790/854;
71-858/873; 71-1409/1416;
73-1056/1115; 73-1654/1658;
74-998/1013; 74-1694/1723;
75-374/385; 75-410/417;
75-424/441; 75-669/680.

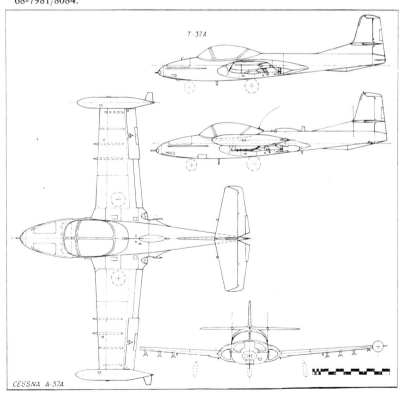

Cessna O-2A in all-grey finish, with white wing stripe for visibility from above (*Cessna photo*).

Cessna O-2

To supplement the Cessna O-1 Bird Dogs operating in the forward air controller (FAC) role in Vietnam, the USAF selected a military variant of the Cessna 337 Skymaster in December 1966. Differences from the commercial model included the communications installation, which was external, and the provision of four underwing hardpoints, used to carry Minigun or rocket pods, flares, etc. Additional windows were provided in the lower fuselage on the starboard side for use by the observer who sat alongside the pilot. A distinctive feature of the O-2A, as the type was designated by the USAF, was the tandem arrangement of the two Continental IO-360-C/D engines, driving tractor and pusher propellers respectively.

The initial contract for O-2As, placed on December 29, 1966, was for 145, and subsequent contracts brought the total purchased for USAF to 501 (plus 12 for Iran).

At the same time the O-2A was ordered, the USAF contracted for 31 O-2Bs. This version, designed for psychological warfare, did not have the wing strong points but was fitted instead with special communications equipment for air-to-ground broadcasting, and a leaflet dispenser in the rear starboard side of the fuselage. Apart from this dispenser, the O-2Bs differed externally from O-2As in having faired propeller spinners like their commercial counterparts.

Cessna O-2A test-painted in overall black for night operations in Vietnam, 1967/68 (*Robert C. Mikesh*).

To speed deliveries of the O-2B, the USAF acquired 31 commercial aircraft built but unsold by Cessna. Deliveries of the O-2B began on March 31, 1967, and of the O-2A a month later. Both types were quickly operational in Vietnam.

TECHNICAL DATA (O-2A)

MANUFACTURER: Cessna Aircraft Company, Wichita, Kansas.
TYPE: Observation and special duties.
ACCOMMODATION: Pilot and observer, side-by-side; two passengers optional.
POWER PLANT: Two 210 h.p. Continental IO-360-C/D piston engines.
DIMENSIONS: Span, 38 ft. 2 in. Length, 29 ft. 9 in. Height, 9 ft. 4 in. Wing area, 201 sq. ft.
WEIGHTS: Empty, 2,848 lb. Gross, 5,400 lb.
PERFORMANCE: Max. speed, 199 m.p.h. at sea level. Cruising speed, 144 m.p.h. at 10,000 ft. Initial climb, 1,180 ft./min. Service ceiling, 19,300 ft.; range, 1,060 st. miles.
ARMAMENT: Four wing hardpoints can carry weapon pods.
SERIAL NUMBERS:
O-2A: 67-21295/21439; 68-6857/6903;   O-2B: 67-21440/21470.
   68-10828/10872; 68-10962/11070;
   68-11122/11173; 69-7601/7669;
   70-1409/1442.

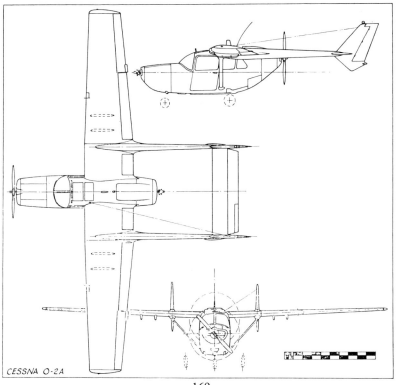

CESSNA O-2A

Dayton-Wright TW-3 with modified tail (*McCook Field photo*).

Consolidated PT-1, PT-3, PT-11, O-17

The long line of Consolidated primary trainers began with the product of a predecessor company. The Dayton-Wright Company had just started producing side-by-side TW-3s, powered with World War I surplus Wright E engines (American built 180 h.p. Hispano-Suiza) when it was closed down by the parent company, General Motors. Its design rights and chief designer, and the TW-3 contract, were acquired by the newly-formed Consolidated Aircraft Corporation of Buffalo, New York in 1923. Subsequent TW-3s were delivered as Consolidated TW-3s.

The first trainer of Consolidated design was the PT-1, essentially a refined TW-3, with the steel tube fuselage changed to tandem seating and the tail surfaces revised. The first of 171 PT-1s used a streamlined nose radiator installation similar to that of the World War I Fokker D-VII, but the remainder used the unfaired installation illustrated. One PT-1 airframe (27-149) was completed as XPT-2 with a 220 h.p. Wright J-5 (R-790) radial.

The XPT-3 (27-177) was almost identical with the XPT-2 except for the tail. One hundred and thirty production PT-3s were ordered, with one (28-229) being completed as the XO-17. These were followed by 120

Consolidated PT-1 with uncowled engine (*Peter M. Bowers*).

Consolidated PT-3A in blue and yellow training colours (*Peter M. Bowers*).

PT-3As with minor changes. The XPT-3 became XPT-5 when fitted with a Curtiss Challenger R-600 two-row six-cylinder radial engine, but was soon converted to PT-3 standard. The XPT-4, never built, was to have been a PT-3 with experimental Fairchild-Caminez engine. One NY-2 (30-421), a Naval equivalent of the PT-3, was obtained for evaluation.

O-17. A parallel development to the PT-3 series was the O-17. The XO-17 was a converted PT-3 with such slight refinements as improved fuselage streamlining, oleo shock absorbers, wheel brakes, balanced elevators, and increased fuel capacity. A removable fairing was provided for the rear cockpit so that it could be fitted with a standard Scarff gun ring or with padded coaming as a trainer cockpit. Twenty-nine O-17s were built, most of them for the National Guard. The XO-17A was a refined O-17 that Consolidated tried to market commercially and for export as the "Courier". It became the XPT-8 when fitted with the experimental Packard diesel radial engine and was scrapped in 1932.

PT-11. The PT-11s were greatly refined PT-3s, retaining the same general

Consolidated Y1BT-7 with blue fuselage and yellow wings, Randolph Field, 1932 (*via Bill Dyche*).

proportions but making much more generous use of curved outlines and streamlining. Four YPT-11s were built with 165 h.p. Continental R-545-1 engines. The last of this quartet (31-596) became PT-11A when fitted with the Curtiss Challenger R-600 engine and PT-11C when this was replaced with a 220 h.p. Lycoming YR-680-1. The third YPT-11 (31-595) became the BT-6 when fitted with a 300 h.p. Wright J-6 (R-975) engine and the other two YPT-11s were converted to PT-11D, with 31-593 serving briefly as the second PT-11C. Five YPT-11Bs with Kinner YR-720-1 engines were converted to PT-11D and a sixth was procured for the Coast Guard.

Twenty-one Y1PT-11Ds were ordered with 220 h.p. Lycoming R-680-3 nine-cylinder radial engines. The service test designation was soon dropped, and these aeroplanes became plain PT-11Ds. Eight additional PT-11Ds

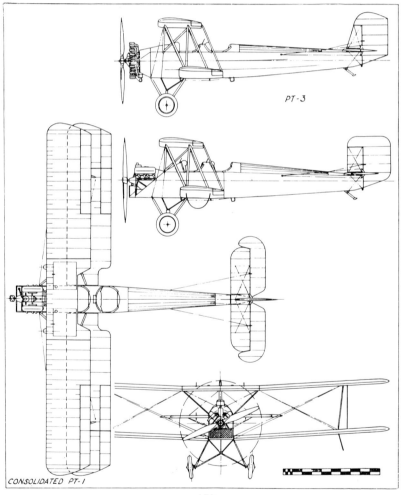

PT-3

CONSOLIDATED PT-1

172

Consolidated O-17 for National Guard (*Peter M. Bowers*).

resulted from conversion of three Y1PT-11s and five Y1PT-11Bs by engine change. The ten Y1PT-12s were identical with PT-11s except for minor equipment changes and the 300 h.p. Pratt & Whitney Wasp Junior R-985A engine. They were redesignated as BT-7 basic trainers.

TECHNICAL DATA

MANUFACTURER: Consolidated Aircraft Corporation, Buffalo, New York.
TYPE: Primary trainer.
ACCOMMODATION: Pupil and instructor in tandem open cockpits.

	TW-3	PT-3A	PT-11D
Power Plant:	180 h.p. Wright E	220 h.p. R-790-AB	200 h.p. R-680A
Dimensions:			
Span, ft., in.	34 9	34 6	31 7
Length, ft., in.	26 9	28 1	26 11
Height, ft., in.	9 0	10 3	9 8
Wing area, sq. ft.	285	300	280
Weights:			
Empty, lb.	1,706	1,785	1,918
Gross, lb.	2,407	2,481	2,585
Performance:			
Max. speed, m.p.h. at s.t.	103	102	118
Cruising speed, m.p.h.	—	81	—
Climb, min. to ft.	12·2/6,500	7·6/5,000	7·4/5,000
Service ceiling, ft.	14,500	14,000	13,700
Endurance, hr.	3·75	3·7	—

SERIAL NUMBERS:

TW-3 (D-W): 22-226, 22-401.
TW-3: (Consol) 23-1302/1319.
PT-1: 23-1253; 25-245/294; 26-226/275;
    26-301/350; 27-108/177.
PT-3: 28-218/228; 28-230/316;
    28-318/347.
PT-3A: 29-38/157.

YPT-11: 31-593/596.
Y1PT-11B: 32-367/371; 32-395 (CG).
Y1PT-11D: 32-372/392.
Y1PT-12: 32-357/366.
XO-17: 28-229.
O-17: 28-360/385; 28-396/397; 30-89.
XO-17A: 28-317.

Consolidated PB-2A (*Bowers collection*).

Consolidated P-30 (PB-2)

Between the two World Wars, only one two-seat monoplane fighter reached operational status with the Air Corps. This was the Consolidated PB-2A, the first aircraft built in that company's factory in San Diego. An all-metal low-wing design with retractable undercarriage, the PB-2A had a long, enclosed cockpit with the pilot and gunner in tandem.

The design originated as a military version of the Lockheed Altair, known as the XP-900, with a Curtiss V-1570-23 engine. This was purchased by the Air Corps as the YP-24 in September 1931, and four more Y1P-24s were ordered, together with four prototypes of a ground attack version designated Y1A-9. Early in 1932, Detroit Aircraft, of which Lockheed was then a subsidiary, withdrew from aviation, but the P-24's chief designer, Robert Wood, joined Consolidated and a new version of the same design was submitted. In place of the eight aeroplanes ordered from Lockheed, the Air Corps ordered from Consolidated two prototypes of the revised design, one Y1P-25 pursuit and one XA-11 attack type. The Y1P-25 had a V-1570-27 in-line engine with turbo-supercharger on the port side of the nose; in the XA-11, the superchargers were not used. Also designated, but not built, were the YP-27 and YP-28 with radial engines—respectively, the 550 h.p. R-1340-21 and 600 h.p. R-1340-19.

The Y1P-25 was tested towards the end of 1932, showing promising performance, but crashed on January 13, 1933. Four examples of an improved version with the supercharged 675 h.p. V-1570-57 engine were then ordered, and were delivered as P-30s for tests in mid-1934. Following these trials, a contract was awarded on December 6, 1934, for 50 P-30As. Shortly after delivery, these aircraft were reclassified in a new category for two-seat fighters, as PB-2As, the two surviving P-30s then becoming PB-2s. The PB-2As had the 700 h.p. V-1570-61 engine and the effect of the turbo-supercharger was to increase the top speed by 60 m.p.h. between sea level and 20,000 ft.

The A-11 series continued with four service test models ordered with the four P-30s, and distinguished by the absence of turbo-superchargers and the use of two-blade propellers. One A-11 became the XA-11A as a flying test-bed for the Allison V-1710 liquid-cooled engine.

TECHNICAL DATA (PB-2A)

MANUFACTURER: Consolidated Aircraft Corporation, San Diego, California.
TYPE: Two-seat pursuit.
ACCOMMODATION: Pilot and gunner in tandem.
POWER PLANT: One 700 h.p. Curtiss V-1570-61 piston Vee in-line.
DIMENSIONS: Span, 43 ft. 11 in. Length, 30 ft. 0 in. Height, 8 ft. 3 in. Wing area, 297 sq. ft.
WEIGHTS: Empty, 4,306 lb. Gross, 5,643 lb.
PERFORMANCE: Max. speed, 274 m.p.h. at 25,000 ft. Cruising speed, 215 m.p.h. Initial climb, 7·78 min. to 15,000 ft. Service ceiling, 28,000 ft. Range, 508 st. miles.
ARMAMENT: Two fixed forward firing 0·30-in. guns and one flexibly-mounted 0·30-in. gun in rear cockpit.
SERIAL NUMBERS:

Y1P-25: 32-321/322.	A-11: 33-208/211.
P-30 (PB-2): 33-204/207.	P-30A (PB-2A): 35-001/050.

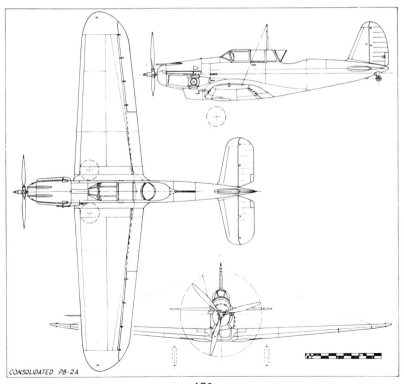

CONSOLIDATED PB-2A

Convair B-24H-5 in O.D. and grey finish (*USAF photo 27752AC*).

Consolidated B-24, C-87, F-7 Liberator

More B-24s were built for the USAAF, USN and the Allied air forces during World War II than any other single type of American aircraft—a remarkable record for a design which was not started until 1939, was in service by the middle of 1941 and was withdrawn from use almost overnight in 1945. The B-24 served in many different roles, but its most important contribution to the ending of the War was as a bomber in the Pacific area. Its design was started early in 1939, when the Air Corps outlined to Consolidated a requirement for a heavy bomber of better performance than the Boeing B-17 then in production. Specifically, a better range was wanted—3,000 miles—together with a speed of more than 300 m.p.h. and a ceiling of 35,000 ft.

Some design studies had already been made at San Diego by Consolidated engineers, who were aware of the growing Air Corps interest in large bombers as indicated by the experimental XB-15 and XB-19 programmes as well as by the orders for B-17s. The company was in a good position to meet the specification, especially insofar as very long ranges were wanted, as it had recently taken up the Davis patents for a wing design which lent itself to this type of aircraft. This wing had high-lift characteristics which allowed a reduction in angle of attack for a given weight, and hence reduced drag and improved range. First used on the Consolidated Model 31 (P4Y-1) flying-boat, the Davis high aspect ratio wing was the basis of the Model 32 bomber, in which it was located high on the deep fuselage. Also borrowed from the Model 31 was the twin-finned tail assembly.

Under Isaac M. Laddon, chief engineer, the design took shape rapidly. Preliminary specifications were ready on January 20, 1939, and construction of a mock-up began the same month. A wind tunnel model was tested in February and Consolidated designers went to Wright Field on

February 21 to discuss the design with Air Corps officers, who recommended nearly 30 changes in the preliminary specifications. A contract for a single prototype and the mock-up was signed on March 30, 1939, and construction went ahead. The wing and fuselage were mated on October 26, and William Wheatley took the XB-24 (39-680) into the air for the first time from Lindbergh Field, San Diego, on December 29, 1939.

Among the unusual features of the Consolidated Model 32 design, which was of conventional structure, were the use of a nose-wheel undercarriage, the main units of which folded sideways to lie in the wings; the high aspect ratio wing already described, and the commodious bomb-bay with its roller-shutter doors. So deep was the Model 32's fuselage that the bombs—up to a total load of 8,000 lb.—were stowed vertically in the two halves of the bomb-bay, which was separated by a catwalk to connect the flight deck and the rear fuselage. Armament, in the XB-24, comprised hand-held 0·30-in. Browning machine guns in the nose, at fuselage waist, dorsal and ventral positions and in the tail.

Three days before the contract for the prototype had been signed, the Air Corps had ordered seven YB-24s for service trials. These aircraft (40-696 to 702) were delivered in 1940, and were similar to the prototype apart from an increase in gross weight from the original 41,000 lb. to 46,400 lb. The engines in both cases were 1,200 h.p. Pratt & Whitney R-1830-33s, but the YB-24 models had wing leading edge slots deleted and de-icing boots added on wings and tail. Further orders were placed in 1940 for 36 of an initial production version to be designated B-24A, but only nine were completed to this standard, with 0·50-in. machine guns in place of 0·30-in. twin guns in the tail, and gross weight increased to 53,600 lb.

The B-24As were delivered in 1941, by which time the XB-24 had become the XB-24B by the substitution of R-1830-41 engines with turbo-superchargers for the mechanically-supercharged -33s. Associated with this change was the relocation of the oil coolers on each side of the radial engines instead of beneath, to produce the characteristic elliptical cowling of all subsequent Liberators. With these modifications, and the introduction of a Martin dorsal turret and a Consolidated tail turret, each with

Convair LB-30 with U.S. markings and British serial AL-535 (*Peter M. Bowers*).

177

twin 0·50-in. guns, nine more of the 1940 batch of 36 were completed as B-24Cs in 1941. The first significant production version for the USAAF was, however, the B-24D, which had R-1830-43 engines and gross weight increased to 56,000 lb. but was otherwise generally similar to the B-24C. The first B-24Ds were the remainder of the original 1940 order (40-2349 to 2368); six of the YB-24s (40-696/701) were also converted to this standard, and production in earnest began with two more orders for 56 and 352 placed before the end of 1940. Additional contracts in 1941 eventually brought the total of B-24Ds built to 2,738, of which 2,409 were by Consolidated Aircraft at San Diego. A second Liberator production line, operated by Consolidated, was started at Fort Worth in 1942 and built 303 of this version, while the third source of B-24s, the Douglas-operated plant at Tulsa, produced ten B-24Ds also in 1942 before going on to B-24Es.

Overtaking the Boeing B-17, which was already in service in the Pacific area, the B-24 was on the point of going into operational use when Japan attacked on December 7, 1941. Destroyed on the ground in the attack on

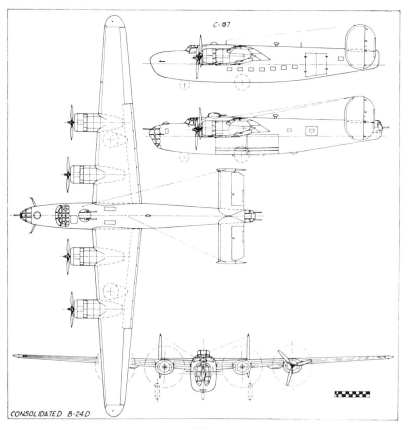

CONSOLIDATED B-24D

Pearl Harbor and adjacent airfields was a B-24 which was one of two specially modified and armed for a flight from Hawaii to the Philippines and subsequent reconnaissance of Japanese bases at Truk and Jaluit.

Immediately following the Japanese attack, the USAAF repossessed 75 Liberator IIs on a contract for 139 then in hand for the RAF. Fifteen of these repossessed aircraft, which retained their British serial numbers and the designation LB-30, were dispatched to the Pacific, but none reached the Philippines before the Japanese occupied the islands. Travelling eastwards through Africa and India, four of these LB-30s eventually reached the 7th Bombardment Group in Java, where it had retreated with the remnants of its B-17 squadrons from the Philippines. On January 16, 1942, three LB-30s and two B-17s from this group made an operational sortie against Japanese shipping and airfields from Singosari, Malang, this being the first Liberator action of the War by USAAF crews. Another 17 LB-30s, fitted with British ASV and Martin dorsal turrets, were assigned to the Canal Zone for shipping patrols and in 1944 six of these were converted to C-87 transports.

Earlier in 1941, B-24As had been issued to the Air Corps Ferrying Command, which was able to make good use of the type's phenomenal range. Operations of this kind began on July 1, when a B-24 flew from Washington to Prestwick, Scotland, via Montreal and Newfoundland. On August 31, the first flight across the South Atlantic was made, and in September two B-24s went to Moscow via Prestwick, one continuing right round the world via the Middle East, India, Australia and Hawaii and the other returning via Egypt, central Africa, the South Atlantic and Brazil. Flights such as these, made before the U.S. entered World War II, provided much information on the aircraft's capabilities which was later put to good use. Early in the war, three Ferrying Command B-24As were diverted from the Washington–Cairo route to the Southwest Pacific, where they flew between Australia, the Philippines and Burma.

Before a policy decision to concentrate B-24 squadrons in the Pacific could take effect, events in the Middle East brought the Liberator into action there. The 10th Air Force had been activated in February 1942 for action in the China–India–Burma theatre, and one of the repossessed LB-30s had joined with four B-17s for the first mission by this Air Force on April 2 in an attack against the Andaman Islands. A detachment of 23 B-24Ds under Col. H. A. Halverson, on its way to join the 10th Air Force, was, however, held in the Middle East where it eventually formed the nucleus of the 9th Air Force. Twelve B-24Ds of the Halverson Detachment attacked the Rumanian oilfields at Ploesti on June 11–12, proving the long-range ability of this aircraft, but achieving little strategic success.

Next in action was the 11th Air Force in Alaska, whose 36th Squadron had one LB-30 with its B-17s at the end of 1941, and received more B-24s by June 1942. It was joined by the B-24-equipped 21st and 404th Squadrons later in the year for attacks on Japanese shipping.

The first complete B-24 unit reached the Southwest Pacific in October

Convair B-24D of 98th Bomb Group, Middle East, in "Desert Pink" camouflage, 1942 (*Howard Levy*).

1942, when aircraft of the 90th Bombardment Group began to arrive in Australia, to serve with the 5th Air Force. This Group and the 380th were both flying long missions to strike at Japanese bases in the Celebes and Java by the beginning of 1943. A special unit of ten Liberators carrying new radar bomb sights joined the 5th Air Force later in 1943, and as the 394th Squadron flew operationally from August. These aircraft were designated SB-24s. Other B-24Ds were in action with the 7th Air Force, whose 307th Group flew a 26-aircraft mission from Hawaii to Wake Island (refuelling at Midway) on December 22, 1942—the first of many such operations. Meanwhile, still more B-24Ds were going into action in the Middle East and Europe, with the 9th and 8th Air Forces respectively. In North Africa, the 98th and 376th Bombardment Groups were serving with the 9th Air Force, while B-24Ds went into action from England for the first time on October 9, 1942, in an attack on Lille.

In June 1943, two B-24 Groups (the 44th and 93rd) were transferred from the 8th to the 9th Air Force, together with the 389th which had just arrived from the U.S., to join with the 98th and 376th Groups in a spectacular second attack on the Ploesti oil refineries. After intensive training, this attack was mounted on August 1, 1943, as a low-level mission by 177 Liberators operating from Benghazi, Libya. The round trip was a 2,700-mile journey, necessarily unescorted, and the fuel load and extra armanent for the mission reduced the bomb-load to 5,000 lb. per aircraft. The loss of the lead navigator en route and late arrival by two groups minimized the effectiveness of the raid, which suffered severe casualties from intense ground fire and defending fighters; 57 aircraft were lost, and the damage to the refineries, though considerable, was soon repaired. Five Medals of Honor were awarded to crews in this raid.

Several changes in armament and fuel capacity were made in the course of production of the B-24Ds, the various standards being indicated by block-number designations. The first Ds carried only five 0·50-in. machine guns—one in the nose and two each in dorsal and tail turrets; the bomb load was 8,000 lb. and tankage 2,364 U.S. gallons. Subsequently, a ventral "tunnel" gun was added, then two more nose guns and two waist guns,

180

to make ten 0·50s in all. The tankage increased eventually to 3,614 U.S. gallons and the bomb load to 12,800 lb. Douglas-built B-24Ds, and the final batches from Fort Worth and San Diego, had R-1830-65 engines which allowed the gross weight to increase to 71,200 lb., and on a few aircraft a retractable Briggs–Sperry ball turret with two 0·50-in. guns replaced the ventral tunnel gun.

At the end of 1942, a fourth B-24 production source was provided by the Ford Motor company in a new factory at Willow Run. The first aircraft built there were 490 Liberators similar to the B-24D but with different propellers and designated B-24E (commencing 42-6976). Consolidated also built 144 B-24Es at Fort Worth and Douglas built 167; the latter had R-1830-43 engines and the remainder had R-1830-65 engines.

A fifth Liberator production line began deliveries early in 1943. This was operated by North American at Dallas, and its first 430 aircraft (from 42-78045) were B-24Gs. The first 25 were similar to the B-24Ds with R-1830-43 engines and no ventral armament, but the remainder (blocks G-1 to G-16) introduced an upper nose turret for the first time. This was an Emerson or Consolidated turret mounting two 0·50-in. guns, fitted above a revised visual bomb-aiming position, and required to resist head-on attacks by enemy fighters to which both the B-17 and the B-24 had proved vulnerable in action. Later B-24Gs had -65 engines.

Variants similar to the "G" were built by Consolidated (at Fort Worth) and by Douglas and Ford as the B-24H. The 738 by Convair had Emerson nose turrets; Douglas built 582 with Consolidated nose turrets and the 1,780 by Ford were similar. Only minor details distinguished the B-24J variant, which was built by all five factories and in greater quantity than any other variant. It had a Motor Products nose turret and later autopilot and bomb-sight, many B-24Gs and B-24Hs being redesignated B-24J when fitted with the latter.

Production of the B-24J totalled 6,678, made up as follows: by Convair at San Diego, 2,792; by Convair Fort Worth, 1,558; by Douglas, 205; by North American, 536, and by Ford, 1,587. These were followed by the B-24L, in which the tail turret was replaced by a Convair-designed gun

Convair B-24D-110, in O.D. and white finish (*Peter M. Bowers*).

station with two manually-controlled 0·50-in. guns; and by the B-24M, which had a Motor Products tail turret but was otherwise similar to the B-24J. Consolidated built 417 B-24Ls at San Diego and Ford built 1,250. These two factories were also the only ones to build the B-24M, of which Convair produced 916 and Ford 1,677.

Examples of most of these later variants of the Liberator reached Europe to serve with the twelve B-24 groups which eventually constituted the 2nd Air Division of the Eighth Air Force. Other groups served with the 9th Air Force in the Middle East but the majority continued to serve in the Pacific. Towards the end of 1944, just over 6,000 B-24s were on operational strength with the USAAF, equipping 45 groups. In September of that year, aircraft with the 5th Air Force in the New Guinea campaign flew on missions against the Borneo oil refineries at Balikpapan which matched in skill and endeavour the earlier attack on Ploesti. The first strike at Balikpapan was made by nine B-24s of the 380th Group in August, on a 17-hour sortie from Darwin. In September, the airfield at Noemfoor, in northwest New Guinea, became available, reducing the flying time to 14 hours and permitting a 2,500 lb. bomb load to be carried.

On September 30, 72 B-24s from the 5th, 90th and 307th Groups made the first of a series of raids in which optimum range was achieved by such devices as moving crewmen from one part of the fuselage to another at specified times, and firing all remaining ammunition soon after leaving the target. Also in 1944, the B-24s of the 5th and 13th Air Forces began to attack the Philippines and supported the island-hopping campaign across the Pacific until, in April 1945, the Japanese mainland came within range. From then until the end of the War, these B-24 units were engaged in explosive and fire raids on Japan and Occupied China.

Several experimental Liberator variants had appeared by this time, one of the first being the XB-24F, a B-24D with a thermal de-icing system. Another was the B-24E (42-7127) which had remotely controlled gun barbettes in the fuselage side and a third was a B-24J with a complete B-17G type front fuselage and nose turret. In 1943, a B-24D (42-40234) was modified into the XB-24K by the Ford factory at Willow Run, by the introduction of a large single fin and rudder. With 1,350 h.p. R-1830-75

Convair B-24J in desert camouflage, with British fin flash, February 1944 (*Howard Levy*).

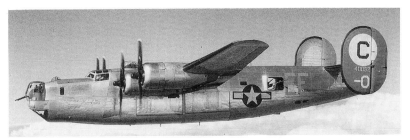
Convair B-24J-145-CO in all-metal finish, European theatre, 1944/45.

engines, this version had improved performance and greater stability and was accordingly adopted for production. With further armament revisions including a ball turret in the nose, Ford built the XB-24N (44-48753) and seven YB-24Ns to initiate production, but 5,168 B-24Ns on order at Willow Run were cancelled on May 31, 1945, when the war in Europe ended.

By conversion, a few RB-24Ls were produced in 1944 to train B-29 gunners. They had chin, dorsal, ventral and tail barbettes and modified noses, and were later redesignated TB-24L, being among the last B-24s in service. Despite the enormous quantity built, the USAAF had declared all its B-24s surplus before the end of 1945. Two post-war experiments produced the XB-24P and XB-24Q (44-49916), respectively conversions of a B-24D and a B-24L, the latter as a test-bed for the General Electric radar-controlled rear turret for the B-47. The last B-24 flying with USAF markings was 44-51228, finally disposed of in 1953 as an EZB-24M.

XB-41. This designation applied to a single B-24D (41-11822) modified in 1942 to serve as a "destroyer" in company with B-24 formations, especially in Europe. A second dorsal turret was fitted, together with a chin turret and additional beam guns to bring the total fire power to 14 0·50-in. guns.

F-7. A photo-reconnaissance version of the Liberator, with this designation, appeared in 1943, the conversion of a B-24D being made by Northwest Airlines at their modification centre at St. Paul, Minnesota. The XF-7 had extra fuel tanks in the forward bomb-bay, and a specially-equipped cabin in the aft portion able to carry as many as eleven cameras. The F-7s used in the Pacific area were similar, and were converted B-24Hs. They were followed by 86 F-7As converted from B-24Js, with three cameras in the nose and three in the bomb-bay, and the F-7B, also a B-24J conversion, with six cameras in the bomb bay.

C-87. Because of its very long range capability, and roomy fuselage, development of the B-24 Liberator for use in a transport role was logical, and the earliest deployment of the B-24A with the USAAC was with the Air Corps Ferrying Command. From these early examples, a transport variant was developed and ordered from Consolidated in 1942. It was based on the B-24D and initial deliveries were from converted B-24D contracts at the Fort Worth factory. Provision was made in the fuselage for 25 passengers and the crew numbered five. Externally this version, designated the C-87, was distinguished by the absence of turrets and a row of windows along the fuselage. A total of 285 C-87s was delivered to the USAAC, which allocated 24 to the R.A.F. under Lend–Lease arrangements and used the others as the principal heavy transport aircraft for the duration of the War. Some operating into China over the "Hump" had two fixed forward firing machine guns. Deliveries were made from both the Convair lines at Fort Worth and San Diego.

The only other C-87 variant produced was the C-87A, which was equipped with ten berths to be used as an executive sleeper. Six were produced in 1943, and had R-1830-45 engines in place of the R-1830-43s of the C-87s.

To enable the C-87 to shoot back if attacked, an armed variant was proposed as the C-87B but was not produced. The C-87C also remained a project, as the transport variant of the single-finned B-24N. Production plans were cancelled at the end of the War, but deliveries of 46 examples

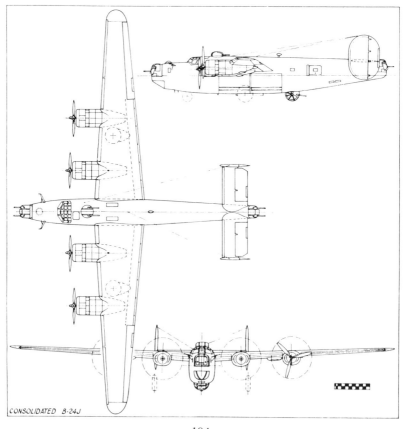

CONSOLIDATED B-24J

Convair C-87, showing fuselage windows (*Peter M. Bowers*).

were made to the U.S. Navy under the designation RY-3, 27 of these being allocated direct to the R.A.F. under Lend–Lease.

AT-22. In 1943, five C-87s were converted to become flying classrooms for flight-engineer training. In this new role they were designated AT-22, and subsequently became TB-24s under revised designating procedure in 1945. They carried a total of 18 persons including pupils, instructors and the flight crew of five.

C-109. Examples of both the B-24 Liberator and B-17 Flying Fortress were hurriedly converted in 1943 to serve as flying tankers with the task of ferrying fuel to advanced China bases for the use of B-29s in their attacks against Japan. The prototype Liberator conversion, designated XC-109, was undertaken by the Ford company and was based on a B-24E. It had light alloy fuel tanks in the nose, in the bomb-bay and over the bomb-bay in the upper fuselage, with a total capacity of 2,900 U.S. gallons, or about double the usual tankage of the B-24. The extra tanks were all filled and emptied through a single point in the fuselage side, and a special system was provided to replace the fuel with an inert gas as the tanks were emptied, to avoid the risk of explosion.

The superior range of the B-24 led to its adoption rather than the B-17 tanker, and further examples of the C-109 were produced for operational use on the route over the "Hump" from India to China. Both B-24D and B-24E models were converted, by Glenn Martin and other companies, and these later conversions had flexible tanks instead of the metal tanks of the prototype.

TECHNICAL DATA (B-24)

MANUFACTURER: Consolidated (later Consolidated-Vultee) Aircraft Corp., San Diego, California (B-24, A, B, C, D, F, J, L, M, P) and Fort Worth (B-24D, E, H, J). Douglas Aircraft Co., Tulsa, Oklahoma (B-24D, E, H, J). Ford Motor Co., Willow Run, Michigan (B-24E, H, J, K, L, M, N, Q). North American Aviation Inc., Dallas (B-24G, J).
TYPE: Medium bomber and reconnaissance aircraft.
ACCOMMODATION: Eight/ten crew.

TECHNICAL DATA (B-24 continued)

	B-24A	B-24D	B-24H/J	B-24M	C-87
Power Plant:	4× 1,200 h.p. R-1830-33	4× 1,200 h.p. R-1830-43	4× 1,200 h.p. R-1830-65	4× 1,200 h.p. R-1830-65	4× 1,200 h.p. R-1830-43, 65
Dimensions:					
Span, ft., in.	110 0	110 0	110 0	110 0	110 0
Length, ft., in.	63 9	66 4	67 2	67 2	66 4
Height, ft., in.	18 8	17 11	18 0	18 0	18 0
Wing area, sq. ft.	1,048	1,048	1,048	1,048	1,048
Weights:					
Empty, lb.	30,000	32,605	36,500	36,000	31,935
Gross, lb.	53,600	60,000	65,000	64,500	56,000
Performance:					
Max. speed, m.p.h./ft.	292/15,000	303/25,000	290/25,000	300/30,000	306
Cruising speed, m.p.h.	228	200	215	215	—
Climb, min. to ft.	5·6/10,000	22/20,000	25/20,000	25/20,000	20·9/20,000
Service ceiling, ft.	30,500	32,000	28,000	28,000	31,000
Range, miles	2,200	2,850	2,100	2,100	2,900
Armament:	6×0·50 in. 2×0·30 in. 4,000 lb.	10× 0·50 in. 8,800 lb.	10× 0·50 in. 8,800 lb.	10× 0·50 in. 8,800 lb.	1×0·50 in.

SERIAL NUMBERS:

XB-24: 39-680.
YB-24: 40-696/702.
B-24A: 40-2369/2377.
B-24C: 40-2378/2386.
B-24D-CO: 40-2349/2368; 41-1087/1142;
   41-11587/11938*; 41-23640/24311†;
   41-24339; 42-40058/41257;
   42-72765/72963.
B-24D-CF: 42-63752/64046.
B-24E-DT: 41-28409/28573;
   41-29007/29008.
B-24E-FO: 42-6976/7464; 42-7770.
B-24E-CF: 41-29009/29115;
   41-64395/64431.
B-24G-NT: 42-78045/78474.
B-24H-DT: 41-28574/29006;
   42-51077/51225.
B-24H-CF: 41-29116/29608;
   42-50277/50451; 42-64432/64501;
B-24H-FO: 42-7465/7769;
   42-52077/52776; 42-94729/95503.

B-24J-CF: 42-50452/50508;
   42-64047/64394; 42-99736/99935;
   44-10253/10752; 44-44049/44501.
B-24J-FO: 42-50509/51076;
   42-51431/52076; 42-95504/95628;
   44-48754/49001.
B-24J-DT: 42-51226/51430.
B-24J-CO: 42-72964/73514;
   42-99936/100435; 42-109789/110188;
   44-40049/41389.
B-24J-NT: 42-78475/78794;
   44-28061/28276.
B-24L-CO: 44-41390/41806.
B-24L-FO: 44-49002/50251.
B-24M-CO: 44-41807/42722.
B-24M-FO: 44-50252/51928.
XB-24N: 44-48753.
YB-24N: 44-52053/52059.
C-87: 42-107249/107275; 43-30548/36027‡;
   44-39198/39298; 44-52978/52987.

* Includes 35 C-87-CF, 8 B-24D-CF and 4 B-24D-DT.
† Includes 6 B-24D-DT, 35 C-87-CF and 3 C-87A-CF.
‡ Includes 3 C-87A.

Convair RB-36E modified from B-36A (*Warren M. Bodie*).

Convair B-36

Development of the biggest bomber, in sheer size, that has ever gone into service with the USAF began in 1941, when almost the whole of Europe was under German domination and the survival of Britain seemed doubtful. The possible need to bomb European targets from U.S. bases led the Army Air Force to outline a requirement for a strategic bomber which could carry a 10,000-lb. bomb-load for 5,000 miles and then return to its base without refuelling, with a maximum speed of 240–300 m.p.h. and a 35,000 ft. operating ceiling. Maximum bomb-load was to be 72,000 lb. The specification was issued to industry on April 11, 1941, and from four designs submitted, the USAAF selected the Consolidated Model 37. This design had a 230-ft. wing span, with slight sweep back; twin fins and rudders; a pressurized fuselage; six engines with pusher propellers on the wing trailing edge; and a gross weight of 278,000 lb.

Two prototypes were ordered in 1941, but development, assigned to the company's Fort Worth division, was slow because of the need to produce B-24s and then B-32s. When, in 1943, it appeared that the B-36 might be needed to attack Japan from bases then in American hands, plans for its production were hastened, and a contract for 100 was placed on July 23, 1943. By the time the first XB-36 (42-13570) was rolled out, on September 8, 1945, the original design had been changed to have a single tail unit and the armament had been increased. The wing, high on the circular section fuselage, was 6 ft. thick at the root and allowed access to the engines in flight. Forward and rear compartments in the fuselage were connected by an 80-ft. long tunnel along which ran a wheeled cart. Powered by Pratt & Whitney R-4360-25 engines, the XB-36 first flew on August 8, 1946.

The second prototype was designated YB-36 (42-13571) and introduced the raised cockpit roof which became a production feature, and additional nose armament. It later became the YB-36A with four-wheel bogie main undercarriage units, each wheel being of 56-inch diameter compared with the 110-inch main wheels of the XB-36.

The first production aircraft was a B-36A, flown on August 28, 1947, and powered by R-4360-25 engines. Twenty-two aircraft were built in this configuration and deliveries to Strategic Air Command began on August 28, 1947; they were unarmed and used principally for training and crew conversion. Production continued with 73 of the B-36B model, the first of which flew on July 8, 1948. The B-36B was fully equipped for operational use, with armament comprising six retractable and remotely controlled turrets mounting two 20-mm. cannon each, and two more 20-mm. guns each in nose and tail turrets. The engines were R-4360-41s and the gross weight 328,000 lb.

The B-36 became the object of bitter inter-Service rivalry leading to a Congressional investigation in 1949, which vindicated the original Air Force decision to buy the B-36. A more important event the same year was the first flight on March 26, 1949, of the B-36D. This model introduced additional power in the form of four turbojets paired in pods under each wing. These boosted the speed to 435 m.p.h., the ceiling to more than 45,000 ft. and the gross weight to 358,000 lb. and led to further production contracts and the eventual establishment of the B-36 as the major SAC deterrent weapon. The maximum bomb-load increased to a possible 84,000 lb., in two 42,000 lb. "Grand Slams", and snap-action bomb doors were introduced. Equipment included the K-3A bombing–navigation system and AN/APG-41A gun-laying radar.

The first B-36D was a "B" conversion, with four Allison J-35 engines, but the standard model (first flown on July 11, 1949) and all subsequent B-36 variants, had General Electric J47-GE-19s in the pods. Of the 73 B-36Bs built, 64 were converted to B-36D and another 22 of the latter type were built from scratch. Deliveries, to Eglin A.F.B., began on August 19, 1950. The RB-36D was a strategic reconnaissance version of the B-36D, first flown on December 18, 1949, and first delivered to SAC on June 3, 1950. Two of the four bomb-bays were deleted in favour of 14

Convair B-36B-5 in Arctic colours and with 8th A.F. insignia on tail (*Peter M. Bowers*).

Convair GRB-36F carrying GRF-84F (*Republic photo*).

cameras, and the crew increased to 22. Convair built 17 RB-36Ds and seven B-36Bs were also converted to this standard. In 1950, all but one of the 22 B-36As, plus the single YB-36A, were converted to RB-36E standard, generally similar to the RB-36D and first flown on December 18, 1949. The B-36F was similar to the "D" but had 3,800 h.p. R-4360-53s. It first flew on November 18, 1950, and 34 were built, plus 24 similar RB-36Fs with increased fuel.

The B-36D entered service with the 7th Bomb Wing at Carswell A.F.B., and was first deployed overseas in January 1951, when six aircraft flew to the United Kingdom on a simulated mission lasting more than 24 hours. With bomb-bay tanks, the B-36 had an unrefuelled endurance of more than 50 hours. The first B-36s to visit the Far East were from the 92nd Bomb Wing, in 1953, and in 1954 this became the first entire B-36 Wing to be deployed overseas, when it went to Guam. In July 1953, the 11th Bomb Wing flew 21 B-36s to North Africa.

The RB-36F was the type used for development of the FICON parasite fighter idea. The McDonnell XF-85 was originally developed for the B-36 but was abandoned after test drops from a B-29, and the Republic GRF-84F was adopted instead. Trials were successfully conducted in May 1953, in which a GRF-84F was dropped from a trapeze beneath the modified GRB-36F, and at least 12 of the Convair bombers were subsequently modified to carry fighters in this way or to serve as carriers and controllers for GAM missile development.

Final production versions of the big bomber were the B-36H and J. The former had improvements to the flight deck and was first flown on April 5, 1952. Convair built 83 of these, and 73 of the similar RB-36H. The B-36J, which had additional fuel tanks in the outer wings and undercarriage strengthened for a gross weight of 410,000 lb., first flew on September 3, 1953, and 33 were built. Some were stripped of all armament but the tail guns and carried only nine crewmen; these were known as "Featherweight" B-36s, for high altitude operation. Convair delivered the last B-36J to SAC on August 14, 1954, and SAC retired the last B-36 on February 12, 1959, becoming an all-jet force on that day.

In 1955, a B-36H (51-5712) was modified for use as a nuclear reactor

189

Convair B-36J-III-CF, with white anti-radiation finish on the undersides. The -III- in the designation indicates a modification programme (*Peter M. Bowers*).

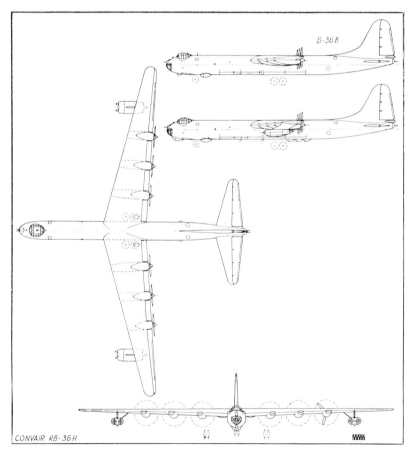

test-bed, and designated NB-36H. The reactors did not contribute to the aircraft's propulsion, the object of the trials being to measure the effect of radiation upon instruments, equipment, and airframe, and to study shielding methods. The first flight was made on September 17, 1955, and the programme totalled 47 flights up to March 1957. A project to build a B-36 using nuclear power for primary propulsion, under the designation X-6, was abandoned.

Other experimental designations were YB-36C, projected with R-4360-51 tractor engines and YB-36G, a swept-wing pure-jet development of the design, two examples of which were built and flown as the YB-60.

TECHNICAL DATA (B-36)

MANUFACTURER: Consolidated-Vultee Aircraft Corporation, Fort Worth, Texas.
TYPE: Heavy strategic bomber and reconnaissance aircraft.
ACCOMMODATION: Normal crew complement 15, including four reliefs.

	B-36B	B-36D	B-36J
Power Plant:	6 × 3,500 h.p. R-4360-41	6 × 3,500 h.p. R-4360-41 and 4 × 5,200 lb. J47-GE-19	6 × 3,800 h.p. R-4360-53 and 4 × 5,200 lb. J47-GE-19
Dimensions:			
Span, ft., in.	230 0	230 0	230 0
Length, ft., in.	162 1	162 1	162 1
Height, ft., in.	46 8	46 8	46 8
Wing area, sq. ft.	4,772	4,772	4,772
Weights:			
Empty, lb.	140,640	158,843	171,035
Gross, lb.	328,000	357,500	410,000
Performance:			
Max. speed, m.p.h./ft.	381/34,500	439/32,120	411/36,400
Cruising speed, m.p.h.	202	225	391
Climb, ft./min.	1,510	1,740	1,920
Service ceiling, ft.	42,500	45,200	39,900
Range, miles	8,175	7,500	6,800 (10,000 lb. bombs)

ARMAMENT: Two 20-mm. M24A1 cannon each in six retractable, remotely controlled fuselage turrets, tail turret and nose mounting, with 9,200 rounds. Maximum bomb load, 86,000 lb. (at restricted gross weight). Normal bomb-load up to 72,000 lb.
SERIAL NUMBERS:

XB-36: 42-13570.
YB-36: 42-13571.
B-36A: 44-92004/92025.
B-36B: 44-92026/92098.
B-36D: 49-2647/2668.
B-36F: 49-2669/2675; 49-2677/2683; 49-2685; 50-1064/1082.
B-36H: 50-1083/1097; 51-5699/5742; 52-1343/1366.

B-36J: 52-2210/2226; 52-2812/2827.
RB-36D: 49-2686/2702.
RB-36F: 49-2703/2721; 50-1098/1102.
RB-36H: 50-1103/1110; 51-5743/5756; 51-13717/13741; 52-1367/1392.

Convair C-131B electronic test bed (*Convair photo A2191*).

Convair C-131 Samaritan, T-29

A total of 472 examples of the Convair 240/340/440 series of twin-engined transports was purchased by the USAF in nine principal versions of two basic types for training and transportation. The trainer came first and the two prototypes, based on the Convair 240, were originally designated XAT-29, this being later changed to XT-29. The first flight was made at Lindbergh Field, San Diego, on September 22, 1949, and a production order for T-29As followed, 46 being built. This variant was unpressurized, had 14 stations in the fuselage for student navigators and four astrodomes; the first was delivered to the Air Force on February 24, 1950. In the T-29B (first flight July 30, 1952; 105 built), the fuselage was pressurized, gross weight increased, provision made for ten student navigators and four student radar operators and only three astrodomes were fitted. The T-29C (first flight July 28, 1953; 119 built) had 2,500 h.p. R-2800-99W engines in place of the -77 or -97 models. Some later became VT-29C staff transports and AT-29C (redesignated ET-29C in 1962) for airways checking.

The distinctive feature of the T-29D (first flown August 11, 1953; 92 built) was the installation of the "K" system bombsight and camera-scoring equipment. The fuselage had no astrodomes and carried six students with their instructor. Some became executive transports as VT-29D and others were ET-29D trainers for electronic warfare officers. Four of the "B" trainers were converted to VT-29Bs in 1952 as 29–32 seat staff transports. The T-29E was projected with Allison T38 turboprops but was not built; however, a single T-29B (51-5171) became the VT-29E executive transport. Also cancelled was the YT-32 with a bombardier nose.

The first transport variant produced for the USAF was the C-131A (or MC-131A) Samaritan (26 built), a version of the Convair 240 delivered in 1954 and equipped for casualty evacuation. It could carry 27 litters or 37 passengers and had a large loading door for stretchers and cargo. The first was delivered to MATS on April 1, 1954. Based on the Convair 340,

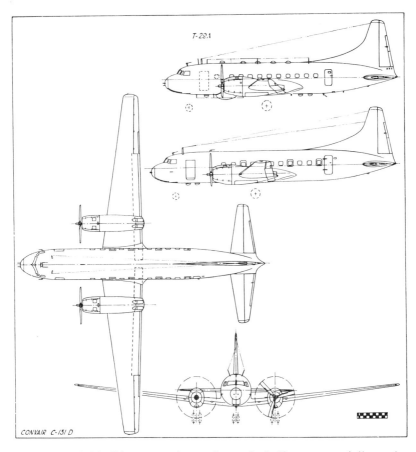

CONVAIR C-131 D

the C-131B (36 built) was an electronic test bed. Six were specially-equipped, as JC-131Bs, for use by the 6560th Operation Group (Range Support) to detect and locate re-entering missile nose-cones.

For use as staff transports by MATS, Continental Division, Convair

Convair T-29B, showing overall glossy grey finish with white top and vertical tail, and "O-for-over 10" on tail serial number (*Jim Sullivan*).

built 33 C-131Ds and VC-131Ds, of which 27 were to commercial 340 standard and another six to commercial 440 standard, with improved sound-proofing. These seated up to 44 passengers. Fifteen C-131Es were built in 1956 and 1957 for use as electronic countermeasures trainers by Strategic Air Command, but some of these were later converted for use by MATS—six as RC-131Fs for photo-survey and charting duties with the Air Photographic and Charting Service and one to the RC-131G for the Airways and Air Communication Service, checking airways aids.

Two Convair 340s were fitted with Allison YT56-A-3 turboprops in 1954 and were used to provide the USAF with turboprop handling experience. They were designated YC-131C and the first flew on June 29, 1954. Four C-131Ds were similarly modified to have T56 engines as VC-131Hs in 1965 for use by the 89th MAW, Special Missions, at Andrews AFB. A single NC-131H, first flown on July 8, 1970, was equipped to simulate the handling of advanced large aircraft projects.

TECHNICAL DATA (C-131, T-29)

MANUFACTURER: Consolidated-Vultee Aircraft Corporation, later Convair Division of General Dynamics Corp., San Diego, California.

TYPE: (C-131) Personnel transport and casualty evacuation. (T-29) Navigator-bombardier trainer.

	T-29B	T-29D	C-131B	VC-131H
Accommodation:	Four crew plus 16	Four crew plus 16	Four crew plus 48	Four crew plus 44
Power Plant:	2,400 h.p. R-2800-97	2,500 h.p. R-2800-99W	2,500 h.p. R-2800-99W	3,750 s.h.p. T56-A-9
Dimensions:				
Span, ft., in.	91　9	91　9	105　4	105　4
Length, ft., in.	74　8	—	79　2	81　6
Height, ft., in.	26　11	—	28　2	29　2
Wing area, sq. ft.	817	817	920	920
Weights:				
Empty, lb.	—	29,000	29,248	—
Gross, lb.	43,575	43,575	47,000	54,600
Performance:				
Max. speed, m.p.h.	296	299	293	—
Cruising speed, m.p.h.	248	286	254	342
Initial climb, ft./min.	1,230	1,370	1,410	2,050
Service ceiling, ft.	23,500	24,000	24,500	—
Range, miles	1,500	760	450	1,605

SERIAL NUMBERS:

XT-29: 49-1910/1911.
T-29A: 49-1912/1945; 50-183/194.
T-29B: 51-3797/3816; 51-5114/5172; 51-7892/7917.
T-29C: 52-1091/1175; 53-3461/3494.
T-29D: 52-1176/1185; 52-5812/5836; 52-9976/9980; 53-3495/3546.

C-131A: 52-5781/5806.
C-131B: 53-7788/7823.*
YC-131C: 53-7886/7887.
C-131D: 54-2805/2825; 55-290/301.†
C-131E: 55-4750/4759; 57-2548/2552.
　* 53-7793 converted to NC-131H.
　† 54-2815/2817 and 55-299 to C-131H.

F-102A of the 327th FIS, George A.F.B. in 1956, with original over-all grey finish, peculiar to F-102/106 until adoption of camouflage. The original short fin and rudder are shown; compared with photographs on following page. (*Peter M. Bowers*).

Convair F-102 Delta Dagger

Deliveries of the F-102 to the USAF, beginning in June 1955, marked the introduction into service of the first delta-wing aircraft the Air Force had accepted. Its design, begun in 1950, was closely related to that of the experimental XF-92A, which Convair had built in 1948 to provide data for the proposed F-92 (Model 7) Mach 1·5 fighter designed in consultation with Dr. Alexander Lippisch, who had done much research on delta wings in Germany. The XF-92A (Model 7-002) was the first powered delta-wing aircraft flown, and the YF-102 (Model 8-80) with which Convair won the 1950 design contest, was basically the XF-92A scaled up by 1·22:1.

The first YF-102 (52-7994) flew at Edwards A.F.B. on October 24, 1953, and the second on January 11, 1954, both being powered by the J57-P-11 turbojet. These aircraft were found deficient in performance, and while a further eight YF-102s (Model 8-82) were being built to the same standard, Convair embarked on a major investigation and redesign programme. The latter occupied only 117 days, and on December 20, 1954, the first YF-102A (Model 8-90) made its first flight. The most prominent new feature was a longer fuselage with a pinched or "coke-bottle" waist—the first application of "area rule" developed at NACA by Richard Whitcomb. The wing leading edge was cambered and the tips were given wash-in. The J57-P-23 turbojet was installed and the cockpit canopy redesigned.

From the outset, the F-102 had been designed as a missile carrier, and it was in fact the first USAF fighter to become operational armed only with guided missiles and unguided rockets. The WS201A weapon system included the Convair F-102 and the Hughes MG-3 fire-control systems and Falcon armament, and was the first Air Defense weapon system to include a piloted aircraft.

The first of four YF-102As achieved supersonic speed on its second flight, and production of the similar F-102A (Model 8-10) proceeded. Between 1953 and 1957, five production contracts were awarded for a total of 875 F-102As, the first going into squadron service in mid-1956 and the last being completed

195

Tall-finned Convair F-102As in their original overall grey finish. (*USAF photo*).

in April 1958. By 1958, 26 Air Defense Command squadrons were flying F-102As, and 32 ADC units flew the type during its deployment. The F-102A also served in Alaska until 1969, with USAF squadrons in Europe until 1970 and with PACAF also until 1950, the latter flying combat missions in Vietnam from 1962 through 1969. By the end of 1970, only two units still flew the F-102 in ADC, but 19 ANG squadrons flew Delta Daggers until the spring of 1976.

To serve as a combat trainer, the Air Force also purchased 63 TF-102As (Weapon System WS201L) which were similar to the F-102A but had a wider front fuselage seating two side-by-side. Full operational equipment and armament was retained. The first TF-102A (Convair Model 8-12) flew on November 8, 1955. In 1957, Convair began a modernization programme for early F-102As to bring them up to the latest standard including a larger tail, MG-10 in place of MG-3 fire control system, fittings for wing drop tanks and provision for 2·75-in., in place of 2-in., rockets. A subsequent programme added an infra-red sighting system and deleted the internal rocket armament.

After being withdrawn from squadron use, 65 Delta Daggers became

Convair TF-102A after modernization, in South-East Asia camouflage (*Roger Levy*).

196

PQM-102A target drones and about 145 more PQM-102Bs were more extensively equipped. Four QF-102A drones retained provision for manned operation.

TECHNICAL DATA (F-102A)

MANUFACTURER: Convair Division of General Dynamics Corp., San Diego, California.

TYPE: Supersonic all-weather fighter-interceptor.

ACCOMMODATION: Pilot only, with upward ejection seat.

POWER PLANT: One 16,000 lb.s.t. (with a/b) Pratt & Whitney J57-P-23A turbojet.

DIMENSIONS: Span, 38 ft. 1 in. Length, 68 ft. 3 in. Height, 21 ft. 2 in. Wing area, 695·1 sq. ft.

WEIGHT: Empty, 19,350 lb. Max. take off, 28,150 lb. clean, 31,276 lb. with drop tanks.

PERFORMANCE: Max. speed, 780 m.p.h. at 36,000 ft. Initial climb, 17,400 ft./min. Combat ceiling, 51,800 ft. Radius of action, 566 nautical miles.

ARMAMENT: Six Hughes AIM-4C or AIM-4D, or two AIM-26B air-to-air missiles plus 24 unguided 2·75-in. FFARs.

SERIAL NUMBERS:

YF-102: 52-7994/7995; 53-1779/1786.
YF-102A: 53-1787/1790.
F-102A: 53-1791/1818; 54-1371/1407;
   55-3357/3464; 56-957/1518; 57-770/909

TF-102A: 54-1351/1370; 55-4032/4059;
   56-2317/2379.

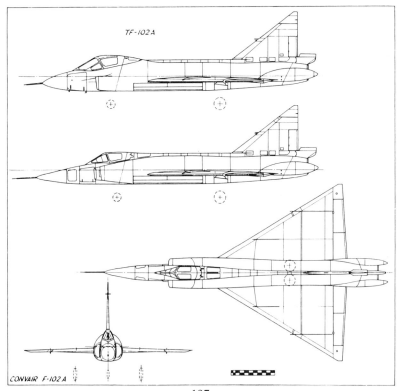

TF-102A

CONVAIR F-102A

A late-production Convair F-106A-135-CO in service with the 194th FIS, California ANG.

Convair F-106 Delta Dart

An extensively modified version of the F-102 Delta Dagger was developed during 1955 under the designation F-102B (Air Defense Weapon System WS201B) but the changes became so extensive that the designation was eventually changed to F-106. The delta wing remained substantially unchanged, but the fuselage was modified to accommodate the 50 per cent more powerful Pratt & Whitney J75 turbojet. Engine intakes were relocated behind the cockpit and closer to the engine; the cockpit was moved forward relatively, and the shape of the fin and rudder changed. A new undercarriage was fitted, including a steerable twin nose wheel, and provision was made for later weapons in the internal bomb bays. To obtain optimum engine performance at all speeds, variable intake ducts were adopted.

The F-106 was fitted with the Hughes MA-1 electronic guidance and fire-control system, which operated with the SAGE (Semi-Automatic Ground Environment) defence system.

The first F-106A (Model 8-24) was flown from Edwards A.F.B. by R. L. Johnson on December 26, 1956, and was built to a production con-

Convair F-106A-125-CO in the markings of the 87th FIS.

The two-seat F-106B in service with the final Delta Dart ANG unit, the 119th FIS from New Jersey (*Howard W. Serig*).

tract placed earlier in 1956. Subsequent contracts kept the F-106 in production until July 1961, and many of the earlier production aircraft were returned to Convair during 1960 and 1961 to be modified to the latest standard with an improved MA-1, supersonic ejection seats and vertical display instrument panels (as Model 8-31). Deliveries of the F-106A to Air Defense Command began in July 1959 and the type entered service with the 498th Fighter Interception Squadron at Geiger A.F.B., Washington. Although plans had existed for production of sufficient F-106As to equip 40 squadrons, successive reductions cut this total to 14, to achieve which a large number of the early test aircraft had to be brought up to full operational standard.

A second version of the Delta Dart was ordered in April 1957 as part of the third contract for F-106s. This was the F-106B (Model 8-27), a two-seat combat trainer variant having the full operational capability of the single-seater, but with a new cockpit containing two seats in tandem. The first F-106B (57-2507) was flown for the first time, also at Edwards A.F.B., on April 9, 1958, and examples served alongside F-106As on all squadrons equipped. Early F-106Bs were eventually modified to tactical standard as Convair Model 8-32. Production totals were 277 F-106As and 63 F-106Bs, completed by December 1960. Between September 1960 and 1963, most F-106As and F-106Bs underwent three updating programmes, which added an infra-red search/track sight ahead of the cockpit, a new canopy offering thermal flash protection, and an upward rotational ejection seat. Later, TACAN and in-flight refuelling receptacles were added. Plans to produce an F-106C with Pratt & Whitney JT4B-22 engine and improved radar, did not proceed beyond the construction of two YF-106Cs, used as radar test-beds. The F-106D, a two-seat version of the F-106C, was also cancelled.

Although at various times from March 1968 onwards, four ADC squadrons of F-106s were deployed in the Far East, the Delta Dart saw no operational service in Vietnam but remained the mainstay of continental United States air defence, equipping 11 squadrons until 1972. By 1974, six ANG squadrons were flying F-106s alongside six ADC units. The last examples were retired from the active Air Force in 1988, when conversion of surplus airframes to QF-106 drones began. ANG units continued to fly the last few F-106As and F-106Bs for a few months after the USAF had relinquished the type.

TECHNICAL DATA (F-106A)

MANUFACTURER: Convair Division of General Dynamics Corp., San Diego, California.

TYPE: Supersonic interceptor.

ACCOMMODATION: (F-106A): Pilot. (F-106B): Pilot and instructor or radar operator.

POWER PLANT: One 17,200 lb.s.t. (24,500 lb. with a/b) Pratt & Whitney J75-P-17 turbojet.

DIMENSIONS: Span, 38 ft. $3\frac{1}{2}$ in. Length, 70 ft. $8\frac{3}{4}$ in. Height, 20 ft. $3\frac{1}{2}$ in. Wing area, 697·8 sq. ft.

WEIGHTS: Empty, 24,315 lb. Max take-off, 39,195 lb.

PERFORMANCE: Max. speed, 1,327 m.p.h. at 35,000 ft. Initial climb, 42,800 ft./min. Service ceiling, 45,000 ft. Combat radius, 730 miles.

ARMAMENT: One AIR-2A or -2B Genie unguided air rocket and four AIM-4F or AIM-4G Falcon AAMs, stowed internally.

SERIAL NUMBERS:

F-106A: 56-451/467; 57-229/246; 57-2453/2506; 58-759/798; 59-001/148.

F-106B: 57-2507/2547; 58-900/904; 59-149/165.

Convair B-58A at take-off (*Convair photo*).

Convair B-58 Hustler

The first supersonic bomber put into production for the USAF, the B-58 was developed from original Convair design studies which won an Air Force competition in 1949. This study showed the feasibility of a manned supersonic bombing system and design work continued until April 1952, when the MX-1964 contract called for development of a flyable bomber under the weapon system concept. The weapon system designations WS102A and WS102L were allotted to bomber and reconnaissance versions respectively.

Features of the B-58 design (Convair Model 4) were its delta wing with four podded engines, area-ruled fuselage and large-scale use of honeycomb sandwich skin panels for the wing and fuselage. To obtain the maximum in performance and mission flexibility, an external pod was adopted rather than internal weapon stowage. This pod contained fuel for the outward journey, and a nuclear weapon; the entire pod could be jettisoned after the target had been attacked. A later development of this idea was a dual pod, with fuel in the larger, lower compartment and a weapon, cameras, electronic countermeasures equipment or other special gear in the upper pod.

The first contract for B-58s was for 13 test aircraft, wih 17 more test examples ordered later. The first of these (55-0660) flew for the first time, without the pod, at Fort Worth on November 11, 1956, piloted by B.A. Erickson, followed by the second on February 16, 1957. The 30 trials aircraft were used for extensive flight testing, at first by the makers and then by the USAF B-58 Test Force comprising 6592th Test Squadron and 3958th Operational, Test and Evaluation Squadron at Carswell A.F.B. Only 55-0660 was designated XB-58, others in the test batch being YB/RB-58 or (No 10 onwards) YB/RB-58A. Early aircraft were powered by YJ79-GE-1 engines until the definitive -5 engines became available.

Production orders for a total of 86 B-58As were placed in 1959-61, the first of these flying in September 1959. On October 15, this aircraft flew 1,680 miles in 80 minutes with one refuelling, maintaining a speed of over Mach 2 for over an hour. The 43rd Bomb Wing at Carswell A.F.B. was selected as the first B-58 unit, and was activated on March 15, 1960; it was joined later by the

201

305th Bomb Wing at Bunker Hill and these two units flew B-58s until they were withdrawn from service in 1970.

To help equip the operational units, 20 of the test batch were brought up to full production standard during 1961. Eight others were converted to TB-58A trainers with dual controls in the two front cockpits and operational equipment deleted; the first (55-670) flew on May 10, 1960.

TECHNICAL DATA (B-58A)

MANUFACTURER: Convair Division of General Dynamics Corp., Fort Worth, Texas.
TYPE: Supersonic medium bomber.
ACCOMMODATION: Pilot, navigator-bombardier and defensive system operator.
POWER PLANT: Four 15,600 lb.s.t. (with a/b) General Electric J79-GE-5A, 5B or 5C turbojets.
DIMENSIONS: Span, 56 ft. 10 in. Length, 96 ft. 9 in. Height, 31 ft. 5 in. Wing area, 1,542 sq. ft.
WEIGHT: Empty (with MB-1C pod), 64,115 lb. Gross, 163,000 lb. (Max. in-flight refuelled weight, 176,890 lb.).
PERFORMANCE: Max. speed, 1,385 m.p.h. at 40,000 ft. Average cruising speed, 579 m.p.h. Max. rate of climb, 38,050 ft./min. Service ceiling, 63,080 ft. Combat radius, 1,550 miles.
ARMAMENT: One 20-mm. General Electric M-61 multi-barrel cannon in radar aimed tail mount. MB-1C pod under fuselage.
SERIAL NUMBERS:
XB-58: 55-660.
YB/RB-58: 55-661/668
YB/RB-58A: 55-669/672; 58-1007/1023

B-58A: 59-2428/2463; 60-1110/1129;
61-2051/2080.

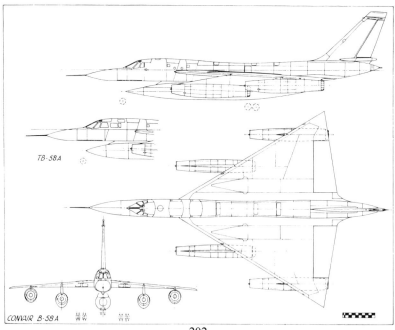

CONVAIR B-58A

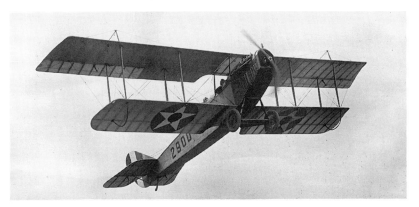

Curtiss JN-4D with clear-doped finish and 1917 markings (*Signal Corps/National Archives photo 9847*)

The Curtiss Jennies

The word "Jenny" (or "Jennie") is one of those entirely unofficial names applied to a particular aeroplane design that was so suited to the subject that it virtually replaced the regular model designation. The name was a logical derivation of the factory model designation JN, itself the result of combining the best structural features of two earlier models, the J and the N. The slurring of the two separate letters into a single feminine name was inevitable. The remarkable double career of the JN series, one as a World War I trainer and the other as a post-war barnstorming/air-show/private owner type, has made the Jenny one of the most widely known "name" aeroplanes in America. Extensive use of the surplus military model in post-war years gave its name to the entire era to such an extent that there is a tendency today to refer to other contemporary designs as Jennies.

The Jenny originated in England, when Glenn Curtiss hired B. Douglas Thomas, then an engineer with Avro, to design a tractor biplane along lines then becoming standardized in England. Thomas completed most of the J design there. The J design was combined with the N early in its career to produce the JN line, but separate development of the N continued to N-9, the last procured by the Army (see page 525) and N-10 for the Navy. The Army tested two Js (29, 30) and an N (35) in 1914 and then ordered eight JN-2s (41/48) with equal span wings and two JN-3s (52, 53) with overhang. The JN-2s were later fitted with JN-3 wings.

Large-scale Jenny procurement began with 94 wheel-control JN-4s in 1916, which were used both as trainers and as observation types on the Mexican Border during General Pershing's punitive campaign against the bandit Pancho Villa. The JN-4, with ailerons only on the upper wing, was practically identical to the N-8 except for the airfoil section and control

Modified Curtiss J (29) with extended upper wing.

system. Curtiss also supplied JN-3s and 4s to England as trainers before the United States entered World War I.

American participation in the War standardized the Curtiss JN-4 series, and the equivalent Standard Aircraft Corporation SJ and J models, as the principal Army primary trainers. Improved Jenny versions with redesigned tails were tested and procured as JN-4A and B but major procurement concentrated on the JN-4D. Powered like its predecessors with the 90 h.p. Curtiss OX-5 engine but featuring stick control instead of the "Dep" wheel control, the JN-4D also had large distinguishing cut-outs in the wings at the fuselage.

Curtiss built 1,412 JN-4A through D and the single JN-4D-2 prototype, while 1,310 Ds were built by six other firms. The JN-4D-2 featured minor refinements and the prototype was outwardly indistinguishable from the Standard D. The 100 production D-2s built by Liberty Iron Works were conspicuous in not having the downward tilt to the engine that was a feature of the JN-4A and D. A Canadian version of the basic JN-4 was built by Canadian Aeroplane Corporation of Toronto, 680 of which were procured by the Army as JN-4Can (for "Canadian"). These were universally referred to as "Canucks" to designate their Canadian origin, and had

Curtiss JN-2 serial 42 after JN-3 wings were fitted (*Boardman C. Reed collection*).

Curtiss JN-4A with high dihedral and ailerons on both wings (*Signal Corps/National Archives*).

rounded tail surfaces similar to the original JN-4, stick control, ailerons on both wings, and the engine was installed with the thrust line level.

Curtiss records list only two JN-4Cs built as experimental models with R.A.F. 6 airfoil, but Army records show 276, with different serial numbers from the "Canucks", on the Air Service inventory in 1919. Several dozen additional "Canucks" with RFC serial numbers were absorbed into the U.S. Air Service from winter flying schools established by Britain in Texas.

The next Jenny variant was the JN-4H, an advanced trainer. The "H" indicated a 150 or 180 h.p. Wright-built Hispano Suiza engine substituted for the OX and did not continue the earlier alphabetical sequence of development. Increased fuel capacity resulted in thickening of the upper wing centre section to accommodate a supplementary fuel tank.

Supplementary designations were applied for specialized use; JN-4HB bomber trainer, JN-4HO observation trainer, and JN-4HG and JN-4HG-2 for one- and two-gun gunnery trainers.

Curtiss JN-4H with Wright-Hispano "A" engine (*Peter M. Bowers collection*).

Canadian-built Curtiss JN-4Can with 1918 US markings (*Signal Corps/National Archives photo 9847*).

The Army converted one JN-4H (41358) to a prototype bomber trainer under the unofficial designation of JN-5 after installing Curtiss Model R vertical tail surfaces to provide control at the higher gross weight. Curtiss then built 1,035 production versions as JN-6H, the first ones with the R tail but the rest with regular JN-4D/H tails. The special JN-4H designations also applied to JN-6s and were expanded to include the JN-6HP pursuit trainer. Principal JN-6 recognition feature over the JN-4H was the use of ailerons on both upper and lower wings and lower wingtip matching the shape of the upper.

The OX-powered Jennies were declared surplus after World War I and were snapped up by the hundreds by civil owners at prices that dropped as low as $50. The Hispano-powered -4s and -6s remaining in Army service went through various modification programmes and emerged as Model JNS for "JN Standardized". A few even acquired steel tube fuselages, and the S in the designation was sometimes taken to mean steel. Suffix letters were added to designate the power plant, as JNS-E for those powered with

Curtiss JN-6 with skis (*Ordnance Dept. 15683/USAF photo 1771A.S.*).

206

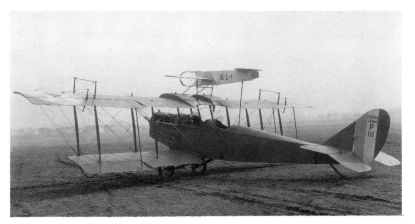

Curtiss JN-6HG-1 with GL-1 target glider (*USAF photo 16893*).

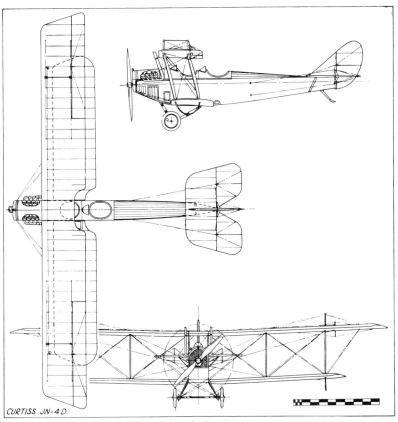

CURTISS JN-4D

Curtiss JNS-1 with new Fiscal Year serial number assigned following rebuild from JN-4H.

the 180 h.p. Wright-Hispano E. Many were powered with the 150 h.p. Wright-Hispano I, which was misread as the figure One and resulted in the aeroplanes sometimes being called JNS-one's on those occasions when they were not "Hisso Jennies". Service modification of the JNs continued as late as 1925, with fiscal year serials being assigned to the rebuilt airframes. The last Army Jennies, then in use by National Guard Units, were withdrawn from service and scrapped in September, 1927.

TECHNICAL DATA (JENNY)

MANUFACTURER: Curtiss Aeroplane and Motor Co., Inc., Garden City, L.I.
TYPE: Trainer.
ACCOMMODATION: Pupil and instructor in tandem open cockpits.
POWER PLANT: (JN-4D) 90 h.p. Curtiss OX-5; (JN-4H, JN-6) 150 h.p. Wright-Hispano A.
DIMENSIONS: Span, 43 ft. 7⅜ in. Length, 27 ft. 4 in. Height, 9 ft. 10⅝ in. Wing area, 352 sq. ft.
WEIGHTS: Empty (4D) 1,580 lb.; (4H) 1,595 lb.; (6H) 1,797 lb. Gross (4D) 2,130 lb.; (4H) 2,150 lb.; (6H) 2,687 lb.
PERFORMANCE: Max. speed (4D) 75 m.p.h.; (6H) 79·2 m.p.h. Climb, 3,000 ft. in 10 min. Service ceiling (4H) 8,000 ft.; (6H) 5,700 ft. Range, 250 st. miles.
ARMAMENT: None.
KNOWN SERIAL NUMBERS:

JN-4: 79-81; 116-125; 130-136; 230-264; 408-461; 682-699; 731-991.
JN-4A: 1059-1136; 1213-1282.
JN-4C: 1200-1212; 1301-1309.
JN-4CAN: 38536/38586; 39155/39193; 39227/39267; 39314/39352; 39868/39906.
JN-4D: 1283-1647; 2405-4075; 4976-5293; 24056-25087; 29105-29210; 33775-34220; 37999-38188; 39868-39869; 39913; 44262-44594; 47340-47576.

JN-4D-2: 47816 (prototype).
JN-4H: 37933; 38013-38079; 38132-38530; 41358; 41412-41724; 41915-41976; 42047-42122.
JN-6H: 41725-41914; 41977-42046; 42391; 44153-44246; 44729-44885; 45000-45287; 49117-49122.

Curtiss PW-8 on skis (*USAF photo 29247*).

Curtiss PW-8

From the successful R-6 racer, which took first and second places in the 1922 Pulitzer Prize race, Curtiss began development of a single-seat fighter as a private enterprise. Official interest was aroused before completion of a prototype, and a contract was placed on April 27, 1923, for three examples of the type, designated PW-8 in the Air Service category for water-cooled pursuits. Delivery of the first (23-1201) was made under a month later, on May 14. This prototype had a semi-split-axle landing gear and the engine cowling was indented between the two cylinder banks. Both these features were later abandoned. After two unsuccessful attempts (by Lt. Russell Maughan) to make a daylight U.S. transcontinental flight, 23-1301 was converted to a two seater and became the CO-X (Corps Observation-Experimental).

The second PW-8 prototype (23-1202) differed from the first in having a divided type of landing gear, with reduced drag; better streamlined cowling; strut connected ailerons and unbalanced elevators. Its weight increased from 2,799 lb. to 3,151 lb. and the better streamlining increased the speed by 9 m.p.h. to 168 m.p.h. In this form, the type went into production, 25 examples of the PW-8 being ordered in September 1923.

A trial installation of a turbo-supercharger was made in the second PW-8, (24-202), and on the fourth (24-204), Lt. Maughan finally succeeded in flying across the U.S. from coast-to-coast in the hours of daylight on June 23, 1924, a year after his earlier attempts.

The third of the XPW-8s originally ordered in 1923 was completed with a number of modifications, of which the most obvious was the 30-ft. span single-bay wing arrangement in place of the standard 32-ft. span two-bay wings. A modified rudder without balance area was fitted and the skin-type radiators were eliminated in favour of a core-type mounted flat in the centre section of the upper wing. When the aircraft was modified for racing, the radiator was installed in a "tunnel" below the engine as on the Boeing PW-9. In this guise, 23-1203 was known as the XPW-8AA.

Later still, the PW-8A was further modified at Air Corps request by the installation of completely redesigned wings of tapered plan form and Clark Y aerofoil, similar to those of the Boeing PW-9. In this guise it was re-designated XPW-8B and was in effect the prototype of the P-1 Hawk.

TECHNICAL DATA (PW-8)

MANUFACTURER: Curtiss Aeroplane and Motor Co., Inc., Garden City, L.I.
TYPE: Single-seat pursuit.
ACCOMMODATION: Pilot in open cockpit.
POWER PLANT: One 440 h.p. Curtiss D-12 piston Vee in-line.
DIMENSIONS: Span, 32 ft. 0 in. Length, 22 ft. 6 in. Height, 8 ft. 10 in. Wing area, 287 sq. ft.
WEIGHTS: Empty, 2,191 lb. Gross, 3,151 lb.
PERFORMANCE: Max. speed, 168 m.p.h. at sea level. Cruising speed, 160 m.p.h. at 10,000 ft. Initial climb, 9 min. to 10,000 ft. Service ceiling, 21,700 ft. Range, 440 st. miles.
ARMAMENT: Two fixed forward firing 0·30-inch guns.
SERIAL NUMBERS:
XPW-8: 23-1201/1203.
PW-8: 24-201/225.

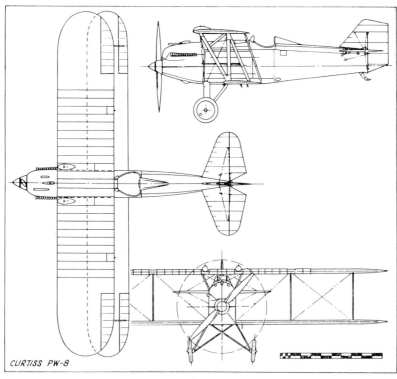

CURTISS PW-8

Curtiss P-1B in training configuration at Kelly Field, with larger tyres and no wheel covers. (*Boardman C. Reed collection*).

Curtiss P-1 to P-23 Hawk Biplanes

When a contract was awarded to Curtiss on March 7, 1925 for 15 production examples of the XPW-8B, the type became the first to qualify for a designation in the newly adopted "P" category for pursuits. It was also the first model of the series (which had begun in 1923 with the prototype PW-8) to be named Hawk. The 15 P-1s were outwardly similar to the XPW-8B apart from an extra strut in the centre section bracing and a change in rudder shape. They served with the 27th and 94th Pursuit Squadrons.

The final five aircraft of the production batch had provision for alternate engine installations—the standard Curtiss V-1150-1 of the P-1 or a 500 h.p. Curtiss V-1400 (D-12). With the latter engine fitted, these five aircraft were re-designated P-2; the first (25-420) had an experimental turbo-supercharger, which increased the absolute ceiling from 22,980 ft. to 32,790 ft. Three other P-2s were later re-converted to P-1A standard for squadron service while the fourth (25-423) with a 600 h.p. Curtiss V-1570-1 engine was re-designated XP-6 as a racer, achieving 189 m.p.h. in the National Air Races in 1927, with an inverted air-cooled Liberty engine. The first P-1 (25-410) was later converted to XP-17 with inverted Wright V-1460-3.

The first Hawk to serve in quantity with Air Corps pursuit squadrons (the 17th, 27th and 94th) was the P-1A, 25 examples of which were ordered in September 1925. Detail changes included a 3-inch lengthening of the fuselage, changed cowling lines and additional service equipment which increased the weight by 20 lb. and reduced the speed by 2 m.p.h. One P-1A (26-296) was temporarily re-engined with a Wright-Hispano E as an advanced trainer designated XAT-4, and another (26-295) was modified into the XP-6A racer, by fitting XPW-8A wings.

211

Curtiss P-1C on skis (*U.S. Army photo*).

A second batch of 25 Hawks was ordered in August 1926 and these appeared as P-1Bs, delivery to the Air Corps beginning on October 28, 1926. The radiator was a little more rounded, and two experimental P-1Bs were flown with further radiator changes. The wheel diameter was increased, and equipment changes increased the weight and reduced the speed further, to 157 m.p.h. A 435 h.p. Curtiss V-1150-3 engine was fitted, and the P-1Bs served with squadrons already flying the earlier Hawks.

In October 1928, the Army ordered its largest single quantity of Curtiss pursuits to date—33. These were delivered, by April 1929, as P-1Cs. Once again the weight increased and the performance decreased. The engine was a 435 h.p. Curtiss V-1150-3, and wheel brakes were fitted. One P-1C (29-238) was fitted with an experimental Heinrich radiator and Prestone cooling system, being re-designated XP-1C.

No more P-1s were built, but a further 71 were delivered to the Army in 1929 by conversion programmes. In October 1926, after trials with the converted P-1A (as the XAT-4), the Army had ordered 40 similar aircraft, of which 35 were delivered in 1927 as AT-4s with 180 h.p. Wright V-720 engines and five as AT-5s with 220 h.p. Wright R-790-1s. In 1929, 25 of the AT-4s became P-1Ds when re-engined with the 435 h.p. Curtiss

Curtiss AT-5A with Bolling Field insignia on fuselage, before conversion to P-1F (*Peter M. Bowers*).

Curtiss P-3A with fuselage data in white or black as standardized 1928-1931. Manufacturer's name and Army model number had previously appeared on the rudder (*Curtiss-Wright photo T3974*).

V-1150-3, becoming similar to the P-1Bs but having only one machine gun. When similarly re-engined, the AT-5s became P-1Es. Both versions served with the 43rd School Squadron at Kelly Field.

On July 30, 1927, the Army had ordered a further 31 trainers as AT-5As. These also were converted to pursuits in 1929, being re-engined with the V-1150-3 and designated P-1F. One other P-1F (28-189) was obtained by the Army by reconverting an XP-21, which in turn had earlier been converted from a P-3A.

P-3. The first radial-engined Hawk was produced by conversion of the last P-1A (26-300). Intended to have the experimental 390 h.p. Curtiss R-1454, it was in fact fitted with a 410 h.p. Pratt & Whitney R-1340-9, flown both uncowled and with various types of deep-chord N.A.C.A.

Curtiss P-5 in 1928 (*Curtiss-Wright photo 34620*).

213

cowls. The lighter engine installation gave the XP-3A, as this conversion was designated, an improved climb and ceiling performance compared with the P-1 series, and a contract was placed in 1928 for five more examples designated P-3A (28-189/193). With R-1340-3 engines, the performance was slightly better than that of the prototype. One P-3A (28-189) was flown with experimental cowlings and re-designated as the second XP-3A. Both it and the original XP-3A were re-designated XP-21 when used to test-fly the 300 h.p. R-985-1 Wasp Junior engine, and 28-189 eventually became a P-1F when it was again re-engined with a Curtiss V-1150-3 in-line engine.

P-5. Five Hawks generally similar to the P-1C were ordered in April 1927 with turbo-supercharged V-1150-3 engines, and were designated P-5s.

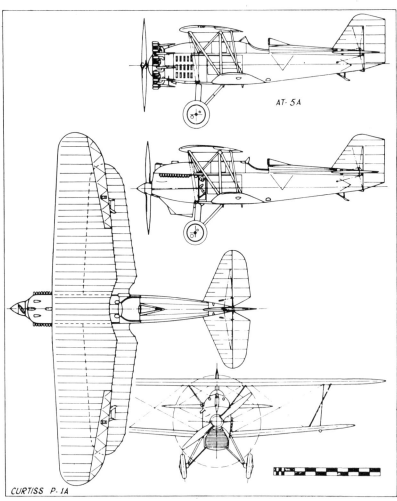

AT-5A

CURTISS P-1A

Top left, Curtiss P-6A (*Peter M. Bowers*); top right, P-6D *Peter M. Bowers*); bottom left, XP-6F (*John C. Mitchell*); bottom right, XP-6H (*David C. Cooke*).

Although the low-level performance was poor, the P-5 achieved 166 m.p.h. at 25,000 ft., which was above the absolute ceiling of the P-1.

P-6. The first aircraft to carry the P-6 designation was one of the five P-2 Hawks (25-423) modified to race for the Air Corps in the U.S. National Air Races, in 1927. At 189 m.p.h., this aircraft took second place in the event, held at Spokane, Washington. It was the first Hawk to be fitted with a Curtiss V-1570, the engine which later became known as the Conqueror. A second aircraft converted for the same event was the P-1A (26-295) re-designated XP-6A with PW-8A-type untapered wings and skin radiators in top and bottom wings. This also had the V-1570-1 engine, and took first place in the 1927 race at 201 m.p.h.

The success of the Curtiss Conqueror engine in these two aircraft led to a contract for a service test quantity of YP-6s placed on October 3, 1928. Two other aircraft subsequently completed as YP-6s (29-367 and 368) were originally ordered as YP-11s with Curtiss H-1640 engines. Generally similar to the P-1 in construction and appearance, the P-6 had a fuselage of revised and more streamlined shape. The rear fuselage was deepened to fair into the bottom of the radiator tunnel and stringers were added to the sides to round out the cross section. Deliveries to the Air Corps were made between October 1929 and December 1930. In service, the first eight aircraft were converted to P-6A by change of engine from V-1570-17 to V-1570-23, the latter being Prestone cooled. In 1931, the first P-6A (29-260) was converted to the XP-6D with a side-mounted turbo-super-charger, and in 1932, all remaining YP-6 and P-6A aircraft (two had crashed) were converted at the Fairfield Air Depot to the same standard with F-2F superchargers; they then became P-6Ds and were assigned to Langley Field, Virginia, for service trials.

Modifications similar to those which distinguished the P-6 were made to the last production P-1C (29-259) which became known as the Hawk Hoyt Special, for use by Captain Hoyt in an attempted flight from the

East U.S. coast to Alaska. With built-in long-range tanks, this aircraft reached Valemont, British Colombia, in July 1929 on its long-range flight, where it made a crash landing. After repair at Fairfield and deletion of the long-range tanks, it was returned to service as the sole XP-6B.

The major production and service version of the P-6 series was the P-6E, the designation P-6C having been tentatively assigned to this model and then cancelled. The prototype P-6E (29-374) began life as the last of three trials aircraft ordered as P-11s, to be powered by the new Curtiss H-1640 Chieftain, which proved unsatisfactory. Two P-11s were converted to YP-6, and the third was refashioned as the YP-20, with a 575 h.p. Wright R-1820-9 radial engine. Other changes included redesigned controls, a

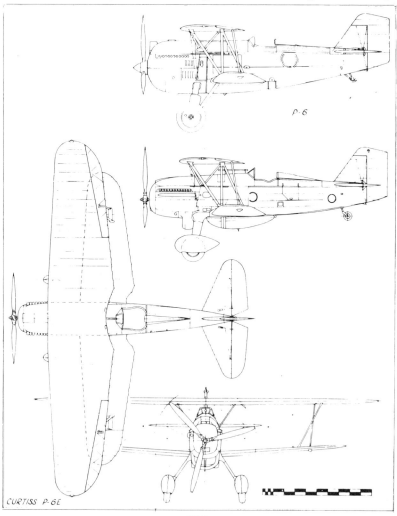

P.6

CURTISS P-6E

216

Curtiss P-6E of 17th Pursuit Squadron with open-sided wheel pants as modified after entering service. In the 1930s the aeroplane-in-group numbers of 1st Pursuit Group aeroplanes matched the last two digits of the Army serial number (*Peter M. Bowers*).

tailwheel in place of skid, re-proportioning of fin and rudder areas and addition of wheel spats. Another series of modifications to the third production P-6A (29-262) produced the XP-22, powered by a 700 h.p. V-1570-23 with Prestone cooling and a completely revised radiator.

A production batch of 46 Y1P-22s was planned, with features similar to those of the XP-22, but because many of the parts were identical with P-6 spares, this designation was dropped in favour of P-6C. Meanwhile, however, features of the XP-22, including the power plant and single-strut undercarriage, had been added to the YP-20 airframe and it was decided that the production aircraft should be to this standard as P-6Es. The YP-20 was then re-designated XP-6E. The fuselage contours were again changed, with the lower fairing removed but the curved side panels retained, and the machine guns were moved from under the top cowl to the fuselage sides, just below the line of the engine exhaust stacks. The production order was placed on July 8, 1931, and delivery of 45 of the 46 aircraft (32-233 to 277) had been made before the end of 1932.

Three P-6Es served in an experimental role during their life and were re-

Left, Curtiss YP-20 (*Curtiss photo*); right, Curtiss XP-23 (*USAF photo*).

designated. They were the prototype (29-374) which became the XP-6F with a fully enclosed cockpit and sliding canopy, and a turbo-super-charged V-1570-23 engine; 32-254 as the XP-6G with a V-1570-51 engine and other small changes; and 32-233 which, as the XP-6H, flew with ex-perimental wings mounting four 0·30-inch machine guns and the V-1570-51 engine. The XP-6G later reverted to P-6E, while the XP-6F and the XP-6H both became P-6Fs with 675 h.p. V-1570-55 engines.

P-23. One other Hawk biplane, although purely experimental, deserves mention as the last biplane fighter procured by the Army Air Corps. This was originally ordered as the last of the P-6Es (32-278), but was modified before delivery into the XP-23. While the original wings were retained, a new all-metal monocoque fuselage was developed, and metal tail surfaces of revised outline were fitted. The engine was a turbo-supercharged, geared, V-1570-23 which gave the XP-23 a top speed of 220 m.p.h. at 15,000 ft., but the supercharger was difficult to cool at high altitudes and was later removed, when the aircraft was re-designated YP-23.

TECHNICAL DATA (Hawk Biplanes)

MANUFACTURER: Curtiss Aeroplane and Motor Co., Inc., Garden City, L.I.
TYPE: Single-seat pursuit.
ACCOMMODATION: Pilot in open cockpit.

	P-1A	P-1C	P-5	P-6E
Power Plant:	435 h.p. V-1150-1	435 h.p. V-1150-5	435 h.p. V-1150-3	600 h.p. V-1570-23
Dimensions:				
Span, ft., in.	31 7	31 6	31 6	31 6
Length, ft., in.	22 10	23 3	23 8	23 2
Height, ft., in.	8 7	8 6	9 3	8 10
Wing area, sq. ft.	250	252	252	252
Weights:				
Empty, lb.	2,041	2,136	2,520	2,699
Gross, lb.	2,866	2,973	3,349	3,392
Performance:				
Max. speed, m.p.h. at s.l.	160	154	146	198
Cruising speed, m.p.h.	128	124	117	175
Initial climb, ft./min.	2,170	1,460	1,110	2,400
Service ceiling, ft.	20,200	20,800	31,900	24,700
Range, miles	—	600	—	570

ARMAMENT: Two fixed forward firing 0·30-inch guns.
SERIAL NUMBERS:
P-1: 25-410/419.
P-1A: 26-276/300.
P-1B: 27-063/087.
P-1C: 29-227/259.
P-2: 25-420/424.
P-3A: 28-189/193.
P-5: 27-327/331.

P-6: 29-260/273; 29-363/366.
P-6E: 32-233/277.
XP-23: 32-278.
AT-4: 27-088/097; 27-213/237.
AT-5: 27-238/242.
AT-5A: 28-042/072.

Curtiss O-1C transport for Secretary Davidson. Note four-star flag of a Cabinet Officer (*Curtiss photo*).

Curtiss O-1 Falcon

For six years after the end of World War I, the Army Air Service relied almost exclusively upon the DH-4B and DH-4M for observation and light bombing duties. By 1924, however, it became apparent that procurement of a more modern type of higher performance could be deferred no longer. Accordingly, two series of trials were arranged at McCook Field to select a new observation aircraft; the first, late in 1924, was for aircraft powered by the Liberty engine while the second, early in 1925, was for those with the Packard IA-1500 engine.

In the 1924 evaluation, in which eleven prototypes competed, the Douglas XO-2 was declared winner (see page 223), while the Curtiss XO-1 was among the unsuccessful types. The latter was forthwith re-engined with the Packard IA-1500 for the 1925 trials, which it won.

Although the design contest won by the XO-1 had been for aircraft based on the Packard, this engine failed to live up to expectation, and the production O-1, of which the Army ordered ten in 1925, had the lower-powered 435 h.p. Curtiss V-1150 (D-12) engine and consequently lower performance. This engine became the standard power plant for all subsequent O-1 variants except the O-1A (25-333), an O-1 conversion which had the 420 h.p. Liberty V-1650-3 and a deeper fuselage.

The 1927 production model of the Falcon, the O-1B with V-1150-5 engine, had several refinements including wheel brakes and fuel dumping provision. Of 25 D-12-powered O-1Bs, four (27-264, 266, 267, 268) were converted to O-1C transports for government officials by deleting armament, widening the rear cockpit, and making it more comfortable. There was no O-1D. Major production was concentrated on 37 O-1Es, which could be distinguished from earlier models mainly by refined engine

Curtiss XO-1 with Packard engine replacing original Liberty engine of 1924 (*McCook Field photo*).

cowling lines, Frise-type ailerons and horn-balanced elevators. The O-1F was an unarmed O-1E, and the XO/Y1O-1G (29-295) was an O-1E refined with better streamlining and a redesigned rear cockpit. Thirty identical O-1Gs followed.

O-11. Production of the Liberty-powered Falcon was concentrated on the O-11, 66 of which were built. The XO-11 was converted from O-1 (25-328). The single O-11A, an O-11 conversion, incorporated the same improvements as the O-1E, but an order for 40 O-11As was cancelled.

There were numerous minor variants of the Falcon, some as experimental conversions of various O-1s and others built under a particular designation. The XO-12 was O-11 27-35 fitted with an air-cooled Pratt & Whitney Wasp while the XO-13 and XO-13A (25-332, -331) were O-1s

Curtiss O-1A 25-333 with Liberty engine at McCook Field (as XP449, marked on rudder) (*McCook Field photo*).

220

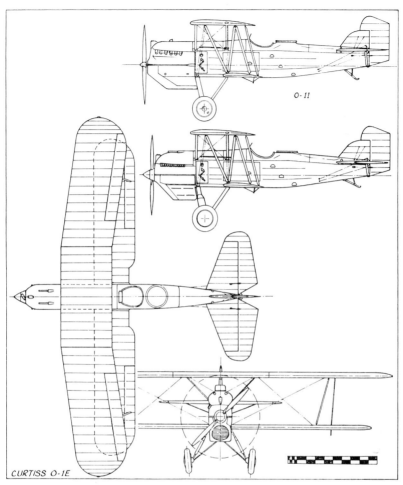

O-11

CURTISS O-1E

fitted with Curtiss V-1570 Conqueror engines for the 1927 national air races. The XO-13A reverted to wing skin radiators similar to the PW-8 and the contemporary XP-6A racer. The O-13B was one of the transport O-1Cs fitted with a water-cooled Curtiss V-1570 Conqueror. Three

Left, Curtiss O-1E (*Peter M. Bowers collection*); right, O-1G (*A. U. Schmidt*).

221

Liberty-engined Curtiss O-11, photographed October 7, 1927, showing markings standardised in 1926 with U.S. Army and serial number on fuselage in white and designation and maker's name in black on white tail stripes. Also note McCook Field designation XP-487 on tail (*Curtiss photo L-3494*).

YO-13Cs were similar to O-1Es but with Conqueror engines while the YO-13D was O-11 28-207 with a supercharged Conqueror. The XO-16 was similar to an O-11 with a Prestone-cooled Conqueror. The XO-18 was O-1B 27-263 fitted with the two-row liquid-cooled Curtiss Chieftain engine but was reconverted to O-1B. The Y1O-26 was similar to O-1E except for a geared GIV-1570A Conqueror and revised cooling system. The XBT-4 was O-1E 29-295 tested as a basic trainer and then converted first to the XO-1G and then the Y1O-1G.

The last observation Falcon was the O-39, essentially an O-1G with Prestone-cooled Curtiss V-1570 Conqueror engine. Ten were built and were easily recognized by their reduced rudder area and small radiators. Some had enclosed canopies for the pilots and a few had wheel pants.

A-3, XA-4. The A-3 was an attack version of the O-1B, differing mainly in having a 0·30-inch machine gun in each lower wing panel to supplement

Curtiss O-39 with original radiator and tail shape (*Wright Field photo 41793*).

222

Left, Curtiss XO-13 (*Curtiss photo M-319*); right, XO-18 (*Wright Field photo 34489*).

the two forward-firing nose guns. Twin Lewis guns were carried on the rear cockpit Scarff ring. Seventy-six A-3s were built. Five A-3As, including 27-306, -310, and -315 were A-3s converted to dual control trainers. The 78 A-3Bs incorporated O-1E structural and aerodynamic improvements. The XA-4 was identical to the A-3 except for installation of a 410 h.p. Pratt & Whitney Wasp R-1340.

TECHNICAL DATA (Falcon)

MANUFACTURER: Curtiss Aeroplane and Motor Co., Inc., Garden City, L.I.
TYPE: (O-1, O-11, O-39) Observation biplane; (A-3) Attack biplane.
ACCOMMODATION: (O series) Pilot and observer; (A-3) Pilot and gunner.

	O-1B	O-1E	O-1G	A-3B
Power Plant:	One 430 h.p. Curtiss D-12	One 435 h.p. V-1150-5	One 435 h.p. V-1150-5	One 435 h.p. V-1150-5
Dimensions:				
Span, ft., in.	38 0	38 0	38 0	38 0
Length, ft., in.	28 4	27 2	27 4	27 2
Height, ft., in.	10 1½	10 6	9 11	10 6
Wing area, sq. ft.	353	353	349	353
Weights:				
Empty, lb.	2,706	2,922	3,143	2,875
Gross, lb.	4,384	4,347	4,488	4,476
Performance:				
Max. speed, m.p.h.	135·5	140·8	145·5	139
Cruising speed, m.p.h.	110·5	110	116·4	110
Initial climb, ft./min.	978	980	1,060	948
Service ceiling, ft.	15,425	15,300	16,750	14,100
Range, miles	—	—	—	628
Armament:	4 × 0·30-in. guns	4 × 0·30-in. guns	4 × 0·30-in. guns	6 × 0·30-in. guns 200 lb. bombs

SERIAL NUMBERS:
XO-1: 23-1252.
O-1: 25-325/334.
O-1B: 27-263/287.
O-1E: 29-282/287; 29-289/318.
O-1F: 29-288.
O-1G: 31-472/501.
O-11: 27-001/035; 27-098/107; 28-197/217.

YO-13C: 29-319/321.
XO-16: 28-196.
Y1O-26: 29-322.
O-39: 32-211/220.
A-3: 27-243; 27-245/262; 27-298/317; 28-083/118.
A-3B: 30-001/028; 30-231/280.
XA-4: 27-244.

223

Curtiss A-12 flying from Oahu in 1936 (*USAF photo 23550AC*).

Curtiss A-8, A-10, A-12 Shrike

The Curtiss XA-8 (30-387) was designed to an Army request for an all-metal low-wing attack monoplane and first flew in 1931. Its direct competitor was the General Aviation/Fokker XA-7. Fuselage was the then-new smooth skin semi-monocoque construction while the conventional two-spar wings were covered with aluminium sheet and braced with wires and introduced an innovation to Army aircraft—trailing edge flaps. Forward firing armament was four 0·30-inch machine guns in the landing gear fairings while the rear gunner had a single flexible 0·30-inch. Four 100-lb. or ten 30 lb. bombs could be carried under the wings. Following testing of the prototype, five service test YA-8s and eight YIA-8s were ordered, powered by Prestone-cooled Curtiss Conqueror engines, in 600 h.p. V-1570-31 and 675 h.p. V-1570-57 versions respectively. The Y1A-8A (32-356) was the last Y1A-8 with revised cooling system and a 675 h.p. Conqueror while the YA-10 (32-344) was the first YA-8 airframe with a

Curtiss Y1A-8 (*A. U. Schmidt*).

625 h.p. Pratt & Whitney R-1620-9 Hornet engine. The radial engine installation proved superior to the liquid cooled, so the 46 production A-12s which concluded the Shrike series used 690 h.p. Wright R-1820-21 Cyclones. Major structural change from the A-8/10 configuration was relocation of the rear gunner to a position just behind the pilot.

The Shrike family served with various USAAC units between 1932 and 1942. Service use began in July 1932 when four YA-8s and six Y1A-8s were assigned to the 3rd Attack Group for testing and were divided between the Group's three squadrons—the 13th, 8th and 90th. After A-12s had been issued to these units, the A-8s were transferred to Barksdale Field and then in 1935 they were assigned to the 37th Attack Squadron of the 8th Pursuit Group at Langley Field. The surviving A-8s were withdrawn from operational use in 1936 and by December 1938 only two remained airworthy.

The A-12s, meanwhile, began to reach the 3rd Attack Group in December 1933. When the USAAC took over responsibility for flying the air mails in the US in February 1934, the 41 A-12s attached to the 3rd Attack Group were all assigned to this task for three months. Later the same year, the 3rd's commanding officer, Lt. Col. Horace W. Hickam was killed while flying an A-12; subsequently, Hickam Field in Hawaii was named after him. More than 20 A-12s were transferred to Hawaii in 1936/37 to serve with the 26th Attack Squadron and nine of these were still at Hickam Field in December 1941 when Japan launched the attack on Pearl Harbor. Surviving Shrikes were assigned as instructional airframes at bases in the US during 1942.

Curtiss Y1A-8 in blue and yellow finish, with Wright Field "arrow-head" symbol on fuselage side (*Curtiss photo C352*).

225

TECHNICAL DATA (A-12)

MANUFACTURER: Curtiss Aeroplane and Motor Co., Inc., Garden City, L.I.
TYPE: Attack.
ACCOMMODATION: Pilot and gunner in tandem.
POWER PLANT: One 690 h.p. Wright R-1820-37 piston radial.
DIMENSIONS: Span, 44 ft. 0 in. Length, 32 ft. 3 in. Height, 9 ft. 4 in. Wing area, 285 sq. ft.
WEIGHTS: Empty, 3,898 lb. Gross, 5,900 lb.
PERFORMANCE: Max. speed, 175 m.p.h. at sea level. Cruising speed, 150 m.p.h. Initial climb, 5·1 min. to 5,000 ft. Service ceiling, 15,150 ft. Endurance, 3·4 hrs. at cruise speed.
ARMAMENT: Four 0·30-inch Browning fixed and one flexible; 400 lbs. bombs (4 × 100 lb., 10 × 17 lb., 10 × 25 lb. or 10 × 30 lb.).
SERIAL NUMBERS:

XA-8: 30-387.
YA-8: 32-344/348.

Y1A-8: 32-349/356.
A-12: 33-212/257.

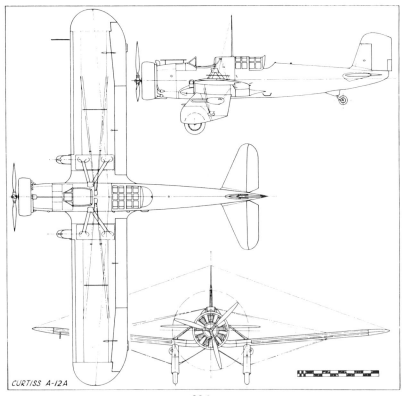

CURTISS A-12A

226

Curtiss P-36A, aeroplane No. 99 of 20th Pursuit Group, with red vertical band of "A" Flight Leader on fuselage (*USAF photo 19555AC*).

Curtiss P-36

A series of design competitions held by the Air Corps in 1935 and 1936 led to orders for the Curtiss P-36 and Seversky P-35 (see pp. 476-477) the first single-seat Army pursuit monoplanes to have such modern features as retractable undercarriages and enclosed cockpits. Destined to be overtaken by the rapid technological advances of the late 'thirties, neither type was produced in large numbers, but they provided a bridge between the old biplane fighters and the World War II generation of high performance monoplanes. The Curtiss company, with a long line of Hawk biplanes already produced for the Air Corps, began work on its Model 75 monoplane in November 1934.

The privately-financed prototype Curtiss 75 (X17Y) was submitted to Wright Field for a May 1935 design competition, and was the only entry at that time. Powered by 900 h.p. Wright R-1670 two-row radial engine, it was an all-metal low-wing monoplane, one of the novel features being the rotation of the main undercarriage legs through 90 degrees as they retracted aft, so that the wheels lay flush in the wings. A second design competition in August 1935 was indecisive, and for the third in the series, in April 1936, an 850 h.p. Wright XR-1820-39 single-row radial engine was installed, and the cockpit canopy was modified. The armament comprised two 0·30-inch guns on the cowling, firing through the airscrew disc.

Three service test models of the Hawk 75 were ordered in July 1936, while the Seversky pursuit won a production order. As Y1P-36s, these were

Curtiss P-36C in 1939 War Games washable paint. Squadron leader stripes, 27th Squadron insignia, and aeroplane number in 1st Pursuit Group retained (*Gordon S. Williams*).

delivered in February 1937 and had the 1,050 h.p. Pratt & Whitney R-1830-13 engine, retractable tailwheel and cockpit modified to improve the view forward and to the rear. Tests with these three aircraft produced, on July 7, 1937, an order for 210 examples; valued at just over $4 million, it was the largest peacetime contract the Air Corps had ever awarded for fighters.

Deliveries to Air Corps pursuit squadrons began in April 1938, the first 178 aircraft being P-36As. The production run was concluded in the first months of 1939 with 31 P-36Cs, which had an additional 0·30-inch gun in each wing and the 1,200 h.p. R-1830-17 engine. During 1940, various teething troubles were overcome, and by February 1941, the P-36 was deployed outside the U.S. for the first time, when the 23rd Pursuit Squadron moved to Elmendorf, Alaska. In the same month, the 46th and 47th Pursuit Squadrons moved with their P-36s to bases in Hawaii. Flying from

Curtiss P-36A, aeroplane No. 9 of 51st Pursuit Group, in O.D. and grey camouflage applied in February, 1941 (*Peter M. Bowers*).

228

Wheeler Field, four P-36As of the 46th intercepted a formation of Japanese bombers in the second phase of the attack on Pearl Harbor on December 7, 1941, and destroyed two of them.

Several experimental conversions were made in 1938 and 1939. These included the XP-36B with a 1,100 h.p. R-1830-25 engine, the fastest of the series; the XP-36D with two 0·50-inch cowl guns and four 0·30s in the wings and the XP-36F, with one 0·30 and one 0·50 on the cowling and a 23 mm. Madsen gun in a fairing under each wing. Others were used for propeller development.

Many Hawk 75s were sold for export by Curtiss, and it was in service with foreign Air Forces that the type saw most service in World War II, flying both for and against the Allies. Among the foreign orders was one from Norway for 30 Hawk 75A-8s with Wright Cyclone R-1820-95 engines. Undelivered when Norway fell, they were used in Canada as advanced trainers until being sold to the USAAF in April 1942, when they were designated P-36Gs. They were later presented to the Peruvian Air Force.

Of the original order for 210 P-36s, one aircraft was completed to a later standard. This (the tenth production airframe) became the XP-40 with a V-1710-19 engine, and the P-36 was thus the immediate forebear of the P-40 series which were to be the mainstay of U.S. fighter strength in the early war years (see pp. 231-237). Another P-36A was redesignated XP-42, and was an attempt to obtain better performance by streamlining

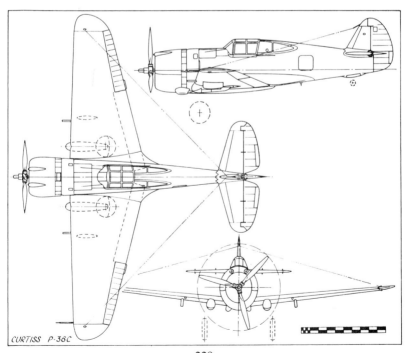

CURTISS P-36C

229

the cowling round the radial engine. It was first tested in March 1939 with a long fairing completely enclosing the R-1830-31, and a large airscoop beneath the spinner. In this form it achieved 315 m.p.h., but this was improved to 343 m.p.h. when a shorter, more conventional cowling and a larger spinner were used.

One other P-36 variant deserves mention. This was the XP-37, the first Air Corps fighter designed around the Allison V-1710-11 engine. Its design was derived from that of the P-36, but the fuselage was lengthened and the cockpit was moved aft to reduce drag. The V-1710-11 engine had side radiators and G.E.C. turbo-superchargers. In Air Corps evaluation which began in April 1937, the XP-37 (37-375) became the first U.S. pursuit to exceed 300 m.p.h., and a service test batch of 13 YP-37s (38-472/484) was ordered in December of that year. These had V-1710-21 engines with a longer nose and modified radiators and superchargers. A top speed of 340 m.p.h. had been expected but was not achieved, and the project was discontinued in favour of the P-40.

TECHNICAL DATA (P-36)

MANUFACTURER: Curtiss Aeroplane Division of Curtiss-Wright Corp., Buffalo, N.Y.
TYPE: Single-seat pursuit and advanced trainer.
ACCOMMODATION: Pilot in enclosed cockpit.

	P-36A	P-36C	P-36G
Power Plant:	1,050 h.p. R-1830-13	1,200 h.p. R-1830-17	1,200 h.p. R-1820-95
Dimensions:			
Span, ft., in.	37 4	37 4	37 4
Length, ft., in.	28 6	28 6	28 10
Height, ft., in.	12 2	12 2	9 6
Wing area, sq. ft.	236	236	236
Weights:			
Empty, lb.	4,567	4,620	4,541
Gross, lb.	6,010	6,150	5,750
Performance:			
Max. speed, m.p.h. at ft.	300/10,000	311/10,000	323/15,100
Cruising speed, m.p.h.	270	270	262
Climb, ft./min.	3,400	4·9 min. to 15,000 ft.	—
Service ceiling, ft.	33,000	33,700	32,700
Range, miles	825	820	1,000
Armament:	2 × 0·30-in. guns	4 × 0·30-in. guns	6 × 0·30-in. guns

SERIAL NUMBERS:
Y1P-36: 37-068/070.
P-36A: 38-001/180*.
P-36C: 38-181/210.

P-36G: 42-38305/38322;
42-108995/109006.

* Includes one XP-40 (38-010), one P-36B (38-020), and one P-36C (38-085).

Curtiss P-40N-20-CU, with a dramatic skull marking on the nose, photographed at Tegguan, India, in April 1944 (*Howard Levy*).

Curtiss P-40 Warhawk

As the last of the Curtiss Hawks, the P-40 was a far cry from the P-1 biplane which was the first to bear the name. Flown on almost all battle fronts in World War II and supplied to many Allied air forces including those of Britain, France, China and Russia, the P-40 was built in greater quantity than any other fighter for the USAAF except the P-51 and P-47. The basis of its inception was the substitution of a 1,160 h.p. supercharged Allison V-1710-19 in-line engine for the R-1830-13 radial in a P-36A; this conversion of the tenth P-36A production model (38-010) in a batch of 210 was redesignated XP-40 (Hawk 81) and first flew on October 14, 1938. As first flown, the XP-40 had the radiator under the rear fuselage, but this was later re-located under the nose in combination with the oil cooler intake. In other respects, the XP-40 was unaltered from the P-36.

Evaluated at Wright Field in May 1939 in competition with other pursuit prototypes, the XP-40 was declared the most acceptable for USAAC requirements, and an order for 524 P-40s was placed with Curtiss-Wright Corporation—worth nearly $13 million, this was the largest order placed, at the time, for a U.S. fighter. As the Hawk 81-A, the first production P-40s were distinguished by intakes for the carburettor above the nose and absence of mainwheel fairing plates. The 1,040 h.p. Allison V-1710-33 was fitted. The original contract was later reduced to 200; of these, the first three served as prototypes, first flight being on April 4, 1940.

Production continued with the P-40B (Hawk 81-A2), similar to the British Tomahawk II. The P-40A designation was not at first assigned and it was generally considered that this designation applied to the improved Model 81As supplied to Britain. The USAAC did use one P-40A, which was a P-40 (40-326) converted in March 1942 as a camera-carrying reconnaissance type. The P-40B first flew on March 13, 1941.

231

Curtiss P-40 in original 1940 colours and markings (*Peter M. Bowers*).

The P-40B introduced armour protection for the pilot and doubled the armament with two wing-mounted 0·30-inch guns, in addition to two 0·50s on the engine cowling. Curtiss built 131 P-40Bs in 1941 before going on to produce 193 P-40Cs, with improved self-sealing fuel tanks and two more wing guns. These production models all had the 1,040 h.p. V-1710-33 engine; the gross weight rose from 6,870 lb. in the XP-40 to 7,215 lb. in the P-40, 7,645 lb. in the "B" and 8,058 lb. in the "C". First flight of the P-40C was on April 10, 1941.

P-40s were first deployed overseas by the USAAC when the 33rd Pursuit Squadron was moved to Iceland on July 25, 1941. Others went to the Philippines where a total of 107 P-40s was present by December. In the first Japanese attack on the Islands on December 8, 1941, four P-40s of the 20th Pursuit Squadron succeeded in taking off from Clark Field before the raid began, and claimed three enemy aircraft destroyed. On December 10, P-40s of the 34th Pursuit Squadrons attacked Japanese shipping but by the end of that day, only 22 P-40s remained intact in the Philippines, and these were withdrawn from combat to be used for

Curtiss P-40C showing markings scheme introduced in March 1941 (*Peter M. Bowers*).

232

reconnaissance duties, until eventually destroyed in the defence of Corregidor. At Pearl Harbor on December 7, 73 P-40Bs and Cs were among the 152 Army aircraft destroyed by the initial Japanese attacks.

Among the first P-40s to see action were those flown by the pilots of General Clair Chenault's American Volunteer Group (AVG) defending China. As initial equipment for the AVG, the U.S. Government financed 100 P-40Bs, diverted from a British contract for Tomahawk IIs (under which name the type was used by the R.A.F.). Flying from Kunming, two of the three squadrons destroyed six Japanese raiders on December 20, 1941, and from then until being absorbed by the USAAF on July 4, 1942 as the 23rd Pursuit Group, the AVG was officially credited with the destruction of 286 Japanese aircraft for the loss of 23 American pilots.

In 1941, the P-40D (Hawk 87-A2) followed the C into production as the first major redesign since the XP-40. A change to the Allison V-1710-39 (F3R) engine with an external spur airscrew reduction gear allowed the fuselage to be shortened by 6 inches, with a reduction in cross area and

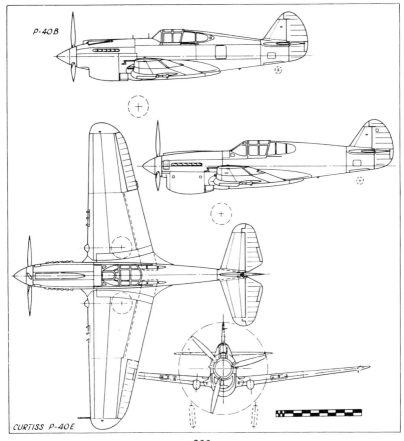

P-40B

CURTISS P-40E

Curtiss P-40E-1 with two underwing drop tanks (*Curtiss-Wright photo 1796*).

shortening of the undercarriage. The nose radiator was moved forward relatively, and deepened, and the fuselage guns were removed. The calibre of the four wing guns was increased from 0·30-inch to 0·50-inch and external racks were introduced, for a 500-lb. bomb or 52-gallon drop tank under the fuselage and for small bombs under the wings. Major production of the P-40D was for the R.A.F., which purchased 560 as Kittyhawk 1s; only 22 went to the USAAF. Similar to the P-40D was the P-40E (Hawk 87-A3) which had the wing armament increased to six 0·50s. With a gross weight of 8,840 lb., the maximum speed of the P-40E was 354 m.p.h. compared with the D's 360 m.p.h. P-40s of this type were the first to serve in Europe with the USAAF, which had a number of squadrons in the Middle East theatre by 1942. Production of the P-40E totalled 2,320, making it the second most-produced variant after the P-40N.

Another 1941 development was the installation of a Rolls-Royce Merlin 28 in a P-40D airframe (40-360) to produce the XP-40F (Hawk 87-D), first flown on June 30, 1941. The greater power of the Merlin boosted the top speed to 373 m.p.h. and improved the performance at higher altitudes. Production models of the Merlin-engined variant made use of the Packard-built Merlin V-1650-1 and could be distinguished from the P-40E by the absence of the carburettor intake on top of the cowling

Short-fuselage Curtiss P-40K with small dorsal fin, in "Desert Pink" camouflage. Many USAAF aeroplanes operating in North Africa had British fin flashes added (*Howard Levy*).

234

Repossessed short-fuselage Curtiss P-40K in original British camouflage, with fuselage drop tank (*Curtiss-Wright photo*).

after revised cooling arrangements had been tested on the third production article as the YP-40F. Of the 1,311 P-40Fs built, approximately the first 260 had the same fuselage as the earlier P-40s, but the P-40F-5 and later models had a 20-inch longer rear fuselage to increase the tail moment and improve directional stability at low speeds. With a 170-U.S. gallon drop tank, the gross weight of the P-40F increased to 9,870 lb.

In parallel with the P-40F came the P-40K, with an Allison V-1710-73 which was powerful enough to boost the top speed to 360 m.p.h. despite the 10,000 lb. gross weight which made this the heaviest of the P-40 variants. Like the P-40Fs, the earlier P-40Ks had the 31-foot fuselage length, but with a small dorsal fin to control a tendency to swing on take-off; this was later overcome by introducing the lengthened fuselage. One thousand three hundred P-40Ks were built, plus another 600 P-40Ms, which had the V-1710-81 engine.

Experimental projects in 1941 and 1942 accounted for two P-40 designations. These were the P-40H, a cancelled designation; and the P-40J, projected with a turbo-supercharged Allison engine but rendered unnecessary by the advent of the Merlin-engined version. In July 1940, one of the original P-40s (39-221) was delivered as P-40G with H81A-2 six-gun wings and at least 58 more P-40s were subsequently so modified.

Further development of the P-40F led to the P-40L, often known as the "Gypsy Rose Lee" because it was partially stripped; removal of two wing guns, armour, some fuel capacity and other items actually saved no more than 250 lb. on the gross weight, but the P-40L followed the P-40F into production and 700 were built, some with the short fuselage and some with the long. A shortage of Merlin spares in 1944 led to installation of Allison V-1710-81s in 300 long-fuselage P-40F and P-40L; these were redesignated P-40R-1 and P-40R-2 as advanced trainers.

Developed from the P-40L and P-40M, the P-40N was the most produced Warhawk variant, occupying the Curtiss production lines from 1943 until production ended the following year. With the 1,200 h.p. V-1710-81 engine, the P-40N was a lightweight variant with only four wing guns, front fuselage fuel tank removed and other weight-saving changes which reduced the weight to 8,850 lb. and allowed a top speed of 378 m.p.h. in the early production models. Later P-40Ns had the wing armament restored to six 0·50s, and shackles for a 1,500 lb. external bomb-load, making it an effective fighter bomber. One thousand nine hundred and seventy-seven P-40Ns were built in the blocks up to -15.

With the P-40N-20, a change was made to the V-1710-99 engine. Three thousand and twenty-three of these were built before a further engine change was made, in the P-40N-40, to the V-1710-115; of 1,000 of this model ordered, only 220 were completed before production ended.

P-40s of these later variants served with USAAF units in the Middle East and Pacific areas, but the greater proportion went under Lend–Lease to Allied nations, notably Britain, Russia, China, South Africa and Australia. Some 2,500 were on USAAF strength in April 1944, but this dwindled to a single operational group in July 1945.

Experiments with the cooling on the P-40 series led to the final prototypes, the three XP-40Qs. These experiments began with a P-40K-10

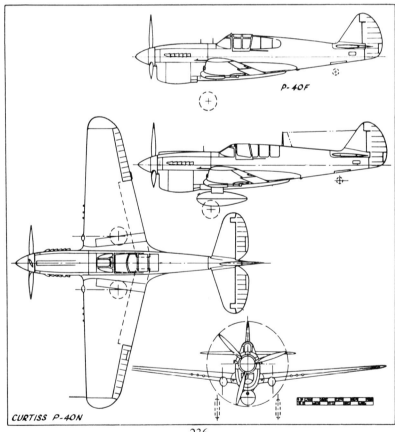

P-40F

CURTISS P-40N

236

(42-10219) modified to have wing radiators for its Allison V-1710-73 engine. These were used with a 1,425 h.p. V-1710-121 engine and four-blade propeller in the first XP-40Q (42-9987), a converted "K". An experimental clear-view bubble canopy which had previously been flown on a P-40L was used on the second and third XP-40Qs (42-45722 and 43-24571), respectively, converted from a P-40K and a P-40N.

After several two-seat conversions of P-40s had been made at various training fields, Curtiss delivered two two-seaters designated P-40ES and 30 two-seat P-40Ns. The latter are often referred to as TP-40N, but this designation may not have been official.

TECHNICAL DATA (P-40)

MANUFACTURER: Curtiss-Wright Corporation, Airplane Division, Buffalo, N.Y.
TYPE: Single-seat pursuit, ground-attack reconnaissance and advanced trainer.
ACCOMMODATION: Pilot in enclosed cockpit.

	P-40	P-40B	P-40F/L	P-40K	P-40N-20
Power Plant:	1,040 h.p. V-1710-33	1,040 h.p. V-1710-33	1,300 h.p. V-1650-1	1,325 h.p. V-1710-73	1,360 h.p. V-1710-81
Dimensions:					
Span, ft., in.	37 4	37 4	37 4	37 3	37 4
Length, ft., in.	31 9	31 9	33 4	33 4	33 4
Height, ft., in.	12 4	12 4	12 4	.12 4	12 4
Wing area, sq. ft.	236	236	236	236	236
Weights:					
Empty, lb.	5,376	5,590	6,590	6,400	6,000
Gross, lb.	7,215	7,600	9,350	10,000	8,850
Performance:					
Max. speed, m.p.h. at ft.	357/15,000	352/15,000	364/20,000	362/15,000	378/10,500
Cruising speed, m.p.h.	277	280	290	290	288
Climb, min./ft.	5·3/15,000	5·1/15,000	7·6/15,000	7·5/15,000	6·7/15,000
Service ceiling, ft.	32,750	32,400	34,400	28,000	38,000
Range, st. miles	950	940	375	350	240
Armament:	2×0·50-in.	2×0·50-in. 2×0·30-in.	6×0·50 in. 1×500lb.	6×0·50-in. 1×500 lb.	6×0·50-in. 1×500 lb.

SERIAL NUMBERS:
XP-40: 38-010.
P-40: 39-156/289; 40-292/357.
P-40B: 41-5205/5304; 41-13297/13327.
P-40C: 41-13328/13520.
P-40D: 40-359/381*.
P-40E: 40-358; 40-382/681;
    41-5305/5744; 41-13521/13599;
    41-24776/25195; 41-35874/36953.
P-40F: 41-13600/13695; 41-13697/14599;
    41-19733/20044.

P-40G: 42-14261/14274; 42-14277;
    42-14278; 42-14281†.
P-40K: 42-9730/10429; 42-45722/46321.
P-40L: 42-10430/11129.
P-40M: 43-5403/6002.
P-40N: 42-104429/106428;
    43-22752/24751; 44-7001/8000;
    44-47749/47968.

* Includes one (40-360) completed as YP-40F.   † Plus 42 converted P-40s.

Curtiss C-46D of U.K.-based Troop Carrier Wing in 1945, showing unit colour markings on nacelles and tip of tail (*Crown Copyright*).

Curtiss C-46 Commando

Widely used in the Pacific theatre during World War II, the C-46 was the largest and heaviest twin engined aeroplane to see operational use with the USAAF. The design originated in 1937 as a 36-passenger commercial transport offering a new degree of luxury and performance. Known as the CW-20, a prototype of this airliner powered by 1,700 h.p. Wright R-2600 engines was built at St. Louis and was first flown there, by Eddie Allen, on March 26, 1940. Army interest was aroused in the CW-20, which had an especially capacious fuselage, and a contract was placed soon after the first flight for 46 examples of a militarized version designated C-46. These were similar to the prototype in most respects, with no special provision for freight carrying but fewer cabin windows. Two thousand h.p. Pratt & Whitney R-2800-43 engines replaced the Wright Cyclones and the gross weight increased from 40,000 lb. to 50,675 lb.

While the first batch of C-46s was being built, the CW-20 prototype was purchased in June 1941 and evaluated under the designation C-55 (41-21041). It was subsequently supplied to Britain under Lend-Lease and operated as G-AGDI "St. Louis". The first C-46 (41-5159) was rolled out of the Curtiss Buffalo factory in May 1942 and delivered in July.

With the successful introduction of the C-46 into service with Air Transport Command and Troop Carrier Command in 1942, coupled with the pressing need to provide the U.S. Army with airlift capability, orders for the C-46 were rapidly multiplied. With a large cargo loading door in the rear fuselage, a cargo floor and folding seats along the cabin walls for 40 equipped troops, the C-46A followed production of 25 C-46s and Curtiss built 1,041 of this model at Buffalo. Additional sources of C-46A were provided at Louisville and St. Louis, where Curtiss built 439 and 10 respectively, and at New Orleans, where Higgins built two of a contract for 500 which was then cancelled.

The C-46As were powered by 2,000 h.p. R-2800-51 engines and grossed 49,600 lb. Because of their greater load-carrying ability and better performance at high altitude, compared with the C-47, the C-46s and C-46As were assigned primarily to the Pacific. There, they made a notable contribution to the success of the supply operation over the "Hump", by which war material was supplied to China from India after the capture of Burma and the Burma road by Japanese forces. The C-46 saw comparatively little service in Europe, although it was adapted in Troop Carrier Command to tow one or two gliders and to drop paratroops.

The first C-46A-CK was modified to XC-46B (43-46953), with 2,100 h.p. R-2800-34W engines and a new "stepped" windscreen. This feature was not adopted, however, on the C-46D, which was the next major production variant. It retained the R-2800-51 engines, had a revised nose and a troop door in the starboard side. Curtiss built 1,410 at Buffalo, and then 234 C-46Fs which were similar with R-2800-75 engines and blunt wing tips.

At St. Louis, Curtiss built 17 C-46Es, which were similar to the F model but had a single cargo-loading door and the stepped windscreen of the XC-46B. Two doors and blunt tips were features of the C-46G, with R-2800-34 engines; only one "G" had been built (at Buffalo) from a contract for 500 when further work was stopped after VJ Day. Also cancelled was the C-46H, with more powerful engines and twin tail wheels. The 2,500 h.p.

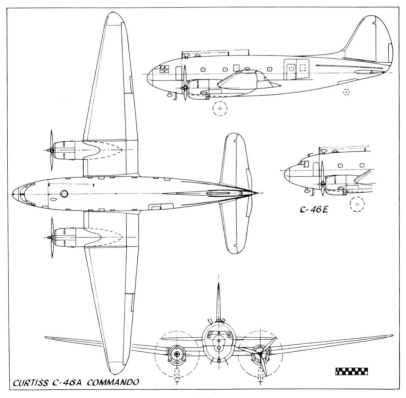

C-46E

CURTISS C-46A COMMANDO

239

Wright R-3350 Double Cyclone engines were planned for the XC-46K, which was not built, and were used in three XC-46Ls.

Many C-46s remained in service after the end of World War II, especially with Troop Carrier Command. They were used for a year or two for experiments in glider towing techniques which included "solid" tows with the glider coupled close behind the tug, as practised in Germany during the war. Flying with Combat Cargo Command, the C-46 was operational in Korea between 1950 and 1952. The C-46E became obsolete in 1953, but the A, D and F models continued in service with Air Force Reserve squadrons, and a few TC-46A and D trainers were used by Air Training Command. The C-46 was given a new lease of life in 1962 when it formed part of the equipment of the 1st Air Commando Group of TAC performing counter-insurgency duties in South-East Asia.

TECHNICAL DATA (C-46A)

MANUFACTURERS: The Curtiss-Wright Corporation, Airplane Division, Buffalo, St. Louis and Louisville. Higgins Aircraft Inc., New Orleans.

TYPE: Troop and freight transport.

ACCOMMODATION: Four crew and 50 troops or 33 litters with four attendants or 10,000 lb. cargo.

POWER PLANT: Two 2,000 h.p. Pratt & Whitney R-2800-51 piston radials.

DIMENSIONS: Span, 108 ft. 1 in. Length, 76 ft. 4 in. Height, 21 ft. 9 in. Wing area, 1,360 sq. ft.

WEIGHTS: Empty, 32,400 lb. Gross, 56,000 lb.

PERFORMANCE: Max. speed, 269 m.p.h. at 15,000 ft. Cruising speed, 183 m.p.h. Initial cimb, 1,300 ft./min. Service ceiling, 27,600 ft. Range, 1,200 st. miles.

ARMAMENT: None. Provision for small arms fire through windows.

SERIAL NUMBERS:

C-46-CU: 41-5159/5183.
C-46A-CU: 41-5184/5204;
  41-12280/12433; 41-24640/24775;
  42-3564/3683; 42-60942/61091;
  42-96529/96828*; 42-101036/101235†;
  42-107280/107399**; 44-77444;
  44-77446.
  *Includes 29 C-46D.
  ‡Includes 10 completed as C-46A-CS.

C-46A-CK: 43-46954/47402‡.
C-46A-HI: 43-43339/43340.
C-46D-CU: 44-77295/77443‡;
  44-77445; 44-77447/78544.
C-46E-CS: 43-47403/47419.
C-46F-CU: 44-78545/78778.
C-46G-CS; 44-78945.
†Includes 133 C-46D.
**All transferred to USN.
§40 transferred to USN.

Curtiss C-46E-1-CS, showing stepped windscreen (*Peter M. Bowers*).

De Havilland DH-4 in early production colours (*Bowers/Williams collection*).

The de Havilland 4 "Liberty Plane"

Since the United States had no acceptable military aircraft at the time of her entry into World War I in April 1917, a decision was made to produce proven European types in American factories rather than lose precious time in designing new types without benefit of combat experience. Of several British and French designs selected by the famous Bolling Commission, only one, the de Havilland 4, was built in true production quantities. The British DH-4 was a large all-wood two seater used primarily for observation and light bombing, but its performance with alternative installations of B.H.P. and Rolls-Royce engines was such as to make it an effective two-seat fighter.

A sample British airframe arrived in the U.S. on August 15, 1917, and was rushed by rail to McCook Field, Dayton, Ohio, to test its compatibility with the brand new 400 h.p. Liberty engine which had been developed for it. With the Liberty installed, it first flew at Dayton on October 29, 1917. Following extensive detail redesign to accommodate American production methods, the DH-4, renamed "Liberty Plane" in keeping with the mood of the times (German Sauerkraut had been renamed "Liberty Cabbage" and patriotic citizens were investing their money in "Liberty Bonds"), was placed in production at the Standard Aircraft Corporation of Patterson, New Jersey, the Dayton–Wright Company of Dayton, Ohio, and the Fisher Body Division of General Motors at Cleveland, Ohio. Between them, these plants turned out 4,846 Liberty Planes to the end of production: 3,106 by Dayton–Wright, 1,600 by Fisher and 140 by Standard. An additional 7,502 on order with these and other firms were cancelled at the end of hostilities.

The American aviation programme of World War I was sorely beset by production problems, and there was much public hue and cry as to why the

De Havilland DH-4B in non-standard silver finish (*McCook Field photo*).

thousands of promised aeroplanes were not at the front on schedule. The DH-4 came in for a major share of this criticism, particularly since many modifications had to be made in France before the aircraft were considered suitable for the front. While the DH-4 was a leading combat machine at the time it was selected for U.S. manufacture, it was at best an obsolescent 1916 model when the Americanized versions were delivered.

The American Expeditionary Force in France flew its first sortie over enemy territory with the DH-4 on August 2, 1918, and the Squadrons equipped with the type in France comprised Nos. 8, 11, 20, 50, 85, 96, 100, 135, 155, 166, 168, 278 and 354.

Combat deficiencies of the American model soon became apparent. The position of the fuel tank between pilot and observer, which had been changed on the later British D.H.9, was particularly vulnerable to enemy fire. With the heavy tank behind him, the pilot was an almost certain fatality in any crash. Another undesirable characteristic was a tendency to nose over during landings on soft or muddy fields. An official report

De Havilland DH-4Amb-2 to carry two stretchers (*McCook Field photo 5913*).

criticized the unorthodox expedient of the observer crawling aft on top of the fuselage to decrease the nose-heaviness.

Some of the complaints were heard in the right places, and extensive redesign resulted in the DH-4B, featuring a re-located landing gear and revised cockpit arrangement with the pilot behind the tank and close to the observer as in the newer British DH-9. Fuselage construction was changed to one continuous unit instead of the three-section structure of the original, and the sides were covered with plywood for the full length in place of the fabric between cockpit and tail of the "Liberty Plane". While 1,213 Liberty Planes were delivered to France, no DH-4Bs were shipped over before the Armistice. After the war, 612 of the DH-4s were returned to the United States; those remaining in France were stacked and burned, along with the obsolete observation and trainer types purchased from the French. The resulting "Billion Dollar Bonfire" raised still another hue and cry about American military aircraft procurement policies.

By the end of 1918, an Americanized version of the later British DH-9A was being prepared for production after 13 pilot models had been started by the Army Engineering Division and Dayton–Wright as USD-9 and 9A. Production was cancelled by the Armistice and post-war requirements were met by existing DH-4s and 4Bs.

While even the revised DH-4B was obsolete in the early post-war years, there were no funds available for the development or procurement of new types. However, "maintenance" funds were available, and these, carefully distributed, kept the struggling American aircraft industry alive during the critical post-war years through extensive modification and rebuilding, starting with the conversion of Liberty Planes to DH-4Bs. This programme, in which at least ten companies and Army depots

Top left, DH-4B with supercharged and geared Liberty (*McCook Field 20906*); top right, Boeing XCO-7A (*McCook Field 20577*); bottom left, DH-4B-4 on skis (*McCook Field 29211*); bottom right, DH-4B-5 "Honeymoon Express" (*McCook Field 178*).

243

The Atlantic XCO-8, combining a DH-4M2 fuselage and tail unit with Loening wings. Note McCook Field number P369 on tail (*McCook Field photo*).

participated, culminated in the Atlantic (Fokker) and Boeing-built DH-4Ms of 1923/24. These utilized the wings, tails, power plants and other hardware of existing DH-4Bs but featured new fuselages of welded steel tube construction as developed by Fokker during the war. The "M" in the designation stood for "modernized".

By the time the Ms were built, new designs had become available, but the old biplanes were kept in service because an enormous investment had been made in them and the taxpayers would not stand for any more bonfires just because the aeroplanes were obsolete. As a result, the last DH-4M-2P was not retired from Army service until 1932.

Because of their carefully recorded performance and ready availability, the DHs were widely used for experimental and test flying at McCook Field, Headquarters of the Air Service Engineering Division, for several years after the War. All sorts of in-line and radial power plants were installed, new wings of various sizes and airfoils were tried, and some of the open-cockpit designs were converted to cabin types.

A number of DH-4Bs were fitted experimentally with Loening COA-1 wings and placed in limited service status. Attempts to extend the service utilization of the basic DH-4 through the use of new wings culminated in the Boeing XCO-7, XCO-7A and XCO-7B (24452/24454) which were standard DH-4M1 fuselages fitted with entirely new thick-section tapered wings, enlarged horizontal tail surfaces, and divided oleo-pneumatic landing gear. The XCO-7B was the most distinctive, featuring an experimental inverted air-cooled Liberty engine. The performance improvement was not sufficient to justify manufacture of the new wings.

An Atlantic-built DH-4M2 became XCO-8 (23163) when fitted with the Loening wings and achieved a degree of fame when used by Captain O. A. Stevens for experiments in high-altitude and long-range photography through 1930. Flight refuelling trials were made in 1923 with a DH-4 receiver, carrying an extra fuel tank, with a large filling point, in the rear fuselage; and the DH-4B-1 tanker which trailed a 50 ft. length of

244

hose with a quick-acting shut-off valve. The first successful contacts were made on June 27, 1923, and on August 27/28, the receiver remained airborne for 37 hours 15 minutes in the first conclusive demonstration of flight refuelling.

While the Liberty Planes and DH-4Bs were originally identified only by their DH-4/DH-4B designations regardless of various minor modifications or change of mission, the original manufacturer's model designation was treated as an official type number after adoption of the letter-and-number system in 1920. Originally, suffix letters were added to indicate straight sequence of design development but other letter-and-number suffixes were added to indicate special purpose modifications or usage of the aeroplanes. In the normal course of reassignment and modification, it was not unusual for one airframe to have carried several different designations throughout its service life. The DHs are impossible to keep track of by serial number, partly because of the incompleteness of the early records and partly because of the practice, not followed consistently, of assigning a new serial number at the time an aeroplane was rebuilt. Some DHs are known to have carried as many as four, the latest being two assigned in 1926 (DH-4BK, 26-29/30).

The following is a partial listing of "Standard" designations officially assigned to DH-4 variants between 1920 and 1925 and includes a few of the purely experimental designations assigned to various research and development models at McCook Field.

Another line of DH-4 development was started by the U.S. Post Office Department in cooperation with the Engineering Division of the Air Service. The DH-4B was standardized for mail service in 1919, and entered service with little modification other than pilot control from the

Boeing DH-4M-1T, the dual-control training conversion of the DH-4M-1, photographed at Brooks Field in 1929 (*Museum of Flight photo*).

DH-4, DH-4B VARIANTS

DH-4	Basic Americanized "Liberty Plane" of World War I.
DH-4A	Single Liberty with revised fuel system, 110 gallon tank; British three-seater.
DH-4Amb-1, Amb-2	One and two-litter ambulance conversions, respectively.
DH-4Ard	Dual-control cross-country version, 165 gallon tank, 7 hour fuel supply as modified at Air Repair Depot, Montgomery, Alabama (Ardmont).
DH-4B	Major redesign of DH-4; 88 gallon main tank, 8 gallon reserve.
DH-4B-1	110 gallon main tank, 8 gallon reserve.
DH-4B-2	76 gallon leak-proof tank, 8 gallon reserve.
DH-4B-3	135 gallon main tank, 8 gallon reserve.
DH-4B-4	Airways Version, 110 gallon main tank, 8 gallon reserve.
DH-4B-5	"Honeymoon Express", 2-seat cabin behind pilot as British DH-4A.
DH-4BD	Standard DH-4B equipped for crop dusting.
DH-4BG	Gas Barrage conversion with chemical smoke tanks.
DH-4BK	Standard DH-4B equipped for night flying.
DH-4BM	Messenger with rear seat and rear baggage compartment only.
DH-4BM-1	Dual-control transport version of DH-4BM, with 110 gallon main tank.
DH-4BM-2	As DH-4BM-1 Transport version with 135 gallon main tank.
XDH-4BP	Experimental single-seat photo plane—cameras in front cockpit.
DH-4BP1	Peacetime photo plane for vertical mapping, oblique and motion pictures.
XDH-4BP-2	Experimental photo plane—135 gallon tank, USD-9A wings.
DH-4BP-3	Similar to DH-4BP-1, 110 gallon main tank.
XDH-4BS	Experimental DH-4B with supercharger, 88 gallon main tank.
DH-4BT	DH-4B modified as dual control trainer with instruments in rear cockpit.
DH-4BW	Test bed for 300 h.p. Wright–Hispano "H" engine.
DH-4C	DH-4B test bed for 350 h.p. Packard 1A-1237 engine, modified fuselage.
XDH-4L	Cleaned-up cross-country racer, 185 gallon, 9 hour fuel supply.

DH-4M VARIANTS

DH-4M	"Modernized" DH-4/DH-4B with new steel tube fuselage. 53 built by Boeing.
DH-4M-1	Boeing-built DH-4M, 76 gallon main tank, arc-welded fuselage. 97 built.
DH-4M-1K	DH-4M-1 equipped as target tug.
DH-4M-1T	Dual-control trainer version. 22 converted DH-4M-1s.
DH-4M-2	Atlantic-built (Fokker) DH-4M, 110 gallon main tank, gas-welded fuselage. 135 built.
DH-4M-2A	Equipped for operation on airways.
DH-4M-2K	Target tug.
DH-4M-2P	Photo plane with 110 gallon main tank.
DH-4M-2S	Supercharged engine, 88 gallon main tank.
DH-4M-2T	Dual control trainer, no armament or radio.

rear cockpit and a 400 lb. capacity mail compartment replacing the forward cockpit. Standard Air Service colouring, markings, and serial numbers were used to about 1923. The Airmail DH-4 soon developed into a standardized postal configuration, however, with modified landing gear, enlarged rudder, clear-varnished plywood-sided fuselage, and a rounded turtledeck similar to that of the Army "Airways" DH-4B. This configuration was to remain standard for virtually all U.S. civil mailplane designs through the Northrop "Gamma" of 1932, prototype of the Army YA-13/XA-16 attack models.

When the government abandoned the airmail routes to private operators in July 1927, 15 airmail DH-4s in the Post Office serial number range of 328/427 were turned over to the Army. Useless for normal military purposes, they were reconverted to two-seaters and used for the Air Corps forest fire patrols in the western states. Since they were not standard purchases, they did not acquire 1927 fiscal serial numbers but merely added the prefix A.C. to the Post Office number, a safe enough procedure since earlier Army models in that serial range were long gone. Standard Army colouring was not applied, either, and the patrol models flew with the airmail silver wings and varnished fuselages. The only markings were U.S. Army and the serial number on the fuselages. These repossessed DHs remained in service until 1931.

The most distinctive of all the many DH-4 variants was the twin-engine model developed in 1919 by Lowe, Willard, and Fowler (L.W.F.) for the Post Office. The single Liberty was removed in favour of increased mail capacity and two 200 h.p. Hall–Scott L-6 engines were installed between the wings. Two extra rudders were required because of the altered air-

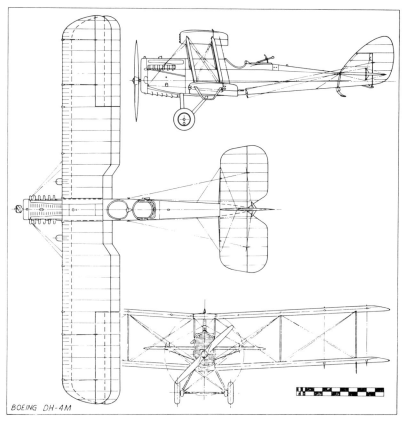

BOEING DH-4M

stream. Twenty were built for the Post Office, and ten more for the Army. Other modifications such as Loening and Bellanca wings, increased wingspans, deep-belly fuselages, etc., were tested on airmail DH-4s at McCook Field but were not adopted.

TECHNICAL DATA (DH-4)

MANUFACTURER: (DH-4): Dayton–Wright Co., Dayton, Ohio; Standard Aircraft Corp., Patterson, N.J.; Fisher Body Division of General Motors, Cleveland, Ohio. (DH-4M): Boeing Airplane Co., Seattle, Washington, and Atlantic Aircraft Corp., Teterboro, N.J.
TYPE: Observation and day bomber.
ACCOMMODATION: Pilot and observer in tandem.

	DH-4	DH-4B	DH-4L	DH-4M-2	Twin DH
Power Plant:	420 h.p. Liberty	416 h.p. Liberty	416 h.p. Liberty	420 h.p. Liberty	200 h.p. Hall-Scott L-6
Dimensions:					
Span, ft., in.	42 5½	42 5½	42 5½	42 5½	52 6
Length, ft., in.	29 11	29 11	29 11	29 11	28 2
Height, ft., in.	9 8	9 8	9 8	10 6	
Wing area, sq. ft.	440	440	440	438·7	548
Weights:					
Empty, lb.	2,732	2,939	1,806	2,952	3,670
Gross, lb.	4,297	4,595	—	4,510	5,490
Performance:					
Max. speed, m.p.h.	124	118	—	123·2	105
Climb, min./ft.	8·5/6,500	11·25/6,500	—	9·3/6,500	—
Service ceiling, ft.	15,800	12,800	—	14,400	—
Endurance, hr.	3·16	3·25	—	3·75	—
Armament:	4×0·30-in. 322 lb. bombs	—	—	—	—

De Havilland Twin DH-4 for the Post Office (*Courtesy Jesse Davidson*).

248

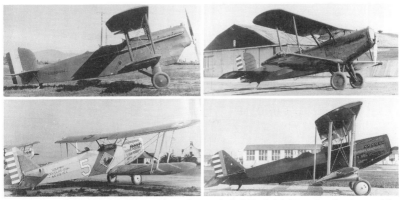

Top left, Douglas O-2B with 1926 rudder stripes and all-O.D. finish (*Douglas photo*); top right, O-2C, all-O.D. with new rudder stripes (*USAF photo*); bottom left, O-2H with early tail, light blue fuselage and yellow wings and tail (*USAF photo*); bottom right, O-2J "plush" version for staff transport (*USAF photo*).

Douglas O-2 Series, O-25, O-38

One of the longest-lived designs of the between-war years was the Douglas biplane series that started with the XO-2 of 1924. A few of the last related model, the O-38E and F, were still in service at the time of the Pearl Harbor attack by Japan. The XO-2 was developed from the Navy DT Torpedo-plane for two Army observation aircraft competitions at McCook Field in 1924, one for Liberty-engined types and one for new designs powered with the Packard 1A-1500 engine. The single XO-2 was designed to accommodate either engine, and was entered in both competitions. An order for 46 Liberty-powered O-2s resulted, while the Packard competition was won by the Curtiss XO-1 (see pp. 192–197).

Construction and layout of the O-2 were conventional, with welded steel tube fuselage and wooden wings. Fuel was carried in extra-thick centre section stubs for the lower wing. After the XO-2 had been tested with two sizes of equal span wings, the production models used the long wings.

Eighteen O-2As were similar to O-2s except for night flying equipment. Six O-2Bs had dual control for training use. The 32 O-2Cs were improved O-2As with revised rear armament and revised noses with radiator above instead of below the propeller shaft. Two O-2Ds were unarmed Cs, and the single O-2E was an improved O-2C with a new tail. There was no O-2F or G.

The 143 O-2Hs were an entirely new design but continued the same basic model number. Major differences were heavily staggered wings, a more compact engine installation with nose radiator similar to O-1C/E, and clean landing gear secured to the fuselage. Vertical tail shape differed

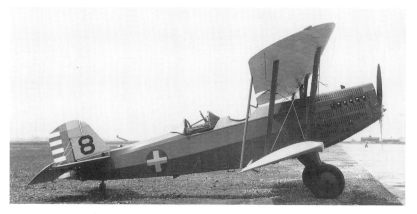

Douglas BT-1 with hood over rear cockpit (*Gordon S. Williams*).

considerably between early and late O-2Hs, with the late design being retained for all subsequent models through the O-38C. Three O-2Js (28-127, 28-188, 29-209) were O-2Hs and an O-2K completed without armament and fitted with extra comforts for use as transports. The 60 O-2Ks were further improvements of the O-2H, and all were converted to dual control basic trainers under the designation of BT-1. The flight of a BT-1 from Fort Clark, Texas, to Kelly Field on September 13, 1935, was the last U.S. Army mission flown with the famous World War I Liberty engine.

Three O-7s (25-405/407) and an O-9 (25-409) were O-2s fitted with Packard 1A-1500 engines, and the O-8 (25-408) was an O-2 with an experimental 400 h.p. Wright R-1454 radial engine. All were later converted, to two O-2s, two O-2As and one O-2C. One O-2 (25-380) was converted to the XA-2 attack plane and fitted with an experimental air-cooled inverted Liberty. The XO-14 was in effect a scaled-down O-2H powered with a 220 h.p. Wright J-5 engine and a wing span of 30 ft. 1 inch. Three YO-22s were identical to

Douglas O-25C (*Gordon S. Williams*).

250

Douglas BT-2C in May 1931, with light blue fuselage used by some trainers and observation types 1928-1935 before blue replaced O.D. service wide (*Douglas photo 2793*).

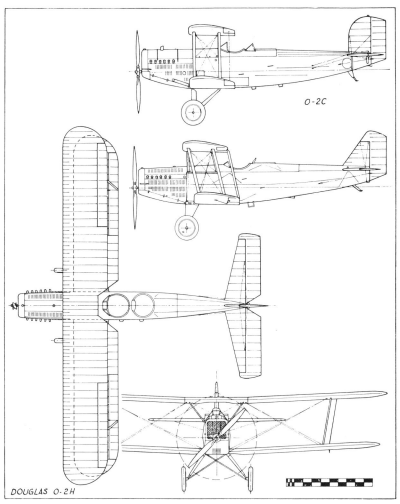

O-2C

DOUGLAS O-2H

251

Douglas O-38E with ski-wheel combination (*Gordon S. Williams*).

O-2Hs except for the installation of a swept-back upper wing and a Pratt & Whitney Wasp engine. The last O-22 (29-373) was completed as YO-34 by substitution of a Curtiss V-1570 Prestone-cooled Conqueror engine.

The single O-25, later to become XO-25A, was essentially a late-type O-2H airframe powered with Curtiss Conqueror engine and a considerably revised nose. Forty-nine O-25As were production versions. The three O-25Bs were O-25As (30-161/163) fitted with dual controls. A major appearance change was made to the 30 O-25Cs by changing to a Prestone-cooled Conqueror that resulted in a further nose contour revision.

The O-29, later designated Y1O-29A, was an O-2K (29-184) fitted experimentally with a 525 h.p. Wright R-1750 Cyclone engine. The single O-32 (a converted O-2K) and 30 O-32As followed the O-29 pattern but used the 450 h.p. Pratt & Whitney R-1340-3 Wasp engine. All O-32 series aircraft were eventually converted to basic trainers and redesignated BT-2 and BT-2A. Later versions were built as BT-2B (146 built) and BT-2C (20 built). Most O-32/BT-2s were later fitted with anti-drag rings and aircraft converted for use as instrument trainers became BT-2BIs (58 converted) and BT-2CIs (13 converted).

Red-and-silver Douglas A-4 target conversion of BT-2B, with no national markings, 1941 (*Peter M. Bowers*).

252

Last of the Douglas observation biplanes was the O-38 series. The 46 O-38s were similar to the O-29/O-32 except for 525 h.p. Pratt & Whitney R-1690-3 Hornet engines. The first one was converted to O-38A with features similar to O-2J and the 63 O-38Bs were improved O-38s. A single O-38C (32-394) was an O-38B procured by the Army for the Coast Guard while the single O-38D (33-001) was a considerably revised design with deeper and more streamlined fuselage, full engine cowling, single strut landing gear, enclosed cockpits for the crew, and new tail surfaces. The 37 O-38Es were production versions of the O-38D and the eight O-38Fs incorporated further minor refinements.

The O-38s were replaced as first line equipment by O-43As, O-46As, and O-47As, but remained the mainstay of National Guard units, some serving into early 1942 for training and tow target work. Beginning in 1940, obsolescent BT-2s were put to the unique task of serving as radio-controlled anti-aircraft targets. To simplify the take-off and landing problems, these aircraft were converted to tricycle configuration by relocating the main landing gear farther aft and adding a steerable nosewheel.

In this form, the converted BT-2s carried a dual designation, A-4 for Aerial Target and BT-2BR for BT-2B with radio control. The con-

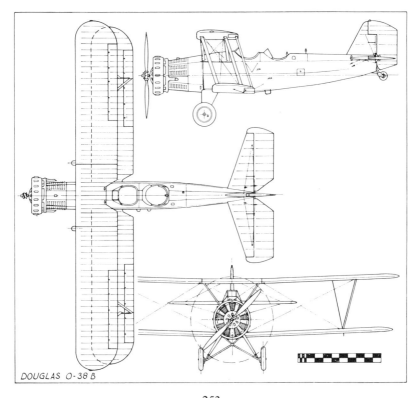

DOUGLAS O-38 B

trolling aircraft were BT-2Cs with designation changed to BT-2CR. For the benefit of gunners on the ground or aboard ship, the BT-2CRs flew in standard Army Air Corps colours of chrome yellow wings with blue fuselage and the conventional national markings on wings and tail, while the A-4 conversions were painted bright red and silver and carried no national markings. The A-6 target designation was reserved in 1940 for O-38s as radio-controlled targets, but this project was cancelled.

TECHNICAL DATA (O-2, O-38, BT-2)

MANUFACTURER: Douglas Aircraft Co., Santa Monica, California.
TYPE (O-2, O-38)*:* Observation. (BT-2) Basic trainer.
ACCOMMODATION: Pilot and observer in tandem open cockpits.

	O-2C	O-2H	O-38B	BT-2B
Power Plant:	400 h.p. Liberty	450 h.p. Liberty V-1650A	525 h.p. R-1690-5	450 h.p. R-1340-11
Dimensions:				
Span, ft., in.	39 8	40 0	40 0	40 0
Length, ft., in.	29 6	30 0	32 0	31 2
Height, ft., in.	10 10	10 6	10 8	10 6
Wing area, sq. ft.	411	367·6	371	364
Weights:				
Empty, lb.	3,026·5	2,817	3,072	2,918
Gross, lb.	4,706	4,484	4,458	3,948
Performance:				
Max. speed, m.p.h.	126·4	133.4	149 at s.l.	133 at s.l.
Cruising speed, m.p.h.	—	107	128	113
Climb,	16·1 min. to 10,000 ft.	1,050 ft./ min.	10·6 min. to 10,000 ft.	12·0 min. to 10,000 ft.
Service ceiling, ft.	14,700	17,100	20,700	19,000
Endurance	3·5 hr.	512 miles	2·2 hr.	—
Armament:	3×0·30-in. Browning	3×0·30-in. Browning	2×0·30-in. Browning 4×100 lb.	Nil

SERIAL NUMBERS:

XO-2: 23-1251.
O-2: 25-335/380.
O-2A: 25-387/404.
O-2B: 25-381/386.
O-2C: 26-386/417.
O-2D: 26-419/420.
O-2E: 26-418.
O-2H: 27-288/297; 28-127/188; 28-349/358; 29-158/178; 29-342/351; 29-375/404.
O-2K: 29-179/218; 29-413/432.
XO-14: 28-194.
YO-22: 29-371/373.
O-25: 30-160.

O-25A: 30-161/195; 30-357/370.
O-25C: 32-181/210.
O-32A: 30-196/225.
O-38: 30-407/419; 31-349/379; 31-406/407.
O-38B: 31-409/438; 32-102/116; 32-325/342.
O-38C: 32-394.
O-38D: 33-001.
O-38E: 33-002/016; 34-001/022.
O-38F: 33-322/329.
BT-2B: 31-001/146.
BT-2C: 31-439/458.

Douglas C-29 with Bolling Field insignia on hull (*Peter M. Bowers*).

Douglas C-21, C-26, OA-3, OA-4

Introduction of the commercial Douglas "Dolphin" twin-engine amphibian aroused immediate interest in the Armed Forces, which needed large capacity transport amphibians to supplement the Loenings then in use by the Army as COA-1 and OA-2 and by the Navy as the OL-series. The Army ordered 10 Dolphins in 1932, eight as 7-place Y1C-21s with 350 h.p. Wright R-975-3 Whirlwind engines and two 8-place Y1C-26s with 300 h.p. Pratt & Whitney Wasp Juniors. Similar models for Navy were designated RD-1 and -2.

Additional orders were placed for eight 8-seat Y1C-26As and six C-26Bs, with 350 h.p. Pratt & Whitney R-985-5s and -9s, respectively. Two C-26Bs were later fitted with 575 h.p. Pratt & Whitney R-1340-29 engines and then redesignated C-29 (33-292/293). Assigned to patrol work on the Mexican border, the Y1C-26As operated for a short while under Treasury Department control as FP-2Bs.

In 1933 and 1934, the C-21s and C-26s were converted from transports to 4-seat observation-amphibians under the designations of OA-3 and OA-4. The same series letters were carried over, the C-26As and Bs becoming OA-4A and B. The two C-29As were not affected. In 1936, both OA-4s, four OA-4As (32-405/408) and one OA-4B (33-295) were fitted with R-985-9 engines and new wings built of stainless steel instead

Douglas OA-4B, previously C-26B (*A. U. Schmidt*).

255

of wood and were redesignated OA-4C. Earlier, one OA-4B had been fitted experimentally with tricycle landing gear to test the suitability of this feature for large aircraft. As a result, this "new" configuration, neglected since the beginning of World War I, was specified for the prototype Douglas DC-4 transport which eventually became the C-54 (see page 262), and for the giant XB-19 of 1937 (see page 556).

TECHNICAL DATA (C-21)

MANUFACTURER: Douglas Aircraft Co., Santa Monica, California.
TYPE: Transport amphibian (and OA-3 observation amphibian).
ACCOMMODATION: Seven seats.
POWER PLANT: Two 300 h.p. Wright R-975E piston radials.
DIMENSIONS: Span, 60 ft. 0 in. Length, 43 ft. 10 in. Height, 14 ft. 1 in. Wing area, 489 sq. ft.
WEIGHTS: Empty, 5,861 lb. Gross, 8,583 lb.
PERFORMANCE: Max. speed, 140 m.p.h. Cruising speed, 119 m.p.h. at 85% power. Range, 550 st. miles.
ARMAMENT: Nil.
SERIAL NUMBERS:

C-21 (OA-3): 32-279/286. YIC-26A (OA-4A): 32-403/410.
C-26 (OA-4): 32-396/397. C-26B (OA-4B): 33-292/297.

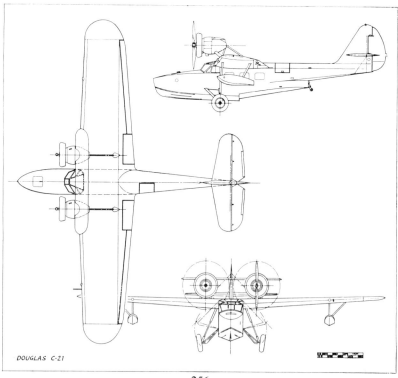

DOUGLAS C-21

256

Douglas O-46A with 1941 War Games marking under wing after repainting from blue and yellow to silver (*Peter M. Bowers*).

Douglas O-31, O-43, O-46

Douglas, major supplier of observation types to the Army from 1925 to 1935, entered the monoplane field with the XO-31 in 1930. This was an all metal gull-wing design powered with the Curtiss Conqueror engine as used in the O-25 biplane. Fuselage construction was similar to that of the Thomas-Morse O-19, using corrugated duraluminum sheet wrapped around formers and stringers. Wing covering was fabric. The YO-31 was identical except for a geared Conqueror that changed the appearance of the nose.

Five service test Y1O-31As, later O-31A, retained the general proportions of the prototypes but differed considerably in structure and

Douglas XO-31 (*Peter M. Bowers*).

257

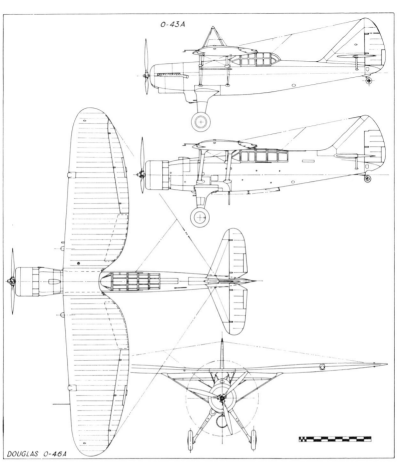

O-43A

DOUGLAS O-46A

Top left, Douglas O-31A with wheel fairings; top right, O-31B; bottom left, Y1O-43; bottom right, O-43A in 1941 War Games (*all photos, Peter M. Bowers*).

258

Douglas O-43A (*Peter M. Bowers*).

outline. The wings were of curved planform, tail shape was changed, and fuselage construction was changed to a built-up semi-monocoque structure of flat sheets. The single YO-31B (32-231) was similar to the A except for modification of the fuselage to fair the cockpit canopy to the tail. Armament consisted of a single 0·30-inch machine gun in the rear cockpit and a single fixed 0·30 in the centre section outside of the propeller arc. The single YO-31C was the final Y1O-31A with a cantilever landing gear and deepened fuselage beneath the observer's cockpit. Five more aircraft tentatively designated Y1O-31C were delivered as Y1O-43 with fully parasol wings and after tests, the Army ordered 24 similar O-43As.

The XO-46 (33-291) was the last O-43A fitted with a 725 h.p. twin-row Pratt & Whitney R-1535-7 engine. The 90 O-46As were identical except that the rear fuselage was built up between the cockpit and the tail in the manner of the O-31B. The XO-46 was to have become XO-48 with a 775 h.p. Wright R-1670-3 engine, but the conversion was not made.

TECHNICAL DATA (O-31A)

MANUFACTURER: The Douglas Aircraft Co., Inc., Santa Monica, California.
TYPE: Observation.
ACCOMMODATION: Pilot and observer in tandem.
POWER PLANT: (O-31A). One 675 h.p. Curtiss GIV-1570-FM (V-1570-53) piston vee in-line. (O-43A). One 675 h.p. Curtiss V-1570-59 piston vee in-line.
DIMENSIONS: Span, 45 ft. 8 in. Length, 33 ft. 10 in. (O-43A, 33 ft. 11 in.). Height, 11 ft. 9 in. (O-43A, 12 ft. 3 in.). Wing area, 340 sq. ft. (O-43A, 335 sq. ft.).
WEIGHTS: Empty, 3,751 lb. (O-43A, 4,135 lb.). Gross, 4,635 lb. (O-43A, 5,300lb.).
PERFORMANCE: Max. speed, 190 m.p.h. at sea level. Cruising speed, 168 m.p.h. (O-43A, 163 m.p.h.). Climb (O-43A) 3·3 min. to 5,000 ft. Service ceiling, 22,700 ft. (O-43A, 22,400 ft.).
ARMAMENT: One fixed and one flexible 0·30 in. Browning m.g. No bombs.
SERIAL NUMBERS:

XO-31: 30-229.	Y1O-43: 32-291/295.
YO-31: 30-230.	O-43A: 33-268/291.
YO-31A: 31-604/608.	O-46A: 35-161/231; 36-128/144;
YO-31B: 32-231.	36-147/148.

Douglas C-39 of 10th Transport Group, 1941 (*Peter M. Bowers*).

Douglas C-32, C-33, C-34, C-39

The first aircraft purchased by the Army with its Fiscal 1936 funds was an example of the Douglas DC-2 commercial transport, which had first flown in April 1934 and was bringing about a revolution in air transport. The Army example was evaluated as the XC-32, the designation later changing to C-32 when it went into service with a transport squadron. Orders followed for 18 C-33s, which were similar but had a larger tail, and a cargo-loading door. Powered by 750 h.p. Wright R-1820-25 Cyclones and grossing 18,560 lb., the C-33s had a top speed slightly better than 200 m.p.h., or some 50 m.p.h. faster than any transport built in quantity for the Army before 1936.

Also purchased with FY1936 funds were two YC-34s, which had the standard DC-2 tail and passenger door, and differed from the XC-32 only in having a different interior arrangement.

In service with Army transport squadrons from 1936, the C-33s were joined in 1939 by the first of 35 C-39s with 975 h.p. R-1820-55 engines and a DC-3-type centre section, tail unit and landing gear. This version, which had no direct commercial counterpart, was developed by way of the single C-38 (36-70), a C-33 converted in 1937 to have a DC-3 tail and sometimes called the DC-2$\frac{1}{2}$. By the end of 1941, the 16-seat C-39s had been absorbed into the Transport Groups and they were called upon to perform many rigorous transport operations in the early days of the War; as for instance, ferrying supplies to Goose Bay, Newfoundland, and flying survivors out of the Philippines to Australia, in December 1941.

Two other Douglas transports of "DC-2$\frac{1}{2}$" type were developed before the U.S. entered World War II. These were the C-41 (38-502),

Douglas C-33 in May 1943 (*Peter M. Bowers*).

which was the fourth C-39 with 1,200 h.p. R-1830-21 Twin Wasp engines and a gross weight of 25,000 lb.; and the C-42, being the fifth C-39 with 1,200 h.p. R-1820-53 Cyclones and a gross weight of 23,624 lb. Both of these machines were converted at the factory before completion as C-39s. Two additional C-42s (38-513, 38-528) were subsequent C-39 conversions. The C-41A designation covered a single DC-3 with plush interior for 23 passengers.

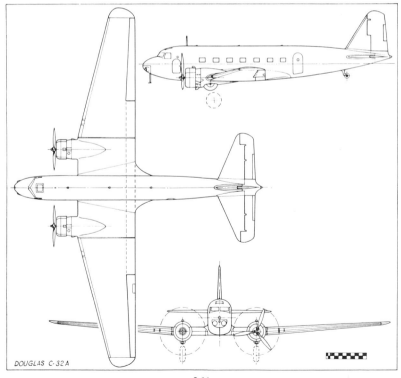

DOUGLAS C-32A

261

During 1942, 24 commercial DC-2s were among the transport aircraft impressed for military service from the fleets of U.S. domestic operators. These were generally similar to the single C-32 and were designated C-32A. They had 740 h.p. SGR-1820-F3A Cyclone engines which were designated R-1820-33 by the Army, and differed from the C-33s in having no special door for large cargo. Two of the C-32As (44-83226/83227) were ex-KNILM aircraft that flew out of Java in 1941 at the time of the Japanese occupation.

TECHNICAL DATA (C-39)

MANUFACTURER: The Douglas Aircraft Co., Inc., Santa Monica, California.
TYPE: Cargo and personnel transport.
ACCOMMODATION: Sixteen seats.
POWER PLANT: Two 975 h.p. Wright R-1820-55 piston radials.
DIMENSIONS: Span, 85 ft. 0 in. Length, 61 ft. 6 in. Height (C-33), 19 ft. 7 in. (C-39), 18 ft. 8 in. Wing area, 939 sq. ft.
WEIGHTS: Empty (C-33), 12,476 lb. (C-39), 14,729 lb. Gross (C-33), 18,200 lb. (C-39), 21,000 lb.
PERFORMANCE: Max. speed (C-33), 202 m.p.h. at 2,500 ft. (C-39), 210 m.p.h. at 5,000 ft. Cruising speed (C-33), 171 m.p.h. (C-39) 155 m.p.h. Climb (C-33), 5 min. to 5,000 ft. (C-39), 4 min. to 5,900 ft. Service ceiling (C-33), 20,000 ft. (C-39), 20,600 ft. Endurance (C-33), 5·35 hrs. (C-39), 5·9 hrs. at cruise.
ARMAMENT: None.
SERIAL NUMBERS:

XC-32; 36-001.	C-33: 36-70/87.
C-32A: 42-53527/53532; 42-57154/57156;	YC-34: 36-345/346.
42-57227/57228; 42-58071/58073;	C-39: 38-499/501; 38-504/535.
42-61095/61096; 42-65577/65579	C-41: 38-502.
42-68857/68858; 42-70863;	C-41A: 40-70.
44-83226/83227.	C-42: 38-503.

Douglas YC-34 with Bolling Field insignia and Cabinet Officer's flag (*Howard Levy*).

262

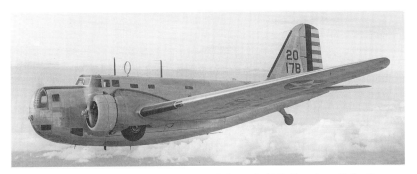

Round-nose Douglas B-18 of 17th Bomb Group in 1940 (*Boardman C. Reed*).

Douglas B-18

To replace the Martin B-10 as its standard bomber, the Army Air Corps wrote a new requirement early in 1934 for an aircraft able to carry double the B-10's bomb load for twice as far. Three industry-financed prototypes were built for the competition to meet this requirement, held at Wright Field in August 1935. Of these three (which included the Martin 146 and—see page 87—the Boeing 299) the Douglas entry was derived from the DC-2 commercial transport, with similar wings, tail unit and power plant. It was designated the DB-1 (Douglas Bomber 1) and was powered by two 930 h.p. Wright R-1820-45 Cyclone engines. The six-man crew included three gunners, one in a nose turret, one in a tail turret and one for the ventral gun firing through a tunnel in the fuselage floor; each had a single 0·30-inch calibre gun.

As the B-18, the DB-1 design was selected for immediate production with a contract for 133 signed in January 1936. Production models resembled the prototype DB-1 (which was itself delivered as the first aircraft of the contract) with some small changes in equipment which added 1,000 lb. to the normal loaded weight. The last aircraft of this order was of

Douglas B-18A of 18th Reconnaissance Squadron (*USAF photo 19992AC*).

modified type with a power-operated nose turret, and was known as the DB-2.

A second large contract for the Douglas bomber was placed in June 1937, for 177 aircraft costing some $12 million. The first of these came off the line at Santa Monica in April 1938 and had a new nose arrangement in which the bomb-aimer's station was extended forward and over the front gun position. The engines were changed to 1,000 h.p. R-1820-53s, and the weight went up to 22,123 lb. This version was the B-18A and a further contract in mid-1938 brought the total procured to 217.

By 1940, B-18s and B-18As equipped most of the Bomber squadrons, and the type was still in front line service when Japan attacked the U.S.

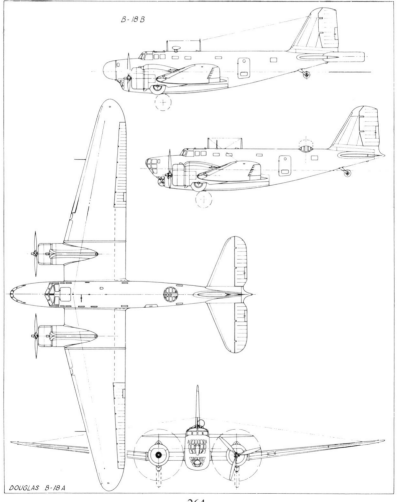

B-18B

DOUGLAS B-18A

Camouflaged Douglas B-18A in 1944. Note use of Army s/n under left wing, a common practice with fixed-base aircraft before post-war adoption of "Buzz Numbers" (*Peter M. Bowers*).

in December 1941; many of the 33 B-18As of the 5th and 11th Bomb Groups then on the Hawaiian airfields were destroyed. Others were in service in Alaska. After being replaced by B-17s, in 1942, 76 became B-18Bs with a remodelled nose and magnetic airborne detection (MAD) gear, for anti-submarine patrols in the Caribbean. Two B-18Cs were similar conversions.

The designation C-58 applied to two B-18As converted for use as transports but many others were used in this role without being re-designated. One B-18A also was used for trials with a 75 mm. cannon in the nose, before this weapon was adopted for use in the B-25.

TECHNICAL DATA (B-18A)

MANUFACTURER: Douglas Aircraft Co., Santa Monica, California.
TYPE: Medium bomber, anti-submarine and trainer.
ACCOMMODATION: Crew of six.
POWER PLANT: Two 850 h.p. Wright R-1820-53 piston radials.
DIMENSIONS: Span, 89 ft. 6 in. Length, 57 ft. 10 in. Height, 15 ft. 2 in. Wing area, 965 sq. ft.
WEIGHTS: Empty, 16,321 lb. Gross, 27,673 lb.
PERFORMANCE: Max. speed, 215 m.p.h. at 10,000 ft. Cruising speed, 167 m.p.h. Initial climb, 1,030 ft. /min. Service ceiling, 23,900 ft.
ARMAMENT: Three 0·30-in. machine guns in nose, ventral and dorsal positions. Maximum of 6,500 lb. bombs.
SERIAL NUMBERS:
B-18: 36-262/343; 36-431/446; 37-001/034; 37-051.

B-18A: 37-458/634; 38-585/609; 39-012/026.

Douglas B-18B with nose radome (*Peter M. Bowers*).

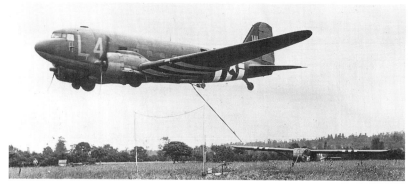

A Douglas C-47B makes the first "snatch" retrieval of a Waco CG-4A glider after the June 6, 1944, invasion of Normandy (*USAF photo*).

Douglas C-47 Skytrain

No aeroplane used by the U.S. Army Air Forces has been more widely known, and probably none has been more widely used for so long an operational life, than the C-47. Produced in greater numbers than any other Army transport, the C-47 was used in every combat area of World War II, and subsequently in the Korean and Vietnam conflicts. Several hundred remained in the USAF inventory in 1970. At the end of the War, the C-47 —"Gooney Bird" or "old bucket seats" to those who flew and flew in it— was nominated by General Eisenhower as one of the four weapons (with the bazooka, the jeep and the atom bomb) that most helped win the conflict.

The aeroplane which was basically the prototype of the C-47 was first flown on December 17, 1935, by Carl Cover, from Clover Field, Santa Monica. Identified by the Douglas type number DC-3 (Douglas Commercial Three) and also known as the DST (Douglas Sleeper Transport), it had been produced for U.S. domestic airlines as a successor for the DC-2. From then until 1940, a total of 430 DC-3s was delivered to the airlines, including more than 100 for export. The Army, which had already bought a number of DC-2 variants (see pp. 234–236) was eager to buy the DC-3 also, and outlined to Douglas the changes that would be needed—stronger cabin floor, strengthened rear fuselage with large loading doors, more powerful engines and provision for carrying large cargo and supply packs externally. Most of the design work on the military version had already been completed for the single C-41 when the first orders were placed, in 1940, for large numbers of C-47s.

By this time, the Santa Monica factory was already committed to the production of other types including the A-20, and the C-47 was in consequence produced in a new Douglas plant at Long Beach. The engines

Douglas C-47D of Air Rescue Service. Black-bordered fuselage bands and outer 6 ft of wings
Douglas C-47A-20-DK (42-93255) with pathfinder radar (*IWM photo*).

of the initial version were 1,200 h.p. Pratt & Whitney R-1830-92 radials, whereas most of the commercial DC-3s had Wright Cyclones. The airline interior gave way to utility bucket-type seats along the cabin walls and the permissible operating weight increased from 25,000 lb. to 29,300 lb. in the C-47 and, eventually, to as much as 35,000 lb. in later models.

Long Beach built 953 C-47s and then changed to the C-47A, which differed significantly only in having a 24-volt in place of 12-volt electrical system. With contracts by this time running into four figures, a second supply source was established in a Douglas-operated factory at Tulsa, Oklahoma, which built 2,099 C-47As while Long Beach built 2,832. The third major production variant was the C-47B, which had R-1830-90 or -90B engines with high altitude blowers and provision for extra fuel, particularly for operation in the China–Burma–India theatre. Long Beach built 300 C-47Bs and Tulsa built 2,808, plus a further 133 TC-47Bs with R-1830-90C engines and equipment for navigational training. In addition to these aircraft for the USAAF, Douglas built 458 more C-47s, under Army contract and with Army serial numbers, for the USN. This total comprised 12 C-47, 200 C-47A-DK, 122 C-47A-DL and 124 C-47B-DK.

In service with the Army Air Force by 1941, the C-47 was deployed as widely as the U.S. forces. It was among the first types of aircraft delivered by air across the North Atlantic to Britain in 1942, and in the same year began operating over the "Hump" route from India to China. The need to fly over Himalayan peaks up to 16,500 ft. high on this route led to development of the C-47B, as noted above. With the formation of Air Transport Command on July 1, 1942, the C-47 became its primary

Douglas AC-47D for Airways checking (*Warren D. Shipp*).

equipment, and proved itself capable of hauling a great variety of military loads into and out of the most primitive of airfields.

Also in 1942 the C-47 joined Troop Carrier Command, formed in the summer of that year to provide aircraft for the movement of airborne troops. This led to development of the C-47 in one of its most important wartime roles, that of paratroop transport and glider tug. In the first large-scale Allied airborne invasion, troop carriers—principally C-47s—dropped 4,381 paratroops over Sicily on July 10, 1943. Thereafter, operations of this kind multiplied rapidly, notable highlights being the first airborne invasion of Burma, which began on March 5, 1944, and involved Troop Carrier Command C-47s towing Waco CG-4A gliders; and the D-Day assault against Normandy (June 6, 1944) in which more than 1,000 C-47s (including those supplied under Lend–Lease to Britain and known as Dakotas) were operational. In the first 50 hours of the operation against Normandy, C-47s carried more than 60,000 paratroops and their equipment into action.

Several other military DC-3 variants, in addition to the C-47 Skytrain were operational during the War. Of these, the C-53 Skytrooper was the most important. This and the other variants are described under their individual designations below. A 1943 experiment produced the single XC-47C (42-5671), a C-47 fitted with twin Edo amphibious floats, each of which contained two retractable wheels and a 300-U.S. gallon fuel tank. Several similar conversions were made at Air Force bases.

After VJ Day, many C-47s were declared surplus and sold to civil operators or foreign governments, but others remained in service with USAF as staff and troop transports and for other special duties. Since the peculiar requirements of the "Hump" operation no longer applied, surviving C-47Bs had the two-speed blowers deleted and were designated C-47D. TC-47Bs similarly became TC-47Ds. Staff transports were designated VC-47A, VC-47B and VC-47D, and a small batch of Skytrains was modified for use by MATS' Air Rescue Service as SC-47B and SC-47D, with provision for carrying a lifeboat under the fuselage. A total of 239 C-47s passed into service with MATS when that service was formed on

Top left, Douglas C-49B (*Peter M. Bowers*); top right, C-52C (*Peter M. Bowers*); bottom left, XC-53A (*Harold G. Martin*); bottom right, C-117C (*Gordon S. Williams*).

268

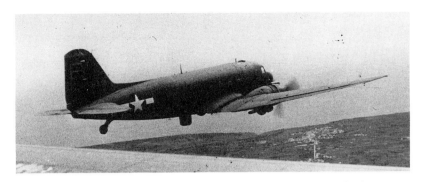

Douglas C-47A-20-DK (42-93255) with pathfinder radar (*IWM photo*).

June 1, 1948, and this type was the first to operate into Berlin on June 26, 1948, carrying supplies when all surface routes were closed by Russia. By the end of July, 105 C-47s were engaged in the Berlin Airlift. Another major MATS operation with C-47s was the evacuation of wounded from Korea, including one notable action in which 4,689 casualties were flown out, in five days, from a battle area surrounded by Chinese troops.

The C-47 also saw service in Korea with Combat Cargo Command, dropping paratroops, bringing in supplies and (as RC-47Ds) dropping flares for night bombing attacks. Other C-47s served, from 1946, with T.A.C. and S.A.C. In 1953, 26 aircraft were converted to AC-47D by Hayes, to be used by the Airways and Air Communication Service (AACS, another component of MATS) for checking the performance of airways navigation aids.

The C-47E designation was reserved in 1951 for a modernized variant with Wright R-1820-80 engines; this programme was cancelled but the designation was revived later for eight aircraft which were modernized for the U.S. Army with R-2000-4 engines. The single YC-47F was similar to the Super DC-3 produced by Douglas for the commercial market in 1950. Originally designated YC-129, it was later transferred to the U.S. Navy as the prototype R4D-8.

Several C-47 variants were re-designated in 1962 to conform with the uniform tri-service system. The SC-47A and SC-47D became HC-47A

Douglas VC-47A in 1961 with curtained, modified windows and integral air-stairs (*Peter M. Bowers*).

Douglas C-47A s/n 42-100536, the personal gift of General "Hap" Arnold to Lord Louis Mountbatten, Supreme Allied Commander, South-East Asia, in India, February 1945. Note three-star marking in fuselage insignia. (*Peter M. Bowers*).

and HC-47D respectively and AC-47D became EC-47D. Also in existence were RC-47A and RC-47D camera-equipped versions.

The Vietnam war brought the C-47 a new role and one of its most aggressive as a heavily armed gunship. Designated AC-47D (not to be confused with the earlier variant with the same designation, changed to EC-47D in 1962), this armed version carried three General Electric 7·62 mm. Miniguns in the fuselage, each having a rate of fire of 6,000 rounds per minute. One gun was mounted to fire through the open door in the port fuselage side, the others through the two windows immediately forward of the door. Armourers flew in the AC-47Ds to load the guns, which were aimed and fired remotely by the pilot using a special gun sight.

Trials with the first AC-47D were made in Vietnam during 1965, after which the type entered service with the 4th Air Commando Squadron and, subsequently, other units. Carrying flares for night operation, the AC-47Ds were able to loiter in target areas for long periods and could bring massive fire power to bear on suspected Viet Cong hide-outs. They quickly earned the nick-name "Puff the Magic Dragon" or simply "Magic Dragon" from the song of that name popular at the time of their introduction. Within the USAF gunship programme, they were known as Spooky. When AC-119s and AC-130s became available in 1970, most of the AC-47Ds were transferred to South Vietnam Air Force units.

Douglas C-47 stripped of original camouflage in India, March 1945. Note open cargo doors and enlarged repetition of last three digits of tail number (*Peter M. Bowers*).

270

Douglas EC-47P in South-East Asia camouflage, with reduced-size national insignia, as used in Vietnam to check navaids and for other special tasks (via *Stephen P. Peltz*).

Also operational in Vietnam were several special electronic reconaissance versions of the C-47, including the EC-47N, modified from the C-47A, the EC-47P, modified from the C-47D, and the EC-47Q, which had R-2000-4 engines.

C-48. This designation applied to 36 DC-3s of various types taken over from U.S. airlines in 1941 for use by USAAF. All had Pratt & Whitney R-1830 engines, like the C-47, but were limited to the commercial gross weight which varied from 22,650 lb. to 26,850 lb. according to type. The aircraft in this series comprised one C-48 from United Air Lines (41-7681), with 21 seats and R-1830-82 engines; three C-48A (41-7682/4) with R-1830-51 engines and 10 seats; 16 C-48B (42-38324/26; 42-56089/91; 42-56098/102; 42-56609/12 and- 4256629) which had been DSTs and had 14 berths; and 14 C-48C (42-38258/60; 42-38327; 42-38332/38; 42-78026/28) 21-seat DC-3s with R-1830-51 engines.

C-49. A total of 138 commercial DC-3s was impressed under this designation. They included 51 acquired from airlines and a further 87 which were under construction and were impressed direct from the factory. The first six aircraft (41-7685/7689, 41-7694) came from TWA. Delta provided a single C-49A (41-7690) and two C-49Cs (41-7715, 41-7721), and from Eastern came three C-49Bs (41-7691/7693) and five C-49Ds (41-7716/7720). Six more C-49Ds (42-38256, 42-43624, 42-65583/65584, 42-68860 and 44-

Former U.S. Navy R4D-6 serving U.S. Army as NC-47J in the 'sixties, in overall white finish with day-glo trim and no national insignia (*Robert Esposito*).

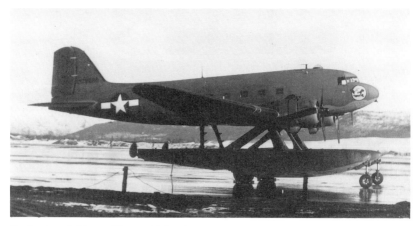

Production C-47s on Edo amphibian floats did not carry the C-47C designation of the prototype. This is a C-47A operating in Alaska (*Alwyn T. Lloyd*).

52999) were impressed while in production, as were all subsequent versions except the 34 C-49Js (43-1961/1994). These other variants comprised 22 C-49Es (42-43619/43623, 42-56092/56097, 42-56103/56107, 42-56617/56618, 42-56625/56627 and 42-56634); nine C-49Fs (42-56613, 42-56616, 42-56620/56621, 42-56623, 42-56628, 42-56633 and 42-56636/56637); eight C-49Gs (42-38252, 42-38255, 42-56614/56615, 42-56630/56632 and 42-56635), 19 C-49Hs (42-38250/38251, 42-38253/38254, 42-38257, 42-38328/38331, 42-57506, 42-65580/65582, 42-68687/68689, 42-107422, 44-83228/83229) and 23 C-49Ks (43-1995/2017). Most of the C-49 variants had 1,200 h.p. Wright R-1820-71 piston engines; the C-49Es had -79 engines and the C-49G and C-49H and -97 engines. The final two C-49Hs listed were ex-KNILM, impressed in Australia after flying out of the Dutch East Indies.

C-50. These were Wright-powered commercial DC-3s, like the C-49 series, but with small differences in interiors, gross weights and engine powers. The USAAF impressed four C-50 from American Airlines (41-7697/7700), with 1,100 h.p. R-1820-85 engines; two C-50A from American Airlines (41-7710/11) with the same engines and trooper seating; three C-50B from Braniff (41-7703/5) with R-1820-81s and starboard door; a single C-50C from Penn-Central Airlines (41-7695) with R-1820-79s and four C-50D also from Penn-Central (41-7696; 41-7709 and 41-7712/13) with -79 engines and trooper seating.

C-51. One impressed DC-3 from Canadian-Colonial Airlines with R-1820-83 engines (41-7702) bore this designation.

C-52. Another series of commercial DC-3s with Pratt & Whitney R-1830-51 engines and 27,700 lb. weight carried this designation. The sub-variants comprised one C-52 from United (41-7708); one C-52A from Western (41-7714), two C-52B from United (41-7706/7) and one C-52C from Eastern (41-7701).

C-53. Named Skytrooper by the USAAF, the C-53 was another production version, based on the airline DC-3 configuration and fitted to carry personnel. Consequently, only a single entry door was provided, in place of the C-47's double door, and the name Skytrooper was assigned. Douglas built 221 C-53s, with R-1830-92 engines; 20 of these were assigned to the Navy. The single XC-53A (42-6480) had full-span slotted flaps. Eight C-53Bs had extra tanks and a navigator's station. The 17 C-53Cs were fitted with side seats, as were the 159 similar C-53Ds.

C-68. Two commercial DC-3s impressed in 1942 took this designation (42-14297/98). They had R-1820-92 engines and 21 passenger seats.

C-84. The four aircraft of this type were 1937-model DC-3Bs impressed (42-57157; 42-57511/13). They had Wright R-1820-71 engines and 28 seats.

C-117. This was a production variant of the C-47B with an airline-type interior for use as a staff transport. Only 17 were built of an order for 131 which was cancelled after VJ Day. Of these, 16 were C-117A from the Tulsa factory, plus a single C-117B from Long Beach. In 1953, 11 non-standard VC-47 staff transports were redesignated C-117C. These were the

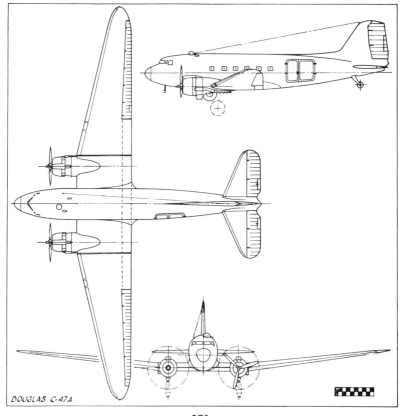

DOUGLAS C-47A

last examples of the DC-3 designated by the U.S. services; they were still in service in 1962, some as VC-117A and VC-117B.

XCG-17. One C-47 (41-18496) was converted to a glider in the course of a series of trials by the Air Technical Service Command at Wright Field in 1944. The programme was intended to develop a troop glider suitable for use behind the C-54, and went through three phases: dead-stick landings with a C-47: towed flights of one C-47 by another, the second aircraft using partial power for take-off: and finally tests of the XCG-17 itself. The latter was a C-47 with engines removed, and was first flown behind a C-47 from Clinton County airfield by Major D. O. Dodd in the summer of 1944. The XCG-17 was also used for some unique experiments in which it was towed off by two powered C-47s in tandem.

It had the flattest glide of any cargo glider tested up to that time, and could have been even better had not the specification required that it be possible to reconvert the XCG-17 to a C-47. In consequence, the engine nacelles were retained on the wing, less engines.

TECHNICAL DATA (C-47)

MANUFACTURER: Douglas Aircraft Co., Long Beach, California and Tulsa, Oklahoma.

TYPE: Troop and supply transport, paratroop transport, glider tug.

ACCOMMODATION: 27 troops or 18–24 litters or 10,000 lb. of cargo.

POWER PLANT: Two 1,200 h.p. Pratt & Whitney R-1830-92.

DIMENSIONS: Span, 95 ft. 6 in. Length, 63 ft. 9 in. Height, 17 ft. 0 in. Wing area, 987 sq. ft.

WEIGHTS: Empty, 18,200 lb. Gross, 26,000 lb.

PERFORMANCE: Max. speed, 230 m.p.h. Climb, 9·6 min. to 10,000 ft. Service ceiling, 24,000 ft. Range, 1,600 st. miles.

ARMAMENT: None. Grommets in cabin windows to permit small arms fire.

SERIAL NUMBERS:

C-47: 41-7722/7866; 41-18337/18699; 41-19463/19499; 41-38564/38763; 42-5635/5704; 42-32786/32923; 43-30628/30639*.

C-47A-DL: 42-32924/32935; 42-23300/24419; 42-100436/101035; 43-15033/16132.

C-47A-DK: 42-92024/93158; 42-93160/93823; 42-108794/108993*; 43-47963/48262.

C-47B-DK: 42-93159; 43-48263/49962†; 44-76195/77294‡; 45-876/1139.

C-47B-DL: 43-16133/16432.
YC-47F: 51-3817.
C-47: 49-2612/2641§.
C-53: 41-20045/20136**; 42-6455/6504††; 42-15530/15569; 42-15870/15894; 42-47371/47382*; 43-14404/14405*; 43-36600‡‡.
C-53C: 43-2018/2034.
C-53D: 42-68693/68851.
C-117A-DK: 45-2545/2547; 45-2549/2561.
C-117B-DL: 45-2548.

* Procured for USN.   † Includes 18 TC-47B.
‡ Includes 115 TC-47B and 124 assigned to USN.
§ Rebuilt aircraft procured for MAP to Greece.
** Includes six for USN and eight C-53B: 41-20047/50, 52, 57/59.
†† Includes one XC-53A: 42-6480.   ‡‡ Douglas staff transport.

Douglas A-24 in A.T.C. markings, 1944 (*USAF photo 32408AC*).

Douglas A-24

Army interest in the single-engined two-seat high-performance dive bomber was aroused in 1940 by the successes then being enjoyed in Europe by the Luftwaffe's Junkers Ju 87 Stukas. Aeroplanes in this category were already in production for the U.S. Navy.

Designated A-24, the Douglas attack bomber was similar to its Navy forerunner apart from the deletion of deck-operating features. Powered by a 1,000 h.p. R-1820-52 engine, the A-24 could carry a 1,200 lb. bomb load and was armed with two fixed forward-firing 0·50-inch machine guns, and two 0·30-inch guns in the rear cockpit. To meet what was considered at the time to be an urgent need, 168 A-24s were ordered and were delivered from the Navy production line at El Segundo between June and October 1941. These were Navy aeroplanes, delivered with the designation SBD-3A (for Army) stencilled on the tail, the deck hook removed and a pneumatic tail wheel tyre in place of the solid one.

In the light of the deteriorating situation in the Pacific in November 1941, 52 of these A-24s were despatched by sea for the Philippines, to be used by the 27th Bombardment Group (L). When the Philippines were attacked, they were diverted to Australia where they arrived in Brisbane in December 1941. In February 1942 the 91st Bombardment Squadron took them to the Netherlands East Indies, where they were first used operationally; both here and subsequently in the hands of the 8th Bombardment Squadron (3rd B Group) in Australia they were found too slow, too short of range and too vulnerable for continued operation.

Nevertheless, further contracts were placed, for 170 A-24As in 1942 and 615 A-24Bs in 1943. The A-24A, equivalent of the Navy's SBD-4, was built at El Segundo and had a 24-volt electric system. The A-24B (SBD-5 equivalent) had a 1,200 h.p. R-1820-60 and was built at Tulsa.

A few A-24s were retained in the Air Force inventory until 1950. When the "A" designation category was dropped, they were re-designated F-24A and F-24B, and were used in trials connected with dive-bombing attacks by fighter-bombers. A single QF-24A was a radio-controlled drone for special tests, controlled from the single DF-24B; these were additional SBDs acquired from the Navy in 1948.

TECHNICAL DATA (A-24)

MANUFACTURER: Douglas Aircraft Co., El Segundo, California and Tulsa, Okl.
TYPE: Dive bomber.
ACCOMMODATION: Pilot and gunner.
POWER PLANT: One 1,000 h.p. Wright R-1820-52 piston radial.
DIMENSIONS: Span, 41 ft. 6 in. Length, 32 ft. 8 in. Height, 12 ft. 11 in. Wing area, 325 sq. ft.
WEIGHTS: Empty, 6,265 lb. Gross, 9,200 lb.
PERFORMANCE: Max. speed, 250 m.p.h. at 17,200 ft. Cruising speed, 173 m.p.h. Initial climb, 7 min. to 10,000 ft. Service ceiling, 26,000 ft. Range, 1,300 st. miles.
ARMAMENT: Two forward firing 0·50-in. guns, two flexible 0·30-in. guns, 1,200 lb. bombs.
SERIAL NUMBERS:
A-24: 41-15746/15823; 42-6682/6771.   QF-24A: 48-044.
A-24A: 42-6772/6831; 42-60772/60881.   DF-24B: 48-045.
A-24B: 42-54285/54899.

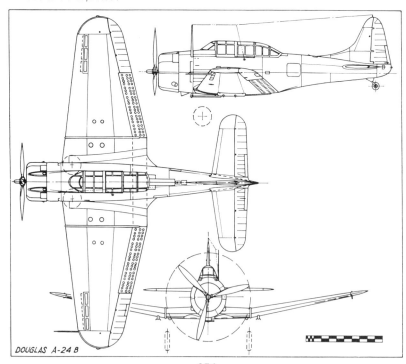

DOUGLAS A-24 B

Douglas A-20B equipped for target towing, in service from Goxhill with 2nd Gunnery & Target Towing Flight, Eighth Air Force, in 1944 (*courtesy Peter H. T. Green*).

Douglas A-20, P-70, F-3 Havoc

Developed from an original Douglas design of 1937 and put into production for foreign air forces in 1938, the A-20 was the most-produced of all the aircraft procured by the USAAF in the "Attack" category, and was the first type of aircraft operated by American crews in the European theatre in World War II. By the time the Army placed its first contract for the A-20, in July 1939, production was well advanced on several hundred examples of the same basic design for the French Air Force (as the DB-7) and for the R.A.F., which eventually took over many of the French contracts. The project had begun with the Douglas Model 7A in 1936, designed at the Douglas El Segundo Division under Ed Heinemann as chief engineer. Although no official requirement existed, the Model 7A was intended to provide the Army Air Corps with a high performance attack bomber. With some revisions this design was built in prototype form as the Model 7B, first flown on October 26, 1938, and this aircraft formed the basis of the first French order for 105.

Modifications required by the French and indicated for European warfare led to an almost complete re-design of the Model 7B as the DB-7, a prototype of which flew on August 17, 1939 from Los Angeles Municipal Airport (El Segundo). The DB-7 featured a comparatively deep fuselage of narrow cross section, and "stepped" cockpit and dorsal gun position; a third crew member in the transparent nose doubled as navigator and bombardier. The wing was mid-mounted on the fuselage and the big Pratt & Whitney Twin Wasp radial engines were faired into long nacelles underslung on the wing. In addition to fixed forward firing guns, there were upper and lower rear defence guns aimed by the dorsal gunner.

Initial Army contracts, for a total of 206 aircraft, were for the A-20

Douglas A-20B of the 85th BS, 47th BG in "Desert Pink" finish, photographed at Sousse, Tunisia, in June 1943 (*Howard Levy*).

and A-20A models, both variants of the French DB-7. The 63 A-20s (Douglas Model DB-7B) had Wright R-2600-7 radial engines with turbo-superchargers and were the fastest of all Havoc variants purchased by the Army, at 390 m.p.h.; they were not, however, used operationally in the attack role, but were converted to F-3 and P-70 variants as described below. The first operational variant for the Army was thus the A-20A, 14 of which made up the balance of the initial Fiscal 1939 contract for 77; total production of the A-20A, including two Fiscal 1940 contracts, was 143. This variant was without the turbosuperchargers, the engines in this form being designated R-2600-3.

The armament was increased by a rearward firing 0·30-inch gun in the back of each nacelle, in addition to four fixed forward firing, one ventral and two dorsal guns. Although lighter than the A-20 at 18,605 lb., the A-20A achieved only 349 m.p.h.

The single XA-20B was an A-20A conversion in 1941, with power-operated twin-gun turrets in the nose and dorsal and ventral locations. Another A-20A became the XA-20F with dorsal and ventral General Electric turrets and a 37-mm. cannon in the nose.

Production of the next Army variant was initiated at a new Douglas plant in Long Beach, as El Segundo was still heavily committed in ful-filling foreign orders. A third source was established by Boeing at Seattle, but the 140 A-20Cs built by Boeing went to the R.A.F. under Lend–Lease. Although orders for the A-20B were not placed until the end of 1940 this version—of which Long Beach built 999—was of an earlier standard than either the A-20 or the A-20A, being basically the Douglas Model DB-7A already produced for the French and British. The engines were R-2600-11s and detail differences in the nose transparency design accounted for a 5-inch greater fuselage length. Seventeen A-20As were converted approximately to A-20B standard as A-20Es with R-2600-11 engines in 1941, and at the end of that year, considerable quantities of DB-7Bs (British) and DB-7Cs (Dutch) were re-possessed by the Army.

New programmes at Long Beach and El Segundo led to the transfer

278

of A-20 production to the main Douglas factory at Santa Monica in 1941, and all A-20 variants from the A-20C on were built there. The A-20C, of which Douglas built 808, represented an attempt to standardize U.S. Army and British R.A.F. requirements and equipment. With 1,600 h.p. R-2600-23 engines, the A-20C had a much higher gross weight—25,600 lb.—and the speed went down to 342 m.p.h. Nacelle guns were deleted and provision was made for a 2,000 lb. torpedo under the fuselage.

Although A-20As were serving overseas with Army squadrons before the end of 1941, the A-20C was the first model to see combat, in the hands of the 15th Bombardment Squadron. This unit arrived in the U.K. in May 1942 and its crews went into action on July 4—flying, for their first few sorties—with No. 226 Squadron, R.A.F. in Boston IIIs supplied to that service. The 15th Bombardment Squadron, and others which followed it to Europe and North Africa, eventually served with the Ninth and Fifteenth Air Forces, achieving considerable success in the tactical and

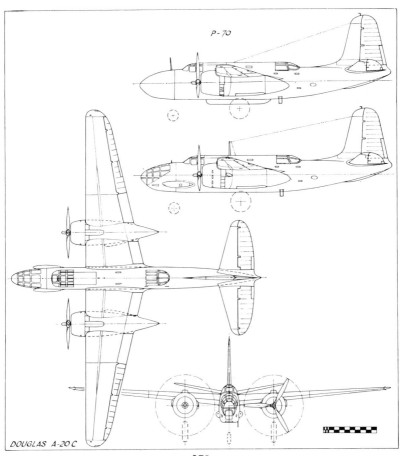

P-70

DOUGLAS A-20C

Douglas A-20G-20-DO with nose gun armament (*USAF photo*).

intruder role. The principal variant used operationally was the A-20G, which followed the A-20C in production at Santa Monica and was the most-built of all DB-7 variants. This version was distinguished by a "solid" gun-carrying nose in place of the transparent bomb-aiming position, and was the first "attack" variant to have this feature, although similar gun batteries had been designed for the P-70 and, independently, in Britain for the R.A.F.'s Havoc night fighter.

In the early A-20G models the nose armament comprised four 20-mm. M2 cannon and two 0·50-inch machine guns; single guns were carried in the dorsal and ventral position. With the new nose, the fuselage length became 48 ft.; the engines were R-2600-23. A second series of A-20Gs had the cannon removed in favour of four more 0·50-inch guns, while a third series (from A-20G-20) was still further modified to have a six-inch wider rear fuselage containing a Martin electrically-powered dorsal turret with two 0·50-inch guns; underwing bomb racks which doubled the bomb load from 2,000 lb. to 4,000 lb., and extra fuel tanks in the bomb-bay which, with a 374-U.S. gallon under-fuselage ferry drop tank gave a maximum endurance of 10½ hours. These final models of the A20G had a maximum gross weight of 30,000 lb., but normally operated at about

Douglas TA-20K-15-DO, with day-glo band round rear fuselage for better visibility on training sorties.

280

26,000 lb., when the speed was 317 m.p.h. Production of the A-20G totalled 2,850, and another 412 A-20Hs were similar apart from having 1,700 h.p. R-2600-29 engines which increased the speed to 322 m.p.h.

In addition to service in Europe and North Africa, the A-20Gs and A-20Hs saw operation in the Pacific theatre, principally in the low-altitude attack role. Flying with the Fifth Air Force from September 1942, A-20s played an important part in the attacks on Japanese targets in the Pacific islands, dropping fragmentation bombs from low altitude, attached to parachutes and with instantaneous fuzes. For these operations A-20Cs had their nose armament increased, in the field, to four 0·30-inch and four 0·50-inch guns. Many A-20C, A-20G and A-20H went to Russia, which received a total of 3,125 Havocs of all types.

To simplify navigation and improve bombing navigation, versions of the A-20G and A-20H were produced in 1943 with bombardier noses, and designated respectively A-20J and A-20K. The transparent nose was

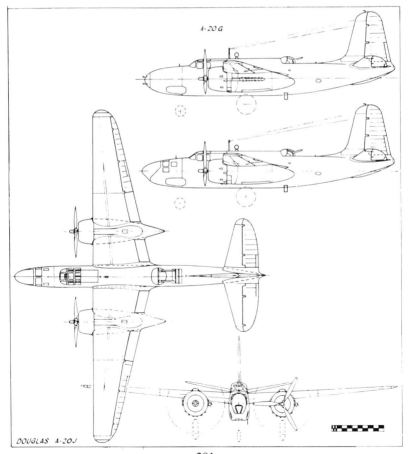

A-20G

DOUGLAS A-20J

Douglas P-70 field conversion of A-20G, operated by 419th NF Squadron in Guadalcanal in 1943 (*courtesy Harry Gann*).

of a new, frameless type, increasing the length by a further seven inches. Production of the A-20J totalled 450 and of the "K", 413; 259 of this total went to the R.A.F. The last Havoc came off the Santa Monica line on September 20, 1944, by which time Douglas had built a grand total of 7,385 DB-7 variants, including those for export.

Most surviving A-20s were discarded by the USAAF before the end of 1945, including some A-20Hs and A-20Js which had been adapted for training as TA-20s. One of these, a TA-20H (44-466), was modified at Wright Field to fly an experimental tracked undercarriage.

F-3. One A-20 (39-741) was converted in 1940 for the reconnaissance role, and designated XF-3, with a T-3A camera in the rear bomb-bay and a five-gun armament. Two other A-20s converted to YF-3 (39-745 and 39-748) had the same camera installations but experimental armament, including a hand-held gun in the extreme tail, and rearward-firing nacelle guns. All three aircraft were later re-designated F-3. In 1944, 46 A-20Js and A-20Ks were fitted with cameras in the rear fuselage in place of the ventral tunnel gun, and designated F-3A. They were used in 1944/45 by the 155th Photographic Squadron (Night), Ninth AF, in the European theatre.

O-53. An observation variant of the A-20B was planned in 1941, but was not produced. Contracts for 1,489 (41-3670/5158) were cancelled.

P-70. To take advantage of British airborne interception radar, then more advanced than U.S. equipment, the first AAC A-20 (39-735) was converted to a night fighter in 1942 and re-designated XP-70. Changes included installation of R-2600-11 engines, a "solid" nose containing the radar, and a gun pack under the fuselage in which the entire armament—four 20-mm. cannon—was concentrated. Primarily to serve as operational trainers in radar-directed night fighting, a further 59 A-20s (39-736/740, -742/744; -746/747, -749/797) were similarly converted to P-70s. With the designation P-70A-1, 13 A-20Cs were converted as night fighters in 1943, carrying six 0.50-in. guns in the ventral tray, and the A.I. radar. Twenty-six A-20Gs were similarly converted to P-70A-2 standard with the armament in the nose. The single P-70B-1 was another A-20G conversion with the six-gun armament in blisters on each side of the fuselage, and SCR-720 centimetric radar. The P-70B-2 designation applied to 105

A-20Gs and A-20Js used as night fighter trainers, with SCR-720 or SCR-729 and provision for armament in the ventral tray. Limited operational use was made of the P-70s by USAAF night-fighter squadrons including the 6th, 418th, 419th and 421st NFS, over Guadalcanal and New Guinea.

TECHNICAL DATA (A-20)

MANUFACTURERS: Douglas Aircraft Co., Santa Monica, El Segundo and Long Beach, California. Boeing Airplane Co., Seattle, Washington.
TYPE: Light bomber.
ACCOMMODATION: Pilot; navigator; bombardier/gunner.

	A-20A	A-20G	A-20K	P-70
Power Plant:	2 × 1,600 h.p. R-2600-3	2 × 1,600 h.p. R-2600-23	2 × 1,700 h.p. R-2600-29	2 × 1,600 h.p. R-2600-11
Dimensions:				
Span, ft., in.	61 4	61 4	61 4	61 4
Length, ft., in.	47 7	48 0	48 4	47 7
Height, ft. in.	17 7	17 7	17 7	17 7
Wing area, sq. ft.	464	464	464	464
Weights:				
Empty, lb.	15,165	15,984	17,266	16,031
Gross, lb.	20,711	27,200	27,000	21,264
Performance:				
Max. speed, m.p.h. at ft.	347/12,400	339/12,400	333/15,600	329/14,000
Cruising speed, m.p.h.	295	272	269	270
Initial climb, min. to ft.	5·1/10,000	7·1/10,000	6·6/10,000	8/12,000
Service ceiling, ft.	28,175	25,800	25,100	28,250
Range, miles	675	1,090	830	1,060
Armament:	7 × 0·30 in. guns 2,600 lb. bombs	8 × 0·50 in. guns 2,600 lb. bombs	5 × 0.50 in. guns 2,600 lb. bombs	4 × 20 mm. guns in ventral pack

SERIAL NUMBERS:
A-20-DE: 39-735/797*.
A-20A-DE: 39-721/734; 40-071/179; 40-3143/3162.
A-20B-DL: 41-2671/3669†.
A-20C-DO: 41-19088/19462; 42-32951/33383.
A-20C-BO: 41-19589/19728.
A-20G-DO: 42-53535/54284; 42-86563/86912; 43-9038/9229; 43-9231/9437; 43-9458/9637; 43-9665/9856; 43-9881/9909; 43-9918/10104; 43-10145/10237; 43-21252/21431; 43-21472/21551; 43-21582/21701; 43-21752/21827; 43-21878/21987; 43-22148/22251.

A-20H: 44-001/008; 44-010/065; 44-199/328; 44-407/536; 44-619/706.
A-20J: 43-9230; 43-9438/9457; 43-9638/9664; 43-9857/9880; 43-9910/9917; 43-10105/10144; 43-21432/21471; 43-21552/21581; 43-21702/21751; 43-21828/21877; 43-21988/22147.
A-20K: 44-009; 44-066/198; 44-329/406; 44-537/618; 44-707/825.

*All converted to F-3 or P-70 variants.
†Includes eight for USN.

Douglas B-26Bs in Korea, 1951 (*USAF photo 51-7521P*).

Douglas A-26, B-26 Invader

Designed to a USAAF requirement written in 1940, the A-26 was developed and put into production with great rapidity, reaching the European theatre of operations before the end of 1944. Although numbers up to XA-45 were assigned, the A-26 also proved to be the last important operational aircraft produced in the "attack" category. The specification called for a multi-purpose light bomber capable of fast attack operations at low level as well as precision bombing from medium altitudes, and carrying a powerful defensive armament.

Three prototypes were ordered in June 1941, and the first of these, the XA-26 (41-19504), was first flown on July 10, 1942. This prototype was completed as the basic bomber, with a bomb-aimer's station in the nose. The second prototype, XA-26A (41-19505) was armed as a night fighter, with four 20-mm. guns in the belly and four 0·50-inch guns in the top turret, remotely sited and fired from a gunner's position amidships. The third prototype, XA-26B (41-19588), included a 75-mm. cannon, nose-mounted, in its armament.

Flight testing of these three prototypes, and combat reports from Europe and the Pacific area, led to adoption of the A-26B as the production model. Like the XA-26B, this had an "attack" nose, but the large-bore cannon gave way to six 0·50-inch machine guns; dorsal and ventral turrets, both remotely controlled, had two more 0·50s in each. The armament could be supplemented by eight more 0·50s in four packages under the wings and two in packages each side of the nose; the top turret guns also could be used for ground attack, with the guns locked to fire forwards and controlled by the pilot. Heavily armoured, to afford protection against ground fire, the A-26B carried a crew of three, comprising pilot, navigator/radio operator and the gunner. Internal stowage was provided for a maximum 4,000 lb. bomb load. Underwing points carried 2,000 lb. of bombs, eight 5-inch rockets and two fuel tanks, or 16 rockets.

The A-26B was put into production by Douglas at the Long Beach and

Douglas A-26C with standard turrets (*Peter M. Bowers*).

Tulsa factories, which built 1,150 and 205, respectively, of this model, deliveries starting in the first half of 1944. Powered by 2,000 h.p. Pratt & Whitney R-2800-27 or -79 engines, the A-26B achieved a maximum level speed of 355 m.p.h. at 15,000 ft., making it one of the fastest bombers used by the USAAF in World War II. Experiments with nose armament continued, with an A-26B mounting a 75-mm. cannon, another with this gun plus two 0·50-inch machine guns and a third with two 37-mm. cannon.

The operational career of the A-26B began on November 19, 1944, with the 9th Air Force in Europe. The A-26 was also operational in the Pacific in the later stages of the campaign against Japan, for which the A-26C joined the A-26B. In the "C", a transparent "bombardier" nose replaced the gun nose, to permit more accurate bombing from medium levels; two forward-firing guns were retained, together with the turret guns. The fuselage was widened, and dual controls were fitted, the second pilot also acting as bombardier. Douglas built five A-26Cs at Long Beach and 1,086 at Tulsa, with deliveries starting in 1945. One XA-26D was also built, as a development of the "B" having eight 0·50s in the nose and six in wing packages. A camera-equipped reconnaissance version which appeared in small numbers was the FA-26C.

Production of 750 A-26Ds was cancelled after VJ Day, but the eight-gun nose was later adopted on the A-26B, as well as the wing packages

All-black Douglas A-26C with radome; turrets deleted (*Warren M. Bodie*).

285

Versions of the B-26K (later, A-26A) with bombardier and "solid" noses.

as noted above. Also cancelled were 445 A-26Bs, 2,809 A-26Cs and 1,250 A-26Es, an advanced development of the A-26C. The single XA-26F, first flown in 1945, was an A-26B airframe (44-34586) used to test-fly a General Electric J31 turbojet mounted in the rear fuselage.

Many hundreds of both B and C models of the A-26 remained in front-line service after the end of World War II, particularly as the primary offensive weapon of Tactical Air Command when it was created in 1946 from the wartime 9th and 12th Air Forces. In June 1948, the Attack category was officially abandoned and the designation changed to B-26B and B-26C, all examples of the Martin B-26 being then out of service. The B-26B returned to Europe when the 38th Light Bomber Wing was assigned to USAFE, and the B-26C and RB-26C also operated from bases in Germany. The latter had no armament but carried cameras, and flash flares for night photography.

The 3rd Bombardment Group, comprising three B-26 squadrons, was early in action in Korea, flying tactical intruder missions from Iwakuni, Japan, for the first time on June 27, 1950. It was later joined by the 452nd (later renumbered 17th) Bomb Group at Itazuki. For these operations, the B-26 operated at considerably higher weights, and with greater loads, than had been achieved in World War II. The B-26B, for instance, mounted eight nose guns and three in each wing (in place of the earlier packages on the wings) with a total of 4,000 rounds; the four turret guns with 500 r.p.g.; 4,000 lb. of bombs internally; fourteen 5-inch HVARs under the wings, or fewer HVARs plus two 165-U.S. gal. fuel tanks, or two 110-gal. Napalm tanks. The gross weight on operations reached 38,500 lb.

The B-26Cs in Korea had the same underwing loads as the "B", and the two turrets, with the bombardier nose and H2S radar in the fuselage between the nose wheel and bomb-bay. The use of radar permitted the B-26Cs to make highly effective bombing attacks by night.

The B-26 remained in service with Air Force Reserve and National Guard units after being retired by TAC, and was available to return to operational service in Vietnam in 1962. Both B-26B and B-26C versions went into action in the counter-insurgency role, and in the light of early operational experience the USAF initiated development of a new COIN variant designated YB-26K (US Navy versions having become B-26Js in 1962). Conversion of an airframe to the prototype YB-26K was completed by On Mark Engineering early in 1963. Major changes were concerned with load-carrying ability and short-field performance. The wing could carry up to 5,500 lb. of external fuel and weapons, or eight pylons in two tip tanks. Fixed forward-firing armament was increased to a maximum of 14 × 0·50 in guns—eight in the nose and three in each wing; the eight-gun nose was interchangeable with the "bombardier" nose. The 2,500 h.p. R-2800-103W engines reduced take-off runs and Hytrol anti-skid brakes reduced the landing run, while provision was also made for six 1,000 lb. JATO units under the fuselage.

The USAF ordered about 70 B-26s to be converted to B-26K standard

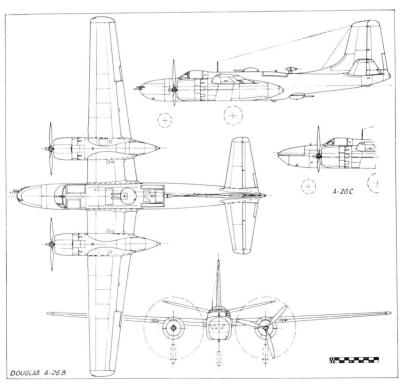

A-26C

DOUGLAS A-26B

287

after evaluating the YB-26K and subsequently redesignated these aircraft as A-26As. Some saw service in Vietnam and others were supplied to foreign countries through the MAP.

In addition to its use as a bomber, the B-26 was adapted for several other roles, among the most important of which were training and staff transport. With the designations TB-26B and TB-26C, the training variants served in Reserve and NG units, while the CB-26B and VB-26B transports were used by Air Force Headquarters. Air Research and Development Command used some DB-26Cs as drone launchers and controllers.

TECHNICAL DATA (A-26)

MANUFACTURER: Douglas Aircraft Co., El Segundo and Long Beach, California, and Tulsa, Oklahoma.
TYPE: Light bomber and reconnaissance.
ACCOMMODATION: Pilot, navigator/bombardier, gunner.
POWER PLANT: Two 2,000 h.p. Pratt & Whitney R-2800-27 or -79 piston radials.

	XA-26	A-26B-1	A-26C
Dimensions:			
Span, ft., in.	70 0	70 0	70 0
Length, ft., in.	51 2	50 0	51 3
Height, ft., in.	18 6	18 6	18 3
Wing area, sq. ft.	540	540	540
Weight:			
Empty, lb.	21,150	22,370	22,850
Gross, lb.	31,000	35,000	35,000
Performance:			
Max. speed, m.p.h.	370	355	373
Cruising speed, m.p.h.	212	284	284
Climb, min./ft.	10·2/20,000	8·1/10,000	8/10,000
Service ceiling, ft.	31,300	22,100	22,100
Range, miles	1,800	1,400	1,400
Armament:	6×0·50-in. in nose, top, ventral turrets. 3,000 lb. bombs	10×0·50-in. in nose, top, ventral turrets. 4,000 lb. bombs	6×0·50-in. in nose, top, ventral turrets. 4,000 lb. bombs

SERIAL NUMBERS:

XA-26: 41-19504.
XA-26A: 41-19505.
XA-26B: 41-19588.
A-26B-DL: 41-39100/39151;
  41-39153/39192; 41-39194;
  41-39196/39198; 41-39201/39599;
  44-34098/34753*.
XA-26D-DL: 44-34776.

A-26B-DT: 43-22252/22303;
  43-22305/22307; 43-22313/22345;
  43-22350/22466.
A-26C-DL: 41-39152; 41-39193;
  41-39195; 41-39199/39200.
A-26C-DT: 43-22304; 43-22308/22312;
  43-22346/22349; 43-22467/22751;
  44-35198/35996†.

* Includes one (44-34586) completed as XA-26F.
† Total of 791 built in this sequence, of which 88 to US Navy.

288

Douglas C-54G in India, 1945 (*Peter M. Bowers*).

Douglas C-54 Skymaster

Chance, rather than deliberate planning, gave the U.S. Army its first four-engined transport in time to serve with distinction for the last three years of World War II. When Japan's attack on Pearl Harbor brought America into the war, no formal requirement existed for a long-range four-engined transport capable of operations across the Atlantic and Pacific, but the Douglas factory at Santa Monica had in production its DC-4A, designed for transcontinental operation by the U.S. domestic airlines. A 65,000 lb. aeroplane powered by four Pratt & Whitney R-2000 radial engines and with seats for 42 passengers, the DC-4A had been developed by Douglas in close collaboration with five U.S. carriers and followed the prototype DC-4E, a larger aeroplane which had been designed, built and flown (on June 21, 1938) to meet similar requirements. Backed by United and American Airlines, Douglas laid down 24 DC-4As in 1940, without building a prototype of the revised design, and nine of these were in various advanced stages of construction by December 1941.

Early in 1942, the Army Air Force commandeered the production line and designated the first 24 aeroplanes C-54s. They were completed in accordance with the original commercial specifications with few changes and had no special provision for military operations. The main cabin seated 26 passengers and four fuselage fuel tanks supplemented the wing tankage; the 1,350 h.p. engines were designated R-2000-3. John F. Martin flew the first C-54 (41-20137) on March 26, 1942 at Santa Monica.

Production orders quickly followed for a militarized version capable of handling heavy freight. As Santa Monica was committed to other priority programmes, Douglas laid down a new C-54 line at Chicago, and this accounted for some two-thirds of the total production of the type. The first military model, built both at Chicago (155) and Santa

Monica (52) was the C-54A, structurally redesigned for heavy cargo loads with a strengthened floor, a large door and a boom hoist and winch. The cabin was convertible for passenger or troop seats, and large cargo could be carried on suspension points beneath the fuselage. The fuel capacity was increased and the engines were R-2000-7s.

In the C-54B, integral fuel tanks in the wings replaced two of the fuselage cells, and cabin fittings were provided for stretcher installation. The normal seating capacity was 50, and the gross weight increased to 73,000 lb. Douglas built 100 at Santa Monica and 120 at Chicago. The C-54D, similar to the "B" model but with R-2000-11 engines, was the most produced variant; as well as the last built at Chicago, which produced 350 in 1944 and 1945.

Also with R-2000-11 engines, the Santa Monica-built C-54E had increased payload flexibility by using combination seat and cargo tie-down fittings in the floor. Extra bag tanks in the wings gave a significant increase in range with a restricted payload of about 20 passengers. Production of this model totalled 75, and Santa Monica then built 76 C-54Gs, similar to the "E" but with 1,450 h.p. R-2000-9 engines and basic accommodation for 40–50 passengers. This brought the total number of C-54s built to 952, plus 211 more on Army contracts for the U.S.N.

Experimental models were the XC-54F, designed as a troop transport for Troop Carrier Command, of which only a mock-up was built; the C-54H, a similar project with R-2000-9 engines, cancelled when the War ended; the C-54J, a variant of the "G" with a new interior, also cancelled; and the XC-54K, a long-range development of the "E" with 1,425 h.p. R-1820-HD engines, of which a single example (42-72484) was built.

The C-54s were operated during World War II by Air Transport Command, which came into being in December 1942, in time to take delivery of the first aircraft from Douglas. Although designed for domestic operations, its service use was world-wide, and in the course of three years of wartime flying an unequalled safety record was achieved. In making 79,642 ocean crossings up to VJ Day, only three C-54s were lost. The C-54 became the first transport aircraft to establish a regular and

The third Douglas C-54 in O.D. and grey finish in 1942 (*USAF photo E-22339AC*).

290

President Roosevelt's C-54C "The Sacred Cow". Grouped flags on fuselage show countries visited (*Peter M. Bowers*).

reliable service across the North Atlantic, over which it averaged more than 20 round trips a day for many months; across the Pacific from the U.S. West Coast to the Philippines and Australia; and across the Indian Ocean from Ceylon to Australia, a 3,100-mile sector. The type served in North Africa, over the "Hump" from India to China, in Alaska and, in fact, in every area where U.S. servicemen were in action.

One C-54A was specially modified to transport President Roosevelt. With an electrically-operated elevator for the President's use, it had four state rooms and a conference room, with provision for 15 passengers and bunks for six. This aircraft, designated the C-54C (42-107451) was later used by President Truman and visited 55 countries between 1944 and 1947. Known as the "Sacred Cow", it was retired to a museum in 1961.

Following the end of the War, a number of C-54s were declared surplus and were purchased by airlines all over the world to give good service for many more years. The USAF retained several hundred C-54s, however, and a number of these were used to equip the troop carrier squadrons of Tactical Air Command upon its formation in March 1946. When the Military Air Transport Service came into existence on June 1, 1948, 234 C-54s still serving with ATC passed to the new service (together with four squadrons of the U.S. Navy version, designated R5D). Less than a month after MATS was formed, the Communist blockade of Berlin became critical and MATS became involved in the Berlin Airlift. By August, eight squadrons of nine C-54s each were in Europe and eventually 319 C-54s, of about 400 still in service, were committed to this operation, including 19 at a special aircrew training school for the airlift. Of the aircraft in use, 38 were stripped of non-essential equipment to carry coal, and had their payload increased by some 2,500 lb.; these were designated C-54Ms.

MATS C-54s played a prominent part, too, in the Korean conflict, and an aircraft of this type was, in fact, the first U.S. aeroplane destroyed in Korea, when it was strafed on Kimpo Airfield on June 25, 1950. From June until November, MATS operated the Pacific Airlift, from the U.S. West coast to Tokyo, using aircraft (largely C-54s) from its own three divisions, and from the C-54-equipped 61st and 62nd Troop Carrier

291

Groups of TAC. To carry wounded to the U.S. from Japan, 30 C-54Es were converted to MC-54Ms in 1951.

Some models of the C-54 remained in service with MATS for several more years, and in 1955, 38 "D"s were modified by Convair for use by the Air Rescue Service, being then re-designated SC-54D. Nine JC-54s were in use in 1960 by the 6560th Operations Group (Range Support) for special duties associated with the recovery of missile nose cones, and a few others became AC-54Ds for use with MATS' Airways and Air Communications Service. Staff transports were designated VC-54C, VC-54D and VC-54G. In 1962, the AC and SC models were re-designated EC-54D and HC-54D respectively. A few TC-54Ds were equipped for training.

A 1947 experiment accounted for the C-54L, which was an "A" temporarily modified to have a new fuel system. In September 1947, a

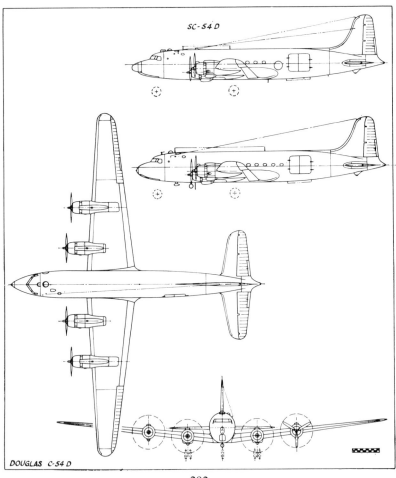

Douglas SC-54 of Air Rescue Service (*USAF photo*).

specially-equipped C-54 (42-72461) from the All Weather Flying Center completed a fully-automatic flight from Newfoundland to England, being at no time controlled by the check pilots on board.

XC-114. This designation applied to a single C-54 variant built in 1946, with four 1,620 h.p. Allison V-1710-131 inline engines. The gross weight was 81,000 lb.

XC-115. A projected variant of the XC-114, with 1,650 h.p. Packard V-1650-209 engines. Not built.

YC-116. Similar to the XC-114, but with thermal de-icers.

TECHNICAL DATA (C-54A)

MANUFACTURER: Douglas Aircraft Co., Long Beach, California.
TYPE: Troop and cargo transport.
ACCOMMODATION: 50 troops.
POWER PLANT: Four 1,290 h.p. Pratt & Whitney R-2000-7.
DIMENSIONS: Span, 117 ft. 6 in. Length, 93 ft. 10 in. Height, 27 ft. 6 in. Wing area, 1,460 sq. ft.
WEIGHTS: Empty, 37,000 lb. Gross, 62,000 lb.
PERFORMANCE: Max. speed, 265 m.p.h. Climb, 14·8 min. to 10,000 ft. Service ceiling, 22,000 ft. Range, 3,900 st. miles.
ARMAMENT: None.
SERIAL NUMBERS:

C-54-DO: 41-20137/20145; 42-32936/32950; 45-59602*.	C-54D-DC: 42-72440/72764; 43-17199/17253‡.
C-54A-DO: 41-37268/37319; 42-107426/107470†.	C-54E-DO: 44-9026/9150§.
C-54A-DC: 42-72165/72319.	C-54G-DO: 45-476/637**.
C-54B-DC: 42-72320/72439.	XC-114: 45-874.
C-54B-DO: 43-17124/17198; 44-9001/9025.	YC-116: 45-875.

* Ex-USN in 1945. † Acquired for USN. ‡ Includes 30 for USN
§ Includes 50 for USN. ** Includes 86 for USN.

Douglas RB-66B, in overall natural metal finish (*Douglas photo SM 207389*).

Douglas B-66 Destroyer

The Douglas Model 1326 was developed from the USN A3D Skywarrior to provide the USAF with a tactical light bomber and reconnaissance aircraft. No prototypes were built, the first aircraft to fly (from Long Beach to Edwards AFB on June 28, 1954, piloted by George R. Jansen) being one of five RB-66A models used for type development. Although resembling the A3D in general layout, the RB-66A differed considerably in detail and was virtually a new design, powered by two Allison YJ71-A-9 turbojets. The RB-66A was designed for all-weather night photographic reconnaissance, with a crew of three and provision for two 450 U.S. gallon underwing tanks and probe-and-drogue flight refuelling.

The RB-66B (Douglas Model 1329) was designed for a similar role to the RB-66A and was the first production model; the first flew in March 1955 and deliveries began on February 1, 1956. Contracts totalled 175, of which 30 were completed as RB-66C. This version eventually equipped

Douglas RB-66C, showing wing-tip radomes (*Douglas photo*).

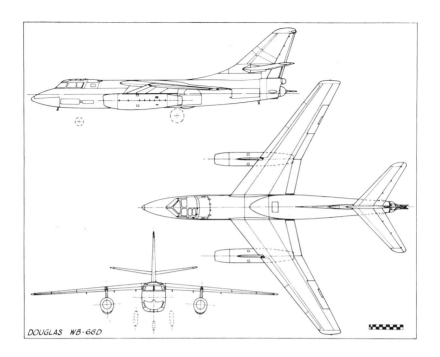

DOUGLAS WB-66D

Nos. 1, 19 and 30 Tactical Reconnaissance Squadrons of the 10th T. R. Wing in Europe, where it first appeared early in 1957. It carried photo-flash bombs in the bomb-bay and a General Electric remotely controlled tail turret with two 20-mm. cannon.

The B-66B (Douglas Model 1327A) first flew on January 4, 1955 and was the only variant in the Destroyer series designed exclusively for the bombing role. Like the RB-66B, it was powered by two 10,200-lb.s.t. Allison J71-A-13 turbojets, and the design gross weight increased from the RB's 70,000 lb. to 78,000 lb. Deliveries of 72 B-66Bs to the USAF began on March 16, 1956.

Produced at the Douglas Tulsa plant, the RB-66C was designed for electronic reconnaissance, with a pressurized ECM compartment between the forward and rear fuselage tanks, in place of the bomb-bay. Carrying four ECM observers, this compartment increased the total crew to seven. The RB-66C had small radomes at the wing tips and a shallow radome under the forward fuselage. Chaff dispensing pods could be carried in place of underwing fuel tanks, and a chaff dispenser could also replace the tail MD-1A fire control system. First flown on October 29, 1955 the RB-66C was first delivered on May 11, 1956. Production totalled 36 including 30 originally ordered as RB-66B.

Final Destroyer version was the WB-66D, of which Tulsa built 36. Designed for electronic weather reconnaissance, this had a weather

295

compartment in the fuselage carrying two observers. Its primary function was to obtain accurate weather data in combat areas, for which reason the tail armament was retained and chaff dispensers were optional, as on the RB-66C. The first WB-66D was flown on June 26, 1957, and production of the Destroyer ended in June 1958.

Many RB-66s were converted to EB-66 electronic jamming and counter-measures aircraft, different standards of equipment distinguishing the EB-66B (13 modified B-66B), EB-66C (RB-66C redesignated with upgraded equipment) and EB-66E (52 modified RB-66B). By the end of 1970, only the EB versions remained in service, primarily in Vietnam with two Tactical Electronic Warfare Squadrons of the 355th Tactical Fighter Wing at Takhli and also with the 39th Tactical Electronic Warfare Squadron in Germany, where the type had been based since 1969.

Two WB-66Ds (55-408 and 55-410) provided the basis for the Northrop X-21A research programme, for which they were fitted with laminar flow wings and rear-fuselage mounted engines.

TECHNICAL DATA (B-66B)

MANUFACTURER: Douglas Aircraft Co., Long Beach, California.
TYPE: Light tactical bomber.
ACCOMMODATION: Three crew.
POWER PLANT: Two 10,000 lb.s.t. Allisoj J71-A-13 turbojets.
DIMENSIONS: Span, 72 ft. 6 in. Length, 75 ft. 2 in. Height, 23 ft. 7 in. Wing area 780 sq. ft.
WEIGHTS: Empty, 42,369 lb. Gross, 83,000 lb.
PERFORMANCE: Max. speed, 594 m.p.h. at 36,000 ft. Range, 1,500 st. miles.
ARMAMENT: Two 20-mm. guns in radar-controlled General Electric tail turret.
SERIAL NUMBERS:

RB-66A: 52-2828/2832.
RB-66B: 53-409/481; 54-417/446; 54-506/547.

B-66B: 53-482/507; 54-477/505; 54-548/551; 55-302/314.
RB-66C: 54-447/476; 55-384/389.
WB-66D: 55-390/425.

Douglas EB-66C conversion of RB-66C for electronic countermeasures.

296

Douglas C-124A Globemaster II modified to C-124C standard (*Douglas photo SM267843*).

Douglas C-124 Globemaster II

Development of the C-124 began in 1947 and was based on the C-74 Globemaster I (see page 636) which was in production from 1945 to 1947. Using the same wing, power plant and tail unit as the C-74, the C-124 had a new deep fuselage with clam-shell nose loading doors and a built-in ramp, but retained the novel elevator hoist amidships which had first featured on the C-74. The prototype C-124 was actually the fifth C-74 with a new fuselage; designated YC-124 (42-65406) it flew on November 27, 1949. Later, this aircraft was fitted with 3,800 h.p. R-4360-35A engines in place of the 3,500 h.p. R-4360-49s and was redesignated YC-124A.

With 3,500 h.p. R-4360-20WA engines, the aircraft went into production as the C-124A (Douglas Model 1129A) at the Long Beach plant, where the first C-124A was completed and delivered to the USAF in May 1950. In all, 204 C-124As were built before a switch was made to the C-124C (Douglas Model 1317), the principal feature of which was a change to 3,800 h.p. R-4360-63A engines. The C-124C also introduced combustion heaters (carried in wing-tip fairings) to heat the cabin and de-ice the wing and tailplane leading edges, and APS-42 weather search radar in a distinctive nose radome. These two features were added retrospectively to most C-124As in service. The C-124C also had increased fuel capacity and higher design gross weight and payload. Total C-124C production was 243, the last aircraft being delivered in May 1955.

Globemaster IIs went into service with squadrons of Tactical Air Command, Military Air Transport Service, Strategic Air Command, Air Materiel Command and Far Eastern Air Force. Early in 1961, C-124s were issued to Troop Carrier Squadrons of the Air Force Reserve.

The single YC-124B (Douglas Model 1182E) was powered by four 5,500 e.h.p. Pratt & Whitney YT34-P-6 turboprops and flew on February 2, 1954 (51-072). This variant had been started in 1951 as a prospective

297

tanker designated YKC-124B, but was subsequently used for engine development flying in connection with the C-133. Another C-124 (52-1069) had a T57 turboprop mounted in the nose for flight trials.

TECHNICAL DATA (C-124C)

MANUFACTURER: Douglas Aircraft Co., Long Beach, California.

TYPE: Heavy cargo transport.

ACCOMMODATION: 68,500 lb. of cargo or 200 passengers or 127 litters and crew of eight.

POWER PLANT: Four 3,800 h.p. Pratt & Whitney R-4360-63A piston radials.

DIMENSIONS: Span, 174 ft. 2 in. Length, 130 ft. 0 in. Height, 48 ft. 4 in. Wing area, 2,506 sq. ft.

WEIGHTS: Empty, 101,165 lb. Gross, 194,500 lb.

PERFORMANCE: Max. speed, 271 m.p.h. at sea level ft. Cruising speed, 230 m.p.h. at 10,000 ft. Initial climb, 625 ft./min. Service ceiling, 18,400 ft. Range, 4,030 st. miles with 26,375 lb. cargo.

ARMAMENT: None.

SERIAL NUMBERS:

C-124A: 48-795; 49-232/259;   YC-124B: 51-072.
   50-083/118; 50-1255/1268; 51-073/182;   C-124C: 51-5188/5213; 51-7272/7285;
   51-5173/5187.   52-939/1089; 53-001/052.

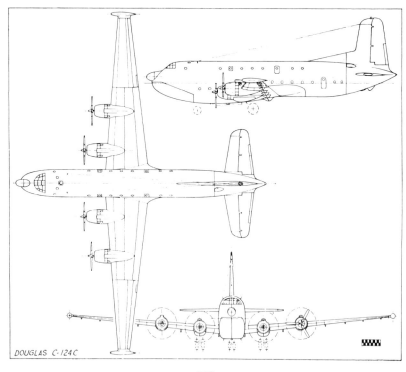

DOUGLAS C-124C

Douglas C-133A over San Francisco Bay (*Douglas photo EST16505*).

Douglas C-133 Cargomaster

An operational requirement for a heavy strategic freighter was drawn up in 1952 following a USAF policy decision to adopt the turboprop engine for its future transport aircraft. The Douglas Model DTS-1333 design was accepted to meet this specification, as the Logistic Carrier Supporting System SS402L, and detail design began in February 1953. No prototypes were built, the type going straight into production as the C-133A against an initial contract for 35 placed in 1954. The engines were Pratt & Whitney T34-P-3 turboprops.

The first C-133A flew on April 23, 1956. Flight tests revealed the need for a few changes, including a larger dorsal fin, and after the first seven aircraft the shape of the rear fuselage cone was changed to a flat "beaver tail" type to improve the airflow. All production C-133s were assigned to MATS, which received the first at Dover A.F.B. on August 29, 1957. At Dover, the 1607th Air Transport Wing's 39th Air Transport Squadron of Eastern Transport Air Force equipped with the Cargomaster, while others went to the 84th Air Transport Squadron of Western Transport Air Force; respectively, these squadrons began operating the C-133As during 1958 on MATS routes to Europe, the Middle East and Africa, and to Honolulu, Wake Island, Japan and Okinawa.

Later production C-133As had 6,500 h.p. T34-P-7W or -7WA turbo-props and the gross weight, originally 255,000 lb., rose to a permissible 282,000 lb; a notable characteristic of the aircraft was that the max. landing weight was also 282,000 lb. The enormous freight hold of the C-133A, with its rear-loading doors, allowed it to transport a wide variety of military stores, including all operational IRBMs and ICBMs such as Atlas, Thor, Jupiter and Titan.

To permit the Titan to be carried in one unit instead of disassembled, clam-shell rear doors, adding 3 ft. to the usable hold length, were introduced on the 33rd production aircraft. Following 35 C-133As, Douglas built 15 C-133Bs (Douglas Model 1430) at the Long Beach factory; this model, in addition to the clam shell doors, had T34-P-9W turboprops, and a gross weight of 286,000 lb. The C-133B first flew on October 31, 1959, and the first was delivered to Travis A.F.B. on March 21, 1960. The C-133s were withdrawn from service in the early 'seventies.

TECHNICAL DATA (C-133A)

MANUFACTURER: The Douglas Aircraft Co., Long Beach, California.

TYPE: Strategic heavy freighter for MATS.

ACCOMMODATION: 13,000 cu. ft. freight volume; 200 passengers optional. Crew of ten comprising three pilots, two navigators, three systems engineers and two loadmasters.

POWER PLANT: Four 6,500 s.h.p. Pratt & Whitney T34-P-7WA turboprops.

DIMENSIONS: Span, 179 ft. 8 in. Length, 157 ft. 6 in. Height, 48 ft. 3 in. Wing area 2,673 sq. ft.

WEIGHTS: Empty, 120,000 lb. Gross, 275,000 lb.

PERFORMANCE: Max. speed, 331 m.p.h. Cruising speed, 300 m.p.h. Initial climb 1,100 ft./min. Service ceiling, 19,400 ft. Range, 3,975 st. miles with 47,000 lb. payload.

ARMAMENT: None.

SERIAL NUMBERS:

C-133A: 54-135/146; 56-1998/2014;   C-133B: 59-522/536.
57-1610/1615.

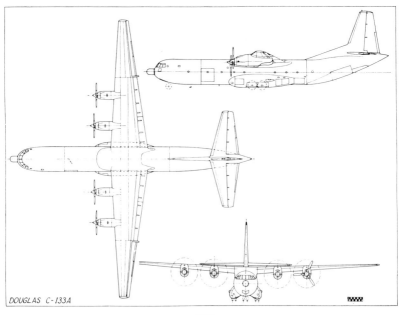

DOUGLAS C-133A

Engineering Division XB-1A (*McCook Field photo 8168*).

Engineering Division XB-1

The Bristol F.2B Fighter, which served the R.F.C. with distinction from April 1917 until the end of World War I, and thereafter remained in service with the Royal Air Force until 1932, was the subject of extensive but less successful design and production development in the U.S. Its adoption for production in the U.S. followed a recommendation in August 1917 by the Bolling Commission, and a sample F.2B arrived in Washington on September 5. Powered by the standard 200 h.p. Hispano-Suiza engine, it was assigned to the Curtiss Aeroplane and Motor Co., which received contracts for 2,000 examples in October and December.

The Curtiss-built Bristols, officially known as U.S.A. O-1s, had 400 h.p. Liberty 12 engines and changes in construction necessary to accommodate the greater power. The first O-1 flew on March 5, 1918, followed by a further batch of 25 with modifications. Further production was cancelled when the re-engined F.2B proved to be over-powered and unsafe, but Curtiss completed and tested one other example—a second British-built specimen imported without an engine and fitted with the 300 h.p. Hispano-Suiza unit. This same engine was also fitted in the first British sample at McCook Field in April 1918, where it was allocated the project number P-30 and became the prototype U.S. B-1. The other British airframe, project number P-37, later flew with the Liberty 8 engine.

At McCook Field, plans were then made to produce four examples each of the O-1 with ply-covered fuselages and the 300 h.p. Wright Hispano and 290 h.p. Liberty 8 respectively. These were to be known as U.S. B-1 and U.S. B-2, while two more examples with each engine and an entirely new plywood fuselage were to be the U.S. B-3 and U.S. B-4 respectively. The original B-1 and B-2 were dropped, whereupon the B-3 and B-4 became the XB-1 and XB-2; the new XB-2 also was eventually abandoned.

The U.S. XB-1 was damaged before its flight test, and was rebuilt with Browning instead of Marlin guns. Redesignated XB-1A, and numbered P-90, it flew on July 3, 1919. With the war over, only small quantities of the aircraft were procured: a production batch of 40 XB-1As, with 300 h.p. Wright Model H engines, was built in 1920-21 by Dayton–Wright.

TECHNICAL DATA (XB-1A)

MANUFACTURER: U.S. Army Engineering Division, McCook Field, Dayton, Ohio.
TYPE: Fighter.
ACCOMMODATION: Pilot and gunner.
POWER PLANT: One 300 h.p. Wright H. piston vee in-line.
DIMENSIONS: Span, 39 ft. 4½ in. Length, 25 ft. 6 in. Height, 9 ft. 9½ in. Wing area, 406 sq. ft.
WEIGHTS: Empty, 2,201 lb. Gross, 3,679 lb.
PERFORMANCE: Max. speed, 121·5 m.p.h. at sea level. Cruising speed, 107 m.p.h. at 15,000 ft. Initial climb 8·4 min. to 6,500 ft. Service ceiling, 16,750 ft. Endurance, 3·8 hr. at 10,000 ft.
ARMAMENT: Two fixed forward firing and two flexible 0·30-in. guns.
SERIAL NUMBERS:

ENG DIV XB-1A: 40124/40125;   D-W USXB-1A: 64156/64193;
   94107/94108.   64300/64301.

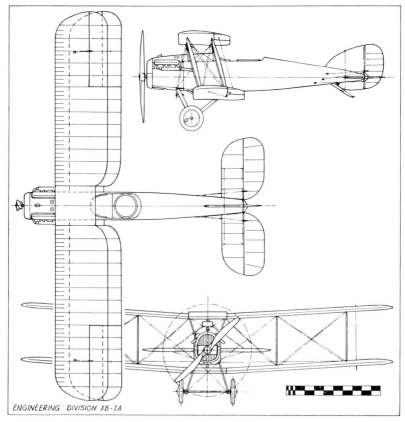

ENGINEERING DIVISION XB-1A

Engineering Division/Sperry Messenger with aerial hook-on device (*USAF photo 11730AC*).

Engineering Division/Sperry Messenger
M-1 and MAT

The Engineering Division Messenger, with no other designation, was designed at McCook Field by Alfred Verville. The little all-wood biplane, smallest aeroplane ever used by the U.S. Army, was intended to serve as the aerial equivalent of a dispatch motorcycle, landing in small clearings in forward areas to deliver and pick up messages from field commanders— hence the name Messenger. The Sperry Aircraft Company of Farmingdale, N.Y., won contracts for the manufacture of 42 Messengers, including prototypes. Since these had not been given a number in the new designation system and were built by Sperry, they became known simply as Sperry Messengers.

The structural simplicity and low cost of the Messenger suited it to experimental work and research. Eight of the first 12 were completed as radio-controlled aerial torpedoes and Sperry was given an additional contract to rebuild three Standard E-1s (page 589) as torpedoes. One Messenger was used to test four sets of wings with different airfoils including a variable-camber type, and two other airfoils were tested on sets of tapered wings. Lawrence Sperry conducted tests of an Army Messenger with jettisonable landing gear; the subsequent landing was made on sprung skids. He also developed a device for hooking-on to an airship in flight and a hand-operated mechanical starter for air-starts. The first drop of a Messenger from the Army blimp TC-7 was made on October 23, 1924; the first hook-on was to the TC-3 on December 12, 1924.

Following revision of the designation system in 1924, the Messengers

303

received the official designations of M-1 and M-1A, and a directive was issued to the effect that reference to the machines as "Sperry" would cease. The torpedoes were to have become AT, but since this would have duplicated the new advanced trainer designation, it was changed to MAT, for Messenger Aerial Torpedo.

TECHNICAL DATA (M-1)

MANUFACTURER: Sperry Aircraft Co., Farmingdale, Long Island, N.Y.
TYPE: Communications.
ACCOMMODATION: Pilot only.
POWER PLANT: One 60 h.p. Lawrance L-4 radial piston engine.
DIMENSIONS: Span, 20 ft. 0 in. Length, 17 ft. 9 in. Height, 6 ft. 9 in. Wing area, 160 sq. ft.
WEIGHTS: Empty, 623 lb. Gross, 862 lb.
PERFORMANCE: Max. speed, 96·7 m.p.h. Minimum speed, 45 m.p.h. Initial climb, 700 ft./min.
ARMAMENT: None.
SERIAL NUMBERS:
M.1: 64223/64227.   22-1/5.
    68472/68477.   22-329/348.
    68528/68533.   22-6 (rebuild of 64227).
              M.1A: 22-329/348

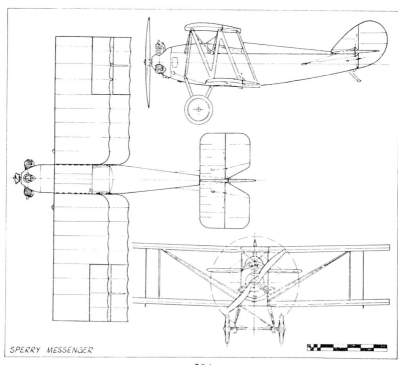

SPERRY MESSENGER

All-silver Fairchild AT-21 showing red border around national marking, used only from July to September 1943 (*Fairchild photo*).

Fairchild AT-13, AT-14, AT-21 Gunner

The introduction of gun turrets on a large scale in combat aircraft brought with it the need to provide adequate air-to-air gunnery training and practice. When the U.S. entered World War II, no specialized gunnery schools existed (by 1944 there were seven) and contracts had been placed by the Army for only two prototypes of a specialized trainer which was to become the first specifically produced for use in these schools.

The first of these prototypes, the Fairchild XAT-13, was designed as a bomber crew trainer, with provision for training all members of a medium bomber crew. It carried a flexibly-mounted nose gun and a second 0·30 gun in a dorsal power turret, and had a small fuselage bomb-bay. Training stations could be provided for a bombardier, navigator, gunner and radio operator, as well as a pilot and instructor. Powered by 600 h.p. R-1340-AN-1 radial engines, the XAT-13 featured Duramold plastic-bonded plywood in its construction.

The similar XAT-14 was powered by 520 h.p. Ranger V-770-6 in-line engines and was later adapted, as the XAT-14A, as a specific bombardier trainer with nose-gun and turret removed.

In 1942, the same basic type was ordered into production as a gunnery trainer, with a two-gun dorsal turret and a single nose gun, and no bomb-bay. In this guise it was designated AT-21 and was powered by 520 h.p. Ranger V-770-11 or -15 engines. Fairchild had built 106—one at Hagerstown and the remainder at Burlington—by the time production ended in October 1944, and two additional production lines were laid down in 1942 to meet the then urgent demand for a trainer of this type. Bellanca built 39 AT-21s at New Castle, Delaware, and McDonnell built a further 30 at their St. Louis plant. Projected production on a much larger scale was cancelled.

AT-21s served at several of the specialized gunnery schools but were eventually replaced by training versions of the operational aircraft on which the gunners were to serve. Many of the AT-21s were then relegated to target-tow duties.

TECHNICAL DATA (AT-21)

MANUFACTURER: The Fairchild Engine & Airplane Corporation, Hagerstown, Md. Burlington, N.C. McDonnell Aircraft Corp., St. Louis, Mo. Bellanca Aircraft Corporation, New Castle, Del.

TYPE: Gunnery trainer.

ACCOMMODATION: Pilot, co-pilot/instructor and three student gunners.

POWER PLANT: Two 520 h.p. Ranger V-770-11 piston vee in-line.

DIMENSIONS: Span, 52 ft. 8 in. Length, 37 ft. 0 in. Height, 13 ft. 1 in. Wing area, 375 sq. ft.

WEIGHTS: Empty, 8,700 lb. Gross, 12,500 lb.

PERFORMANCE: Cruising speed, 195 m.p.h. at 12,000 ft. Initial climb, 10·3 min. to 10,000 ft. Service ceiling, 22,400 ft. Range, 870 st. miles at cruise speed.

ARMAMENT: Three 0·30-in. m.g. No bombs.

SERIAL NUMBERS:

XAT-13: 41-19500.

XAT-14: 41-19503.

AT-21-FA: 42-11679.

AT-21-FB: 42-11680/11753;
  41-76615/76645.

AT-21-BL: 42-48052/48090.

AT-21-MC: 42-48412/48441.

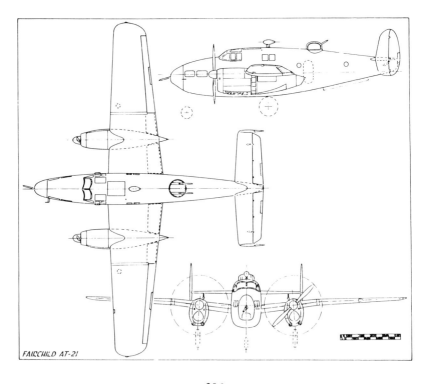

FAIRCHILD AT-21

Fairchild PT-19B in 1943 trainer markings with cockpit canopy used mainly on PT-26 model for Canada (*Fairchild photo 5263*).

Fairchild PT-19, PT-23, PT-26

Although Army policy tended eventually to favour the biplane for primary pilot training programmes in World War II, the Fairchild low-wing trainers were built in almost as large a number as the Boeing-Stearman biplanes, and were widely used in U.S. training schools. Having been developed by Fairchild as the M-62, this design was first purchased by the Army in 1940 as the rapid expansion of the Air Corps got under way, and was designated PT-19. Powered by the 175 h.p. Ranger L-440-1 engine, the PT-19 had tandem seating in open cockpits and a gross weight of 2,550 lb. Production totalled 270.

Massive orders for the Fairchild trainer in 1941 led to a doubling of the company's production facilities, but the demand exceeded capacity at Hagerstown and additional sources were provided by production lines

Fairchild PT-19A in blue and yellow 1941 trainer finish (*Peter M. Bowers*).

put down by Aeronca and St. Louis. All three built the PT-19A version, with the 200 h.p. L-440-3 engine and detail improvements. Production totals were 3,182 by Fairchild, 477 by Aeronca and 44 by St. Louis.

Introduction of equipment for blind-flying instruction, including a hood for the front cockpit, changed the designation to PT-19B. Fairchild built 774 of these, and Aeronca produced a further 143.

With production of the Ranger engine lagging behind airframe output in 1942, Fairchild converted a PT-19A (41-15172) to have an uncowled Continental R-670-5 engine; this prototype was designated XPT-23, and production PT-23s were built by Fairchild (two, with R-670-4 engines); Aeronca (375 with the -4 engine); Howard (199, with -4 or -5 engine); St. Louis (200, with -11 engine) and Fleet in Canada (93, with -4 engine). The PT-23A had blind-flying provision; Howard built 150 and St. Louis 106.

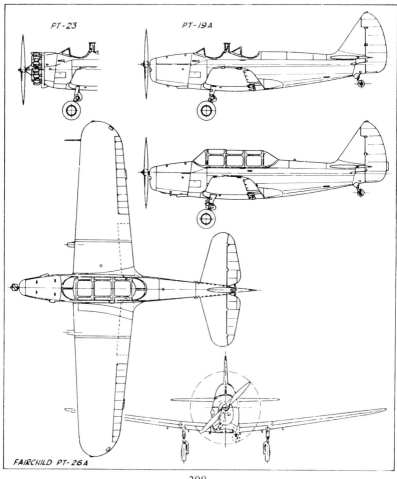

For use in the Commonwealth Air Training Scheme in Canada, a version of PT-19A was fitted with a canopy over the two cockpits and re-designated PT-26. Fairchild built 670 for Lend–Lease to the R.C.A.F., and the Army paid for another 807 PT-26A and 250 PT-26B built by Fleet in Canada.

TECHNICAL DATA (PT-19A, PT-23A)

MANUFACTURER: The Fairchild Engine & Airplane Corporation, Hagerstown; The Aeronca Aircraft Corporation, Middletown, Ohio; The St. Louis Aircraft Corporation, St. Louis, Mo.; Howard Aircraft Corporation, St. Charles, Ill. and Fleet Aircraft Corp., Fort Erie, Ontario.

TYPE: Primary trainer.

ACCOMMODATION: Pupil and instructor in tandem open cockpits.

POWER PLANT (PT-19A): One 175 h.p. Ranger L-440-1 piston in-line.
(PT-23A): One 220 h.p. Continental R-670-4, -5 or -11 piston radial.

DIMENSIONS: Span, 36 ft. 0 in. Length (PT-19A), 28 ft. 0 in. (PT-23A), 25 ft. 11 in. Height (PT-19A), 10 ft. 6 in. (PT-23A), 10 ft. 0 in. Wing area, 200 sq. ft.

WEIGHTS: Empty (PT-19A), 1,845 lb. (PT-23A), 2,045 lb. Gross (PT-19A), 2,545 lb. (PT-23A), 2,450 lb.

PERFORMANCE: Max. speed (PT-19A), 132 m.p.h. (PT-23A), 128 m.p.h. Climb (PT-19A), 17·5 min. to 10,000. (PT-23A), 19·4 min. to 10,000 ft. Service ceiling (PT-19A), 15,300 ft. (PT-23A), 13,200 ft. Range (PT-19A), 400 st. miles (PT-23A), 330 st. miles.

ARMAMENT: None.

SERIAL NUMBERS:

PT-19: 40-2418/2687.

PT-19A-FA: 41-040/139; 41-14600/15172; 41-20146/20590; 41-25197/25201; 42-2514/2961; 42-14708/14712; 42-33384/34418; 42-34420/34513; 42-83366/83662; 43-33665/33844.

PT-19A-AE: 42-47827/47834; 42-47978/48051; 42-65452/65551; 43-31363/31657.

PT-19A-SL: 42-50027/50070.

PT-19B-FA: 42-34419; 42-34514/34583; 42-82663/83365.

PT-19B-AE: 42-47835/47977.

PT-23-FA: 42-2962/2963.

PT-23-AE: 42-47452/47826.

PT-23-HO: 42-49077/49260; 42-49262/49276.

PT-23-SL: 42-49677/49876.

PT-23-FE: 42-70864/70956.

PT-23A-HO: 42-49277/49426.

PT-23A-SL: 42-49877/49982.

PT-26-FA: 42-14299/14498; 42-15330/15529; 44-19288/19557.

PT-26A-FE: 42-65585/66001; 42-70957/71346.

PT-26B-FE: 43-36248/36497.

Fairchild XPT-23 at Wright Field. Tail letters identify Aeroplane No 70 of Materiel Division. Note Wright Field arrow. (*Peter M. Bowers*).

Fairchild C-82A dropping paratroops (*Planet News 217747*).

Fairchild C-82 and C-119 Flying Boxcar

Fairchild undertook the design of a specialized military freighter to meet an Army requirement in 1941. The largest Fairchild project to date, this Model F-78 was designed around the concept of a large, uninterrupted cargo hold, with direct access for loading at near ground level. To achieve the latter, a twin boom layout was adopted, with the wing mounted high on the deep fuselage, which ended in clam-shell doors at the rear providing for straight-in loading of vehicles up ramps, or of freight from trucks at the same height as the fuselage floor. The fuselage cross section was adequate for trucks, howitzers, half-tracks, tanks and other Army vehicles. Two 2,100 h.p. Pratt & Whitney R-2800-85 radial engines provided power.

The F-78 design and a mock-up were approved in 1942 and a contract for one prototype designated XC-82 was placed. This aircraft (43-13202) flew on September 10, 1944, by which time Fairchild had received a contract for 100 C-82A Packets. Deliveries began at the end of 1945, and intensive service tests followed, to prove new features of the design including a wing and tail de-icing system using hot air, and to develop suitable operating technique. For air-dropping of vehicles and other large items, the rear fuselage doors were removed completely and a system was developed in which a drogue parachute was deployed and used to draw the vehicle out of the rear of the hold, after which the main parachute cluster was opened. For paratrooping, with 42 troops, small doors in each side of the rear fuselage were used. The C-82 could carry 34 stretchers, and was suitable for glider towing: in trials early in 1946, a Waco CG-15 and a Waco CG-4A were towed simultaneously.

Fairchild C-119C operating in Europe (*Crown Copyright*).

In 1945, Fairchild received a contract for another 100 C-82As and North American Aviation was asked by the USAF to undertake production also. A second production line was laid down at Dallas and work began on a contract for 792 Packets similar to the Fairchild model and designated C-82N. Only three of these were completed, however, before this contract was cancelled after VJ Day. Fairchild eventually built 220 Packets. Deliveries ended in September, 1948.

The C-82s were assigned to Troop Carrier squadrons of TAC in 1946 and subsequently some were also allocated to MATS. Five were assigned to the Berlin Air Lift, primarily to carry vehicles into the city. One aircraft (45-57746) was tested with Firestone tracked undercarriage units, and was designated EC-82A. The Packet was declared obsolete in 1954.

During 1947, an improved version of the Packet was developed by Fairchild as the XC-82B. The principal modifications from the basic design were the relocation of the flight deck, forward and lower, with new nose contours; removal of the ventral fins; and use of 2,650 h.p. R-4360 engines. One C-82 (45-57769) was modified to this form with R-4360-4 engines, and was eventually redesignated C-119A; it first flew in November 1947. Accepted by the USAF for production as a successor to the C-82, the C-119 Flying Boxcar was further modified from this prototype, to have a fuselage 14 inches wider, and structural changes in the wings to

Fairchild C-119F with Arctic markings (*Peter M. Bowers*).

311

Fairchild C-119J conversion from C-119G, showing beaver-tail [*M. Olmstead*].

permit higher gross weights. The troop capacity went up to 62.

Initial production version of the Flying Boxcar was the C-119B, which had the wide fuselage and R-4360-20 engines. The wing span increased from the C-82's 106 ft. 6 in. to 109 ft. 3 in. and the gross weight went up from 54,000 lb. to 74,000 lb. Deliveries of 54 of this model began in December 1949. It was followed by the C-119C which was powered by 3,500 h.p. R-4360-20WA engines with water injection. This model also introduced as standard the long dorsal fins which were flown experimentally on a C-119B (48-319); associated with this change was the deletion of the tailplane sections outboard of the booms. To speed production of the C-119C during the Korean War, a second production line was established by Kaiser Manufacturing Co. at Willow Run and this company assembled 41 of the 303 C-119Cs built by Fairchild.

Both companies also built the C-119F, in which R-3350-85 engines were used and the gross weight increased to 85,000 lb. Angular ventral fins on each boom were a later modification. Production of this model totalled 139 by Fairchild and 71 by Kaiser. The most-produced Boxcar variant was the C-119G, similar to the F apart from its Aero-products propellers which replaced the Hamilton Standards. Of 396 C-119Gs built by Fairchild, 88 were assigned to foreign air forces under Mutual Defence. Kaiser also built 88 C-119Gs. Some years after delivery, all C-119Bs were converted to C-119Cs, and all C-119Fs became C-119Gs.

The C-119s served principally with Troop Carrier Command wings, and also with MATS. They saw service over Korea, flying from Japan, where the C-119-equipped 314th Troop Carrier Group arrived in August 1950, and participated, from 1953, in ferrying of supplies to the Arctic for construction of the DEW Line. Nine specially-modified JC-119s equipping the 6593rd Test Squadron played a major part in the Discoverer satellite test programme in 1960, successfully using an aerial snatch technique to recover three capsules during their descent from orbit.

The last-mentioned aircraft were re-allocated to the 434th Aerospace Troop Carrier and Capsule Recovery Wing of the Air Force Reserve in 1961, this being the newest of many AFRes units to fly the type:

others included the 94th, 403rd, 435th, 440th, 442nd, 459th, 512th and 514th Troop Carrier Wings. Other units such as the 14th and 183rd Aeromedical Transport Squadrons also were equipped with C-119s.

Among experimental variants of the type tested were the original C-119A, which later flew with wingtip radomes as part of a test programme associated with the XC-120; and the C-119F (51-8119) which had an experimental "beaver" tail with flight operable door and ventral ramp. The "beaver" tail was subsequently introduced as a retrospective modification on a total of 68 C-119Fs and C-119Gs, which were then redesignated C-119Js. The MC-119J designation was used for aircraft equipped for medevac duties, and a small number of EC-119Js were equipped for satellite tracking. The YC-119D and YC-119E designations applied to a version of the C-119 with a detachable fuselage pod and three-wheel main undercarriage units, powered respectively with R-4360 and R-3350 engines. Neither of these variants, for which the designations C-128A and C-128B had also been provisionally reserved, was built.

The YC-119H Skyvan, of which a single prototype (51-2585) was built, was an extensive revision of the design, with a 148 ft. span wing of 40 per cent

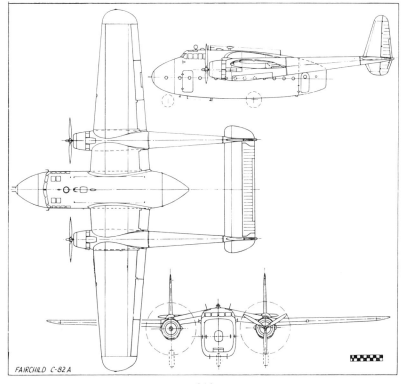

FAIRCHILD C-82A

Fairchild Hiller AC-119G gunship conversion (*Stephen P. Peltz*).

greater area, all fuel in two external tanks under the wings, a larger tail unit and two R-3350-85 engines. The gross weight was 86,000 lb. The YC-119H first flew on May 27, 1952.

Also in the same series was the XC-120 Packplane (48-330), first flown on August 11, 1950. This comprised a C-119B wing and tail unit, with a flight deck in an upper fuselage component. The lower component was a detachable cargo-carrying pod, the XC-120 being flyable with or without this fitted.

The introduction of Lockheed C-130s allowed the C-119s to be gradually withdrawn from the regular squadrons and assigned to AF Reserve units. By 1970, five Reserve units were still flying the C-119Js in the airlift role.

Fairchild Hiller AC-119K. For night operations it has black undersides and vertical tail surfaces, and small national insignia (*Fairchild Hiller photo*).

During May 1966, Fairchild Hiller Corporation (as the company had become two years previously) began the design of a jet-augmented version of the C-119. Identified as the YC-119K, this aircraft made its first flight in February 1967, and was distinguished primarily by the provision of two podded 2,850 lb. s.t. General Electric J85-GE-17 turbojets, one beneath each wing. Uprated R-3350 piston engines were also fitted, and the gross weight increased from 69,000 lb. to 77,000 lb. Five C-119Gs were converted to C-119Ks in 1970.

Development of a gunship version was started by Fairchild Hiller as a matter of extreme urgency late in 1967, to provide a replacement for the Douglas AC-47s in Vietnam. Armament in this aircraft, which was Gunship Three in the USAF programme, comprised four General Electric SUU-11 gun pods, each containing a six-barrel 7·62 mm. GAU-2 Minigun. These guns were mounted along the port side of the fuselage, to fire through square gun ports. Much additional avionics gear was fitted, together with an AN/AVQ-8 airborne illuminator light set and night observation system, and a 60-kva. APU to generate the additional electrical power.

The USAF contracted for 52 of these gunships, converted from C-119Gs. The first 26 were AC-119Gs, with delivery of the first being made to the USAF on May 19, 1968. Following the AC-119Gs were 26 AC-

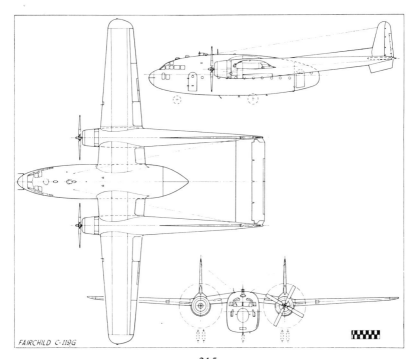

FAIRCHILD C-119G

315

119Ks, similarly converted from C-119Gs but differing from the first batch of gunships in having underwing J85 jet pods and two SUU-16 gun pods each containing a 20 mm. M61A1 gun. These weapons were mounted for and aft of the SUU-11 pods in the fuselage.

The AC-119Gs went into service with the 17th SOS of the 14th Special Operations Wing in Vietnam early in 1969, taking the local soubriquet of Shadow. They were followed later in the year by the AC-119K Stingers used by the 18th SOS. Finally, 22 C-119Gs became C-119Ls when fitted with three-bladed propellers; a few RC-119Ls were specially equipped. The 130th Special Operations Group, West Virginia ANG, flew the last C-119s in service until September 1975.

TECHNICAL DATA (C-82A)

MANUFACTURER: The Fairchild Engine and Airplane Corporation, Aircraft Division, Hagerstown, Maryland.
TYPE: Troop and supply transport.
ACCOMMODATION: Two pilots, navigator and radio operator.
POWER PLANT: Two 2,100 h.p. Pratt & Whitney R-2800-85 piston radials.
DIMENSIONS: Span, 106 ft. 5½ in. Length, 77 ft. 1 in. Height, 26 ft. 4 in. Wing area, 1,400 sq. ft.
WEIGHTS: Empty, 32,500 lb. Gross, 54,000 lb.
PERFORMANCE: Max. speed, 248 m.p.h. at 17,500 ft. Cruising speed, 218 m.p.h. at 10,000 ft. Initial climb, 950 ft./min. Service ceiling, 21,200 ft. Range, 3,875 st. miles.
ARMAMENT: None.
SERIAL NUMBERS:
XC-82: 43-13202.   C-82N: 45-25436/25438.
C-82A: 44-22959/23058; 45-57733/57832;
 48-568/587.

TECHNICAL DATA (C-119G)

As C-82A except as follows:
ACCOMMODATION: Flight crew of two pilots, navigator and radio operator, plus flight mechanic and loadmaster. Up to 62 troops (normally 42) or 35 stretchers plus four attendants.
POWER PLANT: Two 3,500 Wright R-3350-89A piston radials.
DIMENSIONS: Span, 109 ft. 3 in. Length, 86 ft. 6 in. Height, 26 ft. 6 in. Wing area, 1,447 sq. ft.
WEIGHTS: Empty, 40,785 lb. Gross, 72,700 lb.
PERFORMANCE: Max. speed, 281 m.p.h. at 18,000 ft. Cruising speed, 186 m.p.h. at 5,000 ft. Initial climb, 852 ft./min. Service ceiling, 21,580 ft. Range, 1,630 st. miles.
SERIAL NUMBERS:

C-119B: 48-319/355*; 49-101/118.
C-119C-FA: 49-119/199; 50-119/171;
 51-2532/2584; 51-2587/2661.
C-119C-KM: 51-8233/8273.
C-119F-FA: 51-2586; 51-2662/2686;
 51-2690/2717; 51-7968/8052.
C-119F-KM: 51-8098/8168.

C-119G-FA: 51-8053/8097;
 51-17365/17367†;
 52-5840/5954; 52-6000/6058†;
 52-9981/9982; 53-3136/3222;
 53-4637/4662†; 53-7826/7884.
C-119G-KM: 53-8069/8156.

*Includes one static test airframe.
†88 for MAP delivery to Italy, India and Belgium.

Fairchild C-123B in TAC service (*USAF photo*).

Fairchild (Chase) C-123 Provider

Fairchild-built C-123Bs entered service with the 309th Troop Carrier Group of Troop Carrier Command in July 1955 after an interesting, if somewhat protracted, period of development. The basis of the design was the XG-20 cargo glider produced by Chase Aircraft in 1949.

Of all-metal construction, the XG-20 was designed from the start to be adapted as a powered assault transport, and on October 14, 1949, the first prototype (47-786) flew with two R-2800-83 engines in wing nacelles. In this guise it was re-designated XC-123 Avitruc. The second prototype was fitted with four J47 turbojets in paired pods under the wing and became the XC-123A, first flown on April 21, 1951. In 1952, contracts were placed with Chase for five pre-production model C-123Bs, and after Kaiser-Frazer Corporation acquired a majority interest in Chase in 1953, a production contract for 300 was awarded.

Chase built and flew its five C-123Bs (52-1627/31) at Willow Run in 1953, but difficulties encountered by Kaiser-Frazer led to cancellation of their contract on June 24, 1953, in favour of a new contract placed with Fairchild later the same year. Fairchild then assumed responsibility for the continued flight development of the Chase-built C-123Bs, and introduced on these a large dorsal fin which became standard on the production aircraft. The first Fairchild-built C-123 Provider (54-552) flew on September 1, 1954, piloted by E. R. Gelvin. Production totalled 302 on USAF contracts, including one static test airframe and 24 for MAP delivery to Venezuela and Saudi Arabia. The VC-123C command transport version planned by Kaiser was not built.

The C-123 designation was also carried by two versions developed by Stroukoff Aviation, a company formed by the original designer of the aircraft when he was employed by Chase Aircraft. These were the YC-123D (53-8068) which had boundary layer control by means of suction slots in the upper wing surfaces; and the YC-123E (55-4031) with a "Panto-base" undercarriage for sand, snow, ice, water and land operations.

317

Fairchild C-123B support aircraft for the Thunderbirds aerobatic team, in the latter's distinctive markings (*M. Olmstead*).

Stroukoff also modified the first C-123B (52-1627) to the YC-134, intended to test a boundary layer control system. This prototype had Wright R-3350-89A turbo-compound engines with four-bladed propellers, a longer and wider fuselage, and a much-modified undercarriage. Small endplate fins and rudders replaced the dorsal fin, and when Pantobase hydro-skis were fitted it became the YC-134A.

In addition to the production batch of C-123Bs, USAF contracted with Fairchild for a single YC-123H, the principal new feature of which was a wide track undercarriage to overcome the aircraft's tendency to capsize when taxying in a strong cross wind. Subsequently, some C-123Bs were earmarked for conversion to C-123H standard. In 1962, the YC-123H was fitted with two General Electric CJ610 turbojets in underwing pods, to demonstrate improved performance of the aircraft as an assault transport, the first flight in this guise being made on July 30, 1962.

Previously, in 1957, Fairchild had fitted two of its own J44-R-3 turbo-

Fairchild C-123K, showing added underwing jet pods (*Fairchild Hiller photo 42-991*).

318

Fairchild UC-123K in South-East Asia camouflage, with spray bars under the wing for defoliation missions (*MAP photo*).

jets in wing-tip nacelles on a Provider, first flown in this form on October 23, 1957. Ten aircraft were modified to this configuration for the USAF as C-123Js, to serve as support aircraft for DEW-Line installation in the Arctic. Provision for a ski/wheel landing gear was made and these C-123Js were operated by the Alaskan ANG.

A third jet-boost configuration was developed by Fairchild Hiller in 1966 to produce the C-123K. This had 2,850 lb. s.t. J85-GE-17 turbojets pod-mounted under each wing. First flight of the C-123K was made on May 27, 1966, and Fairchild Hiller converted 183 C-123Bs to this standard by September 1969.

Many Providers operated in Vietnam, where special requirements led to the modification of 34 C-123Ks to UC-123Ks with underwing spray bars, for defoliation missions; the last few UC-123Ks eventually served, until 1986, with a Reserve unit. Two NC-123Ks (sometimes called AC-123Ks) had extensive equipment changes and carried sensors, to fly night interdiction/reconnaissance missions in Korea and, later, Vietnam, and a single

Fairchild NC-123K as modified for Project Black Spot in 1968 and operated in Vietnam until 1970, in overall four-tone camouflage (*MAP photo*).

319

VC-123K was the personal transport of General Westmoreland in Vietnam, flown by the 24th Special Operations Wing.

TECHNICAL DATA (C-123B)

MANUFACTURER: The Fairchild Engine and Airplane Corporation, Aircraft Division, Hagerstown, Md.
TYPE: Troop and supply transport.
ACCOMMODATION: Two pilots; 61 troops or 50 litters with six sitting wounded and six attendants.
POWER PLANT: Two 2,300 h.p. Pratt & Whitney R-2800-99W piston radials.
DIMENSIONS: Span, 110 ft. 0 in. Length, 75 ft. 9 in. Height, 34 ft. 1 in. Wing area, 1,223 sq. ft.
WEIGHTS: Empty, 29,900 lb. Gross, 60,000 lb.
PERFORMANCE: Max. speed, 245 m.p.h. Cruising speed, 205 m.p.h. Initial climb, 1,150 ft./min. Service ceiling, 29,000 ft. Range, 1,470 st. miles.
ARMAMENT: None.
SERIAL NUMBERS:
C-123B-CN: 52-1627/1631.   C-123B-FA: 54-552/553; 54-555/715;
YC-123H: 54-2956.   55-4505/4577; 56-4355/4396;
                                                       57-6185/6202; 57-6289/6294.

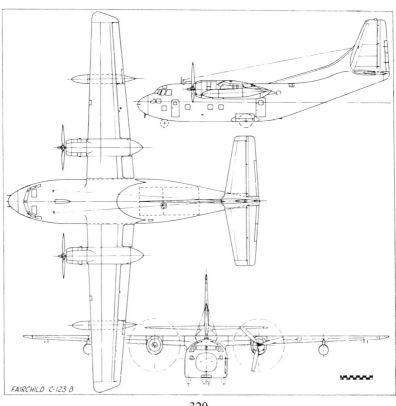

FAIRCHILD C-123 B

Fairchild A-10A in Europe 1 finish and with "SU" tail code indicating the 51st TF Wing at Suwon, South Korea (*Robbie Shaw*).

Fairchild A-10 Thunderbolt II

In 1967 the USAF initiated a design competition for a close air support (CAS) aircraft in a programme then identified as A-X. The concept grew out of experience gained in Vietnam and was for an aircraft that was uncomplicated, easy to maintain in the field and required the minimum of ground support facilities so that it could operate from small forward bases close to the battle line. It was to carry large ordnance loads and to be able to withstand extensive battle damage, but high-speed performance was of less importance.

Northrop and Fairchild received contracts on December 18, 1970, to build two prototypes each of their A-X submissions, and designations YA-9 and YA-10 were assigned, respectively. The two Fairchild YA-10s made their first flights on May 10 and July 21, 1972 and after competitive evaluation with the YA-9s at the end of that year, the Fairchild design was adopted for production on January 18, 1973. The first contract was placed with Fairchild on March 1, 1973, and covered six YA-10As to be used for development, test and evaluation. Small changes distinguished the YA-10As, the first of which flew on February 15, 1975, from the YA-10 prototypes, including a small increase in wing span and area, production TF34-GE-100 engines in place of YTF-34s, an improved windscreen and changes to the flight control and landing gear systems.

Acquisition of a planned total of 739 A-10As began with FY 75 funds but annual increments up to FY 82 brought the production total to only 713, when procurement was brought to an end. The first production A-10A flew on October 21, 1975, and deliveries to TAC began in March 1976, for use by the training squadrons of the 355th TTW. A year later, the 354th TFW at Myrtle Beach, South Carolina, became the first operational unit to receive the A-10A, which became known universally by the nickname "Warthog" before the name Thunderbolt II was officially bestowed in April 1978.

Production deliveries of the A-10A were completed in March 1984, and the type was used to equip the 23rd and 354th TFWs in TAC, the 81st TFW in Europe, the 18th and 25th TFS respectively in Alaska and Korea, four Air Force Reserve and five ANG units within the United States. In 1978, the first YA-10A was modified to YA-10B with a second raised seat for a weapons system operator, to demonstrate the aircraft's night/adverse weather capabilities when suitably equipped. First flight was made on May 4, 1979, but no production ensued.

Development began in 1987 of the OA-10A as a single-seat Forward Air Control aircraft, for deployment from 1989 onwards as a replacement for the Cerrua OA-37Bs in the FAC role.

TECHNICAL DATA (A-10A)

MANUFACTURER: Fairchild Republic Company (division of Fairchild Industries Inc), Farmingdale, Long Island, N.Y.
TYPE: Close support attack aircraft.
ACCOMMODATION: Pilot only.
POWER PLANT: Two 9,065 lb.s.t. General Electric TF34-GE-100 turbofans.
DIMENSIONS: Span, 57 ft. 6 in. Length, 53 ft. 4 in. Height, 14 ft. 8 in. Wing area, 506 sq. ft.
WEIGHTS: Empty, 25,600 lb. Gross, 50,000 lb.
PERFORMANCE: Max. speed, 439 m.p.h. at sea level. Cruising speed, 387 m.p.h. at 5,000 ft. Initial climb, 6,000 ft./min. Service ceiling, 30,500 ft. Radius, (deep strike mission) 620 miles.
ARMAMENT: One 30-mm. General Electric GAU-8A Avenger multi-barrel cannon in nose. Eleven external stores stations (three on fuselage, one each inner wing, three each outer wing), for maximum 16,000 lb. load, including bombs, up to six AGM-65B Maverick missiles and/or four AIM-9L Sidewinder missiles.
SERIAL NUMBERS:
    YA-10A: 71-1369/1370.
    A-10A: 73-1664/1669; 75-258/309; 76-512/554; 77-177/276;
    78-582/725; 79-082/225;   80-140/283; 81-939/998; 82-646/665.

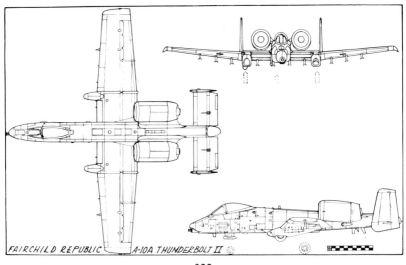

FAIRCHILD REPUBLIC   A-10A THUNDERBOLT II

Fokker C-2, serial 26-204 (*Fokker photo from N.A.A.*).

Fokker C-2, C-5, C-7

In the autumn of 1925 the Army tested the prototype Fokker F-VIIA/3m, which had been rushed to completion in Holland for the first Ford Reliability Tour. As a result of this testing, three similar aircraft were ordered with the designation C-2. These differed from the prototype mainly in the use of 220 h.p. Wright J-5 engines instead of J-4s, a re-designed pilot's cockpit, and a larger fuselage.

It was decided that the first C-2 would be used for an Army trans-pacific flight, so 26-202 was completed as a long-range machine with a special Holland-built wing of 71 ft. 2 in. span in place of the standard 63 ft. C-2 wing. Under the name "Bird of Paradise", this aeroplane made the first transpacific flight, 2,400 miles from Oakland to Honolulu, piloted by Lts. Lester J. Maitland and Albert Hegenberger, on June 1, 1927.

Eight C-2As (28-119/126) were ordered, using a long wing similar to that of the first C-2. By far the best known of these was 28-120, named the "Question Mark", which established an air-refuelling endurance record of 150 hours in January 1929.

A single C-5 (29-405) was a 12-passenger commercial Fokker F-10A with Wright R-975s substituted for Pratt & Whitney Wasps. The XC-7 was a C-2A (28-126) with engines changed to 330 h.p. Wright J-6-9 (R-975). It and four other C-2As similarly re-engined became C-7s. The six production C-7As (29-407/412) had a slightly larger wing, new vertical fins and fuselages patterned after the commercial Fokker F-10As.

TECHNICAL DATA (C-2, C-2A, C-7)

MANUFACTURER: Atlantic Aircraft Corporation, Teterboro Airport, New Jersey.
TYPE: Personnel and cargo transport.
ACCOMMODATION: (C-2) Eight passengers; (C-2A, C-7), ten passengers.

C-2: 26-202/204.	C-5: 29-405.
C-2A: 28-119/126.	C-7A: 29-407/412.

	C-2	C-2A	C-7
Power Plant:	3 × 220 h.p. Wright R-790	3 × 220 h.p. Wright R-790	3 × 330 h.p. Wright R-975
Dimensions:			
Span, ft., in.	63 6	74 2¼	72 10¾
Length, ft., in.	47 6	48 4	48 9
Height, ft., in.	13 1	13 6	13 0
Wing area, sq. ft.	577·75	718	748
Weights:			
Empty, lb.	5,061	6,507	7,033
Gross, lb.	7,646	10,394	11,026
Performance:			
Max. speed, m.p.h.	120	112·8	136·3
Cruising speed, m.p.h.	—	90	110
Climb	16 min. to 6,500 ft.	645 ft./min.	910 ft./min.
Service ceiling, ft.	15,000	—	18,500
Range	5 hours	296 miles	—

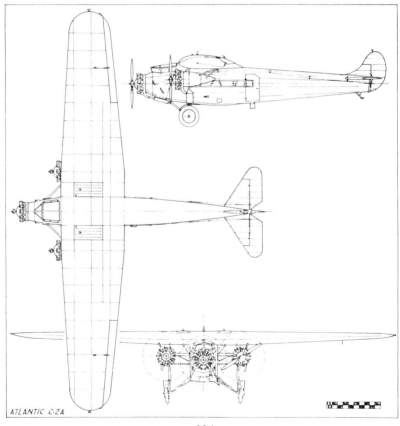

ATLANTIC C-2A

324

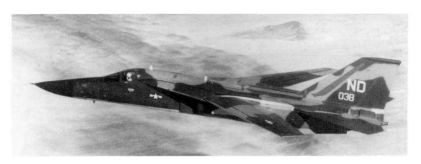

General Dynamics F-111A (*General Dynamics photo 30-45829*).

General Dynamics F-111, FB-111, EF-111

Development of one of the most controversial warplanes which has ever entered service with the USAF began in the late 1950s when the need for a replacement for the Republic F-105 in Tactical Air Command first began to be studied. The aeroplane wanted by the Air Force was to have good short and rough field performance, low level supersonic dash coupled with over Mach 2 speed at high altitude and unrefuelled ferry range sufficient to cross the Atlantic or Pacific.

Known in its formative stages as the TFX, this requirement was combined, at Department of Defense insistence, with a US Navy requirement for an air superiority fighter to replace the F4H Phantom. The combined requirement was issued as SOR (Specific Operational Requirement) 183 in 1960, and in January 1962 General Dynamics and Boeing were selected as finalists in the design competition. Both designs were closely similar at this stage, although based respectively on Pratt & Whitney and General Electric engines, and both featured variable wing sweep-back.

This feature, offered for the first time in an operational air force fighter, made it possible to achieve the slow speeds for good take-off and landing together with the high speeds for combat missions.

The General Dynamics TFX design was selected by the DoD on November 24, 1962, and work proceeded immediately on a development batch of 23 aircraft, designated F-111A for the USAF and F-111B for the USN. Five of the test aircraft were completed as F-111Bs by Grumman, which had been made responsible for the Navy version, but the Navy programme was subsequently cancelled.

First flight of the F-111A was made at Fort Worth on December 21, 1964, by Richard Johnson and Val Prahl, with the remaining aircraft in the development batch coming into the programme in 1965 and 1966.

Initial production contracts had by this time been placed by the USAF, which had indicated an eventual total requirement for 1,469 aircraft. Subsequent problems, changes in operational requirement and cost

325

evaluation led to this planned procurement being reduced to about 520 aeroplanes.

The first production batch totalled 141 F-111As, delivery of which began in October 1967. Whereas the development aircraft had TF30-P-1 engines, the production F-111A switched to the uprated P-3 engine. First unit to receive the F-111A was the 4480th Tactical Fighter Wing, but the normal sequence of introducing a new combat aircraft into the USAF was short-circuited in March 1968 when six F-111As were assigned to the 428th Tactical Fighter Squadron for operational trials in South-East Asia from a base in Thailand. Three of these aircraft were lost in the space of four weeks, apparently through aircraft problems rather than enemy action and the trial then ended.

In the United States, the 474th TF Wing was selected to equip with the F-111A, and became the first of four Wings to fly the F-111 fighter. Among the early development problems with the aircraft were those associated with the engine intake. Production F-111As had a modified intake configuration known as Triple Plow 1 and eventually equipped the 366th TFW at Mountain Home A.F.B., Montana. The introduction of a further intake refinement, the Triple Plow 2, brought a change of designation to F-111E for the next 94 production aircraft. These aircraft were assigned to the second F-111 Wing in TAC, this being the 20th TF Wing, based in the U.K. for service in USAFE. The first two F-111Es reached one of the U.K. bases, at Upper Heyford, on September 12, 1970.

While the F-111A and F-111E were in production, development was proceeding of an updated variant, the F-111D, featuring both the Triple Plow 2 intakes and the so-called MK II Avionics with improved air-to-air capability. Procurement of the F-111D totalled 96 aircraft to equip the third TAC F-111 wing, the 27th TFW at Cannon A.F.B. The fourth wing was assigned to fly F-111Fs, procurement of 106 of which extended F-111 production at Fort Worth to 1975. The F-111F differed from the F-111D in two major respects—the Mark II avionics were simplified in an effort to reduce costs, and the uprated TF30-P-100 engine was introduced. Because of delays in the production of this engine, the first 30 F-111Fs were delivered to the 374th TFW at Mountain Home A.F.B. in 1971 temporarily fitted with TF30-P-9 engines. After serving with the 366th TFW, the F-111Fs were assigned to the 48th TFW in the U.K.

General Dynamics FB-111A (*General Dynamics photo 30-49798*).

The F-111C designation was applied to 24 aircraft ordered by the Royal Australian Air Force, and F-111K was the designation of 50 aircraft ordered by Britain for the RAF but subsequently cancelled. The first two F-111Ks, near to completion at the time of cancellation, were completed as additional USAF test aircraft and designated YF-111A. The 11th trials aircraft of the original batch (63-9776) was fitted with cameras in the weapons bay, reconnaissance radar and infra-red sensors, and first flew in December 1967 as the RF-111A. A production reconnaissance variant was planned as the RF-111D.

On December 10, 1965, the Department of Defense authorized work to start on a version of the F-111A to be operated by SAC as a strategic bomber. This variant, designated FB-111A (rather than BF-111A, as might have been expected to conform with the 1962 DoD designating system), combined features of the F-111A and the F-111B. The latter had been designed to have a longer span wing with extra weapon pylons and could carry a war load of over 40,000 lb. when operating at a gross weight of about 100,000 lb.

The FB-111A was intended as an interim replacement for the B-58 and some B-52s in SAC from 1970 onwards, and procurement of 210 was planned. This quantity was subsequently reduced to 76, to equip two wings. The prototype FB-111A was the 18th of the development F-111As (63-9783), first flown on July 30, 1967. This was followed by the first production FB-111A on July 13, 1968, powered initially by TF30-P-12

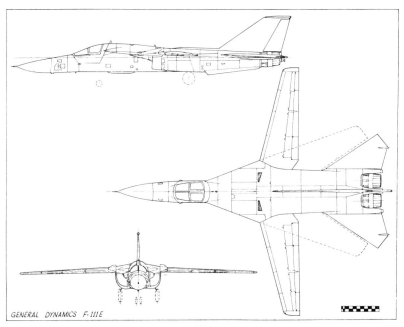

GENERAL DYNAMICS F-111E

Grumman EF-111A Raven conversion of GD F-111A (*Grumman photo*).

engines as used in the F-111B. The definitive engines for the bomber, TF30-P-7s, were introduced in the third production aircraft.

Delivery of the FB-111As to the USAF began on October 8, 1969, when the first aircraft for the 4007th Combat Crew Training Squadron was handed over at Carswell A.F.B. Operational squadrons (four in all) were divided between Plattsburgh A.F.B., N.Y. and Pease A.F.B., New Hampshire. First operational unit activated was the 509th Bombardment Wing at Pease, in the first half of 1970, followed by the 380th Wing at Plattsburgh. During 1988, the designation F-111G was adopted for the FB-111As that were to be converted eventually to serve in the tactical rôle when displaced from Strategic Air Command.

Arising out of experience gained in South-East Asia, the USAF set out in the early 'seventies to acquire a dedicated airborne tactical jamming system—an aircraft that could fly with or ahead of strike aircraft to detect and neutralise enemy radars (whether ground-based or airborne). Performance of this mission called for an unarmed aircraft with performance matching that of the strike aircraft it would accompany, whilst carrying several tons of electronic equipment and the generators needed to energize it. On December 26, 1974, a contract was placed with Grumman Aerospace for the conversion of two F-111As as prototype EW (electronic warfare) aircraft

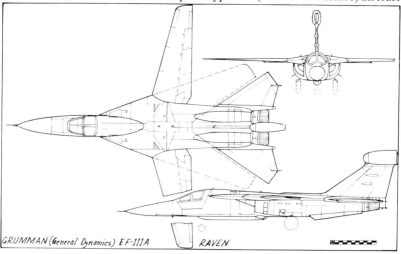
GRUMMAN (*General Dynamics*) EF-111A   RAVEN

to meet this requirement. After full modification, these aircraft flew on March 10 and May 17, 1977, acquiring the new designation of EF-111A.

Retaining the TF30-P-3 engines of the original F-111A, the EF conversions introduced a large fin-tip fairing to house the receiver and antennas of the AN/ALQ-99E tactical jamming system, the transmitters for which were installed in a long canoe-shaped radome under the fuselage. After successful testing, the two prototypes were brought up to full "production" standard and 40 more F-111As were converted by Grumman. With the popular name of Raven, the EF-111As began to enter service in November 1981, and were issued to the 390th Electronic Combat Squadron at Mountain Home A.F.B. and the 42nd ECS at Upper Heyford, in the U.K.

TECHNICAL DATA (F-111A)

MANUFACTURER: General Dynamics Corporation, Fort Worth Division, Fort Worth, Texas.
TYPE: Tactical fighter-bomber.
ACCOMMODATION: Two pilots, side-by-side.
POWER PLANT: Two 18,500 lb.s.t. with a/b. Pratt & Whitney TF30-P-3 turbofans.
DIMENSIONS: Span, 63 ft. 0 in. (31 ft. 11 in., fully swept). Length, 73 ft. 6 in. Height, 17 ft. 0½in. Wing area, 525 sq. ft.
WEIGHTS: Empty, 45,200 lb. Gross, 92,500 lb.
PERFORMANCE: Max. speed, 1,650 m.p.h. (Mach 2·5) at 40,000 ft.; service ceiling, over 60,000 ft; range, over 3,800 st. miles on internal fuel.
ARMAMENT: Internal weapon bay carries one 20-mm. M-61A1 multiple barrel cannon or two 2,000 lb. bombs. Four swivelling and four fixed wing pylons carry total external load of about 30,000 lb. in bombs, missiles, rockets or fuel tanks.
SERIAL NUMBERS:

F-111A: 63-9766/9782; 65-5701/5710;	F-111D: 68-085/180.
66-011/058; 66-9277;	F-111E: 67-115/124;
67-032/114.	68-001/084.
YF-111A: 67-149/150.	F-111F: 70-2362/2419; 71-883/894;
F-111C: 67-125/148 (for RAAF).	72-1441/1452; 73-707/718;
	74-177/188.

TECHNICAL DATA (FB-111A)

MANUFACTURER: General Dynamics Corporation, Fort Worth Division, Fort Worth, Texas.
TYPE: Strategic bomber.
ACCOMMODATION: Two pilots, side-by-side.
POWER PLANT: Two 20,350 lb.s.t. with a/b. Pratt & Whitney TF30-P-7 turbofans.
DIMENSIONS: Span, 70 ft. 0 in. (33 ft. 11 in. fully swept). Length, 73 ft. 6 in. Height, 17 ft. 0½in. Wing area, 550 sq. ft.
WEIGHT: Empty, 47,980 lb. Gross. 119,250 lb.
PERFORMANCE: Max speed, 1,450 m.p.h. (Mach 2·2) at 40,000 ft.; service ceiling over 69,000 ft.; range, 4,100 st. miles with external fuel.
ARMAMENT: Up to six Boeing AGM-69A ASMs in bomb-bay and externally on wing pylons. Provision for up to 37,500 lb. of conventional bombs.
SERIAL NUMBERS:
FB-111A: 63-9783;
67-159/163; 67-7192/7196;
68-239/292; 69-6503/6514.

A General Dynamics F-16A, in Egypt I finish, serving with the 120th FIS, Montana ANG (*Joe Cupido*).

General Dynamics F-16 Fighting Falcon

On April 13, 1972, the USAF ordered two prototypes of the General Dynamics Model 401, a design for a lightweight air combat fighter in response to a January 1972 Request for Proposals in the Lightweight Fighter (LWF) programme. Designated YF-16, the GD prototypes were used for a "fly-off" against the two YF-17s ordered at the same time from Northrop. Competing design proposals from Boeing (Model 908-909), Vought (Model V-1100) and Lockheed (CL-1200 Lancer) were eliminated. The YF-16 emerged as a mid-wing aeroplane with a blended wing/body design and cropped-delta wing having 40 degrees of leading-edge sweepback. The chosen power plant was a single Pratt & Whitney F100-PW-100 and provision was to be made for a single 20-mm. multi-barrel cannon in one wing root, Sidewinder AAMs at the wing tips and additional ordnance on wing pylons.

The YF-16 (70-1567) made an inadvertent first flight on January 20, 1974, during high-speed taxi runs, and a full first flight on February 2, followed by the second aircraft (70-1568) on May 9, 1974. After the evaluation and fly-off, the GD aircraft was selected as the winning LWF on January 13, 1975. Although begun as a technology demonstration programme, the LWF had by this time become a candidate for full-scale service with the USAF in the role of an Air Combat Fighter (ACF). For production, the design was enlarged somewhat, two more weapon stations were added on the wing to give the aircraft nine in all and the nose was enlarged to take Westinghouse AN/APG-66 pulse-Doppler radar. Eight aircraft to this new standard were ordered for Full Scale Development (FSD), six as YF-16As and two as two-seat YF-16Bs. The first YF-16A flew at Fort Worth on December 8, 1976 and the first YF-16B (fourth of the FSD aircraft), on August 8, 1977.

Large-scale production of the Fighting Falcon, as the F-16 was duly

330

General Dynamics F-16A of the 474th TFW, with three drop tanks, embarking on a Red Flag exercise from Nellis A.F.B. (*Frank Mormillo*).

named by the USAF, began with FY 78 funds, and procurement of 1,388 was planned (not counting sales to the four NATO countries in Europe —Belgium, Denmark, The Netherlands and Norway, which selected the F-16 as their F-104 replacement in June 1975—and subsequent sales to a number of other foreign air forces). The first full production F-16A flew in August 1978 and was formally delivered to the USAF later that month. The 388th TFW at Hill A.F.B. began to receive F-16As and F-16Bs in January 1979, initially for use by its 16th Tactical Fighter Training Squadron and then the 4th, 34th and 421st TF Squadrons. Continuing deliveries allowed F-16s to replace F-4s in the 56th TTW at MacDill A.F.B. (to serve as the OTU) and the 474th T.F.W. at Nellis A.F.B., followed in June 1981 by the 8th TFW at Kunsan A.F.B., South Korea, and then the 50th TFW at Hahn A.F.B. in Germany. Further units receiving Fighting Falcons as time went by were the 363rd TFW at Shaw A.F.B. and 58th TTW at Luke A.F.B., the 401st TFW at Torrejon, Spain and—the first Air National Guard unit to fly the type—the 169th TFG at McEntire, South Carolina.

By 1988, the F-16 had undergone extensive development and numerous experimental and research variants had been flown or projected. For USAF

The third production F-16D, with special Digital Flight Control System ("DFLCS F-16D") marking on tail and "ED" codes of the 6512th TS (*Joe Cupido*).

331

F-16A showing insignia of Vermont ANG, the 134th TFS, operating Fighting Falcons in air defence role (*Thomas Hildreth*).

service, the F-16A and F-16B had been succeeded by the F-16C and F-16D, which were distiguished by a number of internal improvements resulting from a Multinational Staged Improvement Programme (MSIP). Deliveries of the C and D models began in July 1984, but external differences from the A and B were minimal. From July 1986 onwards, F-16s were built with a common engine bay that allowed the General Electric F110-GE-100 engine to be used as an alternative to the F100 previously standardised. Uprated PW-229 or GE-129 engines, further avionics improvements and a larger variety of missiles were to be introduced in the late 'eighties and early 'nineties, with the USAF's total production requirement increased to 3,047. Of particular importance was the addition of LANTIRN (Low Altitude Navigation and Targeting Infrared for Night) pods to about 350 F-16s, for enhanced capabilities in the ground attack role.

The designation F-16E was tentatively reserved for a heavily-modified version of the Fighting Falcon that was proposed to meet the USAF requirement for a two-seat dual-role air defence/ground atack fighter. Known to GD as the F-16XL, this featured a "cranked arrow" wing and a lengthened fuselage, with increased fuel capacity and greater weapons-carrying capability. A single-seat F-16XL was flown on July 3, 1982 and the designation F-16F was later reserved for this version. The two-seat F-16XL prototype flew on October 29, 1982, but after selection of the F-15E to meet the USAF's dual-role requirement, work on the F-16XL was discontinued.

As a replacement for the RF-4C in USAF service, a variant of the F-16D was developed, carrying a GD-designed pod containing cameras, video equipment and/or electro-optical sensors. Under an October 1986 contract, 270 F-16As from USAF stocks were being modified by 1992 as air defence fighters (ADF) to replace early F-4s and F-106s in 12 ANG squadrons dedicated to continental air defence. Improved radar, ECM and other uprated avionics were fitted for the ADF role, and provision made for an armament of three AIM-7 Sparrows or six AIM-120 AMRAAMs or AIM-9 Sidewinders.

TECHNICAL DATA (F-16C)

MANUFACTURER: General Dynamics Corp, Fort Worth Division, Fort Worth, Texas.

TYPE: Multi-role fighter.

ACCOMMODATION: Pilot only or (F-16D) pilot and instructor in tandem.

POWER PLANT: One 29,000 lb.s.t. with a/b General Electric F110-GE-100 or Pratt & Whitney F-100-PW-220 turbofans.

DIMENSIONS: Span (over wing-tip missiles), 32 ft. 9¾in. Length, 49 ft. 4 in. Height, 16 ft. 8½ in. Wing area, 300.0 sq. ft.

WEIGHTS: Empty, 16,794 lb. Gross (air-to-air missions), 25,071 lb. Gross (full external load), 37,500 lb.

PERFORMANCE: Max. speed, more than Mach 2, 1,320 m.p.h. at 40,000 ft. Service ceiling, above 50,000 ft. Radius of action, more than 575 miles.

ARMAMENT: One 20-mm. General Electric M61A1 multi-barrel cannon. One AIM-9J or -9L Sidewinder AAM at each wing-tip. One hard point on fuselage centreline and six wing hard point for max. external load of 12,000 lb., including fuel tanks, ASMs, AAMs, bombs, gun pods, sensor pods, etc.

SERIAL NUMBERS:

YF-16: 70-1567/1568

YF-16A: 75-0745/0750

F-16A: 78-0001/0027; 78-0038/0076; 79-0288/0409; 80-0474/0622; 81-0663/0811; 82-0900/1026; 83-1066/1117

F-16C: 83-1118/1165; 84-1212/1318; 84-1374/1395; 85-1398/1505; 85-1544/1570; 86-0207/0371; 87-0217/0362.

YF-16B: 75-0751/0752

F-16B: 78-0077/0115; 79-0410/0432; 80-0623/0638; 81-0812/0822; 82-1027/1049; 83-1166/1173;

F-16D: 83-1174/1185; 84-1319/1331; 84-1396/1397; 85-1506/1517; 85-1571/1573; 86-039/053; 87-0363/0396.

Plus later contracts
(Serial numbers allocated for FMS and other foreign-use F-16s excluded)

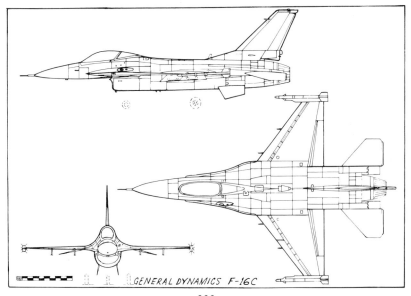

GENERAL DYNAMICS F-16C

Grumman SA-16A in regular A.R.S. finish (*USAF photo*).

Grumman SA-16, U-16 Albatross

Grumman Aircraft Engineering Corp. designed the Albatross (G-64) amphibian in 1946, primarily to meet a U.S. Navy requirement for a general purpose aircraft suitable for use as a transport, trainer or for rescue duties. The prototype, designated XJR2F-1 by the Navy, flew on October 24, 1947, and orders from the USAF followed almost immediately. For the Air Force, the G-64 was delivered specifically for airsea rescue duties, and was designated SA-16. The designation was interesting as the first, as well as the last, in the "A" for amphibian category introduced in June 1948 in lieu of OA; the latter series had then reached OA-15. The "S" in the Albatross designation was a duty prefix for search and rescue.

Powered by two 1,425 h.p. Wright R-1820-76 engines, the SA-16A was of conventional "boat-layout", with a single-step hull, high wing and outrigged wing floats. Accommodation was provided for up to 12 stretchers.

Grumman delivered a total of 297 SA-16As to the USAF; others were obtained on USAF contracts for foreign air forces under Mutual Defense Aid. Most of the SA-16As were assigned to the MATS Air Rescue Service.

In 1953, Grumman developed a "triphibian" Albatross, featuring sprung skis under the hull and on the wing-tip floats, which allowed the SA-16A to operate from land, water, snow or ice without modification. The skis were tested on 48-588, and the USAF purchased 127 conversion kits.

During 1955, an improved version of the design was developed as Grumman Model G-111, with the object of providing greater range, higher speed and better single-engined performance. The modifications comprised a 16 ft. 6 in. increase in wing span, with a cambered leading edge in place of slots, larger ailerons and tail surfaces, and improved de-icing boots. This version was designated SA-16B by the USAF, and SA-16As were converted to the new standard during IRAN programmes at Grumman. The prototype SA-16B flew on January 16, 1956 and the first "production" conversion on January 25, 1957.

In 1962, the "A" for amphibian category was dropped and the Albatross variants were redesignated HU-16A and HU-16B. By 1970, only a few remained in service for ASR duties, plus a few others with the ANG as transports for Army Special Forces.

TECHNICAL DATA (SA-16B)

MANUFACTURER: The Grumman Aircraft Engineering Corporation, Bethpage, Long Island, N.Y.

TYPE: Rescue amphibian.

ACCOMMODATION: Two pilots, navigator, radio operator and two medical attendants.

POWER PLANT: Two 1,425 h.p. Wright R-1820-76A or -76B piston radials.

DIMENSIONS: Span, 96 ft. 8 in. Length, 61 ft. 3 in. Height, 25 ft. 10 in. Wing area, 1,035 sq. ft.

WEIGHTS: Empty, 22,883 lb. Gross, 32,000 lb.

PERFORMANCE: Max. speed, 236 m.p.h. at 18,800 ft. Cruising speed, 150 m.p.h. Service ceiling, 25,000 ft. Range, 3,220 st. miles. Max. endurance (external tanks), 22·9 hours.

ARMAMENT: None.

SERIAL NUMBERS:
SA-16A/B: 48-588/607; 49-069/100; 50-172/182; 51-001/071; 51-471/476; 51-5278/5306; 51-7140/7255; 52-136/137; 60-9301/9310.

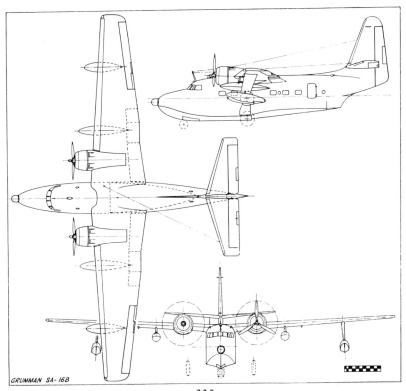

GRUMMAN SA-16B

335

Grumman OV-1D, with SLAR pod under fuselage and wing tanks, in overall grey Army finish (*Grumman photo 83-028*).

Grumman OV-1 Mohawk

The first aircraft with turboprop engines developed for the US Army, the Mohawk was conceived to meet joint Army and Marine Corps requirements for a battlefield surveillance aircraft. Originated in 1956, the Grumman G-134 design was to have STOL performance, rough field capability and equipment for various tactical observation roles. Nine aircraft were ordered in 1957 for test and evaluation, with the USN acting as the programme manager for the Army and USMC, but before the first prototype was completed, the Marines withdrew and their OF-1 version was dropped. The Army Mohawk was designated AO-1 in the category for fixed-wing observation aircraft established in 1958, but this was changed to OV-1 in the designation changes in 1962.

The first YOV-1A (then designated YAO-1A) made its first flight on April 14, 1959, and all nine test aircraft were completed by the end of that year. Also during 1959, the Army placed the first production contracts for OV-1As and OV-1Bs, subsequently ordering the OV-1C version also. Successive orders brought the production totals to 64 OV-1As, 90 OV-1Bs and 133 OV-1Cs.

The OV-1A was the basic visual photographic version with a KA-30 or (later) KS-61 camera in the fuselage providing for horizon-to-horizon coverage. This version entered service in 1961, when it was deployed to Germany with units of the 7th Army. The Mohawk began operation in Vietnam, with the 23rd Special Warfare Aviation Detachment, in July 1962, and in 1964 some specially armed aircraft, designated JOV-1A, were operated by the 11th Air Assault Division. These aircraft had four additional underwing pylons, outboard of the two usually used to carry drop tanks.

In the OV-1B, side-looking airborne radar was carried in a long pod under the forward fuselage. Capable of producing a radar map of the ground on each side of the flight path, this radar was linked to equipment

336

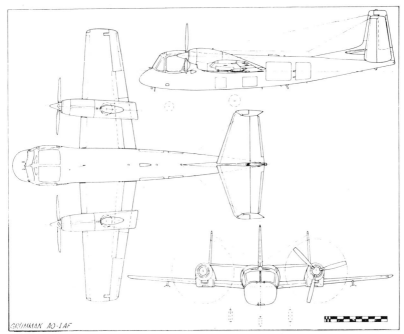

GRUMMAN AO-1AF

in the cockpit which could develop and print a photograph within seconds of the film being exposed. The wing span of this version was increased by six feet.

Generally similar to the OV-1A, the OV-1C had, in addition to the cameras, an infra-red sensor in the underside of the aft fuselage, and single pilot controls instead of dual. A forward-looking panoramic camera was also installed. All three versions were originally powered by 1,000 e.h.p. Lycoming T53-L-3 engines, but 1,150 e.h.p. L-7 or L-15 engines were introduced later in production and as a retrofit.

During 1967, the Army initiated development of the OV-1D by assigning four OV-1C airframes (67-18898/99, 67-18902 and 04) to be completed as pre-production models of the new configuration. The OV-1D incorporated three photographic systems—the standard vertical camera, a new vertical

Grumman JOV-1A for tests with underwing armament such as rocket pods, showing original overall O.D. finish of all Army Mohawks. (*Department of Defense photo APS-63-26*).

337

panoramic camera and a panoramic forward-looking camera. It also had provision for rapid installation of SLAR or IR systems and thus provided in one airframe all the options of the OV-1A, B and C. Following the four YOV-1D conversions, the Army ordered 67 OV-1Ds with FY 1968 and 1969 funds. Subsequently, a total of 72 OV-1B/C Mohawks was brought up to OV-1D standard. A further modernization of the OV-1D was under study in 1988, with plans to modify at least 58 aircraft.

Whilst continuing to serve in the battlefield reconnaissance role for which it was designed, the Mohawk was also adopted as a suitable airframe to carry electronic intelligence-gathering equipment. Trials aircraft carrying ELINT sensors including the ALQ-133 underwing pod were flown as JOV-1B, -C and -1D in the Army's *Quick Look* I programme. These led to the appearance of the RV-1D, an operational system carrying *Quick Look* II. At least 36 OV-1Bs were converted to this standard, with the features of the OV-1D plus ALQ-133 and other sensors. The OV-1E was a projected development of the Mohawk with an enlarged front fuselage and four-man crew. Sixteen EV-1E conversions from OV-1Bs were also ELINT-equipped, to a different standard from the RV-1D, but these saw no service with the U.S. Army.

TECHNICAL DATA (OV-1)

MANUFACTURER: Grumman Aircraft Engineering Corp., Bethpage, Long Island, N.Y.
TYPE: Army STOL observation.
ACCOMMODATION: Pilot and observer side-by-side.

	OV-1B	OV-1C	OV-1D
Power Plant:	2 × 1,150 s.h.p. T53-L-7 or −15	2 × 1,150 s.h.p. T53-L-15	2 × 1,400 s.h.p. T53-L-701A
Dimensions:			
Span, ft. in.	47 10½	42 0	47 10½
Length, ft. in.	41 0	41 0	43 0
Height, ft. in.	12 8	12 8	12 8
Wing area, sq. ft.	360	330	360
Weights:			
Empty, lb.	11,067	10,400	12,054
Gross, lb.	17,018	16,684	18,109
Performance:			
Max. speed, m.p.h.	297	308	289
Cruising speed, m.p.h.	207	207	242
Climb, ft./min.	2,350	2,670	3,618
Service ceiling, ft.	30,300	30,300	25,000
Range, miles	1,230	1,330	1,020

SERIAL NUMBERS:
YOV-1A: 57-6463/6467; 57-6538/6541.
OV-1A: 59-2603/2620; 60-3720/3744;
  63-13114/13134.
OV-1B: 59-2621/2637; 62-5859/5906;
  64-14238/14273.

OV-1C: 60-3745/3761; 61-2675/2728;
  62-5849/5858; 66-18881/18896;
  67-18897/18932.
OV-1D: 68-15930/15965;
  68-16990/16996; 69-16997/17026.

Hiller H-23F in Army white and red finish (*Hiller photo 61-1369*).

Hiller H-23 Raven

The H-23 derived from the original Hiller 360, developed in 1948 to make use of Stanley Hiller's simplified control system with a hanging control column and "Rotor-Matic" aerodynamic control systems. An example of the Hiller 360 was purchased for Army evaluation in 1950 and was designated YH-23. Successful trials with this aircraft led to an order for 100 two-seat H-23As in the 1951 Fiscal Budget, this being the largest Army contract for helicopters up to that time. The majority of H-23As were delivered in air ambulance configuration with two external, totally enclosed panniers for stretchers, on the fuselage sides. The engine was a 178 h.p. Franklin O-335-4. The first five H-23As were delivered late in 1950 and most of the remainder in 1951. Five H-23As also were procured by the Air Force for evaluation.

The H-23B followed in 1952, and differed in having a skid/wheel undercarriage, 200 h.p. O-335-6 engine and detail refinements. This model was the first to serve at Camp Wolters, starting early in 1957 and about half of the 273 built for the Army eventually served there. Deliveries began in 1952. Another 81 H-23Bs were built for Mutual Defense Aid programmes.

In 1956, the H-23C appeared. Army equivalent of the Hiller UH-12C, this model was distinguished by a one-piece moulded canopy, a three-seat cabin, and metal rotor blades. A total of 145 were delivered.

Further development of this model enabled Hiller to guarantee 1,000 hours between airframe overhauls, compared with the 600 hours usually obtained. Prototype flight trials of this new version, designated H-23D, began on April 3, 1956, and production contracts were placed in March 1957. Hiller delivered its first H-23Ds to the Army in December 1957, for utility and training duties. By the end of 1959, 130 H-23Ds had replaced 178 assorted Bs and Ds at the Primary Helicopter School, the

Hiller H-23D, showing prominent display of complete serial number 57-2996 and national insignia under engine bay (*Hiller photo 58-344*).

reduction in numbers having been made possible by the increased overhaul period of the new model. Apart from component changes to achieve this reliability, the H-23D had a 250 h.p. Lycoming O-540 engine and a

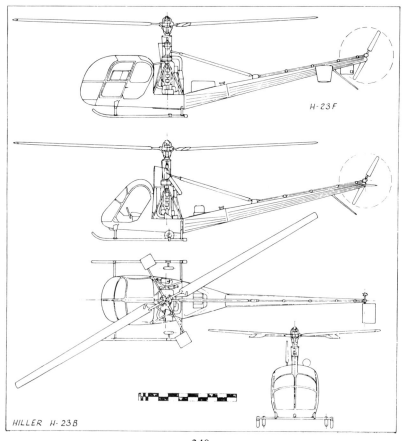

completely new transmission and rotor system.

Starting in 1962, the Army bought 33 of the larger four-seat Hiller Model 12E-4s, for duties with the 937th Engineer Company attached to the Inter-American Geodetic Survey in Central and South America. These were designated H-23F, the H-23E designation having been reserved for a possible Army version of the three-seat Model 12E. The "O" mission prefix was added to the designation of all H-23 models in service in mid-1962. After delivery of a total of 348 OH-23Ds, production switched to the OH-23G, this being a three-seat dual-control version of the H-23F. A total of 793 was delivered to the Army, ending in 1967.

TECHNICAL DATA (H-23D)

MANUFACTURER: Hiller Aircraft Corp., Palo Alto, California.
TYPE: Army light observation helicopter.
ACCOMMODATION: Two pilots and student or passenger side-by-side.
POWER PLANT: One 250 h.p. Lycoming VO-450-23B flat-six piston engine.
DIMENSIONS: Rotor diameter, 24 ft. 5 in. Length, 27 ft. 9½ in. Height, 9 ft. 9½ in. Disc area, 985 sq. ft.
WEIGHTS: Empty, 1,816 lb. Gross, 2,700 lb.
PERFORMANCE: Max. speed, 95 m.p.h. at sea level. Cruising speed, 82 m.p.h. at sea level. Initial climb, 1,050 ft./min. Service ceiling, 13,200 ft. Range, 197 st. miles.
ARMAMENT: None.
SERIAL NUMBERS:

YH-23: 50-1254.
H-23A: 51-3969/4018; 51-16092/16141; 51-15966/15970 (USAF).
H-23B: 51-16142/16414; 54-862/881*; 54-2915/2949*; 54-4009/4034*.
H-23C: 55-4060; 55-4063/4131; 56-2245/2316; 56-4020/4021*; 57-6521*.
H-23D: 55-4061/4062; 57-2982/3077; 58-5398/5505; 59-2675/2786; 61-3085/3114

H-23F: 59-2787/2790; 61-3218/6234; 62-12507/12512; 64-14850/14851; 65-13069; 66-8039; 67-14867/14868.
H-23G: 61-3088/3217; 62-3756/3831; 63-9222/9371; 63-12765/12901; 64-15108/15317; 66-13106/13195.

*These batches assigned to MAP use.

Hiller H-23B serving with Washington National Guard, showing correct presentation of serial 54-2918 (*Peter M. Bowers*).

Huff-Daland LB-1 (*Huff-Daland photo 284 from Curtiss*).

Huff-Daland/Keystone Light Bomber Series

A biplane bomber series that was to span a decade began in 1923, with an order for the Huff-Daland XLB-1 (23-1250), a normal three-place bomber that differed from convention only in being fitted with tapered wings and a single 800 h.p. Packard 1A-2540 engine in the nose instead of the traditional pair of lower-powered engines, one on each side of the fuselage between the wings. Bombs were carried internally, and aiming was done through a window in the belly instead of from the normal nose sighting station. Nine service test LB-1s were identical except for installation of an improved 2A-2540 engine.

This single-engine configuration proved to be unsuitable, and a twin-engined XLB-3 was ordered. This was essentially an LB-1 airframe powered with experimental air-cooled and inverted Liberty engines, one on each side. This power plant installation was abandoned, however, and the same aeroplane became the XLB-3A (27-333), with 410 h.p. air-cooled Pratt & Whitney Wasp R-1340-1 engines. Crew was increased to five, with conventional nose gunnery and bombing stations.

By the time the XLB-3A was delivered, the Huff-Daland Company had been reorganized as Keystone, so the aeroplane was known as a Keystone. The XLB-5 (26-208), similar to the XLB-3A except for conventional 420 h.p. Liberty engines, and 10 production LB-5s were delivered before the company change as Huff-Dalands. Twenty-five LB-5As, however, with twin tails instead of the single large rudder with two smaller rudders on each side as used on the LB-5s, were delivered as Keystones, as were all succeeding variants of the LB family.

A major change took place with the appearance of the XLB-6 (27-344), which was the 10th LB-5 fitted with entirely new straight-chord wings with 525 h.p. Wright R-1750-1 Cyclone engines suspended between the wings instead of resting on the lower. The 17 production LB-6s were the

Keystone LB-7 showing twin tail shape (*USAAF photo*).

same except for minor refinements and a revised angular shape to the twin rudders.

The LB-5s and LB-6s entered service with squadrons of the 2nd Bomb Group, which was the sole US-based bombing unit of the USAAC until 1928. Other aircraft of the same type were used by the 5th Group (Composite) in Hawaii. They were supplemented by 18 LB-7s, produced by Keystone in 1928/29 with Pratt & Whitney R-1690-3 Hornet engines but otherwise identical with the LB-6s.

Changes of powerplant and some variation in tail shape were wholly responsible for a number of different designations applied to the Keystones in this period. The final two LB-7s on the 1929 contract, for example, were completed as the LB-8 (29-9) and the LB-9 (29-10) when fitted, respectively, with geared 550 h.p. Pratt & Whitney R-1860-3 and 575 h.p. Wright R-1750 Cyclone engines.

The last two LB-6s were similarly completed with experimental engine installations, 525 h.p. R-1750-1s in the LB-10 and R-1750-3s in the LB-11. The LB-10 also had a single fin and rudder in place of the twin units which Keystone had standardized in the LB-5As. The LB-11 was converted to

Keystone LB-5A (*Keystone photo 536 from Curtiss*).

343

Keystone B-5A, showing single tail of production model Keystone bombers (*Keystone photo from Curtiss*).

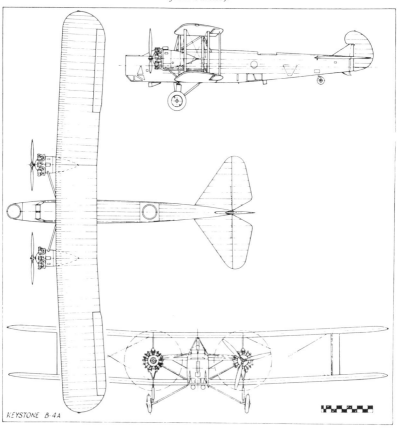

KEYSTONE B-4A

LB-11A when fitted with geared GIR-1750 Cyclones and a single LB-12 was similar to the LB-7.

In 1930, the USAAC abandoned its separate designation categories for light (LB) and heavy (HB) bombers and introduced a single bomber (B) category. At that time, production contracts had been placed for a further 73 Keystone bombers as LB-10A, LB-13 and LB-14, but all were re-designated for delivery in the B category. The 63 LB-10As appeared as B-3As, with the same single fin as the LB-10, and 525 h.p. R-1690-3 Hornet engines. Of seven LB-13s ordered, five were completed as Y1B-4s with R-1860-7 engines and the other two as Y1B-6 with R-1820-1 engines; three more Y1B-6s were converted from B-3As. The three LB-14s were re-designated Y1B-5 before delivery, with R-1750-3 engines, but it is uncertain whether they were ever completed. The B-3, B-4 and B-5 versions all had single fins and rudders, and production quantities of each were ordered; 25 B-4As, 27 B-5As and 39 B-6As, with deliveries concluding in 1932. They flew with units of the 7th and 19th Bomb Groups, formed in 1928, in addition to the original 2nd Bomb Group and units overseas.

TECHNICAL DATA (LB-1 series)

MANUFACTURER: (LB-1) Huff-Daland and Co. Inc., Ogdensburg, New York.
   (LB-3 and subsequent) Keystone Aircraft Corp., Bristol, Pa.
TYPE: Light bomber.
ACCOMMODATION: Two pilots, bombardier, front and rear gunners.

	LB-1	LB-5	LB-6
Power Plant:	One 787 h.p. 2A-2540	Two 420 h.p. V-1650-3	Two 536 h.p. R-1750-1
Dimensions:			
Span, ft., in.	66 6	67 0	75 0
Length, ft., in.	46 2	44 8	43 5
Height, ft., in.	14 11	16 10	18 1
Wing area, sq. ft.	1,137	1,139	1,148
Weights:			
Empty, lb.	6,237	7,024	6,836
Gross, lb.	12,415	12,155	13,440
Performance:			
Max. speed, m.p.h.	120	107	114
Cruising speed, m.p.h.	105	—	95
Climb, ft./min.	530	—	600
Service ceiling, ft.	11,150	8,000	11,650
Range, miles	430	435	632

ARMAMENT: Five 0·30-in. guns, 2,000-lb. bombs.
SERIAL NUMBERS:

XLB-1: 23-1250.
LB-1: 26-377/385.
XLB-3: 27-333.
XLB-5: 26-208.

LB-5: 27-335/344.
LB-5A: 28-001/025.
LB-6: 29-011/027.
LB-7: 28-388/395; 29-001/010.

345

TECHNICAL DATA (B-3 series)

MANUFACTURER: Keystone Aircraft Corp., Bristol, Pa.
TYPE: Light bomber.
ACCOMMODATION: Two pilots, bombardier, front and rear gunners.

	B-3A	B-4A	B-6A
Power Plant:	Two 525 h.p. R-1690-3	Two 575 h.p. R-1860-7	Two 575 h.p. R-1820-1
Dimensions:			
Span, ft., in.	74 8	74 8	74 9
Length, ft., in.	48 10	48 10	48 10
Height, ft., in.	15 9	15 9	17 2
Wing area, sq. ft.	1,145	1,145	1,137
Weights:			
Empty, lb.	7,705	7,951	8,037
Gross, lb.	12,952	13,209	13,374
Performance:			
Max. speed, m.p.h.	114	121	121
Cruising speed, m.p.h.	98	103	103
Climb, ft./min.	650	—	690
Service ceiling, ft.	12,700	14,000	14,100
Range, miles	860	855	363

ARMAMENT: Three 0·30-in. Browning guns, 2,500 lb. of bombs.
SERIAL NUMBERS:
B-3A: 30-281/343.
Y1B-4: 30-344/348.
B-4A: 32-117/141.

Y1B-6: 30-349/353.
B-6A: 32-142/180.

Keystone LB-7 used to test new N.A.C.A. cowlings in 1929. The angular twin-tail shape was shared with LB-6 (*Keystone photo 794*).

346

Hughes OH-6A Cayuse in O.D. finish (*Hughes Tool Co photo*).

Hughes H-6 Cayuse

The U.S. Army design competition for a light observation helicopter initiated in 1960 was one of the most hotly contested in the history of the helicopter industry, with 12 companies submitting 22 alternative designs.

In May 1961, Bell and Hiller were named initial winners of the design contest, but a few weeks later Hughes was made an equal partner in the programme. The Hughes design (Model 369) incorporated a number of new concepts, including a system of attaching the four rotor blades by a novel laminated strap arrangement, and an unusual pod-and-boom fuselage for optimum strength at minimum structural weight.

Five prototypes were ordered for Army evaluation and the designation HO-6 was assigned in the original Army category for observation helicopters. This was changed to OH-6A in the tri-service designation system introduced in July 1962. The first flight of a YOH-6 was made on February 27, 1963 and the Hughes OH-6A was named the winner on May 26, 1965.

An initial order for 714 was placed by the Army immediately following selection, and subsequent contracts brought the total procured to 1,417. Deliveries were completed in 1970 and all remaining OH-6As were transferred to the Army National Guard in 1974-75.

A single OH-6A was acquired by the USAF in March 1969 for general research into VTOL operations. This helicopter (62-4212) was actually the original Army test OH-6, refurbished for Air Force use.

The designations OH-6B,- 6C and -6D covered experimental programmes and proposed developments, including the single OH-6C with an uprated Allison 250-C20 engine and muffler plus other modifications to reduce external noise levels. The OH-6D was an improved Cayuse to meet the Army AHIP requirement, eventually satisfied by the Bell OH-58D. After Hughes

Hughes OH-6A showing serial without Fiscal Year (65) indication (*U.S. Army photo SC647212*).

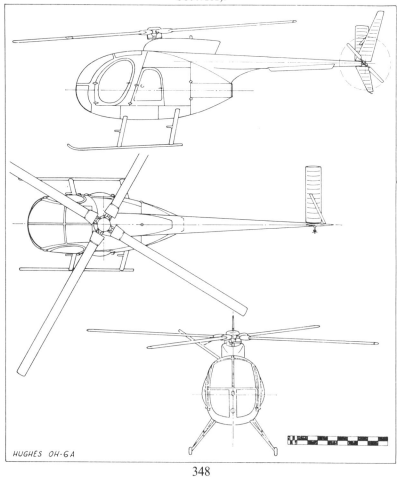

HUGHES OH-6A

had developed the improved Model 500 M-D Defender and Model 530 from the original Model 369/OH-6A, the Army procured a quantity of about 30 for service with the 160th Aviation Group (known as Task Force 160). Featuring the quiet four-bladed tail rotors, mufflers, advanced avionics and mast-mounted sights, these helicopters operated in pairs, with the MH-6E to search and the AH-6F to attack, using armament that could include 7·62-mm. machine gun pods and Hydra-70 rocket pods containing 19 2·75-in FFARs. A single Model 530F (86-141) was also acquired for USAF evaluation.

During 1988, the Mississippi National Guard's Aviation Classification Repair Activity Depot developed a package of improvements for the OH-6A, including modification to the airframe, transmission, electrical and navigation systems, the avionics and radio. Conversion of the 350 Cayuses remaining in Guard service to OH-6B standard was in prospect.

TECHNICAL DATA (OH-6A)

MANUFACTURER: Hughes Tool Company, Aircraft Division, Culver City, California.
TYPE: Light observation helicopter.
ACCOMMODATION: Crew of two and provision for two seated passengers or four equipped troops in rear of cabin.
POWER PLANT: One 317 s.h.p. Allison T63-A-5A turboshaft.
DIMENSIONS: Rotor diameter, 26 ft. 4 in. Length, 30 ft. 3¾ in. Height, 8 ft. 1½ in. Disc area, 545 sq. ft.
WEIGHTS: Empty, 1,229 lb. Gross, 2,700 lb.
PERFORMANCE: Max. speed, 150 m.p.h. at sea level; cruising speed, 134 m.p.h. at sea level; initial climb, 1,840 ft./min.; service ceiling, 15,800 ft.; range, 380 st. miles.
ARMAMENT: None.
SERIAL NUMBERS:

YOH-6A: 62-4212/4216; 62-12624.	67-16000/16686; 68-17140/17369;
OH-6A: 65-12916/13003; 66-7775/7942;	69-15960/16075.
66-14376/14419; 66-17750/17833;	AH/MH-6: 86-0382/0387; 86-141
	(plus other contracts).

Hughes 530MG demonstrator showing mast-mounted sight and other features of OH-6s used by Army's Task Force 160 (*McDonnell Douglas photo*).

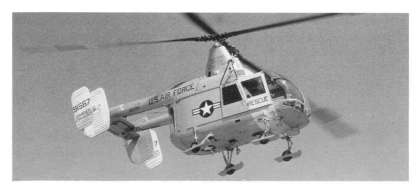

Kaman H-43B for USAF Rescue service (*Kaman photo 3712-1*).

Kaman H-43 Huskie

The H-43 was the first Kaman product purchased in quantity by the USAF and the first helicopter purchased for an airborne fire-fighting and crash rescue role. An Air Force evaluation of existing helicopter designs suitable for this job led to the choice of the Kaman 600, which was in production for the U.S. Navy as the HOK-1. An initial production batch of 18 was ordered, differing only from the Navy model in equipment; the first was flown on September 19, 1958, and they were delivered, as H-43As, from November 1958 to mid-1959. These 18 aircraft, powered by Pratt & Whitney R-1340-48 piston engines, were assigned to Tactical Air Command bases and served until 1961.

To improve the performance, and especially the load-carrying ability of the basic design, the H-43B (Kaman 600-3) was developed with a Lycoming T53-L-1A shaft turbine engine. Experience had been obtained with this power unit when a HOK-1 had been modified, on a USAF contract, to test-fly the XT53, the first flight of this prototype having been made on September 27, 1956. USAF originally ordered 116 of the H-43B version (commencing 58-1841, flown on November 1, 1958) deliveries of which began in June 1959. Further contracts brought the total of this variant built for the USAF to 203, including some for MAP use overseas. The H-43Bs were assigned to bases of all flying Commands throughout the continental U.S. for crash and fire rescue missions. They were operated by detachments of MATS Air Rescue Service.

Use of the H-43 in a crash rescue role was based on Naval practice of using a helicopter for plane guard duties during flying operations on an aircraft carrier. The H-43B could start up and be airborne within 30 seconds of an alert, with another 30 seconds needed to attach a fire suppression kit (foam and water bottle, nitrogen pressure bottle and hose) to the cargo sling beneath the fuselage.

In mid-1962, the USAF Huskie designations were changed to HH-43A and HH-43B to signify the rescue role. The UH-43C, OH-43D, TH-43E and QH-43G designations applied to USN versions. Final model of the Huskie for the USAF was the HH-43F (Kaman 600-5) with uprated T53-L-11A engine for improved performance in high temperatures and at high altitudes. Forty-two were built including 10 for MAP, and many HH-43Bs were brought up to the same standard.

TECHNICAL DATA (HH-43B)

MANUFACTURER: The Kaman Aircraft Corp., Bloomfield, Connecticut.
TYPE: Local crash rescue helicopter.
ACCOMMODATION: Pilot and observer and fire-fighting crew or up to 10 passengers or four stretchers with attendant.
POWER PLANT: One 860 e.h.p. Lycoming T53-L-1B turboshaft.
DIMENSIONS: Span, 51 ft. 6 in. Length, 25 ft. 0 in. Height, 15 ft. 6½ in.
WEIGHTS: Empty, 4,469 lb. Gross, 8,800 lb. with slung load.
PERFORMANCE: Max. speed, 120 m.p.h. Cruising speed, 97 m.p.h. Initial climb, 2,000 ft./min. Service ceiling, 25,700 ft. Range, 235 st. miles. Endurance, 3·2 hr.
ARMAMENT: None.
SERIAL NUMBERS:

H-43A: 58-1823/1840.
H-43B: 58-1841/1860; 58-5524; 59-1540/1593; 60-251/292; 61-2920/2922; 61-2943/2954; 62-4509/4565; 62-5976/5979; 62-12513/12514; 63-9710/9717.

HH-43F: 64-14213/14220; 64-15097/15103; 64-17557/17559; 64-17682; 65-10647/10656; 65-12755/12758; 65-12914/12915; 67-14769/14775.

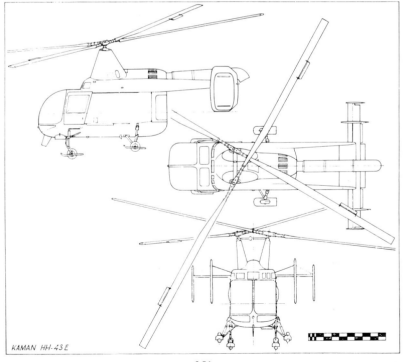

KAMAN HH-43 E

Lockheed C-60 in O.D. and grey finish, with red-bordered insignia (*Lockheed photo V6118*).

Lockheed C-56, C-57, C-59, C-60 Lodestar

First flown early in 1940, the Lockheed Model 18 was designed as a 17-passenger development of the Model 14—itself a continuation of the Model 10 Electra, the Model 12 and the unbuilt Model 16 series. Powered by two Wright Cyclones, the Lodestar proved to be among the fastest aeroplanes of its class, and Air Corps interest crystallized in May 1941 into a contract for one C-56, with the Wright R-1820-89 engines, and three C-57s differing only in having Pratt & Whitney R-1830-53 engines. These were respectively equivalent to the Lockheed Model 18-50 and 18-14, and ten more C-57s were procured later.

When the Air Corps began to requisition commercial transports after the start of the War in December 1941, numerous other Lodestars were pressed into service from the U.S. domestic operators. As many of these differed in engine type and interior fittings, a variety of designations was used. The single C-56A, 12 C-56C and seven C-56D had R-1690-54 or -25 Hornet engines and were Model 18-07 and 18-08. The 13 C-56B were model 18-40 with R-1820-97s; and the two C-56E had 22 seats each.

The single C-57A was a requisitioned commercial Lodestar and seven C-57Bs were equipped for trooping. The C-57C designation was used for three C-60As re-engined with R-1830-43 engines, and one of these became C-57D with R-1830-92s.

Under the first Defense Aid programme, ten C-59s (Model 18-07 with R-1690-25s) and 15 C-60s (Model 18-56, R-1820-87s) were purchased for supply to other countries, principally the U.K. Another 21 C-60s were bought later, and in 1942 production began of 325 C-60As. One was converted to the XC-60B (42-55860) with experimental hot-air de-icing.

One other designation applied to a Lodestar type. This was the C-66, a Model 18-10 with a VIP interior and 1,200 h.p. R-1830-53 engines, purchased in 1942 for delivery to Brazil as a presidential transport.

The designation C-111 applied to the smaller Model 14, built in 1938. Four civil machines owned by KNILM escaped from the Dutch East Indies in 1941 and three of these were impressed for USAAF use in Australia.

TECHNICAL DATA (C-56)

MANUFACTURER: Lockheed Aircraft Corporation, Burbank, California.
TYPE: Personnel, troop and freight transport.
ACCOMMODATION: Seventeen seats.
POWER PLANT: Two 1,200 h.p. Wright R-1820-71 piston radials.
DIMENSIONS: Span, 65 ft. 6 in. Length, 49 ft. 10 in. Height, 11 ft. 1 in. Wing area, 550 sq. ft.
WEIGHTS: Empty, 11,650 lb. Gross, 17,500 lb.
PERFORMANCE: Max. speed, 253 m.p.h. Climb, 7·1 min. to 10,000 ft. Service ceiling, 23,300 ft. Range, 1,600 st. miles.
ARMAMENT: None.
SERIAL NUMBERS:

C-56: 41-19729.
C-56A: 42-38261.
C-56B: 42-38262/38263; 42-68347/68357.
C-56C: 42-53494/53503; 42-68690; 42-57212.
C-56D: 42-53504/53507; 42-57223/57224; 42-62602.
C-56E: 43-3278/3279.
C-57: 41-19730/19732; 41-23164/23170; 43-34921/34923.

C-57B: 43-3271/3277.
C-59: 41-29623/29632.
C-60: 41-29633/29647; 42-32166/32180; 42-108787/108792.
C-60A: 42-32181/32232; 42-55845/56084; 43-16433/16465.
C-66: 42-13567.
C-111: 44-83233/83235.

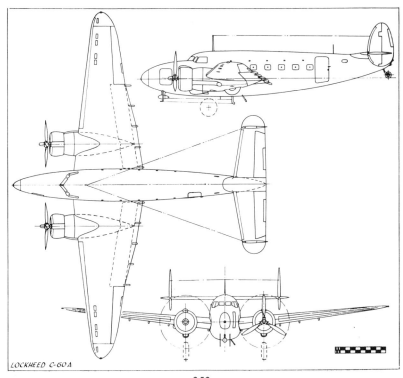

LOCKHEED C-60A

353

Lockheed A-29 with both USAAC and RAF serial numbers. Turret replaced by open cockpit for single 0.50-in calibre machine gun, early 1942 (*Wright Field photo 87274*).

Lockheed A-28, A-29, AT-18

This Lockheed aeroplane is one of the rare examples of a successful military type developed from an existing commercial design. Its origin lay in the Lockheed 14 transport, which in 1938 was the largest of the Lockheed twin-engined line begun with the 10A Electra. Its conversion to a military type was made expressly to meet British requirements for a coastal reconnaissance bomber, at a time when the British Purchasing Commission was spending considerably larger sums with the U.S. industry than was the U.S. Army Air Corps. A contract for 250 was placed in June 1938 after a mock-up fuselage had been produced by Lockheed in a matter of days, and the name Hudson was allocated. The first Hudson flew on December 10, 1938, at Burbank.

Some 1,500 Hudsons were purchased by the R.A.F. and the R.A.A.F. before the type was included in Lend–Lease procurement programmes and in consequence received an Army designation, A-28. All 52 of this model procured by the Army went to the R.A.F., as did 450 A-28A with convertible interiors for troop-carrying. The A-28 and A-28A had Pratt & Whitney R-1830-45 engines, and were Lockheed Model L-414-08.

With Wright R-1820-87 engines, the Model 414-56 was designated A-29 for Lend–Lease purposes; 416 were built, plus 384 A-29As with troop benches for optional transport use. The latter were provisionally designated C-63 before becoming A-29As. All 800 A-29 and A-29A were allocated to the R.A.F. and received R.A.F. serial numbers, but a number were repossessed and, with dorsal turrets deleted, were used for bomber crew training and for anti-submarine duties, in 1942/43 over the Atlantic, Pacific and Indian Oceans, the 13th Bombardment Group (M) being one unit equipped. An A-29 was responsible for the first successful attack on a U-boat by an Army Air Force aircraft in World War II. Also in 1942, 24 of the repossessed Hudsons were converted for photographic reconnaissance and designated A-29B. These were used for survey and charting flights by the 1st Photographic Group until 1942.

A specifically Army variant of the design was the AT-18, similar to the A-29A, with R-1820-87 engines and a Martin dorsal turret; they

354

were used for some time for the training of air gunners, and later as target tugs. Lockheed built 217 of this model, and 83 of the similar AT-18As, which had the dorsal turret removed and were used as navigation trainers.

TECHNICAL DATA (A-29)

MANUFACTURER: Lockheed Aircraft Corporation, Burbank, California.
TYPE: Light bomber, maritime reconnaissance and troop transport.
ACCOMMODATION: Two pilots, navigator/bombardier and gunner.
POWER PLANT: Two 1,200 h.p. Wright R-1820-87 piston radials.
DIMENSIONS: Span, 65 ft. 6 in. Length, 44 ft. 4 in. Height, 11 ft. 11 in. Wing area, 551 sq. ft.
WEIGHTS: Empty, 12,825 lb. Gross, 20,500 lb.
PERFORMANCE: Max. speed, 253 m.p.h. at 15,000 ft. Cruising speed, 205 m.p.h. Climb, 6·3 min. to 10,000 ft. Service ceiling, 26,500 ft. Range, 1,550 st. miles.
ARMAMENT: Two 0·30-in. guns in nose, one in lower rear fuselage, two in optional dorsal turret. 1,600-lb. bombs.
SERIAL NUMBERS:

A-28: 41-23171/23222.
A-28A: 42-6582/6681; 42-46937/47286.
A-29: 41-23223/23638.

A-29A: 41-23639; 41-36968/37267; 42-47287/47369.
AT-18: 42-55568/55784.
AT-18A: 42-55485/55567.

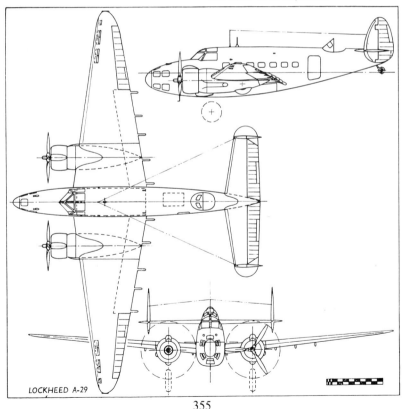

LOCKHEED A-29

355

Lockheed B-37 showing short-lived presentation of national insignia as a white star, with neither red centre nor blue surround (*Lockheed photo V437*).

Lockheed B-34, B-37 Lexington

The considerable success enjoyed by the Hudson (see pp. 354–355) in early wartime operations with the Royal Air Force led Lockheed to develop the design further to meet British requirements. Whereas the Hudson had been based on the commercial Model 14, the new design, named Ventura by the R.A.F., was derived from the larger Model 18. Orders for 675 were placed by the British Purchasing Commission, and the first Ventura flew on July 31, 1941. Resembling the Hudson in overall appearance, the Ventura was heavier and more powerful, and incorporated a ventral gun position giving the under fuselage line a distinctive kink.

When the Ventura was included in Lend–Lease programmes, it was given the Army designation B-34 for procurement purposes. All 200 B-34s were assigned to the R.A.F., but most of a second batch of 250 similar aircraft built at the Lockheed Vega factory were retained by the Army, for use on overwater patrols. Early examples requisitioned from Lend–Lease allocations were known as Model 37, and others were designated B-34A. A small number of B-34Bs were used for navigation training. All models had the 2,000 h.p. Pratt & Whitney R-2800-31 engines, carried a 3,000-lb. bomb load and mounted two 0·50-inch machine guns in the nose and in a dorsal turret, plus another six 0·30-inch guns for use from various fuselage positions.

A version of the Ventura was developed with Wright R-2600-31 engines, and a contract for 550 was placed, the designation being O-56. Only 18 of this contract were delivered, under the revised designation of B-37.

All production of the Ventura was assigned to the U.S. Navy from the end of 1942, after 27 had been requisitioned from the B-34 Lend–Lease contract for Britain. As the PV-1, the type continued in production until May 1944, the Navy receiving 1,600 compared with approximately 875 shared between the Army Air Force and the R.A.F.

TECHNICAL DATA (B-34A)

MANUFACTURER: Lockheed (Vega) Aircraft Division, Burbank, California.
TYPE: Medium bomber, anti-submarine and trainer.
ACCOMMODATION: Crew of four.
POWER PLANT: Two 2,000 h.p. Pratt & Whitney R-2800-31 piston radials.
DIMENSIONS: Span, 65 ft. 6 in. Length, 51 ft. 5 in. Height, 11 ft. 11 in. Wing area, 551 sq. ft.
WEIGHTS: Empty, 17,275 lb. Gross, 27,250 lb.
PERFORMANCE: Max. speed, 315 m.p.h. at 15,500 ft. Cruising speed, 230 m.p.h. Initial climb, 8·2 min. to 15,000 ft. Service ceiling, 24,000 ft. Range, 950 st. miles.
ARMAMENT: Two fixed forward-firing 0·50-in. guns; six flexible 0·30-in. guns in nose, dorsal and ventral positions. 2,500 lb. of bombs.
SERIAL NUMBERS:
B-34: 41-38020/38219.   B-37: 41-37470/37487.

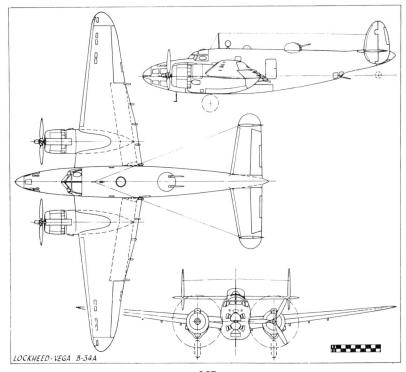

LOCKHEED-VEGA B-34A

357

Lockheed P-38J with distinctive chin radiators (*Lockheed photo*).

Lockheed P-38, F-4, F-5 Lightning

One of the best-known USAAF fighters operational in World War II, the P-38 was already in mass production before the War started. Production continued until 1945, and the Lightning served in every combat area in a variety of roles. The original Lockheed 22 design was drawn to meet an official specification of 1937 for a high altitude interceptor. The required speed, 360 m.p.h. at 20,000 ft. and 290 m.p.h. at sea level, and the required climb of 6 minutes to 20,000 ft., led Lockheed to choose a twin-engined layout for what was, in fact, the company's first military project. A twin-boom arrangement was chosen, with engines, turbo-superchargers, radiator baths and main undercarriage units all carried in the booms.

Judged by existing U.S. fighter standards, the Lockheed proposal was radical, not only in its layout, but also for its armament of one 23-mm. and four 0·50-inch guns in the nose. The gross weight of 14,800 lb. was greater than that of some contemporary bombers. Nevertheless, the project was accepted by the USAAC on June 23, 1937, and one prototype of the Lockheed 22 was ordered as the XP-38 (37-457). The task of detail design went ahead under H. L. Hibbard. Construction started in July 1938, the XP-38 being moved from Burbank to March Field on the last day of the year. Lieutenant B. S. Kelsey made the first flight from March Field on January 27, 1939.

Two weeks after the first flight, on February 11, 1939, the XP-38 was delivered across the continent to Mitchell Field, taking 7 hrs. 2 min. with two refuelling stops, but it undershot on landing and was destroyed. An order had already been placed for a service test quantity of 13 YP-38s

(Model 122) and enough had been learnt with the prototype for some modifications to be made. These included the use of 1,150 h.p. Allison V-1710-27/29 engines in place of the XP-38's 960 h.p. -11/15 models, with a higher thrust line resulting from spur reduction gears instead of epicyclic, revised intakes, and outwardly-rotating propellers. The armament was amended by substituting 0·30-inch Colts for two of the 0·50-in. guns, and changing the 23-mm. Madsen for a 37-mm. Oldsmobile. The first YP-38 flew on September 16, 1940, and was delivered to the USAAC in March 1941 for evaluation; the whole batch was completed by June of that year.

Production contracts for the Lightning had been placed before the first YP-38 flew, first for 66 (in September 1939) and then for another 607. A production line was established at Burbank and the first 30 aircraft were completed as P-38s, (Lockheed Model 222) similar to the YP-38s but with the armament restored to XP-38 standard and some armour plate fitted around the cockpit. The weight of this model, delivered in mid-1941, increased to 15,340 lb. and the speed was 395 m.p.h. The remainder of the initial contract were built as P-38Ds in which the tail-plane incidence was changed to overcome a buffeting problem, self-sealing tanks were introduced and other small changes made. Deliveries of the P-38D began in August 1941 and were completed at the end of the year.

The P-38D was the first "battle-worthy" version of the design and the first to bear the name Lightning (Atlanta having been considered for a brief interim period). Most of the earlier P-38s were used for various experimental purposes, such as the first production article (40-744) which had a second cockpit built into the port boom for Wright Field tests into pilot reactions to asymmetric flight, and 40-762 modified into the XP-38A (Lockheed 622) with a pressurized cockpit.

In November 1941, the P-38E (Lockheed 222) followed the D models off the Burbank line, being distinguished only by the use of a 20-mm. Hispano cannon in place of the 37 mm. Oldsmobile, with greater ammunition capacity and, on later aircraft, Curtiss Electric in place of Hamilton

Lockheed P-322 with British serial AE992 (*Peter M. Bowers*).

Lockheed P-38G operating in Sicily, 1943 (*Howard Levy*).

Standard propellers. Two hundred and ten P-38Es were built. At about the same time, Lockheed completed the first of their Model 322-61 Lightnings for export to Britain on a cash purchase contract signed in March 1940. With a ban on the export of turbo-superchargers and the F2 Model of the Allison engine used in the USAAC's P-38s, the British Lightning Is had unsupercharged Allison C15s as used in the XP-38, and the performance suffered accordingly. The total British order was for 667 aircraft, of which the first 143 were built to the L322-61 standard. Three reached Britain early in 1942 for evaluation, but the others were repossessed by the USAAF after America's entry into the War. As P-322s, they were used as trainers. The other 524 aircraft on British contract were to have been Lightning IIs (Lockheed 322-60) with Allison F2R engines, but none was in fact delivered. All these aircraft were absorbed into USAAF contracts, 150 being completed as P-38F-13 or F-15 and the remainder as P-38G-15.

The P-38F (Model 222) had followed the E in production at Burbank early in 1942, with 1,325 h.p. Allison V-1710-49/53 engines and, for the first time, racks under the inner wings for up to 2,000 lb. of bombs, torpedoes, SCI (smoke curtain installation) or 165 or 310 U.S. gallon drop tanks. The so-called "manoeuvring flap" was introduced on the P-38F-15-LO and subsequent models, and permitted the Fowler landing flaps to be extended 8 degrees at combat speed to increase the wing lift and therefore the manoeuvrability. P-38Fs were also the first Lightnings adapted as two-seat trainers, with a pupil crammed into a small space behind the instructor in place of the radio, to obtain an impression of handling and fighting tactics. Production totalled 527, and was followed by 1,082 P-38Gs, which had equipment changes.

Lightnings had been in action with the 342nd Composite Group from Icelandic bases from the first day of America's entry into the war, but the P-38F was the first to see large-scale active service, with USAAF Fighter Groups in Europe in mid-1942 and in North Africa from November 1942. In action against German fighters for the first time over North

360

Africa, the P-38 gained its German nickname of *Der Gabelschwanz Teufel*—the "fork-tailed devil"—but in fact it did not prove wholly successful in fighter-to-fighter combat and subsequent development tended to be for roles other than that of pure fighter. At this time, P-38s were the only fighters being air-delivered to Europe. In the latter half of 1942, the 1st and 14th Fighter Groups, with B-17 navigation escorts, flew to England and early in 1943 another group flew to North Africa via the south Atlantic.

P-38s were also in service in the Pacific area before the end of 1942, and were instrumental in securing air superiority. P-38Gs of the 339th Fighter Squadron, based on Guadalcanal in April 1943, were responsible for a notable operation which succeeded in intercepting the Mitsubishi transport carrying Admiral Yamamoto, 550 miles from their base. This action, based on an intercepted Japanese plan, was made possible by the use of long-range drop tanks. The underwing capability of the Lightning was further increased on the P-38H (Model 222) to a maximum of 1,600 lb. on each of two pylons. This model, of which Lockheed built 601, had 1,425 h.p. V-1710-89/91 engines, with improved General Electric B33 superchargers in some cases, and an M-2C camera in place of the M-1. Automatically-operated oil radiator flaps were also used on the P-38H, which was in service by May 1943.

Up to this point, all versions of the Lightning were externally similar, but with the P-38J (Model 422) came one obvious change of outline, with the introduction of "chin" radiators under the spinners. The engines were V-1710-89/91 and on later Js the internal fuel tankage was increased and hydraulic power boosting for the ailerons was introduced. With 410 U.S. gallons of internal fuel and two 300-gallon drop tanks, the P-38J had a total ferry endurance of 12 hours and a combat radius sufficient to escort Eighth Air Force bombers on deep penetration raids on Germany. In the Pacific, the P-38s played a prominent part in the island-hopping campaign of 1944, and on this type of aircraft Capt. Richard I. Bong became the USAAF's top-scoring fighter pilot with 40 confirmed victories.

Production of the P-38J totalled 2,970, making it the second most produced model. One "J" was converted to the sole P-38K, with larger diameter propellers on V-1710-75/77 engines. The P-38L (Model 422)

Lockheed P-38L with rocket "Christmas trees" (*Lockheed photo*).

Lockheed P-38E in O.D. finish with grey undersides (*Lockheed photo Z-2671*).

which was numerically the most important Lightning, had 1,600 h.p. V-1710-111/113 engines but was otherwise similar to the "J". Lockheed built 3,810, and a further 113 were built by Vultee at Nashville before a contract for 2,000 was cancelled on VJ Day. The "L" was the first model to carry rocket projectiles, in tiers under the wing.

As the need for fighters in Europe dwindled with the strength of the Luftwaffe, Lightnings were used on a growing scale for ground attack and fighter-bomber sorties. This led to a modification on some P-38Js and Ls to have a transparent nose with a station for a lead bomb-aimer, complete with Norden sight, to control the bombing operation of a whole formation of P-38s. A development of this theme was the use of "Mickey" or BTO (bomb-through-overcast) radar in a bulbous nose. These versions were known colloquially as the Droop-snoot and Pathfinder respectively.

In the final stages of the War, the P-38M reached operational status in the Pacific. This was a night fighter, with an observer in a raised seat behind the pilot and AN/APS-6 radar in a fairing under the nose. The 75 P-38Ms produced were "L" conversions, and a few TP-38J "piggy-back" two-seat trainers converted from P-38Js carried AN/APS-4 radar in an under-wing pod, to train P-38M radar observers.

Post-war, a few Lightnings survived as F-38J and F-38L until declared surplus in 1949.

F-4. A total of about 1,400 P-38s of various models was delivered for reconnaissance duties as the most-used aircraft in this category in World

P-38L-5 with "droop-snoot" bombardier nose, in India, September 1945 (*Peter M. Bowers*).

362

Lockheed P-38M-5-LO two-seat night fighter (*Lockheed photo AD-6547*).

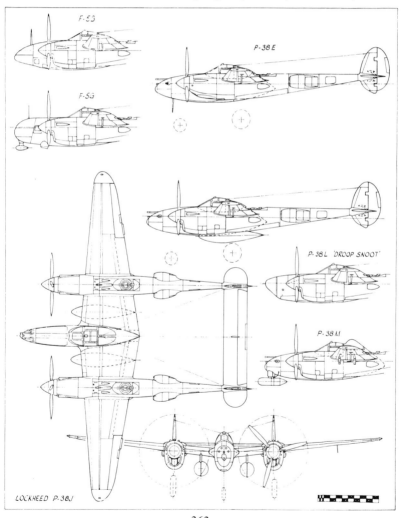

Lockheed F-5B, camera-equipped version of P-38G (*Lockheed photo*).

War II. The first such aircraft, designated F-4, were basically P-38Es with four K-17 cameras, a drift sight and an autopilot. Deliveries of the 99 F-4s began in March 1942, followed by 20 F-4As similar to P-38Fs with later engines.

F-5. Reconnaissance versions of the P-38G were designated F-5A, or, with intercoolers, F-5B. Totals of 181 and 200 were completed, respectively. One F-5A was rebuilt with a second seat for an observer, becoming the XF-5D. The foregoing variants were additional to P-38 production already listed, but the 128 F-5Cs were converted from P-38Hs and a total of 705 P-38J and P-38L were converted to F-5Es. The F-5F and F-5G were also P-38J and P-38L conversions, respectively, with varying camera arrangements.

XP-49. A single prototype (40-3055) of the Lockheed 522 design was ordered in 1940. Basically a P-38 type, it had 1,350 h.p. Continental XIV-1430-13/15 engines, an armament of two 20-mm. cannon and four 0·50-inch machine guns and a pressurized cockpit. First flown in November 1942, it was used for high altitude research and pressure cabin development at Wright Field.

XP-58. The Chain Lightning, as this model was known, was an enlarged two-seat fighter development of the P-38, a single prototype of which (41-2670) was built and flown in June 1944. Powered by two Allison V-3420-11/13 engines, it had a four-gun turret in addition to an interchangeable nose armament of one 75-mm. cannon, or two 20-mm. and

Lockheed F-5G converted from P-38L, in China, 1945 (*Peter M. Bowers*).

four 0·50-inch guns. The span was 70 ft., gross weight 43,000 lb. and maximum speed 430 m.p.h.

TECHNICAL DATA (P-38)

MANUFACTURER: Lockheed Aircraft Corp., Burbank, California, and Consolidated Vultee Aircraft Corporation, Nashville, Tennessee.

TYPE: Single-seat pursuit and long-range escort; two-seat night fighter (P-38M only); unarmed photographic reconnaissance (F-4 and F-5); advanced trainer.

ACCOMMODATION: Pilot in enclosed cockpit (with radar operator in tandem, P-38M only).

	P-38	P-38E	P-38F	P-38J	P-38L
Power Plant:	2×1,150 h.p. V-1710-27/29	2×1,150 h.p. V-1710-27/29	2×1,325 h.p. V-1710-49/53	2×1,425 h.p. V-1710-89/91	2×1,475 h.p. V-1710-111/113
Dimensions:					
Span, ft., in.	52 0	52 0	52 0	52 0	52 0
Length, ft., in.	37 10	37 10	37 10	37 10	37 10
Height, ft., in.	9 10	9 10	9 10	9 10	9 10
Wing area, sq. ft.	327·5	327·5	327·5	327·5	327·5
Weights:					
Empty, lb.	11,672	11,880	12,264	12,780	12,800
Gross, lb.	15,340	15,482	18,000	21,600	21,600
Performance:					
Max. speed, m.p.h./ft.	390/20,000	395	395/25,000	414/25,000	414/25,000
Cruising speed, m.p.h.	310	—	305	290	290
Climb, min./ft.	1/3,200	—	8·8/20,000	7/20,000	7/20,000
Service ceiling, ft.	—	39,000	39,000	44,000	44,000
Range, st. miles	825	500	—	450	450
Armament:	1×37 mm. 4×0·50-in.	1×20 mm. 4×0·50-in.	1×20 mm. 4×0·50-in.	1×20 mm. 4×0·50-in. 2×1,600 lb.	1×20 mm. 4×0·50-in. 2×1,600 lb.

SERIAL NUMBERS:

XP-38: 37-457.
YP-38: 39-689/701.
P-38: 40-744/773.
P-38D: 40-774/809.
P-38E: 41-1983/2292*.
P-38F: 41-2293/2392†; 41-7484/7680; 42-12567/12666; 43-2035/2184‡.
P-38G: 42-12667/12866§; 42-12870/13557; 43-2185/2558‡.

P-38H: 42-13559; 42-66502/67101.
P-38J: 42-12867/12869; 42-13560/13566; 42-67402/68191; 42-103979/104428; 43-28248/29047; 44-23059/23768.
P-38K: 42-13558.
P-38L-LO: 44-23769/27258; 44-53008/53327.
P-38L-VN: 43-50226/50338.
F-5B: 42-67312/67401; 42-68192/68301.

* 99 F-4s as follow: 41-2098/2099, 2121/2156, 2158/2171, 2173/2218, 2220 and one F-5A, 41-2157.

† 20 F-4A, 41-2362/2381.

§ 180 F-5A as follow: 42-12667/12686, 12767/12786, 12967/12986, 13067/13126, 13267/13326.

‡ British contracts absorbed by USAAF.

Lockheed C-121C Constellation in MATS white-top finish (*Lockheed photo*).

Lockheed C-69, C-121 Constellation

First examples of the Constellation (Lockheed L-49) purchased by the USAAF had been laid down as commercial transports for T.W.A. and Pan American. In common with other transports in production at the time of Pearl Harbor, they were requisitioned on the production line, and were designated C-69. Still bearing a civil registration (NX67900), the first C-69 was first flown from Burbank on January 9, 1943. Powered by 2,200 h.p. Wright R-3350-35 engines, it was the largest (82,000 lb.) and fastest (329 m.p.h.) transport built to date for the USAAF, and was distinguished by its clean-lined "turtle-back" fuselage shape and three fins and rudders. The pressurized fuselage had accommodation for 64 passengers.

A total of 22 C-69s was built for USAAF before termination of the military contract after VJ Day. These comprised nine aircraft on which work had already started and 13 of a contract for 180 placed in 1942. All but one were C-69s, the exception being a single C-69C (42-94550) with a V.I.P. interior for 43 passengers. The cancelled contract included 49 more of this model. Also cancelled were the C-69A (Lockheed 49-43-11) to carry 100 troops; the C-69B, also a trooper with bench seats for 94, and the C-69D, with seats for 57 passengers. The prototype C-69 later became the XC-69E with Pratt & Whitney R-2800 engines. The C-69s saw service with Air Transport Command in the final year or so of the War before being declared surplus and resold to the airlines in 1946/47.

In 1948 the USAF ordered from Lockheed 10 examples of the later L-749 Constellation, designating them in the new C-121 series. They were intended for use by MATS on long-range V.I.P. missions and the first (48-608) was a VC-121B, with extra fuel tanks. The other nine (48-609/17) were designated C-121A or VC-121A on delivery, according to the seating standard, but were all later designated PC-121A, indicating that they were permanently employed as passenger carriers. These C-121s included *Columbine I* (48-614) used by General Eisenhower as NATO

366

commander; *Columbine II* (48-610) used as a Presidential transport by Eisenhower; and *Bataan* (48-613) used by General MacArthur.

To increase MATS' long-range transport capability, contracts were placed in 1951 for 33 of the larger L-1049 model Constellation, with the designation C-121C. The gross weight of this model was 135,000 lb. compared with the 107,000 lb. of the PC-121A, and the length increased from 95 ft. 4 in. to 116 ft. 2 in. The 3,500 h.p. R-3350-34 engines replaced 2,500 h.p. R-3350-75s. One other aircraft in this series was a Navy R7V-1 acquired for Presidential use as the VC-121E *Columbine III*. MATS also obtained 32 Navy R7V-1s which were transferred to the Air Force as C-121Gs. After the C-121s had been superseded by turboprop and turbojet types in MAC service they were assigned to ANG units, some of which flew Constellation variants until 1979.

Following U.S. Navy development of the Constellation as an airborne picket plane carrying special electronic gear, a similar USAF variant was produced for airborne early warning operations (the WS214M defence weapon system). The first ten such were designated RC-121C at first, later TC-121C, and then EC-121C. Their special role was indicated by the massive radomes above and below the centre fuselage, which carried a total of 6 tons of electronic gear. They entered service with Air Defense Command in October 1953 (the 552nd AEW & C Wing), operating patrols off the U.S. West Coast. With the delivery of 72 RC-121Ds beginning in May 1954, distinguished by their wing-tip fuel tanks, a second ADC wing (the 551st) in 1955 assumed responsibility for patrols over the Atlantic. One additional RC-121D was a converted C-121C. All were redesignated as EC-121Ds in 1962.

During 1962, additional electronic equipment, including a computer, was added to 42 EC-121Ds operated by the 551st AEW and C Wing to feed information to NORAD SAGE installations, and these were redesignated EC-121Hs. Two EC-121Ds became EC-121Js, with changed electronic equipment. For use as AEW trainers, nine RC-121Cs and four C-121Gs

Lockheed C-69 after being stripped of original O.D. finish, showing CM "Buzz Number" *(Peter M. Bowers)*.

became TC-121Cs and TG-121Gs respectively, whilst four other C-121Cs became VC-121C VIP transports for use by the 1254th Air Transport Squadron (Special Missions) and one of the TC-121Gs later became a VC-121G staff transport.

The K, L, M, N and P variants were U.S. Navy aircraft (and a single JC-121K was an EC-121K used for electronic experiments by the Army). Three EC-121Ps transferred to the USAF as avionics test beds became JEC-121Ps. Four EC-121Gs were conversions of EC-121Ds or Hs with more advanced avionics. Thirty of the Navy's EC-121K and EC-121P AEW aircraft were transferred to the USAF for service with the 553rd Reconnaissance Wing in the Vietnam war, flying with radomes removed in the role of airborne relay stations from Korat A.F.B. in Thailand. Five (or more) conversions of C-121Cs to EC-121S configuration served with the Pennsylvania ANG for ELINT/ECM duty and finally 23 (or more) EC-121D, H and J models were updated to EC-121Ts with improved equipment for the AEW role, were serving with AFRES until late 1978.

Two aircraft in the C-121 series were acquired in 1955 for part of the USAF

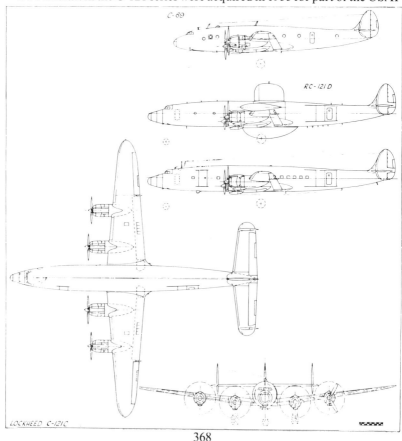

All-grey Lockheed EC-121H airborne early-warning aircraft (*P. J. Bish*).

investigation into turboprop transports. Designated YC-121F (Lockheed 1249A) they were powered by T34-P-6 engines and were evaluated by the MATS Service Test Squadron (Turboprop) at Kelly A.F.B. Apart from the power plant, the YC-121Fs were to C-121C standard and were converted U.S. Navy R7V-2s.

TECHNICAL DATA (C-69, C-121)

MANUFACTURER: Lockheed Aircraft Corporation, Burbank, California.
TYPE: (C-69, C-121) Personnel and cargo transport. (C-121D) Airborne early warning.
ACCOMMODATION: (C-69): 60 troops. (C-121): 72 troops (C-121D): Crew of 27.

	C-69	C-121G	RC-121D
Power Plant:	4 × 2,200 h.p. R-3350-35	4 × 3,250 h.p. R-3350-91	4 × 3,250 h.p. R-3350-34, -91
Dimensions:			
Span, ft. in.	123 0	123 0	126 02
Length, ft., in.	95 2	116 2	116 2
Height, ft. in.	23 8	24 8	27 0
Wing area, sq. ft.	1,650	1,650	1,653·6
Weights:			
Empty, lb.	50,500	72,815	80,611
Gross, lb.	72,000	145,000	143,600
Performance:			
Max. speed, m.p.h./ft.	330	368/20,000 ft.	321/20,000 ft.
Cruising speed, m.p.h./ft.	—	259/10,000 ft.	—
Climb	7·1 min. to 10,000 ft.	1,100 ft./min.	845 ft./min.
Service ceiling, ft.	25,000	22,300	20,600
Range, miles	2,400	2,100	4,600

ARMAMENT: None.
SERIAL NUMBERS:
C-69: 42-94549/94561*; 43-10309/10317.   RC-121D: 52-3411/3425; 53-533/556;
C-121A: 48-609/617.   53-3398/3403; 54-2304/2308; 55-118/139.
VC-121B: 48-608.   VC-121E: 53-7885.
C-121C: 54-151/183.   YC-121F: 53-8157/8158.
RC-121C: 51-3836/3845.   C-121G: 54-4048/4079.

*Final seven of this batch completed but not delivered to USAAF; resold to civil operators.

369

Silver-painted P-80A with underslung tip tanks and original PN "Buzz Number" (*Peter M. Bowers*).

Lockheed P-80, T-33 Shooting Star

As the first jet aircraft accepted for operational service by the USAAF, the Lockheed P-80 is assured of a lasting place in history. Developed in the latter part of World War II, it was one of the first types of aircraft operated by the USAF in the Korean War, with considerable success. Development of the Lockheed jet fighter began in June 1943, when the company was officially invited to design an aircraft around the de Havilland H-1 turbojet newly developed in Britain. Lockheed's design team led by Clarence L. Johnson completed project details in one week and proposed a 180-day schedule for prototype construction, to which the Army Air Force agreed. Contracts were drawn up for three prototypes and a service trials batch of 13.

Built at Burbank, the first prototype, XP-80 (44-83020), was at Muroc Dry Lake 139 days after work started, and four days later, on January 8, 1944, Milo Burcham made the first two flights. The XP-80 was a sleek low-wing monoplane with the centre line of the equi-tapered wing just aft of the fuselage midpoint. A laminar-flow section with a knife leading edge was used. Air intakes for the 3,000-lb. s.t. H-1 turbojet were in the fuselage side forward of the leading edge, and the armament comprised five 0·50-inch guns grouped in the nose.

Production P-80s were intended to be powered by the H-1 engine produced by Allis-Chalmers as the J36, but the failure of this programme led to adoption of the Allison-developed General Electric J33 in all but the first prototype. With this engine, the two other prototypes were designated XP-80A (44-83021/22), and the first was flown on June 10, 1944, by Tony Le Vier. The new engine was rated at 3,750 lb., and the design of the aircraft was altered somewhat to accommodate the greater weight and increased power. Changes included an increase in wing span from 37 ft. to 38 ft. 10½ in. and in fuselage length from 32 ft. 10 in. to 34 ft. 6 in., a stronger undercarriage, taller fin with rounded top and gross weight of

370

Lockheed T-33A from USAF Instrument School (*USAF photo 46714AC*).

13,780 lb. against 8,916 lb. In the 13 YP-80As (44-83023/35), a vigorous attempt to save weight kept the gross down to 11,500 lb. Whereas the XP-80As had the original General Electric I-40 engines, the service trials aircraft had production-model J33-GE-9 or GE-11 engines. Armament was increased to six 0·50s in the nose. The first YP-80A was delivered in October 1944, and two aircraft reached Italy shortly before VE Day.

Plans for production of the Shooting Star were made on a large scale during 1944, and involved North American as well as Lockheed, with contracts for 5,000 either placed or planned. More than 3,000 of these were cancelled after VJ Day, Lockheed actually building 525 of the P-80A model which was similar to the YP-80A in most respects. Deliveries to the USAAF began in Dec. 1945. The addition of wing-tip tanks and underwing bombs or tanks increased the gross weight to an eventual 14,500 lb.; the Allison J33-A-17 became standard in the final batches. A feature of early P-80As was the overall light grey finish used to seal all skin joints. It was too hard to maintain in service and was deleted for the natural metal finish.

The 5,200 lb. s.t. J33-A-21 engine (with water injection), provision for JATO and a thinner wing distinguished the F-80B, which appeared in

All-red Lockheed QF-80A with white lettering and Q-prefix to "Buzz Number" (*Gordon S. Williams*).

Lockheed P-80C in markings of 36th FB Squadron, 8th FB Wing, carrying napalm tanks under wings for mission in Korea. Note FT "Buzz Number" and lack of serial number on tail (*USAF photo AF3138-1*).

1946. A total of 240 of the late production P-80As were either completed as "B"s or converted to this standard. Also in 1946, one aircraft (44-85200) from the first batch of 500 P-80As was specially modified for an attempt on the World Air Speed Record, for which it had a J33-A-23 engine, with water-alcohol injection, clipped wings, a smaller cockpit canopy and a high-speed finish. On June 19, 1947, this aircraft was flown by Colonel Albert Boyd to establish a record at 623·8 m.p.h. At first known as the XP-80B, this aircraft was re-designated XP-80R.

With the same engine as the racer and other small changes, the P-80C was the final production version of the single-seat Shooting Star, with 798 produced in 1948 and 1949. The later production models had the 5,400 lb.s.t. J33-A-35 engine, and a gross weight of 16,000 lb. On June 11, 1948, the designation of all Shooting Stars in service was changed from P-80 to F-80.

Although the P-80 had reached USAAF squadrons too late to see service in Europe or the Far East in 1945, it was on hand in large numbers when the Korean conflict began in June 1950. F-80s were stationed in the Far East at that time as interceptors, but the type was used principally in Korea for tactical ground attack duties. For operation from Japan, enlarged wing-tip tanks were developed, with a capacity of 260 U.S. gallons compared with 165 previously; in addition, four 5-in. RPs were carried or, on short-range missions, eight RPs or two 1,000 lb. bombs or

Lockheed RF-80A (formerly FP-80A) in 1956, with centreline tip tanks and Alabama Air National Guard markings (*Peter M. Bowers*).

372

six Napalm bombs. An F-80 flown by Lieutenant Russel Brown destroyed a MiG-15 over Korea on November 8, 1950, in what is believed to be the first conclusive air combat between two jet fighters.

With the advent of the F-84 and F-86 after the end of the Korean War, most F-80s were assigned to a training role, or were allocated to Air National Guard and Air Force Reserve units. For this purpose, F-80As, RF-80As (see below) and F-80Bs were brought up to partial F-80C standard; when modified, 137 "A"s became F-80C-11s or RF-80C-11s and 117 "B"s became F-80C-12s. Three F-80As and several F-80Cs were eventually modified as drones, designated QF-80A and QF-80C, or when further modernized, QF-80F, as missile targets and to fly into radioactive clouds to collect fall-out samples, while others designated DF-80A were used as directors. Experimental variants included one F-80C (47-171) constructed of magnesium throughout; another (44-85044) with a second, prone-position, cockpit in the nose; an F-80C (49-429) on skis in Alaska; a P-80A (44-85116) with a rocket gun in the nose; a P-80A (44-83027) with a Rolls-Royce Nene engine and P-80A (44-85214) with Marquardt ramjets at the wing-tips.

RF-80 (FP-80, F-14). One of the 13 service trials YP-80As was completed

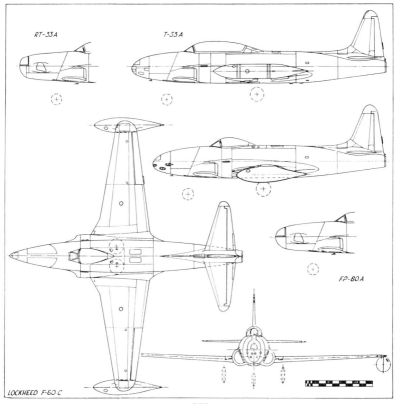

as the XF-14 (44-83024). It was followed by a reconnaissance variant of the production P-80A, the prototype of which was designated XFP-80A (44-85201). With cameras replacing guns in a lengthened and deepened nose, the FP-80A became a service variant 152 being delivered. The designation was changed to RF-80A on June 11, 1948. Seventy F-80Cs were similarly converted to RF-80Cs.

T-33 (TF-80C, RT-33). In August 1947, Lockheed took an F-80C airframe (48-356) and lengthened the fuselage by 38·5 inches to provide space for a second cockpit in tandem with the first. The canopy was extended to cover both cockpits and the armament was deleted. Designated TF-80C, this version flew on March 22, 1948, and was ordered eventually in greater quantities than any other Shooting Star variant. It had the same J33-A-23 or -25 engine as the F-80C. Lockheed built 128 TF-80Cs before the designation was changed to T-33A on May 5, 1949; as the USAF's standard jet trainer, production of the T-33 continued until August 1959.

Included in the USAF procurement of T-33As were several hundred acquired for MAP and delivered to foreign nations qualifying for such aid. The USAF also served as the procurement agency for T-33s acquired by the

TECHNICAL DATA (F-80, T-33)

MANUFACTURER: Lockheed Aircraft Corporation, Burbank, California.
TYPE: (F-80) fighter, fighter-bomber. (T-33) advanced trainer. (RF-80, RT-33) reconnaissance.
ACCOMMODATION: Pilot in enclosed cockpit. (TF-33, pilot and instructor in tandem.)

	F-80A	F-80C	T-33A
Power Plant:	4,000 lb. s.t.	4,600 lb. s.t.	4,600 lb. s.t.
	J33-A-11	J33-A-23	J33-A-35
Dimensions:			
Span, ft. in.	39 11	39 11	38 10½
Length, ft. in.	34 6	34 6	37 9
Height, ft. in.	11 4	11 4	11 4
Wing area, sq. ft.	238	238	238
Weights:			
Empty, lb.	7,920	8,240	8,084
Gross, lb.	14,500	16,856	11,965
Performance:			
Max. speed, m.p.h./ft.	558/0	580/7,000	543/25,000
Cruising speed, m.p.h.	410	439	—
Climb, ft./min.	4,580	6,870	6·5 min. to 25,000 ft.
Service ceiling, ft.	45,000	42,750	47,500
Range	540 miles	1,380 miles	(3·12 hours)
Armament:	6 × 0·50-in.	6 × ·50-in. 2 × 1,000 lb. or 10 × 5 in. R.P.	2 × ·50-in.

U.S. Navy as TV-2s (later T-33Bs), and these also were assigned USAF serials when ordered, although they operated subsequently with BuAer numbers. According to Lockheed records, production of the T-33A for USAF, USN and MAP totalled 5,819, but the record of USAF assigned serial numbers indicates a total of 5,691, of which 699 were for the U.S. Navy and 1,058 for MAP. The T-33A was also built under licence in Japan and Canada for local use.

Included in the MAP contracts were 85 RT-33As. This was a special single-seat reconnaissance version, with the camera-carrying nose of the FP-80A, and electronic equipment occupying the rear cockpit beneath the standard full-length canopy of the T-33A. Some of the USAF aircraft were modified as drone directors, designated DT-33A, and others became AT-33A when fitted with armament for interdiction and close air support, solely for foreign sale. USAF use of the T-33A came to an end in 1988.

SERIAL NUMBERS:

XP-80: 44-83020.
XP-80A: 44-83021/83022.
YP-80A: 44-83023/83035.
P-80A: 44-84992/85491*; 45-8301/8363*.
FP-80A: 45-8364/8477.
P-80B: 45-8478/8717.
P-80C: 47-171/224; 47-525/604;
    47-1380/1411; 48-376/396;
    47-863/912; 49-422/878; 49-1800/1899;
    49-3597/3600.
T-33A: 48-356/375; 48-913/920;
    49-879/1006; 50-320/454;
    50-1272/1276†; 51-4019/4424;
    51-4435/4514; 51-4525/4533;
    51-6497/6577; 51-6588/6664;
    51-6675/6957†; 51-8506/8517;
    51-8542/8635; 51-8652/8728;
    51-8750/8835; 51-8871/8939;
    51-8954/9039; 51-9076/9149;
    51-9168/9310†; 51-16976/16995†;
    51-17388/17556†; 52-9129/9975†;
    53-4886/6152‡; 54-1522/1618†;
    54-2950/2955†; 54-4035/4036†;
    55-2979/2983†; 55-3017/3049†;
    55-3074/3117†; 55-4332/4456†;
    55-4807/4810†; 55-4945/4962†;
    56-1573/1792§; 56-6848/6927†;
    57-530/769; 58-450/710;
    58-2094/2106.

TV-2: 49-2757/2772; 51-4425/4434;
    51-4515/4524; 51-6578/6587;
    51-6665/6674; 51-8518/8541;
    51-8636/8651; 51-8729/8749;
    51-8836/8870; 51-8940/8953;
    51-9040/9075; 51-9150/9167;
    53-2687/2780; 53-5241/5243;
    53-5310/5317; 53-5351/5358;
    53-5360/5363; 53-5375/5383;
    53-5385/5387; 53-5437/5440;
    53-5442/5448; 53-5450/5456;
    53-5458/5460; 53-5505/5507;
    53-5509/5516; 53-5518/5524;
    53-5526/5532; 53-5450/5456;
    53-5458/5460; 53-5505/5507;
    53-5509/5516; 53-5518/5524;
    53-5526/5532; 53-5534; 53-5570/5573;
    53-5575/5580; 53-5582/5586;
    53-5588/5593; 53-5595/5599;
    53-5601/5603; 53-5642/5643;
    53-5645/5649; 53-5651/5655;
    53-5657/5661; 53-5663/5667;
    53-5669/5674; 53-5676/5680;
    53-5682/5686; 53-5688/5692;
    53-5694/5698; 53-5700/5704;
    53-5706/5709; 53-5711/5715;
    53-5717/5719; 54-2689/2728;
    55-2984/3016; 55-3050/3073;
    56-1573/1792§; 56-3659/3694.

*38 from these two batches completed as FP-80A.
†All or part of these batches for MAP use.
‡Includes 176 TV-2s for US Navy, listed separately.
§This batch comprised 184 T-33A and 36 TV-2.

Lockheed F-94C with large centre-line tip tanks, wing-mounted gun pods and Air National Guard markings (*E. M. Sommerich*).

Lockheed F-94 Starfire

Development of the original F-80 Shooting Star jet fighter as a two-seat all-weather radar-equipped fighter began in 1949 and took advantage of the work already done to convert the basic design into a two-seat trainer, the T-33. Two YF-94 prototypes were produced by converting T-33s; the first of these (48-356) had been an F-80C before conversion to the prototype TF-80C, and it first flew as a YF-94 on April 16, 1949. Changes involved the fitting of APG-32 radar in the nose, a radar operator in the rear seat and a 6,000 lb. afterburning J33-A-33 engine. Armament comprised four 0·50-inch M-3 guns in the forward fuselage. As the F-94A (Lockheed Model 780) this variant went into production in 1949 and deliveries to the 317th and 319th All-Weather Fighter Squadrons began in May 1950. One hundred and ten F-94As were built.

The 19th F-94A (49-2497) was converted to the YF-94B prototype in 1950, with larger tip tanks centred on the wings (the F-94A had F-80-type tip tanks beneath the wing), revised hydraulics and a Sperry Zero Reader in the cockpit. First flight was on September 28, 1950, and production of the F-94B, starting in 1951, totalled 357. Two F-94Bs (51-5500 and 5501) served as configuration prototypes for the proposed F-94D (Model 980) single-seat ground attack variant, but a production order for 113 F-94Ds was cancelled in October 1951.

A more fundamental redesign of the type produced the F-94C (Model 880), which was initially designated F-97A, but was redesignated on September 12, 1950. The 8,750 lb.s.t. afterburning Pratt & Whitney J48-P-5 engine was installed, and the wing was redesigned with a thickness/chord ratio of 10 per cent compared with 13 per cent previously and a Hughes E-5 fire control system was fitted. Nose design was altered to mount 24 2·75-in. Mighty Mouse air rockets in a ring round the radome, faired in by a

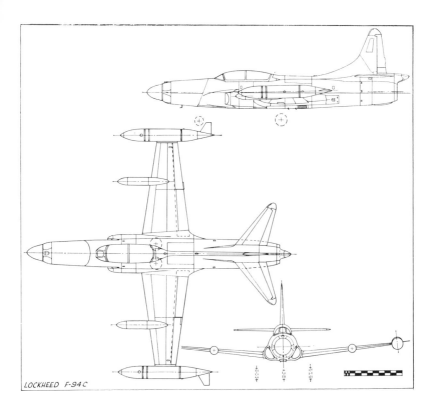

LOCKHEED F-94 C

retractable shield, and a pod carrying 12 more of these missiles could be carried on each wing. The tailplane was swept back, and the critical Mach number increased from 0·80 to 0·85. Gross weight went up from 16,850 lb. to 24,200 lb.

Two YF-94C prototypes were converted from F-94Bs, the first of these (50-955) flying first as the L-188 demonstrator (N94C) on January 19, 1950

Lockheed F-94A with original underslung tanks (*Howard Levy*).

377

with an F-94B-type nose and revised tip tanks. Production of the F-94C totalled 387.

The F-94B entered service in April 1951 with the 61st FIS at Selfridge A.F.B., and the F-94C in March 1953 with the 437th FIS at Otis A.F.B. Service use was principally in CONAC (Continental Air Command), which had been set up in December 1948 to embrace ADC, TAC and the nine fighter squadrons previously assigned to SAC. The Starfire also flew with squadrons of Alaskan Air Command and, in March 1951, F-94As began to reach the 68th FIS at Itazuke, Japan, in FEAF. The 68th took the Starfire into combat service over Korea at the end of 1951 and was joined there in 1952 by the F-94B-equipped 339th FIS and 319th FIS.

Progressively retired from the active USAF from 1954, the A and B models were passed to ANG units, and 21 Guard squadrons eventually flew Starfires, including F-94Cs, until 1959.

During the Korean War, a single-seat ground support and long-range escort version of the F-94C was proposed. One prototype YF-94D was produced by conversion of a "C" in 1951, but a production order for 112 F-94Ds was cancelled.

TECHNICAL DATA (F-94C)

MANUFACTURER: Lockheed Aircraft Corporation, Burbank, California.
TYPE: All-weather fighter.
ACCOMMODATION: Pilot and radar operator in tandem in enclosed cockpit.
POWER PLANT: One 6,350 lb. s.t. (8,750 lb. with a/b) Pratt & Whitney J48-P-5 or P-5A turbojet.
DIMENSIONS: Span (over tip tanks), 42 ft. 5 in. Length, 44 ft. 6 in. Height, 14 ft. 11 in. Wing area, 232·8 sq. ft.
WEIGHTS: Empty, 12,700 lb. Gross 24,200 lb.
PERFORMANCE: Max. speed, 585 m.p.h. at 30,000 ft. Combat speed, 522 m.p.h. at 49,700 ft. Initial climb 7,890 ft./min. Service ceiling, 51,400 ft. Ferry range, 1,200 st. miles.
ARMAMENT: Twenty-four 2·75 in. folding-fin air rockets in nose and twelve each in two wing pods.
SERIAL NUMBERS:
YF-94: 48-356; 48-373. F-94B: 50-805/955; 51-5307/5512.
F-94A: 49-2479/2588. F-94C: 50-956/1063; 51-5513/5698; 51-13511/13603.

Lockheed F-94B with 61st FIS shark's mouth insignia (*Peter M. Bowers*).

378

Lockheed F-104A with Sidewinder missiles at wing tips (*Lockheed photo*).

Lockheed F-104 Starfighter

The "missile with a man in it", as the F-104 has been called, was the first operational interceptor capable of sustained speeds above Mach 2, and the first aircraft ever to hold the World Speed and Altitude records for aeroplanes simultaneously. Its design began in November 1952 as Lockheed Model 83 and the USAF ordered two prototypes in March 1953, as the tactical day fighter weapon system WS-303A. The design concept was radical, with a long, needle-nosed fuselage tightly tailored around a single large turbojet; tiny, thin wings without sweepback and a T-tail. With a span of only 21 ft. 11 in., the F-104 was one of the smallest aircraft ever produced for the USAF.

Lockheed test pilot Tony Le Vier flew the first XF-104 (53-7786) on February 7, 1954. This and the second prototype were powered by the 10,000 lb. s.t. afterburning Wright XJ65-W-6 turbojet; with this engine, an XF-104 reached Mach 1·79 on March 25, 1955. Subsequent aircraft, however, had the 14,800-lb. afterburning General Electric J79-GE-3 engine. A batch of 15 YF-104As (Model 183) was built for service trials with this engine and also introduced the chock-control ramps in the fuselage-side air intakes, forward (in place of rearward) retracting undercarriage and a lengthened fuselage. These were features also of the production model F-104A while later modification introduced a ventral fin and -3B engines. Basic armament was an M-61 20-mm. multi-barrel gun in the fuselage and a Sidewinder AAM at each wingtip.

Mach 2 was first reached in a YF-104A on April 27, 1955, by Joe Ozier. Deliveries of the F-104A to the 83rd Fighter-Interceptor Squadron, at Hamilton A.F.B., began on January 26, 1958, and pilots from this squadron were responsible for the first speed and altitude record flights by the Starfighter. Flying YF-104As from the Lockheed test base at Palmdale, Major Howard C. Johnson reached 91,249 ft. on May 7, 1958, and Captain Walter W. Irwin reached 1,404·19 m.p.h. on May 16, 1958. Later an F-104A set up seven climb-to-height records, taking 41·8 seconds for the first 3,000 m. (9,840 ft.) and 4 min. 26 sec. to reach 25,000 m. (82,000 ft.).

Lockhead F-104C of Tactical Air Command (*Lockheed photo*).

The F-104A was joined in service with Air Defense Command by the two-seat F-104B, with full operational capability but a second (tandem) cockpit to allow its use as an operational trainer. The first F-104B (Model 283) flew on February 7, 1957 and production aircraft had increased fin area and a fully-powered rudder. An order for 18 RF-104A reconnaissance versions of the Starfighter was cancelled early in 1957; production of the F-104A totalled 153 and of the F-104B, 26. The F-104As and Bs were temporarily withdrawn from ADC by 1960, and 24 of these were converted in 1960 and 1961 to target drones designated QF-104. After a period of service with the ANG, some F-104As and Bs returned to service with ADC, and were then joined by some F-104Cs transferrd from TAC.

For use by Tactical Air Command, the F-104C (Model 483) and F-104D (Model 383) were developed, respectively single and two-seaters. With a 15,800 lb. a/b J79-GE-7, they introduced flap-blowing, provision for in-flight probe-and-drogue refuelling, and equipment for the ground-attack role. Deliveries of the F-104C to the 831st Air Division of TAC began on October 16, 1958 at George A.F.B. On December 14, 1959, an F-104C took the altitude record to 103,389 ft. Production totalled 77 F-104Cs and 21 F-104Ds.

Two-seat F-104B, showing use of same FG "Buzz Number" as single-seat Starfighter (*Norman E. Taylor*).

380

The high-altitude capabilities of the Starfighter were further enhanced in 1963 when three NF-104As were produced by modification of F-104As. These aircraft each had a 6,000 lb. s.t. Rocketdyne AR-2 rocket engine fitted in the tail above the jet pipe, a larger fin and rudder, extended wing tips and reaction jet controls at the nose, tail and wing tips. They could reach altitudes of up to 130,000 ft. and were used at the USAF Aerospace Research Pilots' School at Edwards AFB. Other Starfighters were used by NASA for astronaut training, with the designation F-104N.

Additional Starfighter production under USAF contract was undertaken by Lockheed in connection with Mutual Aid Programmes, but none of these later variants served with the USAF. Primary MAP Starfighter was the F-104G (Model 683) which had an uprated engine, strengthened structure and changed operational equipment, and was built in Europe. A two-seat training version, built by Lockheed, with full operational capability was designated TF-104G (Model 583) and a version with a reconnaissance

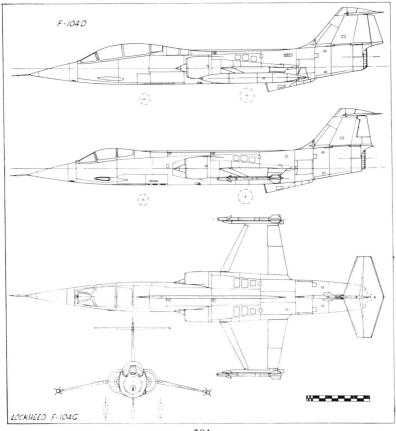

F-104D

LOCKHEED F-104G

pack was designated RF-104G (Model 683). The F-104J and F-104S were versions for production in Japan and Italy respectively.

The USAF also ordered 140 F-104Gs from Canadair for delivery to MAP nations, after Canada had ordered CF-104 Starfighters for her own air force. Included among the aircraft bearing USAF serial numbers were a number of F-104Gs built in Europe and used in USAF markings to train Luftwaffe pilots under USAF direction at Luke A.F.B., Arizona. Lockheed also built for the Luftwaffe 30 F-104Fs (Model 483), two-seaters generally similar to the F-104D.

TECHNICAL DATA (F-104C)

MANUFACTURER: Lockheed Aircraft Corporation, Burbank, California.
TYPE: Fighter-bomber.
ACCOMMODATION: Pilot in enclosed cockpit.
POWER PLANT: One 10,000 lb.s.t. (15,800 lb. with a/b) General Electric J79-GE-7 turbojet.
DIMENSIONS: Span, 21 ft. 11 in. Length, 54 ft. 9 in. Height, 13 ft. 6 in. Wing area, 196·1 sq. ft.
WEIGHT: Empty, 12,760 lb. Gross, 27,853.
PERFORMANCE: Max. speed, 1,150 m.p.h. at 40,000 ft. Initial climb, 54,000 ft./min. Service ceiling, over 55,000 ft. Range, 850-1,500 st. miles.
ARMAMENT: One 20-mm. six-barrel rotary Vulcan gun in nose; two 1,000 lb. bombs or two or four Sidewinder AAMs.
SERIAL NUMBERS:

XF-104: 53-7786/7787.	F-104G*: 61-2601/2623; 62-12214/12231;
YF-104A: 55-2955/2971.	63-13229/13278; 63-13690/13691;
F-104A: 56-730/882.	65-12545; 65-12745/12754;
F-104B: 56-3719/3724; 57-1294/1313.	66-13524/13526; 67-14885/14889;
F-104C: 56-883/938; 57-910/930.	67-22517.
F-104D: 57-1314/1334.	F-104G-CF*: 62-12302/12349;
F-104F*: 59-4994/5023.	62-12697/12734; 63-13638/13647;
RF-104G*: 61-2624/2633; 62-12232/12261;	64-17752/17795.
67-14890/14892.	TF-104G*: 61-3025/3084; 62-12262/12279;
	63-8452/8469; 63-12681/12696;
	64-15104/15106; 65-9415;
	66-13622/13631.

*Purchased by USAF for other users

Camouflaged F-104C, showing fixed (removable) in-flight refuelling probe alongside cockpit
(*Lockheed photo*).

Lockheed C-130A Hercules in early natural metal finish, with nose radome in place of original bluff nose shape (*Peter M. Bowers*).

Lockheed C-130 Hercules

Development of the Hercules (Lockheed Model 82) was started in 1951 after a top USAF policy decision to equip with turboprop transports, a decision which produced the C-130, C-133 and the projected C-132. It was the first transport produced under the weapon system concept, as the SS-400L medium cargo support system. A contract for two prototypes designated YC-130 was placed on July 11, 1951 and was followed by production contracts in September 1952. While the two YC-130s were built at Burbank—where Stanley Beltz made the first flight on August 23, 1954—the production line was laid down at Marietta, Georgia. There, the first C-130A flew on April 7, 1955; like the YC-130s it had 3,750 s.h.p. Allison T56-A-1A turboprops and a bluff front fuselage. Later production C-130As had T56-A-9 engines.

Deliveries of the C-130A to Troop Carrier Command and TAC units began in December 1956 and 204 were purchased to equip four Wings, including the 463rd T.C. Wing and the 322nd Division USAFE. The installation of APS-42 or APN-59 radar changed the nose profile of all but the first 27 aircraft, all of which were eventually retrofitted with the radar, and a later modification programme strengthened the fuselage for 20-ton payloads. The internal fuel capacity of 5,250 U.S. gallons was supplemented by two 450 U.S. gallon underwing pylon tanks.

Several special variants of the C-130A were produced. These included eight GC-130A (later, DC-130A) drone launcher/directors for ARDC, carrying four drones under the wings each, and 16 RC-130A (support system SS-400M) for the 1,370th Photo Mapping Wing of MATS' APCS with special aerial survey equipment. One TC-130A was the prototype of a crew trainer, later modified to an RC-130A; the other photo-survey RC-130As were built as such. During 1967, one Hercules was converted to AC-130A gun-ship by the USAF at Wright-Patterson A.F.B., and was tested in

Vietnam by the 14th SOW. The installation comprised four 20-mm. Gatling-type guns and four 7·62-mm. Miniguns in the fuselage, plus special sensors and night flying aids. Following the success of trials in Vietnam, seven more AC-130E gunship conversions were ordered from LTV in 1968, and entered service in 1970, and a further eight AC-130As were then modified, each with two 7·62-mm., 20-mm. and 40-mm. guns.

Twelve Hercules were delivered for service with the USAF in the Arctic, primarily for DEW-line resupply missions, with combined wheel/ski landing gear. They were designated C-130Ds and followed a prototype conversion of a C-130A, other changes including provision for JATO and for extra fuel in fuselage tanks. Sixteen JC-130As were equipped to track missiles over the Atlantic test range; later, six of these became AC-130As (as mentioned above) and two others were designated RC-130S to serve on night SAR missions in Vietnam, carrying the Battlefield Illumination Airborne System. Ten other Hercules became C-130A-IIs when equipped for electronic reconnaissance.

The C-130A was followed in production by the C-130B (Model 282), which differed primarily in having 4,050 e.h.p. T56-A-7A engines, Hamilton Standard in place of Aeroproducts propellers, more internal fuel and increased weights. The first C-130B flew at Marietta on November 20, 1958, and deliveries to the 453rd TC Wing's 774th Squadron began on June 12, 1959. Of total production of 230 aircraft in this basic configuration, 128 went to the USAF, 33 to other air forces and 69 to the USN and USCG under different designations.

One C-130B was modified as a STOL test-bed with a boundary-layer control system provided by air bleeds from two Allison YJ56-A-6 engines operating as gas producers and carried in pods beneath the wings. It operated as the NC-130B (58-0712), and the designation C-130C was reserved for a possible production version. First flight was made on February 8, 1960.

Five WC-130Bs were delivered for weather reconnaissance duties with the 53rd Weather Reconnaissance Squadron, known as the "Hurricane Hunters". During 1970, one WC-130B and one C-130B were modified to an improved configuration at the Warner Robins Air Materiel Area and

Lockheed C-130D was ski-equipped for operation, by New York ANG squadron, in the Arctic to support DEW-line.

Lockheed C-130E operated by 357th TAS, an AF Reserve unit, showing Europe 1 finish with grey undersides and small size insignia (*Stephen P. Peltz*).

modifications of the other four WC-130Bs and 11 C-130Bs to the new weather reconnaissance standard followed. Fourteen other C-130Bs were delivered from 1961 as JC-130Bs with air snatch satellite recovery gear for use by the 6593rd Test Squadron at Hickam A.F.B., Hawaii, in connection with the Discoverer programme.

Thirteen C-130Bs modified for electronic reconnaissance (ELINT) duty were at first designated C-130B-IIs before becoming RC-130Bs. A single aircraft used temporarily as a staff transport was VC-130B until reconverted to a standard C-130B.

The C-130E (Model 382) was ordered in 1961 in a rush programme to modernize MATS (now MAC) airlift capability, an initial contract for 99 being placed with Lockheed. To meet the strategic requirements of MATS operation, the range was increased by making provision for 1,360 U.S. gallons external fuel tanks between the engines under each wing (compared with the two 450 gallon tanks which could be carried outboard of the engines by the C-130A and C-130B). Higher gross weights were permitted. The first flight by a C-130E was made on August 15, 1961, and deliveries began in April 1962. Nearly 500 aircraft were purchased from Lockheed in the C-130E configuration, of which 377 were for MATS and TAC, the remainder being for the USN (4), USCG (1), FAA (3), and foreign air forces (108).

As with the earlier versions, C-130Es were the basis for a number of modification programmes. Of particular interest were the aircraft for use by the Special Operations Force to recover downed aircrew or agents from behind enemy lines. For this purpose, 18 C-130Es (including one NC-130E used earlier in a test role) were fitted with the Fulton STAR (Surface-To-Air-Recovery) yoke on the nose and other special equipment, and were designated C-130E-Is. These were the first of the *Combat Talon* Hercules, a code-name used for the SOF role, and they passed through a number of modification programmes, whereby two became MC-130E-Y

385

(Yank), one an MC-130E-C (Clamp) and 11 became C-130H(CT)s after the C-130H had appeared as an improved C-130E with uprated engines. Of the C-130H(CT)s, nine still later became MC-130E-Cs and the other two, E-Ys. Another NC-130E was modified to become an MC-130E-S (Swap), the Yank, Clamp and Swap indicators being used for differing equipment fits.

Ten C-130Es equipped for the Airborne Battlefield Command and Control Center (ABCCC) role went into service in Vietnam as C-130E-IIs before being redesignated EC-130Es in 1976. In 1980, some at least of these aircraft were modified to EC-130H standard with the T56-A-15 engines and AAR capability. The EC-130E designation was then assigned to eight aircraft operated by the Pennsylvania ANG in *Coronet Solo II* configuration for electronic surveillance, with large blade antennae under the wings and above the dorsal fin. Eleven AC-130E gunships for service in Vietnam had armament of two 7·62-mm., two 20-mm. and two 40-mm. guns (or one 40-mm. and one 105-mm. howitzer). One was lost in action and the other 10 were converted to AC-130Hs, for operation by the 16th SOS. Seven DC-130Es were equipped to carry, launch and guide drones or RPVs, and six WC-130Es were modified for weather reconnaissance.

Reference has already been made to the C-130H, which appeared in March 1965 as an improved "E" featuring uprated (but usually derated) T56-A-15 engines, some structural improvements, better braking system, optional

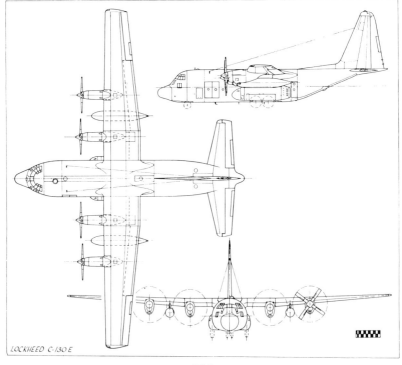

LOCKHEED C-130 E

Lockheed EC-130E, with dorsal "fin" antenna, in South-East Asia camouflage and PA code of 193rd SOS, Pennsylvania ANG (*Robert Ruffle*).

provision for in-flight refuelling and numerous equipment and missions options. First deliveries were for overseas customers but the C-130H replaced the "E" as the basic model as the USAF placed additional contracts for Hercules throughout the 'seventies and 'eighties, and it was still in production in 1988. By then, over 300 had been built for the USAF, AFRES, ANG, USN and USCG, and over 450 had been ordered by more than 40 other nations. In addition, some of the USAF special-purpose C-130E variants had been upgraded to C-130H standard, as noted.

Apart from the C-130H transport variants bought principally for AFRES and ANG units, the USAF procured H-model Hercules in several special variants, starting with the HC-130H versions for the Aerospace Rescue and Recovery Service (earlier, the Air Rescue Service). First flown on November 30, 1964 (as the first in the "H" series), the HC-130H had the nose-mounted Fulton STAR equipment and, in a large fairing above the forward fuselage, the Cook ARD-17 aerial tracking equipment to locate re-entering space capsules. Later in their service lives, most HC-130Hs had the STAR yokes removed, and 15 were then converted to WC-130Hs to serve in the weather reconnaissance role. Two others became DC-130H drone controllers, and the designation JHC-130H applied to two HC-130Hs that were modified for the aerial recovery of re-entering space capsules, before being re-designated NC-130Hs.

The USAF acquired 43 HC-130Hs in 1964/65, and, to allow air-to-air refuelling of the rescue helicopters operated by ARRS, 20 similar HC-130Ps were acquired in 1965/66. These had underwing pods containing hose drum units, and 15 HC-130Ns purchased in 1969 were generally similar to HC-130Hs, but equipped specifically for the recovery of space capsules. The HC-130H, N and P variants were eventually operated by six squadrons of the ARRS within MAC, by two ANG squadrons (California and New York) and three AFRES squadrons. The New York ANG (139th TAS, 109th TAG) also received four LC-130Hs, these being standard transport models fitted with skis (like the U.S. Navy's LC-130Fs) for operation in the Arctic.

To bring the operational force of Hercules in service with the 1st SOW to 38

Lockheed HC-130N in original A.R.S. overall grey finish (*Dr Alan Beaumont*).

(including the 14 updated MC-130Es already described), acquisition of 24 new MC-130Hs began in 1984. These aircraft, known as *Combat Talon* 2s, differed in several respects from the *Combat Talon* 1 standard, including the use of Emerson AN/APQ-170 terrain following/terrain avoidance radar in place of Texas AN/APQ-122; new ECM and Texas AAQ-15 infra-red detecting equipment and a modified air drop system for use at higher than normal speeds. First flight of a fully-equipped MC-130H was made in December 1987.

Another special-duty version of the "H" model Hercules, the EC-130H, served as a communication jamming platform under the *Compass Call* code-name. Ten of these aircraft, modified from standard C-130H airframes, were flown by the 41st and 43rd Electronic Countermeasures Squadrons, and were easily identifiable by the same pale grey finish as used on the GD/Grumman EF-111A Raven jammers, as well as by radomes on the rear fuselage sides and unusual aerials under the tailplane. Four of the EC-130Es used for the ABCCC role were also known as EC-130Hs when modified to have in-flight refuelling receptacles, modernized avionics and uprated engines.

Also based on C-130H airframes were 12 AC-130U gunships, acquisition

Lockheed HC-130P in overall three-tone camouflage, operated by 129 ARRS, California ANG (*MAP Photo*).

of which began in FY87 when a contract was placed with Rockwell to modify and equip basic Lockheed-built C-130H aircraft to the required standard. Armament of the AC-130U included 105-mm., 40-mm. and 25-mm. guns, and the equipment suite included FLIR, low-light-level TV, strike radar, ECM and other items to the latest standards. Deliveries of fully-equipped AC-130Us were to start in 1991, for service alongside the AC-130Hs with the SOF.

TECHNICAL DATA (C-130H)

MANUFACTURER: Lockheed-Georgia Company, Marietta, Georgia.

TYPE: Tactical transport.

ACCOMMODATION: Crew of four plus provision for up to 92 troops or six standard freight pallets.

POWER PLANT: Four 4,910 e.s.h.p. (derated to 4,508 e.s.h.p.) Allison T56-A-15 turboprops.

DIMENSIONS: Span, 132 ft. 7 in. Length, 97 ft. 9 in. Height, 38 ft. 3 in. Wing area, 1,745 sq. ft.

WEIGHTS: Empty, 76,780 lb. Gross, 175,000 lb.

PERFORMANCE: Max. speed, 386 m.p.h. at 25,000 ft. Cruising speed 353 m.p.h. Initial climb, 2,570 ft./min. Service ceiling, 33,000 ft. Range, 2,745 st. miles with max. payload.

ARMAMENT: None.

SERIAL NUMBERS:

YC-130: 53-3396/3397.

C-130A: 53-3129/3135; 54-1621/1640; 55-001/048; 56-468/551; 57-453/497; 57-498/509*.

RC-130A: 57-510/524.

C-130B: 57-525/529; 58-711/758; 59-1524/1537; 59-5957; 60-293/310; 60-5450/5453*; 61-948/972; 61-2634/2649; 62-3487; 62-3488/3491*; 62-4140/4143*.

WC-130B: 62-3492/3496.

C-130E; 61-2358/2373; 62-1784/1866; 63-7764/7899; 63-9810/9817; 63-13186/13189*; 64-0495/0572; 64-17624/17639*; 64-17680/17681; 64-17949*; 64-18240; 65-10686/10689*; 65-12766/12769*; 65-12896/12907*; 66-4114/4115*; 66-4310/4313*; 67-14726/14729*; 68-10934/10951; 69-6566/6583; 69-7706/7710*; 70-1259/1276; 70-1947*; 71-1468*; 72-1288/1299; 73-991*.

C-130H: 64-15094/15096*; 68-8218/8219*; 68-10952/10957*; 71-213/223*; 71-1067/1069*; 71-1374/1375*; 71-1797/1808*; 73-1580/1599; 73-1600/1601*; 73-1678/1680*; 74-1658/1693; 74-2061/2072; 74-2130/2134; 75-0534/0539*; 75-0542/0549*; 76-1598/1603*; 78-0745/0750*; 78-0755/0768*; 78-0806/0813; 79-0473/0480; 80-0320/0326; 81-001; 81-0626/0631; 82-0054/0061; 83-0486/0489; 84-0204/0213; 85-0035/0042; 85-1361/1368; 86-0372/0373*; 86-0374/0389; 86-0410/0415; 86-1391/1398; 86-0418/0419; 87-0137/0138*; 87-9281/9288

LC-130H: 83-0490/0493.

MC-130H: 83-1212; 84-0475/0476; 85/0011/0012; 86-1699; 87-0023/0024.

HC-130H: 64-14852/14866; 65-0962/0987; 65-0989/0990.

HC-130P: 65-0988; 65-0991/0994; 66-211/225.

HC-130N: 69-5819/5833.

AC-130H/U: 87-0125/0128

*For MAP and/or FMS
(Plus later contracts)

Lockheed U-2A, in overall natural metal finish, operated by 4028th SRS, 4080th SRW, in the early 'sixties (*Lockheed photo 1755-18*).

Lockheed U-2, TR-1

Technically one of the most remarkable and operationally one of the most controversial aeroplanes ever to serve with the USAF, the Lockheed U-2 was categorized in the "Utility" class in order to hide its real operational purpose. This, it became known in 1960, was to make unarmed reconnaissance flights over Communist-controlled territory. On May 1, 1960, while the traditional May Day parade was being cheered through the streets of Moscow, a U-2 on such a reconnaissance flight crashed near Sverdlovsk. The pilot survived and was publicly tried in Moscow in August 1960, being sentenced to 10 years' detention. The U-2, which was said to be flying without military markings, had taken off from the Incirlik Air Base near Adana, in Turkey, and was to have landed at Bodo, in Norway, after flying the length of Russia. Operations of this kind over Russian territory—although not always of such ambitious character— were unofficially said to have been conducted by U-2s for some two years prior to the 1960 incident.

Work on the U-2 began in 1954 in great secrecy, with "espionage reconnaissance" as the primary role. This called for an ability to fly for long periods at very high altitudes and dictated the basic design parameters. The U-2 evolved essentially as a powered glider, with a sailplane-like high aspect ratio (14·3:1) wing and lightweight structure. A typical weight-saving device was the use of a single unit, two wheel main undercarriage, with jettisonable wing-tip wheels for take-off stability. Landings were made on the main wheel and tail wheel, and the wing-tips were turned down to serve as skids. A braking parachute was used.

The first U-2 (Lockheed Model CL-282) was flown for the first time by Lockheed test pilot Tony Le Vier on August 1, 1955, at Groom Lake, a secure airfield in the Nevada desert. It had been developed with extreme rapidity in

390

the Lockheed Experimental Department (more colloquially known as the "Skunk Works") under the direction of Clarence L. Johnson. Financed through unconventional channels and partially under the direction of the CIA, the U-2 was quickly brought into production and, considering its unusual characteristics, was soon ready for service. USAF serial numbers have been made public for 53 early-model U-2s and 25 of the later batch of U-2Rs, which were almost a new design, but the first U-2 to fly carried no serial number, and production of between 8 and 12 of the U-2Rs may have been cancelled.

Included in the initial batch of U-2s were about 40 U-2As, with 10,500 lb.s.t. Pratt & Whitney J57-P-37 or 11,200 lb.s.t. J57-P-37A engine and provision to carry cameras or other sensors in the nose and aft of the cockpit in the so-called "Q" bay, and a smaller number (probably seven) U-2Bs which had 15,800 lb.s.t. Pratt & Whitney J75-P-13 or 17,000 lb.s.t. J75-P-13B turbojets and increased internal fuel capacity. Many A and B models later became U-2Cs, with J75 engines, enlarged nose bays and other changes, and five new-build U-2Ds had enlarged Q-bays that allowed for a second crew position, necessary for certain high-altitude missions. One U-2C and one U-2D became two-seat U-2CT trainers, with raised rear cockpits.

Other designations known to have been used were U-2E for about 18 updated U-2A/Bs with ECM and other special equipment; U-2F for a few aircraft with air-to-air refuelling capability and U-2G for two U-2Cs with arrester hooks for operation on and off aircraft carriers.

Most of these early-batch U-2s served with the CIA before passing to the USAF, which operated them primarily for high-altitude reconnaissance and the five-year High-Altitude Sampling Program (HASP) in support of Defense Atomic Support Agency. Those aircraft equipped for HASP were designated WU-2As. USAF operations were initially conducted by the 4028th Strategic Reconnaissance Squadron (part of the 4080th SRW), which added reconnaissance overflights of Cuba to its responsibilities in 1962, to monitor the build-up of Soviet missile forces there. Moving from Laughlin A.F.B., Texas to Davis-Monthan A.F.B., Arizona, in 1963, the 4028th SRS

Lockheed U-2D in overall black finish, operated by 4080th SRW over New Zealand for High Altitude Sampling Program (HASP) (*Lockheed photo LA4958*).

391

Unmarked, all-black Lockheed U-2C operated by 100th SRW (*William Strandberg*).

Lockheed U-2D attached to 6512th TG, with ARDC insignia on tail and olive drab upper front fuselage.

began to operate over Vietnam at the beginning of 1964, and continued that activity for 12 years. As part of the cover for CIA operation of the U-2s, which had begun in June 1956, units known as the 1st and later, 2nd and 3rd Weather Reconnaissance Squadrons, Provisional (WRSP-1, -2 and -3) were set up, but these were not USAF units.

Lockheed U-2s were operated by the Air Research and Development Command from Edwards A.F.B. (the 6512th Test Group) on special missions primarily concerned with the tracking and recovery of Discoverer space capsules and the development of equipment for Midas and Samos satellites. A few were assigned to the Chinese Nationalist Air Force for reconnaissance sorties over the Chinese mainland.

During 1966, Lockheed received a production contract for the completely new U-2R variant of the basic aircraft. This was designed in the light of operational experience to offer improved performance, better payload and somewhat less demanding flight characteristics. It featured a major increase of wing span and area, a larger fuselage and provision for sensor pods on the wing. Span went up from 80 ft. to 103 ft., area from 565 sq. ft. to 1,000 sq. ft., fuselage length from 50 ft. to 63 ft., and maximum take-off weight from 22,542 lb. to more than 40,000 lb. The J75-P-13B engine was retained, and the first flight was made on August 28, 1967.

Continuing to operate over Vietnam, the 4028th SRS was redesignated during 1966 as the 349th SRS in the 100th SRW, and in 1968 its detachment at Bien Hoa became a squadron, the 99th SRS, in its own right. Much of the squadron's activity was concerned with the operation of RPVs to collect

Lockheed U-2C (converted from U-2A) in two-tone grey finish for European deployment in 1975 (*Flight Line photo*).

communications intelligence around and over mainland China, with U-2Rs gradually becoming available (after initial use by the CIA) to replace the earlier variants. The first U-2CT dual control trainer modified from a U-2A that had been updated to U-2C, did not fly until February 13, 1973. A second, similar, aircraft was acquired later, and one of these U-2CTs led the move in March 1976 of the 99th SRS to Beale AFB, there to join the Lockheed SR-71s of the 9th SRW. This became the final permanent base for USAF U-2s, but during the 'seventies and 'eighties many overseas deployments were made, particularly to the U.K.

Late in 1979, production of the U-2 was re-instated, for the second time, when the USAF ordered a small batch of U-2Rs as attrition replacements, and a larger quantity of aircraft designated TR-1s. The latter—single-seat TR-1As and two-seat dual-control TR-1Bs (plus an ER-2 earth resources survey aircraft for use by NASA)—were almost identical, externally, with the U-2Rs. The TR-1A had been designed to carry the Precision Location Strike System (PLSS)—an advanced sensing system to locate and identify hostile radar sites and to direct strike aircraft or ground-based missiles against them. When not operating as part of PLSS, the TR-1As could carry sensors similar

Lockheed U-2R in overall black finish (*Lockheed photo*).

Lockheed TR-1A, all black with red serial number and no national insignia (*Lockheed photo CC2905*).

to those used by the U-2R for high-altitude reconnaissance. First flights of the TR-1A and TR-1B were made on August 1, 1981 and February 23, 1983, respectively, and the new type entered service that year with the 95th Reconnaissance Squadron, part of the 17th RW, at Alconbury in the U.K. The sole ER-2 flew on May 11, 1981, in time to serve as a prototype for the TR-1 series. By 1987, a total of 26 TR-1As and two TR-1Bs had been funded for production, and up to 21 more were planned, but the PLSS system itself had meanwhile been cancelled.

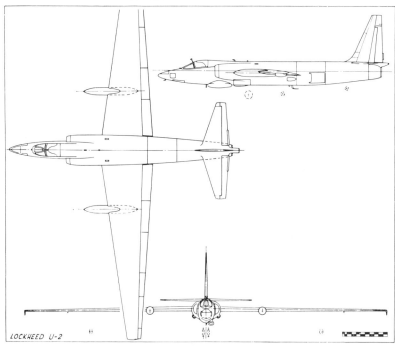

LOCKHEED U-2

394

TECHNICAL DATA (U-2B)

MANUFACTURER: Lockheed Aircraft Corporation, Burbank, California.
TYPE: High-altitude strategic and weather reconnaissance aircraft.
ACCOMMODATION: Pilot only; upward ejection seat.
POWER PLANT: One 17,000 lb.s.t. Pratt & Whitney J75-P-13B turbojet.
DIMENSIONS: Span 80 ft. 2 in. Length, 49 ft. 9 in. Height, 15 ft. 2 in. Wing area, 600 sq. ft. approx.
WEIGHTS: Empty, 13,000 lb. Gross, 23,100 lb.
PERFORMANCE: Max. speed, 528 m.p.h. above 40,000 ft. Cruising speed, 475 m.p.h. above 40,000 ft. Operational ceiling, about 75,000 ft. Range, about 4,500 miles. Endurance, over 10 hours.
ARMAMENT: None.
SERIAL NUMBERS:
U-2A/2B: 56-6675/6722. U-2R: 68-10329/10353.
U-2D: 56-6951/6955.

TECHNICAL DATA (TR-1A)

MANUFACTURER: Lockheed Aircraft Corporation, Burbank, California.
TYPE: High-altitude reconnaissance and stand-off battlefield surveillance aircraft.
ACCOMMODATION: Pilot only or (TR-1B) pilot and instructor in tandem.
POWER PLANT: One 17,000 lb.s.t. Pratt & Whitney J75-P-13B turbojet.
DIMENSIONS: Span, 103 ft. 0 in. Length, 63 ft. 0 in. Height, 16 ft. 0 in. Wing area, about 1,000 sq. ft.
WEIGHTS: Empty, 15,500 lb. Gross, 41,550 lb.
PERFORMANCE: Max. cruising speed, over 430 m.p.h. at 70,000 ft. Operational ceiling, 90,000 ft. Range, over 3,000 miles.
ARMAMENT: None.
SERIAL NUMBERS:
TR-1A: 80-1066/1091 ER-2: 80-1063
TR-1B: 80-1064/1065

The first of the two two-seat TR-1Bs, in overall white finish (*Lockheed photo CC2915*).

Lockheed SR-71 in overall matt black finish, with red serial number on fin and no national insignia (*Lockheed photo C04022*).

Lockheed SR-71

The first Mach 3 aeroplane to enter service with the USAF was the Lockheed SR-71, evolved from the Lockheed A-12 design for strategic reconnaissance duties. Entering service in 1966, the SR-71 could operate at altitudes above 85,000 ft. and at speeds approaching Mach 3.5 for sustained periods. This performance placed it far ahead of any other military aircraft available in the same period, and clearly indicated its value as a successor to such types as the RB-47 and the U-2 on which the U.S. relied heavily during the 1950s for strategic reconnaissance information.

The A-12 design (one of 12 project studies identified by Lockheed as A-1 to A-12), proceeded under a USAF contract placed in August 1959, the role being unarmed reconnaissance in succession to the U-2. Twenty-five aircraft were ordered, of which nine were to be two-seaters, using FY 60 funds, and with the close backing of the CIA. Powered temporarily by Pratt & Whitney J75 turbojets, the first A-12 flew at Groom Lake on April 26, 1962, and was re-engined with the definitive J58s designed to operate on an exotic blend of low volatility fuel known as JP-7, before the end of 1962. Between 1963 and 1968, single-seat A-12s were used on covert operations by the CIA. The two-seater was intended to launch and control Lockheed D-21 drones (similar in general configuration to the A-12 itself) in order to extend the reconnaissance capability over hostile territory, but this technique proved unsuccessful and only two of the planned nine two-seaters were built.

To meet the USAF's SOR-220 for an advanced interceptor, a version of the A-12 was proposed to replace the cancelled North American XF-108 Rapier, and three A-12s already on order were modified under the designation YF-12A. First flown at Groom Lake on August 7, 1963, the YF-12A carried

Lockheed A-12, serial 60-6932, ninth of the development batch of aircraft (*Lockheed photo CC2358*).

Hughes AN/ASG-18 radar from the XF-108 and armament of four AIM-47A missiles, but no funds were made available for production. Later, one SR-71A (64-17951) was redesignated YF-12C for use by NASA, taking the serial (60-6937) previously used on an A-12.

The two-seat SR-71A itself emerged to provide the USAF, rather than the CIA, with a high-performance reconnaissance aircraft. Retaining the configuration of the A-12, it was slightly larger, heavier and slower, but had more internal stowage space for cameras and sensors and for the Reconnaissance Systems Officer, to handle the extensive array of equipment. First flown on December 22, 1964, at Palmdale, the SR-71A entered service in January 1966 with the 4200th Strategic Reconnaissance Wing at Beale A.F.B. This unit was redesignated the 9th SRW later in 1966, with the 1st and 99th SR Squadrons. After the 99th SRS was disbanded, the 1st SRS continued as the sole operator of the SR-71A.

Of 32 SR-71s known to have been built, two were modified to SR-71B two-seat trainers (with raised rear cockpit) and one (the last built) was an SR-71C, also a two-seater. One other became the YF-12C as noted above, and at least four were cancelled from production. By 1988, attrition and funding limitations had reduced the number of SR-71As in operational use with the 9th SRW to six. Although widely used, the name Blackbird was unofficial.

Lockheed SR-71 in original finish, with white serial number and underwing insignia (*Lockheed photo LA 4540*).

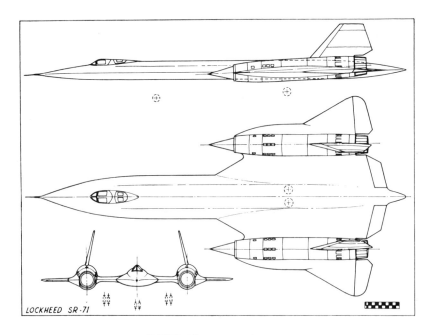

TECHNICAL DATA (SR-71A)

MANUFACTURER: Lockheed-California Company, Burbank, California.
TYPE: High performance strategic reconnaissance aircraft.
ACCOMMODATION: Pilot and reconnaissance systems officer in tandem.
POWER PLANT: Two 32,500 lb.s.t. (with afterburning) Pratt & Whitney J58 (JT11D-20B) turbojets.
DIMENSIONS: Span, 55 ft. 7 in. Length, 107 ft. 5 in. Height, 18 ft. 6 in.
WEIGHT: Empty, 60,000 lb. Gross, 172,000 lb.
PERFORMANCE: Max. speed, over 2,200 m.p.h. at 80,000 ft. Service ceiling, over 85,000 ft. Range, over 3,000 st. miles.
ARMAMENT: None.
SERIAL NUMBERS:

A-12: 60-6924/6933; 60-6937/6941.   SR-71A: 64-17950/17955; 64-17958/17980.
YF-12A: 60-6934/6936.   SR-71B: 64-17956/17957.
     SR-71C: 64-17981.

Two-seat Lockheed SR-71B in service with 4200th SRW (*USAF photo 175896*).

398

Lockheed C-141B conversion of C-141A, operated by 437th MAW (*Lockheed photo RM3514*).

Lockheed C-141 StarLifter

Among its aircraft designed for the USAF, Lockheed can claim a number of "firsts" including, in the case of the C-141A StarLifter, the first pure-jet transport designed for the strategic transport elements of the Air Force. A product of the Georgia branch of the Lockheed company, where the C-130 Hercules was already eastablished in production, the C-141 originated as Lockheed Model 300 in 1960 in response to a Specific Operational Requirement (SOR 182).

The requirement was issued on May 4, 1960, and was intended to modernize the strategic airlift capability of the Military Air Transport Service. After a design competition in which Lockheed competed with Boeing, Convair and Douglas, the Georgia design was named the winner on March 13, 1961. Development proceeded under the designation Support System SS476-L.

To meet the overall needs of the USAF, the new aircraft followed the Hercules in general layout, with a high wing and rear loading, but it was much larger and had a swept-back wing in order fully to utilize the performance increase offered by fitting four Pratt & Whitney TF33 turbofan engines in underwing pods. The size of the fuselage and of the rear loading doors was dictated by the types of military equipment to be carried.

Contractual arrangements were completed on August 16, 1961, for the initial batch of five C-141As, and the first of these flew at Marietta on December 17, 1963. Subsequent contracts brought total C-141A production to 284, with deliveries ending in December 1966. Deliveries began on October 19, 1964, at Tinker AFB and operational service with MATS (later, MAC) units began at Travis AFB on April 23, 1965, and a few months later the StarLifter started a regular supply operation across the Pacific to Vietnam. Subsequently this supply operation was maintained at virtually a daily frequency.

Delivery of the last C-141A was made on February 28, 1968 and 14 squadrons of MAC were equipped, in six Wings. A few aircraft were specially

399

adapted to carry the massive Minuteman ICBMs which, in their special containers, grossed 86,207 lb. In 1975, the USAF contracted with Lockheed to modify one C-141A to have a 23 ft. 4in. lengthening of the fuselage, air-to-air refuelling capability and a new wing root fairing. This aircraft flew as the YC-141B on March 24, 1977; after successful testing, the USAF decided to modify the entire StarLifter force to the new standard. The first "production" C-141B flew at Marietta on November 5, 1979, and the last of the 270 aircraft in the programme was redelivered to MAC on June 29, 1982. Service use continued in the 14 squadrons originally equipped with the C-141As, but a 10-year programme to transfer 80 StarLifters from the active Air Force to ANG and AFRES units began in 1986.

TECHNICAL DATA (C-141B)

MANUFACTURER: Lockheed-Georgia Company, Marietta, Georgia.
TYPE: Strategic transport.
ACCOMMODATION: Crew of four and 154 troops or 123 equipped paratroops or 94,508 lb. of payload.
POWER PLANT: Four 21,000 lb.s.t. Pratt & Whitney TF33-P-7 turbofans.
DIMENSIONS: Span, 159 ft. 11 in. Length, 168 ft. 3½ in. Height, 39 ft. 3 in. Wing area, 3,228 sq. ft.
WEIGHTS: Empty, 144,492 lb. Gross, 343,000 lb.
PERFORMANCE: Max. speed, 571 m.p.h. at 25,000 ft. Cruising speed, 494 m.p.h. Initial climb, 2,600 ft./min. Service ceiling, 41,600 ft. Range, 2,927 st. miles.
ARMAMENT: None.
SERIAL NUMBERS:
C-141A: 61-2775/2779; 63-8075/8090;   66-126/209; 66-7944/7959; 67-001/031;
  64-609/653; 65-216/281; 65-9397/9414;   67-164/166.

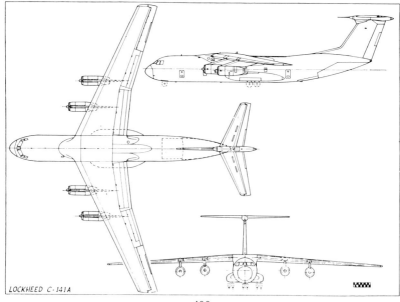

LOCKHEED C-141A

400

Lockheed C-5A in MATS grey with white upper fuselage (*Lockheed photo*).

Lockheed C-5 Galaxy

To supplement the Lockheed C-141 StarLifter and to increase the MATS airlift capability, the USAF began to study very large logistic transports in 1963. An early requirement identified as the CX-4 was for a 600,000 lb. aircraft but this was stepped up in 1964 when the requirement became known as the CX-HLS. This Heavy Logistics System was required to carry a payload of 125,000 lb. over a distance of 8,000 miles, or twice that load over a shorter distance, whilst also being able to operate from the same runway lengths and semi-prepared runways as the C-141.

Following a design competition between Boeing, Douglas and Lockheed, the last-mentioned company was named winner in October 1965, with a design which was a logical extrapolation of the Hercules/StarLifter series. With a gross weight of 764,500 lb., however, the Model 500 dwarfed not only the earlier transports but every other type operated by the USAF.

To power the aircraft, which took the designation C-5A as the first new design included in the post-1962 "C" series, General Electric developed the TF39 turbofan, the largest such engine produced up to that time, with a rating of 41,000 lb. The C-5A incorporated both nose and rear loading, by way of an upwards-hinged nose visor and a ramp and clamshell doors under the rear fuselage. Normal arrangement in the C-5A provided 75 troop seats on an upper rear deck, leaving the entire lower deck clear for freight, but another 270 troops could be carried in the main cabin. Provision was made for in-flight refuelling from KC-135A tankers.

The first C-5A, of five ordered initially for the development programme, flew on June 30, 1968 (with YTF39-GE-1 engines). Total planned USAF procurement for the C-5A was to be 115 aircraft to equip six squadrons, and the first production contract was for 53. The first delivery of a C-5A to MAC

Lockheed C-5B at take-off, revealing 28-wheel undercarriage – four on nose gear, six each on four main legs – and Europe 1 three-tone camouflage in which the "B" models were delivered from the company's Marietta, Georgia, plant (*Lockheed photo*).

was made on December 17, 1969, with the ninth aircraft off the line, and after a training programme, the C-5A became operational in 1970 and took its place alongside the C-141A on supply flights to Europe and South-East Asia.

Because of cost overruns, the six-squadron programme was reduced to four squadrons in 1969 and a second contract for 23 C-5As was then placed to make a total of 81 on order at the end of 1970. Deliveries were completed in May 1973.

During 1980, Lockheed received a contract to manufacture completely new wing torsion boxes for the entire MAC fleet of C-5As (77 at that time), to overcome a structural deficiency that had been discovered during testing of a fatigue specimen, and following ground and flight testing of an example of the new wing on a C-5A. Starting in January 1982, all the C-5As were rotated through the eight-month modification process, at the rate of 18 a year, until the 77th was redelivered in mid-1987.

With the new wing in production, Lockheed was able to offer the USAF a new production batch of C-5s at an attractive price, and at the end of 1982 the company received a contract for one C-5B with options on 49 more over the next four years, all of these options being taken up in due course. With the same basic engines and overall configuration as the re-winged C-5A, the C-5B differed in having higher weights and a better payload/range, a number of equipment and systems improvements and a new avionics fit. In the new "Europe One" camouflage, the first C-5B flew on September 10, 1985, and deliveries to the 443rd MAW at Altus A.F.B. began on January 8, 1986. Production ended in early 1989. For the C-5B, General Electric developed the TF39-GE-1C engine, with a rating of 53,000 lb.s.t., and engines in the C-5A fleet were modified to this standard. The new aircraft were cleared to operate at weights up to 837,000 lb. with even higher figures in prospect, and this meant that the max. payload of 291,000 lb. could be carried for over 3,400 miles.

TECHNICAL DATA (C-5A)

MANUFACTURER: Lockheed-Georgia Company, Marietta, Georgia.
TYPE: Long range logistics transport.
ACCOMMODATION: Crew of five plus provision for 75 troops and 36 standard 463L pallets or assorted vehicles.
POWER PLANT: Four 41,000 lb.s.t. General Electric TF39-GE-1 turbofans.
DIMENSIONS: Span, 222 ft. 8½ in. Length, 247 ft. 10 in. Height, 65 ft. 1½ in. Wing area, 6,200 sq. ft.
WEIGHTS: Empty, 325,244 lb. Gross, 769,000 lb.
PERFORMANCE: Max. speed, 571 m.p.h. at 25,000 ft. Cruising speed, 537 m.p.h. at 30,000 ft. Initial climb, 2,300 ft./min. Service ceiling, 34,000 ft. Range, 3,500 miles with 220,000 lb. payload.
ARMAMENT: None.
SERIAL NUMBERS:
C-5A: 66-8303/8307; 67-167/174;   C-5B: 83-1285; 84-0059/0062;
    68-211/228; 69-001/027; 70-445/467.   85-001/010; 86-011/026; 87-027/045.

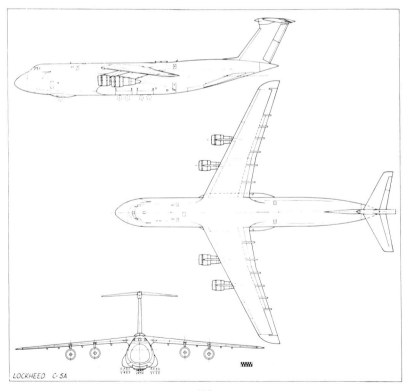

LOCKHEED C-5A

The first official photograph of the Lockheed F-117A, showing its unusual multi-faceted shape to reduce the radar image (*USAF photo*).

Lockheed F-117A

Under the code name *Have Blue*, the Department of Defense, through its Defense Advanced Research Projects Agency (DARPA), together with the USAF, worked with several major contractors to study ways of reducing the detectability of aircraft by radar and other sensors. This work led to a Request for Proposals for an Experimental Stealth Tactical (XST) aircraft demonstrator. From design proposals made by Lockheed, Grumman, Boeing and McDonnell Douglas, the DoD selected those of Lockheed and Grumman for further definition, and then placed a contract with Lockheed-California for five proof-of-concept flying prototypes. Powered by a pair of General Electric J85 engines, the first of these XSTs began flight testing at Groom Lake, Nevada, in late 1977. At least two of the five POC vehicles were lost, but test results proved that various of the design features served to reduce the radar signature and infra-red emissions to a very marked degree.

A contract was then placed with Lockheed for production of a derivative aircraft described as CSIRS (covert, survivable, in-weather reconnaissance/strike). Although widely assumed to be the F-19A (or RF-19A), this aircraft was officially identified as the F-117A when the first photograph was released, in November 1988. First flown in June 1981, the single-seat F-117A was powered by two non-afterburning General Electric F404-GE-400s of about 10,800 lb. s.t. each and its armament was carried internally. Original USAF plans to purchase 100 were cut back to 59 by funding difficulties, of which 52 had been delivered by end-1988. The subsonic F-117A was operated by the 4450th Tactical Air Group at Tonopah Test Range, near Nellis AFB, Nevada. The span was approximately 40 ft., length about 22 ft. and height about 16 ft.

Loening OA-1C with silver-painted fuselage/hull and yellow wings (*USAF photo*).

Loening COA-1, OA-1, OA-2, XO-10

The introduction of the inverted Liberty engine in 1923 made possible the development of a unique form of amphibian aircraft. Where previous amphibians had been flying boats or conventional pontoon seaplanes fitted with retractable landing gear, the Loening COA-1 (adding A-for-Amphibian to the CO designating Corps Observation) utilized the high thrust line of the inverted engine to decrease the distance between the central float and the fuselage of the traditional naval single float seaplane and then faired in the space between with useful working area instead of the conventional struts and wire rigging.

The reduced distance from main float to fuselage also made it possible to fasten the wingtip floats directly to the bottom of the lower wing in the manner of biplane flying boats rather than extending them on the struts of traditional pontoon seaplanes. The retractable landing gear was hinged on the chine line of the hull/pontoon, with the wheel assemblies being rotated upward and inward into recesses in the metal hull. Half of each wheel projected out of the hull when fully retracted. Equipment was normal for an observation type, a synchronized Browning machine gun for the pilot and single or twin Lewis guns and camera and radio installations for the observer.

The XCOA-1 was one of the first aeroplanes in which applied psychology was an important design factor. Knowing the distrust with which all unconventional designs were viewed by pilots and arch-conservative procurement officials, designer Grover C. Loening decided that the radical feature of his new fuselage/hull should be counteracted by a thoroughly familiar feature in which the pilots had full confidence if the design were to be accepted. Consequently, he chose a wooden two-bay biplane wing so similar to that of the ubiquitous DH-4 that the pilots, who could see

405

The second Loening COA-1 (*McCook Field photo*).

the wings from their cockpit but not the lower portion of the unconventional hull, felt right at home.

Following test of the XCOA-1 in July 1924 (the "X" became part of the official designation after the prototype was ordered) a second prototype was ordered and was followed by nine service test COA-1s. Three of these were turned over to the Navy for use by the Navy-MacMillan Arctic Expedition of 1925. Fifteen production OA-1As, with the C-for-Corps

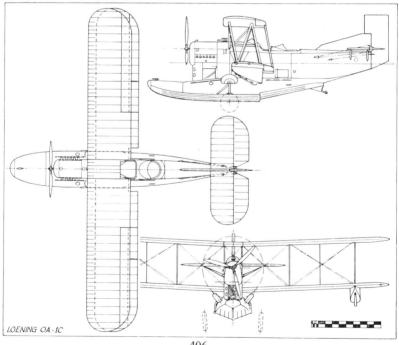

LOENING OA-1C

portion of the designation deleted and featuring extensively redesigned vertical tail surfaces, followed. Of six OA-1As used for a goodwill tour to the tip of South America in 1926, one, named *City of San Francisco* is preserved in the U.S. National Air Museum. Nine OA-1Bs featured minor refinements, but the ten OA-1Cs could be distinguished by a new vertical tail shape that remained standard for all subsequent Army, Navy, and commercial Loening Amphibians of this model.

The designation XOA-1A was originally assigned to an experimental OA-1A variant that featured an experimental inverted Wright V-1640-1 air-cooled engine and a single wheel retracting into the centreline of the hull with ground stability provided by skids on the bottoms of the wingtip floats. This aeroplane was delivered as the XO-10 with no reference in the type designation to its amphibious characteristics.

The eight OA-2s of 1929 were similar to the OA-1Cs except for substitution of the inverted air-cooled Wright V-1460-1 for the obsolescent Liberty. Armament was the same as the OA-1s except that the pilot's gun was relocated in the upper left wing outside of the propeller arc.

TECHNICAL DATA (COA-1)

MANUFACTURER: Loening Aeronautical Engineering Corp., New York, N.Y.
TYPE: Observation amphibian.
ACCOMMODATION: Pilot and observer in tandem open cockpits.
POWER PLANT: One 400 h.p. Liberty V-1650-1 Vee piston in-line.
DIMENSIONS: Span, 45 ft. 0 in. Length, 34 ft. 7 in. Height, 12 ft. 1 in. Wing area, 495 sq. ft.
WEIGHTS: Empty, 3,440 lb. Gross, 5,010 lb.
PERFORMANCE: Max. speed, 119 m.p.h. at sea level. Initial climb, 630 ft./min. Service ceiling, 11,825 ft. Endurance, 3·25 hr.
ARMAMENT: One fixed Browning and two flexible Lewis 0·30-in. guns.
SERIAL NUMBERS:
XCOA-1: 23-1234.   COA-1: 24-008; 25-226/234.

TECHNICAL DATA (OA-2)

MANUFACTURER: Loening Aeronautical Engineering Corp., New York, N.Y.
TYPE: Observation amphibian.
ACCOMMODATION: Pilot and observer in tandem open cockpits.
POWER PLANT: One 480 h.p. Wright V-1460-1 Tornado Vee piston in-line.
DIMENSIONS: Span, 45 ft. 0 in. Length, 34 ft. 10 in. Height, 12 ft. 11 in. Wing area, 504 sq. ft.
WEIGHTS: Empty, 3,766 lb. Gross, 5,325 lb.
PERFORMANCE: Max. speed, 125 m.p.h. at sea level. Cruising speed, 95 m.p.h. Range, 585 st. miles.
ARMAMENT: One fixed Browning and two flexible Lewis 0·30-in. guns.
SERIAL NUMBERS:
OA-1A: 26-428/442.   OA-2: 29-274/281.
OA-1B: 27-318/326.   XO-10: 26-212.
OA-1C: 28-073/082.

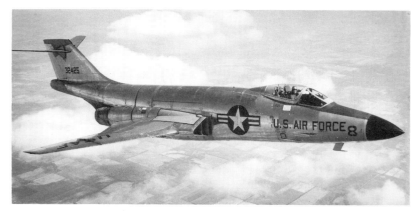

McDonnell F-101A (*McDonnell photo D4E55122*).

McDonnell F-101 Voodoo

Designed to serve with Strategic Air Command as a long-range escort and "penetration" fighter, the F-101 was developed subsequently for both tactical and air defence roles. At the time of its introduction into service it was the heaviest single-seat fighter ever accepted by USAF. McDonnell engineers began design studies of a penetration fighter in 1945, and detail design work started in June 1946. Two prototypes of this design were built as the XF-88 (46-525) and XF-88A (46-526), flight trials starting on October 20, 1948, but a change in tactical requirements and a shortage of funds led to cancellation of the project in 1950.

In 1951, a new USAF requirement for a long-range fighter to serve with Strategic Air Command as a B-36 escort led to a revision of the original XF-88 design, which, with an additional fuselage bay for extra fuel, and J57 turbojets in place of J34s, was ordered as the F-101(McDonnell Model 36). For strategic use, the F-101 was developed as the WS-105A fighter and WS-105L reconnaissance fighter (RF-101) systems. Before the first F-101 (53-2418) flew, on September 29, 1954, SAC cancelled the requirement, but production was continued for Tactical Air Command.

The F-101A was powered by J57-P-13 turbojets and its large internal fuel capacity could be supplemented by three external tanks. Standard armament of four 20-mm. cannon was supplemented by three Falcon AAMs or 12 HVARs on the rotary bomb doors. Production of the F-101A totalled 77, the first delivery being on May 2, 1957, to the 27th Tactical Fighter Wing. This type was followed in production by the F-101C, which had provision for carrying a tactical atomic weapon on the centreline pylon, and a strengthened wing for low level operations. Production of the F-101C totalled 47.

In 1956, two YRF-101As were built as prototypes of a reconnaissance version, the first flight being on May 10, 1956. Deliveries of the production model RF-101A began in May 1957, to the 363rd Tactical Reconnaissance Wing, and an equivalent variant of the F-101C was produced as the RF-101C, first flown on July 12, 1957. Both had a lengthened nose carrying either four KA-2 cameras for day use, or one KA-2 and three K-46 cameras for night photography; two KA-1s were installed in a fuselage bay. Production totals were 35 RF-101A and 166 RF-101C. In addition, 29 F-101As and 32 F-101Cs were later converted to reconnaissance configuration for use by three Air National Guard units from 1966/67 to 1972, being redesignated RF-101G and RF-101H respectively. A small batch of RF-101Cs was transferred to the Nationalist China Air Force, and USAF squadrons equipped with this type were the primary means of tactical air reconnaissance in Vietnam between 1961 and 1965.

For use by Air Defense Command, the F-101B was developed as the long-range interceptor system WS-217A. First flown on March 27, 1957, it was dimensionally similar to the F-101C. but carried an observer behind the pilot in an elongated cockpit. For its primary all-weather mission, it was armed with two Douglas MB-1 nuclear unguided rockets in addition to the three Falcons or bombs carried internally in the bomb-bay. J57-P-55 turbojets in this model had longer afterburners.

Of 480 two-seat Voodoos acquired by the USAF, the final 93 (bought with FY 59 funds) were to a later (Block-115 and -120) standard, including 14 with

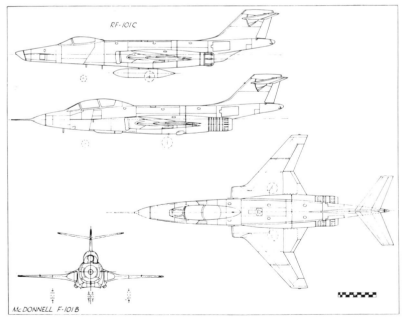

RF-101C

McDONNELL F-101B

409

A trio of McDonnell F-101Bs over Manhattan, with aerobatic team markings (*USAF/Norad photo 110065*).

full dual controls for use as operational trainers whilst retaining full combat capability. The latter took the designation F-101F and in February 1961 this designation was applied retrospectively to 58 (at least) earlier F-101Bs that had been converted by post-production kits to partial dual configuration (but without engine, flap or landing gear controls in the second cockpit). Before becoming F-101Fs, these aircraft had been known simply as "F-101B dual". The designations TF-101B and TF-101F were used unofficially for a few of the dual control aircraft from which all combat equipment was removed.

Service deliveries of the F-101B began early in 1959, to the 60th FIS at Otis AFB, and production ended in March 1961, allowing 17 Fighter Interceptor squadrons in ADC to equip on the type. Active Air Force use ended in 1971, leaving seven ANG squadrons to continue flying the two-seat Voodoo until 1983. From 1972 to 1975, the 192nd TRS, Nevada ANG, used 22 RF-101Bs, converted (plus one prototype) from F-101Bs by LTV to carry cameras in place of the fire control system.

Two-seat McDonnell F-101B-100-MC in 1965, in overall grey finish, showing AIR-2A Genie extended from weapon bay (*Roger Besecker*).

McDonnel RF-101C in landing roll-out (*Peter R. March*).

TECHNICAL DATA (F-101)

MANUFACTURER: McDonnell Aircraft Corporation, St. Louis, Missouri.
TYPE: Interceptor fighter and tactical fighter-bomber.
ACCOMMODATION: Pilot in enclosed cockpit (and radar operator in F-101B).
POWER PLANT: Two 10,100 lb. s.t. (14,880 lb. s.t. with a/b) Pratt & Whitney J57-P-13 (F-101A and C) or 10,700 lb. s.t. (16,900 lb. s.t. with a/b) J57-P-55 (F-101B) turbojets.
DIMENSIONS: Span, 39 ft. 8 in. Length, (F-101A/C) 67 ft. 4 in. (F-101B), 71 ft. 1 in. Height, 18 ft. 0 in. Wing area, 368 sq. ft.
WEIGHT: Empty (F-101B) 28,970 lb. Gross (F-101B) 52, 400 lb.; (F-101C), 47,000 lb.
PERFORMANCE: Max. speed (F-101B) 1,094 m.p.h. at 35,000 ft.; (F-101C) 1,005 m.p.h. at 35,000 ft. Cruising speed (F-101B) 546 m.p.h. at 35,000 ft.; (F-101C) 550 m.p.h. at 36,000 ft. Initial climb (F-101B) 39,250 ft./min.; (F-101C) 33,750 ft./min. Service ceiling (F-101B) 51,000 ft.; (F-101C) 50,300 ft. Combat radius (F-101B) 694 st. miles.; (F-101C) 780 st. miles.
ARMAMENT: (F-101B) Two AIM-4D Falcon AAMs under fuselage, and two Douglas AIR-2A Genie missiles in internal bomb-bay. (F-101C) Four 20-mm. cannon.
SERIAL NUMBERS:

F-101A: 53-2418/2446; 54-1438/1485.   F-101C: 54-1486/1493; 56-001/039.
YRF-10A: 54-149/150.   RF-101C: 56-040/135; 56-162/231.
RF-101A: 54-1494/1521; 56-155/161.   F-101B: 56-232/328; 57-247/452;
 58-259/342; 59-391/483.

McDonnell RF-101G conversion, in service with Kentucky ANG.

411

McDonnell Douglas F-4E from the 347th TFW in 1980, carrying two drop tanks, two AIM-9J
Sidewinders under the right wing, a *Pave Spike* laser designator under the fuselage and a tank
and 2,000 lb. GBU-10 laser guided bomb under the left wing (*USAF photo DF-ST-82-04301*).

McDonnell Douglas F-4 Phantom II

Destined to become the USAF's most significant fighter of the 'sixties and 'seventies and to provide the backbone of the tactical air offensive in Vietnam, the Phantom II originated in 1953 in a completely different guise. The first projects were for a single-seat, twin-engined attack fighter (McDonnell Model 98) for the U.S. Navy, and when the initial development contract was awarded, the aircraft was actually designated in the attack category as the AH-1. This was changed to F4H-1 in the former Navy system, and changed again to F-4 in the joint services scheme in 1962.

Interest in the Phantom II was first shown by the USAF during 1961, when a series of evaluations and comparative trials showed that the F-4 was superior by a large margin to any fighter then serving with the USAF. The USAF decision taken in March 1962 to adopt, with minimum changes, a fighter already in production for the Navy was almost without precedent. The requirement for an aircraft to provide close air support, interdiction and counter air was set out during 1962 in SOR 200, and the aircraft was developed as Weapon System 327A.

Initial contracts were for a single example of the fighter, to be desig-nated F-110A in the "old" USAF fighter series, plus two prototypes of a camera-equipped reconnaissance version, the YRF-110A. A few months later, the unified designation system was introduced and these two variants became the F-4C and RF-4C respectively, the version then in production for the USN becoming F-4B while the Navy's trials batch of 23 aircraft became F-4As. While production of the USAF versions got under way, arrangements were made to borrow F-4Bs from the Navy and these served with the USAF under the same designation; the first two of 29 thus loaned had actually reached Tactical Air Command HQ on January 24, 1962.

The F-4C was purchased primarily as a tactical fighter, with provision for a large external weapon load, including four air-to-air missiles (AIM-7D or -7E Sparrows) recessed into the undersides of the fuselage. No fixed guns

412

A U.S. Navy F-4B in interim USAF service, with Navy serial number and grey and white finish retained (*McDonnell Douglas photo D4C8245*).

were installed but wing stations carried four AIM-9B or -9D Sidewinders or AIM-4D Falcons. Changes from the original USN variant included provision for flying-boom refuelling (in place of probe and drogue), dual controls for the two-pilot crew, an inertial navigation system, improved weapon aiming system, and use of the J79-GE-15 engines with self-contained cartridge starting. The first flight of the F-4C was made at St. Louis on May 27, 1963, and the first two aircraft were delivered on November 20 the same year. Production of this model totalled 583 for TAC, the last delivery being made on May 4, 1966. Of this total, 40 were later transferred to the Spanish Air Force and 36 were adapted for the Wild Weasel defence suppression role in Vietnam, taking the unofficial designation EF-4C.

Service use of the F-4C began in November 1963 at MacDill A.F.B. Florida, initially with the 4453rd CCTW for training and then with the 12th TF Wing early in 1964, achieving initial operational capability (IOC) in October. Three more Wings in TAC received F-4Cs in the following years, these being the 8th, 35th and 366th, and many other units of the USAF and the ANG flew the first Phantom variant before it was retired.

Designed to succeed the RF-101 in the tactical reconnaissance role, the RF-4C (Weapon System 326A to SOR 196) was externally similar to the F-4C but was 33-in. longer and carried forward, oblique and high- and low-altitude panoramic cameras in the nose. Sideways-looking radar and an

McDonnell Douglas F-4C from the Fiscal Year 1963 production batch, with original Navy colour scheme adopted by the USAF.

infra-red line scanner were fitted in the fuselage and other equipment changes were made. Provision for missiles in the fuselage was deleted. The first of the two YRF-4Cs (U.S. Navy F-4Bs modified during production) flew on August 8, 1963, and the first production RF-4C flew on May 18, 1964. Deliveries to TAC began during 1965 and production totalled 503 (of which four went to Spain), ending in December 1973.

The RF-4C began to reach USAF training units in September 1964, but operational capability was not reached until August 1965, with the 16th TRS, with deployment to Vietnam following by year-end. Like the F-4C, the RF-4C was deployed to USAFE in Germany and the U.K. as well as to South-East Asia, and was flown by four Tactical Reconnaissance Wings in TAC as well as numerous ANG squadrons later. Service use continued into the late 'eighties.

Major system changes to improve the Phantom II's weapon accuracy in the air-to-air and air-to-ground roles distinguished the F-4D from the F-4C, which it succeeded in production during 1965. A small reduction had to be made in the fuselage fuel capacity, to accommodate new weapon ranging and release computers. The first F-4D flew on December 8, 1965, and deliveries began in March 1966, initial users being the Fighter Weapons School at Nellis and the 33rd TFW at Eglin. Later that year, F-4Ds were deployed to USAFE bases in Germany for the first time.

Production of the F-4D totalled 793 for USAF and 32 for Iran, with later diversions from the USAF stock to Korea. Some F-4Ds had the same AN/APQ-100 radar as the F-4C, but most had the AN/APA-109 with a similar nose radome. A number of special equipment fits were developed for the F-4Ds operational in Vietnam, where the AIM-4 Falcon, intended as the preferred armament over the F-4C's pylon-mounted AIM-9 Sidewinder, was soon found wanting and was in due course abandoned in favour of the original fit. *Pave Spike* and *Pave Knife* laser designator pods were adopted for Phantoms carrying "smart" bombs and ECM pods were developed. Some F-4Ds operated in EW roles and two were tested in the United States in 1976 as EF-4Ds for the Advanced Wild Weasel programme that led to the F-4G described below.

An F-4D in "Egypt 1" finish, with tail serial number displaced for unit identification of aircraft used by the commanding officer of 465th TFS/507th TFG, a Tinker A.F.B.-based AFRES unit (*Joe Cupido*).

An F-4E of the 4th TFW at Nellis A.F.B. engaged in Red Flag exercise in 1984, with ALQ-131 jamming pod and *Pave Spike* designator under fuselage, and Sidewinders under both wings (*Frank B. Mormillo*).

Deployment of the USAF Phantoms to Vietnam began in early 1965, initially in the F-4C version, and two F-4Cs of the 45th TFS claimed the USAF Phantom's first "MiG kill" on July 10, 1965, destroying two MiG-17s with AIM-9s. The 555th TFS received the first F-4Ds in SEA at Ubon in May 1967. Operational experience showed the need for a built-in gun and armament, although provision had been made for up to three SUU-16A gun pods to be carried externally. A 20-mm. M-61A1 Vulcan multi-barrel gun was therefore located in the nose of the F-4E version, together with AN/APQ-120 fire control radar, the whole installation changing the nose profiles and providing an immediate recognition clue to the "E" model. The first flight of a production model F-4E was made on June 30, 1967, after trial gun installations in the YF-4E (a modification of the original YRF-4C) on August 7, 1965.

Other changes in the F-4E included an additional fuel tank in the rear fuselage and the use of J79-GE-17 engines rated at 17,900 lb.s.t. with reheat. Leading-edge manoeuvering flaps were designed to improve the F-4E's dog-fighting ability, but were not available on the initial production batches. A slotted tailplane also was introduced on the F-4E. Deliveries of the F-4E began immediately following first flight and the 33rd TFW at Eglin, the first TAC combat unit to equip on this model, had its first F-4Es by the end of 1967. Deployment to South-East Asia did not begin until November 1968, as difficulties were encountered with the planned coherent-on-receive doppler

An F-4G Wild Weasel conversion of an F-4E carrying anti-radar missiles and the "WW" codes of the 37th TFW (*McDonnell Douglas photo C22-287-4*).

415

system (CORDS) that was required to give the Phantom an effective look-down capability. The F-4E was in USAFE by July 1969, but Vietnam use took priority and, as with the F-4D, numerous special items of equipment were developed, tested and adopted for that purpose.

The USAF procurement of the F-4E totalled 831, including some for diversion to foreign users, while other foreign contracts accounted for a further 566 F-4Es and 150 RF-4Es, the latter being a reconnaissance variant that was not adopted by the USAF. Production ended in 1981.

The final Phantom variant to enter USAF service was the F-4G, a Wild Weasel derivative of the F-4E airframe (the same designation having previously been used briefly for a U.S. Navy variant). The F-4G carried the AN/APR-38 radar and missile detection and launch homing system, requiring no fewer than 52 aerials located throughout the airframe. Sparrow and Sidewinder AAMs were retained but the nose cannon was deleted, and provision made for specialised anti-radar weapons to be carried, such as AGM-45 Shrike, AGM-78 ARM and AGM-88 HARM. A total of 116 F-4Es was converted, the first flight being made on December 6, 1975, and the F-4G entered service in 1978 with the 37th TFW. It was later issued also to the 52nd TFW in USAFE, Germany, and 3rd TFW at Clark A.F.B., Philippines.

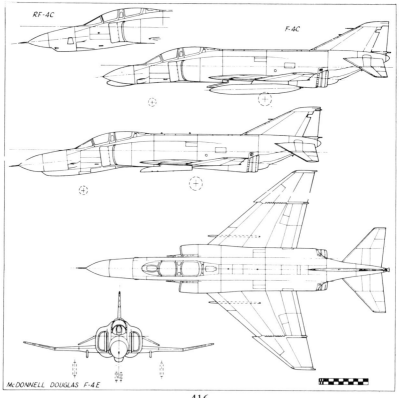

McDONNELL DOUGLAS F-4E

McDonnell Douglas RF-4C of the 30th TRS at Alconbury, in the U.K. (*Stephen P. Peltz*).

TECHNICAL DATA (F-4E)

MANUFACTURER: McDonnell Douglas Corporation, McDonnell Aircraft Company Division, St. Louis, Missouri.

TYPE: Tactical ground support and air superiority fighter.

ACCOMMODATION: Pilot and radar operator, with dual controls.

POWER PLANT: Two 11,870 lb.s.t. (dry) and 17,900 lb.s.t. (with reheat) General Electric J79-GE-15 turbojets.

DIMENSIONS: Span, 38 ft. 5 in. Length, 62 ft. 11½in. height, 16 ft. 5 in. Wing area, 530 sq. ft.

WEIGHTS: Empty, 30,425 lb. Gross, 61,650 lb.

PERFORMANCE: Max. speed, 1,500 m.p.h. (Mach 2·27) at 40,000 ft. Cruising speed, 484 m.p.h. Initial climb 61,400 ft./min. Service ceiling, 62,250 ft. Range, 1,300 st. miles with typical tactical load.

ARMAMENT: One 20-mm. M-61A1 rotary cannon, fixed forward-firing. Provision for up to four AIM-7E Sparrow and four AIM-9D or AIM-9J Sidewinder AAMs, with up to 16,000 lb. assorted external stores.

SERIAL NUMBERS:

F-4B: 62-12168/12196.

F-4C: 62-12199; 63-7407/7713; 64-654/928.

YRF-4C: 62-12200/12201.

RF-4C: 63-7740/7763; 64-997/1085; 65-818/945; 66-384/478; 67-0428/0469; 68-0548/0611; 69-0349/0384; 71-0248/0259; 72-0145/0156.

F-4D: 64-929/980; 65-580/801; 66-226/283; 66-7455/7774; 66-8685/8825.

F-4E: 66-284/382; 67-208/398; 68-0303/0547: 69-0236/0307*; 69-7201/7303*; 69-7547/7589*; 71-0224/0247; 71-1070/1093; 72-0157/1499; 73-1157/1204; 74-0643/0666; 74-1038/1061; 74-1620/1653; 71-1391/1402; 71-1779/1796.

*116 conversions to F-4G from these batches. Many F-4D/F-4E from listed batches diverted to FMS programmes. Additional complete serial batches for FMS or other foreign programmes not listed. RF-4E and F-4F (non-USAF service variants) not listed.

A pair of McDonnell Douglas F-15C Eagles from the Keflavik-based 57th FIS, with Sidewinders on the fuselage-side conformal fuel tanks (*McDonnell Douglas photo C22-402-167*).

McDonnell Douglas F-15 Eagle

The McDonnell Douglas Corporation was named winner on December 23, 1969, of a USAF design competition for a new advanced tactical fighter, following a contract definition phase in which the company competed with the Republic Division of Fairchild Hiller and North American Rockwell. The USAF objective was to obtain, with minimum delay, an air superiority fighter that would counter the threat posed by a new generation of Soviet warplanes. The winning design was for a single-seat aircraft with a shoulder-mounted, low-aspect-ratio wing featuring a modest 38 degrees 42 minutes of sweepback at quarter chord. A pair of Pratt & Whitney F100-PW-100 turbofans side-by-side in the rear fuselage were flanked by tailplane halves and individual fins and rudders. Armament was to comprise a single 20-mm. cannon plus a variety of externally-mounted AAMs—AIM-9 Sidewinders and AIM-7 Sparrows in the first instance.

An initial contract for 20 aircraft for development comprised 18 single-seat F-15As and two two-seat TF-15As, the latter designation changing later to F-15B. First flights of the F-15A and TF-15A took place, respectively, on July 27, 1972 and July 7, 1973. Full-scale production was initiated with an FY 73 contract for 62 Eagles, as the F-15 was duly named, with a total of up to 700 planned for future procurement. By 1987, the total had risen to 1,266 (excluding the 20 FSD Eagles).

After delivery of 361 F-15As and 58 F-15Bs, production switched to the F-15C and F-15D respectively, in June 1979, following first flights of these two new variants on February 26 and June 19, 1979. Retaining the Hughes APG-63 multi-mode pulse-Dopplar radar of the earlier variants, the C and D Eagles introduced numerous enhancements to the avionics and equipment. They also were able to carry conformal fuel tanks attached along the sides of the engine air intake trunks, for use with which McDonnell Douglas

An F-15A of the 405th TTW with belly fuel tank and wing-mounted Sidewinders, taking off from Nellis A.F.B. (*Frank B. Mormillo*).

developed a tangential carriage system that allowed up to twelve 1,000 lb. or four 2,000 lb. weapons to be carried, whilst leaving the wing stations available for drop tanks.

Later F-15Cs and F-15Ds also took advantage of a multi-staged improvement programme (MSIP) that led to the introduction in mid-1985 of the improved APG-70 radar with enlarged memory, provision for more advanced AAMs such as AMRAAM, and various ECM features. The added equipment and weapons provisions called for the take-off weight of the F-15C/D to be increased to a maximum of 68,000 lb. and for progressive increases in engine power, through the use of the F100-PW-220 and eventually the F100-PW-229.

Service use of the Eagle began in 1974 with the delivery on November 14 of a TF-15A to start the training process at the 555th TFTS, 58th TFTW, Luke A.F.B., Arizona. The first operational unit to equip on the new fighter was the 1st Tactical Fighter Wing at Langley A.F.B., Virginia, beginning in January 1976 with the 27th TFS. This and the 71st TFS achieved IOC on the F-15A by the end of 1976, followed by the Wing's third squadron, the 94th TFS, early in 1977. In the same year, Eagles were used to equip the 36th TFW at Bitburg in Germany. Two more TAC wings (the 33rd and 49th) equipped on F-15As

An F-15A (right) and F-15B, showing the changed profile of the latter's two-seat cockpit canopy.

McDonnell Douglas F-15A of the 36th TFW. Note blue border deleted from national insignia on grey-finished aircraft.

before delivery of the F-15C began; Eagles subsequently went to units of the Alaskan Air Command and Pacific Air Forces, Air Defence units of TAC and squadrons of the ANG (starting in June 1985). More than 1,000 Eagles had been delivered by mid-1987, including those for export to Saudi Arabia, Israel and Japan.

Although capable of carrying a variety of ground attack ordnance, the F-15A/B and F-15C/D variants of the Eagle were purchased primarily for use as interceptors and for the air defence rôle. To demonstrate the ground attack capabilities of the Eagle, McDonnell Douglas modified an FSD F-15B (71-291), and this first flew as the Strike Eagle on July 8, 1980. New features either installed or proposed for this dual-rôle version included a redesigned front cockpit, a rear cockpit equipped for use by a weapons officer, APG-70 synthetic aperture radar, FLIR, LANTIRN, structural reinforcement for a max. take-off weight of 81,000 lb. and common engine bays to accept the F100-PW-220 or General Electric F110-GE-120, which the USAF had meanwhile adopted as an alternative fighter engine (AFE) to the F100. Evaluation of the Strike Eagle during 1983 led to a USAF decision, announced on February 24, 1984, to adopt the dual-rôle Eagle as the F-15E, and three prototypes were ordered. The first of these (86-183) flew on December 11, 1986, followed by the first full production F-15E at the end of 1987. Deliveries to the 405th TTW (which had meanwhile replaced the original 58th TFTW at Luke A.F.B.), for training purposes, began during 1988 in preparation for the addition of 392 F-15Es to the USAF inventory.

The first production F-15E, in overall medium grey finish (*McDonnell Douglas photo C22-421-11*).

TECHNICAL DATA (F-15C)

MANUFACTURER: McDonnell Douglas Aircraft Corp, St Louis, Missouri.

TYPE: Air superiority fighter.

ACCOMMODATION: Pilot only or (F-15D) two in tandem.

POWER PLANT: Two 23,830 lb.s.t. (with afterburners) Pratt & Whitney F-100-PW-100 turbofans.

DIMENSIONS: Span, 42 ft 9¾ in. Length, 63 ft. 9 in. Height, 18 ft. 5½ in. Wing area, 608 sq. ft.

WEIGHTS: Empty, 28,600 lb. Normal gross, 44,630 lb.; max. take-off, 68,000 lb.

PERFORMANCE: Max. speed, 1,650 m.p.h. above 36,000 ft. Cruising speed, 570 m.p.h. Initial climb, more than 50,000 ft./min. Service ceiling, over 60,000 ft. Range, over 3,000 miles with maximum fuel, no weapons.

ARMAMENT: One 20-mm. M61A1 rotary barrel cannon with 940 rounds. Normal air-to-air armament comprises four AIM-7F/M Sparrows on fuselage stations and four AIM-9L/M Sidewinders on wing pylons. Up to eight AIM-120A (AMRAAM) later.

SERIAL NUMBERS:

YF-15A: 71-280/289.

F-15A: 72-113/120; 73-085/107;
74-081/136; 75-018/079;
76-008/120; 76-1505/1523*;
77-061/153.

F-15C: 78-468/560; 79-015/081;
79-280/281*; 80-001/053;
80-062/106*; 80-122/130*;
81-002/003*; 81-027/067; 81-068/071*;
82-00 8/038; 82-044/048;
83-010/045; 83-054/062*;
84-001/031; 85-093/128;
88-1667/1708.

YTF-15A: 71-290/291.

F-15B: 73-108/114; 74-137/142;
75-080/089; 76-124/142;
76-1524/1525*; 77-154/168.

F-15D: 78-561/575; 79-004/014;
79-282/287*; 80-054/061;
80-107/121*; 80-131/136*;
81-020/026; 83-048/051; 83-052/053*;
83-063/064*; 84-042/046;
85-129/134; 86-181/182.

F-15E: 86-183/190; 87-169/216;
86-143/180.

(Plus later contracts)
*Foreign deliveries through FMS

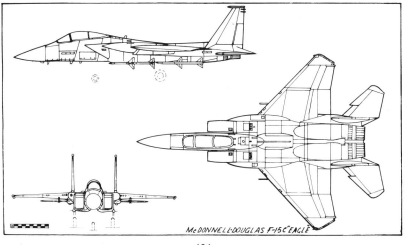

McDONNELL-DOUGLAS F-15C EAGLE

A pair of McDonnell Douglas KC-10As, in low-visibility drab grey with white undersides (*McDonnell Douglas photo G386-6716*).

McDonnell Douglas KC-10 Extender

A USAF requirement for an advanced tanker/cargo aircraft (ATCA) was put to industry in 1976, the proviso being that proposals should be based on certificated freighter variants of wide-bodied aircraft in production. As the Lockheed C-5A was no longer in production and there was no freighter variant of the TriStar, this effectively meant that the ATCA could only be a version of the Boeing 747 or the McDonnell Douglas DC-10. Both were proposed to the USAF, and on December 19, 1977, selection of the latter was announced.

Based on the DC-10 Srs 30CF convertible freighter, the McDonnell Douglas proposal called for a number of modifications that included installation of fuel cells beneath the cabin floor, together with a boom operator's position and an advanced aerial refuelling boom as used on the Boeing KC-135; a hose drum unit for probe and drogue refuelling; an air-to-air refuelling receptacle so that the tanker could itself take on fuel; a cargo handling system and specific military avionics. A side freight loading door and reinforced cargo floor were standard DC-10CF features and allowed the aircraft to carry up to 27 standard cargo pallets without removal of the refuelling provisions. Additional to the DC-10's standard fuel of some 14,000 Imperial gallons the extra tanks had a capacity of about 15,100 Imperial gallons and the entire fuel load could be used by the tanker itself or transferred to other aircraft.

Procurement of the big tankers, designated KC-10As, began in FY 1978 with an order for two, the first of which flew at Long Beach on July 12, 1980. Subsequent contracts brought the total purchased to 60, with the final aircraft delivered early in 1988. Early aircraft were delivered in the standard finish of white top and grey underside, with blue trim and the SAC sash round the fuselage; later, a drab charcoal became standard, with white undersides. Deliveries to SAC began on March 17, 1981, for operational service with the 32nd Air Refueling Squadron at Barkesdale A.F.B., Louisiana. Other user units were the 9th ARS at March A.F.B., California and the 344th and 911th ARS at Seymour Johnson A.F.B., North Carolina. At each base, an Air Force Reserve associate squadron shared duties with the active units, these being the 77th (at Seymour Johnson), 78th (Barkesdale) and 79th (March).

In 1987, the USAF placed a contract for the installation, on the last production KC-10A, of two Flight Refuelling Ltd Mk 32B hose drum units in underwing pods, making the aircraft a three-point tanker for probe/drogue refuelling. All earlier aircraft were subsequently modified to allow them to carry these pods, of which the USAF purchased 40 aircraft sets.

TECHNICAL DATA (KC-10A)

MANUFACTURER: McDonnell Douglas Corporation, Douglas Aircraft Company, Long Beach, California.
TYPE: Tanker/transport.
ACCOMMODATION: Flight crew of three.
POWER PLANT: Three 52,500 lb.s.t. General Electric CF6-50C2.
DIMENSIONS: Span, 165 ft. 4½ in. Length, 181 ft. 7 in. Height, 58 ft. 1 in. Wing Area, 3,958 sq. ft.
WEIGHTS: Empty, 241,027 lb. Gross, 590,000 lb.
PERFORMANCE: Max. speed, 610 m.p.h. Cruising speed, 564 m.p.h. at 30,000 ft. Initial climb, 2,900 ft./min. Service ceiling, 33,400 ft. Range, 4,370 miles with max. cargo. Unrefuelled ferry range, 11,500 miles.
ARMAMENT: None.
SERIAL NUMBERS:
KC-10A: 79-0433/0434; 79-1710/1713;
  79-1946/1951; 82-0190/0193;
  83-0075/0082; 84-0185/0192.

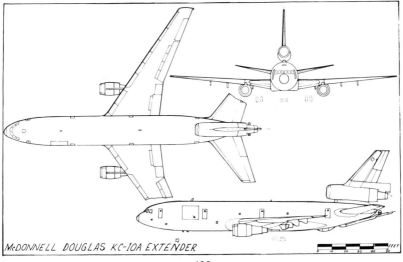

McDONNELL DOUGLAS KC-10A EXTENDER

An artist's impression of the McDonnell Douglas C-17A in action (*McDonnell Douglas L401179*).

McDonnell Douglas C-17

In October 1980, the USAF issued to industry a Request for Proposals for a new cargo airlifter, identified temporarily as the C-X (Cargo Experimental). The requirement was for an aircraft that would fill a shortfall in the Air Force's long-range airlift capability, whilst at the same time providing performance that would allow it to deliver its loads into austere landing fields within an operational theatre. The exacting specification attracted submissions from Boeing, Lockheed-Georgia and the Douglas Aircraft Company division of McDonnell Douglas, and on August 28, 1981 the last-named company was selected by the Air Force to take C-X into the next stage of development.

With the designation C-17 applied to the new design, an initial research and development contract was announced in July 1982, but the decision to buy additional quantities of Lockheed C-5Bs and McDonnell Douglas KC-10As in order to give the USAF airlift strength an urgently-needed boost delayed the implementation of full-scale development of the C-17. The USAF Airlift Master Plan in September 1983 reconfirmed the need for the new aircraft and established a schedule for its development, and a year later the Airlift Total Force Plan added provision for C-17s to be bought for AFRES and ANG units. Full-scale development was launched on a contract dated December 31, 1985, providing for two test specimens and a single C-17A flying prototype, which was to enter testing in August 1990.

Despite its somewhat protracted gestation, the C-17A emerged as the most significant item in Air Force airlift modernization for the 1990s and beyond. The total requirement was established by Military Airlift Command at 210 aircraft, with deliveries starting in the second quarter of 1991 and the first 12 expected to reach IOC in late 1992, serving with the 437th MAW at Charleston A.F.B., South Carolina. Delivery of the 210th aircraft was expected to be made in the year 2000.

The C-17A was designed with a classic configuration for military transport aircraft, with a high wing, fuselage-side stowage for the undercarriage, a T-tail and four engines in underwing pods. Fuselage cross-section was dictated by the size of Army vehicles that had to be carried, and provided a loadable width of 18 ft., height of 13 ft. 6 in. and floor length of 88 ft., including 20 ft. at the rear loading ramp.

To achieve the specified short-field capability, Douglas engineers adopted the externally-blown flap system, in which engine thrust is directed to double-slotted trailing edge flaps to produce additional lift. Other advanced features included winglets and digital avionics system with four CRT displays and two HUDs in the cockpit, allowing the C-17A to be crewed by two pilots and a loadmaster.

TECHNICAL DATA (C-17A)

MANUFACTURER: McDonnell Douglas Corporation, Douglas Aircraft Company, Long Beach, California.
TYPE: Long-range heavy airlifter.
ACCOMMODATION: Flight crew of two pilots, plus one loadmaster. Up to 102 paratroops.
POWER PLANT: Four 37,000 lb.s.t. Pratt & Whitney F117-PW-100 turbofans.
DIMENSIONS: Span, 165 ft. 0 in. Length, 175 ft. 2 in. Height 55 ft. 1 in. Wing area, 3,800 sq. ft.
WEIGHTS: Empty, 259,000 lb. Gross, 570,000 lb.
PERFORMANCE: Max. cruising speed, 403 m.p.h. at low altitude. Normal cruising speed, 508 m.p.h. at 36,000 ft. Range, 2,765 miles with 172,200 lb. payload.
ARMAMENT: Nil.
SERIAL NUMBERS:
YC-17A: 87-0025 (Plus later allocations)

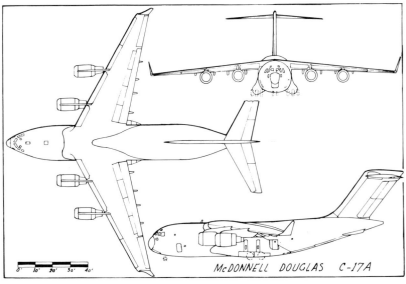

McDONNELL DOUGLAS C-17A

McDonnell Douglas AH-64A Apache in full battle order (*Andrew March*).

McDonnell Douglas (Hughes) AH-64 Apache

Based on rapidly accumulating experience gained in Vietnam with armed examples of the Bell UH-1 family, the U.S. Army formulated in 1964 a requirement for an attack helicopter known as the Advanced Aerial Fire Support System (AAFSS). To meet this requirement, the Army ordered the Lockheed AH-56A Cheyenne into development and production, but early problems proved too expensive and tardy for solution and the AH-56A was cancelled in August 1972. To fill the consequent gap, the Army drew up a new requirement for an Advanced Attack Helicopter (AAH), the primary rôle of which was to be anti-armour attack, by day or night in any weather.

Issued to industry in November 1972, the Request for Proposals (RFP) drew responses from five companies, from which Bell and Hughes were chosen in June 1973 to build two flying prototypes and a ground test vehicle each of their Model 409 and Model 77 designs respectively. These new helicopters were designated YAH-63A and YAH-64A, each being powered—as required by the Army—by a pair of General Electric T700-GE-700 turboshafts.

To meet an exacting operational requirement, the Hughes YAH-64A—which was selected over the Bell YAH-63A in December 1976—was designed to use advanced structural materials and to be able to absorb considerable battle damage whilst continuing to fly and fight. It carried a two-man crew in tandem, the pilot being behind and higher than the co-pilot/gunner in the forward fuselage. To provide all-weather, day/night capability, the helicopter carried a Martin Marietta Target Acquisition Designation Sight and Pilot's Night Vision Sensor (TADS/PNVS), the primary units of which were housed in the nose. Primary armament comprised the specially-developed Hughes

426

30-mm. Chain Gun, mounted, without fairings or housings, under the front fuselage, and eight Rockwell Hellfire laser-guided anti-tank weapons on fuselage-side stub wings. The latter also provided space for a pair of unguided rocket pods.

Testing of the Hughes ground test vehicle (GTV) began on June 22, 1975, followed by first flights of the two prototypes on September 30 and November 22, the same year. Both had fixed tailplanes at the top of the fin and clear of the tail rotor, but a low, movable tailplane was adopted to improve handling at very low altitudes and was first flown on October 31, 1979, on the first of three additional production prototypes ordered in January 1977. This tailplane position was adopted as standard; other changes from the initial configuration included swept tips for the main rotor blades, a taller main rotor mast, larger tail rotor diameter and an improved IR suppression system for the hot engine exhaust. Further changes had to be made to the location and size of the tail rotor to achieve the production configuration, first flown on the last of the pre-production AH-64As on March 16, 1980. First live firings of Hellfire had been made, meanwhile, on March 19, 1979.

A brand new facility was established by Hughes at Mesa, Arizona, in preparation for production of the AH-64A, which was initiated on April 15, 1982, with an order for 11 helicopters, against an anticipated total requirement for 515 to be built by 1990. As annual contract increments increased the number on order by 1987 to 453, the requirement had also gone up to 675, with about 600 more likely to be needed by 1995.

The first production AH-64A was flown at Mesa on January 26, 1984. Early aircraft were used for continued testing and crew training at Fort Eustis, Virginia, and Fort Rucker, Alabama, in preparation for the delivery of the first four AH-64As for an operational unit on February 25, 1986, at Fort Hood, Texas. The first Army unit to train on the Apache was the 6th Cavalry Brigade (Air Combat), which by mid-1986 had brought its 7th Squadron, 17th Cavalry, up to strength; additional units following in sequence included the 1st Squadron, 6th Cavalry; 4th Squadron, 9th Cavalry, and 5th Squadron, 17th Cavalry. During 1987, the Army National Guard also began to receive AH-64As, starting with the 30th Attack

McDonnell Douglas AH-64A, carrying Hellfire missiles (*McDonnell Douglas photo*).

Battalion, North Carolina, and the 51st Attack Battalion, South Carolina. Each ANG unit received 18 Apaches, matching the regular Army establishment of 18 AH-64As, 12 Bell OH-58D Kiowas and three Sikorsky UH-60A Black Hawks in each of its attack helicopter units.

In January 1984, Hughes Helicopters Inc., a subsidiary of the company originally founded by pioneer Howard Hughes, was acquired by McDonnell Douglas Corporation and, on August 27, 1985, the company name was changed to McDonnell Douglas Helicopter Co. During 1987, the company was working on an AH-64B variant, with a number of internal improvements but no major external changes.

TECHNICAL DATA (AH-64A)

MANUFACTURER: McDonnell Douglas Helicopter Company, Mesa, Arizona.
TYPE: Attack helicopter.
ACCOMMODATION: Co-pilot/gunner and pilot in tandem.
POWER PLANT: Two 1,696 s.h.p. General Electric T700-GE-701 turboshafts.
DIMENSIONS: Rotor diameter, 48 ft. 0 in. Length (excluding main rotor), 48 ft. 2 in. Height, 14 ft. 1¼ in. Main rotor disc area, 1,809.5 sq. ft.
WEIGHTS: Empty, 10,760 lb. Gross, 21,000 lb.
PERFORMANCE: Max. speed, 184 m.p.h. Cruising speed, 170 m.p.h. Initial vertical climb, 2,500 ft./min. Service ceiling, 21,000 ft. Range (internal fuel), 300 miles.
ARMAMENT: One 30-mm. McDonnell Douglas M230 Chain Gun under forward fuselage with up to 1,200 rounds. Stub wings to carry, on four hard points, up to 16 Rockwell AGM-114A Hellfires or up to 76 FFARs (2·75-in) in four pods, or combinations of both.
SERIAL NUMBERS:
YAH-64A (GTV): 74-22247
YAH-64A: 74-22248/22249; 77-23257/23259
AH-64A: 82-23355/23365; 83-23787/23834;
    84-24200/24311; 85-25051/25188;
    86-8940/9055; 87-0407/0507.

(Plus later contracts)

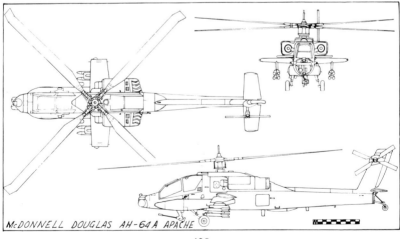

McDONNELL DOUGLAS AH-64A APACHE

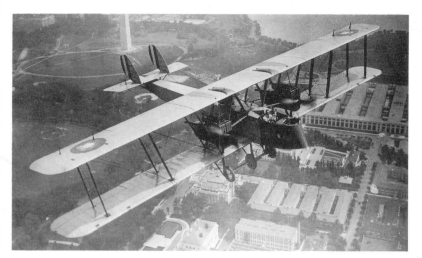

Martin MB-1 in flight (*Martin photo*).

Martin MB-1/T-1

Following his withdrawal from the Wright-Martin combine of 1916, Glenn Martin re-established his own company in Cleveland, Ohio, late in 1917. During conferences held in Washington to unsnarl the World War I aircraft procurement mess, Martin was asked to design a new bomber that would outperform the British Handley-Page. An order for ten aircraft was signed and the first one flew on August 17, 1918. Usually referred to now as MB-1s (as the first Martin Bomber design) they were officially designated GMB by the USAAS.

Powered with two Liberty engines, the GMB was more than just a bomber although it followed the established European four-five seat configuration. High power and relatively small size made the GMB a multi-purpose design. It was also intended to be a long range observation and photographic machine and its 120 m.p.h. top speed combined with three gun stations gave it escort fighter capability.

The first four GMBs were built as observation types and the next three were bombers. The eighth was a special long distance version designated GMT (for transcontinental) with 1,500-mile range while the ninth was a bomber fitted with a 37-mm. cannon on the nose and called GMC (for cannon).

The last aeroplane on the original GMB contract was completed in 1919 as a transport by removing the military equipment, raising the top of the fuselage to provide headroom, and adding cabin windows and seats for ten passengers. The open pilot's cockpit was also converted to a glassed-in enclosure. This version was originally known as GMP for Glenn

Martin Passenger, but was redesignated T-1 in the short-lived T-for-Transport series of 1920/23. Six modified MB-1s were built for the Government Postal Service and some of these were later transferred to the Army.

TECHNICAL DATA (MB-1)

MANUFACTURER: Glenn L. Martin Co., Cleveland, Ohio.
TYPE: Army support reconnaissance and bomber.
ACCOMMODATION: Crew of three.
POWER PLANT: Two 400 h.p. Liberty 12A piston Vee in-line.
DIMENSIONS: Span, 71 ft. 5 in. Length, 44 ft. 10 in. Height, 14 ft. 7 in. Wing area, 1,070 sq. ft.
WEIGHTS: Empty, 6,702 lb. Gross, 10,225 lb.
PERFORMANCE: Max. speed, 105 m.p.h. at sea level. Cruising speed, 92 m.p.h. at sea level. Initial climb, 630 ft./min. Service ceiling, 10,300 ft. Range, 390 st. miles.
ARMAMENT: Five 0·30-in. machine guns in nose and amidships. 1,040-lb. bombs.
SERIAL NUMBERS:
GMB: 39055/39060; 62948.   GMC: 62950.
GMT: 62949.   GMP: 62951.

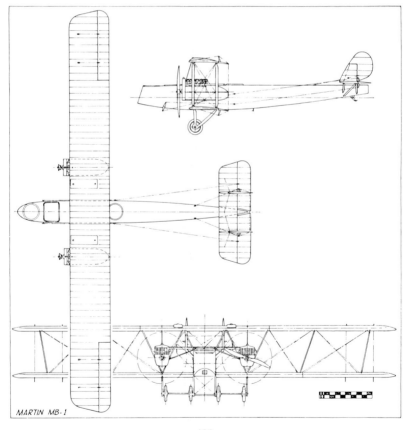

MARTIN MB-1

430

Martin-built NBS-1 with 1,650 lb. bomb (*USAF photo 10025A.S.*).

Martin MB-2/NBS-1

The MB-2 was a direct development of the MB-1 of 1918, and used essentially the same wooden fuselage and tail unit fitted with larger wings and revised power plant and landing gear installations. The non-staggered wings were hinged at the rear spars just outboard of the engines and folded aft in the manner of the British Handley-Page O-400. Except for later naval designs, the MB-2 was the only large U.S.-designed aeroplane to use this feature. The MB-2 was designed specifically as a night bomber, sacrificing the flashing speed and manoeuvrability of the MB-1, which were not considered essential for a night bomber, to greater bomb load.

Twenty MB-2s were ordered from Martin in 1920, the Army accepting, in this case, the manufacturer's designation as the official nomenclature for the type. Under the prevailing Army policy of dividing the meagre procurements of the time among the hard-pressed manufacturers, additional orders were placed with other firms. Lowe, Willard, and Fowler (L.W.F.) got an order for 35 and Curtiss received an order for 50, both these batches of aircraft being designated NBS-1 in the newly introduced designating system, as Night Bombers, Short Range. Upon completion, the first L.W.F. NBS-1 was sent to Aeromarine as the pilot model for another order for 25, and the remainder were shipped overseas. The last 20 NBS-1s on the Curtiss order were fitted with turbo-superchargers and four built by L.W.F. had dual controls for training.

The bomb load varied from 1,800 lb. to a maximum of 3,000 lb., with internal stowage in the fuselage for all but the largest bombs. Defensive armament was a pair of 0·30-inch calibre Lewis guns on Scarff rings around the nose and aft cockpits and a single Lewis firing downward from the bottom of the fuselage. Never used in war, the MB-2/NBS-1's major claim to fame is the sinking of the ex-German battleship *Ostfriesland* in the controversial Billy Mitchell bombing exercises of July 1921. The MB-2/NBS-1 series served with the four squadrons of the 2nd Bomb Group in the U.S. and with units in the Canal Zone, Hawaii, and the Philippines until replaced by Keystone bombers in 1927/28.

TECHNICAL DATA (NBS-1)

MANUFACTURER: Glenn L. Martin Co., Cleveland, Ohio; L.W.F. Engineering Corporation, College Point, N.Y.; Curtiss Aeroplane and Motor Co., Inc., Garden City, N.Y.; Aeromarine Plane and Motor Co., Keyport, N.J.

TYPE: Short distance night bomber.

ACCOMMODATION: Crew of four.

POWER PLANT: Two 420 h.p. Liberty 12 piston Vee in-line.

DIMENSIONS: Span, 74 ft. 2 in. Length, 42 ft. 8 in. Height, 14 ft. 8 in. Wing area, 1,121 sq. ft.

WEIGHTS: Empty, 7,269 lb. Gross, 12,064 lb.

PERFORMANCE: Max. speed, 99 m.p.h. at sea level. Cruising speed, 91 m.p.h. Initial climb, 391 ft./min. Service ceiling, 8,500 ft. Range, 558 st. miles.

ARMAMENT: Five 0·30-in. guns in nose and amidships; 1,800 internal bomb load, up to 2,000 lb. external.

SERIAL NUMBERS:

MB-2 (Martin): 64195/64214. NBS-1 (Curtiss): 68478/68527.
NBS-1 (L.W.F.): 68437/68471. NBS-1 (Aeromarine): 22-201/225.

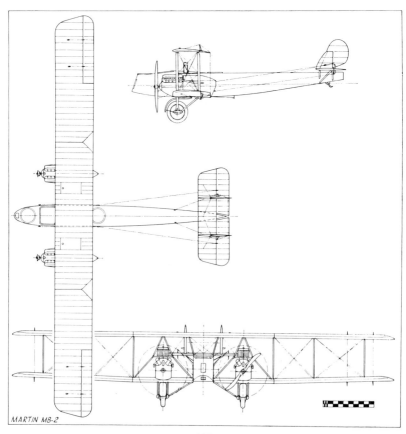

MARTIN MB-2

Martin B-10B (*Gordon S. Williams*).

Martin B-10, B-12, B-14

In the history of Army bombardment aeroplanes, the Martin B-10 and B-12 series has a significant place. Chronologically a little behind the Boeing B-9, which (see page 101) was the Army's first all-metal monoplane bomber, the Martin Model 123 fulfilled the promise inherent in the Boeing project. Like the B-9, it was an all-metal, twin-engined monoplane, with a retractable undercarriage. Unlike the Boeing, it featured internal bomb stowage and—after some initial flying with a blunt, open-cockpit nose—the first gun turret ever fitted to a U.S. bomber. Provision was made for a crew of three.

The prototype Martin 123 was designed and built as a private venture in a calculated attempt by the Glenn L. Martin Co. to get back into the bomber business—the Army's earliest bomb-dropping experiments had been made from a Martin TT (page 606) and the MB-2 (NBS-1) was the main Army bomber from 1921 to 1927. Delivered to the Army on March 20, 1932, the prototype was given the experimental designation XB-907 for its trials at Wright Field, which began in July 1932. It then had a span of 62 ft. 2 in., two 600 h.p. SR-1820-E Cyclone engines with NACA low-drag cowling rings, three open cockpits and three crew positions in the deep fuselage. A top speed of 197 m.p.h. was recorded at 6,000 ft.

During the early autumn of 1932 the Martin 123 was modified to have a front gun turret—a completely transparent, manually-rotated affair with a single 0·303-inch gun. At the same time, 675 h.p. R-1820-19 engines with full cowlings were introduced, and the wing span was increased to 70 ft. 7 in. Despite an increase of nearly 2,000 lb. in the gross weight, to 12,230 lb., the XB-907A now achieved 207 m.p.h. at 6,000 ft. in trials at Wright Field in October 1932. The Martin bomber, which was faster than any U.S. fighter then in service, was ordered on January 17, 1933, when the Army placed a $2,440,000 contract for 48. At the same time, the XB-907A was purchased and took the designation XB-10 (33-139).

Deliveries of the first production aircraft (as Martin 139s) began

433

Martin B-10B in 1934 (*Martin photo*).

in June 1934. External changes included enclosures over the pilot's cockpit and over the rear cockpit, which was modified to accommodate a radio operator and a rear gunner with a 0·30-inch gun. A second gun of this calibre was in the floor behind the bomb-bay and a third in the front turret.

Various engine installations were made in the aircraft on the 1933 order. Thus, the first 14 aircraft, designated YB-10 had 675 h.p. R-1820-25s, giving a similar performance to that of the XB-10. Seven YB-12s were similar with 775 h.p. R-1690-11 Hornet radials and a top speed of 212 m.p.h., while the 25 B-12As with the same engines, had provision for an extra fuel tank in the bomb-bay. This tank had a capacity of 365 U.S. gallons, supplementing the 226 U.S. gallons normal fuel capacity for long range flights. Two experimental models were also included in the 48 aircraft of the original order—the YB-10A with turbo-supercharged R-1820-31 Cyclones boosting the top speed to 236 m.p.h. at 25,000 ft.; and the XB-14 with 950 h.p. YR-1830-9 Twin Wasps. Army records show two more B-10s procured as part of the original contract, with serials 36-347/348. These may have been replacements for the two experimental models, but there is no evidence that they were in fact delivered, or if so, in what particular configuration.

Under the McArthur-Pratt agreement of January 1931, the Army Air Corps had assumed responsibility for Coastal defence around the U.S.

Martin B-12A on ski-wheel combination (*Gordon S. Williams*).

434

mainland, a task which had previously been the U.S. Navy's cherished prerogative. The new Army responsibility led to the adaptation of several YB-10s and B-12As for coastal defence duties, fitted with large floats for operations off water. A later modification programme resulted in the B-10Ms and B-12AMs, for target towing. Also designated was the YB-13 with Pratt & Whitney R-1860-17 engines; ten of these were ordered but cancelled before delivery.

Production of the Martin bomber was continued by 1934 and 1935 procurements of B-10Bs, the primary service version. Of 115 aeroplanes in the Fiscal Year 1934 Air Corps purchase, 88 were B-10Bs and 15 more were ordered in Fiscal Year 1935. One other B-10, serial 42-68358, was an export Model 139 which was used by escapers to Australia from the Dutch East Indies in 1942 and was taken on strength by the USAAF.

The Martin bombers remained in service with Army bombardment squadrons until the advent of the B-17s and B-18s in the late 1930s. Martin also derived considerable business from the export of B-10 variants

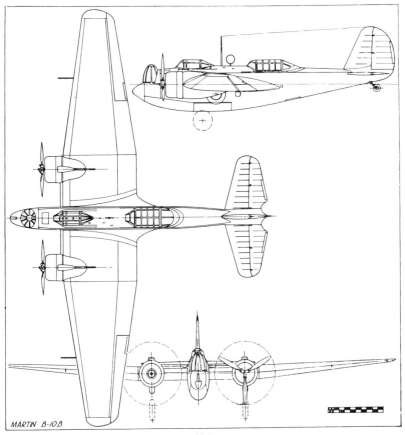

MARTIN B-10B

435

Martin YB-12A for coastal defence duties (*Peter M. Bowers collection*).

and derivatives. Between mid-1936 and 1939, a total of 189 export Model 139W, 146 and 166 bombers was sold, including 120 for use in the Netherlands East Indies. Flown by Dutch crews, the latter were among the first U.S. bombers flown in combat in World War II.

TECHNICAL DATA (B-10 and B-12)

MANUFACTURER: Glenn L. Martin Co., Cleveland, Ohio.
TYPE: Light bomber.
ACCOMMODATION: Pilot, radio operator and two gunners.

	XB-10	B-10B	YB-12
Power Plant:	Two 675 h.p. R-1820-19	Two 775 h.p. R-1820-33	Two 700 h.p. R-1690-11
Dimensions:			
Span, ft., in.	70 7	70 6	70 6
Length, ft., in.	45 0	44 9	45 3
Height, ft., in.	10 4	15 5	11 0
Wing area, sq. ft.	640	678	678
Weights:			
Empty, lb.	7,294	9,681	7,728
Gross, lb.	12,560	16,400	12,824
Performance:			
Max. speed, m.p.h.	207	213	212
Cruising speed, m.p.h.	169	193	170
Climb, ft./min.	1,380	—	1,740
Service ceiling, ft.	21,000	24,200	26,600
Range, miles	600	1,240	524

ARMAMENT: One 0·30-in. Browning gun in nose and rear turrets and one in ventral tunnel; 2,260-lb. bombs.
SERIAL NUMBERS:

XB-10: 33-139.
YB-10: 33-140/153.
YB-10A: 33-154.
B-10: 36-347/348; 42-68358.

B-10B: 34-028/115; 35-232/246.
YB-12: 33-155/161.
B-12A: 33-163/177; 33-258/267.
XB-14: 33-162.

Long-wing Martin B-26B-50-MA of 387th BG in European Theatre colours (*Crown Copyright*).

Martin B-26 Marauder

Army Air Force requirements for a new high-speed medium bomber were circulated to the U.S. aircraft manufacturers on January 25, 1939. Emphasis was placed in the outline specification upon the need for good speed, range and ceiling performance; a crew of five, a 2,000 lb. bomb-load and four 0.30-inch guns were to be carried. By omitting reference to the characteristics at the lower end of the performance range, the AAF tacitly admitted that high landing speeds and long take-offs would be accepted in order to obtain the required speed. A design to meet this specification was submitted to an Army Board at Wright Field by Glenn L. Martin Co. on July 5, 1939, accompanied by a guarantee to build a certain quantity of the bombers in a given time.

In the Army evaluation of the designs submitted by various manufacturers, points were awarded in several categories up to a maximum of 1,000; the Martin 179 design scored 140 points over the next-best project. With World War II imminent in Europe, the AAF took the unprecedented step of ordering its new medium bomber into production immediately the design had been accepted; in September 1939 Martin received a contract for 201 and the type was numbered B-26.

The Martin 179 design had been projected—by Peyton M. Magruder—with the highest wing loading of any aircraft then designed for the AAF, in order to obtain the high speed performance. Associated with the comparatively small wing were two large nacelles for the 1,850 h.p. Pratt & Whitney R-2800 Double Wasp engines and a rotund but beautifully-streamlined fuselage. As specified, one 0.30-inch gun was mounted for tail defence; another 0·30 was hand-operated on a ball-mounting in the nose and two 0·50s equipped the Martin 250CE electrically-operated dorsal turret. The wing was shoulder mounted to leave the centre fuselage free for bomb stowage.

Construction of the first B-26s at the Martin plant in Baltimore was directed by William K. (Ken) Ebel, then Martin's chief engineer, who also piloted the first B-26 (49-1361) on its first flight on November 25, 1940. The next B-26 followed in February 1941. As no prototypes had been ordered, the first few production aircraft were reserved for test purposes. The first 201 aircraft were of the plain B-26 type, with 1,850 h.p. R-2800-5 engines and a gross weight of 30,035 lb.; the maximum bomb load was 5,800 lb., and the speed of 315 m.p.h. was the best of all B-26 models.

Deliveries to the AAF began in 1941 but units were slow to become operational on the type because its high landing speed (inevitable with the chosen wing loading) made conversion training a lengthy, and at times dangerous, process. An increase in gross weight to 32,200 lb. on the B-26A, which followed the B-26 in the second half of 1941, did nothing to improve the problem. The higher weight arose from the introduction of additional optional fuel tanks in the bomb bay, shackles for a 22-inch torpedo beneath the fuselage, 0·50-inch guns in the nose and tail and other additional equipment. A change was made from 12 volt to 24 volt electrical system, and most of the 139 B-26As built had R-2800-9 or -39 engines.

By the end of 1941, the 22nd Bombardment Group had equipped with B-26s, which it took from Langley Field, Virginia, to Australia in February 1942, in one of the first overseas deployments of home-based AAF units of the War. The 22nd took its Marauders into action for the first time in April 1942 in attacks on New Guinea. With fuel in the bomb bays to obtain the necessary range, the bomb-load was limited to 2,000 lb. and these raids were probably of more consequence as morale raisers than for the damage they caused. In June, Marauders of the 38th BG were in action as torpedo bombers at the Battle of Midway and, flown by the 73rd and 77th Bombardment Squadrons from Alaska, in attacks on shipping in the Aleutians.

Martin B-26 of 22nd Bomb Group. Use of fuselage star plus rudder stripes was not standard (*USAAC photo 74181*).

438

Martin B-26B of the initial series with short wing-span, small tail and no package guns on the forward fuselage (*USAF photo 21447AC*).

In May 1942, production of the B-26B began, and this became the most-produced variant, existing in a number of distinct versions. Initially, the changes from the B-26A comprised improved crew protection armour, refined internal equipment, deletion of propeller spinners, revised cowling details, a ventral "tunnel" gun and a new tail gun position with two 0·50-inch guns. The gross weight increased to 36,500 lb. with a 5,200 lb. bomb and torpedo load. The engines were 1,850 h.p. R-2800-5s in the 307 B-26Bs, but these were changed to 1,920 h.p. R-2800-41 or -43 in the second series of Bs (block numbers -2, -3 and -4, production of which totalled 95, 28 and 211 respectively). In the B-26B-4, the length of the nose-wheel strut was lengthened to improve the take-off performance (by increasing the effective wing incidence) and two 0·50-inch beam guns replaced the 0·30-inch tunnel gun of the earlier Bs. A further series of post-production modifications introduced slotted flaps on the B-26B-5.

With the B-26B-10 and subsequent models (also known to the makers

Martin B-26B-10 with long wing-span, larger tail and package guns on the fuselage side, photographed in Tunisia, 1943 (*Howard Levy*).

439

Martin B-26C of the 320th Bomb Group, Tunisia 1943 (*Howard Levy*).

as the B-26-B1), an effort was made to make the Marauder a less tricky
aeroplane on the approach and landing by increasing wing span and area
(65 ft. to 71 ft. and 602 sq. ft. to 659 sq. ft. respectively). In theory, this
reduced the wing loading, but the permissible gross weight was also
increased to 38,200 lb. with the introduction of still more defensive armament. A second gun was added to the nose armament, and two "package"
guns were installed on each side of the lower fuselage just behind the
cockpit; a Martin-Bell power operated tail turret also became standard.
The increased wing span was accompanied by a taller fin and rudder.
Martin built 1,242 of the B-26B-10 and later "B" variants at Baltimore, and
established, later in 1942, a second production source of Marauders at

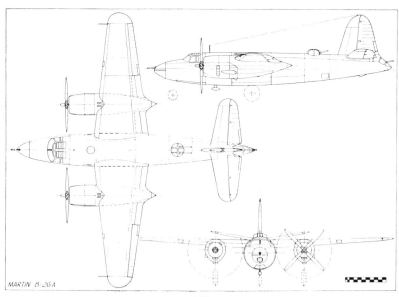

MARTIN B-26A

Martin B-26F-1 in natural metal finish, serving with the 558th Bomb Squadron, 387th BG, in Europe, 1944 (*Crown Copyright*).

Omaha where the same type was built as the B-26C. Omaha built 1,210 bombers of the latter version.

All early B-26 operations were in the Pacific area, but in November 1942, the 17th, 319th and 320th Bombardment Groups of the AAF arrived in North Africa with B-26Bs and B-26Cs, which they took into operation in December. As part of the Ninth Air Force, these Marauder-equipped groups followed the Allied ground forces from North Africa through Sicily to Italy, Sardinia, Corsica and into the South of France.

The first B-26s arrived in the U.K. in February 1943 and flew their first mission with the Eighth Air Force on May 14, 1943, when 12 B-26Bs from the 322nd BG made an inconclusive low-level attack on Ijmuiden; three days later, 11 Marauders attempted a second mission to the same target, from which none returned. More success attended strategic high level operations, started in July with an attack on Abbeville, but the B-26 did not find its optimum employment in Europe until applied to tactical air support duties. In November, all Eighth Air Force B-26 groups, in common with other light and medium bombers, were transferred to the re-formed Ninth Air Force, with which they served with conspicuous success in support of the forthcoming invasion of Europe.

Martin B-26G (*Martin photo P-11496*).

441

Final production models of the Marauder had the wing incidence angle increased by 3·5 degrees in a further attempt to improve the take-off performance. This and other detail changes distinguished the B-26F, of which Martin built 300 in 1943; 200 of these went to the R.A.F. under Lend-Lease in addition to 52 B-26As, 19 B-26Bs and 100 B-26Cs. Minor equipment changes were responsible for a change of designation to B-26G, which was in most respects similar to the B-26F. Martin built 893 B-26Gs (of which 150 went to the R.A.F.) and a further 57 TB-26Gs which were stripped of armament and operational equipment to serve (primarily with the U.S. Navy) as trainers and target tugs. The last B-26G and last Marauder was flown by Martin on April 18, 1945.

The single XB-26D was a B-26 conversion in 1942 with wing de-icing by hot air ducted from the engines. Another experimental type was the single XB-26E, a converted and stripped B-26B with the dorsal turret relocated forward, over the navigator's position. The last Marauder designation was XB-26H, with an experimental installation of a four-wheel bicycle undercarriage of the type then being designed for the Martin XB-48 and the Boeing XB-47. All B-26s were finally declared obsolete by the USAF in 1948, but few survived (as ZB-26Bs) even until that date in an airworthy condition.

The B-26 designation was transferred to the Douglas A-26 in June 1948 after the Martin bomber was withdrawn from service.

AT-23. In 1943, a design modification was initiated to strip B-26s of

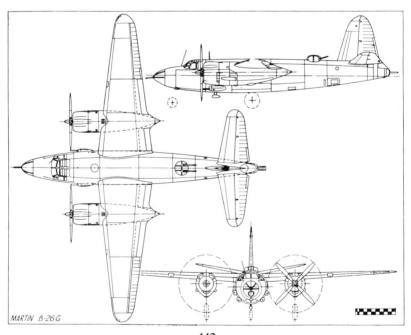

MARTIN B-26G

operational equipment and provide them with target towing gear. In all, 208 B-26Bs were modified and 350 B-26Cs were produced in this way, and re-designated AT-23A and AT-23B in the advanced trainer category. These designations were later changed to TB-26B and TB-26C respectively, and TB-26G models were produced as such, as noted above. Two hundred and twenty-five AT-23Bs went to the U.S. Navy as JM-1s and another 47 TB-26Gs became JM-2s.

TECHNICAL DATA (B-26)

MANUFACTURER: The Glenn L. Martin Co., Baltimore, Maryland (all except B-26C) and Omaha, Nebraska (B-26C only).
TYPE: Light bomber.
ACCOMMODATION: Seven crew.

	B-26	B-26B	B-26C	B-26G
Power Plant:	2 × 1,850 h.p. R-2800-5	2 × 2,000 h.p. R-2800-41	2 × 2,000 h.p. R-2800-43	2 × 2,000 h.p. R-2800-43
Dimensions:				
Span, ft., in.	65 0	65 0	71 0	71 0
Length, ft. in.	56 0	58 3	58 3	56 1
Height, ft. in.	19 10	19 10	21 6	20 4
Wing area, sq. ft.	602	602	658	658
Weights:				
Empty, lb.	21,375	22,380	24,000	23,800
Gross, lb.	32,000	34,000	38,200	38,200
Performance:				
Max. speed, m.p.h./ft.	315/15,000	317/14,500	282/15,000	283/5,000
Cruising speed, m.p.h.	265	260	214	216
Climb, min./ft.	12·5/15,000	12/15,000	24·5/15,000	8/5,000
Service ceiling, ft.	25,000	23,500	21,700	19,800
Range, miles	1,000	1,150	1,150	1,100
Armament:				
	3 × 0·50-in. 2 × 0·30-in. 4,800 lb.	4 × 0·50-in. 2 × 0·30-in. 3,000 lb.	12 × 0·50-in. 3,000 lb.	11 × 0·50-in. 4,000 lb.

SERIAL NUMBERS:
B-26: 40-1361/1561.
B-26A: 41-7345/7483.
B-26B: 41-17544/18334; 41-31573/32072; 42-43260/43357; 42-43360/43361; 42-43459; 42-95738/96228.
B-26C: 41-34673/35560*; 42-107497/107830.
B-26F: 42-96229/96528.
B-26G- 43-34115/34614; 44-67805/67944; 44-67970/68221; 44-68254.

AT-23A: 42-43358/43359; 42-43362/43458; 42-95629/95737.
AT-23B: 41-35371; 41-35373; 41-35516; 41-35539; 41-35541/35547; 41-35552; 41-35561/35872; 42-107471/107496; 42-107831/107855.
TB-26G: 44-67945/67969; 44-68222/68253.

*Includes 12 AT-23B, as listed separately.

443

Martin RB-57D (front) and B-57A (*Martin photo P-56420*).

Martin B-57

As the only aeroplane of non-U.S. design adopted for operational service with the USAF since the end of World War II, the B-57 was unique. It also has a special place in USAF history for its operation, in the RB-57D and RB-57F versions, on clandestine reconnaissance sorties along and across the Soviet borders.

The first example to carry USAF insignia, with the serial number 51-17352, was a British-built English Electric Canberra B.Mk.2 (R.A.F. serial WD932) which was flown to Baltimore on February 21, 1951, becoming the first jet aircraft to complete an unrefuelled Atlantic flight in the process. To establish the production line, Martin built a pre-production batch of eight B-57As (Martin Model 272) patterned closely on the Canberra 2, but with Wright J65-W-1 engines and engineering changes to suit U.S. production methods. The first B-57A flew at Baltimore on July 20, 1953. With cameras in a bay aft of the bomb-bay, the RB-57A was similar in outward appearance. The first of 67 built had been delivered to Shaw A.F.B. by April 1954, and from the end of that year until 1957 this variant equipped the 363rd Tactical Reconnaissance Wing.

Extensive changes were made in the next version produced to suit it for a tactical night intruder mission as Weapon System WS307A. The cockpit was re-modelled to seat two in tandem rather than side-by-side, and fixed wing armament of eight 0·50-in or four 20-mm. guns was introduced. A rotary bomb-door, with the stores mounted on the doors themselves, and wing pylons for HVAR rockets or bombs, were fitted. The first B-57B flew on June 28, 1954 and 202 were built, one more than all the other versions put together. The 461st Bomb Group (Tactical) of TAC received its first B-57B on January 5, 1955, and was fully equipped by the end of the year, followed in 1956 by the 345th BG(T) and the 38th BG(T) in Europe. These Groups were inactivated early in 1958, on April 1, 1958, and June 25, 1959, respectively, the B-57B passing out of TAC service on the latter

444

date. It remained in service, however, with the three squadrons of the 3rd BG(T) of PACAF, which had been the fourth and last Group to equip on the B-57B, in 1957. Based in Japan, this Group was on the point of transferring its B-57Bs to two ANG units in 1964 when the worsening situation in Indo-China brought an abrupt change of plan. Active use of the B-57B began in Vietnam from the first day that jet aircraft were in action there, and the type remained engaged there until 1974, in the hands of the 8th and 13th Tactical Bomb Squadrons. To improve the capabilities of the aircraft in the night intruder role, the B-57G was developed, carrying Texas Instruments AN/APQ-139 forward-looking radar, a low-light-level TV and infra-red sensors and a laser range-finder. Sixteen B-57Bs were converted, after an experimental external installation of the LLLTV on three B-57Bs. The 13th Bombardment Squadron (Tactical), temporarily withdrawn from Vietnam, reformed on the B-57G in 1969 and redeployed to Thailand with the new variant in September 1970. Withdrawn from operations in 1972, the B-57Gs served with the Kansas ANG for a year before being retired.

For use as a transition trainer alongside the B-57B, Martin built 38 B-57Cs with provision for dual controls but retaining full operational capabilities. First flown on December 30, 1954, the B-57C was issued to the four TAC Groups flying the B-57B and to a unit of the 357th Combat Crew Training Wing at Randolph A.F.B., Texas. When eventually dedicated permanently to the training role, the aircraft became known as TB-57Cs. A small number of B-57Bs and B-57Cs later were equipped and redesignated as RB-57Bs and RB-57Cs to serve alongside RB-57As when the latter were issued to ANG squadrons.

The B-57E was a further variant of the basic aircraft, equipped as a target-tug, and was in fact the first aircraft ever built as new for the USAF specifically for this duty. Target containers were fitted on the lower rear fuselage, but the B-57E, which first flew in April 1956, could be converted to a bomber by removing these containers and the internal cable reels and fittings and the cockpit towing controls. Production totalled 68 for service with the Tow Target Squadrons, but a number of these later were modified for other duties as RB-57E, TB-57E and EB-57E (as well as JB-57E and NB-57E in temporary and permanent test roles).

The EB-57E conversions, of which at least 25 were made, served with the

Martin B-57B in original overall black finish, operated by 822BS/38BG at Laon, France, with yellow eagle on tip tanks and yellow rudder (*BAC photo*).

445

Martin B-57E towing a banner target (*Martin photo 22657*).

Defense Systems Evaluation Squadrons, which provided electronic reconnaissance and intercept training for ground and air crews. Among the units flying the EB-57Es were the 4677th, 4713rd, and 4758th DSES, and similar conversions of 12 RB-57As and 22 B-57Bs served in the same role as EB-57As and EB-57Bs respectively.

The non-standard designation MSB-57B, in which MS stood for Missile Simulator, was applied to two B-57Bs that were fitted with the long nose sections of Martin TM-76 Mace SSMs housing Automatic Terrain Recognition and Navigation (ATRAN) radar. Operated by the 38th Tactical Missile Wing, they were later redesignated JB-57Bs in common with others of the same type temporarily assigned to test duties, while some NB-57Bs and at least one NRB-57A had permanent test status.

A major redesign of the B-57 was undertaken in 1955 to produce a high-altitude version designated RB-57D. The fuselage and tail unit remained basically unchanged, but a new wing of much greater span was introduced and the engines were changed to 10,500 lb.s.t. Pratt & Whitney J57-P-37As. The new wing had a span of 106 ft., or 107 ft. 6 in. when optional wing-tip radome pods were fitted. Nose and tail radomes increased the overall length of the fuselage by up to 28 inches. Production of the RB-57D totalled 20, in four distinct versions, according to the primary missions for which they were equipped. Six Group A, or RB-57D-1, aircraft (Martin Model 294) were single-seat photo-reconnaissance aircraft, for operation in the Far East. The seven Group B, or RB-57D-2 aircraft (Model 744) were for European operation, with electronic sensors. A single Group C RB-57D-3 (Model 796) and six Group D RB-57D-4s (Model 797) had different

Martin B-57G with forward-looking radar, LLTV, IR and laser sensors in the front fuselage (*USAF photo 107539*).

446

standards of electronic intelligence gathering equipment, and the latter were two-seaters. All but Group A were equipped for in-flight refuelling.

The RB-57D-1s were first deployed by SAC to Atsugi, Japan, in April 1956. Two years later, Group B aircraft were being used in Europe by the 7407th Support Squadron within USAFE for electronic reconnaissance along and sometimes across the frontiers of Communist territory. Persistent structural problems with the big new wing limited the operational value of the RB-57Ds, but they also were deployed with the 1211th Test Squadron (Sampling), a unit of the Air Weather Service that became responsible for checking the upper atmosphere for evidence of nuclear testing. Wing failures led to the "D" being grounded in 1963, but new wings were manufactured by Martin for nine of the aircraft, which then became EB-57Ds.

To fill the gap left when the RB-57Ds were grounded, a more advanced high-altitude reconnaissance variant was produced by the General Dynamics

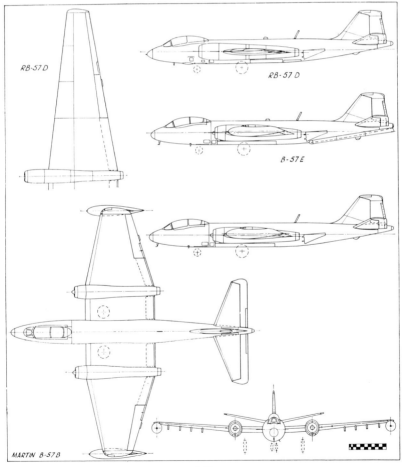

RB-57 D

RB-57 D

B-57 E

MARTIN B-57 B

Martin/General Dynamics RB-57F (*General Dynamics photo 24-12177*).

Fort Worth Division, initial delivery being made in July 1964 only nine months after design work started. The new version, designated RB-57F, had an even larger wing, with a span of 122 ft. 5 in., and new power-plant comprising 18,000 lb.s.t. Pratt & Whitney TF33-P-11 turbofans in the wing nacelles and two 3,300 lb.s.t. J60-P-9 turbojets in underwing pods. The fuselage, based on that of the B-57B, was lengthened by 40 inches to carry new electronic equipment in the nose.

An initial batch of 12 RB-57Fs was made by General Dynamics, based on B-57B airframes but with new FY 63 serial numbers. A second batch of nine was ordered later (although given consecutive serial numbers) and comprised conversions of two B-57Bs, three RB-57As and four RB-57Ds, in that order, to bring the total of this variant to 21. The first RB-57F flew on June 23, 1963, and service use, with the 58th Weather Reconnaissance Squadron, officially began in February 1964. For two to three months prior to this date, however, two RB-57Fs were used by the 7907th Combat Support Wing, from bases in Germany, for intelligence-gathering missions around and over the Eastern Europe bloc boundaries, using passive sensors carried by the aircraft including a massive high-altitude camera (HIAC), as well as electronic devices. In the hands of the 58th WRS, the RB-57Fs had primary responsibility for air sampling to detect and classify nuclear contamination from test explosions. Subsequently, the 56th WRS, based in Japan, also received RB-57Fs for air sampling and weather reconnaissance, and the designation WB-57F came into use when the aircraft became primarily concerned with the latter missions—sometimes accompanied by WB-57B and WB-57C conversions of the earlier models. The USAF retired the last of its WB-57Fs in July 1974, leaving three units flying EB-57Es—the 17 DSES in the active USAF and the 117 DSES (Kansas) and 134 DSES (Vermont) in the ANG. Deactivation of the 117th in 1978 and the 17th in 1979 left the 134th DSES as the very last squadron-sized operator of the type, until it was re-equipped with the F-4 Phantom as a tactical fighter unit in 1982.

TECHNICAL DATA (B-57B)

MANUFACTURER: The Glenn L. Martin Co., Baltimore, Maryland.
TYPE: Light tactical bomber, strategic reconnaissance (RB-57D), trainer (B-57C) and target tug (B-57E).
ACCOMMODATION: Pilot and navigator.
POWER PLANT: Two 7,200 lb.s.t. Wright J65-W-5F turbojets.
DIMENSIONS: Span, 64 ft. 0 in. Length, 65 ft. 6 in. Height, 15 ft. 7 in. Wing area, 960 sq. ft.
WEIGHT: Empty, 27,091 lb. Gross, 58,800 lb.
PERFORMANCE: Max. speed, 598 m.p.h. at 2,500 ft. Average cruising speed, 476 m.p.h. at 36,900 ft. Initial climb, 6,180 ft./min. Service ceiling, 40,100 ft. Range, 2,300 st. miles.
ARMAMENT: Eight fixed forward firing 0·50-in. guns or (from 91st aircraft) four 20-mm. cannon in nose; four underwing pylons with total capacity for 4,000 lb. of bombs or rocket pods, and up to 5,200 lb. of bombs in rotary bomb-bay.
SERIAL NUMBERS:

B-57A: 52-1418/1425.
RB-57A: 52-1426/1492.
B-57B: 52-1493/1594; 53-3859/3935;
  53-3937/3939; 53-3941/3943;
  53-3945/3947; 53-3949/3962.

B-57C: 53-3825/3858; 53-3936; 53-3940;
  53-3944; 53-3948.
RB-57D: 53-3963/3982.
B-57E: 55-4234/4301.

TECHNICAL DATA (WB-57F)

MANUFACTURER: General Dynamics Corp., Fort Worth, Texas.
TYPE: Very high-altitude reconnaissance.
ACCOMMODATION: Pilot and navigator or special equipment operator, in tandem.
POWER PLANT: Two 16,500 lb.s.t. Pratt & Whitney TF33-P-11A turbojets and two 2,900 lb.s.t. Pratt & Whitney J60-P-9 turbojets.
DIMENSIONS: Span, 122 ft. 5 in. Length, 68 ft. 8 in. Height, 20 ft. 5 in. Wing area, 2,000·02 sq. ft.
WEIGHTS: Empty, 36,876 lb. Gross, 63,000 lb.
PERFORMANCE: Max. speed, 483 m.p.h. at 63,500 ft. Cruising speed, 473 m.p.h. Intitial rate of climb, 7,600 ft./min. Service ceiling, 64,000 ft. Typical mission range, 2,950 miles. Ferry range, 3,910 miles.
ARMAMENT: Nil.
SERIAL NUMBERS:
RB-57F: 63-13286/13302; 63-13500/13503.

A preserved EB-57B in the markings of "The Green Mountain Boys", the Vermont ANG's 134th DSES, last unit to operate any B-57 variant (*Thomas Hildreth*).

449

North American BT-12, in blue and yellow training finish, of the 52nd School Squadron, Randolph Field, in June 1941 (*Peter M. Bowers*).

North American BT-9 and BT-14

North American Aviation Inc. entered the training aircraft field in 1935 with a privately financed prototype of its NA-16 design, built and flown in Baltimore with the civil registration marks X-2080.

Evaluated at Wright Field, the NA-16 was regarded as the closest approach to tactical aircraft yet achieved in a trainer. With few changes the North American design was adopted late in 1935 as a standard Army basic trainer, designated BT-9. On the strength of the first order for 42 aircraft North American moved into new production facilities at Inglewood (Los Angeles), California, where the first BT-9 (NA-19) flew in April 1936. The engine was the 400 h.p. Wright R-975-7 Whirlwind.

The first BT-9 contract was quickly followed by a second, for 40 BT-9As (NA-19A), distinguished by the addition of one fixed forward firing gun and a recording camera, and a flexible gun in the rear cockpit.

The 1937 model was the BT-9B (NA-23) again distinguished by only minor changes. North American built 117 of this version, and concluded the series with 67 BT-9C (NA-29) procured for the Organized Reserve.

One BT-9B was converted to the BT-9D (NA-26) in 1938, with new wing panels and tail unit which had by then been developed for the BC-1A. A BT-9C (37-383) fitted with a 600 h.p. Pratt & Whitney R-1340 in 1938 was redesignated Y1BT-10.

Features of the BC-1A, including the new wing and tail shapes, together with a metal-covered fuselage, identified the BT-14 (NA-58), which was ordered in 1940 as an improved BT-9. North American built 251 BT-14s with 450 h.p. Pratt & Whitney R-985-25 engines, and later converted 27 of these to BT-14As with 400 h.p. R-985-11s.

TECHNICAL DATA (BT-9B)

MANUFACTURER: North American Aviation, Inglewood, California.
TYPE: Basic trainer.
ACCOMMODATION: Pupil and instructor in tandem.

450

POWER PLANT: One 400 h.p. Wright R-975-7 piston radial.
DIMENSIONS: Span, 42 ft. 0 in. Length, 27 ft. 7 in. Height, 13 ft. 7 in. Wing area, 248 sq. ft.
WEIGHTS: Empty, 3,314 lb. Gross, 4,471 lb.
PERFORMANCE: Max. speed, 170 m.p.h. at sea level. Operational speed, 147 m.p.h. Climb, 4·7 min. to 5,000 ft. Service ceiling, 19,750 ft. Endurance, 6·0 hr.
ARMAMENT: Two 0·30-in. Browning guns, 200 rounds.
SERIAL NUMBERS:

BT-9: 36-028/069.	BT-9C: 37-383/415; 38-224/257.
BT-9A: 36-088/127.	BT-14: 40-1110/1360.
BT-9B: 37-115/231.	

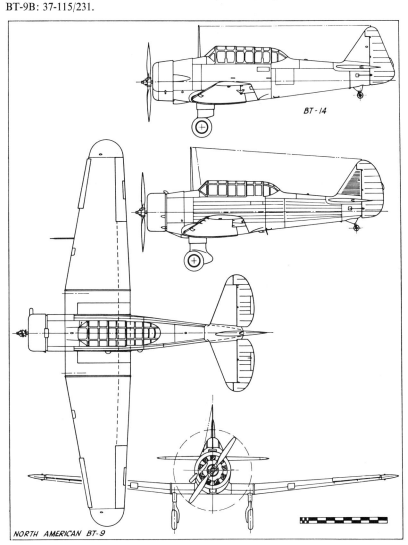

BT-14

NORTH AMERICAN BT-9

451

North American O-47B of California National Guard with O.D. and grey finish added in 1941 (*Peter M. Bowers*).

North American O-47

The North American O-47, standard observation model for Army and National Ground Units from 1937 until Pearl Harbor, originated in 1934 with a predecessor company, General Aviation, itself a successor of the American Fokker Aircraft Corporation which was also known as Atlantic Aircraft. The XO-47 introduced an entirely new concept of observation plane design and broke the tradition of the large heavy two-seater that had been standard since 1915. Even larger and heavier than the two-seaters, the XO-47 was a three-seater, with all crew members sitting in tandem under a long canopy.

The location of the wing was detrimental to observation from this location, so the observer/photographer was provided with a separate station in the deep belly, where windows at the bottom and each side gave him an excellent field of view free of the blanking effect of the wing.

The XO-47 was built in the General Aviation plant at Dundalk, Maryland, and was painted in the then standard observation plane colouring of blue fuselage and chrome yellow wing and tail surfaces. The 164 O-47As (NA-25) with 975 h.p. R-1820-49s, were built in 1937 at the new North American Aviation plant at Inglewood, California, and were finished in natural aluminium. An additional 74 O-47Bs with minor improvements and 1,060 h.p. Wright R-1820-57 engines were delivered in 1939.

Except for those caught at overseas bases by the Japanese attacks of December 1941, the O-47s were not used as combat types in World War II, the long-range photo-reconnaissance function having been taken over by bombers and camera-carrying fighter conversions and the short-range missions by the new "Grasshopper" class of low-powered lightplanes. The O-47s served throughout the War as trainers and in such utility tasks as aerial target towing.

TECHNICAL DATA (O-47A)

MANUFACTURER: North American Aviation, Inglewood, California.
TYPE: Observation monoplane.
ACCOMMODATION: Pilot and observer in tandem.
POWER PLANT: One 975 h.p. Wright R-1820-49 piston radial.
DIMENSIONS: Span, 46 ft. 4 in. Length, 33 ft. 7 in. Height, 12 ft. 2 in. Wing area, 350 sq. ft.
WEIGHTS: Empty, 5,980 lb. Gross, 7,636 lb.
PERFORMANCE: Max. speed, 221 m.p.h. at 4,000 ft. Operational speed, 200 m.p.h. Climb, 6·8 min. to 10,000 ft. Service ceiling, 23,200 ft. Endurance, 2·1 hr.
ARMAMENT: One fixed 0·30-in. Browning (200 rounds) in wing; one flexible 0·30-in. Browning (600 rounds) in rear cockpit.
SERIAL NUMBERS:
XO-47: 36-145.   O-47B: 39-065/138.
O-47A: 37-260/368; 38-271/325.

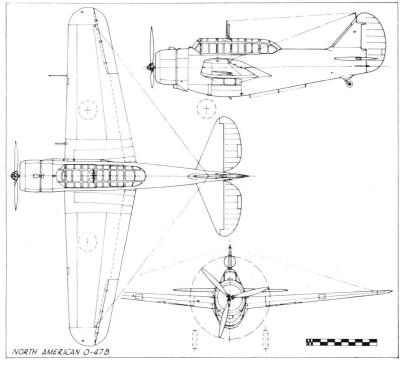

NORTH AMERICAN O-47B

453

All-silver AT-6A of the Harlingen Gunnery School, Texas, in 1941.

North American BC-1, BC-2, AT-6, AT-16

Best known of the North American trainers derived from the original NA-16 design, the AT-6 Texan (or Harvard) was originally a re-designation of the BC-1A type. This, in turn, was derived from the NA-26, an NA-16 variant entered in an Air Corps design competition at Wright Field in March 1937. The competition was intended to produce a new kind of trainer in the "basic combat" category, with the equipment and attributes of operational combat aircraft. Powered by a 600 h.p. Pratt & Whitney R-1340 engine, the NA-26 had a retractable undercarriage and provision for armament, two-way radio and representative navigation and engine instruments. It won the competition and North American was awarded a contract for 41 BC-1s which appeared as NA-36s with R-1340-47 engines. Subsequent contracts swelled the total built to 180. Thirty of these became BC-1Is when equipped for instrument training and the final three were designated BC-2 (NA-54) with R-1340-45 engines, three-blade propellers and metal covered fuselage.

Several changes distinguished the BC-1A (NA-55) including blunter wing tips and a straight trailing edge to the rudder. Production of this version totalled 92 of which one became the BC-1B when fitted with an AT-6A type centre section, and nine were delivered as AT-6s.

The change from BC-1A to AT-6 in 1940 represented a change in policy but virtually no modification to the aeroplane; a further 85 AT-6s (NA-59) were ordered in 1940 to a similar standard for use as advanced trainers.

Production continued with the AT-6A (NA-77) with the R-1340-49 engine and removable metal fuel tanks in place of the AT-6's integral tank in the centre section. As the USAAC re-equipment and expansion programmes got under way in 1940, the need for trainers multiplied rapidly, and the AT-6 became, for the remainder of the War period, the aircraft on which all Air Force pilots received their advanced training. To cope with the demand for these trainers, not only from the Army but also from the

454

R.A.F. in Britain and from other foreign Air Forces, North American established a second production line in 1941 at Dallas, Texas, where 1,210 AT-6As were built, including 298 for the USN. The Inglewood plant built 517 AT-6As and then turned all Texan production over to Dallas, where the next model was the AT-6B, equipped for gunnery training and having the 600 h.p. R-1340-AN-1 engine to common Army/Navy specification.

In the AT-6C (NA-88) of which Dallas built 2,970, a change was made to non-strategic materials, with low-alloy steel and plywood used to save some 1,246 lb. of aluminium alloy per aircraft. When the fears of material shortages proved to be exaggerated, the earlier standard structure was restored in the AT-6D, which changed to a 24-volt electric system. Production of the AT-6D model totalled 4,388, but this included 675 procured on behalf of the USN and many others destined for other nations under Lend–Lease arrangements. A single AT-6D fitted with a high-altitude Ranger V-770-9 engine was designated XAT-6E (42-84241).

Final production version of the Texan was the AT-6F; of 956 built, 931 were assigned to the USN as SNJ-6s. In Canada, the Noorduyn company built 1,800 aircraft of similar design to the AT-6A; financed by the U.S. Government they were all assigned to the R.A.F. under Lend–Lease arrangements for use in the Joint Air Training Plan, and were designated AT-16s.

Well over 2,000 AT-6s remained in service with the USAAF after World War II, to be redesignated T-6A, T-6C, T-6D and T-6F when the AT category was abandoned, along with BT and PT, in June 1948. The following year, while the choice of a new advanced trainer by the USAF was still undecided, a modernization programme was started which eventually covered 2,068 aircraft for the USAF and USN. Each T-6 was re-manufactured with changes in the cockpit to raise the instructor's seat and improve visibility from the front seat; a new cockpit layout, standardized in both cockpits; increased fuel capacity; square-tipped propeller; repositioned aerial masts; F-51-type steerable tail wheel and F-51-type landing gear and flap-actuating levers. Thus modified at the Downey, California, factory, the aircraft were re-designated T-6G (NA-168) and were allocated new serial numbers. A few AT-6Fs converted at

All-yellow North American T-6G, California National Guard, 1950 (*William T. Larkins*),

455

Columbus were temporarily re-designated T-6H but became T-6Gs also. The T-6J designation covered a batch of 50 Harvard 4s built by Can-Car for the Mutual Security Programme.

In July 1950, a number of T-6Fs began flying in Korea on what became

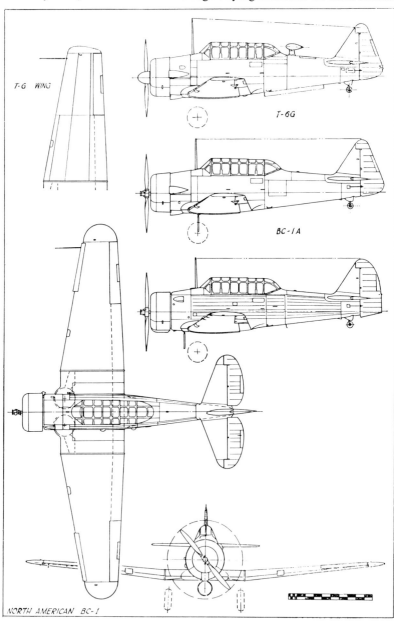

T-6 WING

T-6G

BC-1A

NORTH AMERICAN BC-1

known as Mosquito missions. Carrying trained Army observers in the second seat, these Mosquitos flew from airstrips close behind the front lines to act as "spotters" over U.N. troop movements and ranging up to 50 miles behind the enemy lines at low altitude. For these operations, the 6147th Tactical Air Control Squadron was formed, and 59 LT-6Gs were remanufactured for this role in Korea, replacing converted T-6Fs.

TECHNICAL DATA (BC-1)

MANUFACTURER: North American Aviation Inc., Inglewood, California.
TYPE: Basic combat trainer.
ACCOMMODATION: Pupil and instructor in tandem enclosed cockpit.
POWER PLANT: One 600 h.p. Pratt & Whitney R-1340-47.
DIMENSIONS: Span, 43 ft. 0 in. Length, 27 ft. 9 in. Height, 14 ft. 0 in. Wing area, 225 sq. ft.
WEIGHTS: Empty, 4,050 lb. Gross, 5,200 lb.
PERFORMANCE: Max. speed, 207 m.p.h. Climb, 7·5 min. to 10,000 ft. Service ceiling, 24,100 ft. Range, 665 st. miles.
ARMAMENT: One fixed forward firing and one flexible rear-mounted 0·30-inch machine gun. No bombs.
SERIAL NUMBERS:
BC-1: 37-416/456; 37-636/679; 38-356/447.

BC-1A: 39-798/856; 40-707/716; 40-726/739.
BC-2: 38-448/450.

TECHNICAL DATA (AT-6A)

TYPE: Advanced trainer.
ACCOMMODATION: Pupil and instructor in tandem in enclosed cockpit.
POWER PLANT: One 600 h.p. Pratt & Whitney R-1340-49 piston radial.
DIMENSIONS: Span, 42 ft. 0 in. Length, 29 ft. 0 in. Height, 11 ft. 9 in. Wing area, 254 sq. ft.
WEIGHTS: Empty, 3,900 lb. Gross, 5,155 lb.
PERFORMANCE: Max. speed, 210 m.p.h. Climb, 7·4 min. to 10,000 ft. Service ceiling, 24,200 ft. Range, 629 st. miles.
ARMAMENT: One fixed forward firing and one flexible rear-mounted 0·30-inch machine gun as required. No bombs.
SERIAL NUMBERS:
AT-6: 40-717/725; 40-2080/2164.
AT-6A-NA: 41-149/665.
AT-6A-NT: 41-15824/17033*.
AT-6B-NT: 41-17034/17433.
AT-6C-NT: 41-32073/33072; 41-33073/33819; 42-3884/4243; 42-43847/44411; 42-48772/49069.
AT-6D-NT: 41-33820/34122; 41-34123/34672†; 42-44412/44746; 42-84163/86562‡; 44-80845/81644§.
T-6D: 49-2722/2756††.

AT-6F-NT: 44-81645/82600**.
T-6G: 49-2897/3537; 50-1277/1326; 51-14314/15237; 51-16071/16077; 51-17354/17364; 52-8197/8246; 53-4555/4614.
LT-6G: 49-3538/3596.
T-6J: 51-17089/17231; 52-8493/8612; 53-4615/4636.
AT-16: 42-464/963; 42-12254/12553; 43-12502/13201; 43-34615/34914.

* 298 to USN.   ‡ 100 to USN.   † 300 to USN.   § 275 to USN.
** 931 to USN.   †† remanufactured for Mutual Aid Program, Greece.

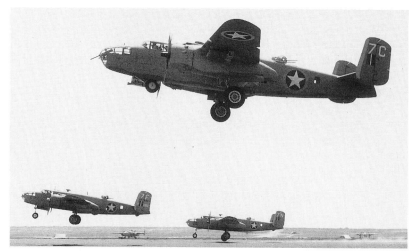

North American B-25Ds of 340th Bomb Group, Tunisia, 1943. Note yellow outlines to wing and fuselage insignia and added British fin flash (*Howard Levy*).

North American B-25 Mitchell

By a happy chance, the aircraft chosen to bear the name Mitchell in memory of Colonel William ("Billy") Mitchell—whose far-sighted views on the significance of air power led to his court martial in 1925—proved to be one of the most outstanding bombers used by the American Forces in World War II. Nearly 11,000 examples were built between 1940 and 1945, of which the USAAF received 9,816, and the Mitchell served on every major front during the War, with the USAAF, the USN, and Air Forces of other Allied Powers.

Design work began in 1938 on a medium bomber to meet an Air Corps requirement, and a prototype of this design was built by North American as a private venture. This was the NA-40-1, a three-seat shoulder-wing aeroplane with a notably deep fuselage, a tricycle undercarriage and twin fins and rudders. For its day, the NA-40 was heavily armed, with hand-held 0·30-inch guns in the nose, dorsal and ventral positions and provision for three more fixed forward-firing guns in the wings. Powered by two 1,100 h.p. Pratt & Whitney R-1830-S6C3-G radial engines, the NA-40-1 was first flown in January 1939 by Paul Balfour. The engines were changed to 1,350 h.p. Wright GR-2600-A71s in February and, as the NA-40-2 or NA-40B, the prototype was delivered to Wright Field in March.

After only two weeks at Wright Field, the NA-40 was destroyed, but its outstanding performance had already been noted and the USAAC requested North American to continue development, and specified a number of design changes. The developed design, as the NA-62, had twice the bomb load of the NA-40; a wider fuselage with side-by-side seating in the cockpit, which was faired into the top line instead of projecting above it, and the wing dropped to a mid position. The crew was increased from three to five, and a tail gun station was added, with a single 0·50-inch hand-held gun.

Basic design work on the NA-62 had been completed by August, 1939, and USAAC approval was indicated by the placing of a production order, that same month, for 184 B-25s. Production began at once and an airframe for static tests was completed in July 1940, followed by the first flying example which flew on August 19, 1940. The engines were 1,700 h.p. R-2600-9s and the gross weight had increased to 27,310 lb. from the original NA-40's 19,500 lb., while the wider fuselage increased the span from 66 ft. to 67 ft. 6 in.

Flight tests indicated that the B-25 was deficient in directional stability, a fault which was cured by reducing the dihedral angle on the outer wing panels to give the Mitchell its distinctive gull-wing appearance. No prototypes of the NA-62 were built as such, but the first nine B-25s were completed with the original full wing dihedral. They were followed by 15 more B-25s with the revised wing before a change was made to the B-25A (NA-62A), in which self-sealing tanks and armour protection for the pilots were introduced.

Forty B-25As were built, and in 1941 began to reach the first Mitchell operational unit, the 17th Bombardment Group (Medium), at McChord Field. Operating on anti-shipping patrols off the U.S. West Coast at the end of 1941, a B-25A of this Group sank a Japanese submarine on December 24 in the first successful attack by this aircraft type.

The original 1939 contract was completed in 1941 with the production of 120 B-25B (NA-62B) variants, one of which (40-2243) crashed before delivery. Changes which distinguished this model of the Mitchell were concerned principally with the armament, which comprised Bendix electric dorsal and ventral turrets, with two 0·50-in. guns in each, with the tail gun removed. The gross weight increased to 28,460 lb. Twenty-three of the B-25Bs went to the R.A.F. under Lend-Lease and a few also went

North American B-25 at March Field, June 1941 (*Peter M. Bowers*).

459

to the Soviet Air Force as forerunners of the large number of later model Mitchells flown to Russia.

Some B-25Bs were also earmarked for the Dutch Air Force in the Netherlands East Indies but these aircraft went instead to the 13th and 19th Squadrons of the 3rd Bombardment Group in Australia. In April 1942, these squadrons went into action against Japanese targets in New Guinea and the Philippines, operating, in some cases, from concealed air strips in the Philippines themselves. Also in April 1942, 16 B-25Bs made an epic raid on Tokyo, flying off the U.S.S. *Hornet* 800 miles away from the target.

The crews for this mission were drawn from the 17th Group and the 89th Reconnaissance Squadron, and the aircraft were modified to have 1,141 U.S. gallons of fuel compared with the standard 694 U.S. gallons. The ventral turret and the Norden bombsight were removed, an auto-pilot was fitted, two wooden guns were fitted in the tail cone to discourage stern attacks, and the gross weight went up to 31,000 lb. These Mitchells, led by Lt. Col. James H. Doolittle, bombed Tokyo, Kobe, Yokohama and Nagoya on April 18. All the aircraft subsequently crashed or forced-landed, but most of the crews survived, including Doolittle, who received the Congressional Medal of Honor.

Deliveries of the B-25C began before the end of 1941, and this same basic model was put into production at a second North American factory at Dallas, Texas, as the B-25D. Identified as the NA-82, the B-25C had an auto-pilot, R-2600-13 engines and external racks under the fuselage and wings. Later batches of both models had additional fuel tanks in the wing and fuselage to bring the standard capacity to 1,100 U.S. gallons, when the gross weight became 33,500 lb. For ferrying, a 585-U.S. gallon tank could be fitted in the bomb bay, and the weight could be increased to 41,800 lb. The external wing racks could carry eight 250 lb. bombs to increase the total load to 5,200 lb., while a 2,000 lb. torpedo was sometimes carried externally beneath the fuselage for attacks on Japanese shipping.

Production of the B-25C totalled 1,619 at Inglewood, and of the B-25D, 2,290 at Dallas, Texas. Many of these were supplied under Lend–Lease

North American B-25C at El Kabrit in 1942 (*Howard Levy*).

460

arrangements to the R.A.F., Russia, Brazil and the Netherlands Indies Air Corps.

During 1942, three B-25Cs were converted into prototypes of later models and were interesting as the first Mitchells to carry "X" designations. The XB-25E had experimental hot-air de-icing of the wing leading edge, while the XB-25F achieved the same results with electric elements. The third prototype was the XB-25G, in which a standard Army 75-mm. field gun was mounted to fire forwards through the nose.

This gun, one of the heaviest pieces of artillery fitted in an aircraft during World War II, was adopted for anti-shipping strikes in the South Pacific, where B-25s with additional 0·50-inch machine guns in the nose were already in action. The M-4 cannon fired 15 lb. shells, and had a 21-inch recoil. It was loaded by the navigator/bombardier and aimed with the help of two 0·50-inch machine guns in the nose. A total of 21 shells was carried, although hand loading reduced the number of shots in a single attack to a maximum of four. As the B-25G (NA-96), 405 of these cannon-armed Mitchells were produced, but did not prove outstandingly successful. They were followed by 1,000 B-25Hs (NA-98), based on the B-25G and the most heavily armed of all the Mitchells.

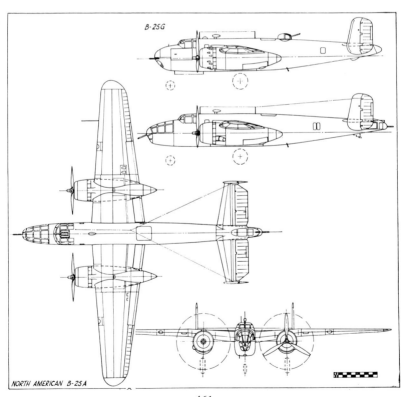

B-25G

NORTH AMERICAN B-25A

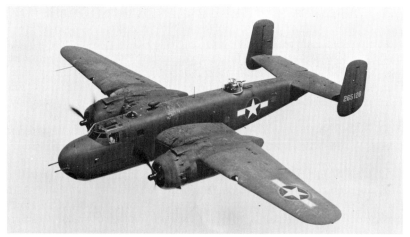

North American B-25G with 75 mm. cannon (*USAF photo 26716AC*).

In the B-25H, the T-13E1 type of 75-mm. cannon was carried, being lighter than the M-4 gun. The crew reverted to five from the B-25G's four, and experience with the G model and with B-25Cs and Ds used for ground strafing led to the introduction as standard of four 0·50-inch "blister" guns, two on each side of the fuselage beneath the cockpit, firing forward. In addition to the cannon, four 0·50s were carried in the fuselage nose itself; new waist hatches were fitted with a 0·50 in each, and a tail gunner was added, with two 0·50s in a power-operated mounting. The ventral turret, which had often been abandoned on earlier operational B-25s, was deleted and the dorsal turret was moved forward to a position just aft the cockpit.

The B-25Hs, with R-2600-13 or -29 engines, were allocated primarily to the U.S. Far East Air Forces, where the first arrived in February 1944 for service with the 498th Squadron. Operationally, the cannon proved a drawback, however, as it limited the flexibility of attack, and the cannon-Mitchell did not serve after August 1944. It was followed by the B-25J (NA-108) which was the most-produced of all the Mitchell variants; between 1943 and 1945, 4,318 B-25Js were built at Kansas.

In the B-25J, the 75-mm. cannon was abandoned in favour of the original type of front fuselage, which was largely transparent and contained a bomb-aiming station in addition to a hand-operated and two fixed forward-firing 0·50-inch guns. The remainder of the fuselage was, however, similar to that of the B-25H, with the forward dorsal turret and tail gun position. The first 150 B-25Js (43-3870 to 4019) had shackles for a 2,000-lb. bomb in the bomb-bay, but this weapon was seldom used, a more normal bomb-load comprising 3,000 lb. of 500-lb. or 1,000-lb. stores.

Most B-25Js which served with the USAAF went to the South-west

462

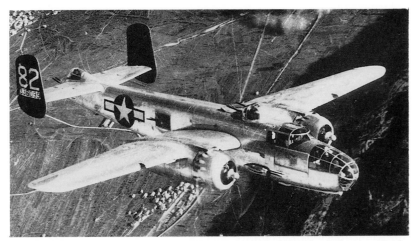

North American B-25J, stripped of camouflage, operated by 319th Bomb Group, with blue tails for Group recognition and cowl ring colours for squadron identity (*USAF photo*).

Pacific to re-equip squadrons flying the B-26; many others were supplied to the Allies under Lend–Lease arrangements. Operational experience in the Pacific from the spring of 1944 showed that most sorties were made at low level and that a bomb-aimer was not therefore needed. Consequently a modification was introduced, at first in the field and later on the production line, to fit a "solid" nose with eight 0·50-inch guns, to make a total of 18 such guns carried by this version of the B-25J. When coupled with eight 5-inch rocket projectiles on racks under the outer wings, these guns made the B-25J one of the most formidable attack bombers of the War.

Because so many Mitchells were supplied to other Air Forces, the USAAF inventory of the type never exceeded 2,700 at any one time during the War. In the Far East Air Force, just over 500 were operational by the autumn of 1944, making the Mitchell the most used type by this Command.

Top left, B-25H in India, 1945; top right, B-25J with eight-gun nose, China 1945; bottom left, CB-25J; bottom right, unarmed B-25C for night courier missions, C.B.I. theatre, 1944/45 (*all pictures, Peter M. Bowers*).

Many hundreds of B-25s passed into post-war service with USAF squadrons, principally in the C, D and J models. A few joined Strategic Air Command upon its formation in 1946; more served with Tactical Air Command units. By 1949, the ZB-25Cs, ZB-25Ds and the single ZXB-25E were obsolete although the latter lingered on until 1952. B-25Js continued to serve in a utility role and as staff transports, designated CB-25J and VB-25J, and about 900 were re-worked for training use, as described below under the AT-24/TB-25 heading. The last staff transport B-25 was retired from the active inventory on May 21, 1960.

F-10. Early B-25s had been issued to the 89th Reconnaissance Squadron before the end of 1941, but the fully-developed reconnaissance version, designated F-10, did not appear until 1943. Ten F-10s were produced by North American as conversions of B-25Ds. All armament was removed, extra fuel tanks were fitted in the bomb bay, R-2600-29 engines were fitted, and cameras were installed in the rear fuselage and in a "chin" fairing for tri-metrogen photography.

AT-24/TB-25. During 1943 and 1944, 60 B-25s were stripped of operational equipment to serve as advanced trainers. Conversions were made from redundant B-25D, B-25G, B-25C and B-25J models, and were re-designated AT-24A, B, C and D respectively. When the AT category was discontinued for converted types, these aircraft were again re-designated as the TB-25D, TB-25G, TB-25C and TB-25J.

Post-war, conversions of the J model to TB-25J continued until a total

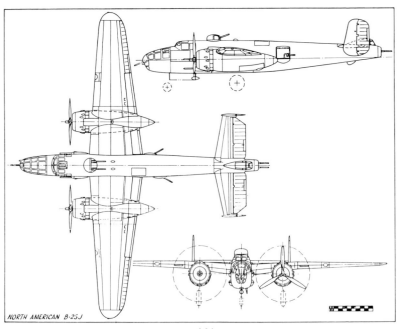

NORTH AMERICAN B-25J

of more than 600 had been completed, although not all TB-25Js were to the same standard so far as equipment was concerned. Most were six seaters with R-2600-29 or -13 engines.

Further training versions of the B-25 appeared between 1951 and 1954, all based on the B-25J. To provide a class-room for instruction in the use of their E-1 and E-5 radar fire control systems, Hughes produced, respectively, 117 TB-25Ks and 40 TB-25Ms. As pilot trainers, the 90 TB-25Ls and 47 TB-25Ns were produced by Hayes Aircraft Corp., the latter having R-2600-29A engines. The TB-25s were last in service for pilot training at Reese A.F.B., being finally retired from service in January 1959.

TECHNICAL DATA (B-25)

MANUFACTURER: North American Aviation Inc., Inglewood, California (B-25 A, B, C, E, F, G, H) and Kansas City, Kansas (B-25D, J).
TYPE: Light bomber.
ACCOMMODATION: Crew of three to six according to mission.

	B-25A	B-25C/D	B-25H	B-25 J
Power Plant:	2 × 1,700 h.p. R-2600-9	2 × 1,700 h.p. R-2600-13	2 × 1,700 h.p. R-2600-13	2 × 1,700 h.p. R-2600-92
Dimensions:				
Span, ft., in.	67 7	67 7	67 7	67 7
Length, ft., in.	54 1	52 11	51 0	52 11
Height, ft., in.	15 9	15 10	15 9	16 4
Wing area, sq. ft.	610	610	610	610
Weights:				
Empty, lb.	17,870	20,300	19,975	19,480
Gross, lb.	27,100	34,000	36,047	35,000
Performance:				
Max. speed, m.p.h./ft.	315/15,000	284/15,000	275/13,000	272/13,000
Cruising speed, m.p.h.	262	233	230	230
Climb, min./ft.	8·4/15,000	16·5/15,000	19/15,000	—
Service ceiling, ft.	27,000	21,200	23,800	24,200
Range, miles	1,350	1,500	1,350	1,350
Armament:	2 × 0·50-in. 3 × 0·30-in. 3000 lb.	6 × 0·50-in. 3000 lb.	14 × 0·50-in. 1 × 75 mm. 8 × 5 m. R.P. 3,000 lb.	12 × 0·50-in. 8 × 5 in. R.P. 3,000 lb.

SERIAL NUMBERS:
B-25: 40-2165/2188.
B-25A: 40-2189/2228.
B-25B: 40-2229/2348.
B-25C: 41-12434/13296; 42-32233/32280;
42-32282/32383; 42-32389/32532;
42-53332/53493; 42-64502/64801.
B-25D: 41-29648/30847; 42-87113/87612;
43-3280/3869.

XB-25E: 42-32281.
B-25G: 42-32384/32388; 42-64802/65201.
B-25H: 43-4105/5104.
B-25J: 43-3870/4104; 43-27473/28222;
43-35946/36245; 44-28711/31510;
44-86692/86897; 45-8801/8899.*
* Includes 72 completed but not delivered.

465

North American P-51D in European camouflage plus invasion stripes (*USAF photo*).

North American P-51, A-36, F-6 Mustang

The Mustang was one of the very small number of aeroplane types which were conceived after the start of World War II, yet saw large scale service in that War. It owed its origin to a British requirement for a fighter for service in Europe, and to the fact that existing U.S. fighters in 1940 could not meet the requirement. In January of that year, North American Aviation undertook to design a new aeroplane in which the early lessons from aerial combat over Europe would be taken account of, and the company accepted a 120-day limit for construction of a prototype. An in-line engine was specified—in keeping with British preference and in contrast with U.S. practice—and the then-standard British armament of eight machine guns was also required.

Despite a comparative lack of fighter design experience, North American engineers under Raymond Rice and Edgar Schmued not only kept inside the 120-day limit, but also succeeded brilliantly in meeting the requirement with their NA-73 design. Its notable features included the use of a laminar-flow wing section, aft-mounted ventral radiator for minimum drag, and simple lines for ease of production. Bearing the civil registration NX19998 (as a privately-financed prototype) the first NA-73 was rolled out at Inglewood, California, minus engine, 117 days after work on the design began. After the installation of a 1,100 h.p. Allison V-1710-F3R engine, it was flown for the first time on October 25, 1940. Production began almost immediately to meet British contracts placed by a Purchasing Commission, and the first production example flew before the end of 1941.

In permitting North American to undertake this work for a foreign buyer, the USAAC had stipulated that two examples of the production model should be supplied, free of charge, for evaluation. This requirement

466

was met by extracting aircraft numbers four and ten from the production line and sending them to Wright Field, where they were tested under the designation XP-51. Despite the excellent performance of these two aircraft, the first of which flew on May 20, 1941, the USAAC did not adopt the P-51 immediately, although the introduction of Lend-Lease did lead to an order for 150 to be supplied to the R.A.F.

These, the first of the type to be built to USAAF order, were designated P-51 (NA-91) and the name Apache was originally proposed, being later changed to Mustang. First flown on May 29, 1942, the P-51 differed from the British Mustang Is (620 of which were built as NA-73 and NA-83) in having an armament of four 20-mm. cannon in the wings, replacing the four 0·30-inch and two 0·50-inch wing guns and two 0·50-inch fuselage guns of the earlier model.

Most P-51s were supplied to the R.A.F. as Mustang IAs, but some Mustang Is were requisitioned for defence of the U.S. after Pearl Harbor, and flew in British camouflage and serial numbers with U.S. stars. It is reputed that only the personal intervention of General "Hap" Arnold secured the acceptance of the Mustang by the USAAF for its own use. The first aircraft ordered as a result of this decision were ground-attack variants of the design, designated A-36A (NA-97) in the attack category (see below).

In the P-51A (NA-99), of which the USAAF ordered 310 in 1942, the armament was reduced to four 0·50-inch wing guns and the performance at higher altitudes, which had been unsatisfactory in the early models, was improved with the introduction of the 1,200 h.p. V-1710-81 (F20R) engine. This model, first flown on February 3, 1943, retained the wing bomb racks of the A-36A, and could carry as an alternative to the bombs, 75- or 150-U.S. gallon drop tanks.

In a further effort to improve the high altitude performance of the type, installation of the Rolls-Royce Merlin engine was proposed in Britain, and four R.A.F. Mustang Is were converted by the engine-makers at Derby. To take full advantage of the improvement offered by this engine, North American undertook a re-design, the most noticeable result of which was a lip intake for the up-draught carburettor. Two P-51s (41-37352 and 41-37421) were retained in the U.S. to serve as prototypes of the new variant and with 1,300 h.p. Packard-built V-1650-3 Merlins were designated XP-78, later changed to XP-51B (NA-101). Retaining the four-cannon armament of the P-51, these prototypes incorporated new ailerons, and streamlined bomb racks which eventually carried 1,000 lb. bombs.

Left, XP-51, serial 41-038 (*Harold G. Martin*); right, repossessed P-51B, British Mustang III serial FB108.

Flight tests starting on November 30, 1942, showed an increase of 50 m.p.h. in maximum speed at optimum altitude to a new high of 441 m.p.h. As the P-51B (NA-102, NA-104) this became the first variant ordered in large quantity by the USAAF, a total of 1,988 being built at North American's Inglewood factory. In addition, a second source was established at Dallas, Texas, where North American built 1,750 of the similar P-51C (NA-103, NA-111), the first of which flew on August 5, 1943. Original production aircraft from both lines had the V-1650-3 engine, with the 1,695 h.p. V-1650-7 introduced later. Some P-51Bs and P-51Cs had the armament increased to six 0·50s in the wings, and the internal fuel capacity was later increased from 184 U.S. gallons to 269 U.S. gallons to give a range of 1,300 miles, or 2,080 miles with the help of two 110-U.S. gallon wing drop tanks.

This range was far in excess of that available in other fighters then serving in the European theatre and the delivery of P-51Bs to the 8th Air Force in Britain, which began on December 1, 1943, was an event of considerable operational significance. These aircraft flew their first mission on December 13, 1943, and on January 15, 1944, they crossed the German border for the first time. In March, P-51Bs flew to Berlin and back for the first time, escorting 8th Air Force B-17s and B-24s. Thereafter, the Mustang played an ever more prominent part in the offensive against "Fortress Europe", and by the time the War ended they equipped all but one of the 8th Air Force fighter escort groups.

A further canopy change distinguished the P-51D (NA-104, NA-106, NA-109, NA-110, NA-111, NA-122, NA-124) which was built in greater quantity than all other P-51s together. The fuselage was redesigned with a lowered rear decking and a large one-piece rearward-sliding "bubble" canopy was fitted to improve the rearward view. The six-gun wing armament became standard, as did the V-1650-7 engine. A small dorsal fin was introduced after delivery of the first few aircraft and was applied retroactively to some P-51Bs and Cs. The P-51D, first flown on November 17, 1943, was built both at Inglewood and at Dallas, the respective totals being 6,502 and 1,454.

North American P-51H showing revised nose, wing root and taller rudder (*Harold G. Martin*).

North American P-51 with cannon armament (*North American photo*).

In addition to its service in Europe, where it arrived in 1944, the P-51D saw operations in the Pacific area. Flying from Iwo Jima in February 1945, P-51Ds escorted B-29s to attack Japan, and on April 7, 1945, penetrated to Tokyo for the first time. After going into service, the P-51D was further modified to allow it to carry rocket projectiles. In some cases the installation comprised three infantry-type Bazookas under each wing, but more normally zero-length launchers for four 5-inch rockets were fitted. With an Aero-products propeller in place of the Hamilton-Standard type, the P-51D became the P-51K (NA-111) of which version the Dallas plant built 1,337. Approximately 600 of these went to the R.A.F.

In 1944, ten two-seat versions of this Mustang model were produced by North American as TP-51Ds (44-84610/84611, 45-11443/11450). The second cockpit, with full dual control, was behind and slightly above the standard position, both being accommodated beneath a modified bubble canopy. One TP-51D was used by General Eisenhower as a high-speed transport round the Normandy beach-heads immediately after the D-Day landings. Other P-51Ds, and some B and C models, were converted to two-seaters in the field, and in post-war years a further quantity was converted by Temco with, in some cases, a heightened fin as used on the P-51H. The TP-51D designation was also later used for some single-seaters assigned as pilot trainers with ANG units.

No P-51E was built, the next models being the XP-51F (NA-105) and XP-51G (NA-105), first flown on February 14 and August 10, 1944, respectively. These were lightweight Mustangs, in the design of which every effort was made to reduce the gross weight. About 2,000 lb. was in fact saved by simplifying the structure, using plastics components where suitable, smaller wheels, only four wing guns and other changes. The three XP-51Fs had the standard V-1650-7 engines while the two XP-51Gs had the 1,500 h.p. Merlin RM-145 and Rotol five blade propellers. At a gross weight of 9,060 lb.

the XP-51F achieved 466 m.p.h., while the XP-51G, still lighter at 8,879 lb., reached 472 m.p.h.

Another lightweight version, similar to the XP-51F, was the XP-51J (NA-105) of which two examples were built. These had Allison V-1710-119 engines which lengthened the fuselage by a few inches and could be distinguished externally by the absence of the "lip" intake for carburettor air under the spinner. The XP-51J first flew on April 23, 1945.

Tests with these lightweight Mustangs led to development of the

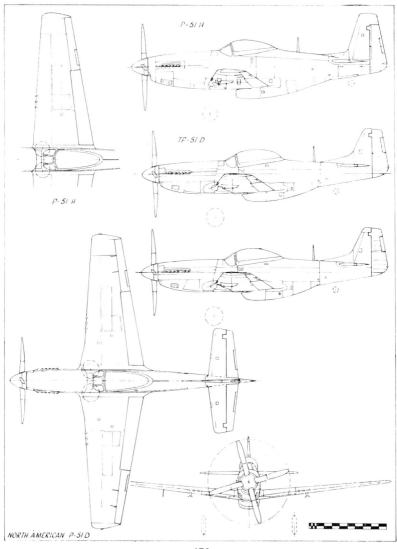

P-51 H

TF-51 D

P-51 H

NORTH AMERICAN P-51 D

470

North American A-36A in North Africa, with yellow borders on insignia and white wing stripes (*Howard Levy*).

P-51H (NA-126, NA-129), the final production version. Based on the XP-51F, this version had a 2,218 h.p. V-1650-9 engine, and differed from the "F" in having a four-blade Aeroproducts propeller, a shorter canopy and increased fuel capacity of 225 U.S. gallons. A taller fin was also fitted. With six wing guns, the weight increased to 10,500 lb., but this was still 1,100 lb. below the top weight of the P-51D. The P-51H, first flown on February 3, 1945, was the fastest of all the Mustangs, at 487 m.p.h. at the optimum rated altitude of 25,000 ft. Of 2,000 ordered, only 555 were completed (at Inglewood) before the end of the War and the termination of contracts. None of these reached the Pacific area in time to serve operationally.

The Dallas plant was to have produced the similar P-51L (NA-129) with a V-1650-11 engine, but all 1,700 on order were cancelled before any had been completed. A further variant ordered from Inglewood, the P-51M (NA-124) had a V-1650-9A; one was built (the final P-51D re-designated) and 1,628 cancelled.

Post-war, many P-51s continued to serve with USAAF units, some with Strategic Air Command until 1949. The P-51B passed out of service in 1949 and the P-51K in 1951, after having been re-designated F-51B and F-51K respectively. The F-51D and F-51H served for several more years primarily with Air Reserve and National Guard units, until jet equipment became available. Consequently, the F-51 became one of the first USA fighters to serve in the Korean War, for which 22 of the 27 Air National

North American TF-51D-30-NA with TF "Buzz Number" instead of FF (*A. U. Schmidt*).

Guard Wings were activated. Equipping the 8th, 18th and 35th Fighter-Bomber Groups, F-51Ds were in Japan by the autumn of 1950 and moved to bases at Kimpo, Pusan and Pohang in October to participate in the first U.N. drive into North Korea.

A-36. As noted above, the first version of the Mustang ordered by the USAAF for its own use was the A-36A (NA-97), a ground-attack variant. It had racks under each wing for a maximum load of one 500 lb. bomb each side, and an armament of six 0·50-inch machine guns, including two in the fuselage. Hydraulically-operated dive brakes were fitted in upper and lower wing surfaces. The first A-36A flew on September 21, 1942, and production of the 500 ordered was completed by March 1943. This version became the first to see operational use in USAAF service, primarily in support of the invasion of Sicily and, later, Italy.

F-6. This designation covered the armed tactical reconnaissance version of the Mustang, produced by conversion of P-51s of various series. The first conversions were of the cannon-armed P-51, a total of 57 of these

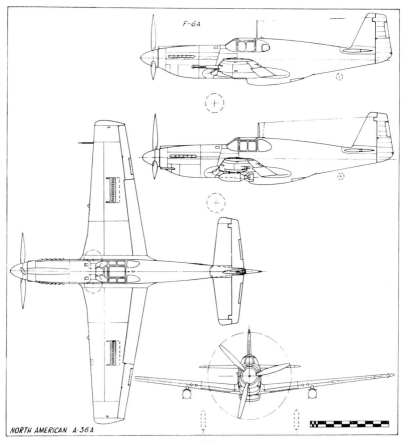

NORTH AMERICAN A-36A

North American RF-51D (later, F-6D), with camera in rear fuselage (*E. M. Sommerich*).

being fitted in 1942 and 1943 with two K-24 cameras in the fuselage and re-designated P-51-1 after the proposed F-6A designation had been cancelled. A similar conversion scheme on 35 P-51As produced the F-6B, while another 91 P-51B and P-51C types became F-6Cs with different camera bays to permit installation of one K-17 and one K-22 as alternatives to the two K-24s. The F-6D was a camera-equipped P-51D, of which 136 were produced by conversion, while the F-6K was the equivalent of the P-51K, 163 being produced. Post-war, some F-6Ds and F-6Ks became RF-51Ds and RF-51Ks, and served in the Korean conflict with the 67th Reconnaissance Wing. A few also became TF-6Ds and then TRF-51Ds.

During 1967, the USAF procured an additional batch of Mustangs from Cavalier Aircraft Corp., which had acquired design rights in the original P-51 from North American. The new aircraft were destined for delivery to South American and Asian nations through MAP but were supplied in full USAF markings with new serial numbers (67-14862/14865, 67-22579/22582, 72-1536/1541). Remanufactured from F-51D airframes, they were fitted with V-1650-7 engines, a new radio fit, tall P-51H-type fins, and a strengthened wing which carried six 0·50 in. guns and a total of eight hardpoints to mount two 1,000 lb. bombs and six 5-inch HVARs. One additional aircraft was a dual control TF-51D (67-14866) with enlarged canopy and only four wing guns; the remainder had the original type of canopy but all had a second seat for an observer behind the pilot. The U.S. Army purchased two F-51Ds from Cavalier in 1968 for use as chase aircraft in the Lockheed Cheyenne test programme. These aircraft, based at Fort Rucker, were unarmed two-seaters and had wing-tip centreline fuel tanks. For the same purpose, the Army also used a genuine F-51D (44-72990) for several years from 1967.

In 1968, Cavalier flight-tested a modified P-51 as the Turbo-Mustang III, powered by a 1,740 e.s.h.p. Rolls-Royce Dart 510 turboprop. With the USAF interested in acquiring a low-cost high-performance close-support aircraft to supply through MAP (under the code-name *Pave Coin*), the company then set about a more ambitious turboprop conversion, using 2,455 s.h.p. Lycoming T55-L-9 engines leased from the USAF. Two airframes were put in hand, one of them a two-seat TF-51D.

First flown on April 19, 1971, this conversion was named Enforcer, and in

O.D. and white finish on two-seat F-51D used by U.S. Army as chase plane (*Cavalier photo*).

that same year Piper Aircraft acquired full rights in the design from Cavalier. The USAF evaluation of one of the Enforcers later in 1971 confirmed the original performance claims but failed to arouse official enthusiasm for the project. Nevertheless, Congressional pressure on the USAF to explore the aircraft's potential more fully led, in September 1981, to a contract placed with Piper for the construction of two new prototypes of what now became the PA-48 (Piper designation) Enforcer.

Although still identifiable externally as a "Mustang", the PA-48 ended up with little more than 10 per cent commonality of parts with the original fighter. Powered by the T55-L-9 engine, it had the fuselage lengthened by 19 inches aft of the wing and larger tail surfaces. A Yankee rocket escape system was fitted in the single-seat cockpit and, as on the Cavalier Enforcers, provision was made for wing-tip tanks and 10 external stores stations, but no built-in guns. The two PA-48s first flew on April 9 and July 8, 1983, and the USAF conducted its evaluation at Eglin A.F.B. and Edwards A.F.B in 1983/1984—more than 43 years after the first flight of the XP-51 from which the Enforcer was derived. With a gross weight of 14,000 lb. the PA-48 achieved a max speed of 403 m.p.h. and cruising speed of 363 m.p.h.; the service ceiling was 37,600 ft. and combat radius (with two gun pods) was 460 miles. No production orders were placed and the prototypes were put into storage by the USAF in late 1986.

End of the Mustang line – the almost unrecognisable Piper PA-48 Cavalier in dual-tone green camouflage for USAF evaluation (*Piper photograph*).

474

TECHNICAL DATA (P-51)

MANUFACTURER: North American Aviation, Inc., Inglewood, California, and Dallas, Texas.

TYPE: Single-seat fighter ground attack and long-range escort; unarmed reconnaissance and two-seat trainer.

ACCOMMODATION: Pilot in enclosed cockpit (pilot and instructor in tandem in TP-51).

	P-51/F-6A	P-51B	P-51D/K	P-51H/M	A-36A
Power Plant:	1,150 h.p. V-1710-39	1,380 h.p. V-1650-3	1,490 h.p. V-1650-7	1,380 h.p. V-1650-9	1,325 h.p. V-1700-87
Dimensions:					
Span, ft. in.	37 0	37 0	37 0	37 0	37 0
Length, ft. in.	32 3	32 3	32 3	33 4	32 3
Height, ft. in.	12 2	12 2	12 2	13 8	12 2
Wing area, sq. ft.	235·7	235·7	235·7	235·7	235·7
Weights:					
Empty, lb.	6,550	6,985	7,125	6,585	6,610
Gross, lb.	8,800	11,800	11,600	11,054	10,000
Performance:					
Maximum speed, m.p.h./ft.	387/15,000	440/30,000	437/25,000	487/25,000	310/5,000
Cruising speed, m.p.h.	307	362	362	380	250
Climb, min./ft.	16/25,000	12·5/30,000	13/30,000	12·5/30,000	—
Service ceiling, ft.	31,350	41,800	41,900	41,600	25,100
Range, st. miles	350	400	950	850	550
Armament:	4 × 20-mm.	4 × 0·50-in. 2 × 1,000lb.	6 × 0·50-in. 2 × 1,000lb.	6 × 0·50-in. 2 × 1,000lb. or 10 × 5-in. R.P.	6 × 0·50-in. 2 × 500lb.

SERIAL NUMBERS:

XP-51: 41-038/039.
P-51: 41-37320/37351; 41-37353/37420; 41-37422/37469.
P-51A: 43-6003/6312*.
XP-51B: 41-37352; 41-37421.
P-51B†: 42-106429/106538; 42-106541/106978; 43-6313/7202; 43-12093/12492; 43-24752/24901.
P-51C‡: 42-102979/103978; 43-24902/25251; 44-10753/11152.
A-36A: 42-83663/84162.
P-51D-NA: 42-106539/106540; 44-13253/15752; 44-63160/64159; 44-72027/75026.

P-51-NT§: 44-11153/11352; 44-12853/13252; 44-84390/84989; 45-11343/11742.
XP-51F: 43-43332/43334.
XP-51G: 43-43335/43336.
P-51H: 44-64160/64714.
XP-51J: 44-76027/76028.
P-51K: 44-11353/12852**.
P-51M: 45-11743.
F-51D (Cavalier): 67-14862/14865; 67-22579/22582; 72-1536/1541.
TF-51D (Cavalier): 67-14866.

*Includes 35 F-6B.   †Includes 71 F-6C.
‡Includes 20 F-6C.   §Includes 146 F-6D   **Includes 163 F-6K.

North American P-82Gs of the 4th All-Weather Squadron over Okinawa.

North American F-82 Twin Mustang

Development of the unusual Twin Mustang began in 1944 with the object of producing a very long-range escort fighter, principally for operations in the Pacific area. The requirements of twin engines, two pilots and a large amount of fuel were matched by using two lengthened P-51H fuselages and modified port and starboard wing halves, joined by a new centre wing and tailplane. Two prototypes of this design (the NA-120) were built and designated XP-82. They were powered by Packard Merlin V-1650-23/25 engines with oppositely-rotating propellers. Two more prototypes as XP-82As had two Allison V-1710-119 engines with common rotation, but did not reach flight test.

The USAAF ordered 500 P-82Bs (NA-123) similar to the XP-82, to follow the F-51H into production at Los Angeles, but only 20 of these were built. During 1946, the tenth and eleventh P-82Bs (44-65169 and 44-65170) were converted to the P-82C and P-82D (NA-123), respectively, as night fighters. A large nacelle under the centre-section carried radar—SCR720 in the P-82C and APS-4 in the P-82D— and the starboard cockpit was modified to be a radar operator's position.

The 1946 Air Force procurement included a batch of 250 new Twin Mustangs, of which 100 were P-82E escort fighters (NA-144); 100 were P-82F night fighters with APS-4 radar (NA-149) and 50 were P-52G night fighters with SCR720 radar (NA-150). During production, the last nine P-82Fs and five P-82Gs were "winterized" to serve in Alaska as P-82Hs, all with SCR720 radar. All the 1946 models had 1,600 h.p. Allison V-1710-143/145 engines, with opposite rotation. The designation of all models from B to H was changed to F-82 in June 1948.

Air Defense Command was the primary operator of Twin Mustangs, and had 225 F-82F and G models on strength at the end of 1948, as replacements for the P-61. The F-82E served as a long-range escort with the 27th FG in SAC, from 1948 to 1950. The F-82Fs were flown, from 1948, by squadrons of the 325th and 52nd Fighter (All-Weather) Groups and the 51st Fighter (Interceptor) Group. The F-82Gs went, in 1949, to the three squadrons of the

347th F (A-W) Group based in Japan and these became involved in the air war over Korea from June 1950. On June 27, two pilots of the 68th F (A-W) Squadron, 1st Lts Hudson and Moran, were each credited with the destruction of a Yak-9, the first USAF "kills" of the Korean conflict. Flown by the 449th F (A-W)S, an ADC unit in Alaska, F-82Hs were also operational during the Korean war, and were the last of the Twin Mustangs to be retired, in mid-1953.

TECHNICAL DATA (F-82G)

MANUFACTURER: North American Aviation Inc., Inglewood, California.
TYPE: Long-range escort and night fighter.
ACCOMMODATION: Pilot and radar-observer in individual enclosed cockpits.
POWER PLANT: Two 1,600 h.p. Allison V-1710-143/145 piston Vee in-line engines.
DIMENSIONS: Span, 51 ft. 7 in. Length, 42 ft. 2 in. Height, 13 ft. 10 in. Wing area, 417·6 sq. ft.
WEIGHTS: Empty, 15,997 lb. Gross, 25,891 lb.
PERFORMANCE: Max. speed, 461 m.p.h. at 21,000 ft. Cruising speed, 286 m.p.h. Initial climb, 3,770 ft./min. Service ceiling, 38,900 ft. Range, 2,240 st. miles
ARMAMENT: Six 0.50-in. guns in wing centre section; two 1,000 lb. bombs or 20 HVARs under wings.
SERIAL NUMBERS:

XP-82: 44-83886/83887.	P-82E: 46-255/354.
XP-82A: 44-83888.	P-82F: 46-405/495.
P-82B: 44-65160/65179.	P-82G: 46-355/383; 46-389/404.
	P-82H: 46-384/388; 46-496/504.

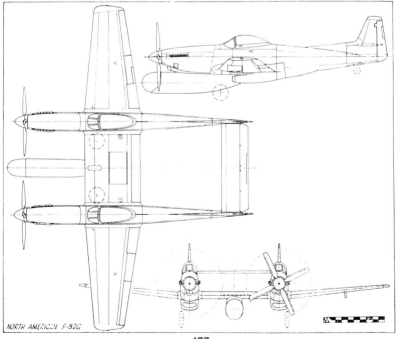

NORTH AMERICAN F-82G

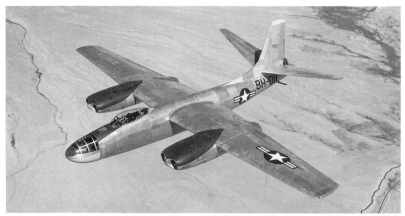

North American B-45A (*A. U. Schmidt*).

North American B-45 Tornado

As America's first four-jet bomber to fly, the B-45 was produced to an official specification which sought to apply jet propulsion to piston-engined bomber techniques. It was a necessary first step in the development of later tactical and strategic jet bombers but was itself of limited operational value. Work on the design began before the end of World War II, and three prototypes were ordered in 1945. The first of these flew from Muroc on March 17, 1947, piloted by George Krebs, by which time a production contract for 96 B-45As had been placed.

The XB-45 (NA-130) was structurally a conventional shoulder-wing monoplane, with the four 4,000-lb. Allison-built General Electric J35-A-4 turbojets paired in large nacelles under each wing. To clear the jet efflux, the tailplane had a large dihedral angle. The crew comprised two pilots in tandem under a fighter-type canopy, a bombardier in the nose and a rear-gunner. A bomb-load of over 20,000 lb. could be carried.

First production models of the B-45A (NA-147), like the prototypes, were fitted temporarily with J35-A-11 engines, but these were later changed to the 4,000 lb.s.t. J47-GE-9s. With these engines, the B-45A went into service in November 1948 with squadrons of the 47th Bombardment Group at Barkesdale A.F.B., Lo., and the type continued to serve with this Wing when it moved to the U.K. to join USAFE in 1952; the last B-45 did not pass out of service until mid-1958. Ninety-six B-45As were built.

The B-45B was a projected variant with new radar and fire-control systems. Deliveries began in 1949 of the B-45C (NA-153) of which only ten were built. With 5,200 lb. J47-GE-13/15 engines, they carried 1,200-U.S. gallon wing-tip fuel tanks and had gross weight increased from 90,000 lb. to 110,000 lb. Intended for tactical support duties the B-45C had a strengthened airframe and canopy.

478

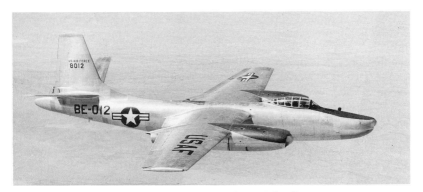

North American RB-45C (*A. U. Schmidt*).

The ten B-45Cs were followed by 33 of the RB-45C model (NA-153) which added photo-reconnaissance capability to the bombing mission of the earlier type. This was achieved by installing a total of 12 cameras in four positions. Four cameras of various types were fitted at the vertical station in the rear fuselage, with four more at the split vertical station and one forward oblique camera. The installation was completed with a tri-metrogen K-17C. The bomb-bay was retained but on photo missions carried only 25 M-122 photo-flash bombs, together with additional fuel tanks to make the total capacity of the aeroplane 8,133-U.S. gallons.

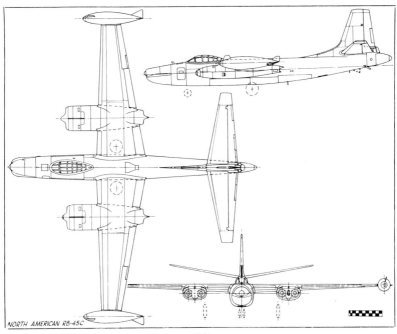

NORTH AMERICAN RB-45C

Provision was made for a 214-U.S. gallon jettisonable water tank to be carried under each nacelle to supply water injection to the engines at take-off. Deliveries of the RB-45C were made from June 1950 to October 1951; the first flight was in April 1950.

The RB-45C entered service with the 91st Strategic Reconnaissance Wing and later saw action over Korea. The type also served with the 19th Tac. R. Squadron in Europe. In 1951, an RB-45C (48-012) was first successfully flight-refuelled (from a KB-29P) using the flying-boom system.

Fourteen B-45As were later modified to target tugs, as TB-45A, with an hydraulically-controlled reel and cable assembly in the bomb bay for a 20 ft. Chance Vought target glider. The DB-45A and DB-45C conversions were used as directors in guided weapon development. Other B-45s served as engine test beds, such as the JB-45A (47-049) for Westinghouse and the JB-45C (48-008) for General Electric.

TECHNICAL DATA (B-45C)

MANUFACTURER: North American Aviation Inc., Inglewood, California.
TYPE: Light tactical bomber.
ACCOMMODATION: Two pilots in tandem, bombardier and tail gunner.
POWER PLANT: Four 5,200 lb.s.t. General Electric J47-GE-13/15 turbojets.
DIMENSIONS: Span (without tip tanks), 89 ft. 0 in. Length, 75 ft. 4 in. Height, 25 ft. 2 in. Wing area, 1,175 sq. ft.
WEIGHTS: Empty, 48,903 lb. Gross, 112,952 lb.
PERFORMANCE: Max. speed, 579 m.p.h. at sea level. Cruising speed, 456 m.p.h. Initial climb, 5,800 ft./min. Service ceiling, 43,200 ft. Range, 1,910 st. miles.
ARMAMENT: Two 0·50-in. Browning M-7 guns in tail turret; up to 22,000 lb. of bombs.
SERIAL NUMBERS:
XB-45: 45-59479/59481.
B-45A: 47-001/096.
B-45C: 48-001/010.

TECHNICAL DATA (RB-45C)

MANUFACTURER: North American Aviation, Inc., Inglewood, California.
TYPE: Day or night photo-reconnaissance, mapping and charting.
ACCOMMODATION: Pilot and co-pilot/radio operator in tandem, tail gunner and photo-navigator.
POWER PLANT: Four 6,000 lb. s.t. (with w.i.) General Electric J47-GE-13/15 or 5,820 lb.s.t. (with w.i.) J47-GE-7/9 turbojets.
DIMENSIONS: Span (with tip tanks), 96 ft. 0 in. Length, 75 ft. 11 in. Height, 25 ft. 2 in. Wing area, 1,175 sq. ft.
WEIGHTS: Empty, 49,984 lb. Gross, 110,721 lb.
PERFORMANCE: Max. speed, 570 m.p.h. at 4,000 ft. Combat speed, 506 m.p.h. at 32,700 ft. Initial climb, 4,340 ft./min. Service ceiling, 40,250 ft. Range, 2,530 st. miles.
ARMAMENT: Two 0·50-inch M-7 guns in tail turret with 400 r.p.g.
SERIAL NUMBERS:
RB-45C: 48-011/043.

North American F-86As of the "Cadillac Flight", part of the Fighter School at Las Vegas A.F.B. (*A. U. Schmidt*).

North American F-86 Sabre

Design work on what was to prove to be the USAF's first swept-wing fighter began in the closing stages of World War II when North American already had a U.S. Navy jet fighter (the XFJ-1 Fury) in the project stage. A variant of this design was proposed to the AAF, which ordered one static test and two flying prototypes in the autumn of 1944, and applied the designation XP-86. Like the XFJ-1, the XP-86 at that time had straight wings and "straight through" jet flow for its Allison TG-180 (J35) turbojet; estimated performance included a top speed of 582 m.p.h., range of 750 miles and ceiling of 46,500 ft.

When the results of German research into swept wings began to become available soon after the end of the War, the decision was taken to change the XP-86 design to have this then-radical feature, at the expense of a year's delay in delivery. A 35 degree sweep angle was adopted, and the fuselage was lengthened. The pressurized cockpit was located well forward of the wing and was above the engine air duct. The aircraft's advanced features included power-boosted ailerons and automatic leading-edge slots.

The first XP-86 (NA-140) flew for the first time on October 1, 1947, and was powered, like the second prototype, by a 3,750 lb.s.t. Allison J35-C-3 turbojet. In the spring of 1948, the first aircraft (45-59597) exceeded Mach 1 for the first time, in a shallow dive, being the first U.S. fighter to do so. A production order—for 221 P-86As—had already been placed by the USAF on December 28, 1947, and for these aircraft the General Electric J47 engine was selected. With a 4,850 lb.s.t. J47-GE-1, the first P-86A flew on May 18, 1948, the designation being changed to F-86A a month later.

Armament in the production model comprised six 0·50-inch machine guns in the nose around the air intake, with provision for 16 5-inch rockets or two drop tanks under the wings. On September 15, 1948, an F-86A established a World Air Speed Record (the first for the U.S. after World War II) at 670·981 m.p.h. Deliveries to the USAF were sufficiently rapid for two full fighter groups—the 4th and 1st—to be equipped by the end of 1949, with the 81st in process of re-equipment. North American built a total of 554 F-86As, later batches of this model being successively fitted with the 5,200 lb.s.t. J47-GE-3, -7, -9, and -13 engine. Included in this total, the USAF received 188 of the F-86A-5 model which had been ordered as P-86Bs (NA-152) intended to have a 7-inch wider fuselage.

The P-86B was cancelled in favour of the F-86C, in which the 6,250 lb.s.t. Pratt & Whitney J48-P-6 engine with afterburner was adopted. The nose intake was replaced by flush NACA-designed side intakes and twin main wheels were fitted; there was a small increase in wing span, to 38 ft. 9 in., and the overall length increased by 6 ft. 7 in. to 44 ft. 1 in. These changes became so extensive that the designation was changed to F-93; the first of two prototype YF-93As (48-317) flew on January 25, 1950, but a production order for 118 F-93As was cancelled in favour of the F-86D described below.

The F-86A was followed in production in December 1950 by a new inter-ceptor model, the F-86E, in which the control system was revised to in-corporate an all-flying tail with linked elevators, power boosting for the tail controls and artificial "feel". Between March 1951 and April 1952, North American delivered 333 F-86Es while a further 60 were purchased from Canadair for the USAF, and 60 for Mutual Defence Aid Programme. Most Canadair-built Sabres had the Avro Canada Orenda engine and the designation F-86J was applicable to this version, but the J47-GE-13 engine was fitted instead in the aircraft for USAF, and the aircraft were

North American F-86E with wing slats and dive brakes open (*A. U. Schmidt*).

North American F-86F-30-NA with "6-3" wing, in blue-and-white stripes of the 390th FBS/366th FBW at Alexandria A.F.B. (*Warrent D. Shipp*).

then designated F-86E-6 (Canadair CL-13). One Orenda-engined F-86J (49-1069) was tested, being a converted F-86A.

While the F-86E was going into production in California, the F-86A was going into action in Korea. The 4th Fighter-Interceptor Wing—one of the earliest Sabre units—arrived in Korea in December 1950 and went into action immediately to overcome the threat represented by the MiG-15 which had appeared on November 1 and was achieving supremacy over the F-51s and F-80s. The first recorded combat between swept-wing fighters—Sabre and MiG-15—occurred on December 17, when the 4th F.I. Wing destroyed four MiGs. In combat, the Russian fighter proved slightly superior to the F-86A, but better flying by the USAF pilots tipped the scales in their favour. Throughout 1951, the 4th F.I. Wing was the only F-86 unit in Korea, being joined there at the end of that year by the 51st F.I. Wing.

Under the impetus of the Korean War, a second Sabre production line was opened by North American at Columbus, where the F-86F was the first model built. This version had a new wing leading edge, extended 6 inches at the root and 3 inches at the tip (and therefore often known as the "6-3" wing) with the slats eliminated and small boundary layer fences fitted for the first time. The 5,970 lb.s.t. J47-GE-27 engine contributed to an overall increase in performance. The first F-86F was flown at Los Angeles on March 19, 1952, by George Smith, and deliveries from Columbus, which built 700 of the F-86F-25 variant, began in the same year.

The "6-3" wing was developed to improve manoeuvrability of the Sabre at high altitudes, where it had been at a disadvantage in combat with MiG-15s in Korea. Deliveries to the USAF began on March 28, 1952, and this version was serving in Korea by the autumn of that year. Early in 1953, the 8th and 18th Fighter-Bomber Wings converted to F-86Fs also, increasing the effective Sabre fighter force in Korea to the point where supremacy over the MiGs could be maintained. Of 2,540 F-86Fs built at Los Angeles and Columbus by the time production ended in 1956, 365 F-86F-40s were for the Mutual Security Programme. An aircraft of this type eventually became the last Sabre to be delivered, at the end of December 1956.

483

North American F-86D operating with USAFE (*USAF photo*).

The F-86F was also the basis of a two-seat Sabre trainer, the TF-86F, produced in 1953. The fuselage was extended by 63 inches to provide space for a second cockpit in tandem, under a single long canopy, and the wing was moved forward 8 inches. Two examples were built, by conversion of F-86Fs; the first (52-5016, NA-204) flew on December 14, 1953 and the second (53-1228, NA-216) with a taller fin and a ventral fin, and two nose guns, was flown in August 1954. Another modification of the "F" model, undertaken locally in Japan, produced the RF-86F, in which two K-22 and one K-17 cameras were installed in the fuselage just ahead of the wing leading edge.

Final production version of the Sabre for the USAF was the F-86H with many new features. Powered by the 9,300 lb.s.t. General Electric J73-GE-3 engine (an improved J47) the F-86H had a two-foot increase in wing span, 14 inch greater length, deeper fuselage, larger tailplane without dihedral, heavier landing gear, and four 20-mm. M-39 cannon in place of the six machine guns in the nose (although the first 116 F-86H were completed with the six-gun armament). The first of two YF-86H prototypes (52-1975) which had a YJ73-GE-3 engine, flew at Los Angeles on April 30, 1953, piloted by Joe Lynch. The F-86H was produced at the Columbus factory, where the first production model (52-1977) was flown by Dan Darnell on September 4, 1953. Deliveries of 473 were made between January 1954 and August 1955.

Development of the Sabre as an all weather interceptor produced the F-86D or "Sabre Dog", in which the nose was re-contoured to carry radar above a lip intake. An afterburner was fitted to the 7,650 lb.s.t. J47-GE-17 engine, and the gun armament was dropped in favour of a retractable tray carrying $24 \times 2 \cdot 75$-inch air rockets. The fuselage was wider and increased in length to 40 ft. 4 in. Originally designated YF-95A, the first of two YF-86Ds was first flown at Muroc by George Welch on December 22, 1949. Delivery of 2,504 production models of the F-86D from the Los Angeles factory began in March 1951. The F-86G designation was provisionally applied to an F-86D development with J47-GE-33 engine and other changes, but 406 of this model on order were completed as F-86D-20 with the new engine.

On November 19, 1952, an F-86D was used by Capt. Slade Nash to establish a World Air Speed Record of 698·505 m.p.h. and in July 1953 Lt. Col. William F. Barnes also used an F-86D to increase the record speed to 715.697 m.p.h.

A total of 981 USAF F-86Ds were converted, starting in 1956, to F-86Ls with a 2 ft. increase in span as used on the F-86H, extended "6-3" and slotted leading edges, and new electronic equipment including Data Link for use in conjunction with SAGE. Another variant of the all-weather Sabre, the F-86K, had four 20-mm. cannon instead of the rocket armament and was intended for use in Europe by NATO countries other than the U.S. North American converted two F-86Ds to YF-86Ks (52-3804 and 52-3630, NA-205), the first of which was flown on July 15, 1954 by Ray Morris. The company produced 120 F-86Ks for European air forces and 221 sets for assembly by Fiat in Italy. Deliveries began early in 1955.

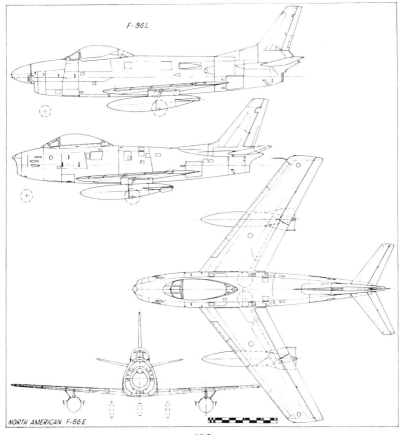

F-86L

NORTH AMERICAN F-86E

North American F-86F-35-NA of the "Skyblazers" aerobatic team provided by the 48th FW based at Chaumont, France, in 1955 (*USAF photo*).

Flight refuelling was developed for the F-86A, successful flying-boom refuelling being demonstrated in mid-1951 by 49-1172 with a receptacle in the fuselage decking ahead of the cockpit, from a KB-29P tanker.

The F-86A had entered service with the 94th Fighter Squadron of the 1st Fighter Group (Fighter-Interceptor Squadron and Group later) in February 1949 and first was deployed to the Korean theatre in December 1950 with the 4th F-I Group. The F-86E entered service with the 33rd F-I Wing in May 1951 and by the end of 1952 had replaced the F-86A in Korea, although the

North American F-86L of the 95th FIS at Andrews A.F.B. (*Howard Levy*).

486

latter version did not begin to reach ANG units from the active Air Force until 1954. Also during 1952, the F-86F began to reach Korea, in the hands of the 51st F-I Wing, joining the "E" to gain air superiority there and helping to achieve a ratio of MiG "kills" to losses of 14 to 1.

In the light of combat experience in Korea, 11 F-86As were converted, under *Project Ashtray*, to RF-86As with cameras for high-speed reconnaissance missions. A small number of RF-86F conversion was also made, these aircraft being used by the 67th Tactical Reconnaissance Wing.

As a tactical fighter-bomber, the F-86H entered service with the 312th F-B Wing at Clovis A.F.B., New Mexico, in the autumn of 1954, but by mid-1958 all F-86Hs had been replaced by F-100s and transferred to the ANG, which also received A, E and a few F models.

Air Defense Command started to use F-86D radar-equipped interceptors in April 1953, and the F-86L updates began to reach the 49th F-I Squadron in October 1956. Both these models also were transferred to the ANG after they had been retired from the active Air Force by June 1960. Final service use of the Sabre by the ANG was in 1965, also in the F-86L model.

A few early aircraft were eventually converted to DF-86As as drone directors for missile tests, and the Army acquired, from 1977 onwards, 24 QF-86Es for testing ground-based air defence systems, these being ex-RCAF Sabres with Orenda engines.

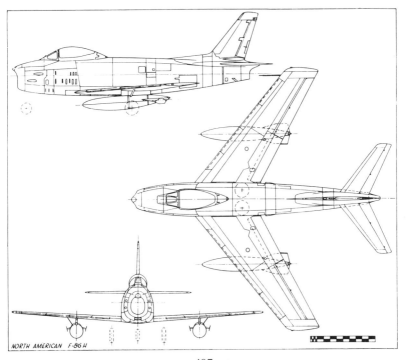

NORTH AMERICAN F-86 H

TECHNICAL DATA (F-86)

MANUFACTURER: North American Aviation Inc., Inglewood, California and Columbus, Ohio. Canadair Ltd., Montreal, Canada.
TYPE: Fighter and fighter-bomber.
ACCOMMODATION: Pilot in enclosed cockpit.

	F-86A	F-86H	F-86F	F-86D
Power Plant:	5,200 lb.s.t.	8,920 lb.s.t.	5,970 lb.s.t.	5,700/ 7,630lb.s.t.
	J47-GE-13	J73-GE-3E	J47-GE-27	J47-GE-17
Dimensions:				
Span, ft., in.	37 1	39 1	37 1	37 1
Length, ft., in.	37 6	38 8	37 6	40 4
Height, ft., in.	14 8	15 0	14 8	15 0
Wing area, sq. ft.	288	313	288	288
Weights:				
Empty, lb.	10,495	13,836	10,950	12,470
Gross, lb.	16,357	21,852	17,000	17,100
Performance:				
Max. speed, m.p.h./ft.	675/2,500	692/0	690/0	707/0
Cruising speed	527 m.p.h.	603 m.p.h./ 43,900 ft.	—	525 m.p.h.
Initial climb, ft./min.	7,630	12,900	10,000	17,800
Service ceiling, ft.	48,300	49,000	50,000	54,600
Range, miles	785	1,040	1,270	836
Armament:	6 × 0·50-in.	4 × 20 mm.	6 × 0·50-in.	24 × 2·75-in.
	2 × 1,000 lb.	2 × 1,000 lb.	2 × 1,000 lb.	FFAR
	or	or	or	
	16 × 5-in. R.P.	16 × 5-in. R.P.	16 × 5-in. R.P.	

SERIAL NUMBERS:
XP-86: 45-59597/59599.
F-86A: 47-605/637; 48-129/316; 49-1007/1339.
YF-86D: 50-577/578.
F-86D: 50-455/576; 50-704/734; 51-2944/3131; 51-5857/6262; 51-8274/8505; 52-3598/4304; 52-9933/10176; 53-557/1071; 53-3675/3710; 53-4018/4090.
F-86E: 50-579/689; 51-2718/2849; 51-12977/13069.
F-86E-6 (CAN): 52-2833/2892; 52-10177/10236*.

F-86F-NA: 51-2850/2943; 51-12936/12976; 52-4305/5271; 53-1072/1228; 55-3816/4030; 55-4983/5117; 56-2773/2882; 57-6338/6457.
F-86F-NH: 51-13070/13510; 52-5272/5530.
YF-86H-NA: 52-1975/1976.
F-86H-NH: 52-1977/2124; 52-5729/5753; 53-1229/1528.
YF-86K-NA: 52-3630; 52-3804.
F-86K-NA: 54-1231/1350; 53-8273/8322; 55-4811/4936; 56-4116/4160.

*Procured through MDAP funds for Britain.

North American T-28A in Air Training Command markings (*A. U. Schmidt*).

North American T-28 Trojan

In 1948, the USAF held a design competition for a trainer to replace the T-6 Texan, which would combine primary and basic training characteristics in a single aeroplane. With the NA-159 design, North American won this competition and obtained a contract to build two prototypes. These were provisionally designated XBT-28 but were reclassified as XT-28 when the former AT, BT and PT categories for trainers were dropped. The first XT-28 (48-1371) flew on September 26, 1949.

Following successful evaluation of the two prototypes, the T-28A was ordered in quantity in 1950, the initial contract being for 266. Subsequent contracts increased the total number of T-28As built to 1,194, deliveries to Air Training Command being made from 1950 to 1953. Used almost exclusively as a primary trainer, the T-28A had provision for carrying two 100-lb. bombs or six 2·25 rockets under the wings, and could be armed with two 0·50-inch machine guns.

In practice, the T-28A was found to be less satisfactory as a primary trainer than had been hoped, and the USAF eventually adopted the lower-powered T-34 to provide a 30-hour *ab initio* course for students before they passed on to the T-28A. The latter served as the standard USAF basic pilot trainer for a number of years at the Air Training Command primary flight schools, being eventually superseded by the T-37.

In 1952, following a policy decision to standardize training aircraft between the U.S. armed forces, the USN also ordered the T-28, which with considerable modifications including the use of a 1,425 h.p. R-1820-86 engine, was produced as the T-28B and T-28C for the Navy. A revised two-part cockpit canopy, introduced on the T-28B, was adopted on the later production T-28As. For counter-insurgency duties, the T-28D was developed in 1962 as an armed counter-insurgency aircraft, while the

489

three YAT-28Es (52-1242), also for ground-attack duties, were re-engined with the Lycoming T55 turboprop. Between 1962 and 1968, the North American Columbus Division received contracts to modify a total of 321 T-28As to T-28Ds, primarily to be supplied through MAP to foreign nations including South Vietnam. Seventy-two similar conversions were made by Fairchild Hiller and referred to as AT-28Ds.

TECHNICAL DATA (T-28A)

MANUFACTURER: North American Aviation Inc., Inglewood, California.
TYPE: Basic trainer.
ACCOMMODATION: Pupil and instructor in tandem.
POWER PLANT: One 800 h.p. Wright R-1300-1 piston radial.
DIMENSIONS: Span, 40 ft. 1 in. Length, 32 ft. 0 in. Height, 12 ft. 8 in. Wing area, 268 sq. ft.
WEIGHTS: Empty, 5,111 lb. Gross, 6,365 lb.
PERFORMANCE: Max. speed, 283 m.p.h. at 5,900 ft. Cruising speed, 190 m.p.h. Initial climb, 1,870 ft./min. Service ceiling, 24,000 ft. Range, 1,000 st. miles.
SERIAL NUMBERS:
XT-28: 48-1371/1372.   T-28A: 49-1491/1756; 50-195/319;
                           51-3463/3796; 51-7482/7891;
                           52-1186/1242; 52-3497/3498.

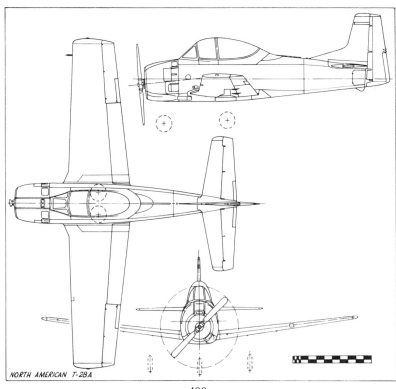

NORTH AMERICAN T-28A

490

Camouflaged North American F-100D-NA operating in USAFE. Notice AAR probe extending forward and above wing leading edge (*M. D. West*).

North American F-100 Super Sabre

The first of the USAF's Century-series fighters and the World's first operational fighter capable of level supersonic performance, the F-100 was evolved from the F-86 Sabre, originally as a North American private venture known as the Sabre 45 because of its 45 degrees of wing sweepback. After two years of project design and development, the Sabre 45 (NA-180) was included in USAF procurement planning with an order for two YF-100 prototypes (later re-designated YF-100A) and 23 F-100A (NA-192) production examples, placed early in 1952. Features of the design, in addition to the low-mounted 45-degree wing, were the slab tailplane located at the base of the rear fuselage, and the oval lip intake for the J57 turbojet. The first YF-100A (52-5754), with an XJ57-P-7 engine, was flown by George Welch at Edwards A.F.B. on May 25, 1953, followed by the second (52-5755) on October 14, 1953.

George Welch flew the first production F-100A (52-5756) on October 29, 1953, on the same day that the first YF-100A set a World Speed Record of 755·149 m.p.h. in the last such record established at low altitude. Initial production aircraft differed from the prototypes in having a shorter fin and rudder of increased chord. The 9,700 lb.s.t. J57-P-7 engine was used and armament comprised four Pontiac M-39E 20-mm. cannon, and a wide variety of underwing stores on six pick-up points. After 70 aircraft had been delivered, the shape of the vertical tail surfaces was again changed to overcome a control difficulty in the roll. Resembling the YF-100A design, the new fin and rudder was made a retrospective modification to all F-100As. The first three production aircraft reached George A.F.B. to begin the re-equipment of the 479th Fighter Day Wing, TAC, before the end of November 1953, and this Wing became operational with the unmodified aircraft on September 29, 1954. Deliveries of the modified F-100As began from the Los Angeles factory in the spring

North American F-100A with early short fin (*North American photo*).

of 1954; with the 104th production aircraft (the first F-100A-20-NA) changes were made to the cockpit equipment, and with the 168th aircraft, the J57-P-39 engine replaced the -7. A total of 203 of this model was built, ending in March 1954. Six were later converted to RF-100As for service with USAFE, with cameras in the front fuselage, which was deepened ahead of the wing leading edge.

The F-100C (NA-214, NA-217, NA-222), following the A, was adapted as a fighter bomber, with a stiffened wing having four pick-up points for bombs, rockets or fuel tanks in each wing half. An F-100A (52-5759) flew with a prototype of this wing on July 26, 1954, and the first production "C" flew from Los Angeles on January 17, 1955, piloted by Al White. A second source of Super Sabres was established at Columbus, Ohio, where the first F-100C flew on September 8, 1955. These two sources delivered 451 and 25, respectively, of this model.

A total of 5,000 lb. of bombs or other weapons could be carried on the external pick-ups, or four large fuel tanks to supplement the internal tankage of 995 Imp. gallons. Provision was made for probe-and-drogue flight refuelling, and buddy refuelling was first demonstrated by F-100s in April 1957. With a gross weight of 28,000 lb. clean, the F-100C had a level top speed of Mach 1·25, as was demonstrated on August 20, 1955. when the first aircraft of this model established a World Speed Record (the first above Mach 1) at 822·135 m.p.h. The F-100C was powered by the J57-P-7 (first few aircraft), P-39 (up to the 100th aircraft) or P-21 (101st onwards) engine. The first AF unit with F-100Cs was the 450th Day Fighter Wing (later the 322nd Fighter Day Group) at Foster A.F.B. By the end of 1956, F-100s were also serving with the 8th Fighter-Bomber Group in the Fifth Air Force in Japan.

In 1956, the F-100D succeeded the "C" at both Los Angeles and Columbus, the first flights from these two lines being made on January 24, 1956 (by Dan Darnell) and June 12, 1956, respectively. Changes in this model (NA-223, NA-224, NA-235, NA-245) comprised an enlarged fin and rudder, a Minneapolis-Honeywell supersonic autopilot, underwing pylons for a maximum load of 7,040 lb., and landing flaps on the inboard wing trailing edges. The final production batches were delivered with equipment for zero-length launching from atom-proof shelters, boosted by a 150,000 lb. thrust Astrodyne rocket; this technique was first demonstrated on March 26, 1958 by an F-100D. The Los Angeles factory built 940 F-100Ds, and 334 were built at Columbus.

Armament trials with six F-100Cs in late 1955 included the carriage of Hughes GAR-1B Falcon and Philco/General Electric AIM-9B Sidewinder AAMs, and in September 1956 the latter was selected as an optional weapon for the F-100D. Provision for the carriage of AIM-9Bs ws made with effect from the 184th F-100D, at the same time that fittings were added for nuclear bombs to be carried on the fuselage centreline pylon. In late 1959, deliveries began of 65 F-100Ds modified to carry Martin GAM-83B Bullpup ASMs, to equip four squadrons. Following trials on the F-100D 55-2793, several hundred F-100s in service were fitted with All American lightweight spring tail hooks for use in emergency landings.

To meet the need for a Super Sabre operational trainer, an F-100C (54-1966) was modified before delivery into a two-seater, with a 36-in. longer fuselage for tandem cockpits under a single long canopy. Designated TF-100C (NA-230), this first flew on August 6, 1956, and served as the prototype for the F-100F, a production combat trainer (NA-243, NA-255, NA-261, NA-262). The F-100F (56-3725) first flew on March 7, 1957, and was fully equipped for operational use but carried only two M-39E cannon. Production of 339 F-100Fs ended in October 1959, and in that year, 15 of the two-seaters were modified to carry GAM-83 Bullpup missiles.

In 1961, the NF-100F (56-3725) was modified for a low altitude, low speed control test programme, with a Rohr thrust reverser in place of the afterburner, a larger airbrake, blown flaps and faired radar altimeter aerials under the nose intake and rear fuselage.

Despite a succession of in-service difficulties and problems, (with more than 500 F-100Ds lost between mid-1956 and mid-1970) the Super Sabre was used extensively in the air war in South-East Asia. Operations over North Vietnam began in 1965, and F-100s were based in South Vietnam for the first time in February that year. By June 1967, only five squadrons of F-100s remained at home in the U.S. Numerous modification programmes were necessary to give F-100Ds and F-100Fs the required combat capabilities, and these included the first Wild Weasel aircraft to enter service with the USAF in

North American F-100C of "Thunderbirds" aerobatic team (*Peter M. Bowers*).

the specialised role of detecting, locating and destroying the radars that guided ground-launched anti-aircraft missiles.

With high priority and in the minimum of elapsed time, Applied Technology Inc (ATI) adapted equipment it had developed for use on the Lockheed U-2, and North American flight tested the installation on an F-100F. Four of the two-seaters were then fitted with this Wild Weasel I equipment that included AN/APR-25, AN/APR-26 and IR-133 receivers and a KA-60 panoramic camera. Assigned to the 6234th TF Wing, the Wild Weasel F-100Fs arrived in the South-East Asia area in November 1965 and the first combat mission was flown on December 3. Code-named *Iron Hand*, the anti-radar missions were usually mounted by one F-100F accompanied by four Republic F-105 Thunderchiefs. Three more Wild Weasel-equipped F-100Fs were converted early in 1966 and all seven aircraft were quickly adapted to carry AGM-95A Shrike anti-radar missiles, the first combat use of which occurred on April 18, 1966. Having proved the concept, the WW Super Sabres were soon replaced by the more capable Republic F-105Gs. Another major commitment for F-100Fs in Vietnam, which did not require modification of the aircraft, was to fly high-speed *Misty* FAC (Foward Air Control) missions.

The USAF plans to phase the F-100 out of service quickly in favour of a more advanced type had to be amended to meet commitments in Vietnam, where four regular Air Force fighter wings deployed 13 squadrons of Super

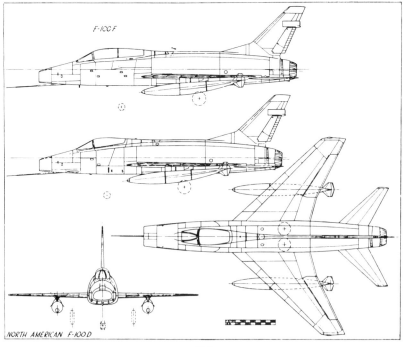

F-100 F

NORTH AMERICAN F-100 D

Sabres. The transfer of F-100As to ANG units had begun as early as April 1958, however, with F-100Cs following in mid-1959 and F-100Fs a little later. Flying these aircraft, four Guard Squadrons (from Colorado, New York, Iowa and New Mexico) also served with distinction in Vietnam. By mid-1972, the ANG was flying 335 F-100Ds, and in the 21 years that the Guard operated Super Sabres (ending in November 1979) 23 tactical fighter or interceptor units flew the type.

Starting in 1979, Sperry Flight Systems developed a pilotless drone conversion of the Super Sabre as the QF-100. The initial programme comprised two YQF-100 prototypes (which retained manual controls), three QF-100s in standard USAF target configuration, three equipped for Army multiple-target missions and one F-100F conversion. Sperry then made 72 production conversions of F-100Ds, and Tracor/Flight Systems Division turned out a further 209 QF-100Ds and QF-100Fs.

F-107. Originally designated F-100B, the F-107 (NA-212) was so extensively redesigned to meet General Operational Requirement (GOR) 68 that the designation was changed before the first YF-107A (55-5118) flew on September 10, 1956. Designed as a tactical fighter bomber, the YF-107A had radar in the nose and the air intake (for a 24,500 lb. a/b Pratt & Whitney J75-P-9 engine) above and behind the cockpit. Provision was made for four 20-mm. cannon and 10,000 lb. of underwing stores, and the max. speed was Mach 2.2. Two other examples were built: 55-5119 flown on November 28, 1956, and 55-5120 flown on December 10, 1956. Production plans were cancelled on March 22, 1957, in favour of the Republic F-105.

TECHNICAL DATA (F-100D)

MANUFACTURER: North American Aviation Inc., Inglewood, California and Columbus, Ohio (C & D).
TYPE: Supersonic interceptor, fighter-bomber and advanced combat trainer.
ACCOMMODATION: Pilot in enclosed cockpit; pilot and instructor (F-100F only).
POWER PLANT: One 10,200 lb.s.t. (16,000 lb. with a/b) Pratt & Whitney J57-P-21A turbojet.
DIMENSIONS: Span, 38 ft. 9 in. Length, 47 ft. 5in.; length (over pitot boom), 54 ft. 2½ in. Height, 16 ft. 2½ in. Wing area, 400·2 sq. ft.
WEIGHTS: Empty, 20,638 lb. Gross, 38,048 lb.
PERFORMANCE: Max. speed, 892 m.p.h. at 35,000 ft. Cruising speed, 587 m.p.h. at 36,000 ft. Initial climb, 18,100 ft./min. Service ceiling, 39,600 ft. Range, 1,200 miles.
ARMAMENT: Four fixed forward firing 20-mm. M-39E cannon in front fuselage; underwing pylons for up to 7,040 lb. of bombs, two Sidewinder or Bullpup AAMs; FFAR pods etc.
SERIAL NUMBES:

YF-100A: 52-5754/5755.
F-100A: 52-5756/5778; 53-1529/1708.
F-100C-NA: 53-1709/1778; 54-1740/2120.
F-100C-NH: 55-2709/2733.

F-100D-NA: 54-2121/2303; 55-3502/3814; 56-2903/3346.
F-100D-NH: 55-2734/2954; 56-3351/3463.
F-100F-NA: 56-3725/4019; 58-1205/1233; 58-6975/6983; 59-2558/2563.

North American T-39A (*North American photo*).

North American T-39

Development of the T-39A Sabreliner was unusual in that the USAF issued a specification but required the manufacturers to design and fly a prototype as a private venture, with no guarantee of a production order. The requirement of August 1956 was one of two issued at that time, and was known as the UTX (utility trainer experimental); the other was the UCX to which the Lockheed C-140 (page 657) was designed. North American was already studying the design of a small jet transport when the UTX requirement was circulated, and on August 27, 1956, announced that it would build a prototype of its NA-246 design to the specification.

Design effort occupied most of 1957, and in this period, the engine location was changed from a wing root buried installation to the rear-fuselage position. The prototype was completed early in May 1958, but the non-availability of suitable engines delayed the first flight until September 16, 1958. This prototype bore the civil registration N4060K, had a six-seat transport interior and flew with two 2,500 lb. General Electric J85 turbojets. It completed USAF Phase II evaluation at Edwards A.F.B. in December 1958, and the following month an initial production order for seven examples (59-2868/74) was placed. Subsequent development was covered by Weapon System SS452L.

The first production T-39A flew on June 30, 1960, and was delivered to the USAF in October. The power plant was changed from the prototype's J85s to two 3,000 lb. s.t. Pratt & Whitney J60-P-3s and internal modifications were made. Two further contracts brought the total number of Sabreliners on order by the end of 1960 to 94, and 55 more were ordered at the end of 1961. Several early production T-39As went to Randolph A.F.B. for service with Air Training Command; others were delivered to USAF Headquarters for command duties and to SAC and Systems Command.

Six Sabreliners—the sixth to eleventh production aircraft—were delivered as T-39Bs, specially equipped with the NASARR all-weather search and range radar used in the Republic F-105. The T-39D and T-39E designations applied to USN versions. Three T-39As were converted to T-39Fs to train pilots and electronic warfare officers in the use of fighter-borne radar homing and warning systems.

TECHNICAL DATA (T-39A)

MANUFACTURER: North American Aviation Inc., Los Angeles, California.
TYPE: Utility jet trainer and transport.
ACCOMMODATION: Two pilots and four–six passengers.
POWER PLANT: Two 3,000 lb.s.t. Pratt & Whitney J60-P-3 turbojets.
DIMENSIONS: Span, 44 ft. 5 in. Length, 43 ft. 9 in. Height, 16 ft. 0 in. Wing area 342 sq. ft.
WEIGHTS: Empty, 9,300 lb. Gross, 17,760 lb.
PERFORMANCE: Max. speed, 595 m.p.h. at 36,000 ft. Cruising speed, 452 m.p.h. at 40,000 ft. Initial climb, 5,550 ft./min. Service ceiling, 39,000 ft. Design range, 1,725 st. miles.
ARMAMENT: None.
SERIAL NUMBERS:
T-39A: 59-2868/2872; 60-3478/3508;   T-39B: 59-2873/2874; 60-3474/3477.
  61-634/685; 62-4448/4502.

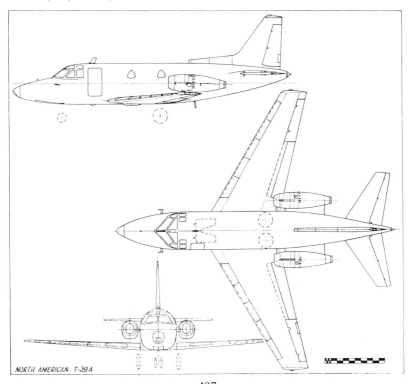

NORTH AMERICAN T-39A

Rockwell OV-10A of the 51st TWF at Osan A.B., Korea, in 1988 (*Robbie Shaw*).

North American Rockwell OV-10 Bronco

The USAF's OV-10A Bronco battlefield support aircraft was developed as a by-product of a U.S. Marine Corps requirement for a light armed reconnaissance aircraft (LARA). The requirement arose after the USMC dropped its plans to use a version of the Grumman Mohawk and was closely related to operational experience in Vietnam. Following a design competition in which several companies participated, the North American NA-300 project was selected in August 1964 for prototype evaluation.

The programme proceeded as a tri-service venture, although the different services saw the aeroplane in rather different roles. So far as the USAF was concerned, primary interest was in the possibility of using the North American aircraft for Forward Air Control duties. The Marine Corps on the other hand, was interested in the aircraft's attack capability as a counter-insurgency (COIN) type. Procurement of seven prototypes was put in hand in 1964, with the U.S. Navy acting as procurement agency and these aircraft therefore carried USN serial numbers.

Designated OV-10A in both Navy and Air Force versions, the new aircraft was designed for simplicity of manufacture and servicing. Pilot and observer sat in tandem beneath a large transparency for maximum all-round visibility and two Garrett AiResearch T76 turboprops were adopted as the standard power-plant. The first YOV-10A prototype flew on July 16, 1965, at Columbus and the seventh and last of the development batch flew on October 7, 1966, being fitted experimentally with Pratt & Whitney YT74 turboprops.

Production contracts were placed in October 1966 and covered 157 for the USAF (built as NA-305 and -321) and 118 for the USMC and USN. The Air Force OV-10As entered service in Vietnam during 1968, the initial evaluation with six aircraft being completed in October. Eventually, 126 OV-10As were assigned to Vietnam, equipping the 19th, 20th and 23rd

Tactical Air Support Squadrons for forward air control duties. Initially they flew unarmed, but later machine guns and HVAR rockets were added. During 1970, LTV Electrosystems modified 15 OV-10s for night FAC duties under the *Pave Nail* code name, with Martin laser rangefinder and target illuminator, night periscope sight and other equipment to allow the weapons systems operator to detect targets and give accurate bearings to accompanying strike aircraft.

TECHNICAL DATA (OV-10A)

MANUFACTURER: North American Rockwell Corporation, Columbus Division, Columbus, Ohio.

TYPE: Forward Air Controller.

ACCOMMODATION: Pilot and observer.

POWER PLANT: Two 715 s.h.p. Garrett-AiResearch T76-G-10 (port)/12 (starboard) turboprops.

DIMENSIONS: Span, 40 ft. 0 in. Length, 39 ft. 10 in. Height, 15 ft. 1 in. Wing area, 291 sq. ft.

WEIGHTS: Empty, 6,893 lb. Gross, 14,444 lb.

PERFORMANCE: Max. speed, 281 m.p.h. at sea level. Cruising speed, 223 m.p.h. at 18,000 ft. Initial climb 2,600 ft./min. Service ceiling, 28,800 ft. Range, 450 st. miles with max. weapon load.

ARMAMENT: Four fixed forward firing M60C 0·30-in. machine guns; four external weapon strong points for rockets, bombs etc to maximum of 3,600 lb.

SERIAL NUMBERS:

OV-10A: 66-13552/13562;
    67-14604/14701; 68-3784/6831; 87-0405/0406*

*Transfer from USMC.

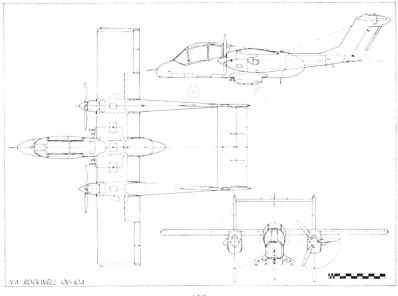

N.A. ROCKWELL OV-10A

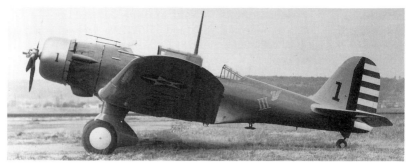

Northrop A-17 in yellow and blue colours of 1935–1940 (*Gordon S. Williams*).

Northrop A-17, A-33

The Northrop company entered the military market with a development of its Gamma and Delta all-metal monoplanes. As a private venture, the prototype Model 2-C was completed in August 1933 and flown with the registration X12291. In June 1934 it was purchased by the Army and designated YA-13; successful evaluation was followed by a $2-million contract for 110 examples in December 1934. The YA-13 was powered by a 710 h.p. Wright R-1820-37 engine, but it was proposed to use the 800 h.p. Pratt & Whitney R-1830-7 in the production models and in March 1935 the prototype flew with this engine. In this guise it was the XA-16.

Flight trials with the XA-16 were disappointing, largely because it was overpowered, and the production version was changed to have the smaller 750 h.p. Pratt & Whitney R-1535-11 radial, as the A-17. The undercarriage was simplified, with the wheels exposed instead of being totally enclosed in large pants. Four fixed forward-firing 0·30-inch guns were located in the wings, and a flexibly-mounted 0·30 in the rear cockpit.

Delivery of the 110 A-17s began in August 1935, and they became standard equipment in attack units, such as the 3rd and 17th Attack Groups, during 1936. Further contracts were awarded in December 1935 to continue production with the A-17A, which had the 825 h.p. R-1535-13 engine and a retractable undercarriage.

Orders for the A-17A totalled 129, but 93 of these served with the Army for only 18 months. In June 1940 they were returned for re-sale to Britain and France; the majority were eventually re-assigned by Britain to South Africa. Two examples known as A-17AS were delivered to the Army in 1937 as three-seat command transports, with 600 h.p. Pratt & Whitney R-1340-45 engines.

The basic Northrop design was developed by Douglas as the Model 8A, for export to several foreign nations. In 1942, 31 Douglas 8A-5s of a batch of 34 ordered by Peru were commandeered by the Army as A-33s with 1,200 h.p. R-1820-87 engines.

TECHNICAL DATA (A-17A)

MANUFACTURER: Northrop Corporation (later, Douglas), El Segundo, Calif.
TYPE: Attack.
ACCOMMODATION: Pilot and gunner in tandem.
POWER PLANT: One 825-h.p. Pratt & Whitney R-1535-13 piston radial.
DIMENSIONS: Span, 47 ft. 9 in. Length, 31 ft. 8 in. Height, 12 ft. 0 in. Wing area, 362 sq. ft.
WEIGHTS: Empty, 5,106 lb. Gross, 7,543 lb.
PERFORMANCE: Max. speed, 220 m.p.h. at 2,500 ft. Cruising speed, 170 m.p.h. Initial climb, 3·9 min. to 5,000 ft. Service ceiling, 19,400 ft. Range, 732 st. miles.
ARMAMENT: Four fixed and one flexible 0·30-in. Browning m.g. Four 100-lb. bombs.
SERIAL NUMBERS: YA-13: 34-027.   A-17AS: 36-349/350.
            A-17: 35-051/160.   A-33: 42-109007/109019;
            A-17A: 36-162/261; 38-327/355.   42-13584/13601.

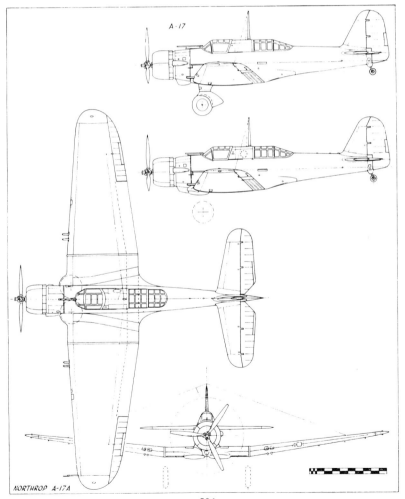

NORTHROP A-17A

501

Glossy black Northrop P-61C in 1945 (*Peter M. Bowers*).

Northrop P-61 Black Widow

U.S. Army interest in the true night-fighting aeroplane was aroused in 1940 by events in Europe and in particular the experience of the Royal Air Force in combating German night attacks. To meet a general Army requirement, Northrop offered in November 1940 a twin-engined twin-boom aeroplane, large enough to carry the new radar equipment, second crewman and adequate offensive armament. Two prototypes of this design were ordered as XP-61s on January 11, 1941, and production orders soon followed: for 13 YP-61s on March 10, 1941, 150 more on September 1, 1941, and 410 on February 12, 1942.

The first XP-61 was flown for the first time on May 26, 1942, and the second prototype and 13 YP-61s had followed by September 1943. In keeping with their nocturnal role, they were finished in black overall, lending emphasis to the popular name taken from that of the poisonous North American spider. Provision was made in the nose of the fuselage nacelle for A.I. radar, developed from original British designs.

The first of 200 P-61As appeared towards the end of 1943. After the first 37, the top turret was deleted because of buffeting, and with the 46th aircraft a change was made from R-2800-10 to -65 engines. This model reached operational units including the 18th Fighter Group in the South Pacific area in 1944, where the first "kill" by a P-61A was recorded on July 7. In the same month, delivery of 450 P-61Bs began. This version could carry four 1,600-lb. bombs, or 300-gallon drop tanks under the wings, and the final 250 had the dorsal turret restored. As aircraft became available, the P-61s replaced the interim P-70s in all USAAF night-fighter squadrons. During 1945, 16 P-61Bs were converted to P-61Gs for weather reconnaissance, with armament deleted.

The final production batch comprised 41 P-61Cs with 2,800 h.p. R-2800-73 engines. The two XP-61Ds were converted "As" with R-2800-77 engines; the two XP-61Es were converted "Bs" as day fighters with radar and turret deleted and a new cockpit seating two in tandem. A similar cockpit was used on the F-15A Reporter, a reconnaissance aircraft of which 36 examples were built in 1946, after one XP-61E and one P-61A had been converted as prototypes designated, respectively, the XF-15 and XF-15A. The F-15As were re-designated RF-61C in 1948 and were out of service by 1952.

TECHNICAL DATA (P-61B)

MANUFACTURER: Northrop Aircraft Inc., Hawthorne, California.
TYPE: Night fighter.
ACCOMMODATION: Pilot, radar operator and gunner in central nacelle.
POWER PLANT: Two 2,000-h.p. Pratt & Whitney R-2800-65 piston radials.
DIMENSIONS: Span, 66 ft. 0 in. Length, 49 ft. 7 in. Height, 14 ft. 8 in. Wing area, 664 sq. ft.
WEIGHTS: Empty, 22,000 lb. Gross, 29,700 lb.
PERFORMANCE: Max. speed, 366 m.p.h. at 20,000 ft. Climb, 12 min. to 20,000 ft. Service ceiling, 33,100 ft. Range, 3,000 st. miles (ferry).
ARMAMENT: Four fixed forward firing 0·50-in. guns and four 20-mm. guns in remote-controlled top turret. Four 1,600 lb. bombs under wings.
SERIAL NUMBERS:

XP-61: 41-19509/19510.	P-61B: 42-39398/39757; 43-8231/8320.
YP-61: 41-18876/18888.	P-61C: 43-8321/8361.
P-61A: 42-5485/5634; 42-39348/39397.	F-15A: 45-59300/59335.

NORTHROP P-61 B

503

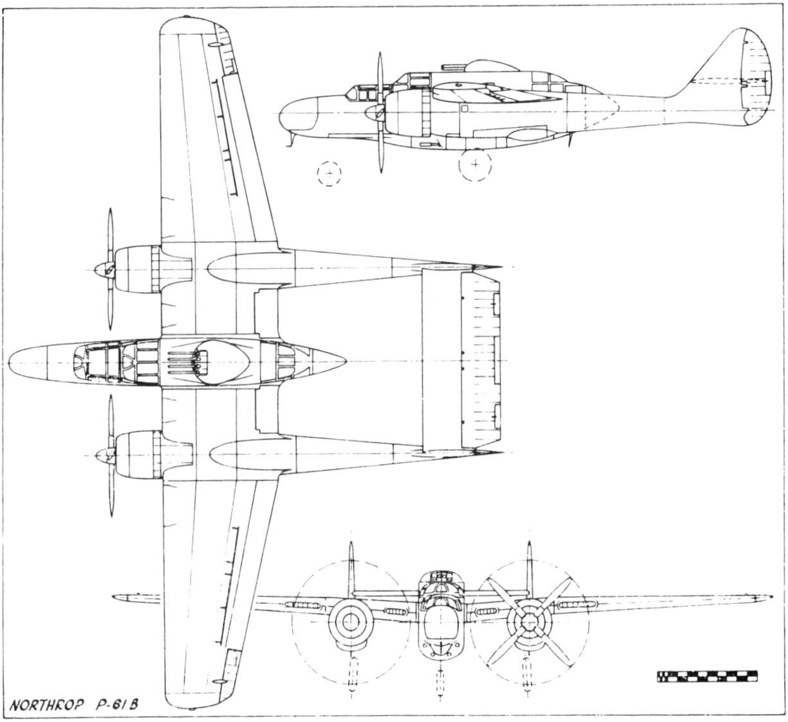

Northrop F-89J conversion serving with the Iowa ANG.

Northrop F-89 Scorpion

Designed around a proposal made by Northrop in December 1945, the F-89 became the first USAF multi-seat jet fighter capable of all-weather operation. The Air Force accepted the Northrop proposal and issued a development contract on May 3, 1946, following this with a firm order for two prototypes in December 1946. Between 1949 and 1956, 1,050 production examples of the F-89 series were built by Northrop.

The Scorpion was of conventional construction, with a shoulder-mounted wing and two Allison J35 engines side-by-side in the fuselage under the cockpit floor. As originally designed, the aircraft had a basic wing span of 52 ft. with tip-mounted fuel tanks which were removable on the first prototype but were subsequently fixed. Armament of four cannon was grouped in the nose together with A.I. radar, and the pilot and radar operator were in tandem beneath a long cockpit canopy.

The first of the two prototypes ordered as XF-89 (Northrop Model N-24) was flown by Fred Bretcher on August 16, 1948 from Edwards A.F.B. For the first 32 flights it had conventional wing ailerons but on February 1, 1949, a new series of trials began with Northrop "decelerons" which were to be a standard feature of all production Scorpions. The "deceleron" was a split surface which operated in one piece as an aileron but which could be opened out to serve also as a dive brake.

The XF-89 was lost on its 102nd flight on February 22, 1950. By that time, the second prototype was in flight test, having first flown on November 15, 1949. Modifications introduced when the airframe was about 90% complete led to a change of designation to XF-89A (N-49). The changes were intended to prove in flight features of the F-89A production model. External differences between the two prototypes included the silver finish of the XF-89A instead of black, and more pointed nose shape which lengthened the fuselage from 50 ft. 5½ in. to 53 ft. 5½ in.

504

Engines were 4,000-lb. s.t. J35-A-9s in the XF-89 and 5,200-lb. s.t. J35-A-21s with afterburners in the XF-89A, which flew on June 27, 1950.

Deliveries of the F-89A Scorpion, a contract for which had been approved on July 14, 1949, began in July 1950. Generally similar to the YF-89A, the F-89A (N-35) had J35-A-21 engines, six 20-mm. T-31 (M-24) guns in the nose with 200 r.p.g. and provision under the wings for two bombs of up to 1,600 lb. each plus a maximum of sixteen rockets. The engines were subsequently changed to· J35-A-21A, rated at 5,100 lb. s.t. dry and 6,800 lb. with afterburner. The lines of the rear fuselage behind the jet pipes were altered to overcome excessive turbulence encountered on the YF-89A at high speeds.

After 18 F-89As had been delivered, production changed to the F-89B (N-35), distinguished by internal equipment changes including the introduction of Lear F-5 autopilot, an ILS system and a Zero-reader system. The armament and radar (AN/APG-33) were unchanged and like the F-89As, the 30 F-89Bs were built with J35-A-21 engines which were later changed to J35-A-21As. All F-89As and F-89Bs had externally mass balanced elevators, adopted to overcome a severe high-frequency, low-amplitude flutter induced by the jet exhaust, but elevators with internal mass balance were fitted retroactively after being developed for the F-89C.

Apart from the new tailplane, the F-89C (N-35) incorporated numerous equipment changes. The first few carried a fuel system purge generator in an external fairing under the starboard engine, and another interim feature was an alcohol tank on the port wing bomb shackle, to provide for engine air inlet de-icing. To overcome a wing structural problem on this model, fins were added to the tip tanks and were then applied retroactively to the F-89A and F-89B. Production of the F-89C totalled 164; the first 34 were delivered with J35-A-21 engines followed by 30 with the -21A engine, 45 with the 5,400 lb. s.t. (7,400 lb. with a/b) -33 engine and 55 with the 5,500 lb. s.t. -33A.

Armament and radar remained unchanged in the F-89C, but work was proceeding meanwhile on a new wing-tip installation containing 52 2·75-inch FFARs in addition to fuel. The pods were first flown during 1951 on a modified F-89B re-designated YF-89D (49-2463) and were a standard

Northrop F-89A showing externally hinged elevators (*Northrop photo 38808*).

Northrop F-89D with wing-tip rocket pods (*Northrop photo R20627*).

feature of the 682 production model F-89Ds. The F-89D (N-68) also had equipment changes, extra fuel in the nose and underwing pylon tanks to increase the total capacity by 862 U.S. gallons, and later engines. The first 27 aircraft had the J35-A-33A, the next 130 had the -41 engine and the remainder had the -35.

Installation of two Allison YJ71-A-3 engines in an F-89C (50-752) accounted for the YF-89E (N-71), used as an engine test bed. A production

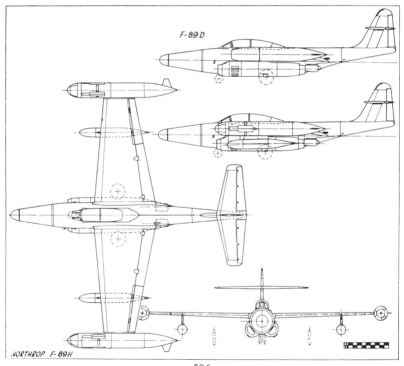

version with these engines and "D" armament was to have been the F-89F but was cancelled. So also was the F-89G, with revised armament and fire control. The final production version of the Scorpion therefore was the F-89H (N-138), in which the wing-tip pods were redesigned to carry three Hughes GAR-1, -2, -3 or -4 Falcon AAMs with 21 FFARs. Up to six more FFARs could be carried under the wings. The engines were J35-A-35s. Production totalled 156, in addition to three F-89Ds (53-2449, 52-1830 and 52-1938) modified to test the new features but not re-designated.

A further change of armament was made in 1956 to introduce the Douglas MB-1 Genie unguided, nuclear-tipped rocket on underwing pylons, one each side. Additional pylons could carry up to four GAR-2A AAMs, and the wing-tip installation could be either FFAR pods or 600 U.S. gallon fuel tanks. So modified as Weapon System 205G, the aircraft were designated F-89J (N-160); 350 were delivered by conversion from F-89Ds, with J35-A-35 or -35A engines, and Hughes MG-12 fire control system.

The F-89A and B began to reach A.D.C. in mid-1951, first to equip being the 84th FIS at Hamilton A.F.B., followed by the F-89C with the 74th FIS at Presque Isle A.F.B. in January 1953, the F-89D with the 18th FIS at Minneapolis-St. Paul in January 1954, the F-89H with the 445th FIS at Wurtsmith A.F.B. in March 1956 and the F-89J with the 84th FIS in January 1957. These aircraft served not only in the U.S. but also in Alaska, where the F-89D became operational in 1954, followed by F-89Hs until replaced during 1957 by the F-102. Some F-89Bs were later allocated to Air Training Command, and the "D", "H" and "J" passed to squadrons of the ANG. As missile and drone control aircraft, some early Scorpions served A.R.D.C. as the DF-89A and DF-89B.

TECHNICAL DATA (F-89D)

MANUFACTURER: Northrop Aircraft Inc., Hawthorne, California.
TYPE: All-weather interceptor fighter.
ACCOMMODATION: Pilot and radar operator in tandem.
POWER PLANT: Two 5,440-lb.s.t. (7,200 lb. with a/b) Allison J35-A-35 (or -33A, -41 or -47) turbojets.
DIMENSIONS: Span, 59 ft. 8 in. Length, 53 ft. 10 in. Height, 17 ft. 7 in. Wing area, 562 sq. ft. (650 sq. ft. including tip pods).
WEIGHTS: Empty, 25,194 lb. Gross, 42,241 lb.
PERFORMANCE: Max. speed, 636 m.p.h. at 10,600 ft. Combat speed, 523 m.p.h. at 46,500 ft. Initial climb, 8,360 ft./min. Service ceiling, 49,200 ft. Range (ferry) 1,370 st. miles.
ARMAMENT: Fifty-two 2·75-in. folding fin air rockets each in wing tip pods; provision for GAR-1 Falcon missiles in place of FFAR.
SERIAL NUMBERS:

XF-89: 46-678.	F-89D: 51-400/446; 51-11298/11443;
YF-89A: 46-679.	52-1829/1961; 52-2127/2165;
F-89A: 49-2431/2448.	53-2447/2686; 54-184/260.
F-89B: 49-2449/2478.	F-89H: 54-261/416.
F-89C: 50-741/804; 51-5757/5856.	

Northrop AT-38B of the 479th TTW, in blue camouflage (*MAP*).

Northrop T-38A Talon

Put into production as the first supersonic trainer for the USAF, the T-38A was a derivative of the Northrop N-156, a lightweight military aircraft originally developed as a private venture. The N-156 concept began in 1954 with a study of European and Asian needs for a lightweight and inexpensive fighter of high performance, achieved in the Northrop design by the use of two small, efficient turbojets with afterburners, advanced aerodynamic principles and new structural techniques. After two years of private development, Northrop obtained USAF interest in a trainer version, the N-156T. Construction of three prototypes was authorized in December 1956 and development proceeded under the weapon system designation SS-420L for a jet basic trainer support system to GOR 94. The contract was later revised and when finally concluded in June 1958 covered seven test YT-38s including one static test airframe.

The first prototype (58-1191) was flown from Edwards A.F.B. on April 10,

TECHNICAL DATA (T-38A)

MANUFACTURER: Northrop Corporation, Norair Division, Hawthorne, California.
TYPE: Supersonic basic flying trainer.
ACCOMMODATION: Pupil and instructor in tandem.
POWER PLANT: Two 2,680 lb.s.t. (dry) and 3,850 lb.s.t. (with afterburners) General Electric J85-GE-5A turbojets.
DIMENSIONS: Span, 25 ft. 3 in. Length, 46 ft. 4½ in. Height, 12 ft. 10 in. Wing area 170 sq. ft.
WEIGHTS: Empty, 7,410 lb. Gross, 11,761 lb.
PERFORMANCE: Max. speed, 805 m.p.h. at 36,089 ft. Average cruising speed, 578 m.p.h. at 43,400 ft. Initial climb, 28,500 ft./min. Service ceiling, 45,000 ft. Range, 860 st. miles (ferry range, 975 miles).
ARMAMENT: None.
SERIAL NUMBERS:
YT-38: 58-1191/1193.
T-38A: 58-1194/1197; 59-1594/1606; 66-4320/4389; 66-8349/8404;
60-547/596; 61-804/947; 67-14825/14859; 67-14915/14958;
62-3609/3752; 63-8111/8247; 68-8095/8217; 69-7073/7088;
64-13166/13305; 65-10316/10475; 70-1549/1591; 70-1949/1956.

1959, by Lew Nelson. This and the second aircraft (58-1192), flown on June 12, 1959, had YJ85-GE-1 turbojets without afterburners; subsequent YT-38s in the operational test batch had 3,600 lb.s.t. YJ85-GE-5s with afterburners while production aircraft had the 3,850 lb.s.t. J85-GE-5 engines.

With Fiscal 1959 funds, the USAF ordered 13 T-38As, and the first of these (59-1594) flew in May 1960. Follow-on contracts were included in successive annual budgets until a total of 1,189 had been contracted by the beginning of 1970, all but 75 of these being for USAF training schools. Included in the total were 46 operated in USAF markings but purchased by the German government and used for advanced training of Luftwaffe pilots in the U.S.A. The first T-38A was delivered to Randolph A.F.B. on March 17, 1961, where it went into service with the 3510th Flying Training Wing.

Among major users of the T-38A was the 465th Tactical Fighter Training Squadron at Holloman A.F.B., giving fighter lead-in training to hundreds of pilots each year. To give the T-38 greater weapons training capability, an AT-38A prototype (60-576) was fitted with an 7·62-mm. SUU-11 gun pod on the fuselage centreline, after which more than 130 Talons were modified similarly to AT-38Bs to serve with four squadrons of the 479th Tactical Training Wing.

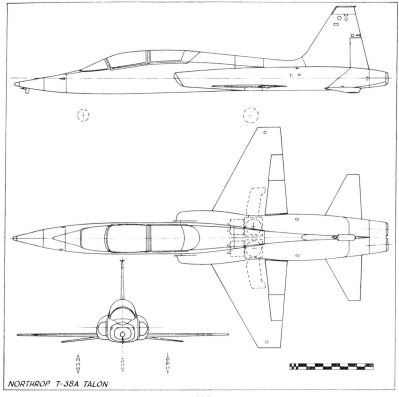

NORTHROP T-38A TALON

Northrop F-5E of 527th Aggressor Squadron, in low-visibility grey finish (*Dr. Alan Beaumont*).

Northrop F-5 Tiger II

In May 1958, the Department of Defense backed construction by Northrop of prototypes of its N-156F design for a lightweight, low-cost fighter which had been projected in parallel with the N-156T trainer (produced as the T-38A Talon). The first N-156F flew on July 30, 1959, and in May 1962 the aircraft was adopted by the DoD as the "Freedom Fighter", to be supplied to approved nations through the Military Assistance Program. Powered by two 4,090 lb.s.t. General Electric J85-GE-13 turbojets, the first aircraft in the YF-5A configuration flew on July 31, 1963. A two-seat conversion trainer was ordered at the same time as the F-5B, first flown in February 1964. Although all F-5 production was intended for MAP, first deliveries were to USAF's 4441st Combat Crew Training Squadron in September 1964, this unit serving as the training squadron for foreign users. In 1965, 12 F-5As were "borrowed" from MAP supplies by the USAF and used for the *Skoshi Tiger* combat evaluation in South Vietnam, flown by the 4503rd TFS. Modified to have in-flight refuelling probes and other differences, they were designated F-5C for their service with the USAF. More than 4,000 combat hours were totalled in 3,500-plus sorties for the loss of two aircraft, but the F-5Cs were then passed to the Vietnam Air Force, and the F-5D (two-seat) version was not acquired by the USAF. Production of the F-5A/B totalled more than 1,100, ending in June 1972.

To meet a DoD requirement for an International Fighter Aircraft as a successor to the F-5A, Northrop successfully proposed the F-5A-21, an improved version of the Freedon Fighter powered by 5,000 lb.s.t. J85-GE-21B engines (which had entered flight test on March 28, 1969, in the YF-5B-21). After selecting the F-5A-21 as the winning IFA proposal in November 1970, the USAF applied the designation F-5E and F-5F to single and two-seat versions, first flights of which were made on August 11, 1972, and September 25, 1974. The name Tiger II was adopted to perpetuate the role of the earlier aircraft in the *Skoshi Tiger* evaluation.

As was the case with the F-5A and F-5B, the new variants were produced

Northrop F-5E of 57th FWW (the same aircraft that is shown on page 510), in original high-visibility camouflage.

primarily for supply through MAP or export on direct purchase contracts. As successor to the 4441st CCTS, the 425th TF Training Squadron at Williams A.F.B., Arizona, received F-5Es and Fs for the training role, from early 1973. In addition, the USAF adopted the F-5E as a specialized aircraft for dissimilar air combat training (DACT), in which they were flown in the aggressor role against other combat types in USAF service. For this purpose, 70-odd F-5Es were diverted from MAP contracts intended for South Vietnam and entered service in a variety of colourful camouflage schemes, with the 64th and 65th Fighter Weapons Squadrons of the 57th FWW at Nellis A.F.B., Nevada, the 527th Aggressor Squadron, 10th TRW, in the U.K. and the 26th AS, 3rd TFW, in the Philippines. A small number of F-5Bs and F-5Fs was also acquired by the USAF, which was upgrading the radars in its 74 Tiger IIs in 1988, from APQ-153 to APQ-159.

Production of the F-5E/F came to an end in late 1986, with about 1,500 of these variants built. Northrop also built three prototypes of the F-20 Tigershark, developed from the F-5 and at first designated F-5G, with a single 18,000 lb. General Electric F404-GE-100 turbofan, but no production ensued.

Northrop F-5C for "Skoshi Tiger" evaluation in Vietnam (*Northrop photo*).

TECHNICAL DATA (F-5E)

MANUFACTURER: Northrop Corporation Aircraft Group, Los Angeles, California.
TYPE: Light tactical fighter.
ACCOMMODATION: Pilot only or (F-5E) two in tandem.
POWER PLANT: Two 5,000 lb.s.t. with afterburning General Electric J85-GE-21B turbojets.
DIMENSIONS: Span, 26 ft. 8 in. Length (over nose probe), 47 ft. 4 in. Height, 13 ft. 4 in. Wing area, 186·0 sq. ft.
WEIGHTS: Empty, 9,723 lb. Gross, 24,722 lb.
PERFORMANCE: Max. speed, Mach 1·64, equal to 1,082 m.p.h. at 36,000 ft. Cruising speed, 646 m.p.h. at 36,000 ft. Initial rate of climb, 34,500 ft./min. Service ceiling, 51,800 ft. Combat radius, 656 miles with max. fuel.
ARMAMENT: Two M39A2 20-mm. cannon in nose. Wing-tip launchers for two AIM-9 Sidewinder AAMs. One centreline and four wing stations for up to 7,000 lb. of ordnance.
SERIAL NUMBERS (incomplete)

F-5A/RF-5A/F-5B: 63-8367/8451;
63-13692; 64-13306/13388;
65-10476/10595; 65-13071/13074;
66-9119/9244; 66-14457/14466;
67-14894/14909; 67-21153/21231;
67-21236/21258; 67-21272/21284;
67-22548/22557; 68-9043/9133;
68-10489/10490; 69-7089/7177;
70-1373/1407; 70-1608/1622;
70-1948; 71-260/279; 71-1029/1038;
71-1377/1390; 72-436/449;
72-1337/1356; 73-1602/1613;
74-775/786; 74-1576/1581;
74-2097/2112; 74-2114/2129.

F-5E/F-5F: 71-1417/1421*; 72-1386/1406*;
73-846/990*; 73-1626/1646*;
74-958/997; 74-1362/1575*;
74-1582/1617; 75-314/373;
75-442/527; 75-562/617*; 75-681/731;
75-735/742; 75-753/755; 76-471/490;
76-1526/1597; 76-1611/1686;
77-328/350; 77-359/379; 77-1767/1779;
78-028/037; 78-770/787; 78-789/805;
78-814/829; 78-865/884; 78-2435/2436;
78-2444/2447; 79-1681/1709; 79-1717/1726;
79-1916/1945; 80-296/319; 80-3501/3537;
81-006/019; 81-558-625; 81-632/642;
81-823/863; 82-004/055; 82-062/065;
82-089/091*; 82-187/189; 82-634/645;
83-072/074*; 84-183/184; 84-194/203;
84-456/457*; 84-490/491; 85-043/044;
85-053/058; 85-1586/1595; 86-090/091;
86-388; 86-405/409.

*Some or all of these batches for USAF use

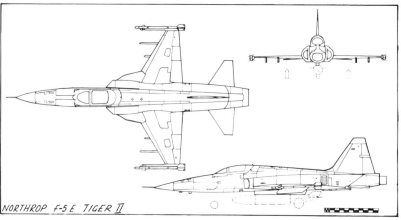

NORTHROP F-5E TIGER II

512

Northrop B-2, in an artist's impression (*USAF photo*).

Northrop B-2

During 1981, the USAF completed plans to initiate the development of an advanced technology bomber (ATB), intended to complement and perhaps eventually replace the Rockwell B-1B as a low-level penetration bomber. After evaluation of design proposals from several manufacturers, the USAF selected Northrop as the prime contractor for the ATB, to which the designation B-2 was duly assigned. Boeing Aerospace and LTV (Vought) were named as major sub-contractors, and General Electric was chosen as the engine supplier. While mock-up and prototype construction proceeded, the aircraft remained subject to intensive security restrictions, and the first official illustration—an artist's impression—was released for publication only in April 1988, a few months before the prototype's roll-out at Palmdale, California, where final assembly was located.

The B-2 was designed in accordance with "stealth" principles, to minimise its chances of detection by enemy radar, and was of all-wing configuration, following Northrop's lengthy experience with this type of layout. Four F118-GE-100 engines rated at about 19,000 lb.s.t. each were semi-buried in the inner wing, with their intakes above the upper surface, alongside the central "fuselage", which was fully blended into the wing. This fuselage housed the two-man crew, the major mission avionics and at least part of the weapon load, which could include advanced cruise missiles such as the AGM-129, as well as nuclear and conventional bombs. An extensive suite of electronic defence equipment was included in the avionics. The large wing area provided stowage for the bulk of the fuel load, which was sufficient to give the subsonic B-2 a range of several thousand miles. A sophisticated flight control system was incorporated in the aircraft, which had no vertical control surfaces.

The USAF plans provided for acquisition of 132 B-2As to make up the core of the strategic bomber force in the first part of the 21st century, with entry into service in the first half of the 'nineties. Whiteman A.F.B., Missouri, was chosen as the first base to receive B-2As, the flight testing of which began early in 1989, up to a year behind the original schedule. Approximate dimensions were span, 172 ft., length, 69 ft. and height, 17 ft.

Piasecki H-21 in service with ARDC (*Ryan photo 2-4061*).

Piasecki (Vertol) H-21 Workhorse

United States Air Force ordered an evaluation and service trials batch of 18 YH-21s from Piasecki Helicopter Corporation in 1949. Based on the U.S. Navy's HRP-2, the YH-21 (Piasecki Model PD-22) was the first tandem-rotor helicopter delivered to the USAF; its first flight was made on April 11, 1952. Following successful trials with these aircraft, 32 H-21As were ordered to serve with MATS Air Rescue Service, principally in the Arctic. Like the YH-21, the H-21A (Piasecki Model 42) was powered by a Wright R-1820-103 engine de-rated to 1,250 h.p. The first H-21A flew in October 1953 and the USAF bought 38, including six for Canada under MAP.

Production of the Workhorse continued with the H-21B, ordered for service with Troop Carrier Command as an assault transport, and delivered from 1953. Apart from an increase in fuselage accommodation for 20 troops, the H-21B had the R-1820-103 re-rated at 1,425 h.p. to cope with the increased gross weight of 15,000 lb. This version did not normally have pontoons, but was fitted with an auto-pilot, provision for external fuel tanks under the fuselage and for armour protection for important components. Production of the H-21B for the USAF totalled 163.

Most produced version of the H-21 was the H-21C (Model 43) similar in most respects to the H-21B but delivered to the U.S. Army for use as cargo and personnel transport, with the name Shawnee. Production of this version, started by Piasecki, was continued after the company name was changed to Vertol, a total of 334 being built. The first flew in June 1953 and deliveries were made from September 1954 to March 1959. For Army operations, the side winch gave way to an external sling hook under the fuselage for loads of up to 4,000 lb. The Army also ordered development of the H-21D (Model 71) in which the piston engine was replaced by two General Electric T58 shaft turbines. Two were converted from H-21Cs, the first flight being made in September 1957.

In 1962 the designations were changed to CH-21A, B and C, while the SH-21B, in MATS' service in the rescue role, became the HH-21B.

514

TECHNICAL DATA (H-21)

MANUFACTURER: Piasecki Helicopter Corporation, Morton, Pennsylvania.
TYPE: Troop and cargo transport helicopter.
ACCOMMODATION: Two pilots, 14 troops or 12 litters.
POWER PLANT: One 1,425 h.p. Wright R-1820-103 piston radial.
DIMENSIONS: Rotor diameter, 44 ft. 6 in. Overall length, 86 ft. 4 in. Height, 15 ft. 5 in.
WEIGHTS: Empty, 8,000 lb. Gross, 13,300 lb.
PERFORMANCE: Max. speed, 131 m.p.h. at sea level. Cruising speed, 98 m.p.h. at
sea level. Initial climb, 1,080 ft./min. Service ceiling, 9,450 ft.
ARMAMENT: Nil
SERIAL NUMBERS:

YH-21: 50-1231/1248.
H-21A: 51-15238/15269; 52-8487/8492.
H-21B: 51-15854/15880; 52-8665/8679;
52-8681/8709; 53-4322/4402;
54-4000/4008; 55-5127/5131*;
57-2610/2611.

H-21C: 51-15881/15913; 52-8613/8664;
52-8680; 55-4132/4221; 56-2015/2160;
56-4343/4354.

* Five for MAP

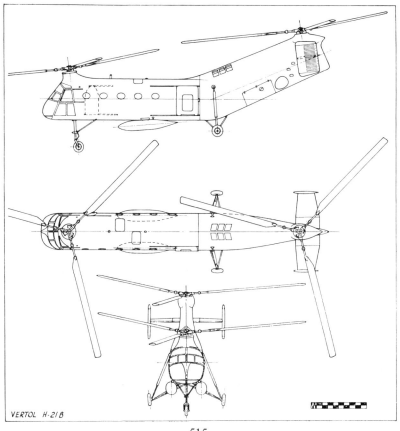

VERTOL H-21B

515

Piper L-4A in Army olive drab, 1943 (*MAP photo*).

Piper L-4, L-18, L-21 Grasshopper

Of the three types of commercial lightplane selected by the Army in 1941 for evaluation in the then-new role of artillery spotting, gun-laying and front line liaison, the Piper Cub was eventually produced in the greatest numbers. Its origins as an Army Grasshopper were exactly similar to those of the Aeronca L-3 (see pages 37–39) and the Taylor-craft L-2 (pages 500–502) with four examples of the Cub J3C-65 purchased in mid-1941 for preliminary investigation, and designated YO-59. This was followed almost immediately by a contract for 40 similar aircraft as O-59s, which were used by the Army in its annual manoeuvres at the end of 1941. Powered by the 65 h.p. Continental O-170-3 engine, the O-59s effectively demonstrated their usefulness in support of ground actions and for rapid staff communications between Army units.

The O-59A was evolved to meet Army requirements more specifically, with a modified cabin enclosure offering better all-round visibility. Orders for this version eventually totalled 948, of which 649 were completed as O-59As before the type was re-classified in the liaison category as the L-4A. The YO-59 and O-59 already in service then became the L-4 after a brief period as L-59. In mid-1942, a contract for 980 Grasshoppers was placed, these being delivered as L-4Bs with less radio than the L-4A.

Small improvements and changes in operational equipment brought a change of designation on the next production series, the L-4H. This variant was the subject of the largest single order for liaison aircraft placed during the War, for 1,301 examples. A second batch of L-4Hs brought the total of this model built to 1,801 before production switched to the L-4J with a controllable pitch propeller. Two contracts, each for 800 L-4Js, were completed and work was in progress on another 350 when the War ended. Only 80 of this final batch were delivered.

516

The L-4 performed its first combat mission for the Army in 1943, when four of these lightplanes flew off the deck of an aircraft carrier to spot for ground units going ashore in the invasion of North Africa. Thereafter, the Piper L-4s and the L-2s and L-3s which shared the official name of Grasshopper, operated with the Army in every campaign and on every front. In the later stages of the War, L-4s made extensive use of the Brodie rig, an overhead cable and harness from which the aircraft could operate without contact with the ground in take-off or landing.

More than 100 Piper Cubs of assorted types also joined the Army by impressment after the U.S. entered the War at the end of 1941, and these were also designated in the L-4 series. They were used principally to give preliminary flight instruction to Army glider pilots. The impressed Cubs comprised eight L-4C (J-3C-65); five L-4D (J-3F-65); seventeen L-4E (J-4E); forty-three L-4F (J-5A) and thirty-four L-4G (J-5B).

One of the three-seat J-5As was impressed by the Air Force for use as a communications aircraft and was designated UC-83, but this was later transferred to the Army as an L-4F. Six other J-5s were acquired for the Mutual Aid Program in 1951 (51-16086/16091).

TG-8. Like Aeronca and Taylorcraft, the Piper company was asked in 1942 to evolve a training glider from the L-4. This was simply achieved by removing the engine and the undercarriage and substituting a new front fuselage with an extra seat for the instructor, and adding a simple cross-axle landing gear, with hydraulic, individually actuated brakes and a steerable tailwheel. The fin area was increased and full controls provided at each of the three seats. Three of these gliders were produced for Navy evaluation under the designation XLNP-1 and a production batch of 250 for the Army as TG-8s.

L-14. When the War ended, Piper had in production a new liaison monoplane, the L-14. Larger than the L-4 series, it was a three-seater with a 130 h.p. Lycoming O-290-3 and a gross weight of 1,800 lb. Five YL-14s (45-55525/29) were completed but another 845 were cancelled (45-55530/56374).

L-18. In 1949, the L-4J design was revised, as the L-18A, for the Mutual Security Programme, but none was built. Instead, 105 standard Cub 95s

All-yellow Piper L-21A for Army Aviation (*Gordon S. Williams*).

517

were purchased as L-18Bs, and allocated to the Turkish Army. The U.S. Army also procured 838 similar L-18Cs, 108 of which went to foreign nations. At the same time, two examples of the larger PA-18 Cub 135 were evaluated by the Army as YL-21s; these were similar to the 243 PA-18s already being used by the Air Force in civil markings for contract training at civilian schools. A single PA-18 received a USAF serial number in 1955.

L-21. The Army Field Forces procured 150 L-21As in 1951 for utility duties. These were Piper PA-18s powered by the 125 h.p. O-290-11 engine and with a gross weight of 1,500 lb. Some later became TL-21As. The L-21B was similar with the 135 h.p. O-290-D2 engine, and a total of 568 was purchased by the Army, in addition to 14 for supply overseas under Mutual Aid. After tests on an YL-21, a new undercarriage with tandem wheels on each main leg was fitted to many L-21Bs for rough field operations. The designation was changed to U-7A in 1962.

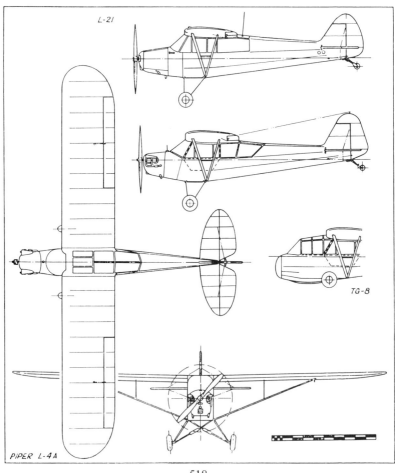

L-21

TG-8

PIPER L-4A

TECHNICAL DATA (L-4/L-18/L-21)

MANUFACTURER: Piper Aircraft Corp., Lock Haven, Pennsylvania.
TYPE: Liaison.
ACCOMMODATION: Pilot and observer in tandem.

	L-4	L-18A	L-21A
Power Plant:	65 h.p. Continental O-170-3	90 h.p. Continental C90-8F	125 h.p. Lycoming O-290-D
Dimensions:			
Span, ft., in.	35 3	35 3	35 3
Length, ft., in.	22 0	22 4½	22 7
Height, ft., in.	6 8	6 7	6 6
Wing area, sq. ft.	179	179	179
Weights:			
Empty, lb.	730	800	950
Gross, lb.	1,220	1,500	1,580
Performance:			
Max. speed, m.p.h.	85	110	123
Cruising speed, m.p.h.	—	100	115
Climb	14 min. to 5,000ft.	624 ft./min.	1,000 ft./min.
Service ceiling, ft.	9,300	13,500	21,650
Range, st. mi.	190	—	770

ARMAMENT: Nil.
SERIAL NUMBERS:

O-59: 42-460/463; 42-7813/7852.
L-4A: 42-15159/15329; 42-36325/36824;
   42-38380/38457; 43-29048/29246.
L-4B: 43-491/1470.
L-4C: 42-79557/79558; 43-2923;
   43-2925; 42-2932; 42-2959; 42-2967.
L-4D: 43-2914; 43-2924; 43-2992;
   43-2995/2996.
L-4E: 42-79555; 43-2941; 43-2954/2958;
   42-2973/2974; 43-2989/2990;
   43-3003/3008.
L-4F: 42-57505; 42-79551/79554;
   42-107425; 43-2909; 43-2911/2912;
   43-2915/2920; 43-2922; 43-2926;
   43-2930/2931; 43-2934/2935;
   43-2937/2939; 43-2947/2949;
   43-2952/2953; 43-2964/2966;
   43-2968/2970; 43-2978; 43-2980;
   43-2991; 43-2999/3002; 44-52988.
L-4H: 43-29247/30547; 44-79545/80044.
L-4J: 44-80045/80844; 45-4401/5200;
   45-55175/55267*.

L-4G: 43-2910; 43-2913; 43-2921;
   43-2928/2929; 43-2933; 43-2936;
   43-2940; 43-2942/2946; 43-2948;
   43-2950/2951; 43-2963; 43-2971/2972;
   43-2975/2977; 43-2979; 43-2981/2988;
   43-2994; 43-2997/2998.
TG-8: 43-3009/3258; 43-12499/12501.
YL-14: 45-55525/55529.
L-18B: 49-2774/2878.
L-18C: 50-1745/1812†; 51-15272/15653;
   52-2376/2539; 53-4665/4848;
   54-719/758†.
YL-21: 51-6495/6496.
L-21A: 51-15654/15803†.
L-21B: 52-6220/6294; 53-3738/3784;
   53-4849/4877; 53-7718/7779;
   54-2309/2663; 54-2826/2835†;
   55-4578/4581†.
PA-18: 55-4749.

* 80 completed in this batch, including 20 for Navy.
† These batches for foreign nations through Mutual Defence Programmes.

519

Republic P-43 (*Peter M. Bowers*).

Republic P-43 Lancer

Tests were conducted at Langley Field in 1939 with the single Seversky XP-41 (see page 547), the last production model P-35 fitted with a turbo-supercharged engine. As a result of these tests, Republic engineers under Alexander Kartveli developed a slightly improved model which was ordered by the AAC in 1940 to the extent of a trials batch of 13 YP-43s. The elliptical wing planform of the P-35 was retained but the flat centre section was deleted and the landing gear retracted inward instead of aft, with the projecting half-wheels streamlined by fixed fairings under the wings. The 1,200 h.p. R-1830-35 turbo-supercharged engine led to a small lengthening of the nose. Although the weight of the YP-43 went up to 7,800 lb., the speed of 351 m.p.h. was far in excess of the best performance of the P-35. The turbo-supercharger gave the YP-43 a considerable advantage in operating ceiling, this being one of the most important factors in the AAC decision to purchase the type.

A contract for 54 P-43s was placed in 1940 and deliveries began in 1941. The P-43 had a 1,200 h.p. R-1830-35 engine and the same armament as the YPs—two 0·30-inch and two 0·50 inch machine guns.

In parallel with the P-43, Republic worked on the P-44 design (Republic AP-4J), with an R-2180-1 engine of 1,400 h.p. and an estimated top speed of 386-400 m.p.h. At a review of Army fighters held in June, 1940 at Wright Field, however, it was concluded that the P-44 would need many changes and much additional equipment if it was to be suitable for operations of the kind being fought in Europe. Rather than embark on development of this type, the Army Air Corps decided to substitute an order for 80 P-43As for the 80 P-44s which had been ordered. These had the R-1830-49 engine but were otherwise the same as the P-43s.

This contract was followed in 1941 by another for 125 P-43A-1s. These had a still later engine variant, the R-1830-57, and the four-gun armament was concentrated in the wings. At 360 m.p.h., the P-43A-1 had the highest speed of any Lancer variant.

In 1942, most of the surviving Lancers were converted to a reconnaissance role, with cameras in the rear fuselage. According to the camera installation, these were re-designated P-43B (150 converted); P-43C (2 converted); P-43D and P-43E. Some were delivered to the Chinese Air Force and saw service against the Japanese while carrying Chinese markings.

TECHNICAL DATA (P-43)

MANUFACTURER: Republic Aviation Corp., Long Island, New York.
TYPE: Single-seat pursuit.
ACCOMMODATION: Pilot in enclosed cockpit.
POWER PLANT: One 1,200 h.p. Pratt & Whitney R-1830-47 piston radial.
DIMENSIONS: Span, 36 ft. 0 in. Length, 28 ft. 6 in. Height, 14 ft. 0 in. Wing area, 223 sq. ft.
WEIGHTS: Empty, 5,654 lb. Gross, 7,935 lb.
PERFORMANCE: Max. speed, 349 m.p.h. at 25,000 ft. Cruising speed, 280 m.p.h. Initial climb, 2,850 ft./min.; Service ceiling, 38,000 ft. Range, 800 st. miles.
ARMAMENT: Two 0·50-in. and two 0·30-in. fixed forward firing guns.
SERIAL NUMBERS:

YP-43: 39-704/716.	P-43A: 40-2891/2970.
P-43: 41-6668/6721.	P-43A-1: 41-31448/31572.

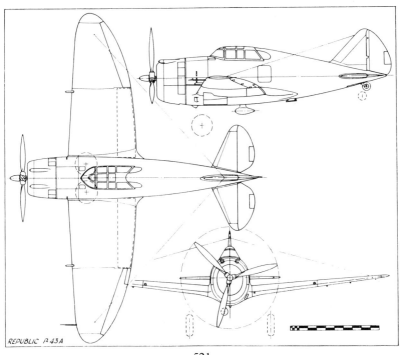

REPUBLIC P-43A

521

Republic P-47D-30 with bubble hood and dorsal fin (*Republic photo H-8771*).

Republic P-47 Thunderbolt

One of the three outstanding USAAF fighters of World War II, the Thunderbolt established the reputation of the Republic Aviation Corp. and provided a sound basis of experience in fighter-bomber design and operation on which the Thunderjet, Thunderstreak, Thunderflash and Thunderchief have subsequently been based. It was itself an outgrowth of a design series which began with Major Alexander P. Seversky's P-35 and included the P-43 and P-44. Like its contemporary, the North American P-51, the Thunderbolt was conceived, tested, produced and put into action wholly within the period of World War II.

The Thunderbolt became the last radial engined fighter to serve in quantity with the USAAF, although the first aircraft to bear the P-47 designation was actually designed around the liquid-cooled Allison V-1710-39. This, the XP-47 of 1940, was an attempt to produce, to official requirements, a lightweight interceptor armed with only two 0·50-inch machine guns. The XP-47A designation covered a still lighter variant which, minus some equipment, had an estimated gross weight of 6,400 lb. Both these prototypes were expected to achieve 400 m.p.h. but Republic engineers under their chief, Alexander Kartveli, undertook a redesign in search of still higher speeds.

As the XP-47B, the new fighter was based on the 2,000 h.p. Pratt & Whitney R-2800 radial engine and no special effort was made to produce a lightweight aeroplane. In fact, at a little over 12,000 lb., this prototype (40-3051) was the heaviest single-seat fighter then adopted by the USAAF. It was first flown on May 6, 1941, by L. L. Brabham. Noteworthy aspects of its design were the deep fuselage, with a duct from below the engine to the supercharger in the rear; the elliptical wing plan form and the telescopic landing gear, required to give ground clearance to the large-

522

Republic P-47D-10 in Italy, 1943 (*Howard Levy*).

diameter four-bladed propeller. The armament of eight 0·50s in the wings
was among the heaviest then fitted to a fighter, and followed the trend
toward eight-gun fighters in Europe and specified by the R.A.F. for the
North American Mustang. With a 2,000 h.p. XR-2800-21 engine, the
XP-47B achieved 412 m.p.h. This performance made the Thunderbolt the
most promising of fighters available to the USAAF, and an initial contract
was placed in September, 1940, for a total of 773 examples.

Only small external details—a sliding cockpit hood and raked forward
aerial—distinguished the prototype from the first production model, the
P-47B, of which 171 were built. Internal changes brought the gross
weight to 13,356 lb. but better performance from the production model
R-2800-21 engine boosted the top speed to 429 m.p.h. Deliveries of the
P-47B began in 1942 and by November the three squadrons of the 56th
Fighter Group were fully operational, followed by the 78th Fighter Group.
Both these groups moved to Europe in January 1943 to join the Eighth
Air Force in the U.K. From bases in England, these squadrons took the
P-47B into action for the first time on April 8, 1943, flying escort to B-17s

Republic P-47M for European service, 1944 (*Republic photo H-7582*).

Curtiss-built P-47G-15-CU, in use as a taxi trainer (*Howard levy*).

and undertaking fighter sweeps. Experience with this first Thunderbolt model revealed inadequate climb and manoeuvrability, but an excellent diving performance and an ability to survive battle damage which was later to prove one of the P-47's most outstanding attributes. The need for more fuel was also revealed in early operations, if escort missions were to be flown all the way to targets inside Germany itself.

In the P-47C, which followed the P-47B on Republic's production line at Farmingdale on Long Island before the end of 1941, provision was made for a 200-U.S. gallon drop tank under the fuselage. Other changes included a 13-inch lengthening of the fuselage to improve manoeuvrability. The initial Thunderbolt contract was completed with the P-47C, 602 of which were built. Most of these went to Europe, where they were flying long-range escort missions by the middle of 1943.

The next Thunderbolt contract was for 850 aircraft of the P-47D type, on which water injection was adopted to boost engine power at higher altitudes. With this addition, the top speed increased to 433 m.p.h. at 30,000 ft. The R-2800-21 engine was later replaced by the R-2800-59 in this model, of which 6,315 were eventually built in versions up to the P-47D-23 (including 2,350 at a second Republic factory at Evansville). The addition

Republic P-47N for Pacific service with rockets and bombs (*Republic photo H-7582*).

524

of wing pylons for two 150-gallon drop tanks again increased the range of the P-47D, and these were later modified to permit their alternative use as bomb racks. With two 1,000 lb., three 500 lb. bombs (one under the fuselage) or, eventually, 2,500 lb. in various combinations, the P-47D proved to be an effective fighter bomber, serving in this role in Europe from the end of 1943. It had, by then, gone into service also in the Pacific area, flying first with the 348th Fighter Group from Australia on long missions to strike at Japanese targets in New Guinea. Other P-47Ds were issued to units of the Ninth and Fifteenth Air Forces in the U.K. and Italy, 240 went to the R.A.F. under Lend–Lease and 103 to Russia.

To improve the rearward vision from the cockpit and remove a dangerous blind spot, a "bubble" type cockpit canopy was designed and tested on a converted P-47D (42-8702) re-designated XP-47K. This new feature distinguished P-47Ds with block numbers of 25 and above, some of which had R-2800-63 engines and a stronger fuselage rack to carry a 110-gallon tank, in addition to the two 150 gallon wing tanks and the internal capacity

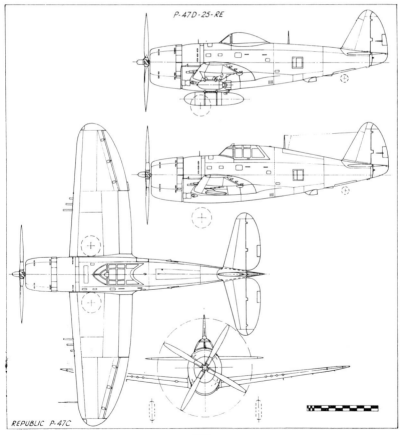

P-47D-25-RE

REPUBLIC P-47C

Republic P-47N-1-RE, carrying nickname "The Repulsive Thunderbox" (*William Larkins*).

of 270 gallons. On the P-47D-27 and later models, a small dorsal fin was fitted. The Farmingdale plant built 2,550 P-47Ds of the later series and Evansville built 3,743 for a total of 6,291, and a grand total of 12,608 P-47Ds of all varieties. A further 354 D-type Thunderbolts were built as P-47G by Curtiss-Wright at Buffalo, and two of these were converted to TP-47G by the addition of a second seat forward of the first in a lengthened cockpit replacing one of the fuselage tanks.

In addition to serving with the USAAF in all active theatres except Alaska, and with the R.A.F., the P-47D flew in the colours of the Soviet Air Force and the Free French forces. Five hundred and ninety of the second-series Ds were supplied to the R.A.F. and 100 to Russia. Operationally the P-47D was of more consequence in a ground attack role than as an escort fighter, and its effectiveness in this respect was enhanced on the P-47D-30 and later models by the introduction of shackles for 10 rocket projectile launchers beneath the wings.

Several prototype models of the Thunderbolt appeared between 1942 and 1944, including one which exceeded 500 m.p.h. in level flight. The last of the P-47Bs (41-6065) was fitted with a pressurized cabin and re-designated XP-47E, and another B (41-5938) was provided with a pair of laminar-flow wings as the XP-47F. Two P-47Ds (42-23297 and 42-23298) served as test-beds for the 2,300 h.p. Chrysler XIV-2220-1 sixteen-cylinder inverted-Vee engine and were designated XP-47H. The single XP-47J (43-46952) was a careful attempt to obtain the highest possible performance from the Thunderbolt, using the 2,100 h.p. R-2800-57 engine, fan cooled and with the intake for the CH-5 supercharger separated from the engine cowling and moved aft. To keep the weight down, two guns were removed. On August 4, 1944, this aircraft reached 504 m.p.h., the highest then recorded by a piston-engined aircraft. An attempt to obtain greater range on internal tankage produced the XP-47L (42-76614), a P-47D with a larger fuselage tank.

For service in Europe, where the advent of German jet and rocket-propelled fighters and V-1 Flying Bomb attacks on Britain in 1944/45 demanded higher performances from Allied fighters, Republic converted three P-47Ds at the end of 1944 into YP-47Ms (42-27385, 86 and 88). These had "sprint" engines, the R-2800-57 with a CH-5 turbo-super-charger to boost the power to 2,800 h.p. above 30,000 ft. Underwing racks were removed as this was intended only as a fighter, and with the weight at 14,700 lb., a top speed of 470 m.p.h. at 30,000 ft. was recorded. Production of 130 P-47Ms was completed in 1945, and most of these reached Europe for action in France and Germany in the closing stages of the war.

The final version of the Thunderbolt was produced solely for service in the Pacific area, and had the greatest range of any P-47 model. The prototype of this version, XP-47N, was also a P-47D conversion (42-27387). The significant difference between the "M" and "N" lay in the wing, which in the latter had an 18-inch greater span and was strengthened to carry two 93-gallon tanks internally in addition to the two drop tanks. Including the internal fuselage tankage and the 100-gallon belly drop tank, the P-47N had a total tankage of 1,266 gallons and a range of 2,350 miles. The engine was an R-2800-77, the dorsal fin was larger than that on the P-47D, and the weight rose to 21,200 lb. It reached squadrons in the Pacific area in 1945, and flew escort missions with B-29 Superfortresses attacking the Japanese mainland in the closing stages of the War.

Republic built 1,667 P-47Ns at Farmingdale, and another 149 at Evansville before the VJ Day cancellation of 5,934 Thunderbolts brought

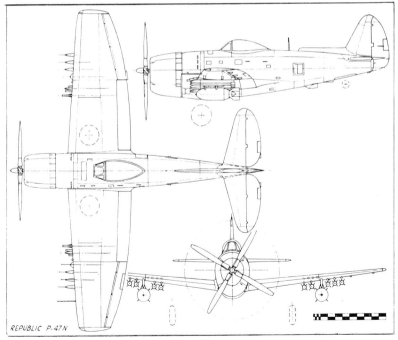

REPUBLIC P-47N

production of the type abruptly to an end. Of the grand total of 15,683 P-47s built, approximately two-thirds reached operational commands overseas, and 5,222 were lost in action including 1,723 non-combat losses. In 1·35 million combat hours flown, the combat loss rate per sortie was less than 0·7 per cent, an exceptionally low figure.

Thunderbolts of the P-47D and P-47N variety remained in service with USAF units for a number of post-war years, as initial equipment for some SAC, TAC and ADC squadrons. Eventually they reached Air National Guard squadrons, from which, after being redesignated F-47D and F-47N in 1948, they finally passed out of service in 1955.

TECHNICAL DATA (P-47)

MANUFACTURER: Republic Aviation Corp., Long Island, New York; and Evansville, Indiana. Curtiss-Wright Corp., Buffalo, N.Y.
TYPE: Single-seat escort fighter and fighter-bomber.
ACCOMMODATION: Pilot in enclosed cockpit.

	P-47B	P-47C/D/G	P-47D-25	P-47M	P-47N
Power Plant:	2,000 h.p. R-2800-21	2,000 h.p. R-2800-21	2,300 h.p. R-2800-59	2,800 h.p. R-2800-57	2,800 h.p. R-2800-77
Dimensions:					
Span, ft., in.	40 9	40 9	40 9	40 9	42 7
Length, ft., in.	35 0	36 1	36 1	36 4	36 1
Height, ft., in.	12 8	14 2	14 2	14 9	14 8
Wing area, sq. ft.	300	300	300	308	322
Weights:					
Empty, lb.	9,346	9,900	10,000	10,423	11,000
Gross, lb.	13,360	14,925	19,400	15,500	20,700
Performance:					
Max speed, m.p.h./ft.	429/27,800	433/30,000	428/30,000	473/32,000	467/32,500
Cruising speed, m.p.h.	335	350	—	—	300
Climb, min./ft.	6·7/15,000	11/20,000	9/20,000	13·4/32,000	14·2/25,000
Service ceiling, ft.	42,000	42,000	42,000	41,000	43,000
Range, st. miles	550	—	475	530	800
Armament:	8 × 0·50-in.	8 × 0·50-in. 1 × 500 lb.	8 × 0·50-in. 2 × 1,000lb.	8 × 0·50-in.	8 × 0·50-in. 2 × 1,000lb.

SERIAL NUMBERS:

XP-47B: 40-3051.
P-47B: 41-5895/6065.
P-47C: 41-6066/6667.
P-47D-RA: 42-22250/23299;
   42-27389/29466; 43-25254/25753;
   44-32668/33867; 44-89684/90483;
   45-49090/49554.

P-47D-RE: 42-7853/8702;
   42-25274/27388; 42-74615/76614;
   44-19558/21107.
P-47G-CU: 42-24920/25273.
XP-47J: 43-46952.
P-47M-RE: 44-21108/21237.
P-47N-RA: 45-49975/50123.
P-47N-RE: 44-87784/89450.

Republic YP-84A (*Harold G. Martin*).

Republic F-84 Thunderjet, Thunderstreak and Thunderflash

The Thunderjet—conceived as a jet successor to the Thunderbolt in 1944—was the last of the subsonic straight-wing fighter-bombers to see operational service with the USAF. In addition to giving valuable service in Korea, it was the aircraft with which flight-refuelling techniques for fighters were developed, and the first single-seat fighter-bomber capable of carrying a tactical nuclear weapon. As the Republic AP-23, it was designed around the General Electric TG-180 (J35) turbojet.

Three prototypes and 100 production models of the Republic fighter, which had been designated the P-84, were ordered early in 1945, and the first XP-84 first flew from Muroc A.F.B. on February 28, 1946. The second XP-84 flew in August 1946 and a month later established a U.S. national speed record of 611 m.p.h. Both these aircraft had a 3,750 lb. s.t. General Electric J35-GE-7 turbojet. This engine was also specified for the first 25 of the first production batch, which were to have been known as YP-84, but the 4,000 lb. s.t. Allison-built J35-A-15 was fitted instead in the third prototype as XP-84A and in all the initial production aircraft, and the first 15 were allocated as service trials aircraft designated YF-84A. These were similar to the prototypes but had provision for wing-tip fuel tanks, and mounted six 0·50-inch M2 machine guns, four in the upper front fuselage and two in the wings.

In the P-84B, which was the first operational model, the M3 machine guns were used, with a higher rate of fire, and the armament was supplemented by eight retractable rocket launchers beneath the wing after the first 85 aircraft had been built. This model, of which Republic built a total of 226, also had an ejection seat for the pilot; the engine was a 4,000 lb. s.t.

Republic P-84B in Germany (*Victor D. Seely*).

Allison J35-A-15C and the gross weight 14,100 lb. Delivery of the P-84B began in the summer of 1947 to the 14th Fighter Group at Dow Field, and the designation was changed to F-84B on June 11, 1948.

Small changes distinguished the second production model, the P-84C (later F-84C), which was powered by the 4,000 lb. s.t. J35-A-13C engine and had a new electrical system. Production totalled 191, followed by 154 F-84Ds in which a number of new features were introduced. These included a thicker skin gauge on wings and ailerons, winterized fuel system suitable for JP4, and mechanical linkages instead of hydraulic in the landing gear to shorten the shock strut during retraction. The gross weight increased to 16,100 lb. in the F-84C and 16,800 lb. in the F-84D, and the "C" entered service with the 20th FG, Shaw A.F.B. in 1948.

The F-84E was the first version of the Thunderjet to arrive in Korea, where it was in service with the 27th Fighter-Escort Wing by December 1950, joined later by F-84Ds. The F-84E (843 built, of which 100 were for NATO air forces) had a radar gun-sight, improved wing-tip tanks for combat use and a 12-in fuselage extension to increase comfort in the cockpit. The fuel system was modified to allow a 230 U.S. gallon tank to be carried under each inner wing on the bomb shackles and the 5,000 lb.s.t J35-A-17D engine was used. Although serving primarily as fighter-bombers with TAC from 1947 onwards, the F-84s were initially assigned B-29 escort duties in Korea, in the course of which they engaged in frequent combat with MiG-15s. Later in the Korean War, the F-84s engaged increasingly in ground attack operations, flying with the 136th Fighter-Bomber Wing. Fifty-nine F-84s were used on

Republic P-84E in Korea with 136th FB Wing (*USAF photo 8139AC*).

May 13, 1953, for an attack on the Toksan irrigation dam, and on May 16, 90 Thunderjets struck the Chusan irrigation dam—two attacks described as "perhaps the most spectacular of the War."

In November 1950, TAC began development of the F-84 to carry nuclear bombs for tactical warfare, and by the spring of 1952 the Thunderjet was the first single-seat fighter-bomber with atomic capability. The variant developed for this purpose was the F-84G, deliveries of which began in 1951. Apart from its revised armament, with up to 4,000 lb. of external stores, it introduced the 5,600 lb.s.t. J35-A-29 engine and had provision for Boeing-developed boom refuelling, with a receptacle in the port wing. Because longer missions were to be flown by the F-84G, an auto-pilot was fitted. The gross weight of both the F-84G and the 'E' model increased to 22,000 lb.

Having converted to a nuclear force, the 49th Air Division with one wing (the 20th FBW) of F-84Gs deployed overseas (to the U.K.) in 1952. In the same year came development of the low-altitude bombing system (LABS) to allow safe delivery of nuclear bombs from low altitudes. The F-84G also served with SAC, in whose hands it began making long-range refuelled flights in 1952. In the first such operation, Fox Peter One, F-84Gs of the 31st Fighter

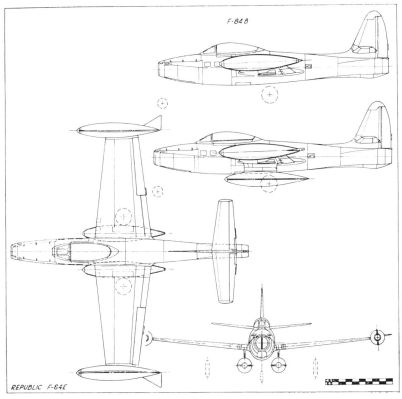

F-84 B

REPUBLIC F-84E

Republic F-84F (*Republic photo 3-8328*).

Escort Wing deployed from Turner A.F.B., Georgia, to the Far East in July 1952, refuelling twice from KB-29Ps en route. Fox Peter Two followed in October 1952 with the 27th Fighter Escort Wing, and in August 1953 as part of Operation Longstride the 508th F.E. Wing flew from Turner A.F.B. to the U.K. and the 31st F.E. Wing went to French Morocco, refuelling from KC-97s.

SAC's Flying Boom refuelling method had limitations for tactical use, and the development of the probe and drogue system by Flight Refuelling in England proved of great interest to TAC, which eventually adopted this system as standard on its fighters and converted B-29 and B-50 tankers. The first TAC fighters with probe equipment were two EF-84Es, converted in England; on September 22, 1950, Col. David C. Schilling completed the first non-stop jet Atlantic crossing in one of these aircraft (49-2091). The probe was located at mid-span on the port wing.

Production of the F-84G totalled 3,025 to bring the grand total of straight-wing Thunderjets to 4,455. Like the 100 F-84Es, 1,936 of the G models were purchased by the Air Force using MAP funds and went straight to NATO Air Forces on delivery. The "G" had been retired from SAC by 1956 but was still serving in considerable quantities with TAC. Most of the F84Es in FEAF and USAFE were eventually returned to the U.S. to equip ANG and AF reserve units.

Development of a swept-wing fighter-bomber based on the F-84 Thunderjet was begun by Republic at the end of 1949, at a time when USAF funds for new aircraft development were limited. By using some 60 per cent of Thunderjet tooling and a standard F-84E fuselage, a high-performance aircraft was offered by Republic at low cost, and the USAF sanctioned construction of a prototype, initially under the designation YF-96A. This aircraft (49-2430) flew on June 3, 1950, piloted by O. P. Hass, and had a 5,200-lb. s.t. Allison XJ35-A-25 engine. The designation was changed to YF-84F on September 8, 1950, and the name Thunderstreak was adopted.

When the Korean War made more funds available, the USAF took a new interest in the Republic venture, and suggested it should be redesigned round the Wright J65 Sapphire engine. A second YF-84F, with an imported YJ65-W-1 engine, flew on February 14, 1951. Production contracts had already been prepared and the first F-84F flew on November 22, 1952; deliveries to the USAF began in 1954, and units of both TAC and SAC were equipped, beginning with the 506th Strategic Fighter Wing in January. Production aircraft had the J65-W-1A or W-3 engine and, in later batches, an all-flying tail; the cockpit fairing was also re-designed. Production totalled 2,713, of which 237 were by General Motors at Kansas City and 1,301 were for NATO Air Forces.

Early in 1952 Republic developed a reconnaissance version of the Thunderstreak, with wing-root intakes and cameras in the nose. The new air intake arrangement was first flown on the third YF-84F, and then

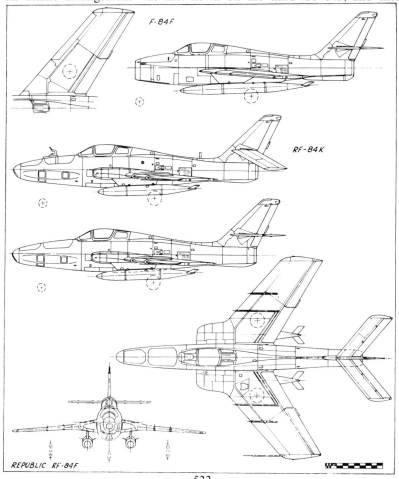

F-84F

RF-84K

REPUBLIC RF-84F

Republic RF-84F serving with the Arkansas ANG.

on the YRF-84F (51-1828), which retained the old Thunderjet-type canopy. This prototype flew in February 1952, piloted by Carl Bellinger; deliveries of the RF-84F to SAC and TAC reconnaissance units began in March 1954. Production of the RF version totalled 715 including 386 purchased by the Air Force for Mutual Defense programmes.

In 1953, the RF-84F was adapted for carriage by a B-36 in the FICON (Fighter Conveyor) project. Modifications comprised a retractable hook in the nose to contact the B-36 trapeze, and anhedral on the tailplane to clear the B-36 bomb bay. Early trials were made with the first YF-84F, and 25 RF-84Fs were subsequently modified, at first under the designation GRF-84F, which was later changed to RF-84K (52-7254/7278). These aircraft equipped the 91st Strategic Reconnaissance Squadron in 1955.

Another experimental programe in 1952/53, also aimed at increasing the range of escort fighters, involved the attachment of the fighters, wing tip to wing tip, to the bombers they were escorting. Two EF-84Bs (46-641 and 661) were adapted to link up with an ETB-29A (44-62093) but this three-plane combination crashed on April 24, 1953. Trials continued for a few months using two RF-84Fs (51-1848 and -1849) with an RB-36F (42-2707), but the project was abandoned before the end of 1953.

After F-84F and RF-84F operations by regular USAF squadrons ended, respectively in 1964 and 1958, many of these aircraft passed into service with

Republic RF-84K in SAC colours (*Howard Levy*).

534

the ANG, which finally disposed of its aircraft of this type during 1971 and 1972 respectively.

Experimental variants, extracted from F-84F production for modification, were two YF-84Js (51-1708/1709) with XJ73-GE-5 engine (first flight by Russell Roth on May 7, 1954) and two XF-84Hs (51-17059/17060). The latter—Republic Model AP.46, tentatively known as XF-106—each had a 5,850 h.p. XT40-A-1 turboprop and supersonic propeller for a joint USAF/USN research programme; the first flew on July 22, 1955, piloted by Henry G. Beaird.

TECHNICAL DATA (F-84, RF-84)

MANUFACTURER: Republic Aviation Corp., Long Island, New York and General Motors Corp., Kansas City.
TYPE: (F-84) Fighter, fighter-bomber.
    (RF-84) Reconnaisance.
ACCOMMODATION: Pilot in enclosed cockpit.

	F-84B	F-84G	F-84F	RF-84F
Power Plant:	3,750 lb. s.t. J35-A-15	5,600 lb. s.t. J35-A-29	7,220 lb. s.t. J65-W-3	7,800 lb. s.t. J65-W-7
Dimensions:				
Span, ft., in.	36 5	36 5	33 $7\frac{1}{4}$	33 $7\frac{1}{4}$
Length, ft., in.	37 5	38 1	43 $4\frac{3}{4}$	47 $7\frac{3}{4}$
Height, ft., in.	12 10	12 7	14 $4\frac{3}{4}$	15 0
Wing area, sq. ft.	260	260	325	325
Weights:				
Empty, lb.	9,538	11,095	—	14,025
Gross, lb.	19,689	23,525	28,000	27,000
Performance:				
Max. speed, m.p.h./ft.	587/4,000	622/0	695/35,000	620/0
Cruising speed, m.p.h.	436	483	—	542
Climb	4,210 ft./min.	9·4 min./ 35,000 ft.	8,200 ft./min.	8,000 ft./min.
Service ceiling, ft.	40,750	40,500	44,300	46,000
Range, miles	1,282	2,000	2,300	2,200
Armament:	4 × 0·50-in. 32 × 5-in. RP	6 × 0·50-in. 32 × 5-in. RP 2 × 1,000 lb.	6 × 0·50-in. 6,000 lb.	4 × 0·50-in.

SERIAL NUMBERS:
XP-84: 45-59475/59477.
YP-84A: 45-59482/59496.
P-84B: 45-59497/59581; 46-533/673.
F-84C: 47-1412/1602.
F-84D: 48-641/794.
F-84E: 49-2022/2429; 50-1111/1230; 50-1813/1837; 51-477/691; 51-9548/9622.
F-84G: 51-692/1343; 51-9623/11249; 51-16643/16751; 52-2893/3329; 52-8287/8486.

YF-84F: 49-2430; 51-1344/1345.
F-84F-RE: 51-1346/1827; 51-17059/17088; 52-6355/7228; 52-8767/9128; 52-10510/10538; 53-6532/7230.
F-84F-GK: 51-9311/9547.
RF-84F: 51-1828/1958; 51-11250/11297; 51-16996/17058; 52-7229/7475; 52-8717/8766; 53-7521/7697.

Republic F-105Ds in service with the 355th TFW in 1969 (*USAF photo*).

Republic F-105 Thunderchief

Declared operational in January 1959, the Thunderchief was the first supersonic tactical fighter-bomber developed from scratch, and was designed to succeed the F-84F. By 1961 it had become the primary equipment of Tactical Air Command in the combat strike role and was serving also in USAFE in Germany. Subsequently, the F-105 became one of the most important USAF weapons in Vietnam. Serving with the 388th and 355th TF Wings until late in 1970, the F-105 was used primarily in bombing attacks against North Vietnam.

First contracts for the F-105 were placed in 1954, and development was undertaken under the WS-306A weapon system designation. From the outset the aircraft was planned on massive lines, with an internal bomb-bay able to accommodate up to 8,000 lb. of nuclear or other weapons; in addition, as much as 4,000 lb. could be carried externally on four wing pylons and under the fuselage. A 20-mm. cannon provided the fixed armament. The wing was highly swept and incorporated low-speed ailerons and high-speed spoilers for lateral control and a droop-snoot leading edge. An unusual feature of the F-105 design (Republic AP-63) was the arrangement of the speed brakes as four segments of the rear jet-pipe fairing. All fuel was carried in the fuselage, with supplementary tanks in the bomb-bay or on the wing pylons as required.

With a gross weight of at least 45,000 lb., the F-105 required the most powerful engine available. At the time of prototype construction this was the J57-P-25, but only two aircraft of an initial test batch of 15 were completed with this engine before a change was made to the J75-P-3. Designated YF-105A, the first Thunderchief (54-0098) was flown by Russell M. Roth on October 22, 1955, exceeding Mach 1 on this flight. The second YF-105A (54-0099) was similar.

536

Introduction of the J75 changed the designation to F-105B. Other changes were made in this model too, including the use of a unique type of swept-forward air intake to control the shock-wave, and introduction of "area rule" on the fuselage. The first F-105B (54-0100) was flown on May 24, 1957, by Henry G. Beaird, Jr. and the remainder of the initial batch were delivered as F-105Bs, with varying standards of equipment. Three of this batch (Nos. 54-0105, 8 and 12) were completed as RF-105B (subsequently changed to JF-105B) with cameras in a redesigned nose to conform to the tactical photo-reconnaissance WS-306L system.

A total of 75 F-105Bs was built in addition to the three JF-105Bs, the first being delivered to the USAF on May 27, 1958. The first unit equipped was the 335th Tactical Fighter Squadron of the 4th T.F. Wing, which worked up on the type at Eglin A.F.B. before taking its aircraft to its permanent base at Seymour Johnson A.F.B. The other squadrons of the 4th T.F. Wing had been equipped by the end of 1960.

Following the F-105B in production in 1960, the F-105D was the definitive service version, with added all-weather capability derived from its General Electric FC-5 fully integrated automatic flight and fire control

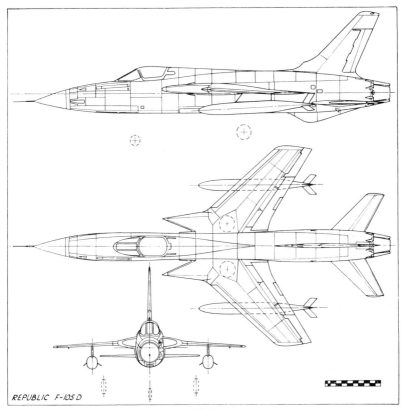

REPUBLIC F-105 D

Republic F-105D in original natural metal finish, with bombs on wing and fuselage racks (*Republic photo*).

system. This system comprised a toss bomb computer, a sight system, a doppler navigator, an air data computer, missile launch computer, autopilot and search and range radar (NASARR). The initial contract for 59 F-105Ds was increased to nearly 300 by the end of 1961, and "D" model Thunderchiefs were issued to the 4th Wing squadrons in addition to serving with the 4520th Combat Crew Training Wing at Nellis A.F.B. In mid-1961 F-105s began to reach squadrons of the 36th T.F. Wing at Bitburg, Germany, and in 1962, the 49th T.F. Wing in Germany and the 355th T.F. Wing in California re-equipped with the F-105D.

The F-105 had a retractable probe for in-flight refuelling from TAC KB-50s, and was one of the first types of aircraft to fly trial refuelling missions with a KC-135A adapted for the probe and drogue system. It could also carry tanks and equipment to serve as a tanker itself in buddy-buddy refuelling.

By the time President Johnson called a halt to the bombing of North Vietnam, seven squadrons of F-105Ds controlled by the 355th and 388th TFWs had borne the brunt of the *Rolling Thunder* campaign, and from the beginning of January 1965 to November 1, 1968 some 350 Thunderchiefs had been lost in combat or to operational causes. In 1969, the 388th TFW gave up its F-105Ds and the 355th returned with its aircraft to the U.S. in November 1970, bringing to an end the combat use of the single-seat version.

Still operating in Vietnam, however, were two-seat F-105Fs. Several two-seat versions of the Thunderchief had been projected, including the F-105C trainer and the F-105E fighter-bomber, but neither of these was built. The USAF did order, in May 1962, a fully operational mission trainer with an additional cockpit in a lengthened fuselage, and a taller fin. By contract amendment, the last 143 F-105Ds on order were changed to two-seat F-105Fs, reducing the total of "Ds" completed to 610, and the first "F" flew on June 11, 1963. Service introduction followed in December with the 4520th Combat Crew Training Wing at Nellis and the 4th TFW at Seymour-Johnson.

T-Stick II conversion of Republic F-105D (*Republic photo B17001*).

The successful deployment in Vietnam of a handful of *Wild Weasel* North American F-100Fs equipped to locate, classify and attack enemy ground-based radar sites led to a more ambitious programme to equip F-105Fs for the *Wild Weasel* role. Starting in 1965, 86 of the 143 F-105Fs built were modified to *Wild Weasel* III configuration, and the first 13 of these were deployed to Vietnam in mid-1966. Fourteen of the WW F-105Fs were further modified to carry and launch Standard ARM Mod0 anti-radar missiles, and then between November 1968 and June 1969 another 16 aircraft were modified to launch the General Dynamics AGM-78B, an improved ARM. In other programmes, a few F-105Fs code-named *Combat Martin* carried QRC-128 VHF jammers to block communications between MiGs and their GCI centres, and others under the *Commando Nail* programme had modified R-14A radar for sharper target definition and flew hazardous all-weather low-level bombing missions. Six each of these two groups of F-105Fs were brought into the *Wild Weasel* programme in mid-1971, by which time 60 of the two-seaters were being modified to F-105G standard with AGM-78B capability plus other improvements.

Republic F-105F, with tandem cockpits.

539

Another modification to improve the Thunderchief's visual bombing accuracy began in 1966, and involved 30 F-105Ds. Fitted with AN/ARN-92 LORAN for more precise navigating, these aircraft were known as Thunderstick (or T-Stick) IIs and could be identified by a long dorsal spine from the canopy to the fin. The first flight was made on August 9, 1969. They served with the 23rd TFW in the U.S. but did not see combat.

Phase-out of the F-105Ds by the active Air Force allowed more ANG units to receive the Thunderchief, two squadrons having equipped on F-105Bs in 1964. One AFRES squadron also flew "Bs" and two more received "Ds". When the ceasefire in Vietnam ended operational use of the WW F-105Fs and F-105Gs by the 17th WW Squadron, the remaining examples of the latter variant were operated in the U.S. by the 35th TFW until they also passed to the ANG. Guard use of the two-seat Thunderchief ended in 1983 and the last AFRES unit to operate the F-105D, the 466th TFS, made the last flight with the type on February 25, 1984.

TECHNICAL DATA (F-105D)

MANUFACTURER: The Republic Aviation Corporation, Farmingdale, Long Island, New York.

TYPE: Long range tactical fighter-bomber.

ACCOMMODATION: Pilot in enclosed cockpit.

POWER PLANT: One 16,100 lb. (dry) or 24,500 lb.s.t. (with a/b) Pratt & Whitney J75-P-19W turbojet.

DIMENSIONS: Span, 34 ft. 11 in. Length, 64 ft. 5 in. Height, 19 ft. 8 in. Wing area, 385 sq. ft.

WEIGHTS: Empty, 26,855 lb. Gross, 52,550 lb.

PERFORMANCE: Max. speed, 1,390 m.p.h. at 38,000 ft.(cruising speed, 584 m.p.h. at 38,000 ft.) Initial climb, 34,500 ft./min. Service ceiling, 41,200 ft. Tactical radius, 780 miles.

ARMAMENT: One General Electric 20-mm. M-61 Vulcan multi-barrel gun and over 14,000 lb. of external stores including ASMs, bombs, rocket pods, etc.

SERIAL NUMBERS:
YF-105A: 54-098/099.
F-105B: 54-100/112; 57-5776/5840.
F-105F: 62-4412/4447; 63-8260/8366.

F-105D: 58-1146/1173; 59-1717/1774; 59-1817/1826; 60-409/535; 60-5374/5385; 61-041/220; 62-4217/4411.

Republic F-105G "Wild Weasel", 561st TFS (*MAP photo*).

540

Rockwell B-1B at take-off, wings fully forward (*Rockwell photo*).

Rockwell B-1

In June 1970, the USAF selected, from a number of design submissions, a proposal by Rockwell International to meet its requirement for an Advanced Manned Strategic Aircraft (AMSA). This acronym had been adopted in 1965, in succession to several others used in the preceding few years, to identify a new bomber to succeed the Boeing B-52. As conceived in 1965, it was to have the ability to penetrate enemy defences and deliver stand-off or lay-down weapons, with supersonic performance at high altitude and high subsonic low-altitude penetration speed. Comprehensive offensive and defensive avionics were to be carried, as well as a large internal weapons load including rotary launchers for the Boeing SRAM. General Electric was selected to provide the power plant, a new turbofan designated F101.

Plans to order five prototypes of the Rockwell B-1, as the new bomber was to be designated, were modified in January 1971 in a cost-cutting exercise that eliminated two of the flying prototypes as well as one static test specimen, and 13 of the 40 test engines. Later, one of the prototypes was restored, allowing work to proceed on four, while plans were made to order 240 operational B-1s.

In its day the largest aircraft to feature variable wing sweepback, the first B-1 made its maiden flight at Palmdale, California, on December 23, 1974. First flight dates for the other three aircraft were April 1 (the No. 3 B-1) and June 14, 1976 (No. 2), and February 14, 1979 (No. 4). In June 1977, however, the B-1 production programme had been cancelled in its entirety following the election of President Carter. Research and development flying by the four prototypes was allowed to continue, and the ability of the aircraft to fly at Mach 2.2 was demonstrated in October 1978. This programme came to an end on April 29, 1981 with a final flight by No. 4, by which time the combined total of test hours flown had reached 1,895 hours.

Interest in a long-range manned bomber re-emerged in the late 'seventies and a variant of the original B-1 design gained favour to meet the USAF's

Rockwell B-1B with wings swept back (*Rockwell photo*).

requirement for a Long-range Combat Aircraft (LRCA). The inclusion of such an aircraft in a Triad of strategic nuclear forces (together with ground-launched and submarine-launched ballistic missiles) became one of the planks of Ronald Reagan's presidential campaign in 1981 and following his election, a go-ahead was announced on October 2, 1981 for production of 100 Rockwell B-1Bs. The four B-1 prototypes then were retrospectively designated B-1As, and aircraft Nos. 2 and 4 were brought into the B-1B development programmes. First flights of these aircraft in their new rôle, and after modification, were made on March 23, 1983 and July 30, 1984 respectively, but No. 2 was lost on August 29, 1984.

Few external differences distinguished the B-1B from the B-1A, but the operational concept was quite different. Whereas the latter had been expected to be able to penetrate defended enemy airspace to deliver nuclear or conventional bombs, the B-1B was to be primarily a cruise missile carrier, launching its missiles a considerable distance from the target and perhaps even outside of the ring of defences. Less emphasis was placed on supersonic performance, the max. speed being reduced to Mach = 1.25. This made it possible to design for a higher gross weight and to adopt fixed, rather than variable, engine inlets. Much greater flexibility of weapons loading was provided through internal modifications and the addition of external hard points for missiles, bombs or tanks. Careful attention to external detail allowed the radar cross-section of the B-1B to be reduced to only one tenth of that for the B-1A, despite its identical dimensions. General Electric F101 engines were retained, in an imroved variant.

Built to production standards from the outset, the first B-1B flew at Palmdale on October 18, 1984 and was permanently assigned as a test aircraft. The second aircraft flew on May 4, 1985, and service induction began on July 7, 1985, when this aircraft arrived at Dyess A.F.B., Abilene, Texas. At Dyess, the 337th Bombardment Squadron of the 96th Bomb Wing received the first 15 B-1Bs, in order to bring the aircraft up to IOC status, achieved in

September 1986. Fourteen more B-1Bs made up the complement of the 96th BW, with remaining aircraft shared between the 28th BW at Ellsworth A.F.B., Rapid City, South Dakota (35 aircraft), the 319th BW at Grand Forks A.F.B., North Dakota (17 aircraft) and the 384th BW at McConnell A.F.B., Wichita, Kansas (17 aircraft). Production of the B-1B was completed in 1988.

TECHNICAL DATA (B1B)

MANUFACTURER: Rockwell International Corp., North American Aircraft Operations, El Segundo and Palmdale, California.

TYPE: Long-range strategic bomber.

ACCOMMODATION: Pilot, co-pilot and two systems operators (offensive and defensive).

POWER PLANT: Four 30,750 lb.s.t. (with reheat) General Electric F101-GE-102 turbofans.

DIMENSIONS: Span (swept), 78 ft. 2½ in. Span (spread), 136 ft. 8½ in. Length, 147 ft. 0 in. Height, 33 ft. 7¼ in. Wing area, 1,950 sq. ft.

WEIGHTS: Empty, 192,000 lb. Gross, 477,000 lb.

PERFORMANCE: Max. speed, 792 m.p.h. at 50,000 ft. Cruising speed, over 500 m.p.h. at 200 ft. Combat ceiling, about 60,000 ft. Range, 7,455 miles.

ARMAMENT: Three internal weapons bays to carry up to eight Boeing AGM-86B ALCMs or 24 Boeing AGM-69B SRAMs, or 12 B-28 or 24 B-61 or B-83 free-fall nuclear bombs or 84 Mk 82 (500-lb) or 24 Mk 84 (2,000 lb) bombs. Eight external store stations under fuselage to carry 14 AGM-86B or AGM-69B, eight B-28, 14 B-61/B-83, 14 Mk 84 or 44 Mk 82.

SERIAL NUMBERS:
B-1A: 74-0158/0160; 76-0174.
B-1B: 82-0001; 83-0065/0071;
84-0049/0058; 85-0059/0092;
86-0093/0140.

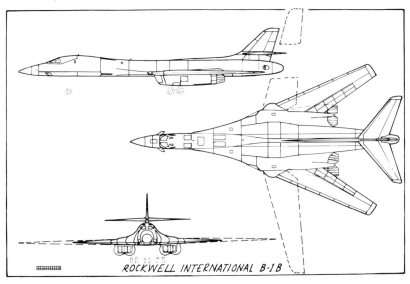

ROCKWELL INTERNATIONAL B-1B

Ryan PT-21 for civilian-operated training school (*Ryan photo*).

Ryan PT-16, PT-20, PT-21, PT-22

When the U.S. embarked upon the massive expansion of its Army and Navy air forces in 1940/41, three companies—Ryan, Stearman and Vultee —were designated to produce the standardized primary and basic trainers upon which the new flying personnel were to receive their training. The Ryan aeroplane for this programme was the PT-22, one of a series of low-wing trainers built by the company for the Army. The first of the series was the PT-16, a militarized version of the Ryan S-T which, in turn, was the aeroplane with which T. Claude Ryan re-entered the aircraft manufacturing business in 1933 after a six-year absence.

The Ryan S-T was a low-wing monoplane with external wire bracing to the top of the fuselage and to the main undercarriage legs. Open cockpits in tandem had dual controls and duplicated basic flight instrumentation. Construction was primarily of metal, with wooden wing spars. Until 1939, all Army primary trainers had been biplanes; the purchase of a single Model STA-1 as the XPT-16 (39-717) was therefore a significant event.

To permit a more thorough evaluation of the Ryan trainer, 15 YPT-16s were purchased a few months later. Like the prototype, they were delivered with the 125 h.p. Menasco L-365-1 in-line engine, with the addition of an engine starter.

The success of trials with the YPT-16s, which were used at the Ryan-operated school at San Diego during the latter months of 1939, led to a further contract in 1940 for 40 of a basically similar model designated PT-20. The principal outward difference was a larger cockpit with external stiffening in the cockpit area. Both the PT-16 and the PT-20 used the standard S-T wheel and tail fairings. These were very troublesome in

544

Ryan PT-20 in original form (*Ryan photo*).

service and were soon removed.

During 1941 the Menasco engine was discarded by the Army in favour of the Kinner R-440 radial. The installation of the new engine in the Ryan trainer, in a streamlined nose fairing with projecting, uncowled cylinders, resulted in the Model ST-3, ordered in 1941 as the PT-21; 100 were purchased. The PT-21s had the 132 h.p. Kinner R-440-3 engine. Some earlier Ryan trainers in service were re-engined with R-440-1s of similar power, these being designated PT-16A (14 delivered) and PT-20A (27) respectively when so re-engined. Three PT-20Bs, also modified PT-20s, retained Menasco D-4 commercial engines.

The advent of the Army–Navy trainer standardization programme co-incided with the development by Ryan of a more powerful variant, the ST-3, with a 160 h.p. Kinner R-540-1. Orders for this new model, desig-nated PT-22 and named Recruit under the World War II practice of applying popular names to military aircraft, totalled 1,023, all placed in 1941. These were delivered without the wheel spats used on earlier models, and also without the complete main leg fairings, but were otherwise identical with the PT-21. The PT-22s went into service at civilian-operated schools throughout the country, including the Ryan-operated schools at San Diego and Tucson.

Quantities of the Ryan trainers were also built for export and one export contract, for 25 ST-3s for the Netherlands, was taken over by the Army in 1942, these aircraft being designated PT-22A. The designation PT-22C applied to 250 PT-22s modified after delivery to have R-540-3 engines.

Production of the PT-22 ended in 1942. In that year, Ryan was asked to investigate the production of a version of the trainer constructed of non-strategic materials. The resultant design, the ST-4, was virtually a new aeroplane, and was built almost wholly of plastic-bonded wood. Five examples were delivered to the Air Force in 1942/43 as YPT-25s.

545

TECHNICAL DATA (YPT-16)

MANUFACTURER: Ryan Aeronautical Co., San Diego, California.
TYPE: Primary trainer.
ACCOMMODATION: Pupil and instructor in tandem open cockpit.
POWER PLANT: One 125 h.p. Menasco L-365-1 piston Vee in-line.
DIMENSIONS: Span, 30 ft. 0 in. Length, 21 ft. 6 in. Height, 10 ft. 1 in. Wing area, 124 sq. ft.
WEIGHTS: Empty, 1,100 lb. Gross, 1,600 lb.
PERFORMANCE: Max. speed, 128 m.p.h. Climb, 15·0 min. to 10,000 ft. Service ceiling, 15,000 ft. Range, 350 st. miles.
ARMAMENT: None.
SERIAL NUMBERS:

XPT-16: 39-717.
YPT-16: 40-040/054.
PT-20: 40-2387/2416.
PT-21: 41-1881/1980.

PT-22: 41-15173/15745; 41-20591/21040.
PT-22A: 42-57479/57503.
YPT-25: 42-8703/8707.

Below, top side view shows PT-20

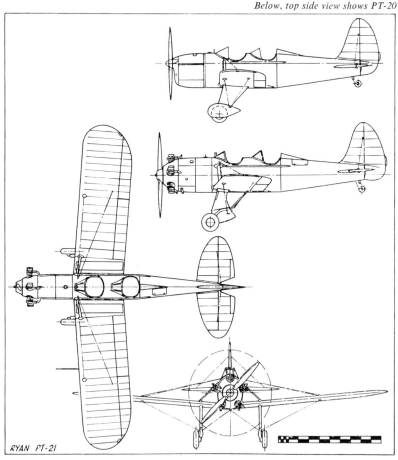

RYAN PT-21

Camouflaged Seversky P-35 in 1943 (*Peter M. Bowers*).

Seversky P-35

Seversky had produced, in 1935, a privately-financed experimental fighter, the two-seat SEV-2XP. First flown early in 1935, it was rebuilt after an accident as a single-seater (SEV-1XP) and submitted in August 1935 for Army Air Corps evaluation. Redesigned by Alexander Kartveli, the company's chief designer, as the SEV-7 or AP-1 it was again tested at Wright Field in April 1936, with a Twin Wasp engine replacing the original Cyclone. In this form, the AP-1 was accepted and a production contract for 77 P-35s was placed at the end of 1936.

The design of the P-35 was based on a low-mounted elliptical wing. The main wheels of the undercarriage retracted backwards into the wings with the lower half projecting and the Pratt & Whitney R-1830-9 two-row radial engine was tightly cowled. The armament comprised one 0·50-inch and one 0·30-inch machine gun in the engine cowling. Seversky delivered 76 P-35s and the last aircraft on the contract (36-430) was completed as the XP-41, having a revised wing and a 1,200-h.p. R-1830-19 engine with a turbo-supercharger. Delivered in 1938, the XP-41 (Seversky AP-4) was in effect the prototype for the Republic P-43 (see page 520).

Following completion of the P-35 production, the company (as Republic) developed an export version of the P-35 and in June 1939 it succeeded in selling this variant to the Royal Swedish Air Force, which ordered 120. This aircraft was identified as the EP-1-06 and was designated J9 by Flygvapnet. Delivery to Sweden began in 1939 but was suspended in the middle of 1940 when restrictions were imposed on the export of arms. Republic continued production of the EP-1-06, however, and on October 24, 1940, President Roosevelt signed an order requisitioning all the undelivered EP-1-06s—a total of 60. These were designated P-35A.

The P-35A differed from the P-35 in having a 1,200-h.p. R-1830-45 engine and one 0·30-inch gun in each wing. Despite the higher gross

547

weight (6,035 lb. compared with 5,600 lb.) the P-35A was nearly 30 m.p.h faster than the P-35.

By the end of 1941, 48 of the P-35As had reached the Philippines, where they were surprised on the ground in the first Japanese attack on December 8. Forty of the P-35As were lost in two days, mostly on the ground but a few in air combat, and this action marked both the operational debut and the last action of the type.

TECHNICAL DATA (P-35A)

MANUFACTURER: Republic Aviation Corporation, Long Island, New York.
TYPE: Single-seat pursuit.
ACCOMMODATION. Pilot in enclosed cockpit.
POWER PLANT. One 1,050-h.p. Pratt & Whitney R-1830-45 piston radial.
DIMENSIONS: Span, 36 ft. 0 in. Length, 26 ft. 10 in. Height, 9 ft. 9 in. Wing area, 220 sq. ft.
WEIGHTS: Empty, 4,575 lb. Gross, 6,723 lb.
PERFORMANCE: Max. speed, 290 m.p.h. at 12,000 ft. Cruising speed, 260 m.p.h. Initial climb, 1,920 ft./min. Service ceiling, 31,400 ft. Range, 950 st. miles.
ARMAMENT: Two 0·50-in. and two 0·30-in. fixed forward-firing guns. 350 lb. of bombs beneath wings.
SERIAL NUMBERS:
P-35: 36-354/429.   P-35A: 41-17434/17493.

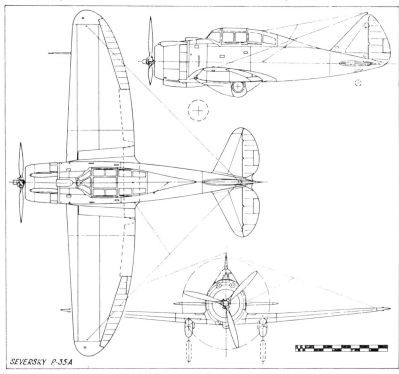

SEVERSKY P-35A

Sikorsky R-4B in all-yellow finish (*Peter M. Bowers*).

Sikorsky R-4

As the first helicopter produced for any of the U.S. armed forces in other than experimental quantities, the R-4 (Vought Sikorsky Model 316A) is historically significant although its achievements in service were far outshone by later Sikorsky machines. A contract for the development of an experimental helicopter, designated XR-4, was awarded to the Vought-Sikorsky Division of United Aircraft in 1941 following Igor I. Sikorsky's successful demonstration of helicopter flight in his VS-300 from September 14, 1939. The XR-4 design retained the single-rotor layout of the VS-300 but introduced a faired fuselage with side-by-side seating for the crew of two and full dual controls.

A 165 h.p. Warner R-500-3 engine was mounted in the fuselage of the XR-4, and drove both the main rotor and the anti-torque tail rotor through transmission shafts and gear boxes. Flying controls set a standard from which there has been little deviation in subsequent helicopters; they comprised the cyclic pitch lever, which controlled variation of the pitch of the main rotor blades in the course of a single revolution for forward or backward flight; the collective pitch lever, varying the pitch of all main rotor blades simultaneously for vertical flight control; and the rudder pedals controlling the pitch of the tail rotor blades.

The XR-4 made its first flight on January 14, 1942, and was subsequently flown in easy stages from Stratford, Conn. to Wright Field, Dayton—the World's first long-distance helicopter cross-country flight. In 1943 it was re-engined with a 180 h.p. Warner R-550-1 engine and the original 36-ft. diameter main rotor was replaced by one of 38 ft. diameter; the designation was then changed to XR-4C.

For further service trials, the USAAF ordered 30 more R-4s, of which the first three were designated YR-4A and the remainder YR-4B. These models introduced the 38-ft. diameter rotor and 180 h.p. R-550-1 engine. Gross weight increased from the prototype's 2,450 lb. to 2,900 lb. and the top speed fell from 102 m.p.h. to 75 m.p.h. The YR-4Bs were extensively tested under many and varied conditions, including tropical trials in

Burma and winterization trials in Alaska. After trials in May 1943 with an AAF YR-4B operating from a small platform on a tanker three aircraft were allocated to the U.S. Coast Guard, and seven more were sent to Britain for use by the R.A.F.

Final variant of the series was the R-4B, AAF contracts for which totalled 100. This production variant had the 200 h.p. R-550-3 engine and greater range but was otherwise similar to the YR-4B. Twenty were supplied to the Coast Guard and 45 to Britain.

TECHNICAL DATA (YR-4B)

MANUFACTURER: Sikorsky Aircraft Division, United Aircraft Corporation, Bridgeport, Conn.
TYPE: General purpose helicopter.
ACCOMMODATION: Crew of two side-by-side in enclosed cabin.
POWER PLANT: One 180-h.p. Warner R-550-1 or -3 piston radial.
DIMENSIONS: Rotor diameter, 38 ft. 0 in. Length, 48 ft. 2 in. Height, 12 ft. 5 in. Disc area, 1,134 sq. ft.
WEIGHTS: Empty, 2,020 lb. Gross, 2,535 lb
PERFORMANCE: Max. speed, 75 m.p.h. Climb, 45 min. to 8,000 ft. Service ceiling, 8,000 ft. Range, 130 st. miles.
ARMAMENT: Nil.
SERIAL NUMBERS:
XR-4: 41-18874.
YR-4A: 42-107234/107236.
YR-4B: 42-107237/107248; 43-28223/28235; 43-28247; 43-47953.
R-4B: 43-46500/46599.

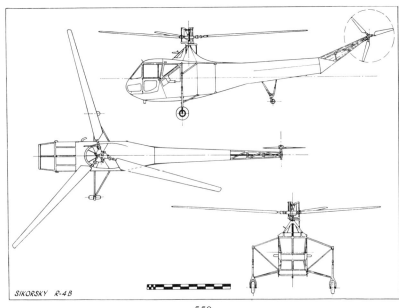

SIKORSKY R-4B

550

All-yellow Sikorsky R-5D for Air Rescue Service, with loudspeaker horn on rear fuselage
(*William Larkins*).

Sikorsky R-5

Based on the successful development and flight trials of the R-4 training helicopter, the USAAF wrote a requirement for a rather larger type capable of performing a useful military job as an observation machine. The Vought-Sikorsky Model 327 which was designed to this specification followed closely the general layout of the R-4, with main and tail rotors shaft-driven from an engine in the fuselage, but it was a completely new design in detail. Four prototypes were ordered early in 1943 with the designation XR-5 and a fifth was ordered later. The first XR-5 flew on August 18, 1943, at Bridgeport, Conn. Powered by a 450-h.p. Pratt & Whitney R-985-AN-5 engine, it had a 48-ft. diameter rotor and grossed 4,850 lb. The crew of two was seated in tandem. Two of the five prototypes were later fitted with British equipment and designated XR-5A.

For service trials, USAAF ordered 26 YR-5As, similar to the prototypes, and 100 R-5As, of which only the first 34 were built. The R-5As had provision for litter carriers on each side of the fuselage, and were the first helicopters to go into use with the Air Rescue Service. Twenty-one R-5As (43-46606 and 43-46640/59) became R-5Ds when modified to carry a second passenger and fitted with a rescue hoist, auxiliary external fuel tank, and a nose-wheel. The five YR-5Es (43-46611/15) were YR-5As modified to have dual control.

From the R-5 design, Sikorsky evolved the S-51 commercial helicopter (first flown on February 16, 1946), with a 49-ft. rotor, four seats in the cabin, nose-wheel in place of tail wheel and gross weight increased to 6,200 lb. USAF procured 11 aircraft of this type in 1947, designated R-5F.

In June 1948, USAF helicopters were re-categorized with "H" in place of "R" designations, resulting in YH-5A, H-5A, H-5D, YH-5E and H-5F designations appearing for the Sikorsky types. To supplement the H-5As used by the Air Rescue Service and to expand this work, 39 more helicopters were purchased in 1948. Designated H-5G, they were similar

551

to the H-5F with rescue hoist and other equipment for their specialized role. The 16 H-5Hs purchased in 1949 had a combination wheel/pontoon undercarriage and gross weight of 6,500 lb.

In service until the mid-fifties, the H-5 was used in a variety of roles of which rescue was the most prominent.

TECHNICAL DATA (R-5B)

MANUFACTURER: Sikorsky Aircraft Division of United Aircraft Corporation, Bridgeport, Connecticut.
TYPE: Rescue and general purpose helicopter.
ACCOMMODATION: Crew of two in tandem; two external litter carriers.
POWER PLANT: One 450 h.p. Pratt & Whitney R-985-AN-5.
DIMENSIONS: Rotor diameter, 48 ft. 0 in. Length, 57 ft. 1 in. Height, 13 ft. 0 in. Disc area, 1,810 sq. ft.
WEIGHTS: Empty, 3,780 lb. Gross, 4,825 lb.
PERFORMANCE: Max. speed, 106 m.p.h. Climb, 15 min. to 10,000 ft. Service ceiling 14,400 ft. Range, 360 st. miles.
ARMAMENT: Nil.
SERIAL NUMBERS:
XR-5: 43-28236/28239; 43-47954.
YR-5A: 43-46600/46625.
R-5A: 43-46626/46659.
R-5F: 47-480/490.
H-5G: 48-524/562.
H-5H: 49-1996/2011.

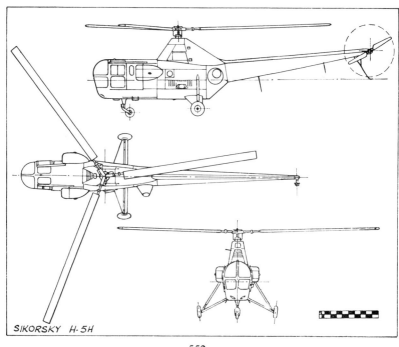

SIKORSKY H-5H

Sikorsky H-19B for MATS (*Sikorsky photo*).

Sikorsky H-19 Chickasaw

In continuation of the series of military helicopters begun with the R-4, Sikorsky designed a larger utility type during 1948, and secured a USAF contract to produce five for evaluation. These were designated YH-19 (Sikorsky S-55) and the first made its first flight at Bridgeport on November 10, 1949. Similar in general layout to the final models in the H-5 series, the H-19 had a novel engine arrangement, with the 550 h.p. R-1340 located in the nose so that the long extension shaft could be carried straight up to the main rotor gear drive.

As first flown, the YH-19's fuselage ended in a sharp step up to the boom carrying the tail rotor. This step was later filled by a triangular fin. Production model H-19As, ordered by the USAF in 1951, had two small fins forming an inverted V beneath the tail boom, whereas the YH-19s had a horizontal tailplane half with an endplate fin on the starboard side only.

After 50 H-19As, the USAF acquired 270 H-19Bs, in which the engine was changed from a 600-h.p. R-1340-57 to a 700-h.p. Wright R-1300-3. The H-19B was also the first model to have a new tail configuration with the boom angled down slightly, a wide-chord arm carrying the tail rotor, and small horizontal tabs without endplates. The diameter of the tail rotor was reduced. These changes were applied retroactively on many H-19As.

USAF used its H-19s primarily to equip MATS Air Rescue Squadrons, for which they were designated SH-19. For the rescue role, the SH-19s had a hydraulic-electric hoist mounted on the starboard side of the fuselage just above the door, with a 100-ft. cable and sling attached. Five Navy HO4Ss assigned to MATS were given USAF serials as H-19As; similarly, four HRS-3s became H-19Bs.

Starting in 1952, the U.S. Army obtained 72 H-19Cs and 338 H-19Ds, these two models being equivalent, respectively, to the USAF H-19A and H-19B. The name Chickasaw was given in the series of Indian tribal names used by the Army.

Mission prefixes were added to H-19 designations in 1962. The H-19B, C and D became UH-19B, C and D respectively and MATS' SH-19Bs became HH-19Bs.

TECHNICAL DATA (H-19B)

MANUFACTURER: Sikorsky Aircraft Division of United Aircraft Corporation, Stratford and Bridgeport, Conn.

TYPE: Utility helicopter.

ACCOMMODATION: Two crew and ten troops or six litters.

POWER PLANT: One 800-h.p. Wright R-1300-3 piston radial engine.

DIMENSIONS: Rotor diameter, 53 ft. 0 in. Fuselage length, 42 ft. 3 in. Height, 13 ft. 4 in. Disc area, 2,206 sq. ft.

WEIGHTS: Empty, 5,250 lb. Gross, 7,900 lb.

PERFORMANCE: Max. speed, 112 m.p.h. at sea level. Cruising speed, 91 m.p.h. Initial climb, 1,020 ft./min. Range, 360 st. miles.

SERIAL NUMBERS:

YH-19: 49-2012/2016.

H-19A: 51-3846/3895; 51-17662/17666.

H-19B: 51-3896/3968; 52-7479/7588; 52-7589/7600; 52-10991/10994; 53-4404/4464; 53-4878/4885; 56-6673/6674;

H-19C: 51-14242/14313.

H-19D: 52-7601/7625; 54-1408/1437; 55-3176; 55-3183/3228; 55-4937/4944; 55-4462/4504; 55-5235/5240; 56-1519/1568; 56-4246/4283; 57-1616/1641; 57-2553/2558; 57-5926/5982; 59-4973/4974.

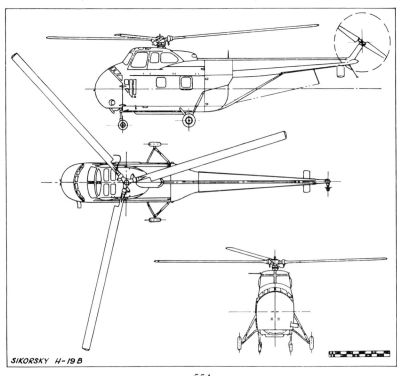

SIKORSKY H-19B

Sikorsky H-34A for Army Aviation (*Sikorsky photo 19356A*).

Sikorsky H-34 Choctaw

Many features of the H-19 were retained in the larger H-34 (Sikorsky S-58) which was originally developed to meet a U.S. Navy anti-submarine requirement. As the XHSS-1, the Navy prototype flew on March 8, 1954. The angled, front-fuselage mounting of the engine was retained, but the engine itself was the 1,425 h.p. Wright (Lycoming-built) R-1820. The fuselage design was wholly new, as were the transmission system and four-blade main and tail rotors.

Flight demonstration of the XHSS-1's performance, including the ability to carry 16 passengers or eight stretchers in the cabin, or a 5,000 lb. load slung under the fuselage, confirmed the U.S. Army's interest in the same basic type, for which preliminary contracts had been placed in 1953. No prototypes were built for the Army, which accepted its first ten H-34As at Bridgeport in April 1955 and delivered them to a number of bases in the U.S. for crew familiarization.

The first Army unit to be fully equipped with the H-34A was the 506th Helicopter Co. at Fort Benning in September 1955, with a complement of 21 helicopters. Other units followed, as several hundred H-34s were delivered. They were powered by the 1,425 h.p. R-1820-84 engine and operated at gross weights up to 13,600 lb. During 1960 and 1961, the H-34B and H-34C variants appeared, distinguished by small equipment changes and production line modifications. The mission prefix "C" was added to the designations in 1962.

By 1958, the H-34 was the principal Army transport helicopter and towards the end of that year it was deployed overseas with the U.S. Seventh Army Aviation Group in Germany. This Group, comprising two Battalions (the 56th and 8th) each with two H-34-equipped Light Helicopter Transportation Companies (the 36th, 59th, 110th and 111th) together with the only H-37A Medium Helicopter Transport Company (the 4th) outside the U.S., controlled all aviation units in the Seventh Army. Its H-34s provided mobility and flexibility on an unprecedented scale, and also became responsible for maintaining a constant patrol along the West German border with Czechoslovakia and East Germany.

Some Air Force Reserve units received ex-USN HH-34Ds (originally HUS-1s), which were given FY60, 61 and 63 serials, and HH-34Js (originally HSS-1s) which used the five-digit BuNo serials. For supply through MDAP, 21 H-34As were modified to CH-34Cs and given new serials, a few of these being eventually repossessed by the U.S. Army. Also for MDAP were 23 ex-USN UH-34Ds and six ex-USN SH-34Gs, and these were also given USAF serials.

TECHNICAL DATA (H-34)

MANUFACTURER: Sikorsky Aircraft Division of United Aircraft Corporation, Stratford and Bridgeport, Connecticut.
TYPE: Troop-carrying assault helicopter.
ACCOMMODATION: Two pilots, 18 troops or 8 litters.
POWER PLANT: One 1,525 h.p. Wright R-1820-84 piston radial.
DIMENSIONS: Rotor diameter, 56 ft. 0 in. Length, 46 ft. 9 in. Height, 15 ft. 11 in. Disc area, 2,460 sq. ft.
WEIGHTS: Empty, 7,630 lb. Gross, 13,000 lb.
PERFORMANCE: Max. speed, 123 m.p.h. Cruising speed, 98 m.p.h. Initial climb, 1,100 ft./min. Service ceiling, 9,500 ft. Range, 182 st. miles.
ARMAMENT: None.
SERIAL NUMBERS:

H-34A: 53-4475/4554; 54-882/937; 54-2995/3050; 55-5241/5261; 56-4284/4342; 57-1684/1770; 58-1721.
CH-34C: 63-13190/13210.

HH-34D: 60-6913; 60-6923; 61-4488/4491; 64-4529; 63-7972/7974.
UH-34D: 63-8248/8259; 63-13006/13014; 63-13139/13140.
SH-34G: 60-5424/5429.

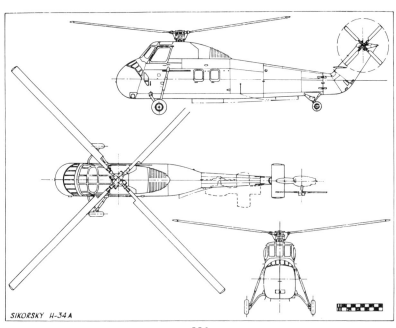

SIKORSKY H-34A

556

Sikorsky H-37A for Army Aviation (*Sikorsky photo 26315*).

Sikorsky H-37 Mojave

The largest helicopter to become operational with the U.S. military forces up to the end of 1961 was the H-37, known to the Army as the Mojave. This massive aircraft, the Sikorsky S-56, was originally developed to meet a U.S. Navy/Marines requirement for an assault transport and the prototype designated XHR2S-1 made its first flight on December 18, 1953. Although it retained the familiar Sikorsky single-rotor layout, the S-56 used two engines (the first Sikorsky design to do so) and these were carried in nacelles on each side of the fuselage close to the rotor head.

In 1954, the Army tested an S-56 with the designation YH-37. A production order for H-37As ensued, the first of which was delivered in 1956. The first 30 were delivered without auto-stabilization equipment, which was fitted retroactively in 1960.

Several changes distinguished the production H-37As from the prototype of the design. The shape of the fairing beneath the rotor head changed considerably, and a dorsal fin was fitted. The Army conducted trials with the H-37A at Fort Rucker, and then used the type to equip some of its Transportation Companies, of which the first was the 4th Medium Helicopter Transportation Company, equipped with H-37s on February 1, 1958. This unit was also the first to take the H-37 overseas when it moved to Germany in 1959.

The cabin of the H-37A is 30 ft. 1 in. long and 7 ft. 3 in. by 6 ft. 7 in. in cross section. The fuselage nose comprises clamshell doors which open to give free access to the cabin at truck-bed height. Normal accommodation is for 23 passengers or 36 equipped troops; the cargo capacity is 1,325 cu. ft.—big enough for two jeeps. A traversing electric hoist is fitted in the cabin roof to facilitate loading, and there is provision for an external cargo sling beneath the fuselage for loads of up to 10,000 lb. capacity. Two 300-U.S. gallon fuel tanks can be carried externally on the fuselage sides.

557

Of a total of 148 S-56 built, the Army received 94, including the last air-craft of the series, delivered in May 1960. Work then began on a pro-gramme to modernize 90 H-37As by installing automatic stabilization equipment, redesigned cabin door and cargo hatch, crash-resistant fuel cells and other changes. The first modified helicopter, re-designated H-37B, was returned to the Army in June 1961. The mission prefix "C" was added to the designations in 1962.

TECHNICAL DATA (H-37)

MANUFACTURER: Sikorsky Aircraft Division of United Aircraft Corporation, Stratford and Bridgeport, Conn.
TYPE: Troop and supply transport helicopter.
ACCOMMODATION: Two crew and 23 troops or 24 litters.
POWER PLANT: Two 2,100-h.p. Pratt & Whitney R-2800 piston radials.
DIMENSIONS: Rotor diameter, 72 ft. 0 in. Fuselage length, 64 ft. 3 in. Height, 22 ft. 0 in.
WEIGHTS: Empty, 20,831 lb. Gross, 31,000 lb.
PERFORMANCE: Max. speed, 130 m.p.h. at sea level. Cruising speed, 115 m.p.h. Initial climb, 910 ft./min. Service ceiling, 8,700 ft. Range, 145 st. miles.
ARMAMENT: None.
SERIAL NUMBERS:
H-37A: 54-993/1001; 55-610/650; 57-1642/1661; 58-983/1006.

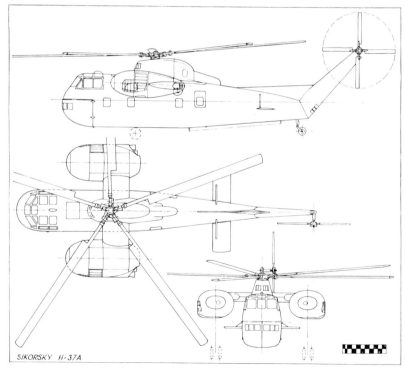

SIKORSKY H-37A

Sikorsky HH-3E, showing refuelling probe (*Sikorsky photo S48409-B*).

Sikorsky H-3 Jolly Green Giant

USAF interest in the Sikorsky S-61 helicopter, which had been developed initially for the U.S. Navy, originated in April 1962. In that month, three Navy HSS-2s were borrowed from the Navy to fly USAF re-supply missions to radar outposts in the Atlantic known as "Texas Towers". Three more were obtained later in 1962, by which time the basic model in service with the U.S. Navy had been redesignated SH-3A, and the six USAF versions then became CH-3Bs.

The success of the CH-3Bs led the USAF to order the same basic design in November 1962 to meet a requirement for a long-range transport helicopter, and the CH-3C version was produced. With the same powerplant, rotors and transmission as the basic S-61, the CH-3C had a new rear fuselage design incorporating a loading ramp for vehicles. The initial contract for 22 was followed by others after the CH-3C had been formally named as winner of a competition for a long-range rotary-wing support system in July 1963. The first flight was made on June 17, 1963 and 75 were built.

Substitution of 1,500 s.h.p. T58-GE-5 engines for the 1,300 s.h.p. GE-1s in the CH-3C changed the designation to CH-3E in February 1966. Forty-five were built in this form and 41 CH-3Cs were updated. A similar version adopted by the USAF Aerospace Rescue and Recovery Service was designated HH-3E; eight were built as such and 50 CH-3Es were modified. The HH-3E had armour protection, a retractable inflight refuelling probe, self-sealing fuel tanks, defensive armament and jettisonable auxiliary fuel tanks, and was extensively used for combat rescue missions in Vietnam, where it first became known as the "Jolly Green Giant". The HH-3E also equipped a USAF detachment which provided a stand-by rescue service at Cape Kennedy during the launching of manned spacecraft.

Two of the eight VH-3As operated by the Executive Flight Detachment to provide a Presidential and VIP transport and emergency evacuation

559

service operated in U.S. Army markings (the remainder being USMC aircraft). The VH-3A was similar to the Navy SH-3A. Service use of HH-3Es by AFRes and ANG units continued into the late 'eighties.

TECHNICAL DATA (HH-3E)

MANUFACTURER: Sikorsky Aircraft Division of United Aircraft Corporation, Stratford, Connecticut.
TYPE: Combat rescue helicopter.
ACCOMMODATION: Crew of two or three and up to 25 troops.
POWER PLANT: Two 1,500 s.h.p. General Electric T58-GE-5 turboshaft engines.
DIMENSIONS: Rotor diameter, 62 ft. 0 in. Length, 73 ft. 0 in. Height, 18 ft. 1 in. Rotor disc area, 3,019 sq. ft.
WEIGHTS: Empty, 12,423 lb. Gross, 22,050 lb.
PERFORMANCE: Max. speed, 164 m.p.h. Cruising speed, 154 m.p.h. Initial climb, 1,520 ft./min. Service ceiling, 13,600 ft. Range, 480 st. miles (internal fuel), 760 st. miles (external fuel).
ARMAMENT: Provision for 0·50-in. machine guns firing through windows.
SERIAL NUMBERS:

CH-3A: 62-12571/12573.
CH-3B: 62-12574/12576.
CH-3C: 62-12577/12582; 63-9676/9691; 64-14221/14237; 65-5690/5700; 65-12511; 65-12777/12800.

CH-3E: 66-13291/13296; 67-14702/14725; 69-5798/5812.
HH-3E: 66-13284/13290; 68-8282.

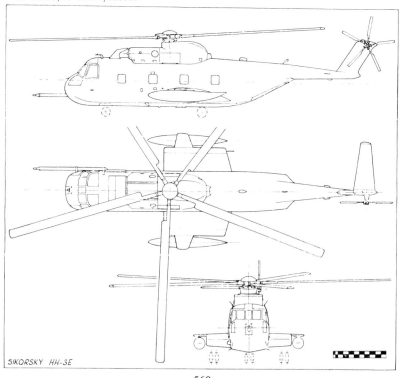

SIKORSKY HH-3E

The first Sikorsky HH-53B (*Sikorsky photo*).

Sikorsky H-53 Super Jolly

Introduction of the Sikorsky S-65 helicopter into USAF service was as a direct result of urgent needs for an aircrew rescue aircraft in Vietnam. The requirement was for an aircraft which could patrol close to the North Vietnam border during periods when combat aircraft were operating against North Vietnam targets, ready to make a rescue dash to pick up crews who had been shot down over enemy-held territory.

While the smaller HH-3E was being brought into service in this role, plans were prepared by the USAF to develop a new combat aircrew rescue aircraft (CARA). However, availability of the S-65, which was in production for the U.S. Marine Corps as the CH-53A Sea Stallion, made development of the CARA unnecessary, since it appeared unlikely that a new design could improve substantially on the H-53's performance.

Procurement of eight HH-53Bs was therefore put in hand as a major priority in 1966, and two CH-53As were borrowed from the USMC to allow crew training to begin in December 1965. New features of the HH-53B included the use of 1,200 lb. of armour plate to give protection against ground fire, installation of three 7·62-mm. Miniguns firing one to each side and one to the rear; addition of a retractable flight-refuelling probe, 3,080 s.h.p. T64-GE-3 engines and two external 650 U.S. gallon fuel tanks to stretch the range. The two pilots were provided with ejection seats and uprated avionics were fitted.

First flight of the HH-53B, called the "Super Jolly", was made on March 16, 1967, and the type entered service with the 37th ARR Squadron in South-East Asia in September 1967. The HH-53B was followed by the

561

Sikorsky HH-53H *Pave Low* in low-visibility camouflage, showing nose radome alongside refuelling probe (*Sikorsky photo*).

HH-53C, which had 3,925 s.h.p. GE-7 engines, 450 U.S. gallon jettisonable fuel tanks on cantilever mounts and increased lifting capability, to handle Apollo space capsules. Assigned to the 48th ARR Squadron at Eglin A.F.B., Florida, from August 1968, HH-53Cs flew precautionary patrols during Apollo launches from Cape Kennedy, and the 6594th Test Group of AFSC used the type to recover returned military satellites from the ocean around Hawaii. Other units continued to use the Super Jolly to good effect up to the end of the Vietnam conflict. Production totalled 44, and USAF also purchased 30 CH-53Cs heavy lift helicopters which lacked the armament and rescue provision of the HH-53C.

In June 1975, an HH-53C was modified in the *Pave Low* II programme to have improved night/all-weather flying capability. This was bestowed by a complex avionics fit, including AN/AAQ-10 FLIR and AN/APQ-158 TF radar. Successful testing of this YHH-53H led to conversion of eight more HH-53G to HH-53H *Pave Low* configuration for use by the U.S. Special Operations Forces. In keeping with SOF custom, these aircraft, plus two attrition replacements, were later redesignated MH-53Hs, delivered in 1979/1980. In 1985, the conversion of the 31 remaining HH-53B/Cs to the

Sikorsky HH-53C (*Dr. Alan Beaumont*).

MH-53J *Pave Low Enhanced* standard began, the first of these being delivered to SOF during 1987. The MH-53H and J had engines improved to T64-GE-415 standard.

TECHNICAL DATA (HH-53C)

MANUFACTURER: Sikorsky Aircraft Division of United Aircraft Corporation Stratford, Connecticut.
TYPE: Rescue helicopter.
ACCOMMODATION: Two pilots, crew chief and two para-medics. Provision for 38 equipped troops or 24 stretchers.
POWER PLANT: Two 3,925 s.h.p. General Electric T64-GE-7 turboshaft engines.
DIMENSIONS: Rotor diameter, 72 ft. 3 in. Length, 88 ft. 2 in. Height, 24 ft. 11 in. Rotor disc area, 4,070 sq. ft.
WEIGHTS: Empty, 23,125 lb. Gross, 42,000 lb.
PERFORMANCE: Max. speed, 186 m.p.h. at sea level. Cruising speed, 172 m.p.h. at sea level. Initial climb, 1,625 ft./min. Service ceiling, 18,550 ft. Range, 540 st. miles.
ARMAMENT: Three 7·62-mm. Miniguns.
SERIAL NUMBERS:
HH-53B: 66-14428/14435.   CH-53C: 68-10922/10933; 70-1625/1632.
HH-53C: 67-14993/14996; 68-8283/8286;   CH-53A: 63-13693/13694.*
   68-10354/10369; 69-5784/5797;
   73-1647/1652.

*Confiscated in FY87, ordered for Iran Navy.

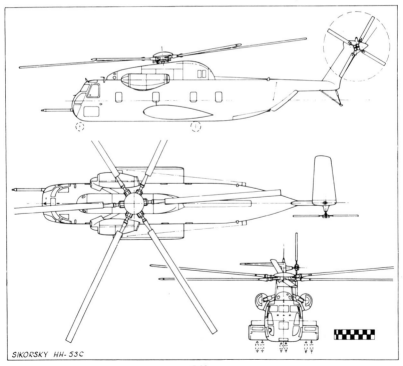

SIKORSKY HH-53C

Sikorsky UH-60A dropping paratroopers over Fort Bragg (*Sikorsky photo*).

Sikorsky H-60 Black Hawk

Responding to a U.S. Army requirement for a Utility Tactical Transport Aircraft System (UTTAS) to replace the Bell UH-1 in the combat support aviation companies, circulated to industry in January 1972, Sikorsky offered its Model S-70. Featuring the classic Sikorsky single-rotor layout and powered by two General Electric T700 engines, the S-70 was one of two designs selected for prototype construction and a fly-off. The designation YUH-60A was given to the three prototypes (plus a ground test vehicle) ordered from Sikorsky, the competing Boeing Vertol Model 179 becoming the YUH-61A.

Sikorsky flew its three prototypes on October 17, 1974, January 21 and February 28, 1975. The YUH-60A featured a fully-articulated four-bladed main rotor with swept-back tips, a fixed undercarriage and a roomy cabin to accommodate an 11-man infantry squad. Flight testing led to a number of modifications that included raising the main rotor by some 15 inches above the fuselage and adopting an all-moving tailplane in place of the original fixed surface. An eight-month period of Government Competitive Testing (GCT) culminated with the selection of the S-70 for production in a decision announced on December 23, 1976. An initial contract for 15 UH-60A Black Hawks was placed as the start of procurement, and 1,184 had been contracted through FY91.

The first production UH-60A flew on October 17, 1978, and deliveries to the U.S. Army began on the 31st of that month, initially to equip the 101st Airborne Division (Air Assault) at Fort Campbell, Kentucky. By 1987, Black Hawks were serving also with the 82nd Airborne and the 9th and 24th Infantry Divisions and with Army units in Hawaii, Panama, South Korea and West Germany, as well as with Army National Guard units in several of the U.S. states, including Alaska. Significant developments after the UH-60A entered production included a hover infra-red suppressor sub-system (HIRSS), a mine delivery system (to dispense anti-tank and anti-personnel sub-munitions), and the external stores support system

564

(ESSS). The last-named comprised removable pylons at shoulder height on the fuselage, from which a variety of weapons could be suspended, or up to four fuel tanks for long ferry flights. Weapon loads could include 16 Hellfire anti-armour missiles (with 16 more in the cabin, for reloading), gun pods, rockets or mine dispensing pods, and other loads included ECM pods or assorted cargo items. The UH-60A was succeeded in production in 1990 by the UH-60L, which introduced 1,857 s.h.p. T700-GE-701C engines. A year later, the UH-60M, also with these engines, added numerous other updates and improvements, including a 1 ft. longer fuselage with increased fuel capacity.

Special Army requirements led to the early development of variants of the Black Hawk equipped for other missions. The first of these was the EH-60A, carrying the *Quick Fix* IIB electronic countermeasures kit to jam enemy communications on the battlefield. A YEH-60A prototype (converted from a UH-60A) flew on September 24, 1981, and showed its special role by an array of four dipole aerials on the rear fuselage plus a deployable whip aerial on the underside. Up to 80 EH-60A conversions were to be made for the Army, Tracor Aerospace being the prime contractor. The first "production" EH-60A was delivered on July 28, 1987, but the programme ended with the 66th aircraft, delivered in November 1988, by which time the *Quick Fix* Black Hawks had been redesignated EH-60C. The YEH-60B, also a UH-60A conversion, flew on February 6, 1981 carrying a large box-like rotatable antenna under the fuselage as part of the Stand-Off Target Acquisition System (SOTAS). Work on this programme was suspended in September 1981, and conversion of seven more YEH-60Bs was cancelled.

For the Army's Special Operations Forces, a version of the Black Hawk was under development in 1988 as the MH-60K. Its features included maximum external fuel on the ESSS, uprated engines, folding rotor blades and tail unit for air and ship transportation, provision for air-to-air refuelling with a detachable probe, additional armament, a rescue hoist and advanced avionics in the cockpit. The latter was to include night vision imaging, moving map, HUD, and multifunction CRT displays.

Intended for clandestine, deep penetration missions and battlefield rescue,

Prototype Sikorsky EH-60C with ventral whip aerial extended (*Sikorsky photo*).

565

Sikorsky HH-60D prototype with long-range tanks and (instrumented) refuelling probe (*Sikorsky photo*).

the MH-60K incorporated some of the features planned for the HH-60D Night Hawk combat rescue helicopters that the USAF intended to acquire. The HH-60D was to have been operated by a crew of four, and a comprehensive avionics suite by IBM including terrain following/terrain avoidance radar and a helmet-mounted display system, as well as FLIR and AAR. A single HH-60D prototype, converted from a UH-60A, flew on February 4, 1984, but the Army's plan to buy 243 Night Hawks proved too expensive, as did an alternative proposal to buy 89 Ds followed by 66 less comprehensively-equipped HH-60Es. The final alternative proposal was to buy 90 HH-60As, using the uprated engines and transmissions of the Navy's SH-60B Sea Hawk variant of the S-70, and avionics of approximately the same sophistication as had been proposed for the HH-60E. However, no funding of the HH-60A had been authorised up to FY 88. Operation of the Sikorsky Black Hawk by the USAF was, consequently, limited to 11 UH-60As that had been procured in 1982-83 and issued (with the exception of one converted to HH-60D), to the 55th Aerospace Rescue and Recovery Squadron. All 10 helicopters were later brought up to Credible Hawk standard by installation of the refuelling probe, an extra internal fuel tank and a fuel management system, and nine more UH-60As were procured to the same standard. Redelivery of the Credible Hawks to the 55th ARRS began in February 1987.

Sikorsky UH-60A in USAF low-visibility finish (*Sikorsky photo*).

566

Further modification of all 19 helicopters brought a change of designation to MH-60G Pave Hawk, with the installation of *Pave Low* III FLIR, additional navaids and communications equipment and 0·50-in guns.

TECHNICAL DATA (UH-60A)

MANUFACTURER: Sikorsky Aircraft Division of United Technologies Corporation, Stratford, Connecticut.
TYPE: Combat assault squad transport helicopter.
ACCOMMODATION: Two pilots and crew chief/gunner plus 11 fully-equipped troops, or 14 in high-density configuration.
POWER PLANT: Two 1,560 s.h.p. General Electric T700-GE-700 turboshafts.
DIMENSIONS: Rotor diameter, 53 ft. 8 in. Length, 64 ft. 10 in. Height, 16 ft. 10 in. Rotor disc area, 2,261 sq. ft.
WEIGHTS: Empty, 10,624 lb. Gross, 20,250 lb.
PERFORMANCE: (At 16,260 lb. mission weight.) Max. speed, 184 m.p.h. Cruising speed, 167 m.p.h. at 4,000 ft. Initial vertical climb, over 450 ft./min. Service ceiling, 19,000 ft. Range, 373 miles. Ferry range, 1,380 miles.
ARMAMENT: Provision for one or two side-firing M-23D 0·30-in machine guns in side doors. Up to 10,000 lb. of assorted weaponry on ESSS pylons, including 16 Hellfire AGMs, rockets, machine guns or mine dispensers.
SERIAL NUMBERS:
YUH-60A: 73-21650/21655.
UH-60A: 77-22714/22728; 78-22961/23015;
    79-23262/23370; 80-23416/23509;
    81-23547/23647; 82-23660/23761;
    83-23837/23932; 84-23933/24028;
    85-24390/24490; 85-24746/24750; 86-24491/24566.

(Plus later contracts)

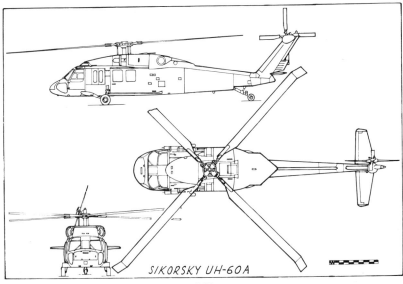

SIKORSKY UH-60A

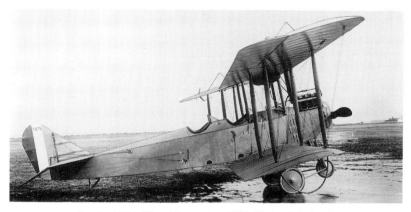

Standard SJ-1 (*Signal Corps photo 5119, National Archives*).

The Standard J Series

The Standard SJ of 1916 was a direct development of the earlier Sloan biplanes and the Standard H series, all designed by Charles Healey Day. Upon American entry into World War I, the Standard SJ was ordered in quantity as a primary trainer to supplement Curtiss JN-4 production. There was little difference between the two designs, the Standard being recognizable mainly by swept-back wings, somewhat wider gap, and a 4-cylinder Hall-Scott A-7 engine with a narrow vertical radiator mounted on top of the fuselage and ahead of the upper wing. The SJ had a small auxiliary wheel ahead of the main wheels to help prevent noseover in soft ground or bouncy student landings.

While the SJ was entering production, Standard introduced a revised and beefed-up model JR, a two-seater with a 175 h.p. 6-cylinder Hall-Scott A-5 that the company optimistically named the "Pursuit". This machine was entirely unsuited to European military operations and the Army bought only six as advanced trainers. Certain features of the JR were incorporated into the major production version of the SJ, which became known as the J-1. Principal differences from the previous models were deletion of the nose-over wheel and a change from the Deperdussin wheel control system to the more popular stick. The main drawback to the J-1 was the Hall-Scott A-7 engine, which was extremely troublesome and frequently caught fire in the air. Because of this, service use of the Standards diminished as adequate numbers of JN-4s became available. Standard revised the JR-1 in 1918 and produced a considerably different model, the JR-1B, with 150 h.p. Wright-Hispano, nose radiator, equal span wings with the lower wing below the fuselage, and new tail surfaces. The Army bought only six (42111/42116) and used them as single-seat mailplanes during the short period from May 15 when the Army flew the air

568

mail. Additional JR-1Bs were brought by the Post Office Department. A further variant was the E-4, identical to the JR-1B except for a lengthened upper wing.

TECHNICAL DATA (SJ)

MANUFACTURER: Standard Aircraft Corporation, Plainfield, New Jersey.
TYPE: Trainer.
ACCOMMODATION: Pupil and instructor in tandem open cockpit.
POWER PLANT: One 100 h.p. Hall-Scott A-7A piston in-line.
DIMENSIONS: Span, 43 ft. 10 in. Length, 26 ft. 7 in. Height, 10 ft. 10 in. Wing area, 429 sq. ft.
WEIGHTS: Empty, 1,557 lb. (1,660 lb.). Gross, 2,070 lb. (2,206 lb.).
PERFORMANCE: Max. speed, 69·5 m.p.h. (85 m.p.h.). Initial climb, 70 ft./min. (590 ft./min.). Service ceiling, 5,800 ft. (15,000 ft.).
ARMAMENT: None.
KNOWN SERIAL NUMBERS:
SJ, J-1: 193/208; 960-1056; 1660/2403;   JR-1B: 42111/42116.
4477/4994; 22403/22803; 41208/41357.

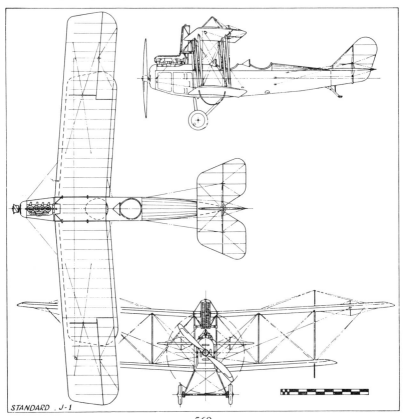

STANDARD . J-1

Stearman PT-17 in silver finish with late 1942 markings (*Peter M. Bowers*).

Stearman PT-13, -17, -18, -27 Kaydet

During 1934, the Stearman Aircraft Company produced as a private venture a training biplane for use by the Army. Known as the X70, it was first powered by a 225 h.p. Wright radial and later by a 215 h.p. Lycoming. Although Army tests were slow in completion, the success of the X70 eventually resulted in production of nearly 5,000 Stearman trainers for the Air Force and many more for the Navy and export. The first Army order, in 1936, was for 26 PT-13s with 215 h.p. Lycoming R-680-5 engines.

Orders for another 92 were placed in 1937, these being delivered as PT-13As with 220 h.p. R-680-7 and improved instruments. Between 1939 and 1941, the Army purchased 225 PT-13Bs with 280 h.p. R-680-11 engines, and six were converted for night and instrument flying with the designation PT-13C. In 1942, when the decision was taken to standardize Army and Navy trainers, the PT-13D appeared as the first completely standardized primary. The Army received 895, with R-680-17 engines.

A change to the Continental R-670-5 engine in 1940, in what was otherwise the PT-13A airframe, brought a change of designation to PT-17, and this version of the Kaydet became the most widely used. Production for the Army alone totalled 2,942, with others built for the Navy and for export. A total of 136 PT-17s with blind-flying instruments were re-designated PT-17A, and three with hoppers for pest-spraying became PT-17Bs. The single PT-17C was a standardized Army/Navy model leading to production of the PT-13D.

In the period immediately before and after America's entry into the War, engine production failed to keep pace with the output of the Stearman trainers, and another alternative version appeared, with the Jacobs R-755-7 radial. This was designated the PT-18, 150 being built, of which six became PT-18A when fitted with blind-flying instruments. Final designation in the series—and the last PT designation used by the Air Force—was the PT-27, built for supply to the Royal Canadian Air Force.

TECHNICAL DATA (PT-17)

MANUFACTURER: Stearman Aircraft Division, Boeing Aircraft Co., Wichita, Ka.
TYPE: Primary trainer.
ACCOMMODATION: Student and instructor in tandem.
POWER PLANT: One 220-h.p. Continental R-670-5 piston radial.
DIMENSIONS: Span, 32 ft. 2 in. (lower wing, 31 ft. 2 in.). Length, 24 ft. 9 in. Height, 9 ft. 8 in. Wing area, 298 sq. ft.
WEIGHTS: Empty, 1,931 lb. (PT-13A, 1,946 lb.). Gross, 2,635 lb. (PT-13A, 2,638 lb.).
PERFORMANCE: Max. speed, 135 m.p.h. (PT-13A, 125 m.p.h.) at sea level. Cruising speed, 96 m.p.h. Initial climb, 17·3 min. (PT-13A, 19·6 min.) to 10,000 ft. Service ceiling, 13,200 ft. (PT-13A, 13,500 ft.). Endurance (PT-13A), 3·9 hr.
SERIAL NUMBERS:

PT-13: 36-002/027.
PT-13A: 37-071/114; 37-232/259; 38-451/470.
PT-13B: 40-1562/1741; 41-787/861.
PT-13D: 42-16846/16995; 42-17057/17063; 42-17080/17095; 42-17097/17101; 42-17115/17134; 42-17150/17182; 42-17184/17190; 42-17200/17219; 42-17227/17863; 49-1458/1490*; 51-16084/16085*.

PT-17: 40-1742/1891; 41-862/1086; 41-7867/9010; 41-25202/25736; 41-25741/25747; 41-25749/25801; 42-15896/16723.
PT-18: 40-1892/2041.
PT-27: 42-15570/15869§.

* From storage for MAP.

§ Lend–Lease for RAF.

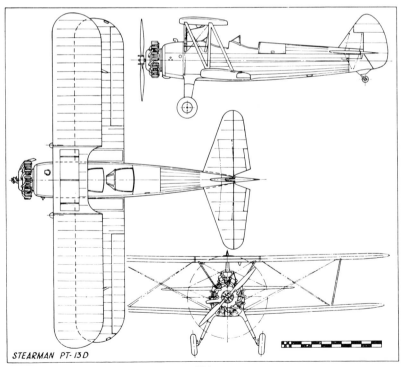

STEARMAN PT-13D

571

Stinson L-1A repossessed from original British contract (*Peter M. Bowers*).

Stinson L-1 Vigilant

Until 1940, the Air Corps' observation aircraft with few exceptions followed in the tradition of World War I corps reconnaissance types, but in that year attention turned for the first time to lighter, unarmed aircraft. Emphasis was placed in the 1940 requirement upon the field performance, to permit operations close to the battle-line in the role of artillery spotter and army co-operation type. Three types of aircraft of generally similar layout and appearance were purchased during 1940 by the Air Corps, which ordered three examples each of the extensively-flapped Bellanca YO-50 and Ryan YO-51, and 142 Stinson O-49s.

Although having less advanced high-lift devices than its competitors, the Stinson Model 74 was well equipped for short-field operation, with full-span automatic slots on the wing leading edge, and pilot-operated slotted flaps on the trailing edge. Powered by a 295 h.p. Lycoming R-680-9 engine, the O-49 grossed 3,325 lb. and carried a crew of two in tandem. A combination of the high-wing layout and the outward sloping sides of the cabin made for a good downward view, and helped to establish the usefulness of the type in service. A further batch of 182 Vigilants with detailed refinements was ordered in 1941. These were designated O-49A and had a small increase in gross weight and a 13-inch lengthening of the fuselage.

The Vigilant was overtaken by the development of the really lightweight Grasshoppers (Aeronca, Piper and Taylorcraft), and no further production occurred. Nevertheless, the type saw widespread service throughout the War, in both the European and the Pacific theatre, after redesignation as the L-1 and L-1A. Eight L-1s were assigned to the Royal Air Force under Lend–Lease, as were more than 100 L-1As; many of the latter, however, were retained by USAAF and operated in a combination of British and U.S. markings.

Four O-49s modified for ambulance duties in 1941 were redesignated O-49B and, later, L-1B. Another ambulance conversion with different internal arrangement became the L-1C, of which 113 went into service.

Fourteen L-1As modified to train pilots in glider pick-up techniques in 1943 were re-designated L-1D. Seven other ambulance conversions from the L-1 were fitted with amphibious floats and became the L-1E and five similar conversions of the L-1A became L-1Fs.

<h2 style="text-align:center">TECHNICAL DATA (L-1A)</h2>

MANUFACTURER: Stinson Aircraft Division of Aviation Manufacturing Corporation, Wayne, Mich.

TYPE: Light liaison, observation and ambulance.

ACCOMMODATION: Pilot and observer in tandem in enclosed cockpit.

POWER PLANT: One 295-h.p. Lycoming R-680-9.

DIMENSIONS: Span, 50 ft. 11 in. Length, 34 ft. 3 in. Height, 10 ft. 2 in. Wing area, 329 sq. ft.

WEIGHTS: Empty, 2,670 lb. Gross, 3,400 lb.

PERFORMANCE: Max. speed, 122 m.p.h. Climb, 24·5 min. to 10,000 ft. Service ceiling, 12,800 ft. Range, 280 st. miles.

ARMAMENT: Nil.

SERIAL NUMBERS:

L-1: 40-192/291; 40-3101/3142.   L-1A: 41-18900/19081.

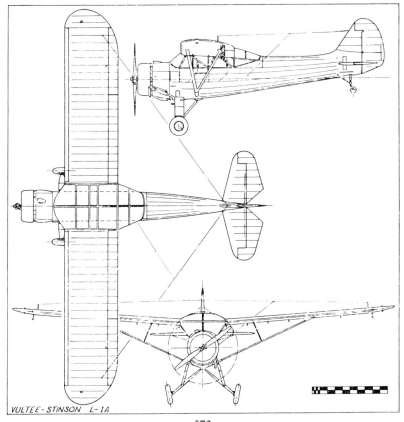

VULTEE - STINSON L-1A

Stinson L-5 in original O.D. and grey finish.

Stinson L-5 Sentinel

Once the idea of using light aircraft for Army liaison and communications duties had been established—largely by their use in large-scale manoeuvres towards the end of 1941—contracts were negotiated for a number of different types. Among them was a developed version of the Stinson 105 Voyager, then in production as a three-seat commercial light-plane. The Army version, procured in 1942 under the designation O-62, had a larger fuselage, was heavier and operated at considerably higher weights, but was based on the same 34-ft. span wing. It used the 185 h.p. O-435-1 engine. Trials had previously been made with six commercial Voyagers purchased in 1941 and designated YO-54.

Deliveries of the initial version of the Sentinel totalled 1,731, and orders for later variants, bringing the total to over 3,000, made this type the second most-used of all Army aircraft in the liaison category. The designation was changed from O-62 to L-5 after the first 275 had been delivered. In 1943, 688 of the L-5s were converted to L-5A with 24-volt electrics, and the undercarriage leg fairings were removed from all L-5s.

A modification to the fuselage to introduce an upward-hinged hatch aft of the cabin and provision for a stretcher made the L-5 a useful ambulance for front line operations and in this role the Sentinel served particularly in the Pacific Theatre during World War II, and in the Korean conflict. The ambulance version was designated L-5B and 679 were built. The 200 L-5Cs also had provision for a K-20 reconnaissance camera in the fuselage, and the 558 L-5Es were like the Cs but had drooping ailerons which operated in conjunction with the flaps.

The single XL-5F had an O-435-2 engine and other changes. Final production version, with 115 built, was the L-5G with a 190 h.p. O-435-11. A single L-5G acquired for the Air Force Academy in 1957 was redesignated U-19B in 1962.

A few commercial Voyagers were commandeered in 1941. Eight were provisionally AT-19As and then became L-9As, with 90 h.p. Franklin O-200-1 engine, while 12 Model 10-As with the 90 h.p. Franklin 4AC-199-EJ engine became L-9Bs rather than AT-19Bs as originally proposed.

574

TECHNICAL DATA (L-5)

MANUFACTURER: Stinson Aircraft Division of Consolidated Vultee Aircraft Corporation, Wayne, Mich.

TYPE: Light liaison.

ACCOMMODATION: Pilot and observer in tandem in enclosed cabin.

POWER PLANT: One 185-h.p. Lycoming O-435-1 piston flat-four.

DIMENSIONS: Span, 34 ft. 0 in. Length, 24 ft. 1 in. Height, 7 ft. 11 in. Wing area, 155 sq. ft.

WEIGHTS: Empty, 1,550 lb. Gross, 2,020 lb.

PERFORMANCE: Max. speed, 130 m.p.h. Climb, 6·4 min to 5,000 ft. Service ceiling, 15,800 ft. Range, 420 st. miles.

ARMAMENT: Nil.

SERIAL NUMBERS*:

L-5: 42-14798/15072; 42-98036/99573.

L-5B: 42-99574/99735; 44-16703/17102; 44-17104/17252.

L-5C: 44-17253/17452.

L-5E: 44-17453/18202.

XL-5F: 44-17103.

L-5G: 45-34911/35025; 57-6278.

L-9A: 42-88666/88673.

L-9B: 42-94130; 42-94136; 42-97051; 42-97430; 42-97432; 42-97434; 42-107278; 42-107406/107410.

* Includes procurement for U.S. Navy/Marine Corps.

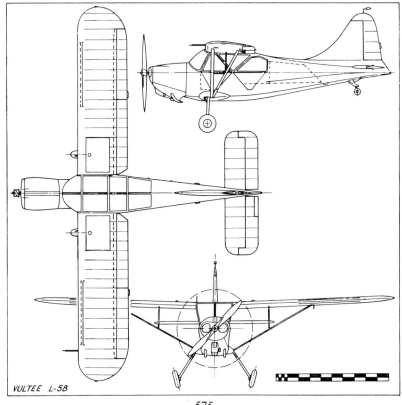

VULTEE L-5B

Camouflaged Taylorcraft L-2A (*John C. Collins*).

Taylorcraft L-2 Grasshopper

With the designation YO-57, four examples of the commercial Taylorcraft Model D (a high-wing lightplane with tandem seats and dual controls)
were obtained by the U.S. Army in 1941. Together with an equal number
of Aeronca and Piper lightplanes, they were used to evaluate the use of
light liaison and observation aircraft in the direct support of Army
operations. Production quantities were ordered for a large-scale test in
the 1941 manoeuvres, and the aircraft continued in production until the
spring of 1944.

The four YO-57s were powered by Continental YO-170-3 engines,
and there were no significant differences in the 70 O-57s. For the fully-
militarized O-57As, similarly powered, the cabin was modified to improve
vision, and the wing-root trailing edge was cut away for the same reason.
The observer's seat behind the pilot could be rotated to face aft, and two-
way SCR-585 radio was fitted.

When, in 1942, these Army aircraft were reclassified in the "L" category,
the YO-57 and O-57 became the L-2, and the O-57A became the L-2A.
To the 336 O-57As redesignated were added 140 L-2As built as such to
make a total of 476. Production continued with 490 L-2Bs which had
special items of equipment for service with the Field Artillery.

The final production version was the L-2M, of which Taylorcraft
built 900. This model incorporated a number of refinements, most important of which were the closed cowling of the engine and the use of wing
spoilers to increase the angle of descent for landing in restricted areas.

Several pre-War Taylorcraft lightplanes were commandeered in 1942,
principally for use in the Army programme of training glider pilots, all of

whom received a primary course in powered flying. The impressed aircraft were of nine different models and received individual designations in the L-series, as follow:

L-2C. Nine DC-65 with Continental A-65-8.
L-2D. One DL-65 with Lycoming O-145-B2.
L-2E. Seven DF-65 with Franklin 4AC-150.
L-2F. Seven BL-65, side-by-side seats with Lycoming O-145-B1.
L-2G. Two BFT-65, tandem seats, Franklin 4AC-150.
L-2H. Nine BC-12-65, side-by-side, Continental A-65-7.
L-2J. Four BL-12-65, side-by-side, Lycoming O-145-B1.
L-2K. The BF-12-65, side-by-side, Franklin 4AC-150.
L-2L. One BF-50, side-by-side, Franklin 4AC-150.

Of these variants, the Taylorcraft BL-65s had originally been taken over

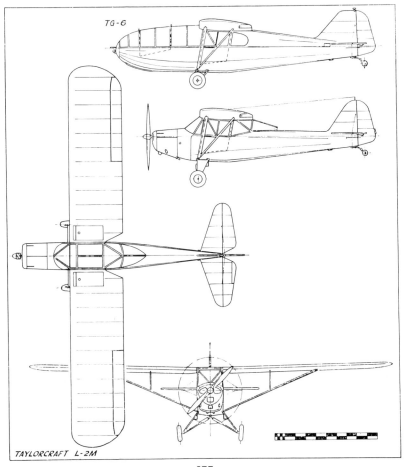

TG-6

TAYLORCRAFT L-2M

by the Air Corps and were designated UC-95 as light communications aircraft, the designation changing later to L-2F.

TG-6. Like Aeronca and Piper, Taylorcraft was asked to produce a light training glider for Army use, based on the L-2. The conversion involved a new front fuselage with a third seat for the instructor, and a simplified undercarriage, with a skid under the nose; wing spoilers were fitted and the fin area increased. This model was known as the Taylorcraft ST-100 and designated TG-6. The Navy purchased three for evaluation and a production batch of 250 was built for the Army.

TECHNICAL DATA (L-2A)

MANUFACTURER: Taylorcraft Aviation Corporation, Alliance, Ohio.
TYPE: Light liaison.
ACCOMMODATION: Pilot and observer in tandem in enclosed cabin.
POWER PLANT: One 65-h.p. Continental O-170-3 piston flat-four.
DIMENSIONS: Span, 35 ft. 5 in. Length, 22 ft. 9 in. Height, 8 ft. 0 in. Wing area, 181 sq. ft.
WEIGHTS: Empty, 875 lb. Gross, 1,300 lb.
PERFORMANCE: Max. speed, 88 m.p.h. Climb, 14·2 min. to 5,000 ft. Service ceiling, 10,050 ft. Range, 230 st. miles.
ARMAMENT: Nil.
SERIAL NUMBERS:

YO-57: 42-452/455.
L-2: 42-7773/7792; 43-2859/2908.
L-2A: 42-15073/15158; 42-35825/36074; 42-38498/38537; 43-25754/25853.
L-2B: 43-001/490.
L-2C: 43-2860, 43-2862; 43-2868/2873, 43-2901.
L-2D: 43-2902.
L-2E: 43-2859, 43-2861, 43-2867; 43-2890/2892, 43-2903.
L-2F: 42-79556, 43-2881/2883; 43-2889, 43-2893, 43-2908.

L-2G: 43-2888, 43-2907.
L-2H: 43-2874, 43-2879/2880; 43-2885/2886; 43-2895/2897, 43-2900.
L-2J: 43-2875/2877, 43-2898.
L-2K: 43-2878, 43-2884, 43-2887, 43-2894.
L-2L: 42-79559.
L-2M: 43-25854/26753.
TG-6: 42-58561/58810; 43-12496/12498.

Taylorcraft TG-6 (*Wright Field photo*).

578

Boeing MB-3A in typical 1920 markings (*Boeing photo*).

Thomas-Morse and Boeing MB-3/R-Series

When the problem of producing new aircraft of American design instead of building current European types was handed to the U.S. aircraft industry in the spring of 1918, Thomas-Morse was asked to develop a single-seat fighter superior to the French Spad. Four MB-3 prototypes were ordered. Power plant was the new 300 h.p. Wright "H", American production version of the French Hispano–Suiza, and the general appearance of the MB-3 showed heavy Spad influence. The first prototype did not fly until February 21, 1919, but even with the War over the Army was sufficiently impressed to order 50 service models.

A further order for 200 improved MB-3As was won by Boeing in 1920, under the competitive bidding system which then prevailed. The MB-3As, which retained the old manufacturer's model number in spite of the new designating system then in effect, differed from the MB-3 mainly in a revised cooling system, with radiators on each side of the fuselage by the cockpit instead of in the upper wing. Armament consisted of one 0·30-inch and one 0·50-inch machine gun or two 0·50s firing through the propeller. Two- and four-blade propellers were used interchangeably on MB-3As, and some Boeing-built four-bladers were installed on the earlier MB-3.

The MB-3As got off to very inauspicious beginnings at the Boeing plant in Seattle. A Thomas-Morse model provided as a sample had flipped onto its back during a landing at the nearest military airfield, so the first of the Boeing-built MB-3As was taken by road to a more suitable field at Camp Lewis, 50 miles south of Seattle. The flight was successful but the Army test pilot did not see a small ditch in a portion of the field. His wheels encountered this during his landing roll and the first MB-3A, too, ended upon its back. Later, Army pilot Tyndall pulled the wings off an MB-3A flown from a short runway near the factory and parachuted to safety after a spectacular low-level bail-out. Boeing made minor structural

Thomas-Morse MB-3 second prototype (*McCook Field photo*).

refinements, and designed and built completely new tail surfaces for the last 50 machines delivered.

The design was constantly plagued by loosening of the structural members as a result of vibration of the heavy engine in its wooden mount, and mechanics complained of poor access to the engine and its accessories. Boeing dissatisfaction with traditional wooden fuselage construction, where the various members were joined through metal fittings, led directly to research that resulted in the arc-welded steel tube fuselage introduced on the Boeing PW-9 and the DH-4M.

One of the first units supplied with the MB-3A was the 94th Pursuit Squadron of World War I fame, then based at Selfridge Field, Michigan. Some MB-3As were also shipped directly from the factory to overseas bases. As MB-3As were replaced in service by newer models, they were relegated to advanced training duties under the designation of MB-3M at Kelly Field, Texas, where they served into 1928.

When the Army became interested in postwar air racing, various manufacturers were asked to produce suitable designs. Thomas-Morse took the simplest course and modified the MB-3 into the MB-6 (68537) by clipping the wings and installing a hotted-up Wright "H" engine of 400 h.p. This plane was re-designated R-2 in the Army Racer series and entered in the 1921 Pulitzer Race. A more extreme racing variant of the MB-3 was the MB-7 (64373) with the same fuselage and power plant but a major change to strut-braced parasol monoplane configuration.

Two R-5 racers were ordered from T-M for the 1922 Pulitzer race. Powered with special 600 h.p. Packard 2A-2025 V-12 engines, these were all-metal TM-22 parasol monoplanes developed from a combined primary trainer and pursuit model that B. Douglas Thomas was trying to sell to the Army. The pursuit version, MB-9, was a relatively conventional single-seat all-metal parasol monoplane while the trainer, MB-10, was the same airframe with a new section spliced into the fuselage to accom-

580

modate the second cockpit and a longer nose that placed the 80 h.p. Le Rhône rotary engine farther forward than the fighter's Curtiss D-12 for balance purposes. The R-5s were notably unsuccessful, as was the trainer-cum-fighter, and the only significant design feature to survive was the wrap-round corrugated metal fuselage construction, which finally won official acceptance on the production O-19 series (see page 508).

TECHNICAL DATA (MB-3A)

MANUFACTURER: Boeing Airplane Co., Seattle, Washington.
TYPE: Single-seat fighter.
ACCOMMODATION: Pilot in open cockpit.
POWER PLANT: One 300-h.p. Wright H-3 piston Vee in-line.
DIMENSIONS: Span, 26 ft. 0 in. Length, 20 ft. 0 in. Height, 8 ft. 7 in. Wing area, 229 sq. ft.
WEIGHTS: Empty, 1,716 lb. Gross, 2,539 lb.
PERFORMANCE: Max. speed, 141 m.p.h. at sea level. Cruising speed, 125 m.p.h. Initial climb, 1,235 ft./min. Service ceiling, 19,500 ft. Endurance, 2¼ hours.
ARMAMENT: Two fixed forward-firing 0·30-inch guns.
SERIAL NUMBERS:
MB-3: 40092/40095; 63331/63370.
MB-3A: 68237/68436.

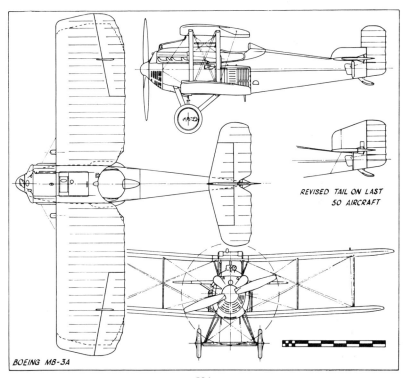

REVISED TAIL ON LAST
50 AIRCRAFT

BOEING MB-3A

Thomas-Morse S-4C with camera gun (*U.S. Navy photo 6389*).

Thomas-Morse S-4 Series

The Thomas S-4, designed by B. Douglas Thomas, was conceived late in 1916 as a Scout to be powered with the 100 h.p. French Gnome rotary engine then being manufactured in the U.S. The single prototype was evaluated by the Army but was rejected as a combat type in favour of more up-to-date European designs. However, the training requirements of the expanding aviation programme of 1917 resulted in production orders from the merged Thomas-Morse Company. The 100 S-4Bs were identical to the prototype except for a considerably shortened fuselage. Structure was all wood with fabric covering. S-4Bs on small twin floats and a tail float were supplied to the Navy as S-5s.

The S-4C was an improved B, the outward differences being straight instead of swept-back trailing edges to the ailerons, and aileron control by push rods and torque tubes in the manner of the French Nieuport 17, an example of which had been sent to the Thomas-Morse Ithaca factory. The first 50 S-4Cs used the 100 h.p. Gnome, but this troublesome power plant was replaced by the 80 h.p. Le Rhône when it became available. Armament was a single 0·30-inch Marlin machine gun or a camera gun. The S-4C contract for 1,050 aircraft was cancelled after the Armistice by which time 497 had been delivered, the final S-4C being numbered 44674.

The large size of the S-4 ailerons resulted in an odd marking situation. Under the initial specifications, the U.S. insignia was to be applied to the wing inboard of the ailerons. This resulted in the top wing markings almost touching at the centre section. Later 1918 applications were moved outward on the aileron.

The last variant, which the Army did not buy, was the speedy taper-winged S-4E. In post-war years this prototype was fitted with a 135 h.p. Aeromarine V-8 engine and used for racing. The S-4s were extremely popular on the surplus market and were widely flown as sport planes until grounded by the increasing stringency of safety regulations in the late

1920s. A few were converted to 3-place Dycer Sport Models by installation of a 90 h.p. Curtiss OX-5 in place of the rotary and the addition of a second 2-seat cockpit. S-4C upper wing panels were also used on the first models of the popular motorcycle-engined Heath "Parasol" lightplane of 1927. S-4Cs saw wide use in Hollywood war films of the 1930s, and a number have been restored by the antique aeroplane fans in the years since World War II.

TECHNICAL DATA (S-4C)

MANUFACTURER: Thomas-Morse Aircraft Corp., Ithaca, New York.
TYPE: Advanced trainer.
ACCOMMODATION: Pilot only.
POWER PLANT: 80-h.p. Le Rhône piston radial.
DIMENSIONS: Span, 26 ft. 6 in. Length, 19 ft. 10 in. Height, 8 ft. 1 in. Wing area, 145 sq. ft.
WEIGHT: Gross, 1,330 lb.
PERFORMANCE: Max. speed, 97 m.p.h. Initial climb, 10 min. to 7,500 ft.
ARMAMENT: One Marlin 0·30-in. machine gun, or camera gun.
KNOWN SERIAL NUMBERS:
S-4B: 4276/4372 (plus three).
S-4C: 38637/38979; 39882; 41359/41408; 44608/44674. (plus six).

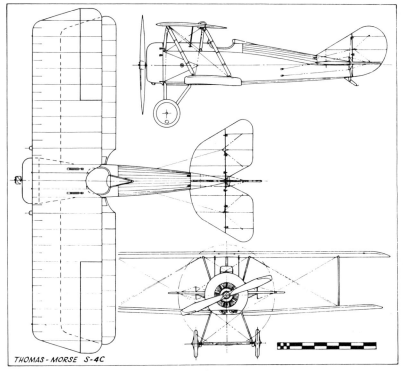

THOMAS-MORSE S-4C

583

Thomas-Morse O-19B at Scott Field in 1930 (*National Archives*).

Thomas-Morse O-19

Nine years of experimentation with all-metal construction finally paid off for the Thomas-Morse Company when orders for 180 O-19s and variants were placed between 1928 and 1931. The Wasp-powered O-19 was an improved version of the unofficial XO-6B built on the experimental XO-6 contract (page 591) and featured the same wrap-around corrugated sheet metal fuselage construction that Thomas-Morse had used on all designs since the S-9 of 1919. Wings and fixed tail surfaces were of metal frame construction with fabric covering while movable surfaces were corrugated aluminium sheet. The initial order was for four examples, one XO-19 and an O-19 with the Wasp and two identical airframes to test the suitability of other power plants—YO-20 with Pratt & Whitney R-1690-1 Hornet and XO-21 with Curtiss H-1640-1 Chieftain (which later became XO-21A with R-1750-1 Cyclone). Three additional service test aeroplanes were then ordered, one O-19 and one O-19A with Wasps and an O-23 with water-cooled Curtiss Conqueror.

Production orders were placed for 70 O-19Bs differing from the Wasp-engined test models mainly in having new cockpits with later gun mounts than the World War I Scarff mount, and 71 O-19Cs were delivered with minor refinements and a Townend drag ring around the engine. The O-19D was the second O-19C fitted out as a V.I.P. transport and production was completed with 30 O-19Es. The first O-19B was converted to Y1O-33 with revised tail surfaces and Prestone-cooled Conqueror engine.

The last Thomas-Morse design, tentatively designated Y1O-41, was essentially a revised Y1O-33 with geared Conqueror and new sesquiplane wings and was tested on Bailment Contract as the XO-932.

TECHNICAL DATA (O-19B, E)

MANUFACTURER: Thomas-Morse Aircraft Corp., Ithaca, New York.

TYPE: Observation biplane.

ACCOMMODATION: Pilot and observer in tandem open cockpits.

POWER PLANT: One 450 h.p. Pratt & Whitney R-1340-7 (O-19B) or R-1340-15 (O-19E) piston radial.

DIMENSIONS: Span (O-19B), 39 ft. 9 in. (O-19E), 40 ft. 0 in. Length (O-19B), 28 ft. 4 in. (O-19E), 28 ft. 10 in. Height, 10 ft. 6 in. Wing area (O-19B), 348 sq. ft. (O-19E), 359 sq. ft.

WEIGHTS: Empty, 2,722 lb. Gross (O-19B), 3,800 lb.

PERFORMANCE: Max. speed (O-19B), 137 m.p.h. (O-19E), 156 m.p.h. Climb, (O-19B), 11·1 min. to 10,000 ft. (O-19E), 10·7 min. to 10,000 ft. Service ceiling (O-19B), 20,500 ft. (O-19E), 23,300 ft.

ARMAMENT: One fixed and one flexible 0·30-in. Browning guns with 350 rounds and 600 rounds respectively.

SERIAL NUMBERS:

XO-19: 28-400.	O-19B: 30-090/159.	YO-20: 28-402.
O-19: 28-401; 29-369.	O-19C: 31-278/348.	XO-21: 28-403.
O-19A: 29-370.	O-19E: 31-523/552.	YO-23: 29-352.

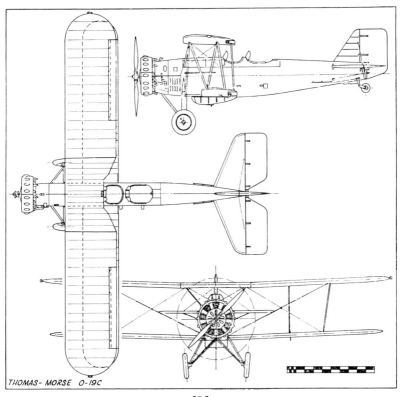

THOMAS-MORSE O-19C

Vought A-7D in original camouflage, and markings of the 354th TFW based at Myrtle Beach A.F.B. (*LTV photo*).

Vought A-7

A USAF decision in 1966 to order a version of the Ling-Temco-Vought Corsair II marked the second occasion within a decade when a Navy-inspired combat aircraft was adopted by the Air Force virtually off-the-shelf. (The precedent had been set by the McDonnell F-4 Phantom II, see page 412). The Corsair II had been designed in 1963 to meet the U.S. Navy's VAX requirement for a relatively cheap, subsonic attack aircraft which, under the terms of the specification, had to be based on an existing design. The winning design, from Ling-Temco-Vought's Aerospace Division (now operating as the Vought Aeronautics Company) was based on the F-8 Crusader and was selected for production in February 1964.

An attempt by the Department of Defense to have the USAF combine with the Navy and USMC to write a common VAX specification failed, but following successful testing of the prototype Navy A-7As (starting on September 27, 1965), USAF interest in the design grew steadily and a formal request to buy A-7s was included in the FY 1967 Air Force budget.

To meet USAF requirements, the Corsair was modified in several respects, the most significant being the use of a version of the Rolls-Royce Spey turbofan in place of the Pratt & Whitney TF30 used by the Navy. The Spey engine was developed jointly with Allison as the TF41-A-1 for the USAF's A-7D, and offered an increase of 2,000 lb. thrust over that of the TF30. Other changes, several of which were later adopted by the USN in its A-7E version, included installation of a 20-mm. multi-barrel cannon, and a new, advanced nav/attack system including a digital computer, head-up display, projected map display and laser rangefinder.

To start flight development of the systems, two YA-7D prototypes were completed with TF30-P-6 turbofans, and the first of these flew on April 6, 1968. The first aircraft to fly with the TF41 Spey took to the air on September 26, 1968, and was the third of the five aircraft ordered as YA-7Ds, all of which were eventually brought up to A-7D standard. Provision for boom flight refuelling, in place of the Navy's probe/drogue system, was introduced on the seventeenth production aircraft, with the receptacle on the top of the fuselage behind the cockpit and offset to port.

Production orders for the A-7D grew steadily, with annual increments from 1968 to 1975 taking the total procured to 459 (including the YA-7Ds). The process of service introduction began during 1970 in the hands of the 57th Fighter Weapons Wing at Luke A.F.B. and, early in 1971, the 354th TF Wing, which had been flying Douglas A-1s in Vietnam, returned to Myrtle Beach A.F.B., South Carolina, to convert onto the A-7D. This Wing took its A-7Ds back to South-East Asia in October 1972, and was soon flying close support missions as well as the "Sandy" (search and rescue) operations previously mounted by A-1s. Two other wings, the 23rd and 355th, also equipped on A-7Ds before converting, like the 354th, to the Fairchild A-10, making A-7Ds available to equip 15 ANG units, starting in October 1975.

In 1979, Vought received a contract to convert one A-7D to two-seat TA-7D configuration, this designation later changing to A-7K. The objective was to provide ANG with a combat-capable aircraft that would also be used for pilot familiarisation. Combining features of the A-7D with those of the U.S. Navy's TA-7C conversion trainer, the A-7K made its first flight in November 1980, and in addition to the prototype, Vought built 30 new A-7Ks for delivery to ANG units, starting in 1981. Production ended in September 1984.

During 1987/88, a total of 78 ANG A-7Ds and A-7Ks was fitted to carry a low-altitude night attack system (LANA), integrating AN/AAR-49 FLIR, AN/APQ-126 radar and the automatic flight control system. In May 1987,

Two-seat Vought A-7K flown by 174th TFS, Iowa ANG, in 1985 (*Peter H. T. Green*).

Vought received a USAF contract to modify two A-7D airframes to what it called A-7D Plus configuration, later designated YA-7F by the Air Force. In keeping with the Tactical Fighter Modernization Attack Plan, the A-7D Plus was a candidate for updating the ANG fleet of 337 A-7D/Ks. The YA-7F introduced the 26,000 lb.s.t. Pratt & Whitney F100-PW-220 engine in a fuselage lengthened by 4 ft., a taller fin and rudder, leading-edge root extensions (LERX), and many other systems improvements. The YA-7Fs were scheduled for delivery to USAF, for full evaluation, after a first flight in April 1989.

TECHNICAL DATA (A-7D)

MANUFACTURER: Vought Aeronautics Division, LTV Aerospace Corporation Dallas, Texas.
TYPE: Attack fighter.
ACCOMMODATION: Pilot only.
POWER PLANT: One 14,500 lb.s.t. Allison TF41-A-1 turbofan.
DIMENSIONS: Span, 38 ft. 9 in. Length, 46 ft. 1½ in. Height, 16 ft. 0 in. Wing area 375 sq. ft.
WEIGHTS: Empty, 19,490 lb. Gross, 42,000 lb.
PERFORMANCE: Max. speed, 698 m.p.h. at low level. Service ceiling, 51,000 ft. Combat radius, 890 st. miles. Ferry range, over 4,000 st. miles.
ARMAMENT: One fixed forward-firing M-61 A1 20-mm. Vulcan cannon. Two fuselage and six wing weapon stations with total combined capacity of 20,000 lb. (maximum external ordnance load, 15,000 lb.).
SERIAL NUMBERS:
YA-7D: 67-14582/14586.
A-7D: 68-8220/8231; 69-6188/6244;
  70-929/1056; 71-292/379; 72-169/265;
  73-992/1015; 74-1737/1760; 75-386/409.

A-7K: 79-460/471; 80-284/295;
  81-072/077.

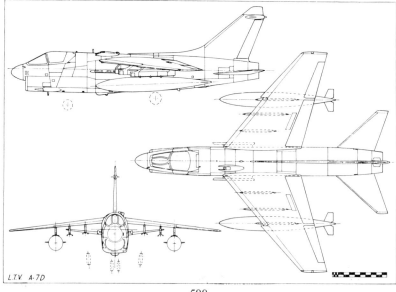

LTV A-7D

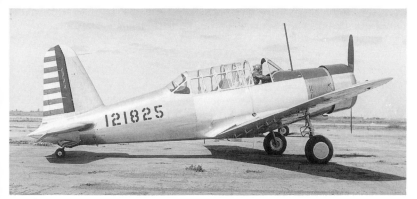

Silver Vultee BT-13A in March 1942, before rudder stripes were deleted. Tail Number is in non-standard location on fuselage (*Peter M. Bowers*).

Vultee BT-13, BT-15 Valiant

The series of Vultee low-wing trainers produced from 1940 to 1944 by far outnumbered all other aircraft in the basic training category, and served almost exclusively as the basic type for all aircrew trained in the U.S. during World War II. The basic trainer represented the second of the three training stages—primary, basic and advanced—which were common to all training programmes. The BT-13 was a docile low-wing monoplane developed in the first place as a private venture (the Vultee Model 54).

Selection of the Vultee 54 by the Army in September 1939 followed tests with a single BC-3 (39-720), a version of the Vultee trainer with a retractable undercarriage and a 600 h.p. R-1340-45 engine. This, incidentally, was the last aeroplane designated in the short-lived Basic Combat category, which overlapped the advanced training role. The Vultee 54 was similar to the BC-3 but had a 450 h.p. R-985-25 engine and fixed undercarriage. The Army order for 300 (40-810/1109) was at the time the largest placed for basic trainers and among the largest for any aircraft type; it was followed, however, in 1941 by two larger contracts, one of which alone was for 2,000 aircraft. These contracts were for the BT-13A, with a R-985-AN-1 engine and small refinements. Production of this, the principal version, eventually totalled 6,407 for the USAAF. Also procured were 1,125 BT-13Bs, having a 24-volt electric system.

So rapid was the build-up of Valiant production that engine production could not keep pace. Consequently, during 1941 and 1942, 1,693 aircraft were built with the 450 h.p. Wright R-975-11 engine. This version was designated BT-15. One BT-13A was rebuilt by Vidal in 1942 with an all-plastic fuselage and was designated XBT-16.

By 1945, the place of the basic trainer in Army programmes was being taken by advanced types, such as the AT-6. The BT-13s and -15s were retired quickly after the War and no more basic trainers were procured.

TECHNICAL DATA (BT-13A)

MANUFACTURER: Vultee Aircraft Inc., Nashville, Tenn.
TYPE: Basic trainer.
ACCOMMODATION: Pupil and instructor in tandem in enclosed cockpit.
POWER PLANT: One 450 h.p. Pratt & Whitney R-985-AN-1.
DIMENSIONS: Span, 42 ft. 0 in. Length, 28 ft. 10 in. Height, 11 ft. 6 in. Wing area, 239 sq. ft.
WEIGHTS: Empty, 3,375 lb. Gross, 4,496 lb.
PERFORMANCE: Max. speed, 180 m.p.h. Climb, 9·2 min. to 10,000 ft. Service ceiling, 21,650 ft. Range, 725 st. miles.
SERIAL NUMBERS:

BT-13: 40-810/1109.
BT-13A: 41-1411/1710; 41-9587/9979; 41-10410/11586; 41-21162/23161; 42-1164/1743; 42-42201/43257; 42-88674/89573; 41-1211/1710*.

BT-13B: 42-89574/90698; 44-31511/32160*.
BT-15: 41-9980/10279; 41-10280/10409; 42-1744/2063; 42-41258/42200.

* These batches procured for USN.

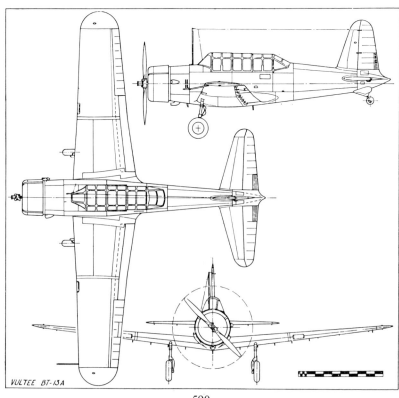

VULTEE BT-13A

Vultee A-31 (*USAF photo*).

Vultee A-31, A-35 Vengeance

Among the types of aircraft ordered from the U.S. in 1940 by the British Purchasing Commission was the Vultee V-72 Vengeance single-engined dive bomber. Like several other types picked to meet the urgent needs of the Royal Air Force, then confronted by an enemy-occupied Europe, the V-72 had not been procured by the Army. To meet British orders, two production lines were established, one at the Vultee factory in Nashville and another by Northrop at Hawthorne.

After passage of the Lend–Lease Bill through the Senate and its signature by President Roosevelt on March 11, 1941, further contracts for the Vengeance were placed by the Army, to be added to those already ordered by Britain. For procurement purposes, the type was then designated A-31, with 100 ordered from Vultee and 200 from Northrop. Deliveries were in progress when the U.S. entered the War; thereafter a number of the aircraft intended for Britain were repossessed (including 243 which had been ordered on the British cash contract, and were in consequence known to the Army as V-72s rather than A-31s).

One A-31 airframe was built by Vultee in 1942 at Downey (where the first two V-72s had been built) as the XA-31A; when fitted with a 3,000 h.p. XR-4360-1 Wasp Major for test-flying it became the XA-31B. Five more aircraft were used as YA-31Cs to develop the Cyclone 18 engines for the B-29, flying with the 2,200 h.p. R-3350-13 and -37 versions.

Equipped to full Army standards, the Vengeance was redesignated A-35A, with four 0·50-inch guns in the wings and a single gun of the same calibre in the rear cockpit. Ninety-nine were built by Vultee at Nashville, followed by 831 of the A-35B version which had the 1,700 h.p. R-2600-13 engine and six wing guns. Of this total, 562 were assigned to Britain and 29 to Brazil under Lend–Lease.

The A-35s saw little service with the Army, many being reassigned for

591

target-towing by the Groups mentioned above and other units. It enjoyed the dubious distinction of being described in 1943 by an Army general as "a shining example of the waste of material, manpower, and time in the production of an aeroplane which this office (Directorate of Military Requirements) has tried to eliminate for several months."

TECHNICAL DATA (A-35B)

MANUFACTURER: Vultee Aircraft, Inc., Nashville and Northrop Aircraft, Hawthorne, California.
TYPE: Dive bomber.
ACCOMMODATION: Pilot and gunner.
POWER PLANT: One 1,700-h.p. Wright R-2600-13 piston radial.
DIMENSIONS: Span, 48 ft. 0 in. Length, 39 ft. 9 in. Height, 15 ft. 4 in. Wing area, 332 sq. ft.
WEIGHTS: Empty, 10,300 lb. Gross, 16,400 lb.
PERFORMANCE: Max. speed, 279 m.p.h. at 13,500 ft. Cruising speed, 230 m.p.h. Initial climb, 11·3 min. to 15,000 ft. Service ceiling, 22,300 ft. Range, 2,300 st. miles.
ARMAMENT: Six forward-firing 0·50-in. machine guns in wings, 2,000 lb. of bombs.
SERIAL NUMBERS:
A-31-VN: 41-31048/31147.
A-31-NO: 41-30848/31047.
A-35A-VN: 41-31148/31246.

A-35B-VN: 41-31247/31447;
42-94149/94548; 42-101236/101465.

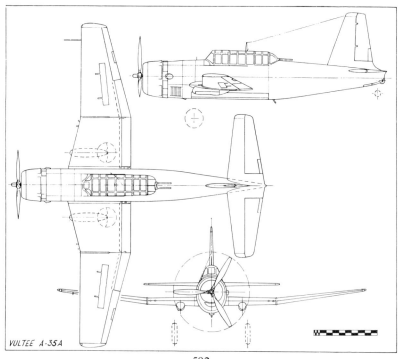

VULTEE A-35A

Waco CG-4A-NW in Sicily, 1943 (*Howard Levy*).

Waco CG-4, CG-15 Hadrian

Army development of troop-carrying gliders began in 1941, with experimental contracts for a series of prototypes to meet two separate specifications. The first requirement was for an 8–9 seat transport, and contracts were placed for single prototypes of the Frankfort Model TCC-41 as the XCG-1 (41-29615); the Waco NYQ-3 as XCG-3 (41-29617); the St. Louis XCG-5 (41-29619) and the Bowlus XCG-7 (41-29621). The second type was to be a larger, 15-seat glider, and the same four companies each received contracts for a single prototype of this type as follows: Frankfort TCC-21 as XCG-2 (41-29616); Waco XCG-4 (41-29618); St. Louis XCG-6 (41-29620) and the Bowlus XCG-8 (41-29622).

Of the eight prototypes ordered, all but the XCG-1, XCG-2 and XCG-6 were completed and test-flown but no further development of the St. Louis or Bowlus designs occurred, only the two Waco types reaching quantity production. The CG-3A, which was used principally for training, is illustrated on page 595. The CG-4 became the first and most-widely used U.S. troop glider of World War II.

After trials with the XCG-4 in 1942, a second prototype was ordered (42-53534) and plans were made for large scale production in which, eventually, sixteen different assembly lines participated, to deliver 13,906 examples of the CG-4A. Of mixed wood and metal construction, mostly fabric covered, the CG-4A was of conventional troop-glider design, with a high wing, a box-section fuselage and an upward-hinged nose section to permit direct loading of vehicles into the cabin. The hinged portion of the nose contained the cockpit with its dual control for two pilots side-by-side, and the tow attachment.

As required by the specification, the CG-4A could accommodate 15 equipped troops, including two serving as pilots. Among other tactical loads which could be carried were a standard Army Jeep, Ford or Willys $\frac{1}{4}$-ton truck with four-man crew, or a 75-mm. howitzer and crew. Its

Waco CG-15A landing (*Howard Levy*).

gross weight of 7,500 lb.–9,000 lb. and towing speed of 150 m.p.h. made it suitable for operations behind the C-46 and C-47.

Companies which were included in the CG-4A programme, and the numbers built by each, were as follows: Babcock, 60; Cessna, 750; Commonwealth, 1,470; Ford, 4,190; G. and A. Aircraft, 627; General, 1,112; Gibson Refrigerator, 1,078; Laister-Kaufman, 310; National, 1; Northwestern, 1,510; Pratt & Read, 956; Ridgefield Manufacturing, 156; Robertson, 170; Timm, 434; and Ward Furniture Co., 7. Waco built 1,075. Included in these totals are four airframes converted to other configurations, as noted below.

The CG-4A went into operation, rather disastrously, in the Allied invasion of Sicily in July 1943. A series of misadventures, none of them attributable to the design of the aircraft, minimized the effectiveness of the glider attack. Greater success attended their participation, in March, 1944, in the second Wingate Chindit operation in Burma, involving landing in a jungle clearing by night 150 miles behind the main Japanese lines. Subsequently these gliders participated in other major airborne operations of which the most significant were the D-Day landings in France on June 6, 1944, the landings in southern France in August 1944, the action at Arnhem and the crossing of the Rhine.

Although the CG-4A was unable to carry some of the larger items of military equipment, it performed its designed mission satisfactorily, and little design development occurred. One of the subcontractors, Timm Aircraft Corp., built in 1943 the sole XCG-4B (42-46394), in which metal was excluded from the structure. Another sub-contractor, Northwestern, converted one CG-4A to the sole XPG-1 (43-27315) in 1943;

Northwestern PG-2A, powered version of CG-4A (*Howard Levy*).

594

this had two Franklin 6AC-298-N3 flat-four engines in nacelles beneath the wings, the object being to allow the glider to return under its own power after completing a mission. A similar conversion was made by Ridgefield to produce the XPG-2 (42-58090) with two Ranger L-440-1 engines. After tests with this prototype, a service trials batch of ten PG-2As was ordered from Northwestern with L-440-7 engines, in 1944. A proposed XPG-2B with R-755-9 radial engines (45-14044) was cancelled in 1945.

Waco, meantime, developed an improved model of the CG-4A as the XCG-15 (Waco Model NEU). The prototype (43-37082) was a CG-4A conversion, the changes comprising a reduction in wing-span from 83 ft. 8 in. to 62 ft. 2 in., elimination of wing spoilers, a cantilever type under-carriage, better nose shape, and internal changes including standard Air Force tie-down fittings and floor spacing. The normal gross weight increased by 500 lb. and the towing speed went up to 180 m.p.h. Waco built two prototype XCG-15As and had delivered 427 of total contracts for 1,000 CG-15As when production was terminated at the end of the

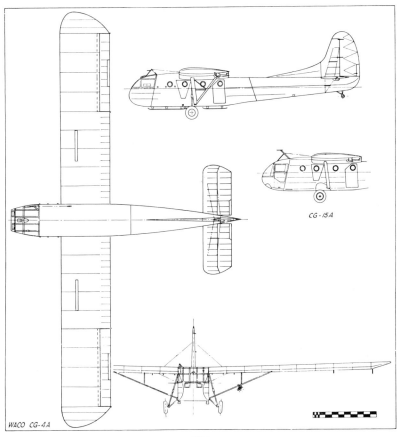

CG-15A

WACO CG-4A

War. The first 385 were 15-seaters, the remainder of the batch having 16 seats each. The CG-15As saw limited service alongside the CG-4As.

One XCG-15A was converted in 1945 to the XPG-3 (44-90986), with two Jacobs R-755-9 radial engines, for use as a low-cost troop or cargo transport which could also be towed as a glider. Fuel was carried for three hours' duration.

In June 1948, the Air Force discarded the CG, PG and TG designations in favour of a simple G category. A number of the Waco types were re-designated as follows: the PG-2A to G-2A; the CG-4A to G-4A; the CG-15A to G-15A and the XPG-3 to G-3. In 1947, 35 G-4As were converted to G-4C with a Navy-developed tow bar.

TECHNICAL DATA (CG-4A)

MANUFACTURER: The Waco Aircraft Company, Troy, Ohio.
TYPE: Cargo and troop glider.
ACCOMMODATION: 15 troops.
POWER PLANT: None.
DIMENSIONS: Span, 83 ft. 8 in. Length, 48 ft. 4 in. Height, 12 ft. 7 in. Wing area, 852 sq. ft.
WEIGHTS: Empty, 3,700 lb. Gross, 7,500 lb.
PERFORMANCE: Max. speed, 120 m.p.h. Stalling speed, 44 m.p.h.
ARMAMENT: Nil.
SERIAL NUMBERS:

XCG-4: 41-29618; 42-53534.
CG-4A-WO: 42-78923/79422;
   43-37009/37508; 45-5201/5275.
CG-4A-BB: 42-47392/47441;
   42-57517/42-57526.
CG-4A-CE*: 42-61101/61460;
   42-61821/62210.
CG-4A-CM: 42-53132/53281;
   42-74313/74612; 43-42829/43328;
   45-14543/15062.
CG-4A-FO: 42-77015/78014;
   43-39579/40778; 45-5976/6700;
   45-15143/16239; 45-16242/16263;
   45-16266/16272; 45-16274/16409;
   45-16412/16414.
CG-4A-GA: 42-43784/43843;
   42-57527/57618; 42-79426/79545;
   43-36809/37008; 45-13233/13387.
CG-4A-GE: 42-45647/75721;
   42-73596/73749; 43-19674/19957;
   43-40779/41278; 45-17243/17341.
CG-4A-LK: 42-43649/43678;
   42-73516/73595; 43-42129/42228;
   45-17143/17242.
CG-4A-(NA): 42-52852.

CG-4A-GN: 42-46552/46611;
   42-46619/46631; 42-52853/52881;
   42-55785/55844; 42-68306/68335;
   42-73750/74112; 43-41279/41778;
   45-27936/27948; 45-27962/27971.
CG-4A-NW: 42-43754/43783;
   42-56643/56696; 43-27254/27469;
   43-36609/36708; 43-42229/42728;
   45-5661/5975; 45-13683/13949;
   45-14094/14121.
CG-4A-PR: 42-52777/52851;
   42-56108/56607; 43-41779/42128;
   45-26436/26466.
CG-4A-RI: 42-46917/46936;
   42-58074/58109; 43-36709/36808.
CG-4A-RO: 42-43628/43647;
   42-78795/78844; 43-42729/42828.
CG-4A-TI: 42-46322/46551;
   42-62609/62812.
CG-4A-WA: 42-46612/46618.
PG-2A-NI: 45-14034/14043.
XCG-15A-WO: 44-90987/90988.
CG-15A-WO: 45-5276/5660;
   45-12743/12784.

* Sub-contracted to Boeing-Wichita.

APPENDIX A

AIRCRAFT PRIOR TO WORLD WAR I

Included in this appendix are details and illustrations of the principal types of aircraft acquired by the U.S. Army from the original Wright Model A up to the time the U.S. entered World War I in 1917. In this period, nearly every aeroplane purchased differed in some detail from others of the same type. A few unimportant types are not illustrated, including the Burgess F (a Wright design) and the Burgess J (also a Wright design modified).

Burgess Model I at Corregidor in the Philippines (*USAF photo 12926AC*).

BURGESS I SCOUT

In 1910, the W. Starling Burgess Co. of Marblehead, Mass., a manufacturer of speedboats, produced a Curtiss pusher type seaplane with the assistance of Greely S. Curtis (no relation of Glenn H. Curtiss). The success of this machine encouraged further activity, and the firm obtained a licence to build established Wright designs, starting with the Models B and C (respectively Burgess Models F and J, Army Serials 5 and 18). The 1913 Burgess Model I (serial 17) illustrated above was a single example for the Army using Wright features and a single 60 h.p. Stutevant engine. The I was used as a scout in the Philippines and crashed in 1915. Span, 39 ft. 10 in.; length, 31 ft. 4 in.; gross weight, 2,038 lb.; speed, 59 m.p.h.; rate of climb, 210 ft./min.

597

(*Erickson collection/USAF*).

BURGESS H

Six Burgess Model H trainers were bought in 1912 as the Army's first tractor designs. Three were converted to seaplanes by removing the wheels from the combination skid-wheel undercarriage and bolting twin pontoons to the skids. The Burgess Hs retained many earlier Wright features, notably the warping-wing method of lateral control and the Wright Model B type of landing gear. The skid under the twin rudders was merely to protect them, and not a true tailskid. The Hs were troublesome, and along with the Wright and Curtiss pushers, gave the Army Training School at North Island, San Diego, a bad reputation.

Four Burgess Hs (Serials 24, 28 and two others) were redesigned and rebuilt by Grover C. Loening, at San Diego. The 70 h.p. French Renault engine was retained, as was the basic fuselage. The wings were rebuilt to use aileron control, and the Wright control levers were replaced by Curtiss controls with wheel for rudder and shoulder yoke for the ailerons. The new tail used a single enlarged rudder with fixed vertical fin and the skid-type landing gear was replaced by an entirely new cross-axle type that Loening patented and which in its essential form was used on all subsequent American designs.

The rebuilt Burgess H No. 28, fitted with extra tanks and flown by student Q. B. Jones, set a world's endurance record for three persons of 7 hours 5 minutes on March 12, 1915.

Modified Burgess H (*Signal Corps photo 1082/National Archives*).

(*Erickson collection/USAF*).

BURGESS–DUNNE TAILLESS

The Dunne Tailless biplane developed in England was manufactured in the U.S. by the Burgess Company of Marblehead, Massachusetts. A single landplane example (serial 36) was evaluated by the Army at North Island, San Diego. Powered by a 200-h.p. water-cooled Canton-Unne radial engine the Burgess–Dunne achieved longitudinal stability by extreme sweepback of the wings, which put the elevators an effective distance aft of the centre of gravity. Span, 46 ft. 6 in.; length, 23 ft.

Army Aeroplane No 6, a 1911 Curtiss Model E (*USAF photo*).

CURTISS D & E

The Army's second aeroplane was a Curtiss Model D (s/n 2) similar to the standard Curtiss pusher with tripod landing gear and interplane ailerons then in production. Distinguishing military feature was multi-panel wings for easy transport on army wagons. The single Army Model D was followed by three improved Model E's (s/n 6, 8 and 23) with double-surface wings and monoplane forward elevator (eventually eliminated). One similar Navy model (s/n AH-8, a dual-control trainer) was obtained from the Navy and was still in Army hands in 1919.

CURTISS F-BOAT

The Curtiss Model F was a single-engined pusher flying boat developed in 1912 and supplied to pre-war private owners as well as to the Army which bought three (15, 34, 49), and the Navy. In keeping with most trainers of the 1910/14 era, the F was a side-by-side two seater. The hull was built up of cross-lapped wood veneer strips formed over wooden longerons and bulkheads. Wing details varied between individual machines, some having equal span wings and interplane ailerons while others had an overhanging upper wing with integral ailerons. Span, 43 ft. 10 in.; length, 27 ft. 9¾ in.; area, 387 sq. ft.; gross weight, 1,860 lbs.; speed, 69 m.p.h.

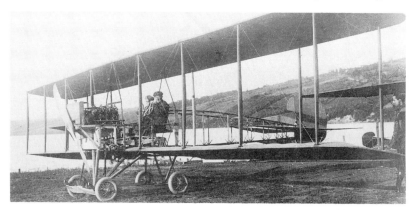

CURTISS G TRACTOR

The two 1913 Curtiss Model G's for the Army (21, 22) were the first Curtiss tractors designed as such and the first Curtisses, other than flying boats, to use an enclosed fuselage or hull. The side-by-side two seaters differed considerably in detail. The first had a tricycle landing gear, a chain reduction drive to the propeller, and 38-foot wings of equal span. The second had the four-wheel undercarriage shown and a direct-drive engine. The lower wing was later shortened and the ailerons were relocated to the upper wing. Data: (s/n 22) Span, 41 ft., length, 25 ft., gross weight, 2,400 lb., high speed, 53 m.p.h.

600

CURTISS J

The Model J was the first Curtiss tractor design after the Model G, and the preliminary design was undertaken in England when Glenn Curtiss hired B. Douglas Thomas from Avro. The original version of the J delivered to the Army (number 29, illustrated) had equal span wings with ailerons on both and the landing gear shown. A modified version (30) had a shorter lower wing, ailerons on the upper only, and deleted the skids. No. 30 developed into the JN-1 while 10 production JN-2s (41/50) with modified landing gear evolved from No. 29. Model J (Number 29): Span, 40 ft. 2 in.; length, 26 ft. 4 in.; gross weight, 1,345 lb.; high speed, 84 m.p.h.

CURTISS TWIN JN

The two-seat Curtiss Twin JN, tentatively designated JN-5, was developed from existing components, with standard JN-4 wings on a wider centre section and JN landing gear. While the prototype used the same dihedral as the JN-4, the other six on the Army order (serials 102-107) had increased dihedral and circular radiators. One additional Twin JN (serial 428) was bought and used with the others on the Mexican border in 1916. One Twin JN was presented to the New Mexico National Guard by the Aero Club of America. Span, 52 ft. $9\frac{3}{8}$ in.; length, 29 ft. 4 in.; height 10 ft. $8\frac{1}{2}$ in.; wing area, 450 sq. ft.; gross weight, 3,150 lb.; high speed, 85 m.p.h.

Curtiss N with extra dihedral (*Erickson collection/USAF*).

CURTISS N SERIES

The Curtiss N was a contemporary of the British-designed J (page 176) and differed from it mainly in airfoil section and the location of the ailerons between the wings in the manner of earlier Curtiss models. The single model N (serial 35) procured by the Army in 1914 was tested both with straight wings and the high degree of dihedral illustrated. Four improved N-8s (60/63) were essentially JN-3s with 10 ft. wing extensions. They later became trainers with the wing extensions removed. The single Curtiss Model O was identical except for being a side-by-side two seater.

Fourteen Army N-9s of 1917 (serials 429–442) were standard Navy trainers, single-float versions of the Army JN-4A fitted with longer span three-bay wings. Filled-in areas on the upper wing kingposts were "skid plates". Span, 53 ft. 4 in.; length, 32 ft. $7\frac{1}{4}$ in.; wing area, 488 sq. ft.; empty weight, 1,860 lb.; gross weight, 2,390 lb.; high speed, 65 m.p.h.

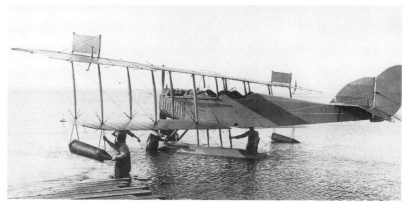

Curtiss N-9, 1917 model with 100 h.p. Curtiss OXX-3 engine.

Curtiss R-4L with two bay wings (*McCook Field photo 79*).

CURTISS R SERIES

The Curtiss Rs were designed as 2-seat heavy-duty workhorses in 1915, and were initially powered with the 150 h.p. Curtiss VX engine. The Army bought 12 R-2s (64/75) in 1916, followed by 55 improved R-4s (including 177/187 and 281/316) in 1916, with 200 h.p. Curtiss V2-3 engines. The R-4s were used on the Mexican border and later as trainers and utility hacks. 12 R-4Ls (incl. 39956, 39369) with Liberty engines were ordered early in 1918. Six of these were converted to R-4LM mailplanes when the Army carried the airmail. 18 R-6s (incl. 505/508) were delivered in 1917 after being ordered as R-3s; some operated as twin-float seaplanes. In 1918, 10 R-9s (incl. 39035/39042, 33748), which were bomber versions of the R-6 using Curtiss V2-C10 engines, were received from the U.S. Navy. Data for R-4: Span, 48 ft. $4\frac{1}{4}$ in.; length, 28 ft. $11\frac{3}{4}$ in.; wing area, 545 sq. ft.; empty weight, 2,225 lb.; gross weight, 3,272 lb.; high speed, 90 m.p.h.

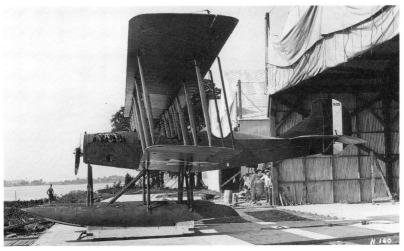

Curtiss R-6 with three-bay wings (*Signal Corps photo 338/National Archives*).

603

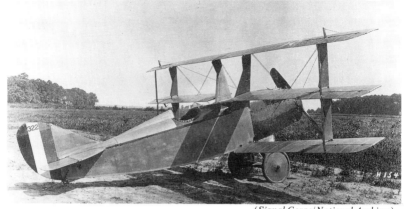

(*Signal Corps/National Archives*).

CURTISS S-3

The four Curtiss S-3s (serials 322/325) of 1916/17 were developed from two earlier Curtiss single-seaters that were not bought by the Army. The S-1, known as the Baby Scout, was the smallest aeroplane that could be built around the 90–100 h.p. Curtiss OX-series engine, with a 20-ft. span. The S-2 had a larger upper wing and a unique "wireless" system of wing bracing. The S-3 substituted wire-braced triplane wings but was otherwise identical to the S-2. Although tested with an armament of two forward-firing Lewis guns, the S-3s were unarmed in service and were used only as trainers.

(*U.S. Navy photo 15829*).

CURTISS L-2

The four Curtiss Ls (473/476) of 1917–18 were derived from the 1916 commercial model L triplane, a type noted for its docile handling characteristics; production of the militarized versions was shared with the Navy. The L-1 was a refinement of the original L, retaining its side-by-side seating but using refined streamlining. The L-2, one a seaplane as illustrated, used a lower wing equal in span to the two uppers and it was rigged without dihedral. Powerplant for all but one L was the 100 h.p. Curtiss OXX; the other used the 90 h.p. OX-5.

604

GALLAUDET D-2

Great aerodynamic efficiency was claimed for this aeroplane, with its two 150 h.p. Hall-Scott engines buried in the fuselage. Both were connected to a four-blade propeller that was mounted on a ring completely encircling the fuselage aft of the wing. Company advertising claimed a cruising speed of 100 m.p.h. on two engines and 70 m.p.h. on one. While the Army bought only four, similar models were also sold to the Navy, which developed the design further, replacing the twin Hall-Scotts with a single Liberty. This improved D-4 model was used as a Naval racer in early post-war years.

LWF V-3 (*L.W.F. photo*).

L.W.F. V AND F

The L.W.F. Engineering Co., Inc. (the initials standing for Lowe, Willard and Fowler) was formed in 1915 at College Point, Long Island, and first produced a two-seat observation and training design called Model V. The Army bought 23 variants of this design before World War I (112/113, 447/467) as trainers and for observation, and another 112 in 1917 and 1918 (inc. 705, 2268/2304, 2509/2518, 12883/12894 and 39920/39950). The V-1 had a 140-h.p. Sturtevant engine in place of the 135-h.p. Thomas; the V-2 had a 165-h.p. Hall-Scott and radiator under the upper wing; the V-3 had a 200-h.p. Sturtevant. The Model F was a special V-2 to test the original 8-cylinder Liberty engine, which made its first flight on June 16, 1917.

605

Martin S.

MARTIN MODELS T AND S

The first of an eventual 17 Martin Model T and TT Trainers were sold to the Army between 1914 and 1916 as the result of a request from Grover Loening, in charge of the Army Aviation School at San Diego, to adapt the current production tractor to dual control as a replacement for the Army's unairworthy pusher trainers. The initial Ts were procured without engines, the Army installing its own 90 h.p. Curtiss OXs removed from other aeroplanes. A later version of the basic T design featured improved streamlining and a large wing with three bays of struts and used a variety of power plants including Curtiss OX, 125-h.p. Hall-Scott, and 135-h.p. Sturtevant.

The Model S was a direct development of the T, the major changes being the use of the 125-h.p. Hall-Scott A-5 engine and the ailerons built into the upper wing instead of being between the wings. Appearance was distinctive due to the location of the fuselage above the lower wing instead of on it. The Army bought six as observation seaplanes late in 1915 and ordered eight more in June 1916.

Martin TT at North Island (*Erickson collection/USAF*).

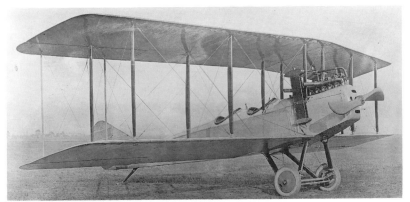

Standard H-3 (*Standard photo*).

SLOAN/STANDARD H-2 & H-3

The Sloan H-2 of 1916 was a reconnaissance biplane designed by Charles Healey Day, formerly of Martin, and was distinguished by the 10-degree sweepback of the equal-span wings. The Army bought three, powered with 125 h.p. Hall-Scott A-5 engines. Nine improved versions known as H-3 (82/89 and one other) were bought and used as trainers. When the Sloan Aircraft Co., Inc., became the nucleus of the Standard Aero Corporation, the aeroplanes in service became known as Standards. H-3: Span, 40 ft. 1 in.; length, 27 ft.; gross weight, 2,700 lb.; maximum speed, 84 m.p.h.

Sturtevant Model S (*Erickson collection/USAF*).

STURTEVANT S AND S-4

In 1915, Grover Loening left the employ of the Army at San Diego and joined the Sturtevant Aeroplane Co. of Boston, Mass., as chief engineer. He developed a series of trainers and observation types for both the Army and Navy. Two Model S advanced trainers (110 and 111) were followed by four S-4 seaplanes (126, 127, 214 and 215). An advanced feature of the Sturtevant designs was the all-metal structure. Model S: 150 h.p. Sturtevant; span, 48 ft. 8 in.; length, 29 ft. 0 in.; gross weight, 3,100 lb.; high speed, 75 m.p.h.

THOMAS D-5

The two-seat Thomas D-5 observation design, powered by a 135-h.p. Thomas engine, was designed for the Thomas Brothers Aeroplane Company of Bath, N.Y., by B. Douglas Thomas, (no relation) who had designed the Model J for Curtiss while still in England after leaving the employ of Avro. His first Thomas Bros. design, the T-2, was an attempt to improve on the Curtiss J. Work was started at Bath in 1914, but was completed following a move to Ithaca, N.Y. The British Thomas became chief designer for Thomas Brothers, and retained the position after the aeroplane and engine manufacturer merged with the Morse Chain Company of Ithaca. Two D-5s (serials 114/115) were bought by the Army for evaluation. Span, 52 ft. 9 in.; length, 29 ft. 9 in.; empty weight, 1,300 lb.; gross weight, 2,500 lb.; high speed, 86 m.p.h.

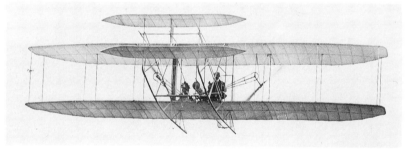

WRIGHT MODEL A

On February 10, 1908, a contract was signed by the U.S. government for one two-seat Wright Model A at a price of $25,000, with bonus and penalty clauses applying to the performance guarantees. The demonstration took place later in the year, on the Parade Ground at Fort Meyer, Virginia, just outside Washington. By September 17, 1908, all tests had met the requirements. The twin pusher propellers had been changed prior to one of the last flights, on which Lt. Thomas B. Selfridge was to be Orville Wright's passenger. These were of slightly larger diameter than the originals, and a diagonal wire, normally clear of the adjacent propeller, vibrated excessively in a certain airspeed range and fouled it. Selfridge was killed in the resulting crash and Wright was injured. The Model A (Serial 1) was rebuilt and was accepted by the Army the following year. When the Smithsonian Institution requested the world's first military aeroplane for a display item, the Wright factory restored it as near to the original configuration as was possible. The aeroplane hangs today in one of the main halls of the Smithsonian, almost in sight of the still-extant original flying site. Span, 36 ft. 4 in.; length, 28 ft.; empty weight, 740 lb.; gross weight, 1,200 lb.; high speed, 44 m.p.h.

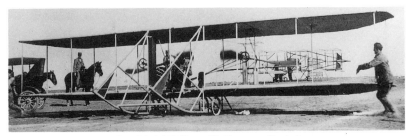

Wright Model B (*Peter M. Bowers collection*).

WRIGHT MODELS B AND C

The Model B was a greatly improved A, the major change being re-location of the elevators from a position ahead of the wings to a rearward position in contemporary "Tractor" configuration. The wing-warping, two-lever controls, and chain-driven propellers behind the wings were retained but wheel landing gear replaced the skids of the original A, which was launched down a rail by a falling weight. The two Bs (serials 3 and 4) were used as trainers, with instructor and student sharing some of the controls, which were not completely duplicated. The seven Model Cs (serials 7, 10-14, 16), practically identical to the B, eliminated this by installing full dual controls. Span, 38 ft.; length, 30 ft.; empty weight, 930 lb.; gross weight, 1,380 lb.; high speed, 54 m.p.h.

WRIGHT F

After the Wright Brothers conformed to the general trend of design by putting the empennage in the rear with their model "B" in 1910, their next step was to abandon open work tail booms in favour of a fuselage that enclosed the two-man crew and the engine. The single Model F produced for the Army by the Wrights (serial 39) retained the old features of warping wing control and chain-drive pusher propellers. An improved Model HS, with shorter wings and a 60 h.p. Wright replacing the 90 h.p. Austro–Daimler of the F, was tested by the Army at San Diego but was

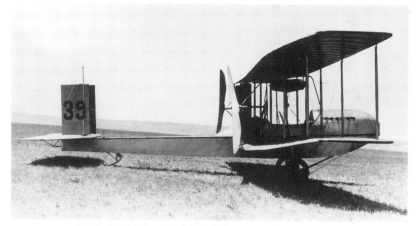

Wright Model F at North Island (*Erickson collection/USAF*).

not purchased. Model F data: Span, 42 ft.; length, 29 ft. 6 in.; gross weight, 2,100 lb.; high speed, 60 m.p.h.

WRIGHT-MARTIN R

In September 1916 the Glenn L. Martin Company and the various Wright interests combined with the Simplex Automobile Company and the General Aeronautical Corporation to form the Wright–Martin Company. Martin retained the Los Angeles factory to complete earlier Army contracts, including two 125 h.p. Hall–Scott powered Model Rs (108, 109) with one-piece round rudders, under his own name. The following 12 Rs (522/533) powered by the 150 h.p. A-5A and with fixed vertical fin, including the last three on pontoons, were delivered as Wright–Martin.

(*Signal Corps/National Archives photo 5121*).

MINOR TYPES, 1917 TO DATE

This appendix includes illustrations of those aircraft of American design or manufacture which served with the Army or Air Force since 1917, but were not significant enough to merit lengthier treatment in the main portion of this volume. Also included here are a few types which remained experimental but were significant in the development of operational techniques, such as the pressure-cabin Lockheed XC-35 and the Douglas XB-43 jet bomber. Purely experimental prototypes are not included; nor are some types purchased in evaluation quantities but not used in service. Conversely, aircraft of which only single examples were procured are illustrated if they served in an operational capacity.

RU-9D (*Aero Design photo*).

AERO COMMANDER L-26, U-4, U-9

Several examples of the Aero Design Commander light twin went into service with USAF and U.S. Army. Service trials were made with three YL-26 (Army) and one YL-26A (AF), equivalents of the commercial 520 and 560 respectively. AF purchased 15 L-26B (commercial 560A) for staff transports, and the Army bought one. Equivalent of the 680 Super, the two AF L-26Cs were allocated for Presidential use; Army obtained four similar models. Army also evaluated two RL-26D, in which Motorola side-looking radar was carried, faired into the lower fuselage. USAF versions were redesignated U-4A and U-4B in 1960; Army versions became U-9B, U-9C and RU-9D in 1962. Span, 49 ft. 6 in.; length, 35 ft. 11¼ in.; gross weight, 7,000 lb.; max. speed, 250 m.p.h.; range, 1,500 miles.

American Y1C-24 (Peter M. Bowers).

AMERICAN Y1C-24

The four Y1C-24s (32-287/290), nicknamed "Yics" by their crews, were unarmed military variants of the commercial American Pilgrim single-engine transport then in use on some American airlines. Powered by a 575 h.p. Wright R-1820-1 Cyclone engine, the ten-place Pilgrim was one of the largest single-engine monoplanes in Army service. The Y1C-24s were distributed throughout various squadrons as utility aircraft for such purposes as transport of needed spare parts and personnel and were redesignated C-24 upon completion of service testing. Span, 57 ft.; length, 39 ft. 2 in.; wing area, 459 sq. ft.; empty weight, 4,195 lb.; gross weight, 7,070 lb.; high speed, 135 m.p.h.

Beech AT-10 (*Beech photo 3257*).

BEECH AT-10

The Beech AT-10 resulted from a programme undertaken in 1941/42 to conserve essential metals for combat aircraft by building the trainer types out of non-strategic materials. The AT-10, powered by the same 295 h.p. Lycoming R-680-9 radial engines used in the Cessna AT-8 and Curtiss AT-9, was designed to serve the same transition trainer function but the entire airframe, except for engine nacelles, was of wooden construction. Beech built 1,771 AT-10s at Wichita and Globe (which became Temco after World War II) built 600 in Dallas, Texas. Span, 44 ft.; length, 34 ft. 4 in.; gross weight, 6,465 lb.; max. speed, 190 m.p.h.

Beech T-34 (*Beech photo 1-18562-30*).

BEECH T-42 COCHISE

The US Army picked the Beech B55 Baron as its new fixed-wing twin-engined instrument trainer in February 1965, following evaluation of suitable types for an off-the-shelf purchase. A single batch of 65 Barons was ordered, with the designation T-42A (65-12679/12733, 66-4300/4309) for service at the Army Aviation School and five more (71-21053/21057) in 1971 for MAP. The T-42A was powered by two 260 h.p. Continental IO-470-L engines. Span, 37 ft. 10 in.; length, 27 ft. 0 in.; gross weight, 5,100 lb.; cruising speed, 195 m.p.h.

Beech QU-22B (*Beech photo 35880-17*).

BEECH U-22

Between 30 and 40 Beech 36 Bonanzas were procured by the USAF in 1969 for service over Vietnam as electronic intelligence-gathering drones in the *Pave Eagle* project. Modification of the basic commercial aircraft, by Univac Division of Sperry Rand, included installation of remote control equipment and an electronic package. Six YQU-22A (Beech Model PD. 1079) prototypes (68-10531/10536) were followed by 27 QU-22B production models (69-7693/7705, 70-1535/1548), which operated over South Vietnam from bases in Thailand, carrying a one-man crew to monitor the electronic equipment in the cabin. The QU-22 engine was a 285 h.p. Continental IO-520-B. Single YAU-22A (70-7859) was Beech Model PD.249 with 345 h.p. GIO-520 and six wing pylons for light close support rôle. Span, 32 ft. 10 in.; length, 26 ft. 4 in.; gross weight, 3,600 lb.; max. speed, 204 m.p.h.

Bell YFM-1B (*Peter M. Bowers*).

BELL YFM-1 AIRACUDA

Only aircraft produced in the FM (fighter, multiplace) category, the Bell XFM-1 (36-351) had a crew of five including two gunners in wing nacelles, and two 1,150-h.p. V-1710-13 pusher engines. It first flew on September 1, 1937, and was followed on September 28, 1939, by the first of nine YFM-1s (38-486/491, 493/495) with -23 engines, heavier armament and bomb-racks. Three YFM-1As (38-496/498) delivered late 1940 had tricycle undercarriage and two of the -1s (38-489/490) became YFM-1Bs with -41 engines. Span, 70 ft.; length, 46 ft.; gross weight, 18,000 lb.; max. speed, 270 m.p.h. at 12,600 ft.

(*Howard Levy*).

BELL R-12/H-12

Thirteen Bell Model 48 five-seat general utility helicopters were ordered by the Air Force in 1946, and the first two were completed as XR-12s (46-214/215) with 600-h.p. R-1340 engines. The third prototype was enlarged to seat a maximum of ten persons and designated XR-12B (46-216). Ten YR-12Bs (46-217/226) were similar with R-1340-55 engines and were used for a variety of test programmes. A production contract for 34 R-12A (47-491/524) was cancelled in 1947 and the R-12s became H-12s in 1948. Rotor diameter, 47 ft. 6 in.; length, 41 ft. 7 in.; gross weight, 6,800 lb.; max, speed, 100 m.p.h.

614

Bell/Boeing V-22A prototype prior to first flight, in Marine Corps grey and green camouflage (*Bell photo*).

BELL/BOEING V-22 OSPREY

One of the most radical aircraft selected for production and service with the USAF, the V-22A Osprey featured a tilting-rotor configuration based on the successful testing of two Bell XV-15 prototypes from 1977 onwards. The V-22 design was selected in April 1983 to meet a requirement for a Joint Services Advanced Vertical Lift Aircraft (the JVX), in which all four services had an interest. The Army dropped out of the programme in 1988, but a USAF requirement for 80 CV-22As for use by the SOF remained. Powered by two Allison T406-AD-400 turboshafts, the CV-22As could carry 12 troops or 2,800 lb. of cargo. Flight testing of the Osprey began in 1989. Span (between rotor centres), 46 ft. 6¾ in.; length, 57 ft. 4 in.; gross weight, 59,000 lb.; max. cruising speed, 391 m.p.h.

C-27C (*W. L. Swisher*).

BELLANCA C-27 SERIES

The Bellanca C-27 was an example of an existing civil design adapted to military cargo/transport requirements. Its origin was the civil Airbus. Four 12-seat Y1C-27s (32-399/402) with large cargo loading doors and 550-h.p. Pratt & Whitney R-1860 Hornet engines were ordered for service test and were followed by 10 C-27As (33-18/27) with 650-h.p. R-1860-19. The single C-27B (33-19) was the second C-27A with engine changed to the slightly smaller but more powerful Wright R-1820-17 Cyclone of 675 h.p. Improved performance with the Cyclone resulted in all Y1C-27s and the remaining C-27As being converted to C-27Cs with 750-h.p. R-1820-25 power plants. Span, 65 ft.; length, 42 ft. 9 in.; wing area, 737 sq. ft.; empty weight, 5,402 lb.; gross weight, 9,655 lb.

PB-1 in War Games camouflage (*Gordon S. Williams collection*).

BERLINER–JOYCE PB-1

In 1929 the Army ordered a two-seat pursuit prototype, for the first time since 1923. After trials with this prototype, the Berliner–Joyce XP-16 (29-326), a batch of 25 similar Y1P-16s was ordered (31-502/515, 31-597, 32-221/230). After delivery, they were re-designated PB-1, as the first aircraft in the pursuit, biplace, category. The engine was the 600-h.p. Curtiss V-1570 (supercharged in the XP-16). Span, 34 ft. 0 in.; length, 28 ft. 10 in.; gross weight, 3,996 lb.; max. speed, 175 m.p.h. at sea level.

BOEING C-73

Twenty-seven of the total of 75 Boeing 247s built were drafted by the Army in 1942, receiving these serial numbers: 42-38274/5, -56642, -57153, -57208/11, -57508/9, -61094, -68336, -68363/73, -68853/4, -68859 and -78017. The first 60 had been built as plain Model 247 but were later modified to 247D standard. The small airline cabin and doors precluded their use for heavy cargo and troop carrying so they were relegated to crew ferrying and later to training. The Army replaced 550 h.p. Pratt & Whitney Wasp S1H-1G engines with 600-h.p. R-1340-AN-1s. Span, 64 ft.; length, 51 ft. 7 in.; gross weight, 13,650 lb.; high speed, 200 m.p.h.

Boeing C-75 (*Imperial War Museum CH 17805*).

BOEING C-75

All five of the TWA Boeing SA-307B Stratoliners of 1939/40 were drafted into the Air Transport Command in 1942 (42-88623/88627). Flown by TWA crews, they were used principally on the North and South Atlantic routes where their range and altitude capability combined with the first pressurized passenger cabins used on commercial aircraft suited them to the carriage of the highest-ranking military and civilian personnel. Power plant, 900-h.p. Wright GR-1820; span, 107 ft. 3 in.; length, 74 ft. 4 in.; wing area, 1,486 sq. ft.; gross weight, 45,000 lb.; high speed, 246 m.p.h. at 17,300 ft.

XB-15 serving with 2nd Bomb Group (*Gordon S. Williams*).

BOEING XB-15

Plans for a bomber with a 5,000-mile range, capable of hitting targets in Alaska or Hawaii, were drawn up at Wright Field in 1933. Boeing and Martin tendered design studies, the Boeing Model 294 design being accepted for prototype construction and ordered in July 1935. The original XBLR-1 designation was changed to XB-15 before the first flight on October 15, 1937, by Eddie Allen. The single XB-15 (35-277) was converted in 1943 to the XC-105 transport with cargo doors and hoist, the gross weight increasing to 92,000 lb. Span, 149 ft. 0 in.; length, 87 ft. 11 in.; gross weight, 70,700 lb.; max. speed, 195 m.p.h.

YL-15 (*James C. Fahey*).

BOEING L-15

The Boeing Model 451 was designed to meet a U.S. Army requirement for an observation and liaison aircraft. Powered by a 125 h.p. Lycoming O-290-7, the L-15 could operate on wheels, floats or skis. The company's Wichita division built the two prototype XL-15s (46-520/521) in 1947 and ten YL-15s (47-423/432) in 1948; a further 47 (47-433/479) were cancelled. The YL-15s went eventually to the Forestry Service. Span, 40 ft.; length, 25 ft. 10 in.; gross weight, 2,111 lb.; max. speed, 104 m.p.h.

618

Boeing T-43A (*Boeing photo R496*).

BOEING T-43A

On May 27, 1971, the USAF announced that it had selected the Boeing 737-253 for an off-the-shelf buy to meet its requirements for a navigation trainer replacing the Convair T-29. The contract was for 19 aircraft designated T-43A (71-1403/1406, 72-282/288; 73-1149/1156), and deliveries were to start in 1973. Powered by two Pratt & Whitney JT8D-9 turbofans, the T-43A had 19 navigator stations in the fuselage—12 for students, 4 for advanced students and 3 for instructors. They were assigned to the 323rd FTW at Mather A.F.B., California, with four transferred later to Colorado ANG. Span, 93 ft.; length, 100 ft.; gross weight, 114,500 lb.; max. cruising speed, 568 m.p.h. at 21,000 ft.

Boeing C-22B, DC Air National Guard (*Donald S. McGarry*).

BOEING C-22

During 1983, four Boeing 727s were purchased by the DoD and were issued to the Air National Guard, to be operated by Detachment 1 of the District of Columbia ANG, based at Andrews A.F.B., Maryland. Replacing T-43As, the aircraft were for use to carry inspection and training teams and various delegations from Washington to other points throughout the U.S. Designated C-22Bs (83-4610, 4612, 4615/4616), these aircraft were ex-commercial 727-100s originally owned by National Airlines and then Pan American, and they became operational on April 23, 1986. Another 727-100 was acquired as the sole C-22A (84-0193) for use as the personal transport of Commander U.S. Southern Command, and was operated by the 310th Military Airlift Squadron. The C-22s were powered by 14,500 lb.s.t. Pratt & Whitney JT8D-7 turbofans. Span, 108 ft. 0 in.; length, 116 ft. 2 in.; wing area, 1,700 sq. ft.; empty weight, 81,534 lb.; gross weight, 142,000 lb.; max speed, 630 m.p.h. at 22,300 ft.

619

Penguin (*Signal Corps photo 26944/National Archives*).

BREESE PENGUIN

The Breese Penguin was built to apply the peculiar French technique of pre-flight ground training to the admirably suited open Texas Prairies. The aircraft used, called "Roleurs" by the French, were low-powered machines with normal aeroplane features except that the wings were too small to permit flight. They got up enough speed, however, for the student to raise the tail and get the "feel" of the controls. The Breese and the ground-running method were not adopted, possibly due to the rough-running 28 h.p. Lawrance two-cylinder engine, and 296 of the 301 Penguins (inc. 33475/33759) were placed in storage until after the war.

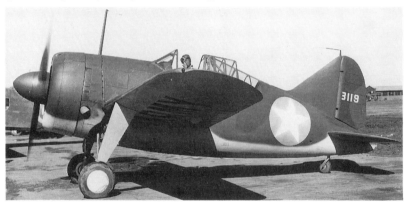

Ex-Dutch B339D in Australia.

BREWSTER B-339D

The Brewster B-339 was an export model of the single-seat fighter designed by the Brewster company under U.S. Navy contract as the F2A-1. The Dutch purchased, for operational use in the Dutch East Indies, 72 B-339Ds, and 20 B-439s with longer fuselages and extra fuel capacity. After the Japanese occupation of the Dutch East Indies early in 1942, the 20 B-439s and a single B-339D arrived in Australia, where all were assigned immediately to the USAAF. Span, 35 ft. 0 in.; length, 26 ft. 7½ in.; wing area, 208·9 sq. ft.; empty weight, 4,216 lb.; gross weight, 6,627 lb.; max. speed, 290 m.p.h. at 16,500 ft.

620

LC-126A (*Cessna photo*).

CESSNA LC-126

Fifteen Cessna 195 commercial aircraft were purchased "off-the-shelf" by the USAF in 1949 at the request of the Army for evaluation in the light cargo and liaison role. These were designated LC-126As. A further order was placed in 1951 for 63 similar aircraft designated LC-126C, for use as instrument trainers. Five LC-126Bs were used by the Air National Guard, from 1950. The LC-126 variants, like the Model 195, were powered by the 300 h.p. Jacobs R-755-11 radial engine. Span, 36 ft. 2 in.; length, 27 ft. 2 in.; gross weight, 3,300 lb.; cruising speed, 140 m.p.h.

Cessna U-3A, Iowa NG (*MAP photo*).

CESSNA U-3

USAF selected the Cessna 310 in 1957 under the designation L-27A; 160 were eventually procured, with the designation changed to U-3A (57-5846/5925, 58-2107/2186). The 35 U-3Bs had swept fins, more cabin windows, and a longer nose. Engines were 240-h.p. Continental O-470-M. Span, 35 ft. 9 in.; length, 29 ft. 7 in.; gross weight, 4,830 lb. (U-3A), 4,990 lb. (U-3B); max. speed, 230 m.p.h.

Cessna T-41As with combined military/civil markings (*Cessna photo GMN-27*).

CESSNA T-41 MESCALERO

In July 1964, the USAF decided to reintroduce a piston-engined primary trainer as a means of eliminating unsuitable pilot trainees before they progressed to the more expensive T-37 which had been in use since 1961 for "all-through" jet training. The Cessna Model 172 was picked off-the-shelf to meet this requirement, and an order was placed on July 31, 1964, for 170 aircraft with the designation T-41A. A second batch of 34 was ordered in July 1967. The first T-41As were delivered between September 1964 and July 1965 and went into service at eight civilian contract flight schools, each located close to one of Air Training Command's Undergraduate Pilot Training bases. Because of their civil operation, the aircraft carried FAA registrations in addition to the USAF serial numbers, the "N" numbers being chosen to coincide with the serials (65-5100/5269, 67-14959/14992). For use at the USAF Academy, Colorado, the USAF acquired 52 T-41Cs (68-7866/7910, 69-7750/7756), these being equivalent to the commercial R172E with 210 h.p. Continental IO-360-D engines and fixed pitch propellers. Also similar to the R172E were 255 T-41Bs (67-15000/15254) acquired by the U.S. Army as trainers and for installation support duties, and the 238 T-41Ds acquired for export to a variety of nations through MAP. Span, 35 ft. 9½ in.; length, 26 ft. 11 in.; wing area, 174 sq. ft.; gross weight, 2,300 lb.; cruising speed, 117 m.p.h.

622

Cessna U-17C (*Cessna photo*).

CESSNA U-17

Starting in 1963, the USAF has purchased more than 450 examples of the Cessna 185 Skywagon with the designations U-17A, B and C. These six-seat utility aircraft have been supplied to many countries eligible for aid under the US Military Assistance Programme, but were not operated by the USAF. Among the recipients of the U-17 were Bolivia, Costa Rica, Greece, Laos, Nicaragua, Turkey and the South Vietnamese Air Force. Procurement included 262 U-17As and 205 U-17Bs with 300 h.p. Continental IO-520-D engine, and seven U-17Cs with 230 h.p. O-470-L engine. Span, 36 ft. 2 in.; length, 25 ft. 9 in.; gross weight, 3,300 lb.; max. speed, 178 m.p.h.

YC-122 (*William T. Larkins*).

CHASE YC-122

The Chase Aircraft Company of New York and, later, Willow Run built two XCG-14 cargo gliders (Chase Model MS-1), followed by two XCG-18A all-metal versions. Five YG-18As followed, and the second (47-641) was converted to the prototype YC-122 light assault transport by the addition of two R-2000-11 radial engines. Two YC-122As were built in 1949 (48-1369 and 70) and the second became YC-122B with R-1820-101 engines. A service trial batch of nine similar YC-122Cs served with the 18th Air Force, TAC for some years from 1950. Span, 95 ft. 8 in.; length, 61 ft. 8 in.; gross weight, 32,000 lb.; top speed, 220 m.p.h.; normal range, 2,900 miles.

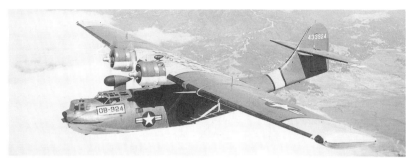

OA-10A with high visibility ASR markings (*William T. Larkins*).

CONSOLIDATED OA-10

Initial procurement of 56 Consolidated OA-10s was a straight transfer of PBY-5A amphibians built for the Navy. They served primarily in search and rescue work throughout World War II and for several years thereafter, some fitted with droppable lifeboats under each wing. The 230 OA-10As were built by Canadian Vickers. Sixty-five OA-10Bs were Consolidated products identical to the improved PBY-6A and could be identified by their taller tails. The Army also operated 16 PB2B-2s, pure PBY-5 flying boats, retaining their original Naval designations and serial numbers.

Convair B-32 (*USAF photo B-29894A*).

CONVAIR B-32 DOMINATOR

Prototypes of the B-32 were ordered in September 1940 at the same time as the B-29, to meet a similar requirement. The first of three XB-32s flew on September 7, 1942; the second, flown on July 2, 1943, changed to a stepped-down cockpit and the third, flown on November 9, 1943, changed from a twin to a single tail. Production models dispensed with pressurization and remote turret controls and had 2,200 h.p. R-3350-23 engines. Convair built 114 B-32s at Fort Worth and one at San Diego; 1,588 were cancelled. Fifteen saw limited action in the Western Pacific in 1945, and 40 were completed as TB-32 for training. Span, 135 ft.; length, 82 ft. 1 in.; gross weight, 111,500 lb.; max. speed, 357 m.p.h.

XC-99 after refit with production B-36 undercarriage (*Peter M. Bowers*).

CONVAIR XC-99

A single XC-99 (43-52436) was built as the transport counterpart of the B-36, retaining the same wings and tail unit and R-4360-41 engines but with a new two-deck fuselage able to accommodate 400 equipped troops, 300 stretchers or 101,000 lb. of freight. The project was approved for construction on December 31, 1942; first flight was made by Russell R. Rogers on November 23, 1947, and the aircraft was delivered to the USAF on May 26, 1949. Based at Kelly A.F.B. and later fitted with nose radar and bogie undercarriage, it operated special transport missions until retired in 1957. Span, 230 ft.; length, 185 ft.; gross weight, 320,000 lb.; max. speed, 300 m.p.h.

L-13B (*Boardman C. Reed*).

CONVAIR L-13

Consolidated Vultee developed the L-13 in the closing stages of World War II as a general liaison, observation, photographic and ambulance aircraft. It was powered by a 245-h.p. Franklin O-425-5 flat-six engine. Two XL-13s (45-58708/09) were built at the Vultee plant in Wayne in 1945. Delivery began in 1947 of 300 L-13A (46-68/213, 47-267/420), including 48 for the ANG, with O-425-9, folding wings and tail and six seats. Twenty-eight L-13Bs were winterized "A"s for Arctic use, on skis, floats or wheels. Span, 40 ft. 6 in.; length, 31 ft. 9 in.; gross weight, 3,500 lb.; max. speed, 115 m.p.h.

PQ-8A (*Harold G. Martin*).

CULVER A-8/PQ-8

Among the aircraft types adapted for use as radio-controlled targets in 1940/41 was the Culver Cadet, a two-seat light monoplane with a Continental O-200 engine. The first tested by the Army was originally A-8 and later XPQ-8 (41-18889). A production batch of 200 PQ-8s was followed by an equal quantity of PQ-8As (later Q-8As) with the 125-h.p. Lycoming O-290 engine and higher performance. Span, 26 ft. 11 in.; length, 17 ft. 8 in.; gross weight, 1,305 lb.; max. speed, 116 m.p.h.

PQ-14B (*Warren M. Bodie*).

CULVER PQ-14, PQ-15

The successful use of the PQ-8 targets led to the development in 1942 of a larger version of the same design. A prototype was ordered as the XPQ-14 with a Franklin O-300 engine, and 75 YPQ-14As were similar. The Army procured a total of 1,348 PQ-14A (Q-14A later) of which 1,198 were assigned to the USN as TD2C-1s. The YPQ-14B (25 built) and PQ-14B (594 built) were heavier. One had an O-300-9 engine and became the PQ-14C. Four drone versions of the post-war commercial Culver "V" were XPQ-15. Span, 30 ft.; length, 19 ft. 6 in.; gross weight, 1,830 lb.

Curtiss 18-B (*McCook Field photo*).

CURTISS 18-B and 18-T

In the spring of 1918, when the only American-designed aircraft in production for the Army were trainers, Curtiss developed an entirely new two-seat fighter powered by an equally new all-American engine, the 400-h.p. Kirkham K-12. The design was introduced in two forms, the Model 18-B Hornet biplane and the 18-T Wasp triplane. The pilot was provided with two 0·30-in.-calibre Marlin machine guns and the observer/gunner with the standard twin Lewis guns. Two additional Lewises could be mounted to fire downward through the floor. Performance of the 18-T exceeded that of contemporary single-seat fighters, and for a while a stock model with full military load held the world's speed record at 163 m.p.h. The war ended before the Army Model 18s were delivered; wartime tests were run on 18-T A-3325 borrowed from the Navy. Two 18-Bs (40058, 40064) and two 18-Ts (40054, 40059) were delivered in 1919. Data, 18-B and (in parentheses) 18-T: Span, 37 ft. 5¾ in. (31 ft. 11 in.); length, 23 ft. 4 in. (23 ft. 3 in.); wing area, 337 sq. ft. (309 sq. ft.); gross weight, 3,001 lb. (2,901 lb.); high speed, 160 m.p.h. (163 m.p.h.).

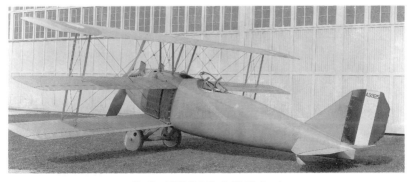

Curtiss 18-T (*McCook Field photo*).
627

Eberhart S.E.5E with plywood-covered fuselage (*U.S. Army photo*).

CURTISS S.E.5A/EBERHART S.E.5E

One of the best known designs selected by the Bolling Commission for U.S. production was the S.E.5A, designed by H. P. Folland in Britain. Planned mass production by Curtiss did not materialize but the company modified and assembled 57 British-built airframes (which retained their British serials). In 1922 and 1923, the Eberhart Steel Products Co. rebuilt 50 S.E.s with 180-h.p. Wright-Hispano Es for use as advanced trainers under the designation of S.E.5E (22-276/325) Span, 26 ft. 9 in.; length, 20 ft. 10 in.; area, 247 sq. ft.; weight, 2,060 lb.; high speed, 122 m.p.h.

(*Curtiss photo*).

CURTISS EAGLE

Three examples (64242/64244) of the Curtiss Eagle 10-seat cabin biplane transport were sold to the Army, but differed from the three-engined commercial model in having only a single Liberty engine in the nose. One of the Army Eagles was evaluated as a four-litter ambulance. Span, 64 ft. 4¼ in.; length, 36 ft.; height, 12 ft. 11 in.; wing area, 800 sq. ft.; gross weight, 7,423 lb.; high speed, 100 m.p.h.

R-6 serial 68563 (*U.S. Army photo*).

CURTISS R-6

Two Curtiss R-6s (68563/68564) were built for the 1922 Pulitzer race. Lt. Russell Maughan won in '64 and Lt. Lester J. Maitland was second in '63. Four days after the race Gen. Billy Mitchell used '64 to set a world one-km. speed record of 224·28 m.p.h. This was raised to 236·587 m.p.h. by Maughan in March 1923. Both R-6s were flown in subsequent Pulitzers, but one shed its wings on a diving start in the 1924 race. Span, 19 ft. 10 in.; length, 18 ft. 10½ in.; area, 135·9 sq. ft.; empty weight, 1,615 lb.; gross weight, 2,120 lb.; max. speed, 239·95 m.p.h.

R3C-1, 1925 Pulitzer winner (*Curtiss photo*).

CURTISS R-8/R3C-1

The R-8 of 1924 (23-1235), bought from the Navy for $1.00, was one of the two Curtiss R2C-1s built for the Pulitzer Race of 1923. Following the crash of the R-8 before the 1924 race, the Army and Navy joined in development and purchase of three improved R3C-1s for the 1925 races. Flying one of these with the Navy designation, Lt. Cyrus Bettis won the 1925 Pulitzer for the Army. With the same aircraft on floats as R3C-2, Lt. Jimmy Doolittle won the 1925 Schneider contest and then set the world seaplane record at 245·713 m.p.h. R3C-1: 590 h.p. V-1400 engine; span, 22 ft.; length, 19 ft. 8½ in.; wing area, 149 sq. ft.; gross weight, 2,150 lb.

Curtiss B-2 in War Games camouflage (*Peter M. Bowers collection*).

CURTISS B-2

The 12 Curtiss B-2 Condors (28-398/399, 29-28/37) were production versions of the single XB-2 (26-211) which itself was a direct development of the Curtiss-built Martin MB-2 (NBS-1) through the two Curtiss XNBS-4s. Principal changes were use of steel tubing instead of wood for fuselage construction, Curtiss Conqueror engines instead of Liberty, and use of thicker Curtiss C-72 airfoil. The outstanding feature of the B-2 was the location of a machine gunner in the rear of each engine nacelle. One B-2 became B-2A when fitted with full dual controls. Span, 90 ft.; length, 47 ft. 6 in.; gross weight, 16,500 lb.; max. speed, 133 m.p.h.

Curtiss A-18 (*U.S. Army photo*).

CURTISS A-14, A-18 SHRIKE

In 1934 Curtiss submitted its Model 76 to the Army as XA-14 in response to a requirement for a new two-seat twin-engine attack design. The XA-14 was tested at Wright Field with experimental Curtiss XR-1510 twin-row engines, and was then purchased by the Army. It was re-delivered in standard Army markings (36-146) with 735 h.p. Wright R-1670-5 engines. Thirteen service test Y1A-18s (37-52/64) ordered in 1936 were virtually identical except for installation of the 600 h.p. Wright R-1820-47 Cyclone engines. Span, 59 ft. 6 in.; length, 42 ft. 4 in.; wing area, 526 sq. ft.; gross weight, 12,679 lb.; high speed, 238 m.p.h. at 3,500 ft.

(*Peter M. Bowers*).

CURTISS O-52

The Curtiss Model 85 Owl drew heavily on experience with 1934/1939 Naval models, using the Hawk III (BF2C-1) landing gear and the collapsible rear turtledeck structure of the SOC and SO3C Seagulls and the SB2C-1 Helldiver that gave the observer/gunner a clear field of fire for his single 0·50-inch calibre machine gun. The 203 all-metal O-52s (40-2688/2890) were not used in combat in World War II, but served as trainers. Power plant was a 600-h.p. R-1340-51. Span, 43 ft. 10 in.; length, 25 ft. 5 in.; wing area, 210 sq. ft.; empty weight, 4,230 lb.; gross weight, 5,307 lb.; high speed, 208 m.p.h.

(*Peter M. Bowers*).

CURTISS AT-9

The AT-9 was designed as a twin-engine pilot transition trainer at a time when there was a need for a "hot" trainer with light bomber landing characteristics. The original AT-9 prototype (Curtiss-Wright Model 25) used a steel tube fuselage and fabric covered wings, but the production version was all stressed skin, as illustrated. The 491 AT-9s and 300 AT-9As, useful for pilot transition only, were phased out of service as production tactical models and more versatile trainers for full crew integration training became available. Engines were 295 h.p. Lycoming R-680-9. Span, 40 ft. 4 in.; length, 31 ft. 8 in.; wing area, 233 sq. ft.; empty weight, 4,600 lb.; gross weight, 6,000 lb.; high speed, 197 m.p.h.

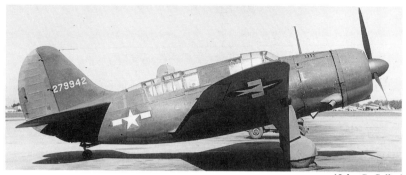

(*John C. Collins*)

CURTISS A-25

Orders for the Curtiss Helldiver were placed in April 1941 at the same time as the Douglas A-24. As the A-25A, the Air Corps ordered a total of 900 Curtiss bombers, closely similar to the USN SB2C-1. Naval gear and wing-folding mechanism were deleted and additional Army equipment specified, but most of the A-25s were re-assigned to the U.S. Marines as SB2C-1As. The engine was a 1,700 h.p. R-2600-8. Span, 49 ft. 9 in.; length, 36 ft. 8 in.; gross weight, 16,000 lb.; max. speed, 275 m.p.h.

TA-3 (*McCook Field photo*).

DAYTON-WRIGHT TA-3

The Dayton-Wright TA-3, marketed commercially as the Chummy, was submitted to the Army in 1921 as a replacement for the OX-5-powered Curtiss JN-4D, which had been withdrawn from service as unsuitable for primary training by post-war standards. Three test models (64390/64392) were ordered, and were unusual in that they reverted to the pre-war side-by-side seating and were the last design submitted to the Army with rotary engines. Even with the lighter airframe, the 80-h.p. Le Rhône was not adequate for the job, so the 10 production TA-3s (22-266/275) were fitted with 110-h.p. Le Rhônes. Eighty-h.p. Model: Span, 30 ft. 11½ in.; length, 22 ft. 7 in.; area, 235 sq. ft.; weight, 1,693 lb.; high speed, 83·8 m.p.h.

TA-5 with test u/c (*McCook Field photo*).

DAYTON-WRIGHT TA-5

In spite of acceptance of the TA-3s, the Army wanted still higher power for primary trainers, so Dayton-Wright developed new models to meet the demand. The TA-5, using the same airframe as the TW-3 (see page 170), was essentially an enlarged TA-3 using the new 200 h.p. Lawrance J-1 radial engine and retaining the same side-by-side seating. The Army bought only a single TA-5 (68583), with the two Dayton-Wright TW-3s. The TA-5 was used for test work, including the unique single-wheel landing gear illustrated. Span, 34ft. 9 in.; length, 25 ft. 8 in.; gross weight, 2,214 lb.; max. speed, 104 m.p.h.

Douglas C-1 (*USAF photo*).

DOUGLAS C-1 SERIES

The C-Class of 1924 was a new series of combined cargo and personnel transport to replace the older T-for-Transport class. First of the new designs was the Douglas C-1, essentially an enlargement of the DWC/O-2 configuration to an 8-seat cabin biplane with two pilots side-by-side in an open cockpit ahead of the wing leading edge. Ten Liberty-powered C-1s were ordered (25-425/434), one being converted to C-1A (25-426) with a geared and supercharged Liberty. A nine-seat version was designated C-1C and 17 were built (26-421/427, 27-203/212). Span, 60 ft.; length, 36 ft.; gross weight, 7,440 lb.; max speed, 121 m.p.h.

DWC for World Flight (*Douglas photo 7574*).

DOUGLAS DWC/DOS/O-5

Four large Douglas two seaters based on the DT series of Navy torpedo planes were built for the Army round-the-world flight of 1924, after a single prototype (23-1210) had been delivered 45 days after the order was placed in July 1923. Four machines (23-1230/1233) started from Seattle on April 6, and two of these completed the westward journey on September 28, having covered 27,553 miles in a total of 175 days. One had been lost in Alaska and another lost in the North Atlantic was replaced by the spare. The flight was conducted alternately on wheels and on twin wooden floats built and installed in Seattle by Boeing. Two of the DWCs, the letters being the official Air Service designation for Douglas World Cruiser, are preserved today, one in the Smithsonian Institution in Washington and the other in the Air Force Museum at Wright-Patterson A.F.B., Ohio. Five militarized near-duplicates of the DWCs were ordered under the initial designation of DOS for Douglas Observation Seaplane, which was changed to O-5 under the new designating system adopted in May 1924. Principal changes were addition of standard military equipment and a reduction of the fuel capacity from 600 to 110 gallons. The O-5s were delivered as twin-float seaplanes for overseas service. Span, 50 ft.; length, 35 ft. $2\frac{1}{2}$ in.; wing area, 694 sq. ft.; empty weight, 4,268 lb.; gross weight, 8,827 lb.; cruising speed, 80 m.p.h.

DWC with armament (*McCook Field photo*).

Y1B-7 (*R. R. Martin*).

DOUGLAS O-35, B-7 SERIES

Douglas produced two nearly identical monoplane prototypes in 1931, the XO-35 (30-227) and the XB-7 (30-228, formerly XO-36). These were of advanced structural concept in that they were all metal, with corrugated wrap-around sheet metal fuselages similar to the Thomas-Morse O-19, and featured retractable landing gear and 600-h.p. Curtiss V-1570 Conqueror engines. Service test orders were placed for five Y1O-35s (32-315/319) and seven Y1B-7s (32-308/314). These were outwardly identical to the prototypes except for substitution of smooth fuselage skin for the original corrugated sheet. The B-7 carried 1,200 lb. of bombs and both were armed with two 0·30 calibre machine guns. Y1B-7: Span, 65 ft. 3 in.; length, 46 ft. 7 in.; area, 621 sq. ft.; gross weight, 11,177 lb.; max. speed, 182 m.p.h.

(*Douglas photo 31105*).

DOUGLAS B-19

Work on the B-19 began early in 1935 under Army auspices as an exercise in large bomber design. Initially designated XBLR-2, it was first flown, after redesignation as XB-19 (38-471), by Major Stanley M. Ulmstead on June 27, 1941. The engines were 2,000 h.p. R-3350-5 radials, the armament totalled two 37-mm., five 0·50-inch and six 0·30-inch guns, and the bomb load totalled 37,100 lb. Max. range was 7,710 miles in 55 flying hours. With 2,600 h.p. Allison V-3420-11 in-line engines, it was redesignated XB-19A and was used during World War II as a transport. Span, 212 ft.; length, 132 ft. 4 in.; gross weight, 162,000 lb.; max. speed, 224 m.p.h.

Douglas B-23 (*Boardman C. Reed*).

DOUGLAS B-23, UC-67

The B-23 Dragon was a development of the B-18A Bolo, with a considerably refined fuselage and—for the first time in a U.S. bomber—a tail gun position. In addition to the 0·50-inch tail gun there were 0·30s in the nose and dorsal and ventral positions. A single contract for 38 B-23s (39-27/39-64) was placed, the first flying on July 27, 1939. Dragons served briefly on coastal patrols on the Pacific coast before being relegated to training. Twelve were converted to transports and for glider towing as UC-67 in 1942. The engines were 1,600 h.p. Wright R-2600-3 radials. Span, 92 ft.; length, 58 ft. 4 in.; gross weight, 30,500 lb.; max. speed, 282 m.p.h. at 12,000 ft.

(*Douglas photo C20429-4*).

DOUGLAS C-74 GLOBEMASTER

Design of the C-74 (Douglas Model 415A) was started during World War II to give USAF a long range heavy transport aircraft. A development of the DC-4 (C-54) it had a circular-section fuselage and its advanced features included an A-12 autopilot, an electric cargo lift in the rear fuselage, integral fuel tanks in the wings, and separate cockpits side-by-side, later replaced by a single canopy. The first C-74 (42-65402) was delivered on October 11, 1945, and the last of 14 built (36 more were cancelled) was delivered on April 28, 1947. Power was provided by four 3,500-h.p. R-4360-49 engines. Span, 173 ft. 3 in.; length, 124 ft. 2 in.; gross weight, 145,000 lb. (overload 165,000 lb.); cargo, 31,486-55,586 lb. or 125 passengers; cruising speed, 176 knots.

(*Douglas photo A51-9-6*).

DOUGLAS C-118A

A total of 101 military versions of the DC-6A was obtained by USAF between 1951 and 1955, for use by MATS Atlantic and Pacific divisions. The C-118A carried 74 passengers or 60 stretchers or 27,000 lb. of cargo, and was powered by 2,500-h.p. R-2800-52W engines. In 1947, one DC-6 was acquired for Presidential use and became the VC-118 Independence, with 25 seats and 12 bunks in a V.I.P. interior. The first DC-6 was built as a developed C-54 and first flew on February 15, 1946, designated XC-112A (45-873). Span, 117 ft. 6 in.; length (C-118A), 106 ft. 10 in., (XC-112, VC-118), 100 ft. 7 in.; gross weight, 107,000 lb.; cruise speed, 307 m.p.h.

Second Douglas XB-43 in flight (*Douglas photo*).

DOUGLAS XB-43

As the first Air Force jet bomber, the XB-43 is historically important although it did not go into production. Its design, begun in 1944, was based on the unconventional XB-42 (originally XA-42) with two piston engines in the fuselage driving pusher contraprops. The XB-43 (44-61508) had two 3,750 lb.s.t. J35-GE-3 turbojets one above the other in the deep fuselage, and first flew on May 17, 1946. A second example (44-61509) was completed as the YB-43 and subsequently served as an engine test-bed. Span, 71 ft. 2 in.; length, 51 ft. 5 in.; gross weight, 40,000 lb.; max. speed, 507 m.p.h.

Douglas A-1E in USAF service (*Wide World Photo*).

DOUGLAS A-1

The USAF's need for a simple and rugged ground attack aeroplane for operations against elusive ground targets in South Vietnam led to the adoption of the US Navy's A-1 Skyraider. An initial batch of 50 A-1Es was acquired by Tactical Air Command and issued to the 1st Air Commando Group, with further batches obtained subsequently including EA-1E, A-1G, A-1H and A-1J versions. These aircraft, known by the popular name of "Spad", remained in USAF operation after the USN had withdrawn its last Skyraiders from Vietnam in 1967. The engine was a 2,700 h.p. Wright R-3350-26W. Span, 50 ft. 0 in.; length, 38 ft. 2 in.; gross weight, 18,263 lb.; max. speed, 321 m.p.h.

(*McCook Field photo*).

DRIGGS DART

In 1926 the Army bought a single Driggs Dart from the Driggs Aircraft Corporation of Lansing, Michigan. This was a production version of the 1924 Driggs-Johnson DJ-1 built in Dayton for the 1924 National Air Races as an ultra-light racer powered with a Henderson motor-cycle engine. The production version used the 28 h.p. Wright-Morehouse opposed twin. The structural simplicity and low cost of light plane types suited them to extensive but easy major modification, and the Dart was used to test wings with variable camber airfoils. Power plant was a 28 h.p. Wright-Morehouse. Span, 27 ft.; area, 70 sq. ft.; gross weight, 511 lb.

FVL-8 (*McCook Field photo 2953*).

ENGINEERING DIVISION—POMILIO FVL-8 and BVL-12

Among the aeronautical talent sent to the United States by the allies in 1917/18 to help the aviation programme was the Italian designer Ottorino Pomilio, whose firm of Pomilio Brothers in Turin had been notably successful in the manufacture of two-seat observation and bomber models. At the request of the Engineering Division at McCook Field, Pomilio undertook the design of a single seat fighter, the FVL-8, around the new 280-h.p. Liberty 8-cylinder engine and a bomber, the BVL-12, designed around the later 400-h.p. 12-cylinder Liberty.

Both were of conventional all-wood construction, although the plywood fuselages were relatively new to American practice. The outstanding feature of both models was the location of the fuselage above the lower wing instead of on it. The FVL-8 radiator was in the centre section of the lower wing while the BVL-12 used a nose radiator. Six FVL-8s (40080/40085) and six BVL-12s (40086/40091) were built in Indianapolis, Indiana, but were not completed before the Armistice. Data for the FVL-8 and the BVL-12 (in parentheses) follow: Span, 26 ft. 8 in. (45 ft. 3 in.); length, 21 ft. 8 in. (31 ft. 10 in.); wing area, 284 sq. ft. (621·5 sq. ft.); empty weight, 1,726 lb. (2,824 lb.); gross weight, 2,284 lb. (4,552 lb.); high speed, 133 m.p.h. (111 m.p.h.).

BVL-1Z (*McCook Field photo 2691*).

639

R-3 in 1924 racing configuration (*McCook Field photo*).

ENGINEERING DIVISION—SPERRY R-3

In 1922, Alfred Verville of VCP-R/R-1 fame designed a new monoplane racer while still employed by the Engineering Division. A contract for three of the racers was given to Sperry under the designation of R-3 (22-326/328). Powered with hopped-up Wright H-3s of 400 h.p., the R-3s did not do very well in the 1922 Pulitzer race. Re-engined with a 500-h.p. Curtiss D-12, 22-328 won it in 1924 at 216·55 m.p.h. Span, 29 ft. 3 in.; length, 22 ft. 5 in.; area, 144·3 sq. ft.; weight, 2,380 lb.

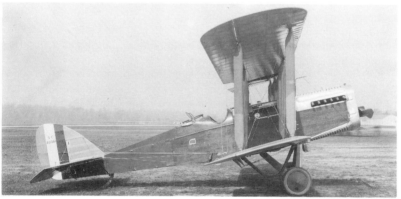

(*McCook Field photo 1596*).

ENGINEERING DIVISION USD-9

The USD-9 was an American redesign of the British DH-9 in the same manner that the "Liberty Plane" was an Americanization of the original DH-4. Principal outward difference between the -4 and -9 was the relocation of the pilot's cockpit, which was moved aft while the fuel tank, originally between the cockpits, was moved forward. All USD-9s as well as 9As used the Liberty. The Armistice ended production after nine had been built at McCook Field (40060/40068) and four by Dayton Wright (40044, 40118, 40119 plus one). Span, 46 ft.; length, 30 ft. $2\frac{7}{8}$ in.; wing area, 508 sq. ft.; empty weight, 2,815 lb.; gross weight, 4,322 lb.; high speed, 126 m.p.h.

VCP-R (*McCook Field photo*).

ENGINEERING DIVISION VCP-1/VCP-R/R-1

The VCP-1 was designed in 1918 and built at McCook Field as a fighter, the initials standing for Verville-Clark Pursuit, from the designers' names. Power for the VCP-1 was the 300-h.p. Wright-Hispano. Two were built (40126, 40127), but only the first was flown. It was modified for the 1920 Pulitzer race—which it won—as VCP-R by installation of a 12-cylinder 660-h.p. Packard 1A-2025 engine and enlarged tail surfaces. The designation was changed to R-1 in 1922. VCP-1 data: Span, 32 ft.; length, 22 ft. 6½ in.; wing area, 269 sq. ft.; empty weight, 2,014 lb.; gross weight, 2,669 lb.; high speed, 154 m.p.h.

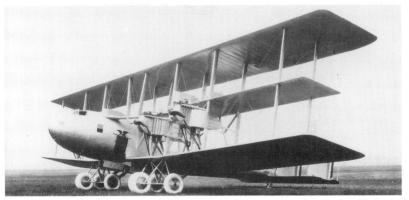

(*McCook Field photo*).

ENG. DIV./WITTEMAN LEWIS/"BARLING" NBL-1

The Witteman-Lewis Company of Teterboro, N.J., won a competitive contract to build two 6-engine NBL-1 triplanes (64215, 64216) designed by the Engineering Division. The second was cancelled, and the first became known as the "Barling Bomber" because the chief designer was Walter Barling, who had designed the Tarrant "Tabor" bomber in England. The first flight (by Lt. H. R. Harris) was on August 22, 1923, and several record flights were made before it was dismantled; it was scrapped in 1928. Span, 120 ft. 0 in.; length, 65 ft.; wing area, 4,017 sq. ft.; empty weight, 27,132 lb.; gross weight, 42,569 lb.; high speed, 95·5 m.p.h.

PW-1 (*McCook Field photo*).

ENGINEERING DIVISION VCP-2/PW-1

The two VCP-2s (64349, 64350) were refinements of the original VCP-1, using the same wings but a more conventional longeron-and-fabric fuselage and a Packard 1A-1170 engine. By the time 64350 was ready for flight (64349 was static tested), a later 350-h.p. Packard 1A-1237 was installed. A unique feature of this installation was the mounting of the radiator in a "tunnel" underneath the engine. When the Army standardized the designating systems in 1920, the VCP-2 became PW-1 for "Pursuit, Watercooled". New straight-chord wings with a thick Fokker airfoil were fitted to the PW-1 fuselage as PW-1A, but were unsuccessful. Span, 32 ft.; length, 22 ft. 6 in.; wing area, 269 sq. ft.; empty weight, 2,069 lb.; gross weight, 3,005 lb.; high speed, 134 m.p.h.

(*Courtesy Arthur Price*).

ENGINEERING DIVISION/BOEING GA-1

The GA-1 was designed at McCook Field by I. M. Laddon, and the prototype was built there as G.A.X. (Ground Attack Experimental). Boeing won a contract for 20 production articles designated GA-1, with gunners stationed in the front of each nacelle ahead of the two 435 h.p. pusher Liberty engines. Additional fixed guns were mounted in the fuselage to fire downward. The GA-1 proved unsatisfactory, and the order was reduced to ten (64146/64155). Span, 65 ft. 6 in.; length, 33 ft. 7½ in.; wing area, 1,016 sq. ft.; gross weight, 9,740 lb.; high speed, 105 m.p.h.

C-8 (*Chester Phillips*).

FAIRCHILD C-8/F-1/C-96

The commercial Fairchild Model 71 seemed to lead a double life in the Army, the same aeroplanes carrying both cargo and photographic designations. The XC-8 of 1929 (29-325) was redesignated XF-1, and eight service test models were ordered as YF-1 (30-388/395). These were followed by six production F-1As (31-463/468). All were later redesignated as C-8 and C-8A. Even when using the "C" designation, the primary mission of these aeroplanes was photography. Normal photographic crew was three while the passenger configuration could accommodate seven. An unusual feature of the F-1/C-8 was the folding wing, first used on an Army plane since the Martin MB-2/NBS-1 of 1920. Power plant was the 410-h.p Pratt & Whitney R-1340-1 Wasp.

In the draft of civil aircraft that took place in 1941/42, three 1929 Fairchild Model 71s were obtained and designated UC-96 (42-78032, 42-88617/8). These aircraft, used for photo survey duties, were the oldest aircraft in Army service at the time in spite of their late designation and serial numbers. Span, 50 ft.; length, 33 ft.; wing area, 335 sq. ft.; empty weight, 3,296 lb.; gross weight, 5,500 lb.; high speed, 142 m.p.h. at 5,000 ft.

C-8 floatplane (*Gordon S. Williams*).

643

Fairchild UC-61A (*Peter M. Bowers*).

FAIRCHILD UC-61

Production of the Fairchild 24W-41 light transport (Warner R-500-1 engine) was initiated for the Army in 1941. Of 163 of the initial UC-61 model built, all but two were assigned to Britain on Lend-Lease. The UC-61A was similar with new radio, and the Air Force retained for its own use 148 of the 512 built. Commercial Model 24s were impressed as UC-61B through UC-61J. The 306 UC-61Ks had Ranger L-440-7 in-line engines. Span, 36 ft. 4 in.; length, 23 ft. 9 in.; weight, 2,800 lb.; speed, 130 m.p.h.

Fairchild T-46A prototype, in overall white finish (*Fairchild photo*).

FAIRCHILD T-46

The USAF completed its five-year search for a New Generation Trainer (NGT) to replace the Cessna T-37A in 1982 and announced that Fairchild Republic was the winner. Initial contracts covered two prototypes and plans were made for procurement of up to 650 of the new trainers, to be designated T-46A. The two prototypes flew on October 15, 1985 (at Edwards A.F.B.) and on July 29, 1986 (at Farmingdale, New York). Production was initiated against a contract for the first 10 aircraft and the first of these flew at Farmingdale on 14 January 1987, but on March 13 that year the USAF terminated all further work on the T-46A programme because of production delays and escalating costs. The T-46A was powered by two 1,330 lb.s.t. Garrett F109-GA-100 turbofans. Span, 38 ft. 7½ in.; length, 29 ft. 6 in.; gross weight, 7,307 lb.; max. speed, 450 m.p.h.

644

Fairchild Metro 3 in USAF markings (*Fairchild photo*).

FAIRCHILD C-26A

In March 1988, the USAF placed a contract with the Fairchild Aircraft Corporation for six of its 19-seat Metro 3 twin turboprop transports, for use as operational support transport aircraft by the Air National Guard. Previously, six Beech C-12Js (Super King Air 200s) had been ordered in the same rôle. With deliveries spread from March to August 1989, the C-26As were allocated to serve with the California, Idaho, Illinois, Missouri, Philadelphia and Texas Air National Guard units. The Metro 3 was powered by two 1,000 s.h.p. Garrett TPE331-11U-612G turboprops. Span, 57 ft. 0 in.; length, 59 ft. $4\frac{1}{4}$ in.; gross weight, 14,500 lb.; max. speed, 285 m.p.h.

Fleet PT-6 (*USAF photo*).

FLEET PT-6

The PT-6, product of the Fleet Aircraft Corporation of Buffalo, N.Y., an offshoot of Consolidated, was introduced in 1928 and was originally known as "Husky Jr." The XPT-6 (30-88) and the 10 YPT-6s (30-372/381) were identical with Kinner-powered commercial Fleet Model 2s except for compliance with military requirements. Five YPT-6As (30-382/386) were identical except for slightly enlarged cockpits. Span, 28 ft.; length, 21 ft. 5 in.; gross weight, 1,580 lb.; max speed, 100 m.p.h.

YO-27 (*Peter M. Bowers*).

FOKKER O-27/B-8

Two XO-27s (29-327/328) were built to an Army requirement for a three-place observation monoplane. The second prototype was redesignated XB-8 before completion. Six service test YO-27s (31-587/592) and six YB-8s (31-598/603) were ordered, but the YB-8s were redesignated Y1O-27 prior to manufacture. The XO-27 was modified to XO-27A by the installation of geared Conqueror engines like those of the YOs, revision of the vertical tail surfaces, and the addition of an enclosed canopy to the pilot's cockpit. XB-8 data: Span, 64 ft.; length, 47 ft.; wing area, 619 sq. ft.; empty weight, 6,861 lb.; gross weight, 10,545 lb.; high speed, 160 m.p.h.

C-14 (*Peter M. Bowers*).

FOKKER C-14, C-15

The Fokker F-14 was designed in 1929 to an obsolete airline specification with a six-place cabin under a parasol wing. The Army placed an order for 20 as Y1C-14s (31-381/400) powered with 525-h.p. Wright R-1750-3 Cyclones. The last aircraft was fitted with the larger R-1820-7 Cyclone of 575 h.p. and delivered as Y1C-14A. The first, meanwhile, was fitted with the 525-h.p. Pratt & Whitney R-1690-5 Hornet as Y1C-14B while the ninth was converted to a specialized all-white ambulance as Y1C-15. The single C-15A (32-398) was a commercial F-14 acquired from General Aviation, with an R-1820 Cyclone engine. Span, 59 ft.; length, 43 ft. 3 in.; wing area, 551 sq. ft.; empty weight, 4,529 lb.; gross weight, 7,200 lb.; high speed, 133 m.p.h.

C-4A (*Peter M. Bowers*).

FORD C-3, C-4, C-9

Thirteen Ford Tri-Motors of different types were acquired by USAAC. The first, in 1928, was a commercial 4-AT-B type designated C-3 (28-348). Seven C-3As (29-220 to 226) were similar with 235-h.p. R-790-3 engines; all were later re-engined with 300-h.p. R-975-1s and designated C-9. A single 5-AT-B type in 1929 was the C-4 (29-219) followed in 1931 by four C-4As (31-401 to 404) similar to the civil 5-AT-D. Engines were 450 h.p. R-1340-3 and -11 respectively and one C-4A was re-designated C-4B when fitted with R-1340-7s. Span (C-3, C-9), 73 ft. 11 in.; (C-4), 77 ft. 11 in.; length (C-3A, C-9), 50 ft.; (C-4), 51 ft.; gross weight (C-3, C-9), 9,950 lb. (C-4), 13,500 lb.; max. speed (C-3), 115 m.p.h.; (C-4), 145 m.p.h.; (C-9), 131 m.p.h.

(*Frankfort photo*).

FRANKFORT TG-1

Procurement of gliders by the Army began in April 1941, in the wake of successful use of troop-carrying gliders by the Luftwaffe. The first contract was for three examples of the civilian Frankfort Cinema, designated XTG-1 (41-29609/29611). A production batch of 40 TG-1As (42-52884/923) was ordered, plus two single examples (42-57159 and 42-57198); these had SCR-585A radio added. The Army also acquired some civilian Cinemas, as TG-1B (four Cinema I Model A); TG-1C (three Cinema II Model B) and TG-1D (one Cinema II Model PC-2). Span, 46 ft. $3\frac{1}{4}$ in.; length, 23 ft. $2\frac{1}{4}$ in.; gross weight, 920 lb.; top speed, 80 m.p.h.

Learjet C-21A (*Gates Learjet photo C2250-60BW*).

GATES LEARJET C-21A

The USAF selected the commercial Gates Learjet Model 35A in September 1983 as the replacement for North American CT-39s. The latter were operated by MAC throughout the world for delivery of high-priority and time-sensitive cargo, passenger transport and medevac. A contract provided for the lease of 80 Learjet aircraft under the C-21A designation, and these aircraft (84-0063/0142) were then purchased outright in September 1986. The first C-21A was completed in March 1984 and deliveries were completed in October 1985. Four more C-21As (86-0374/0377) were purchased for ANG use at Andrews A.F.B. in 1987. The power plant comprised two 3,500 lb.s.t. Garrett TFE731-2-2B turbofans. Span, 39 ft. 6 in.; length, 48 ft. 8 in.; gross weight, 18,300 lb.; max. speed, 542 m.p.h. at 25,000 ft.

Grumman OA-12 with 10th ARS in Alaska (*Lt.-Col. R. B. Hamel*).

GRUMMAN OA-12/A-12

In 1942 a single J2F-5 Duck (Bu No 0660) was transferred from the USN to the USAAF as the OA-12 (serial 42-7771) for evaluation. Then, in 1948, the USAF took on charge five more J2F-5s as A- (for amphibian) 12s (48-563/567) and three J2F-6s as A-12As (48-1373/1375). Some were for military aid to the Colombian Air Force but at least two entered service with the USAF's 10th Air Rescue Squadron at Elmendorf Field, Alaska, painted in Arctic finish with red outer wings and tail units. The A-12 was powered by the 850 h.p. Wright R-1820-50; the A-12A had a 900 h.p. R-1820-54. Span, 39 ft. 0 in.; length, 34 ft. 0 in.; gross weight, 6,710 lb.; high speed, 181 m.p.h.

648

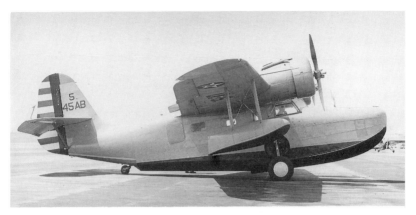

OA-9 *(Peter M. Bowers)*.

GRUMMAN OA-9, OA-13, OA-14

The 26 OA-9s of 1938 (38-556/581) were commercial Grumman G-21 six-place amphibians with slight modifications to adapt them to military operations. Similar models were produced for the Navy as the JRF series. In 1942, three commercial G-21As were purchased from private owners as OA-13A (42-38214/38215, 97055) and five additional OA-9s (42-106979/106983) were procured. Two JRF-5s were obtained from the Navy in 1945 as OA-13B (45-49088/49089). The sixteen OA-14s of 1942/44 (42-38216/38223, 38265, 38339, 38340, 38355, 38356, 43460, 53003, 44-52977) were adaptations of the five-place G-44 commercial amphibian, similar to the Navy J4F-1, powered with in-line inverted Ranger L-440-5 engines of 200 h.p.

Data for the OA-9, with 450-h.p. R-985-17 engines, are: Span, 49 ft.; length, 38 ft. 4 in.; wing area, 375 sq. ft.; empty weight, 5,900 lb.; gross weight, 8,000 lb.; high speed, 195 m.p.h.

Data for the OA-14 with 200-h.p. L-440-2 engines, are: Span, 40 ft.; length, 31 ft. 1 in.; wing area, 245 sq. ft.; empty weight, 3,215 lb.; gross weight, 4,500 lb.; high speed, 150 m.p.h.

OA-14A *(Don Walsh)*.

Gulfstream C-20C with 89th MAW, 1987 (*MAP photo*).

GULFSTREAM C-20A

The Gulfstream III business jet, powered by two 11,400 lb.s.t. Rolls-Royce Spey Mk 511-8 turbofans, was selected by the USAF in June 1983 to meet a requirement to replace Lockheed VC-140A and C-140B special mission support aircraft. Three aircraft, initially leased and then purchased outright, were designated C-20As (83-0500/0502) and assigned to Ramstein A.B. in Germany; at least one became EC-20A when equipped for electronic surveillance. Eight more Gulfstreams were ordered in 1986 and delivered in 1987 as C-20Bs and C-20Cs (86-0200/0207) with some systems changes, for operation by the 89th MAW at Andrews A.F.B. The Army acquired two similar C-20Es (87-0139/0140). Span, 77 ft. 10 in.; length, 83 ft. 1 in.; gross weight, 69,700 lb.; max. cruising speed, 561 m.p.h.

Helio U-10A in South-East Asia camouflage (*via Steve Peltz*).

HELIO L-24, L-28, U-10

Three Helio Model H-395 Super Couriers were purchased by the USAF in 1958 for evaluation of operational techniques and suitability for supplying isolated missile sites. They were designated L-28A and later redesignated U-10A (58-7025/7027). A single example of the earlier H-391 was obtained for U.S. Army evaluation as the YL-24. Over 100 U-10s were subsequently purchased by the USAF for duties in Vietnam, including 26 U-10As, 57 of the extended range U-10Bs and 36 higher weight U-10Ds. Span, 39 ft.; length, 30 ft. 9 in.; wing area, 231 sq. ft.; STOL gross weight, 3,000 lb.; cruising speed, 160 m.p.h.; range, 670 miles.

Hiller YH-32 (*Peter M. Bowers*).

HILLER YH-32

The U.S. Army purchased two examples of the two-seat ultra-light Hornet helicopter in 1953 under the designation YH-32 (53-4663/4664). Twelve more were ordered in 1955 (55-4963/4974) to permit a more thorough evaluation. The YH-32 was generally similar to the civil Hornet prototype, which had first flown in 1950, with the addition of two small tailplanes in the form of an inverted "V". The two-blade rotor was powered by a 38 lb.s.t. Hiller 8RJ2B ramjet at each blade tip. Rotor diameter, 23 ft.; gross weight, 1,080 lb.; cruising speed, 69 m.p.h.

UC-70B (*Peter M. Bowers*).

HOWARD UC-70

Twenty civil Howard DGA-15 models were impressed in 1942. They included 11 UC-70 five-seat DGA-15P (R-985-33 engines); two U-C70A four-seat Model DGA-12 (R-915-1); four UC-70B five-seat DGA-15J (R-915-1); one UC-70C, a four-seat Model DGA-8 (R-760-1) and two UC-70D, four-seat Model DGA-9s (R-830-1). Span, 38 ft.; length, 24 ft. 10 in. to 26 ft. 5 in. according to engine; gross weight, 3,600–4,350 lb.; max. speed, 168–192 m.p.h.

AT-1 (*McCook Field photo*).

HUFF-DALAND TA-6, TW-5, AT-1, AT-2

The single TA-6 (68584), was powered with the 200-h.p. Lawrence J-1. Five TW-5s (23-1211/1215) with 180 h.p. Wright-Hispano E engines were ordered. Since the TW designation was dropped in 1924, ten additional advanced trainers were ordered as AT-1 (25-235/244). A single AT-2, was tested in a number of single and two-seat versions. AT-1: Span, 31 ft. 1 in.; length, 24 ft. 8 in.; gross weight, 2,358 lb.; high speed, 112 m.p.h.

Hughes TH-55A in overall red finish (*Hughes photo 66-271*).

HUGHES H-55 OSAGE

The U.S. Army purchased an evaluation batch of five Hughes Model 269A helicopters in 1958, and tested them at Fort Rucker with the designation YHO-2HU (58-1324/1328) as observation helicopters. The same basic type (Model 269C) with different equipment, was selected by the Army in 1964 as its new standard helicopter primary trainer for service at Fort Wolters, Texas, with the designation TH-55A, and procurement totalled 792 (64-18001/18020, 64-18025/18239, 65-18240/18263, 66-18264/18355, 67-15371/15445, 67-16686/17002, 67-18356/18404). The engine was a 180 h.p. Lycoming HIO-360-B1A. Rotor diameter, 25 ft. $3\frac{1}{2}$ in.; length 28 ft. $10\frac{3}{4}$ in.; gross weight, 1,670 lb.; max. speed, 86 m.p.h.

XL-6 (*Interstate photo*).

INTERSTATE L-6 GRASSHOPPER

In the Army's search in 1941 for a light liaison and observation aircraft for use with and by the Ground Forces, the Interstate S-1B Cadet tandem-seat cabin monoplane was picked for evaluation. The Army prototype was the last aircraft with an Observation designation—XO-63 (42-15895). It was later redesignated XL-6, and was powered by a 100-h.p. Franklin XO-200-5 engine. A production batch of 250 L-6s (43-2559/2808) were used alongside the other Army Grasshoppers. Span, 35 ft. 6 in.; length, 23 ft. 5½ in.; wing area, 174 sq. ft.; gross weight, 1,650 lb.; max. speed, 104 m.p.h.

YG-1B (*William T. Larkins*).

KELLETT YG-1, XR-2, XR-3, YO-60

The Army's first rotary-wing aircraft (other than the service-financed De Bothezat and Berliner helicopters of 1921/23) were autogyros tested for suitability as observation types. One commercial Kellet KD-1 wingless autogyro ordered in 1935 as YG-1 (34-278) was followed by one YG-1A (36-352) and seven YG-1Bs (37-377/382 and 37-635). One "B" became YG-1C (37-378) to test a constant-speed rotor and later became XR-2; another (37-380) became the XR-3. Seven more Kelletts similar to the XR-2 were ordered as XO-60 in 1942 (42-13604/13610); the first six became YO-60. YG-1B: 225-h.p. Jacobs R-775-1; rotor diameter, 40 ft.; length, 28 ft. 10 in.; gross weight, 2,254 lb.; high speed, 125 m.p.h.

653

XTG-4 at Wright Field (*Wright Field photo 90228*).

LAISTER-KAUFFMAN TG-4

To meet the urgent Army need in 1941 for a training glider, Laister Kauffman adapted its Yankee Doodle mid-wing design. Three examples were ordered for evaluation as XTG-4 (42-14705/707), and two production contracts followed, each for 75 TG-4s (LK-10A) (42-43679/753 and 42-53022/096) with SCR-585 radio to permit communication between the glider and towing aircraft. The Army also purchased one commercial model, and designated it TG-4B (42-57191). Span, 50 ft.; length, 22 ft. 0 in.; wing area, 166 sq. ft.; gross weight, 875 lb.

YIC-17 (*U.S. Army photo*).

LOCKHEED Y1C-12, Y1C-17, UC-101

Three of the famous commercial Lockheed "Vega" monoplanes served the Army at widely separated times. The Y1C-12 (31-405) was procured in 1931 to test the small all-wood single-engine civil transport design fitted with the 450 h.p. Pratt & Whitney Wasp R-1340-7 engine. The single Y1C-17 (31-408) was a special "Speed Vega" with metal fuselage, wire-braced single-strut landing gear, NACA cowling, and wheel pants. The UC-101 (42-94148) was a civil Lockheed Model 5 similar to the C-12 and was obtained in the 1941/42 draft of civil aircraft. Span, 41 ft.; length, 20 ft. 7 in.; gross weight, 4,402 lb.; max. speed, 179 m.p.h.

654

Y1C-23 (*Gordon S. Williams*).

LOCKHEED C-23, C-25

Two commercial Lockheed "Altair" designs were purchased in 1932 as high-speed personnel transports. The Y1C-23, later C-23 (32-232), was of composite construction, featuring the famous Lockheed cantilever wood wing and tail but a metal fuselage that resulted from Lockheed's affiliation with the Detroit Aircraft Co. in 1929. The Y1C-25 (32-393) was a stock all-wood Altair otherwise indistinguishable from the C-23. The two-man crew rode in separate cockpits under a single plastic sliding canopy. Span, 42 ft. 9 in.; wing area, 293 sq. ft.; empty weight, 3,235 lb.; gross weight, 4,896 lb.; high speed, 207 m.p.h.

XC-35 (*Gordon S. Williams*).

LOCKHEED XC-35

The XC-35 (36-353) was a special variant of the standard Lockheed 10E Electra transport (Army C-36 & C-37), produced for the specific purpose of conducting experiments in cabin pressurization and engine supercharging for high-altitude flight. Principal outward difference from the standard "Electra" was the completely circular fuselage and the absence of the normal windows. The Army was awarded the Collier Trophy for 1937 for having sponsored the development of the XC-35 and used it for valuable research. Power, two 550-h.p. turbo-supercharged Pratt & Whitney XR-1340-43; span, 55 ft.; length, 39 ft. 8 in.; wing area, 460 sq. ft.; gross weight, 10,500 lb.; high speed, 240 mp.h.; service ceiling, 32,000 ft.

655

UC-36A in 1944 (*Peter M. Bowers*).

LOCKHEED C-36, C-37

Airline success with the all-metal Lockheed Model 10 Electra light transport prompted Army purchase of four "off-the-shelf"—three Y1C-36 (37-65/67) and one Y1C-37 (37-376) all equivalent to the ten-place commercial 10A and powered with the 450-h.p. Pratt & Whitney R-985-13. The "Y1" designation was dropped following service evaluation of the aircraft. In 1942, 15 later 12-place 10As were drafted as C-36A and 4 similar 10Es powered with 600-h.p. Pratt & Whitney R-1340 Wasps became C-36B. Seven ten-place 10Bs with 450 h.p. Wright R-975 Whirlwinds became C-36C. The C-36s and C-37 were redesignated UC-36 and -37 in January, 1943. C-36: Span, 55 ft.; length, 38 ft. 7 in.; wing area, 460 sq. ft.; gross weight, 10,100 lb.; high speed, 205 m.p.h.

C-40A (*Peter M. Bowers*).

LOCKHEED C-40

Three examples of the Lockheed 12-A light transport were purchased in 1938 and designated C-40 (38-536/538). Simultaneously, an order was placed for ten C-40As (38-539/548) with seats for only five instead of seven passengers. The designation of these aircraft was later changed to UC-40 and UC-40A respectively. The single experimental C-40B (38-582) had a fixed tricycle undercarriage. Ten commercial Model 12-As impressed in 1942 were designated UC-40D. All C-40 variants had 450-h.p. R-985-17 engines. Span, 49 ft. 6 in.; length, 36 ft. 4 in.; gross weight, 9,600 lb.; max. speed, 220 m.p.h.

656

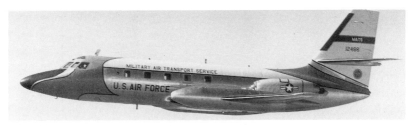

Lockheed VC-140B (*Lockheed photo RF8644-2*).

LOCKHEED C-140

The Air Force outlined a requirement for a utility transport (UCX) to industry in 1956 and invited industry-financed prototypes to be built. Lockheed built two Model 1329 JetStars, and the first flew on September 4, 1957. In October 1959 the USAF announced this design had been adopted as the C-140 with two J-60 turbojets, and in June 1960 five C-140As (59-5958/5962) were ordered for MATS Airway and Air Communications Service. Additional contracts followed for five C-140B (62-4197/4201) mission support aircraft and six VC-140B (61-2488/2493) staff transports for MATS. Span, 53 ft. 8 in.; length, 60 ft. 5½ in.; gross weight, 40,000 lb.; high speed, 540 m.p.h.

Lockheed YO-3A (*Lockheed photo*).

LOCKHEED O-3

Through its Missiles and Space Company, Lockheed began development in 1966 of an ultra-quiet light aircraft for use in Vietnam to carry sensors for tracking Viet Cong guerillas. Two prototypes of this two-seat QT-2 design were modified Schweizer X-26A sailplanes and were tested over Vietnam in the *Prize Crew* project. Fourteen YO-3As (69-18000/18013) for the U.S. Army were similar, apart from the nose-mounted 210 h.p. Continental IO-360D engine, and were operated in Vietnam, 1970/1972, by the 1st Army Security Agency Company. Span, 57 ft.; length, 29 ft. 4 in.; gross weight, 3,800 lb.; max. speed, 138 m.p.h.

Lockheed RP-2E in Army service (*Robert C. Mikesh*).

LOCKHEED B-69, P-2

The RB-69A designation was applied in 1954 to five electronic-surveillance versions of the Neptune patrol bomber built for the USAF plus two Navy P2V-7Us modified to the same standard (54-4037/4043). For operations in Vietnam, the Army acquired six SP-2E Neptunes as electronic-surveillance platforms and used by the 1st Radio Research Company. Two were equipped for passive EW, three for active EW and one was used for training. Redesignated RP-2E at the time of conversion, they later became known as AP-2E (with A indicating Army). Two 3,500 h.p. Wright R-3350-36W engines were supplemented by 3,400 lb.s.t. Westinghouse J34-WE-34 booster jets. Span, 104 ft. 0 in.; gross weight, 77,850 lb.; max. speed, 353 m.p.h.

PW-2A modified for racing (*McCook Field photo*).

LOENING PW-2 SERIES

In 1920, the design concept of the Loening M-8 of 1918 was incorporated into a new single seater, the PW-2, built around the same Wright H engine. Three prototypes were built (64139/64141), retaining the flat knife-edge rear fuselage design of the M-8. The first used the twin rudder arrangement of the original M-8 prototype but soon converted to the conventional single unit. Ten production PW-2As were ordered (22-246/255), the major difference being in redesign of the fuselage. Structural and aerodynamic inadequacies caused the last six to be cancelled. One PW-2B (64389) was similar to the PW-2A but was fitted with shorter wings and a 350 h.p. Packard 1A-1237 V-12 engine. PW-2A: Span, 39 ft. 9 in.; length, 26 ft. 0½ in.; gross weight, 2,799 lb.; max. speed, 136 m.p.h.

S-1 (*Bowers collection*).

LOENING S-1 AIR YACHT

The Air Yacht was a post-war commercial design based on a pusher monoplane flying boat that Grover Loening had designed in 1912. The Army bought nine Liberty-powered Air Yachts, (23-1/8, 24-1) under the designation of S-1 (for seaplane, applied only to this model). The pilot and four passengers rode in a single open cockpit ahead of the wing, and other than the monoplane design, the only unconventional feature of the S-1 was the extremely low aspect ratio of the strut-braced wing. Span, 43 ft. 0 in.; length, 29 ft. 3 in.; wing area, 330 sq. ft.; gross weight, 3,550 lb.; high speed, 125 m.p.h.

M-8 (*Bowers collection*).

LOENING M-8

The M-8 design originated in the spring of 1918, when Grover C. Loening was unofficially asked to produce a two-seat fighter superior to the British Bristol F.2B, and initial procurement was expedited by having the Wright-Martin Company request the Loening Aeronautical Engineering Corporation to build two prototypes (40121, 40122) as test beds for the Wright "H" engine, an Americanized version of the 300-h.p. French Hispano-Suiza. The M-8 met all performance expectations, and in spite of certain structural and aerodynamic problems, was slated for a production order which was cancelled by the Armistice. Fifty-four improved M-8-O and M-81 models were built for the Navy after the war. Span, 35 ft. 0 in.; length, 25 ft. 0 in.; wing area, 290 sq. ft.; gross weight, 2,600 lb.; high speed, 151 m.p.h.

C-9 with Red Cross ambulance marking.

McDONNELL DOUGLAS C-9 NIGHTINGALE

The USAF announced selection of the McDonnell Douglas DC-9 on August 31, 1967, to fulfil a requirement for aeromedical evacuation aircraft. Powered by 14,000 lb.s.t. Pratt & Whitney JT8D-9 turbofans, the DC-9 entered service as the C-9A Nightingale in August 1968 for operations with the 375th Aeromedical Airlift Wing of MAC. Procurement totalled 21 (67-22583/22586, 68-8932/8935, 68-10958/10961, 71-0874/0882) and three similar C-9Cs (73-1681/1683) equipped as VIP transports and used by the 89th MAW at Andrews A.F.B. Span, 93 ft. 5 in.; length 119 ft. 4 in.; gross weight, 108,000 lb.; cruising speed, over 500 m.p.h.

P-64 in Royal Thai Air Force camouflage (*Peter M. Bowers*).

NORTH AMERICAN P-64

Early in 1939, North American developed a single-seat fighter version of the NA-16 design. Seven were sold to Peru as NA-50s and six similar NA-68s were ordered by Siam. When ready for shipment in November 1940, they were commandeered by the Army because of the proximity of Siam to Japan's sphere of influence. Designated P-64 because of their single-seat configuration, these six aircraft (41-19082/19087) were used only as advanced trainers. They were powered by 875 h.p. Wright R-1820-77 engines. Span, 37 ft. 3 in.; length, 27 ft., wing area, 227·5 sq. ft., gross weight, 6,800 lb.; max. speed, 270 m.p.h.

Ryan-built L-17B in O.D. finish (*Peter M. Bowers*).

NORTH AMERICAN L-17, U-18

The Air Force purchased 83 North American NA-154 Navions with Fiscal 1947 Funds, including 47 for use by the National Guard and the remainder for the Army. They were designated L-17A (47-1297/1379), and some were converted to QL-17 drones. After Ryan had acquired the design, an order for 158 more was placed as L-17Bs (48-921/1078) of which 34 were for the National Guard. Five more were acquired in 1949 (49-1961/65). Thirty-five L-17Cs were converted L-17As in 1949 with new brakes and fuel tanks. All had O-470-7 engines; the designations were subsequently changed to U-18A, U-18B and U-18C. The three XL-17Ds were Super Navions with O-435-17. Span, 33 ft. 5 in.; length, 27 ft. 8 in.; gross weight, 3,050 lb.; max. speed, 150 m.p.h.

C-125A (*A. U. Schmidt*).

NORTHROP C-125 RAIDER

The N-23 Pioneer commercial design won a USAF design contest for a short-field light transport and 23 YC-125 were ordered in March 1948. Thirteen were completed as YC-125A (48-628/640) for light assault transport duties and ten as YC-125B (48-618/627) for Arctic rescue duties. Deliveries began in 1950 and the aircraft were assigned to Sheppard A.F.B. for mechanical training, where they remained until declared surplus in 1955. The three engines were 1,200 h.p. Wright R-1820-99. Span, 86 ft. 6½ in.; length, 67 ft. 1 in.; gross weight, 40,900 lb.; max. speed, 207 m.p.h.

XB-35 (*A. U. Schmidt*).

NORTHROP B-35, B-49

Development of a long-range flying-wing bomber began in 1941 as part of a general Northrop programme on this configuration, the design being first submitted to the USAAF in September 1941. USAAF approval for development was obtained, with a contract for one prototype, and detail design began early in 1942. As part of the development programme, Northrop built four 7,100-lb. scale models, a little more than one third the size of the B-35; these were two N9Ms, one N9M-A and one N9M-B. The XB-35 mock-up was approved on July 5, 1942, and the prototype XB-35 (42-13603) was first flown on June 25, 1946 (by Max Stanley) from Hawthorne to Muroc. Powered by two R-4360-17 and two R-4360-21 engines driving pusher contraprops it had a 4,000-sq. ft. wing and a gross weight of 209,000 lb. A second XB-35 (42-38323) and 13 YB-35s (42-102366/78) followed, with the same engines but single-rotation propellers. A contract for 200 B-35A placed with Martin was cancelled. Two YB-35 (42-102367/68) were converted to YB-49 (originally YB-35B) with eight 4,000 lb. Allison J35-A-5 turbojets buried in the wing; the first of these flew on October 21, 1947.

An order for 30 reconnaissance RB-49s was placed in 1948 but was cancelled in April 1949. At the same time, conversion of nine YB-35s to jet power was ordered, but only one of these conversions was completed when the programme was dropped in November 1949. This aircraft was designated YRB-49A and had four 5,600-lb. J35-A-21 turbojets in the wing and two more in external pods. It first flew on May 4, 1950, and had a gross weight of 206,000 lb. Span, 172 ft. 0 in.; length, 53 ft. 1 in.; gross weight (XB-35), 209,000 lb.; (YB-49), 213,000 lb.; max. speed (YB-49), 520 m.p.h.

YB-49 (*Gordon S. Williams*).

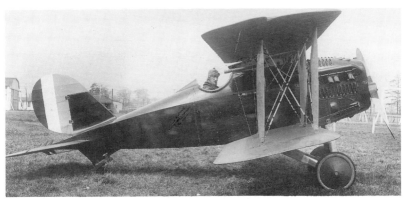
First Curtiss-built Orenco D (*Curtiss photo*).

ORENCO/CURTISS D

The Model D fighter was designed by the Ordnance Engineering Company of Baldwin, Long Island, around the 300 h.p. Wright-Hispano-engine. Four all-wood prototypes (40107/40110) were built during World War I and the Army ordered 50 production models from Curtiss (63281/63330). The production models had increased-span upper wing, balanced ailerons, wing dihedral and a revised installation for the engine. Production Model Ds had one 0.30-in. and one 0.50-in. guns each. Production model: Span, 32 ft. 11$\frac{5}{8}$ in.; length, 21 ft. 5$\frac{1}{2}$ in.; gross weight, 2,820 lb.; max. speed, 139 m.p.h.

Le Pere LUSAC-11 in France (*U.S. Army photo E-5046*).

PACKARD-LE PERE LUSAC-11

The Packard-Le Pere LUSAC-11 was designed for the Engineering Division by Captain Le Pere of the French Aviation mission to the U.S. and built by the Packard Motor Car Co. The LUSAC-11 showed heavy French and Italian design influence, with the 400-h.p. Liberty engine carried in a plywood fuselage. Out of 25 production models and two prototypes built, two LUSAC-11s reached France. The LUSAC-21 (40024) was the same airframe with a 16-cylinder 420-h.p. Bugatti engine and the LUSAC-25 (40025) was another variant. LUSAC-11: Span, 39 ft. 0$\frac{1}{4}$ in.; length, 25 ft. 4$\frac{5}{8}$ in.; wing area, 415·6 sq. ft.; gross weight, 3,655 lb.; high speed, 136 m.p.h.

(*Gordon S. Williams*).

PIASECKI H-25 ARMY MULE

Large quantities of helicopters were included in the 1951 procurements by the Air Force on behalf of the Army. Among them was a contract for 70 Piasecki H-25A (51-16572/16641) tandem-rotor utility helicopters, of the type then in production for the USN as the HUP-2. Powered by a 525-h.p. R-975-42 engine, the H-25A accommodated five passengers or three stretchers. Rotor diameter, 35 ft. 0 in. each; length, 31 ft. 10 in.; gross weight, 6,000 lb.; max. speed, 115 m.p.h.

(*Peter M. Bowers*).

REPUBLIC AT-12

The 50 AT-12s (41-17494/17543) were part of an order for Republic Model 2PA fighter-bombers from Sweden. The 2PA Guardsman was a development of the earlier U.S. Army P-35 and its export equivalent expanded to a two-seater. The Army had no operational requirement for a machine of this type but acquired them when exports were blocked early in World War II. It used them for advanced trainers and assigned the designation of AT-12. The engine was a 1,050-h.p. R-1830-45. Span, 41 ft.; length, 27 ft. 8 in.; wing area, 250 sq. ft.; empty weight, 4,750 lb.; gross weight, 6,433 lb.; high speed, 285 m.p.h.

YPT-15 (*Peter M. Bowers*).

ST. LOUIS PT-15

In its search for a primary trainer on which to base its expanding pilot training programmes in 1939/1940, the Air Corps evaluated several types designed for the civil market. Among them was the St. Louis Model PT-1W, a conventional training biplane with tandem open cockpits and a 225-h.p. Wright R-760-1 uncowled radial engine in a monocoque metal fuselage. One example, the XPT-15 (39-703) was bought in 1939, followed by an evaluation batch of 13 YPT-15s (40-1/13) ordered in 1939. Span, 33 ft. 10 in.; length, 25 ft.; gross weight, 2,770 lb.; max. speed, 124 m.p.h.

XTG-3 at Wright Field (*USAF photo 21157*).

SCHWEIZER TG-3

The Army ordered three examples of a new Schweizer SGS 2-12 high performance two-seat sailplane in 1942, which was developed as a military training glider under the designation XTG-3 (42-14702/704). After evaluation, the type was ordered for use in the Army glider pilot training programme, with contracts for 110 TG-3A (42-52924/998 and 42-53097/53131). A single example of the TG-3A (42-91974) was also built by Air Glider, Inc., but the remainder of a contract for 50 was cancelled. Span, 54 ft.; length, 27 ft. 7 in.; wing area, 237 ft.; gross weight, 1,200 lb.; max. speed, towed or free, 100 m.p.h.

665

All-yellow TG-7A at the Air Force Academy (*MAP photo*).

SCHWEIZER TG-7A

Backed by a 1981 contract for five examples (81-886/890) from the USAF, the Schweizer Aircraft Corporation initiated development of its Model SGM 2-37 motor glider, the first flight of which was made on September 21, 1982. Following certification in February 1983, these aircraft were delivered to the Air Force Academy, Colorado Springs, followed by at least six more (82-039/043 and 87-761). The TG-7As, powered by the 112 h.p. Avco Lycoming O-235-L2C piston engine and seating two side-by-side, were used for voluntary "motivational" flight training, up to solo, by the academy cadets. The TG-7 designation (as a training glider) was in the "G" series adopted in 1962. Span, 59 ft. 6 in.; length, 27 ft. 5 in.; wing area, 195·7 sq. ft.; gross weight, 1,850 lb.; max. speed (unpowered), 133 m.p.h.; max. cruise (powered), 114 m.p.h.

(*Gordon S. Williams*).

SEVERSKY BT-8

The Seversky BT-8 was a direct development of the Seversky 1XP model that served as the prototype of the P-35 series. The basic all-metal airframe was de-rated to a two seater with a fixed faired landing gear and a 450-h.p. Pratt & Whitney Wasp Jr. R-985-11 engine. While it was built in relatively small numbers (a total of 30, numbered 34-247/276). the BT-8 was a significant design in that it was the first Army basic trainer specifically built for the purpose instead of being a converted observation type or a beefed-up primary trainer. It was also the first production monoplane trainer, introduced just at the time that the biplane was being phased out of the pursuit and observation categories. Span, 36 ft.; length, 24 ft. 4 in.; wing area, 220 sq. ft.; empty weight, 3,017 lb.; gross weight, 4,050 lb.; high speed, 175 m.p.h. at sea level.

C-6 (*Wright Field photo*).

SIKORSKY C-6

Army Air Corps purchased an example of the 12-place S-38A sesqui-plane amphibian in 1929 and tested it as the C-6 (29-406) at Wright Field (where it was numbered XP-588). It later went to Bolling Field for service, and 10 more were ordered as C-6As (30-397/406). These served between 1930 and 1933 at various Fields in the U.S., the Canal Zone, and in the Philippines for transport and target-towing duties. The engines were 450-h.p. R-1340-7 radials. Span, 71 ft. 6 in.; length, 40 ft. 3 in.; gross weight, 10,200 lb.; cruising speed, 112 m.p.h. at sea level.

Y1OA-8 (*A. U. Schmidt*).

SIKORSKY Y1OA-8, OA-11

The five Y1OA-8s of 1937 (37-370/374) were commercial 11-seat Sikorsky S-43 amphibians modified slightly for Military Transport Service. The seats could be removed and the entire cabin used for cargo. Since Sikorsky was one of the firms that managed to stay with United Aircraft Corporation after the trust-busting of 1934 that took Boeing and United Air Lines out of it, the OA-8s naturally used Hamilton Standard propellers and Pratt & Whitney engines, the 750-h.p. R-1690-23 Hornet. In July 1941 the Army obtained a civilian S-43 under the designation of OA-11 (42-1) as a personnel transport. It was short-lived, crashing on a trip to Trinidad. Y1OA-8: Span, 86 ft.; length, 52 ft. 1 in.; wing area, 782 sq. ft.; gross weight, 20,000 lb.; high speed, 185 m.p.h.

Sikorsky R-6A (*Harold G. Martin*).

SIKORSKY R-6

Developed in parallel with the R-5, the R-6 (VS-316B) was a refinement of the R-4, having the same rotor and transmission system with an improved fuselage. Sikorsky built one XR-6 prototype (43-47955) with a 225 h.p. Lycoming O-435-7 engine, first flown on October 15, 1943 and five XR-6A (43-28240/44) with a 240 h.p. Franklin O-405-9 engine. Nash-Kelvinator built 26 similar YR-6A and a production run of 193 R-6A. Rotor diameter, 38 ft.; length, 38 ft. 3 in.; weight, 2,590 lb.; speed, 96 m.p.h.

Sikorsky CH-54A flying crane (*Steve Peltz*).

SIKORSKY H-54 TARHE

The U.S. Army acquired six Sikorsky S-64A flying cranes in 1964/65 to investigate the heavy lift helicopter concept, and designated them YCH-54As (64-14202/14207). Powered by two 4,500 s.h.p. Pratt & Whitney T73-P-1 turboshaft engines, they were followed by 54 CH-54As (66-18408/18413, 67-18414/18431, 68-18432/18461) assigned to the Army's 478th Aviation Company and operated primarily in Vietnam to transport heavy equipment and retrieve crashed aircraft. The CH-54B had 4,800 s.h.p. T73-P-700 engines and a gross weight of 47,000 lb. Production totalled 37 (69-18462/18498), with deliveries to the 291st Aviation Company in 1970/71. Rotor diameter, 72 ft. 0 in.; length, 88 ft. 6 in.; gross weight, 42,000 lb.; max. speed, 127 m.p.h.

(*Alfred Cellier*).

SPARTAN UC-71

First produced in 1935 for the U.S. domestic light aircraft market, the Spartan Executive five-seat low-wing monoplane was among the aircraft types commandeered for military service in 1942 soon after the U.S. entered the War. In all, 16 privately-owned examples of the Executive were impounded and all were designated UC-71 for the duration of the War. They served as staff transports and station "hacks" within the U.S. The engines were 400-h.p. Pratt & Whitney R-985-33 radials. Span, 39 ft. 0 in.; length, 26 ft. 10 in.; gross weight, 4,400 lb.; max. speed, 210 m.p.h.

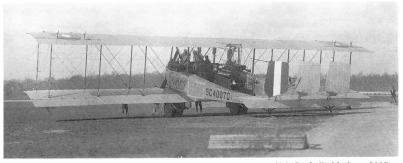

(*McCook Field photo 2187*).

STANDARD/CAPRONI

In addition to French and British designs, the unique twin-fuselage trimotor Italian Caproni biplane and triplane bombers were also selected for production in America in 1917/1918, by the Standard Aircraft Corp. of Elizabeth, N.J., and the Fisher Body Works of Cleveland, Ohio. By war's end, only two Capronis had been built by Standard (40070, 40071) and one (42119), which was not accepted, by Fisher. Two Italian-built samples were sent to America, and the U.S. Forces in France obtained at least one other from the French. Span, 76 ft. 10 in.; length, 41 ft. 2 in.; wing area, 1,420 sq. ft.; empty weight, 7,700 lb.; gross weight, 12,350 lb.; high speed, 103 m.p.h.

Standard-built H.P O-400 in USAAF service (*Bowers/Williams collection*).

STANDARD/HANDLEY-PAGE O-400

The Standard Aircraft Corporation of Elizabeth, New Jersey, was chosen in 1917 to build the Handley-Page O-400, and to deliver sets of components for assembly in the U.K. The first set was assembled in the U.S. by Standard, fitted with Liberty engines, and christened "Langley" in July 1918 for publicity purposes. By the end of World War I, sets of spares equivalent to over 100 complete O-400s had been delivered. After the Armistice, eight Liberty-powered O-400s (inc. 62445-62451) were assembled for the U.S. Army. Span, 100 ft.; length, 62 ft. 10 in.; wing area, 1,655 sq. ft.; empty weight, 8,721 lb.; gross weight, 12,425 lb.; high speed, 96 m.p.h.

Standard E-1 with 100 h.p. Gnome engine (*Bowers/Williams collection*).

STANDARD E-1/M-DEFENSE

Two prototypes (33769/33770) of the Standard E-1, a 1917 design, were tested as fighters but production orders were placed for 460 E-1s as advanced trainers. Thirty-three (44542-44574) were delivered with Gnome 100 h.p. rotary engines, followed by 60 designated M-Defense (44575/44577, 49156/49212) and 75 identical E-1s (49133/49207) with the 80 h.p. Le Rhône. After the war, Sperry converted three E-1s, which were given new serial numbers (64228/64230), to radio-controlled aerial torpedoes by lengthening the fuselage and making other essential modifications. This work was part of a contract for the similar conversion of several Sperry M-1 Messengers (page 303) and the resulting Sperry MAT designation was also attached to these aeroplanes.

670

Stearman YBT-3 (*Boeing Aeroplane Company photo*).

STEARMAN PT-9, BT-3, BT-5

In 1931, Army interest in replacements for the obsolete 180 h.p. PT-1 and its direct successor, the 220 h.p. PT-3, resulted in a flurry of new designs developed for lower horsepowers, starting with the 100 h.p. Fleet PT-6 and ranging to the 165 h.p. Consolidated PT-11. Stearman was awarded a contract for four service test YPT-9s (31-459/462), powered with the 165 h.p. Wright R-540-1 (J-6-5) five cylinder radial engines. The aeroplane was structurally identical with Stearman's commercial Model 6, known as the "Cloudboy". Although the J-6-5 engine was widely used in commercial aviation, it proved unsuitable for military use, and all were removed from the YPT-9s.

Since the Army was also interested in new basic trainers that were built as such instead of being converted observation types, and the Stearman airframe was rugged enough to take increased power without structural reinforcement, a 300 h.p. Wright R-975-1 (J-6-9) was installed in the YPT-9 31-461, which then became YBT-3, and a 300 h.p. Pratt & Whitney R-985-1 Wasp Junior was fitted in 31-462, which became the YBT-5. On both machines, the engine was enclosed in a Townend anti-drag ring. A service test Continental YR-545-1 engine of 165 h.p. was tried in the YPT-9 31-459 converted as YPT-9A. This was soon replaced by a 200 h.p. Lycoming R-680-3 and this aeroplane, along with 31-460 which was fitted with the same engine, became YPT-9B. The YBT-3 underwent a further engine change to become a primary trainer again with a 7-cylinder 170 h.p. Kinner YR-720-1, as the YPT-9C, but the Army picked the Consolidated PT-11 (see page 144) for production. Span, 32 ft. 0 in.; length, 24 ft. 8 in.; wing area, 272 sq. ft.; gross weight, 2,814 lb.; max. speed, 135 m.p.h.

UC-81 (*Lockheed photo Z-1775*).

STINSON UC-81, AT-19

Upon America's entry into World War II, production of the Stinson Reliant four/five seat cabin monoplane ceased in favour of other types, but a total of 47 privately-owned Reliants were impounded for military service under the designation UC-81. Variants included the SR-8, SR-9 and SR-10 types, with Lycoming, Wright and Pratt & Whitney engines; designations up to UC-81N were allocated. The same basic type was later put back into production and 500 were built, as AT-19s, for Lend–Lease delivery to the Royal Navy. Span, 41 ft. 11 in.; length, 27 ft. 11 in.; gross weight, 3,700 lb.–4,680 lb.; max. speed, 145–178 m.p.h.

XO-6. (*McCook Field photo*).

THOMAS-MORSE O-6 SERIES

As a result of competitive bidding, Thomas-Morse was given a contract to build six metal versions of the Douglas O-2 under the designation of XO-6 (25-435/440). The first two were delivered as XO-6s and the next three became standard O-6. At the request of Thomas-Morse, who saw much room for improvement in a machine designed from scratch to capitalize on metal structure, the firm was allowed to build a smaller original design designated XO-6B in place of the final O-6 (25-440). This aeroplane was not accepted and the serial number was cancelled, but an improved version was bought as the O-19 (see page 584).

VICTOR (HEINRICH) ADVANCED TRAINER

Two single-seat "scouts" built in 1917 by the Victor Aircraft Corporation of Freeport, L.I., (539, 540), powered with the 100 h.p. Gnome rotary engine, were also known as Heinrich Pursuits, after the designer, Albert S. Heinrich. They were inadequate by European military standards and were considered only as advanced trainers. Two improved versions (40007, 40008) were built in 1918, powered with the more reliable 80 h.p. Le Rhône rotary and using lighter structure. Span, 26 ft. 0 in.; wing area, 162·5 sq. ft.; gross weight, 1,235 lb. (Gnome), 1,065 lb. (Le Rhône); high speed, 115 m.p.h. (Gnome), 110 m.p.h. (Le Rhône).

VE-9 (*McCook Field photo 12382*).

VOUGHT VE-7, VE-9

The Lewis and Vought VE-7 of 1917 was designed specifically as an advanced trainer, with a 150 h.p. Wright-Hispano "A" engine behind a Spad VII-type radiator. Plans were made for large-scale production, but the demand for advanced trainers was met by converting the Curtiss JN-4 to the Hisso-powered JN-4H, so VE-7 production for the Army was terminated after 14 (inc. 19898/19902) had been delivered by Vought. Two additional improved 180-h.p. models (inc. 40072) were built at McCook Field and four similar models were delivered by Springfield. Two 180-h.p. VE-9 variants (64310, 64316) were procured at the end of the war and an additional 21 (23-379/400) were procured in 1923. Span, 34 ft. 1½ in.; length, 24 ft. 5½ in.; wing area, 284·5 sq. ft.; empty weight, 1,559 lb.; gross weight, 2,095 lb.; high speed, 114 m.p.h.

Vultee YA-19 (*Bowers collection*).

VULTEE A-19

Between 1935 and 1938, the Vultee company achieved considerable success exporting examples of its V-11 light bomber to China, the U.S.S.R., Turkey and Brazil. In June 1938, seven examples were ordered by the Air Corps for evaluation as YA-19s (38-549/555) with 1,200-h.p. R-1830-17 engines. Span, 50 ft. 0 in.; length, 37 ft. 10 in.; wing area, 384 sq. ft.; gross weight, 10,421 lb.; max. speed, 230 m.p.h. at 6,500 ft.

Vultee P-66 (*USAF photo*).

VULTEE P-66

Vultee completed a prototype of its Model 48 Vanguard in September 1939 and obtained an order from Sweden for 144. When deliveries to Sweden were barred, the aircraft were in turn assigned to Britain, Canada and China, under Lend–Lease arrangements. With the Army designation P-66, and R-1830-33 engines, 129 eventually reached China and the remainder served with the Air Force. Span, 36 ft.; length, 28 ft. 5 in.; wing area, 197 sq. ft.; gross weight, 7,384 lb.; max. speed, 340 m.p.h. at 15,100 ft.

674

Gordon S. Williams).

WACO PT-14

The Waco Model UPF-7, one of the range of Waco biplanes produced for civil use in the U.S., participated with the St. Louis PT-1W (see page 584) in Air Corps tests in 1939 to find a new primary trainer. It was an orthodox biplane with open cockpits in tandem and an uncowled 220 h.p. Continental R-670-3 engine. The Army purchased one XPT-14 (39-702) and 13YPT-14s (40-14/26). The latter became PT-14s and one other UPF-7 impressed in 1942 was designated PT-14A. Span, 30 ft. 0 in.; length, 23 ft. 6 in.; gross weight, 2,650 lb.; max. speed, 138 m.p.h.

(John C. Collins).

WACO UC-72

Waco biplanes of many different types were among the most popular of U.S. lightplanes produced in the decade before World War II. A total of 44 examples were impressed for Army service under the designation UC-72. Sixteen different models were represented, including some with tricycle undercarriages, and designations up to UC-72Q were applied. They served throughout the War as staff transports and station ferries. Span, 33 ft. 3 in.; or 34 ft. 9 in. according to model; length, 25 ft. 4 in. to 27 ft. 10 in.; gross weight, 3,100–4,200 lb.; max. speed, 144–200 m.p.h.

CG-3A at Wright Field (*Wright Field photo*).

WACO CG-3

America's first troop glider to reach production was the Waco CG-3, or Model NYQ, of wood and fabric construction. One XCG-3 (41-29617) was delivered in 1942 and was an eight-seater. The production model CG-3A had nine seats. Commonwealth built 100 for use as trainers during 1942, of 300 ordered (42-43518/43617). A contract for 200 placed with Waco was cancelled. Span, 73 ft. 1 in.; length, 43 ft. 4 in.; empty weight, 2,044 lb.; gross weight, 4,400 lb.; towing speed, 120 m.p.h.

CG-13A.

WACO CG-13

Development of troop gliders with twice the capacity of the CG-4A (pages 516–519) began in 1942, the 30-seat Waco XCG-13 being among the designs ordered. Two prototypes (43-28245/6) were tested in 1942/3, with one XCG-13 built by Ford (43-43864) and one by Northwestern (43-43915). The XCG-13A had a tricycle undercarriage, modified tail and 42 seats; Ford built one (43-43865) and Northwestern two (43-43914/916). Production orders were placed for 350 and 50, respectively, but Ford delivered only 85 (43-43866/913 and 44-85942/978) and Northwestern only 47 (43-43917/963). The designation changed to G-13A in 1948. Span, 85 ft. 7 in.; length, 54 ft. 3 in.; empty weight, 8,700 lb.; gross weight, 18,900 lb.; towing speed, 209 m.p.h.

APPENDIX C
FOREIGN AIRCRAFT

Included in this section are details and illustrations of aircraft of foreign design and manufacture operated by the Army or Air Force of the United States. Foreign types constructed in the U.S. are treated as American types and included in other sections of this work as appropriate.

For the most part, the types included in this Appendix were purchased for use in Europe during World War I, or were acquired from Britain under "Reverse Lend-Lease" or other arrangements during World War II. Also during the latter conflict, several British types were operated in the U.K. in USAAF markings; some are illustrated here but photographs of others (such as the D.H.82A Tiger Moth, Miles Master and Percival Proctor) remain singularly elusive to this day.

Many German and Japanese types were flown during and shortly after World War II for technical evaluation after capture as War booty; more recently some Soviet types have been similarly investigated. Such types fall outside the scope of this Appendix.

Airspeed Oxford used by 4th FG in the U.K. (*via G. Fry*).

AIRSPEED OXFORD

Between early 1942, when units of the USAAF first arrived in the U.K., and the middle of 1944, substantial numbers of Airspeed Oxfords were made available to the 8th Air Force for communications duty. At least 132 Oxfords flew in U.S. markings (and with British serial numbers retained), including a few used by the Blind Approach Training (BAT) Flights. The six-seat Oxford was powered by two 395 h.p. Armstrong Siddeley Cheetah X engines. Span, 53 ft. 4 in.; length, 34 ft. 6 in.; gross weight, 8,250 lb.; max. speed, 190 m.p.h.

Airspeed Horsa (*USAF photo 51742A.C.*).

AIRSPEED HORSA

Britain's standard troop carrying glider in World War II, the Airspeed Horsa, was first used operationally, by the Glider Pilot Regiment, in the airborne invasion of Sicily. Under equipment interchange arrangements between Britain and the U.S., many Horsas were operated in USAAF colours and by American troops in the D-Day assault on France, and in Burma and India. Span, 88 ft.; length, 66 ft. $11\frac{3}{4}$ in.; gross weight, 15,500 lb.

Ansaldo S.V.A.5 at McCook Field (*U.S. Army/McCook Field photo 144*).

ANSALDO S.V.A.-10

The S.V.A. 9 and 10 were two-seat versions of the famous S.V.A. (Societa Verduzio Ansaldo) 5, the outstanding Italian fighter of World War I. Unique features of the basic design were the Warren truss bracing of the wings and the abrupt changes in cross section of the plywood fuselage, which became triangular aft of the cockpit. One S.V.A.-5 was sent to the U.S. for test in 1917, and at least one S.V.A.-10 was purchased after the Armistice for use of the American Air Attaché in Rome.

British Avro 504s used for AEF training at Issoudon, with AEF numbers on fuselage (*R. R. Martin*).

AVRO 504K

The Avro 504 was a pre-war design, notable as a light bomber in the early days of World War I but whose greatest fame was earned as Britain's principal primary trainer of the World War I years. The A.E.F. bought 52 504Ks for training in England after several had been sent to the U.S. for evaluation. At least seven were shipped to the U.S. at war's end and given U.S. serial numbers 62953/62959. Span, 36 ft.; length, 29 ft. 5in.; wing area, 330 sq. ft.; gross weight, 1,829 lb.; high speed, 87 m.p.h.

Messerschmitt Bf 108 in R.A.F. markings (The Aeroplane *photo*).

B.F.W. (MESSERSCHMITT) XC-44

The B.F.W. 108B, built by the Bayerische Flugzeug Werke of Augsburg, Germany, but commonly called Messerschmitt after its designer, was the last of a series of miscellaneous European military and commercial aircraft procured throughout the 1920s and 1930s for the use of U.S. Military Attachés in Europe. One was procured in 1939 for the Air Attaché in Berlin as XC-44 (39-718), the only time that a standard U.S. designation was assigned to such a foreign procurement. It was impressed into the Luftwaffe in 1940 and no photo of it in U.S. markings is known to exist. Span, 34 ft. 5 in.; length, 27 ft. 2 in.; wing area, 172 sq. ft.; gross weight, 2,970 lb.; high speed, 189 m.p.h.

Breguet 14A-2 (*USAF photo*).

BREGUET 14

Two versions of the 1917 French Breguet 14 combined with the French Salmson 2A-2 to form the main two-seater strength of the A.E.F. until the "Liberty Planes" went into action in August 1918. The Breguet 14A-2 was a "Corps d'Armée", an observation type, while the 14B-2 was a day bomber. The two were easily distinguishable by the longer lower wing on the B, which was also fitted with a spring-loaded full-span automatic flap that acted as a camber-changing device. Unorthodox by prevailing French standards was the bolted aluminium tube fuselage construction, but the negatively-staggered wings, generally considered unorthodox, were fairly common to several French designs. Two different power plants were used, the 6-cylinder Italian Fiat of 285 h.p. and the 300-h.p. French Renault V-12. A few Breguets sent to McCook Field for test were fitted with Liberty engines. Data for Breguet 14A (Liberty engine): Span, 47 ft. 3 in.; length, 29 ft. 2 in.; wing area, 527 sq. ft.; empty weight, 2,392 lb.; gross weight, 3,771 lb.; high speed, 129 m.p.h.

Breguet 14B-2 of 96th Bomb Squadron, with flap down (*Signal Corps photo 17781/National Archives*).

680

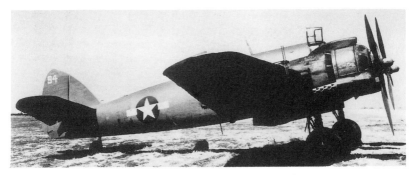

Bristol Beaufighter VIF in Middle East (*Howard Levy*).

BRISTOL BEAUFIGHTER

Widely used by the R.A.F. as a day and night fighter and heavily-armed ground- and sea-attack aircraft, the Beaufighter was one of the operational types interchanged in the field between the R.A.F. and the USAAF. The latter received enough to equip the 414th, 415th, 416th and 417th NF Squadrons in Twelfth AF in the Middle East in June-August 1943. They were retained until the war ended. Power plant, 1,670 h.p. Hercules VI or XVI; span, 57 ft. 10 in.; length, 41 ft. 8 in.; gross weight, 21,600 lb.; high speed, 333 m.p.h.

Artist's impression of C-29A (*British Aerospace photo*).

BRITISH AEROSPACE C-29

In April 1988, the USAF confirmed that it had selected the British Aerospace 125 Srs 800A biz-jet to meet its C-FIN (Combat Flight Inspection and Navigation) requirement. Six aircraft were to be ordered under the C-29A designation, for delivery June-December 1989 as replacements for T-39s and C-140s used in a similar rôle. Powered by two 4,300 lb.s.t. Garrett TFE731-5 turbofans, the C-29A carried computerized equipment to analyze the performance and accuracy of military ground-based navigational facilities, this equipment being supplied by LTV Missiles and Electronics Group. Span, 51 ft. $4\frac{1}{2}$ in.; length, 51 ft. 2 in.; gross weight, 27,400 lb.; max. speed, 525 m.p.h. at 29,000 ft.

Le Rhone powered G-III at A.E.F. school in France (*Signal Corps photo 3235*).

CAUDRON G-IIIE-2 AND G-IVA-2

Two separate but related French Caudron models were used by the A.E.F. as trainers. The G-IIIA-2, originally an observation, or "Corps d'Armée" type of 1914/15, was a single-engined two seater used in 1918 as a primary trainer. The pilot and student sat in tandem in a "bath tub" nacelle behind an 80-h.p. Le Rhône 9-cylinder rotary engine or a 90-h.p. 10-cylinder twin-row Anzani radial. The tail surfaces were supported by tail booms in the manner of contemporary pusher types, but in the Caudron designs the lower booms formed part of the main landing gear and also served as the tailskids. The airfoil was single-surface aft of the rear spar, and late versions of the 192 A.E.F. G-IIIE-2s ("E" indicated "École", sometimes "Entrainment", or trainer, in French nomenclature) used ailerons in the upper wing in place of the original wing warping.

The 10 Caudron G-IVs procured by the A.E.F. had been built as "Corps d'Armée" types and retained their original G-IVA-2 designations while serving as American trainers. In design concept the G-IV, the first twin-engine military airplanes to go into action in World War I, was merely a G-III expanded to a twin-engine type using the same Le Rhône engines. As with the majority of obsolete aircraft obtained from the French, the Caudrons were delivered with French markings. The American colour arrangement was painted over the French on some, while others were flown as received.

Caudron G-IV (*Signal Corps photo/National Archives*).

682

D.H. 94 Moth Minor "Sand Fly" in Egypt (*Howard Levy*).

DE HAVILLAND D.H. 89B DOMINIE

The Army's single DH-94 Moth Minor was a standard British primary *(ab initio)* trainer purchased in 1942 for communications work before quantities of British-built aircraft were supplied under a "Reverse Lend-Lease" programme. As a result, the Moth Minor carried a standard USAAF serial number, 42-94128, while the later types were flown under their original R.A.F. serials. Power plant, 90 h.p. D.H. Gipsy Minor; span, 36 ft. 7 in.; length, 24 ft. 5 in.; wing area, 162 sq. ft.; gross weight, 1,550 lb.; high speed, 118 m.p.h.

D.H. 89A Dragon Rapide (*De Havilland photo via M. Hooks*).

DE HAVILLAND D.H.89B DOMINIE

The Dominie was produced as a military variant of the D.H. 89 Dragon Rapide, an eight-seat light transport, the prototype of which first flew on April 17, 1934. More than 530 were built for the R.A.F. in trainer (Mk I) and communication (Mk II) variants and at least six were made available to the USAAF 8th Air Force in the U.K. between December 1942 and August 1944. They were used for communications, principally by the 27th Transport Group. The Dominie was powered by two 200 h.p. de Havilland Gipsy Queen 3 engines. Span, 48 ft. 0 in.; length, 34 ft. 6 in.; gross weight, 5,500 lb.; max. speed, 157 m.p.h.

683

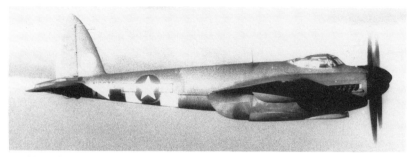

Mosquito P.R. Mk XVI from BAD 2 at Warton in 1944 (*Jack Knight via H. Holmes*).

DE HAVILLAND F-8 MOSQUITO

Nearly 200 examples of the de Havilland Mosquito were acquired by the USAAF between 1943 and 1945, from British and Canadian production lines. Only the 40 Canadian-built examples received a designation, however, as F-8s. Equivalent to the British B Mk IV bomber variant, they were wanted—like those acquired in Britain—primarily for photo-reconnaissance duties, but their performance proved inferior to their British counterparts, and of 40 purchased only 16 were delivered to the U.K. (in the second half of 1944) and none was used operationally.

Starting in early 1944, the 8th Air Force in England began to receive Mosquito PR Mk XVIs, initially to equip two squadrons of the 802nd Reconnaissance Group (later in 1943, the 25th Bomb Group). From well over 100 supplied, about half were also used at some time between May 1944 and May 1945 by a light weather reconnaissance squadron, the 653rd BS. Twelve were converted to carry H2X for radar reconnaissance flights and 12 others were equipped for night photographic work. Twelve of the LWR Mosquitoes were fitted to dispense chaff, for use by the 653rd BS, and seven suitably-equipped PR Mk XVIs (under the code *Red Stocking*) were used by 654th BS to communicate with agents in occupied territory. A few Mosquito T Mk IIIs were supplied to the 802nd RG for use as conversion trainers.

The Mosquito PR Mk XVI was powered by 1,710 h.p. Rolls-Royce Merlin 72/73 engines. Span, 54 ft. 2 in.; length, 41 ft. 6 in.; gross weight, 25,917 lb.; max. speed, 408 m.p.h. at 30,000 ft.

Canadian-built Mosquito F-8 (*NASA photo*).

684

YL-20 Beaver in original overall silver finish (*Peter M. Bowers*).

DE HAVILLAND L-20, U-6 BEAVER

An original product of the de Havilland company in Toronto, Canada, the DHC-2 Beaver became the second non-U.S. design purchased in quantity since World War II when it won a joint USAF/Army design competition for a new liaison aircraft held early in 1951. For evaluation and testing, the Air Force purchased four, and the Army two, examples in 1950 of the Canadian aircraft off-the-shelf, and designated them YL-20. Its subsequent purchase on a large scale required special Congressional action, and deliveries began in 1952.

Only minor changes were made to the basic Canadian design to meet U.S. requirements; these were concerned primarily with equipment and instrumentation. The design had been laid out from the start for rugged operations in Northern Canada, and the sturdy construction, wide track undercarriage and simple maintenance all helped the L-20 in its military operations. The Pratt & Whitney R-985-AN-1 or AN-3 engine was retained. Accommodation in the cabin totalled seven, including the pilot, and provision was made for the fitting of dual control.

By the end of 1960, 968 L-20As and six L-20Bs had been delivered to the U.S., the majority of these being for the Army Air Corps. Those used by the USAF (more than 200) served in all theatres.

The U.S. Army operated more L-20As than any other single type of fixed wing aircraft. The type was used on a large scale during the Korean War, as a command transport and ambulance, and for liaison duties. Because it was used regularly by Generals Van Fleet, Ridgeway and Mark Clark it became known as "The General's Jeep", but its biggest task was the transport of casualties from the front.

Operations on wheels, skis or floats are possible with the L-20, and the Army used some on skis for service in Alaska, after conducting trials in 1951. These were painted in Arctic colours, white overall with red wing-tips and tails; the more usual Army finish was drab olive, while the USAF Beavers were usually in natural metal finish. The designation was changed to U-6A in 1962 and these aircraft continued to give effective service in Vietnam, including 20 RU-6As equipped for airborne radio direction finding (AROF). Some TU-6As were modified for use as trainers.

685

TECHNICAL DATA (L-20A)

MANUFACTURER: de Havilland Aircraft of Canada Ltd., Downsview, Toronto.
TYPE: Army communications and light transport.
ACCOMMODATION: Pilot and seven passengers.
POWER PLANT: One 450 h.p. Pratt & Whitney R-985-AN-1 piston radial.
DIMENSIONS: Span, 48 ft. 0 in. Length, 30 ft. 3 in. Height, 9 ft. 0 in. Wing area, 250 sq. ft.
WEIGHTS: Empty, 2,850 lb. Gross, 5,100 lb.
PERFORMANCE: Max. speed, 163 m.p.h. at 5,000 ft. Cruising speed, 143 m.p.h. at 5,000 ft. Initial climb: 1,020 ft./min. Service ceiling, 18,000 ft. Range, 455 st. miles.
ARMAMENT: Nil.
SERIAL NUMBERS:
YL-20: 51-5110/5111; 51-6263/6266.
L-20A: 51-16463/16863; 52-6059/6161;   56-351/426; 56-4397/4447;
     53-2781/2846; 53-3711/3737;   57-2559/2588; 57-6137/6182;
     53-8159/8170; 53-7888/7967;   57-6522/6525; 58-1978/2077;
     54-1666/1739; 55-681/708;   58-7020/7024; 59-5916/5918.
     55-3481/3489; 55-4582/4612;   L-20B: 53-7780/7785.

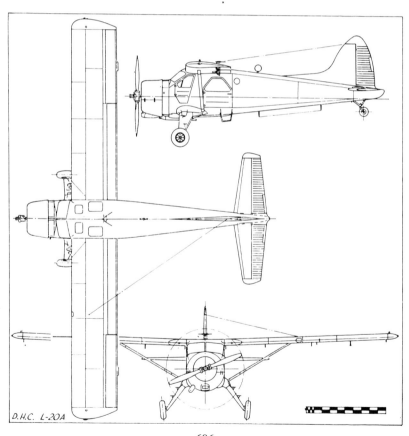

D.H.C. L-20A

YU-1 Otter in all-white Arctic "camouflage", but with red outer wings and tail unit to ensure good visibility against snow (*Harry S. Gann*).

DE HAVILLAND U-1 OTTER

Designed as a "big brother" for the Beaver, the DHC-3 Otter was of similar configuration and retained the same STOL capability and rugged construction. The Otter, powered by a 600-h.p. Pratt & Whitney R-1340 radial engine, first flew at the de Havilland Canada plant near Toronto on December 12, 1951, and first deliveries were to the RCAF and Canadian civil operators.

During 1953, an Otter demonstrator flew to Fort Bragg, N.C., to participate in the Army evaluation exercise *Operation Skydrop*. This was intended to assess the relative efficiency of helicopters and fixed-wing aircraft, and in the light of the Otter's performance—especially its ability to fly substantial loads from small unprepared fields—the Army made plans to purchase the type in quantity. It became the first aircraft designated in a new utility category, as the U-1, and the first six trials aircraft, designated YU-1 (55-2973/2978) were handed over to the Army on March 14, 1955. Subsequent aircraft were designated U-1A; those intended for service in Alaska had Arctic white and red finish, as did the YU-1s; others were finished in drab olive.

Deliveries of the U-1A continued in 1956 and 1957, a total of more than 170 being procured to equip Army Aviation Transport Companies, including the 1st and 2nd AACs. Used in conjunction with helicopters, they made possible a new concept of tactical mobility for Army troops, on which subsequent Army planning has been based. Each U-1A could airlift nine fully equipped troops or about 3,000 lb. of supplies. They were used in Army exercises from 1957 onwards to airlift troops from their operating base to points behind the enemy lines. A typical action was the transportation by 17 Otters of the 2nd Army Aviation Company of 305 infantrymen 35 miles in 100 minutes.

Most Army Otters operated as landplanes although the basic type could be equipped with wheels, floats or skis. One U-1A (55-3318) was flown experimentally with the All-American Engineering Universal Landing Gear, permitting operation from land, swamp, sand, water, ice or snow without modification of the gear. The YU-1s, assigned to Alaska for topographical survey duties, operated from skis as required. Another U-1A (55-3250) was used in air refuelling experiments as a tanker to refuel an H-21 helicopter.

TECHNICAL DATA (U-1A)

MANUFACTURER: de Havilland Aircraft of Canada Ltd., Downsview, Toronto.
TYPE: Army utility transport.
ACCOMMODATION: Two pilots and nine passengers or six litters.
POWER PLANT: One 600-h.p. Pratt & Whitney R-1340 piston radial.
DIMENSIONS: Span, 58 ft. 0 in. Length, 41 ft. 10 in. Height, 12 ft. 7 in. Wing area, 375 sq. ft.
WEIGHTS: Empty, 4,168 lb. Gross, 8,000 lb.
PERFORMANCE: Max. speed, 160 m.p.h. at 5,000 ft. Cruising speed, 138 m.p.h. at 5,000 ft. Initial climb: 735 ft./min. Service ceiling, 18,800 ft. Range, 960 st. miles.
ARMAMENT: Nil.
SERIAL NUMBERS:
YU-1: 55-2973/2978.   U-1A: 55-3244/3327; 57-6107/6136; 58-1681/1720; 58-7019; 59-2207/2227.

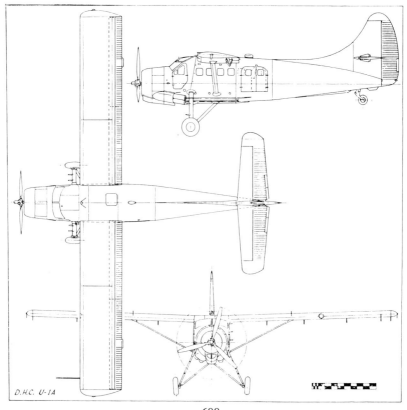

D.H.C. U-1A

688

YAC-1 Caribou in Arctic white-and-red, and with wheel/ski gear (*DHC photo*).

DE HAVILLAND AC-1, CV-2, C-7 CARIBOU

Continuing its reliance on Canadian aircraft in the light transport role, the U.S. Army selected the DHC-4 Caribou as its new standard STOL transport in 1957. Having already gained experience of U.S. Army operational requirements through the supply of large numbers of L-20s and U-1s, the Canadian de Havilland company had had the military applications much in mind when design of the Caribou began, in 1956, as a "twin Otter". It evolved as a utility transport suitable for rough field operation, and at an all-up weight of 26,000 lb. was the heaviest fixed-wing aeroplane purchased to date by the U.S. Army Air Corps.

The initial batch of seven pre-production Caribou included two for the Canadian Government followed by five YAC-1s ordered off-the-shelf by the U.S. Army in 1957. The first Caribou flew on July 30, 1958, followed by the first YAC-1 (57-3079) in March 1959. At a ceremony at the D.H. plant in Downsview, near Toronto, on October 8, 1959, three of the five YAC-1s were delivered to the Army; these and the other two delivered in November were used for evaluation trials at various U.S. Army installations.

An initial order for seven production-type AC-1s was placed early in 1960 and deliveries of these began in January 1961, followed by a further batch of 15 starting in May 1961, and another 137 in subsequent years bringing total procurement to 159, of which the last 103 were to AC-1A standard with increased gun weight.

In its military role, the Caribou was intended primarily to provide rapid mobility for troops, equipment and supplies in forward battle areas. It would be used for instance to fly personnel and supplies from major airports behind the lines, to forward landing strips, from which helicopters would ferry them to their ultimate destination. The payload capacity of up to three tons could be made up of a wide variety of military supplies ranging from 32 combat troops to two jeeps.

The designations of the Caribou variants were changed to CV-2A and CV-2B respectively in 1962. On 1 January, 1967, the US Army was required, under a change of policy towards its operation of fixed-wing tactical transports, to transfer its Caribou to the USAF, whereupon the designations changed again, to C-7A and C-7B.

TECHNICAL DATA (C-7A)

MANUFACTURER: de Havilland Aircraft of Canada Ltd., Downsview, Toronto.
TYPE: Army STOL utility transport.
ACCOMMODATION: Crew of 2–3 plus 32 combat troops, 24 paratroops or 14 litters.
POWER PLANT: Two 1,450-h.p. Pratt & Whitney R-2000-7M2 piston radials.
DIMENSIONS: Span, 96 ft. 0 in. Length, 72 ft. 7 in. Height, 31 ft. 9 in. Wing area, 912 sq. ft.
WEIGHTS: Empty, 16,795 lb. Gross, 26,000 lb.
PERFORMANCE: Max. speed, 216 m.p.h. at 5,000 ft. Cruising speed, 182 m.p.h. at 7,500 ft. Initial climb, 1,575 ft./min. Service ceiling, 27,700 ft. Range, 200–1,400 st. miles.
ARMAMENT: None.
SERIAL NUMBERS:
YAC-1: 57-3079/3083.
CV-2A: 60-3762/3768; 60-5430/5444; 61-2384/2407; 61-2591/2600;

CV-2B: 62-4144/4196; 62-12583/12584; 63-9718/9765.

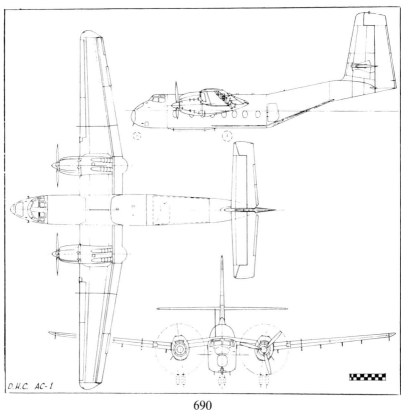

D.H.C. AC-1

UV-18B for Air Force Academy use (*DHC photo*).

DE HAVILLAND V-18 TWIN OTTER

The fourth of the family of DHC STOL transport types acquired to serve with the U.S. Army, two DHC-6 Twin Otters were handed over on October 22, 1976. Designated UV-18A (78-22565/22566) they entered service with the Scout Battalions of the Alaska Army National Guard to provide command, administrative, logistic and personnel flights within Alaska, operating on wheels, floats or skis. Four more were acquired later (79-23255/23256, 82-23835/23836). The 19-seat Twin Otter, powered by two 620 s.h.p. Pratt & Whitney PT6A-27 engines, was subsequently acquired by the USAF, which assigned two UV-18Bs (77-0464/0465) for service at the Air Force Academy. Span, 65 ft. 0 in.; length, 51 ft. 9 in.; gross weight, 12,500 lb.; max cruising speed, 210 m.p.h. at 10,000 ft.

E-9A showing long radome on fuselage side (*LTV Sierra photo*).

DE HAVILLAND E-9

The USAF selected in 1985 the de Havilland Canada DHC-8, a commercial transport powered by two 1,800 s.h.p. Pratt & Whitney PW120A turboprops, to provide the airborne platform for a surveillance system required in support of drone and missile testing out of Tyndall A.F.B., Florida. Two aircraft were converted to E-9As by LTV's Sierra Research Division to carry a steerable phased-array antenna in a starboard-side fuselage fairing, AN/APS-128D sea surveillance radar in a radome under the forward fuselage and a special avionics fit. The two aircraft entered service in 1988. Span, 85 ft. 0 in.; length, 73 ft. 0 in.; gross weight, 33,000 lb.; max. cruising speed, 309 m.p.h. at 15,000 ft.

691

Dorand A.R.1 (*Bowers collection*).

DORAND A.R.1 & A.R.2

The Dorand A.R.1 and 2, with nose and wing radiators for 200 and
190 h.p. Renault engines, respectively, were direct 1917 developments of a
pre-war design by Colonel Dorand of the Section Technique d'Aviation
of the French Army and were built in French Government shops at
Chalais-Meudon. Unconventional features of the design were negatively-
staggered wings and a lower wing set well below the fuselage. The A.E.F.
bought 22 A.R.1s and 120 A.R.2s, and used them as trainers rather than
combat observation types. A.R.1: Span, 43 ft. 7 in.; length, 30 ft.; wing
area, 540 sq. ft.; gross weight, 2,900 lb.; high speed, 92 m.p.h.

AEF Farman F-40P-2 at Ford Aerodrome in the U.K., October 1918 (*Signal Corps
photo 32308*).

FARMAN F-40

The 30 examples of the F-40 used in the A.E.F. were trainers flown
under their original designations of F-40A-2 and F-40P-2 ("P" for
Photographic). The Model 40 was a cleaned-up version of the classic
Farman "Boxkite" pusher of pre-war and early World War I years. The
nacelle of the F-40 was of laminated wood veneer instead of the earlier
framework boxes and almost completely enclosed the 130-h.p. Renault
V-12 engine. No A.E.F. Farmans were flown in the U.S. after World War I.

Federal AT-20 (*USAF photo*).

FEDERAL AT-20

Federal Aircraft Ltd. was a Government-owned company in Montreal set up in 1940 to supervise construction of the Avro Anson trainer in Canada. Fifty of the Canadian production versions were obtained by USAAF (43-8181/8230) under the AT-20 designation. They were basically Anson Mk. IIs, differing from the original British Mk. I in having 330-h.p. Jacobs L-6BM engines, hydraulic u/c and Canadian equipment. Span, 56 ft. 6 in.; length, 42 ft. 3 in.; gross weight, 7,660 lb.; high speed, 178 m.p.h.

Fieseler Storch captured in Sicily, 1943 (*Howard Levy*).

FIESELER Fi-156 STORCH

In the course of World War II, many enemy aircraft were captured by the U.S. forces in Europe, North Africa and the Pacific. At least one example of each type captured was usually flight tested, in USAAF markings, either locally where captured, or at a base in the U.S. In other cases, transports or light liaison types were pressed into service to fill local shortages. The Fieseler Storch, illustrated, is a typical example of a North African war prize in use with USAAF.

693

Single-seat Fokker D.VII with 220 h.p. Hall-Scott engine and original German s/n shortened to 8323 from 8323/18 (*McCook Field photo*).

FOKKER D.VII

Of 347 surrendered German aeroplanes shipped to the U.S. in 1919, 142 were 160-185 h.p. Fokker D.VII biplane fighters. These were widely used by the USAAS as secondary aircraft in fighter squadrons and squadron hacks (of which some were converted to two seaters). Eight, still in their German markings, were sent to Kelly Field as trainers. At least 12 were used at McCook Field for experimental work, some with 290 h.p. Liberty-8 engines and some with 12-cylinder 375 h.p. Packard 1A-1237 engines. As a tribute to Tony Fokker's salesmanship, he was able to sell the Army several more D.VIIs from stocks in his Dutch factory. These had 160 h.p. Mercedes DIII engines. Span, 29 ft. 3½ in.; length, 22 ft. 11⅝ in.; wing area, 221 sq. ft.; gross weight, 1,870 lb.; high speed, 116 m.p.h.

Fokker D.VII converted to two-seater with 290 h.p. Liberty-8 engine and Air Service s/n 94034 (*McCook Field photo 17989*).

The eighth PW-5, s/n A.S.68554 (*McCook Field photo 17622*).

FOKKER V.40, PW-5

In spite of a prevailing "Buy American" policy when World War I ended, General Billy Mitchell was able to procure some foreign designs under available experimental funds. Among these were two Dutch Fokker V.40 parasol monoplane fighters (AS64231/64232) powered by 300 h.p. French Hispano-Suiza engines. These created a good enough impression to be followed by 10 production versions designated PW-5 (AS68547/68556) and powered by 320 h.p. American Wright H-2 engines. The loss of one PW-5 and its pilot through in-flight wing failure led to the requirement that all Army pilots would henceforth wear parachutes. Span, 39 ft. 4½ in.; length 26 ft. 1¼ in.; wing area, 246 sq. ft.; gross weight, 2,686 lb.; high speed, 144 m.p.h.

The first PW-7 with plywood-covered wings and V-struts (*McCook Field photo 20321*).

FOKKER PW-6, PW-7

General Mitchell was sufficiently impressed with Fokker construction to order the sole Dutch-built D-IX as the PW-6 (AS68575). This was essentially a modified D.VII with 300 h.p. Hispano-Suiza engine. He then ordered three new Fokker fighters to be powered with the 435 h.p. Curtiss D-12 engine. Fokker unsuccessfully tried to adapt the existing D-XII design to the bigger engine, then enlarged his taper-winged D-XI design to take it and delivered three PW-7s (AS68580/68582). The first had plywood-covered wings and V-struts; the others fabric-covered wings and N-struts. Span, 38 ft. 4 in.; length, 23 ft. 11 in.; wing area, 250 sq. ft.; gross weight, 3,176 lb.; high speed, 151 m.p.h.

A-2 (*McCook Field photo*).

FOKKER T-2/A-2

One of the largest single-engined aeroplanes built at the time, the Liberty-engined Fokker F-IV was purchased from the Dutch factory together with a second prototype, both to be known as T-2s (AS64233/64234). After delivery to McCook Field, 64234 was converted to a two-litter ambulance and designated A-2. The other T-2 was fitted with extra fuel tanks, and made several record-breaking flights. Span, 79 ft. 8 in.; length, 49 ft. 1 in.; area, 958 sq. ft.; weight, 10,750 lb.; high speed, 95 m.p.h.

CO-4A (*McCook Field photo*).

FOKKER CO-4 SERIES

The Fokker C-IV was the first military two-seater designed at the Dutch Fokker works after the 1919 move from Germany, the C-II and III being variants of the wartime C-I. During a tour of European aircraft plants in 1921, General Billy Mitchell was impressed by the C-IV and arranged for purchase of the prototype as CO-4 (68557) and two more refined versions (68565, 68566) that were also known as CO-4. Following tests, four additional CO-4As (23-1205/1209), identical with the third CO-4, were ordered. Span, 41 ft. 10 in.; length, 29 ft. 8 in.; wing area, 410 sq. ft.; empty weight, 3,030 lb.; gross weight, 4,505 lb.; high speed, 128 m.p.h.

One of two confiscated Fokker F27s in Army service (*Fokker photo*).

FOKKER F27

The Fokker F27 was a commercial twin-engined airliner developed and built in The Netherlands. Two examples confiscated by the U.S. Government in 1984 were made available to be used as primary dropping aircraft by the U.S. Army's Golden Knights parachute display team; they bore USAF serial numbers (85-1607/1608) and Army identifiers GK-001/GK-002, but were not given DoD designations. An example of the longer-fuselage Fairchild-built FH-227 used by the U.S. Navy was known as the "UC-27" (not in the DoD designation series). The F27 was powered by two Rolls-Royce Dart RDa7 Mk 536 turboprops. Span, 95 ft. 2 in.; length, 77 ft. 3$\frac{1}{2}$ in.; gross weight, 45,000 lb.; cruising speed, 298 m.p.h.

Heinkel He 22 used by US military attaché in Berlin (*Bowers collection*).

HEINKEL He 22

The single Heinkel 22 (30-420) was procured in Europe for use of the U.S. military attaché in Germany. Like other types used for the purpose, the Heinkel carried standard U.S. Army markings and was serviced by German technicians. An earlier Heinkel had been exported to the U.S. and entered in the Corps Observation competition by Cox-Klemin. He 22: Power plant, 230 h.p. B.M.W. IV; span, 39 ft. 5 in.; length, 27 ft. 3 in.; wing area, 375 sq. ft.; gross weight, 3,740 lb.; high speed, 126 m.p.h.

Morane 30E1 (*U.S. Army photo*).

MORANE-SAULNIER 30 E1

The unique strut-braced Morane MS-30 was typical of much of the second-line and sub-standard combat equipment procured from the French government that was used for training the A.E.F. While earlier versions with the 160-h.p. Gnome rotary engine had been developed as fighters, the one-gun MS-27 and the two-gun MS-29, the type proved unsuited to combat and the lower-powered MS-30 was built strictly as an advanced trainer as shown by the E-for-Entrainment designation. Power was the 120 h.p. Le Rhône. Fifty-one were procured for the A.E.F. Span, 28 ft. 7 in.; length, 18 ft. 8 in.; gross weight, 1,155 lb.; high speed, 120 m.p.h.

Morane 12R2 (*Signal Corps photo 10317/National Archives*).

MORANE-SAULNIER MS-12 ROLEUR

While most A.E.F. pilots were trained in the conventional American and British way on dual-control two-seaters, some were started out with a modified form of the French "grass-cutting" technique. For this purpose, the Army bought 138 two-seat Morane-Saulnier MS-12s powered with either 50-h.p. Gnome rotary engines or Anzani radials. MS-12s were used for dual instruction and differed from the Baby Bleriots used by the French in being fitted with ailerons.

Morane Saulnier MS-234 (*Bowers collection*).

MORANE-SAULNIER MS-234

The single MS-234 of 1932 (32-419) was procured for the U.S. Military Attaché in Paris as a replacement for an earlier MS-43. Both designs followed a "Morane Parasol" tradition dating to before World War I, and were open-cockpit tandem two-seat advanced training types. The 234 was a partly-Americanized design since it was powered with a 330-h.p. Wright J-6-9 Whirlwind (R-975) engine built under license by Hispano-Suiza. Span, 35 ft. 2 in.; length, 22 ft. 9 in.; wing area, 212 sq. ft.; gross weight, 2,533 lb.; high speed, 127 m.p.h.

Nieuport 80E-2 (*U.S. Army photo E-5058*).

NIEUPORT TWO-SEAT TRAINERS

The Nieuport Model 10 was one of the first armed tractor two-seaters, with the gunner in the front cockpit standing up with his shoulders through a hole in the upper wing in the pre-synchronized gun days of 1914/15. The famous single-seat Model 11 "Bebe" followed and the Model 12 was a typical armed two-seater of 1915/16, with the gunner in the rear cockpit. Three trainers derived from the Model 12 were procured in quantity by the A.E.F.:—147 model 80E-2 two-cockpit single control, 173 81D-2 two-cockpit dual control (D meant "double command", or dual control) and 244 83E-2 with semi-dual controls in a single two-seat "Buddy" cockpit. All used the 80-h.p. Le Rhône 9-C engine.

Nieuport 24bis (*Signal Corps Photo 3295/National Archives*).

NIEUPORT ONE-SEAT TRAINERS

For advanced training purposes, the A.E.F. procured a total of 870 obsolescent V-strut Nieuport single seaters from the French. These included 76 Model 17C-1 (C designated "Chasse", literally Chaser, or pursuit, in French nomenclature) of 1916 and 198 of the de-rated Model 21 trainer version, which used an 80-h.p. Le Rhône instead of the 110 h.p. engine in the same airframe. Fifty Model 23s were almost identical to the 21s. The Model 24, a Model 17 with improved streamlining and 130 h.p. engine, had been intended as a fighter design, but even the French relegated it to training duties, designated 24E-1. The A.E.F. procured 121 standard and 140 improved versions. The standard 24 used the two-piece fin and rudder assembly of the later 27 while the modified Model 24bis used the one-piece square rudder of the 17. The Model 27 was another actual fighter, a greatly cleaned up 17 and the last of the V-strut single seaters. The 120 delivered to the A.E.F. were used only as trainers. Standard armament was a 0·303-in. Vickers and a single Lewis gun.

Nieuport 27 in French markings and with U.S. school number on fuselage (*U.S. Army photo E-4348*).

700

Nieuport 28C-1, showing roundels under upper wing (*Courtesy Danny Grecco*).

NIEUPORT 28C-1

The first fighter to see action with the A.E.F. was the two-gun Nieuport 28, powered by the 160 h.p. Gnome rotary engine. The A.E.F. obtained 298 Model 28s straight from the factory, and 94th and 95th Pursuit Squadrons were the first to be equipped. The first A.E.F. victories were scored in Nieuports on April 14, 1918, and Douglas Campbell became the first American ace while flying this type. Span, 26 ft. 3 in.; length, 20 ft. 4 in.; gross weight, 1,625 lb.; high speed, 122 m.p.h.

Noorduyn UC-64A seaplane (*Logan Coombs*).

NOORDUYN C-64

Designed before the War by Noorduyn Aviation in Canada, the Norseman was adopted by the USAAF in 1942 after trials with seven YC-64s (42-5044/5049, 42-13602). Orders for 746 C-64As, operated on wheels or skis, kept the Norseman in production throughout the War. Three others were bought for the U.S. Navy, plus six C-64Bs on floats for the Corps of Engineers. Power plant, 600 h.p. R-1340-AN-1; span, 51 ft. 6 in.; length, 32 ft. 4 in.; gross weight, 7,440 lb.; high speed, 162 m.p.h.

Pilatus UV-20A in U.S. Army service in Germany (*Pilatus photo*).

PILATUS V-20A CHIRICAHUA

The U.S. Army purchased in 1979 two examples of the Swiss-designed and built PC-6 Turbo Porter, for operation as UV-20As (79-23253/23254) by the Aviation Detachment of the Army's Berlin Brigade. Replacing U-6A Beavers, the Chiricahuas were required for utility and routine training missions in Berlin and West Germany. The Turbo Porter, powered by a 680 s.h.p. Pratt & Whitney PT6A-27 turboprop, was a light STOL transport seating 6 to 11 passengers, derived from an original piston-engined version first flown on May 4, 1959. The V-12 designation had earlier been reserved for proposed Turbo Porter production by Fairchild, and the latter company also developed the AU-23A from the Porter, supplying 20 to Thailand through MAP. Span, 52 ft. 0¾ in.; length, 36 ft. 1 in.; gross weight, 6,173 lb.; cruising speed, 132 m.p.h.

American-operated, British-marked B.E.2E (*Signal Corps photo 32282/National Archives*).

R.A.E. B.E.2E.

The B.E.2 series was introduced by the British Royal Aircraft Factory (later Establishment, or R.A.E.) in 1912. The B.E.2E, of which 12 were bought by the A.E.F. for training in England, differed from early versions in having modified wings with a single bay of struts and extensive over-hang on the upper instead of two-bay equal-span wings. Power plant was a 90 h.p. R.A.E. 1A air-cooled V-8 engine. Span, 40 ft. 9 in.; length, 27 ft. 3 in.; wing area, 360 sq. ft.; gross weight, 2,100 lb.; high speed, 90 m.p.h.

British-marked F.E.2B (*Crown Copyright*).

R.A.E. F.E.2B

The F.E.2 was another pre-war official British design. The initials were originally considered to stand for "Farman Experimental" to associate the pusher configuration with the contemporary French Farman pushers. These letters later stood for "Fighting Experimental". The "Fee's" were used into 1918 as bombers and observation planes. The A.E.F. bought 30 F.E.2Bs powered with 160-h.p. Beardmore engines for training in England. Span, 47 ft. 9 in.; length, 32 ft. 3 in.; wing area, 494 sq. ft.; gross weight, 3,037 lb.; high speed, 91 m.p.h.

Salmson 2A-2 (*U.S. Army photo E-5111*).

SALMSON 2A-2

The Salmson 2A-2 was a standard French "heavy" observation design pressed into service with the A.E.F. along with the equivalent Breguet 14 when it became apparent that the American-built "Liberty Planes" would not be available for service when scheduled. Unconventional features of the Salmson were the installation of the 230–270-h.p. Salmson (formerly Canton-Unne) 9-cylinder water-cooled radial engine and the absence of a fixed fin and tailplane. Armament was a single 0·303-in. Vickers and twin Lewis guns. The A.E.F. acquired 705 Salmsons.

703

Shorts C-23A in European camouflage (*Shorts photo 84498-20*).

SHORTS C-23

The USAF selected the Shorts 330 as the basic aircraft to meet its requirement for a European Distribution System Aircraft (EDSA), required to fly urgent freight from the main distribution centres at Zweibrucken, Kemble and Torrejon to all operational bases within the USAFE area. The version proposed by Shorts and named Sherpa by the company, differed from the civil airliner in having a freight interior with reinforced floor, hydraulic loading winch, full-width rear door and ramp and no cabin windows. The first C-23A of 18 ordered (83-0512/0513, 84-0458/0473) flew at Belfast on December 23, 1952, and deliveries began in November 1984, for use by the 10th MAS. Ten more C-23s were ordered in 1988 for use by the Army National Guard. The C-23A was powered by two 1,198 s.h.p. Pratt & Whitney PT6A-45R engines. The U.S. Army operated four generally similar ex-civil Shorts 330s (85-25342/85345) as C-23Bs for support duties in the Kwajalein area of the Pacific. Span, 74 ft. 8 in.; length, 58 ft. 0½ in.; gross weight, 22,900 lb.; max. cruising speed, 218 m.p.h. at 10,000 ft.

Army-operated Shorts C-23B in Marshall Islands (*Shorts photo 86551-1*).

704

S.I.A.7B at Hampton Air Field in 1917 (*Signal Corps photo 3433/National Archives*).

S.I.A. 7B

In 1917, the Italian Government sent a pair of S.I.A. 7B reconnaissance-bombers to the United States for evaluation and consideration for production under the prevailing plan to mass-produce established European designs. Developed by the Societe Italiano Aviazione of Turin, the S.I.A. 7B was powered with a 300-h.p. Fiat engine and used the standard Italian structural feature of plywood-covered fuselage. The 7B was not put into production in the U.S. but 19 were bought in Italy for use by A.E.F. units sent there. Span, 43 ft. 8 in.; length, 29 ft. 9 in.; wing area, 460 sq. ft.; gross weight, 3,454 lb.; high speed, 111 m.p.h.

American-marked Camel (*U.S. Army E-5014*).

SOPWITH CAMEL

Because of the American shortage of combat aircraft in 1918, 143 Camels powered with 130-h.p. Clerget rotary engines were purchased in England. The majority of these were used as advanced trainers although some were intended to be night fighters. Only one A.E.F. squadron had them at the front at the time of the Armistice, and then only a few. The A.E.F. Camels flew with non-standard markings in that the British roundels, including fuselage marking and white outlining rings, were merely painted over with the colours in the American order, as illustrated.

705

Sopwith 1½-Strutter in A.E.F. service (*Signal Corps/National Archives*).

SOPWITH 1A2

The Sopwith "1½ Strutter", so named by the British because of its extra centre section struts, was a notable military aircraft before American entry into World War I. The French obtained large quantities of the two-seat observation version, which they named Sopwith 1A2, and the single-seat bomber version 1B1, by purchase and license manufacture. When the A.E.F. desperately needed aeroplanes in 1917/18, the French sold 514 Sopwiths (384 As and 130 Bs) to the Americans. Span, 33 ft. 6 in.; length, 25 ft. 4 in.; area, 353 sq. ft.; weight, 2,061 lb.; speed, 95 m.p.h.

British-built Spad VII at Kelly Field, Texas (*Edgar Deigan collection*).

SPAD VII

The Spad VII, (with the model number appearing both in Roman and Arabic figures) was one of the most famous French fighters of World War I. The letters formed the abbreviation of the name "Societe Pour Aviation et ses Derivees." It was designed in 1916 around the new 150-h.p. Hispano-Suiza motor and carried a single 0·303-in. Vickers gun in a trough on the nose. The 103rd Pursuit Squadron used Spad VIIs briefly and repainted them with American markings before re-equipping with Spad XIIIs. Some Spad VIIs built in England by Mann-Egerton remained in service as trainers at Kelly Field, Texas, until 1926.

706

Photo version of Spad XIII, with vertical camera behind cockpit (*USAF photo*).

SPAD XIII

The Spad XIII C-1 was a direct development of the single-gun 150 h.p. Spad VII of 1916, and was one of the European designs selected by the famous Bolling Commission for mass production in the United States. Orders for 2,000 to be built by Curtiss were cancelled and all of the 893 XIIIs delivered to the A.E.F. were procured from the French. A number of XIIIs were fitted with fixed aerial cameras for photo missions.

Principal differences from the Spad VII were the use of the 220-h.p. geared Hispano engine, twin guns, and a general beefing up along with improved streamlining and rounded wingtips.

Significant numbers of XIIIs were shipped to the U.S. after the Armistice and served for a while as first line fighter equipment. They were soon relegated to training duties and the troublesome 220-h.p. Hispano was replaced by an ungeared 180-h.p. Wright-Hispano E. The lower thrust line of the direct-drive engine necessitated a new and revised radiator and nose design. This was the principal recognition feature of the redesignated Spad 13E of 1923 (23-938/948). Span, 26 ft. 4 in.; length, 20 ft. 4 in.; wing area, 227 sq. ft.; gross weight, 1,811 lb.; high speed, 138 m.p.h.

Rebuilt Spad 13E in 1922 (*USAF photo 10653AS*).

General Mitchell's Spad 16A-2 (*USAF photo*).

SPAD 11A-2 and 16A-2

The Spad 11 and 16 were fast two-seat reconnaissance types developed from the Spad VII. Retaining the same short nose of the single seater made it necessary to sweep back the wings of the two seater for balance purposes. Thirty-five 11A-2s were procured, and have erroneously been referred to ever since as Spad 112 because the caption on the most-used photo released by the Office of Public Information in World War I inadvertently left the letter A and the dash out of the designation 11A-2. The Model 16, of which there were six in the A.E.F., was an identical airframe with a 250-h.p. direct drive Lorraine engine.

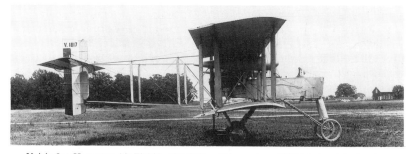

Voisin 8 at Hampton Air Field in 1917 (*Signal Corps photo 3288/National Archives*).

VOISIN 8 AND 10

Even though the basic Voisin design dated back to 1912, the French government tried to sell the U.S. Army later versions as combat types after U.S. entry into World War I. The Model 8 shown was sent to the U.S. for testing in 1917. Ten other examples of the old pusher, with its unique quadricycle landing gear, were purchased in France and used as trainers by the A.E.F., eight Model 8s with 220 h.p. Peugeot engines and two Model 10s with 300 h.p. Renaults.

Spitfire VA, 496th Fighter Group at Goxhill in 1944 (*via Peter H. T. Green*).

SUPERMARINE SPITFIRE

Although no Spitfires were procured by the USAAF, a quantity reported to total 600 operated in U.S. service under "Reverse Lend-Lease" arrangements. Before U.S. insignia appeared on Spitfires, however, they were being flown by American pilots who had volunteered to serve with the Royal Air Force in Britain. In October 1940, the R.A.F. formed No. 71 (Eagle) Squadron to be wholly manned by these pilots, and after several months operating Hurricanes, this unit received 14 Spitfire IIAs on August 20, 1941.

As the flow of volunteers grew, it became possible to form a second Eagle squadron, No. 121, on May 14, 1941, and a third, No. 133, on August 1, 1941. All three Eagle squadrons flew Spitfire IIs with eight 0.303-in. machine guns in the wings and Merlin XII engine. Later they were equipped with the Merlin 45-engined Spitfire VA or Spitfire VB, the latter having two 20-mm. cannon replacing four of the wing guns.

After the U.S. entered the War, further Spitfires were made available on "Reverse Lend-Lease" to equip the first two fighter units of the 8th Air Force in England, the 31st and 52nd Fighter Groups. The USAAF's white star appeared for the first time on the Spitfires of these two units. In September 1942, it also replaced the R.A.F.'s red-white-and-blue cockades on the aircraft of the Eagle Squadrons, which were transferred to the 8th Air Force as the 4th Fighter Group's 334th, 335th and 336th Squadrons.

Following a comparatively short period of service in England, the pilots of the 31st and 52nd Fighter Groups embarked aboard a merchant vessel for transfer to the Mediterranean. They picked up Spitfire VCs in Gibraltar and flew into action in the Operation Torch landings in French North Africa in November 1942. The Spitfires left in the U.K. by these two Groups were used by the 67th Observation Group, which served as the training unit for USAAF Spitfire pilots.

For reconnaissance duties, Spitfires were also issued to the 7th Photo Reconnaissance Group with the 8th Air Force in England, serving from November 1943 until 1945. Spitfire Vs used initially were later replaced by the specialized Spitfire PR Mk XI, an unarmed camera-equipped version which made deep-ranging penetrations of enemy territory to obtain target pictures. In all, 21 of the Mk XIs were used by the 7th PRG.

A few other units of the 8th Air Force had Spitfires attached in small numbers, including a Fighter Training Squadron and the H.Q. Squadron. At least one Spitfire, a Mk. VC (AA963), was despatched to the U.S. in February 1942.

TECHNICAL DATA (SPITFIRE VB)

MANUFACTURER: Vickers-Armstrongs (Supermarine) at Woolston, Hants, and Castle Bromwich Aircraft Factory, Birmingham.
TYPE: Fighter.
ACCOMMODATION: Pilot only in enclosed cockpit.
POWER PLANT: One 1,470 h.p. Merlin 45 V-in-line piston engine.
DIMENSIONS: Span, 36 ft. 10 in. Length, 29 ft. 11 in. Height, 9 ft 11 in. Wing area, 242 sq. ft.
WEIGHTS: Empty, 5,065 lb. Gross, 6,750 lb.
PERFORMANCE: Max. speed, 369 m.p.h. at 19,500 ft. Cruising speed, 320 m.p.h. at 20,000 ft. Climb $7\frac{1}{2}$ min. to 20,000 ft. Service ceiling, 36,200 ft. Range, 470 st. miles (without external tanks).
ARMAMENT: Four 0·303-in. Browning machine guns (350 r.p.g.) and two 20-mm. Hispano cannon (60 r.p.g.).

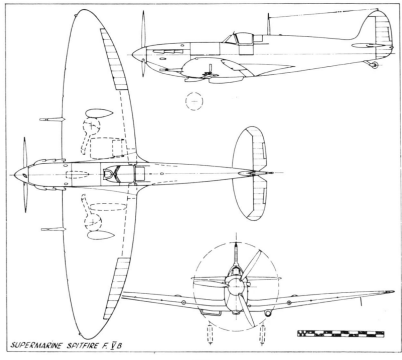

SUPERMARINE SPITFIRE F. VB

Westland Lysander used by 3rd Gunnery & Tow Target Flight in U.K., 1944 (*L. Redman*).

WESTLAND LYSANDER

About two dozen examples of the Lysander in its TT Mk IIIA target-towing version were supplied to units of the 8th Air Force from mid-1942 onwards. They served, until replaced by Vultee A-35s in the first half of 1944, with various Gunnery and Tow Target Flights, wearing U.S. insignia and retaining R.A.F. serials. The Lysander TT Mk IIIA was powered by an 870 h.p. Bristol Mercury XX engine. Span, 50 ft.; length, 30 ft. 6 in.; gross weight, 6,318 lb.; max. speed, 212 m.p.h.

CONFISCATED AIRCRAFT

Under the laws applied from the start of the 'eighties to combat drug-running across U.S. borders, the Drug Enforcement Agency (DEA) was able to confiscate aircraft used by smugglers. As a result, several aircraft were added to the inventories of the USAF and the U.S. Army. Among the types acquired in this way were a single Cessna 206 (82-667); two Fokker F27s (75-1607/1608); a Piper PA-31T Cheyenne (85-1609); three Beechcraft King Air 90s (86-0092, 86-1683 and 87-0142), a Cessna 185 (86-0142), a Gulfstream I (86-0402) and a Learjet 35 (87-0026). Also listed officially as "confiscated" were two Sikorsky CH-53As (63-13693/13694), part of an order for the Iran Navy that was embargoed before delivery.

BALLOONS AND AIRSHIPS

The British and Germans were the principal users of airships in World War I and the U.S. Navy was the exclusive user in World War II. After an early start in 1908, the U.S. Army abandoned airship development from 1910 until after the end of World War I. From 1920 to 1937, however, it was the world's leading operator of military airships. So little has been heard of this programme that it is the Army Lighter-than-Air (LTA) programme, not the Navy's submarine fleet, that should be called "The Silent Service".

The U.S. Army had made limited use of balloons for observation purposes since the American Civil War and used them in Cuba during the Spanish-American war. It accepted its first airship, the SC-1, in 1908. Not until after the Armistice, when several U.S. Navy, British and French designs were taken over, were additional Army airships acquired. In the intervening years, the Army LTA programme was limited to free balloons and captive observation balloons.

The Army airship programme developed rapidly in the 1920s, particularly after an agreement was reached with the Navy regarding respective LTA roles. It was decided that the Army would conduct coastal and inland patrols in non-rigid and semi-rigid types while the Navy would scout at sea with rigid airships. Naval use of non-rigids was limited to training.

To support its airship programme, the Army established training and development bases at Scott Field, Illinois, Brooks Field, Texas, and Ross (later Crissy) Field, California, and an operational base at Langley Field, Virginia. In 1935, after the loss of the Navy's rigid airship U.S.S. *Macon*, the Army took over the Naval airship base at Moffet Field, California. The principal captive balloon training centre from World War I on was at Fort Sill, Oklahoma, with other training at Pope Field, Fort Bliss, Texas.

While most of the World War I and early postwar designs were still serviceable in 1923, these were replaced by newer models designed to use helium gas for lift. The burning of the Army airship *Roma* in 1922, plus the recent availability of non-flammable helium in quantity at reasonable cost (approximately $7.50 per 1,000 cubic feet) resulted in helium being specified for all U.S. military airships, but the change-over took several years. Free and captive balloons continued to use hydrogen into the mid-1930s. Because of its lesser lift, helium could not be substituted for hydrogen without reducing the payload of the airship. For example, the 10-man crew of a TC-series airship had to be reduced to six.

The Army airship programme reached its peak in the late 1920s. From 1920 to 1932, the funds for LTA operation were specifically mentioned in the Air Service and Air Corps appropriation bills, and averaged about two percent of the total appropriation, approximately $258,000 per year from 1920 to 1935. The economic depression that started late in 1929 had a drastic effect on Army LTA appropriations; no funds for airship procurement were left. In 1932, $299,000 was voted for the procurement of two TE-3s and the TC-13 and -14, but the allocation dropped to $45,000 in 1934. After 1933, LTA funds were left out of the appropriations but funding for observation balloons continued through 1939, while barrage balloons were funded to the end of World War II.

Only four new airships were delivered after 1930, and a single 1926 model was taken over from the Navy. The reduced funds made it impossible to conduct an effective LTA programme, so General Oscar Westover, the Chief of Air Corps, terminated the Army's use of airships in 1936. Five operable airships, the TC-10, -11, -13, -14, and the former Navy J-4, were transferred to the Navy in 1937. Army use of LTA during World War II was limited to captive barrage balloons.

LTA Procurement. The Army's LTA craft were obtained in the same manner as aeroplanes—by direct purchase of existing proprietary items, by transfer from other services, or as the result of competitive bidding from industry in response to published specifications. In some cases, airships were designed by the Air Service Engineering Division and were built by private industry that bid for the work. Frequently, an order for a series of similar airships or balloons was split among several manufacturers. It was also a practice to order an airship from one manufacturer and then order a spare envelope for it from another.

LTA Designations. As originally procured, Army LTA craft had no specific designations. Free balloons of the early 1900s were referred to by number, such as "Signal Corps Balloon No. 6". Similarly, the first Army airship was simply "Signal Corps Dirigible Balloon No. 1", and was later referred to as the SC-1, for Signal Corps No. 1. The term "airship" did not come into general use in the U.S. until late in World War I.

U.S. Navy and foreign airships taken over by the Army after World War I were operated under their original designations. The Navy and British system of numbering individual airships consecutively within a model designation was followed by the Army after it adopted a designation system of its own in 1922. Previously, Army-designed series were identified by letters generally applicable to the airship type or mission, preceded by the letters U.S. to indicate a U.S. government design. The U.S.M.B. was an Army-designed motorized observation balloon. A few airship models were produced in sufficient quantity to utilize sequential designations: OB-1 to -4, TA-1 to -5, TC-1 to -14, etc, although the final TCs were somewhat the exception (see page 728).

The airships were always referred to by specific identity or name, as TC-5 or *Roma* rather than by a manufacturer's model number or name. The fact that several manufacturers built nearly identical designs of the same model made the use of builder's names impractical. There were so few Army airships relative to service aeroplanes that each became a highly

Two U.S. Army free balloons and one civilian balloon (centre) ready to take off for a balloon race.

individualistic piece of equipment and virtually assumed a personality of its own.

In the 1920s, balloons were given series-and-model designations, such as A-6, A-7, and A-8 free balloons and C-3 and C-6 observation balloons. These numbers indicated the model within the series, as for aeroplanes, not consecutively-numbered examples of a single model as for the airships.

Some apparent designation discrepancies appeared on a few TC, TE, and TF models in the late 1920s and early 1930s: TC-10 was seen with C-52 painted on the envelope, and TC-11 carried C-71. The "C" was a contraction of TC, and the number was the last two digits of the airship car serial number (252 for TC-10 and 271 for TC-11). On some airships, the designation and serial were painted on the side of the car, as TC-12-264 and TE-3-301.

As in Navy practice, Army airships took their identity from the car; the big envelope was actually only an accessory. Car and balloon basket serial numbers were issued consecutively from World War I days independently of the fiscal year system adopted for aeroplanes in 1921 (page 28).

BALLOONS

Balloons can be divided into two general categories, free and captive. Both have been used by the U.S. Army as described below.

Free Balloons. Spherical free balloons ranged in size from small one-man types of 9,000 cubic feet displacement up to 12-man types of 80,000 cubic feet. Free balloons were used to the end of the Army's observation balloon programme in 1939, mostly for routine short-distance training flights. Their main public notice came from Army participation in the free-balloon races

714

that were popular in World War I and during the 1920s.

Captive Balloons. The first observation balloons, both free and captive, were simply the well-known gas balloons adapted from civil exhibition flights to military use. When held by a cable, their spherical shape made them unstable in a wind and unsuitable for precise observation. The Germans solved this problem near the end of the 19th century by developing an elongated captive balloon with stabilizing fins and a kite-like tail at the rear. Called "dragon" *(Drachen)* in Germany, it was quickly nicknamed "sausage" *(Wurst)* there and in the other countries that adopted it.

Some of the stability of the "sausage" derived from that fact that it flew at a positive angle of attack at the end of its cable, thereby deriving additional lift and keeping the cable taut through a kiting action that earned it the additional designation of kite balloon.

U.S. manufacturers soon developed kite balloons of their own based on the German *Draken*. During World War I, the French developed a greatly improved kite balloon called the *Caquot,* and this soon became the standard for all the warring powers. Three tail fins were inflated by the wind entering an air scoop at the front of the bag on some models, while on others the fins were filled by the lifting gas.

With the observers in communication with the ground by telephone, kite balloons proved to be very effective on the Western Front for spotting artillery fire and troop movements. Their effectiveness is emphasized by the efforts made on both sides to shoot down the enemy's balloons and the heavy anti-aircraft gun concentrations that were set up to defend

An early model U.S. Army observation kite balloon (*Western Newspaper Union photo*).

715

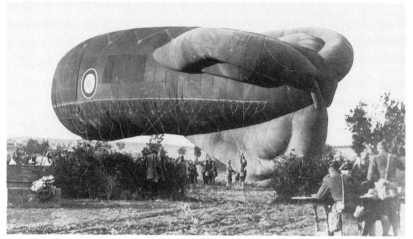

Caquot Modell "R" observation balloon with French markings, used by U.S. Third Army in France, October 1918 (*US Signal Corps 24855/National Archives*).

them. As a result of this activity, the balloon crews were the first in any military aircraft to use parachutes as standard equipment.

Caquot-type "M" and "R" models were manufactured in quantity in the U.S. and were eventually supplied to the other Allies. However, until production was achieved, the A.E.F. used approximately twenty French-supplied Caquots. Caquots remained in service in the U.S. through the late 1930s under the designation C-3 and were used primarily at Army artillery schools.

Army use of captive balloons was revived during World War II when thousands, somewhat smaller than the manned types, were used as barrage balloons over factories, convoys and other targets vulnerable to attack by low-flying aeroplanes.

Motorized Balloons. The captive feature of the C-3 observation balloon limited its movement from point-to-point when inflated, so the C-3s were supplemented by motorized observation balloons. Army experiments along this line began in 1920 with the U.S.M.B. design (for U.S. Motorized Balloon) and the Navy conducted tests with its H-1 "Towing Airship". Goodyear built a similar OB-1, which was evaluated by the Army at McCook and Scott Fields in 1923. The motorized balloons, with displacements somewhat greater than the C-3s, could be flown either as dirigibles or captive balloons. Power was supplied by one or two small air-cooled engines, and the crew was two or three men. Motorized balloon development culminated in the C-6, C-8 and C-9 types, which were put into service in small numbers in 1937. Just before the outbreak of World War II, aeroplanes took over completely the observation function of this closing phase of the Army's manned LTA activity.

Non-Rigid Airships. Non-rigid airships, which came to be called "Blimps" during World War I, are known as "pressure airships". Gas pressure within the envelope maintains the aerodynamic form of the airship. The car or gondola containing the crew and powerplant is suspended from the envelope (or attached to it in later models), and the tail surfaces are attached to the rear of the envelope. All hydrogen-filled non-rigids had suspended cars; the adoption of helium eliminated the fire hazard and encouraged the development of attached cars, but none was seen on U.S. Army non-rigids until 1930.

The earliest non-rigids were merely streamlined gas bags, subject to noticeable sag in the middle if too much gas leaked or was valved out. This situation was soon remedied by the development of one or more air-filled balloonets for installation within the main envelope. In flight these were pressurized by ram air from the airship's forward speed. While the ship was at rest, powered blowers maintained balloonet pressure and kept the envelope taut. Non-rigids were the principal type of U.S. Army airship, with 36 known examples (excluding motorized balloons) in service 1920/36.

Semi-Rigid Airships. The semi-rigid airship, with a stiff keel running the length of the airship under or through the centre of a pressure envelope, never underwent extensive development in the U.S. The world's best-known semi-rigids were developed in Germany prior to and during World War I and in Italy afterward. The U.S. Army bought one semi-rigid from Italy in 1921 and ordered one other from an American manufacturer in 1923.

U.S. ARMY LIGHTER-THAN-AIR CRAFT

The following list of U.S. Army LTA craft is arranged alphabetically by complete designation regardless of chronology or airship type and model.

A-SERIES

A-4. Only this one A-series is known to be a bona-fide airship; the A-5 was a Goodyear motorized balloon and A-6, -7, and -8 were type designations for free balloons. The A-4 was a hydrogen-filled training airship built by Goodyear in 1919 and was similar to the Navy's Goodyear-built E-1 and F-1. The single 90 h.p. Curtiss OX-5 engine was mounted as a pusher at the rear of the suspended car. Length, 162 ft.; diameter, 33 ft. 6 in.; volume, 95,000 cu. ft.; crew, 3; high speed, 46 m.p.h.; range, 382 miles at high speed, 430 miles at cruise speed.

AC-1. Built by Goodyear in 1922 as its Model MA and sometimes called such in contemporary references, the AC-1 was a patrol blimp powered with two 130 h.p. Aeromarine U6D water-cooled engines. These were installed in tandem in the control car and drove a pair of out-rigged pusher propellers through shafts and gearing. The plane of the propellers could be rotated to provide vertical thrust components during take-off and landing. The AC-1 appeared to have its control car attached directly to the envelope, but such was not the case. The cable-suspended car was unusually close to the envelope and the narrow gap was sealed with fabric.

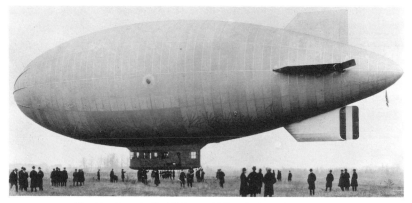

The Goodyear-built AC-1 patrol blimp (*USAF photo 877AS*).

Length, 169 ft.; diameter, 48 ft.; volume, 180,000 cu.ft.; crew, 6; max. speed, 65 m.p.h.; endurance, 20 hrs. (1,300 miles) at high speed, 30 hrs. (1,650 miles) at cruising speed.

C-SERIES

Hydrogen Cs. The original U.S. Army C-type airships were the hydrogen-filled C-2 (Goodrich) and C-4 (Goodyear) obtained from the U.S. Navy in 1921. The Army also obtained the car of C-1 from the Navy and ordered a new envelope for it on an Army contract. The C-2, with a new car built by the Army at Langley Field, achieved fame by making the first airship voyage entirely across the U.S. in September-October, 1922.

The original Cs were a milestone design and established the pattern for most of the following American non-rigid designs. With a crew of up to

The single-engined A-4 after landing on the roof of the Statler Hotel in Cleveland, Ohio, on May 23, 1919 (*USAF photo 10-802*).

The C-2, transferred from the Navy, that made the first coast-to-coast airship flight in the United States (*USAAS photo*).

ten in open cars, all of which were built by Burgess, the C-ships mounted two 200 h.p. Hall-Scott L-6 engines as pushers on outriggers at the mid-point of the car. Shock-absorbing landing gear, which could double as flotation gear for water landings, was in the form of two rubber air-bags under the car. Developed for naval convoy and coastal patrol, the original C-ships had provision for one 1,100 lb., four 700 lb., or eight 100 lb. bombs. Length, 192 ft.; diameter, 42 ft.; volume, 181,000 cu. ft.; crew, 6-10; max. speed 60 m.p.h.; range, 10 hours. at full speed.

Helium Cs. One helium-filled C-ship was a hybrid; C-14, assembled in 1922, was the C-4 redesignated and fitted with a new envelope of 10,000 cu. ft. greater capacity for use with helium gas. Some other high-number C-types seen were not actually such. They were TC-types with the letter C on the envelope instead of TC, followed by the last two digits of the car serial number. The identity of the airship was determined by the car; the large envelope was merely an accessory. In its final years C-14 was seen with the marking C-64.

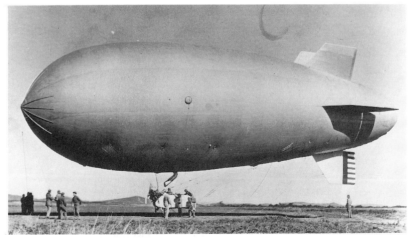
The C-6 motorized observation balloon.

719

Army C-14 utilized the car of C-4 fitted with an enlarged envelope to compensate for the increased lifting capability of helium gas (*USAF photo 10971 A.S.*).

C-3. Post-war Army designation for the World War I French-designed Caquot "R" kite balloon, which was widely used during the war and to a decreasing degree until 1938. U.S. production of Caquots to the end of the World War I contracts totalled 642 complete balloons. Length, 91 ft.; volume, 32,850 cu. ft., later increased to 37,500 cu. ft.; crew, 2.

C-Type Motorized Balloons. The development of motorized observation balloons culminated in limited production of the open-basket C-6, C-8, and C-9 series starting in 1936. These had streamlined envelopes and rigid-frame tailfins in the manner of airships instead of the inflated-cloth fins of the kite balloon. The C-6s were two-seaters with single pilot controls, the C-8s were dual control, and the C-9s were single-seaters for low-cost training. All were fitted with a single 75 to 90 h.p. Lambert air-cooled radial engine at the front of the car that could be removed to lighten the ship when flown as an observation balloon. There were also C-7 motorized balloons, which were the two small TE-3 airships converted. In 1942, five C-6s, seven C-8s, and four C-9s were turned over to the U.S. Navy. C-6 data: Length, 104 ft.; diameter, 30 ft.; volume, 52,000 cu. ft.; crew, 2; cruising speed, 54 m.p.h.

Navy J-4 in flight near Moffett Field, California. J-Cars were normally open, but an enclosure was built for J-4 in 1933 at time of change to air-cooled engines (*Navy photo 80-CF-41267-1/National Archives*).

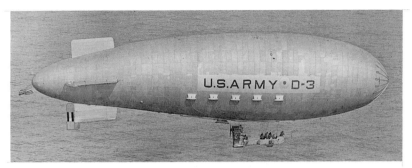

Obtained from the Navy in 1921, D-3 was one of four D-ships used by the Army (*USAF photo 10126 A.S.*).

D-SERIES

In 1921, the Army obtained all but the first and last of the six D-ships built for the U.S. Navy. The D-2 and D-3 were built by Goodyear, the D-4 and D-5 by Goodrich. The Ds were essentially World War I C-types with their envelopes lengthened by adding a six-foot section in the centre and with the 120 h.p. Union pusher engines installed opposite the rear of the car instead of amidships. The distinctive feature of the D-ships, adapted from British practice, was the suspending of ten small fuel tanks from the sides of the envelope. Length, 198 ft.; diameter, 42 ft.; volume, 189,000 cu. ft.; crew, 8-10; max. speed, 56 m.p.h.; range, 12 hours at full speed.

J-4

The single J-4 was a 1926 Navy training blimp similar to the contemporary Army TC-type. The Army obtained it on loan from the Navy when it took over Moffett Field, where the J-4 was stationed, in 1935, and returned it when the Army airship programme was terminated in 1937. After a short period of additional Navy service, it was scrapped in 1940. Since the J-ships were so similar to the original C-ships of 1918, it can be said that this basic blimp design saw service during the period of both World Wars. Originally fitted with 150 h.p. water-cooled Wright-Hispano pusher engines,

Motorized MB balloon (formerly the U.S.M.B.) spraying insecticide.

721

The U.S. Army acquired four Goodyear Model AA "Pony Blimps" with the designations OA-1 through OA-4 (*Goodyear photo*).

the J-4 was fitted with 265 h.p. air-cooled Wright J-6-7 (R-760) tractor engines in 1934. Length, 196 ft.; diameter, 45 ft.; volume, 210,000 cu. ft.; crew, 6; max. speed, 60 m.p.h.; range at full speed, 1,070 miles.

MB

This was a revised designation for the twin-engined U.S.M.B. motorized balloon, designed by the Air Service Engineering Division at McCook Field. It was originally to have been designated OA-1, which has caused some confusion among historians. That designation was transferred to four "Pony Blimps" procured from Goodyear (see OA-Series entry, below). The MB was built by Airships, Inc., and delivered in June, 1921. After test as an observation balloon it was fitted with a hopper for insecticide and loaned to the Department of Agriculture in the summer of 1923 to combat an infestation of gypsy-moths in New Hampshire. Length, 106 ft.; diameter, 29 ft.; volume, 47,000 cu. ft.; crew, 2-3; max. speed 55 m.p.h.; range, 560 miles with 60 h.p. Lawrance L-4 engines.

OA SERIES

The four OAs, -1 through -4, were essentially off-the-shelf commercial airships, the Goodyear Model AA "Pony Blimp", powered with a single tractor 50 h.p. Lawrance engine. Length, 95 ft.; diameter, 28 ft.; volume, 35,000 cu. ft.; crew, 2; max. speed, 40 m.p.h.; range, 400 miles.

The motorized balloon OB-1.

722

French-built RN-1 after modernization and re-designation from ZDUS-1 (*USAF photo 12055 AS*).

OB

The single Model OB was an Army version of the U.S. Navy H-1 "Towing Airship", which could be towed by a ship then cut loose to scout on its own. It was built by Goodyear in 1923. The OB was a single-engined pusher, with the same 60 h.p. Lawrance L-4 engine. The original volume of the OB, 40,000 cubic feet, was increased to 55,000 to compensate for the decreased lift of helium gas compared to the hydrogen for which it was originally designed. Length, 94·8 ft.; diameter, 38.8 ft.; crew, 2; max. speed, 49.5 m.p.h.; range, 346 miles at full speed.

RN-1

The RN-1 was one of three examples of a French Zodiac design ordered by the U.S. Navy in June, 1918. The original designation assigned by the Army was ZDUS-1, later DZ-1, but it is best known by its final designation of RN-1. At the time, it was the largest non-rigid design in the world. The Navy contract was reduced to two ships after the Armistice. Both were delivered to the Navy. The first was turned over to the Army and the second was stored and later scrapped without ever having been flown. ZDUS-1 was erected in the U.S. at Langley Field and was flown by the Army with the original pair of 250 h.p. Renault engines. The ZDUS-1 was unique in carrying armament; a 75-mm. cannon in the bow of the car and a Lewis machine gun in a nest on top of the envelope that was reached by a vertical ladder enclosed in a gas-proof shaft. After service as a patrol ship, the ZDUS-1 was sent to Scott Field for refurbishment with a new envelope and replacement of the Renault engines with Packard IA-1237 engines. In its revised form, the ZDUS-1 became the RN-1. ZDUS-1 data: length, 264 ft.; diameter, 49·5 ft.; volume, 326,500 cu. ft.; crew, 10-12; max. speed, 49 m.p.h.; range, 588 miles at full speed.

ROMA

The *Roma* was originally the Usuelli T-34, a semi-rigid built by the Italian Government Airship factory. Sold to the U.S. Army in 1921 for $195,000, it was then the world's largest semi-rigid and was identified in the U.S. only by the original name of *Roma*. Following shipment to the U.S. and erection at Langley Field, the *Roma* was extensively modified, the principal change being the replacement of the six original 500 h.p.

723

The Italian-built semi-rigid dirigible Roma (*USAAF photo 7761 AS*).

Italian SVA engines with Liberties. The *Roma* was destroyed by fire after the nose collapsed during high-speed flight near Langley Field in April 1922. Reaction to the loss of life in this hydrogen fire hastened the mandatory use of helium in all U.S. military airships. Length, 410 ft.; width, 82 ft.; height, 92 ft.; volume, 1,200,000 cu. ft.; crew, 18; max. speed, 80 m.p.h.; range, 2,796 miles on two engines, 1,709 miles on six engines.

RS-1

The RS-1 was the only American-built semi-rigid airship. Ordered from Goodyear in 1923, it was a four-engined helium airship. Some of the unique power transmission components were designed and built by the Air Service Engineering Division at McCook Field and some were built by Allison. The four Liberty engines, choked to deliver only 202 h.p., were mounted as staggered tandem pairs in two power cars, with the shafts of the forward engines laying alongside the rear engines to drive a single pusher propeller through a common gearbox. The RS-1 was delivered late in 1925 and was assembled at Scott Field by Goodyear and Army crews. First flight was made on January 8, 1926. In 1927, the RS-1 was fitted with two Packard 2A-1500 engines of 400 h.p. in place of the de-rated Liberties. This change

The RS-1 was the only semi-rigid dirigible built in the US (*USAF photo 6402AS*).

The first U.S. Army dirigible balloon acquired the unofficial designation of SC-1 (*USAF photo 3943 A.S.*).

increased the useful load of the airship from 12,840 lb. to 15,740 lb. Speeds did not change, but range at cruising speed increased from 1,722 miles to 2,588 miles. Length, 282 ft.; diameter, 74 ft.; volume, 719,000 cu. ft.; crew, 10; max. speed limited to 50 m.p.h. from 70 m.p.h. because of weakness in the nose cap.

SC-1

This was not a bona-fide model designation but identified the U.S. Army's first airship as Signal Corps No. 1. It was built at Hammondsport, N.Y., by Thomas Baldwin, who won the Signal Corps contract for a two-man dirigible balloon with a payload (including 100 lb. of ballast) of 450 lb. against nine other bidders. His quoted price was $6,740. Power was a special 20 h.p. Curtiss motor driving a single tractor propeller through an extension shaft. In the absence of Signal Corps funds for the purchase of aircraft in 1908, the SC-1 was procured indirectly through the Army Board of Ordnance and Fortifications, which had funds available for the evaluation of new weapons.

Glenn Curtiss was the second crew member when Baldwin flew the SC-1 acceptance tests at Fort Myer, Virginia, on August 12-15, 1908.

The SST was a British World War I scouting blimp obtained from the U.S. Navy.

The contract specified that two Army officers would be trained to fly the dirigible. After checkout, these trainees flew the SC-1 on exhibition and further training flights in 1908 and 1909. Length, 96 ft.; diameter, 19 ft. 6 in.; volume 20,000 cu. ft.; crew, 2; max. speed, 20 m.p.h.; endurance, 2 hours.

SST-SERIES

The SST was a British World War I model built for the Royal Naval Air Service. The designation stood for Sea Scout Twin, meaning twin engines. Three SSTs were obtained by the U.S. Navy and were turned over to the Army in 1920. These were flown in their original British markings as illustrated. Length, 170 ft.; diameter, 35 ft.; volume, 100,000 cu. ft.; cruising speed, 57·5 m.p.h. with two Rolls-Royce Hawk pusher engines.

TA-SERIES

The first U.S. Army airships designed specifically to use helium gas were the five TAs. Built by Goodyear in 1923-25, these were trainers intended to replace the OAs and the OB for pilot training. They departed

TA-1, with tractor engine mounted at the aft end of the car (*Air Force Museum photo*).

somewhat from contemporary practice in having tractor instead of pusher engines and installing them opposite the rear end of the car instead of amidships in an attempt to improve crew comfort by decreasing the powerplant noise. The engines were 90 h.p. Curtiss OX-5s. TA-3, -4, and -5 differed in having their engines moved forward, a mechanics' seat added at the rear of the car, and changes to the fuel system and the positioning of the two internal ballonets. Length, 162 ft.; diameter, 39·3 ft.; volume, 130,160 cu. ft.; crew, 4-5; max. speed, 45 m.p.h.; range, 390 miles at full speed, 520 miles at cruising speed.

TC-SERIES

TC-1/11. Designed originally in 1922, the TCs were helium-filled replacements for the hydrogen-filled C and D-types then in service and which they closely resembled. However, the early models were flown with hydrogen. TC-1 to -3 and -7 to -9 were built by Goodyear from 1923-25. TC-4 to -6 were built by Airships, Inc., in 1923-24 from Goodyear drawings. Over their relatively long years of service, these underwent many

The TC-7 during aeroplane hook-on tests with an Engineering Division/Sperry M-1 hanging beneath the car (*National Archives*).

individual modifications, including changes of power plant from water-cooled pusher engines to air-cooled tractors, addition of removable canopies, and sometimes the installation of entirely new cars. TC-6, with 200 h.p. Wright J-4 engines, was the only one of the early TC-ships to use radial air-cooled engines as original equipment; this installation saved 400 lb. and all were eventually converted to air-coooling.

The designation TC-10 became virtually a model number rather than a sequential designation for a TC-type airship, since there were no fewer than five Army airships designated TC-10. These were TC-10-242, -243, -252, -253, and -254. These were identified by lettering on the nose, rather than on the side of the envelope in the traditional position, as C-42, -43, -52, -53, and -54. Three TC-10s (only one inflated) went to the Navy in 1937.

One TC-10 was used to test a "cloud car", developed from the World War I Zeppelin device, in which an observer could be lowered for observation from below the clouds while the airship remained hidden above. TC-11 was the first TC to use metal construction for the car, which, although suspended in the traditional way, was now completely enclosed. The TC-11 was transferred to the Navy in 1937. Early TC data, with two 150 h.p. Wright-Hispano I engines: Length, 195 ft. 9 in.; diameter, 44 ft. 6 in.; volume, 200,600 cu. ft.;

Confused identity: the car of the TC-10-253 fitted to the envelope of TC-8. (*Air Force Museum photo*).

TC-12 was not built as such but resulted from fitting the car of the AC-1 to a spare TC envelope.

crew, 10 (hydrogen), 6-7 (helium); max. speed, 52 m.p.h.; range, 780 miles at high speed.

TC-12. This was not ordered as a new airship but was created by mating the car of the AC-1 of 1922, complete with internally-mounted Aeromarine engines, to a spare TC envelope that had been modified to have the car attached directly to the envelope instead of being suspended as in standard TC practice. By its creation from existing parts, the TC-12, completed in 1927, preceded TC-10 and TC-11 into service. TC-12 flew with the designation TC-12-264 on the car and C-64 on the envelope.

TC-13, TC-14. These were similar twin-tractor designs built in the early 1930s to entirely different requirements from preceding TC-ships. The TC-13 was built by Goodyear and delivered in 1933 while TC-14, with envelope built by Air Cruisers, Inc., and the car built by Mercury Corporation, was delivered in 1935. TC-14 originally had a third engine at the rear of the car but this was soon deleted, leaving both airships powered by two 325 h.p. Pratt & Whitney R-985 Wasp Junior engines. The distinguishing feature of both airships, other than their bulk as the world's largest non-rigids at the time, was their five-fin tail arrangement. Both were fitted with a "cloud car" and had provision for being refuelled while aloft. Both were deflated

The five-finned TC-13, delivered in 1933, was the U.S. Army's next-to-last airship. It was transferred to the Navy in 1937 (*USAF photo 18083AC*).

C-71 was a refurbished TC ship, not a separate C-class model (*USAF photo 16598 AC*).

at the end of Army airship operations but were soon turned over to the Navy. TC-14 was reinflated in 1938, TC-13 in 1940, and the latter was scrapped in 1943. TC-14, after being used without engines for mooring mast tests at Lakehurst, was scrapped in mid-1944. TC-13 and TC-14 were the last airships built for the U.S. Army; only a few motorized balloons followed them. Length, 233 ft.; diameter, 54 ft.; volume, 360,000 cu. ft.; crew, 8; max. speed, 65 m.p.h.

TE-SERIES

TE-1. A small motorized balloon with two 60 h.p. Wright "Gale" (formerly Lawrance L-4) engines. It was designed by the Army, the envelope and control surfaces were built by Airships, Inc., and the all-metal car was built by Aircraft Development Co. TE-1 was used as a primary trainer. Length, 136 ft.; diameter, 34 ft.; volume, 80,200 cu. ft.; crew, 4; max. speed 45 m.p.h.; range, 315 miles at full speed.

TE-2, TE-3. These were twin-engined airships designed by the Air Corps Materiel Division (formerly Air Service Engineering Division) as TA replacements. With two 70 h.p. Lambert engines, they were built in 1928-29 by Goodyear.

There were two TE-2s, TE-2-288 and 2-816, both with all-metal suspended cars. The two TE-3s, TE-3-301 with metal car by Mercury and -321 with

TE-3, with eight-finned tail assembly, parked crossways ij Scott Field airship hangar, November 1934 (*National Archives*).

729

TF-61 motorized observation balloon in August 1932.

metal car by Goodyear, were the first Army airships to have the cars flush-mounted to the envelope and suspended from catenary curtains inside the envelope. TE-3-301 was later fitted with a new all-metal car and an eight-fin tail built by the Aircraft Development Corporation, a firm best known as the designer and builder of the Navy's metal-clad ZMC-2 airship.

In 1937 both TE-3s were converted to type C-7 motorized balloons and the old cars and one spare envelope were turned over to the Navy. Both C-7s went to the Navy in 1943. As TE-3: length, 139 ft. 6 in.; diameter, 34 ft.; volume, 83,038 cu. ft.; crew, 4; max. speed, 55 m.p.h.; range, 400 miles.

TF-1

This was a motorized balloon built in 1928 by Meadowcroft Balloon and Airship Co. It was intended as a primary trainer. The designation appeared on the car in combination with the serial number as TF-1-261; on the envelope it appeared as F-61. All published references identify the single pusher engine as a 60 h.p. Lawrance L-4, but the photo shows a five-cylinder engine, probably an early Lambert. Length, 106 ft.; diameter, 31 ft.; volume, 52,290 cu. ft.; crew, 2; max. speed, 40 m.p.h.; range, 320 miles.

U.S.M.B.

This was the original designation of the motorized balloon designed by the Air Service Engineering Division at McCook Field in 1920. It had the interim designation of MB-1 before becoming the MB (which see).

ZDUS-1

This was the original operating designation of the French Zodiac airship that became the RN-1 (which see).

DESIGNATION INDEX

The purpose of this section is to provide a quick guide to every aircraft type designated by the USAF or its predecessors since 1919 (see page 10). Every primary designation category used since then to date is included here in alphabetical order, with all the aircraft designated in each category listed in numerical sequence.

References are given in bold type to the page(s) in this volume where information on a particular aircraft can be found. For those experimental types not described in the main body of this work, brief details are given in the Designation Index itself.

To find any aircraft in this index, status prefixes (E, J, N, X, Y and Z) should be ignored. Thus, XB–70A is listed here simply as B–70. Similarly, modifying duty prefixes should be ignored—the AC–47C can be found by referring to C–47, the YRF–101A by referring to F–101 and so on.

In the 1962 tri-service designation scheme, some combinations of duty letter and type number were re-used, but many of the new allocations were for Navy aircraft. In the following index, all post-1962 designations are listed for those duty categories used by both USAF/Army and the USN/Marines. The prefix S had been used only for USN/Marines aircraft up to the time this work went to press, and this category is therefore not listed.

A—AMBULANCE, 1919–1924

A-1	COX-KLEMIN	Two XA-1 ambulances, 23-1247/8. Liberty 12-A
A-2	FOKKER	T-2 conversion as ambulance. **Page 696**

A—ATTACK, 1924–1948

A-1	—	Designation not used in Attack category
A-2	DOUGLAS	Attack prototype from O-2. **Page 249**
A-3	CURTISS	Attack versions of O-1 Falcon. **Page 219**
A-4	CURTISS	A-3 variant, engine change. **Page 219**
A-5	CURTISS	A-3 variant, cancelled.
A-6	CURTISS	A-3 variant, cancelled.
A-7	FOKKER (ATLANTIC)	Low-wing. 30-226 only. V-1570-27. Jan. 1931
A-8	CURTISS	Low-wing Shrike prototype. **Page 224**
A-9	DETROIT (LOCKHEED)	Attack project from P-24. Not built. **Page 174**
A-10	CURTISS	A-8 variant, engine change. **Page 224**
A-11	CONSOLIDATED	Attack version of P-25. **Page 175**
A-12	CURTISS	A-10 improved. **Page 224**
A-13	NORTHROP	Model 2-C Gamma variant. **Page 500**
A-14	CURTISS	First twin-engined attack. **Page 630**
A-15	MARTIN	Attack project from B-10. Not built
A-16	NORTHROP	Revised A-13. **Page 500**
A-17	NORTHROP	Developed A-16. **Page 500**
A-18	CURTISS	Improved A-14. **Page 630**
A-19	VULTEE	Model V-11-GB. **Page 674**
A-20	DOUGLAS	Model DB-7B Havoc. **Page 277**

A-21	STEARMAN	Model X-100 40-191 only. Two R-2180-7
A-22	MARTIN	Model 167F. 40-706 only. Two R-1830-37. British Maryland
A-23	MARTIN	Model 187, project cancelled. British Baltimore
A-24	DOUGLAS	Navy SBD for AAF. **Page 275**
A-25	CURTISS	Navy SB2C for AAF. **Page 632**
A-26	DOUGLAS	Invader, improved A-20. **Page 284**
A-27	NORTH AMERICAN	Ten NA-69 (similar to AT-6) for Siam impounded by AAF. 41-18890/18899.
A-28	LOCKHEED	Model 414. **Page 354.** British Hudson
A-29	LOCKHEED	Model 414. Similar to A-28. **Page 354**
A-30	MARTIN	Model 187B Baltimore. Lend-Lease for Britain, Russia
A-31	VULTEE	Model 72, British Vengeance, repossessed. **Page 591**
A-32	BREWSTER	Dive bomber prototypes, April 1943, 42-13568/9 only R-2800-37
A-33	DOUGLAS	A-17 variant. **Page 500**
A-34	BREWSTER	Navy SB2A projected for AAF. Cancelled
A-35	VULTEE	Improved A-31. **Page 591**
A-36	NORTH AMERICAN	P-51 with bombs and dive brakes. **Page 466**
A-37	HUGHES	Duramold project 1942, two R-2800-49. Cancelled
A-38	BEECH	Model 28 Destroyer, 43-14406/7 only, f.f. 7-5-44. Two R-3350-43
A-39	FLEETWINGS (KAISER)	Project, one R-2800-27. Cancelled
A-40	CURTISS	Dive bomber version of SB3C, one R-3350-8. Cancelled
A-41	VULTEE (CONVAIR)	Model 90, 43-35124 only, f.f. 11-2-44. XR-4360-9
A-42	DOUGLAS	Became B-42, which see. **Page 637**
A-43	CURTISS	Became P-87, which see
A-44	CONVAIR	Became B-53, which see
A-45	MARTIN	Became B-51, which see

A—ATTACK, 1962–

A-1	DOUGLAS	USN AD Skyraider redesignated. **Page 638**
A-2	NORTH AMERICAN	USN AJ redesignated. No USAF use
A-3	DOUGLAS	USN A3D redesignated. One RA-3B Army test-bed
A-4	DOUGLAS	USN A4D redesignated. No USAF use
A-5	NORTH AMERICAN	USN A3J redesignated. No USAF use
A-6	GRUMMAN	USN A2F redesignated. No USAF use
A-7	VOUGHT	Corsair II attack bomber. **Page 586**
A-8	McDONNELL DOUGLAS	USMC Harrier V/STOL, as AV-8A. No USAF use
A-9	NORTHROP	Two YA-9A prototypes with ALF-502 engines for A-X competition in 1972
A-10	FAIRCHILD	Two YA-10A prototypes with TF-34 engines for A-X competition in 1972
A-11	—	Not used in attack category; possible confusion with Lockheed A-11 (company designation)
A-12	McDONNELL DOUGLAS/GD	Advanced Tactical Aircraft (ATA) for USN as A-6 replacement and prospective USAF ATA.
A-16	GENERAL DYNAMICS	Prospective designation (in 1988) for close air support (CAS) version of F-16 as A-10 replacement in 1991.
A-26	DOUGLAS	B-26K Invader redesignated. **Page 284**
A-37	CESSNA	T-37 variant, redesignated from YAT-37D. **Page 164**

A—POWERED TARGET, 1940–1941

A-1	FLEETWINGS	20-ft. span target with 80 h.p. engine
A-2	RADIOPLANE	12-ft. span target, with 5–10 h.p. engine
A-3	CURTISS	Navy N2C as AAF drone
A-4	DOUGLAS	BT-2 as drone. **Page 253**
A-5	BOEING	P-12 conversion project. Cancelled. **Page 94**
A-6	DOUGLAS	O-38 conversion project. Cancelled. **Page 254**
A-7	BELL	P-39 drone. **Page 64**
A-8	CULVER	Drone version of civil Culver Cadet. **Page 626**

A—AMPHIBIAN, 1948–1955
A-9	GRUMMAN	OA-9 redesignated June 1948. **Page 649**
A-10	CONVAIR	OA-10 redesignated June 1948. **Page 624**
A-12	GRUMMAN	Navy J2F-6 for tests, 48-1373/75; also OA-12 redesignated. **Page 648**
A-16	GRUMMAN	Model G-64 Albatross (SA-16 rescue amphibian). **Page 334**

AC—FIXED-WING CARGO (ARMY AVIATION)
AC-1	DE HAVILLAND	Canadian-built Caribou. To CV-2, 1962. **Page 689**
AC-2	DE HAVILLAND	DHC-5 Buffalo for evaluation (63-13686/13689). To CV-7, 1962

AG—ASSAULT GLIDER, 1944
AG-1	CHRISTOPHER	8-place, turret-armed. Two ordered, 44-84153/4. Cancelled
AG-2	TIMM	8-place, turret-armed. Two ordered, 44-90991/2. Cancelled.

AO—ARTILLERY OBSERVATION, 1919–1924
AO-1	FOKKER (ATLANTIC)	CO-4 variant projected for Artillery Observation-Surveillance

AO—FIXED WING OBSERVATION (ARMY)
AO-1	GRUMMAN	Model G-134 Mohawk Army observation. **Page 336**
AO-2	GOODYEAR	Model 466 Inflatoplane for trials. Two seat, 65 h.p. McCulloch, 57-6537 only
AO-3	GOODYEAR	Model 468 Inflatoplane for trials. One seat. 44 h.p. Nelson. 57-6532/6 only

AT—ADVANCED TRAINER, 1924–1948
AT-1	HUFF-DALAND	Refined TW-5. **Page 652**
AT-2	HUFF-DALAND	AT-1 variant for test. Cancelled. **Page 652**
AT-3	BOEING	One PW-9A conversion, V-720 engine. **Page 93**
AT-4	CURTISS	P-1 Hawk trainers. **Page 211**
AT-5	CURTISS	As AT-4. different engine. **Page 213**
AT-6	NORTH AMERICAN	Model NA-16 derivative. **Page 454**. British Harvard
AT-7	BEECH	Model 18. C-45 variant. **Page 50**
AT-8	CESSNA	Model T50 adapted. **Page 158**. British Crane
AT-9	CURTISS	Jeep transition trainer. **Page 631**
AT-10	BEECH	Non-strategic construction. **Page 612**
AT-11	BEECH	AT-7 variant. **Page 50**
AT-12	REPUBLIC	Model 2-PA for Sweden, impounded by AAF. **Page 664**
AT-13	FAIRCHILD	Duramold construction. **Page 305**
AT-14	FAIRCHILD	AT-13 variant. **Page 305**
AT-15	BOEING	Plywood bombing trainer. 41-23162/3 only. Two R-1340-AN-1
AT-16	NOORDUYN	Canadian-built AT-6. **Page 454**
AT-17	CESSNA	AT-8 improved. **Page 158**
AT-18	LOCKHEED	A-29 variant. **Page 354**
AT-19	VULTEE	Stinson SR-8 for lend-lease. British Reliant. **Page 672**
AT-20	FEDERAL	Canadian-built Avro Anson. **Page 693**
AT-21	FAIRCHILD	Developed AT-13/14. **Page 305**
AT-22	CONSOLIDATED	C-87 for engineer training. **Page 176**
AT-23	MARTIN	B-26 for target towing and training. Became TB-26. **Page 437**
AT-24	NORTH AMERICAN	B-25 for training. Became TB-25. **Page 458**
AT-29	CONVAIR	Became T-29. **Page 192**

B—BOMBER, 1924–1962
B-1	KEYSTONE	Heavy bomber prototype, 27-334. Two V-1570-5
B-2	CURTISS	Condor biplane. **Page 630**
B-3	KEYSTONE	LB-10A redesignated with engine change. **Page 342**
B-4	KEYSTONE	LB-13 redesignated with engine change. **Page 342**

B-5	KEYSTONE	LB-14 redesignated with engine change. **Page 342**
B-6	KEYSTONE	LB-13 and B-3 redesignated with engine change. **Page 342**
B-7	DOUGLAS	Was XO-36. **Page 635**
B-8	FOKKER	Was second XO-27. **Page 646**
B-9	BOEING	Models 214, 215 and 246. **Page 101**
B-10	MARTIN	Model 139. **Page 433**
B-11	DOUGLAS	Projected amphibian bomber, two R-1690-11. Became YO-44, then YOA-5
B-12	MARTIN	B-10 with engine change. **Page 433**
B-13	MARTIN	Projected B-10 variant, cancelled. **Page 433**
B-14	MARTIN	B-12 variant. **Page 433**
B-15	BOEING	Originally XBLR-1; became XC-105. **Page 618**
B-16	MARTIN	Six engine project, 105,000lb. weight. Never ordered.
B-17	BOEING	Model 299 Flying Fortress. **Page 103**
B-18	DOUGLAS	DB-1 based on DC-3.
B-19	DOUGLAS	Originally XBLR-2. **Page 635**
B-20	BOEING	Model 316-D project, 80,000 lb., 152 ft. span. Never ordered
B-21	NORTH AMERICAN	Model NA-21, 38-485 only, two R-2180-1, 40,000 lb.
B-22	DOUGLAS	B-18A with R-2600-1 engine, not built
B-23	DOUGLAS	Improved B-18. **Page 636**
B-24	CONSOLIDATED	Model 32 ordered August 1939. **Page 176**
B-25	NORTH AMERICAN	Model NA-62 Mitchell. **Page 458**
B-26	MARTIN	Model 179 Marauder. **Page 437**
B-26	DOUGLAS	A-26 Invader redesignated in June 1948. **Page 284**
B-27	MARTIN	Model 182 project; pressure cabin; not built
B-28	NORTH AMERICAN	Model NA-63. Pressure cabin, two R-2800-11,f.f. 4-42. 40-3056 and 40-3058
B-29	BOEING	Model 345 Superfortress. **Page 113**
B-30	LOCKHEED	Four-engined bomber project with R-3350-13. Never ordered
B-31	DOUGLAS	Four-engined bomber project with R-3350-13. Never ordered
B-32	CONSOLIDATED	Dominator, ordered Sept. 1940. **Page 624**
B-33	MARTIN	Projected with two R-3350 or four R-2600. Not built
B-34	LOCKHEED	British Ventura designated for Lend-Lease. **Page 356**
B-35	NORTHROP	Flying wing ordered Nov. 1941. **Page 662**
B-36	CONSOLIDATED	Ordered Nov. 1941. **Page 187**
B-37	LOCKHEED	B-34 variant, O-56 redesignated. **Page 356**
B-38	BOEING	B-17 with V-1710-89 engines. **Page 103**
B-39	BOEING	B-29 with V-3420-11 engines. **Page 113**
B-40	BOEING	B-17 as escort fighter. **Page 103**
B-41	CONSOLIDATED	B-24 as escort fighter. **Page 176**
B-42	DOUGLAS	Originally A-42. Mixmaster pusher, two V-1710-125 f.f. 6-5-44. 43-50224/5 only
B-43	DOUGLAS	B-42 variant with two J-35. **Page 637**
B-44	BOEING	B-29 with R-4360-33. **Page 113 and 120**
B-45	NORTH AMERICAN	First production jet bomber. **Page 478**
B-46	CONSOLIDATED	Four J35-C-3. f.f. 2-4-47. 45-59582 only. Gross weight, 91,000 lb.
B-47	BOEING	Stratojet. **Page 130**
B-48	MARTIN	Six J35-A-5. f.f. 14-6-47. 45-59585/6 only. Gross weight, 102,600 lb.
B-49	NORTHROP	Jet version of B-35. **Page 662**
B-50	BOEING	Developed B-29. **Page 120**
B-51	MARTIN	Was A-45; three J47-GE-13, gross 55,923 lb. f.f. 28-10-49, 46-685/6 only
B-52	BOEING	Stratofortress. **Page 136**
B-53	CONVAIR	Was A-44. Canard layout, three J35. Cancelled
B-54	BOEING	B-50 variant. **Page 124**
B-55	BOEING	1948 project with four T-40 turboprops, based on XB-47 design. Beoing Model 474. Not built.
B-56	BOEING	B-47 variant. **Page 135**

B-57	MARTIN	British Canberra for USAF. **Page 437**
B-58	CONVAIR	Hustler delta. **Page 201**
B-59	BOEING	1953 design studies, eg Model 701 delta with four J73-GE turbojets. Not built.
B-60	CONVAIR	Jet version of B-36. **Page 187**
B-61	MARTIN	Matador SSM. Became TM-61
B-62	NORTHROP	Snark SSM. Became SM-62
B-63	BELL	Rascal ASM. Became GAM-63
B-64	NORTH AMERICAN	Navaho SSM. Became SM-64
B-65	CONVAIR	Atlas SSM. Became SM-65
B-66	DOUGLAS	Destroyer tactical bomber. **Page 294**
B-67	RADIOPLANES	MX2013 ASM. Became GAM-67
B-68	MARTIN	Titan SSM. Became SM-68
B-69	LOCKHEED	Seven P2V-5U on loan (54–4037/43) in 1954
B-70	NORTH AMERICAN	Valkyrie Mach 3 delta.
B-71	—	Number used for Lockheed A-12 ("A-11") reconnaissance model. SR-71A. **Page 396**
B-72	McDONNELL	Quail ASM. Became GAM-72
B-73	FAIRCHILD	Bull Goose SSM. Became SM-73
B-74	—	No information
B-75	DOUGLAS	Thor SSM. Became SM-75
B-76	MARTIN	Mace SSM. Became TM-76
B-77	NORTH AMERICAN	Hound Dog ASM. Became GAM-77
B-78	CHRYSLER	Jupiter SSM. Became SM-78
B-79	—	No information
B-80	BOEING	Minuteman SSM. Became SM-80
B-81	—	No information
B-82	—	No information
B-83	MARTIN	Bullpup ASM. Became GAM-83
B-84	—	No information
B-85	—	No information
B-86	—	No information
B-87	DOUGLAS	Skybolt ASM. Became GAM-87

B—BOMBER, 1962–

B-1	ROCKWELL	Swing-wing strategic bomber. **Page 541**
B-2	NORTHROP	Flying wing advanced tactical bomber (ATB). **Page 513**

BC—BASIC COMBAT TRAINER, 1936-1940

BC-1	NORTH AMERICAN	Variant of BT-9. **Page 450**
BC-2	NORTH AMERICAN	Version of BC-1. **Page 450**
BC-3	VULTEE	Variant of BT-13. **Page 589**

BG—BOMB GLIDER, 1942-1944

BG-1	FLETCHER	Ten PQ-8 (42-46892/901) with 2,000 lb. bomb replacing engine
BG-2	FLETCHER	Three converted CG-1 (42-46902/4) ordered, not built
BG-3	CORNELIUS	One ordered (42-46911) similar to BG-1. Not built

BLR—BOMBER, LONG RANGE, 1935–1936

BLR-1	BOEING	Became B-15. **Page 618**
BLR-2	DOUGLAS	Became B-19. **Page 635**
BLR-3	SIKORSKY	Project dropped 1937

BQ—GROUND-LAUNCHED CONTROLLABLE BOMB, 1942-1945

BQ-1	FLEETWINGS	Twin-engined missile; 42-79561 only
BQ-2	FLEETWINGS	As BQ-1 with engine change. 42-79562 only
BQ-3	FAIRCHILD	AT-21 variant with 4,000 lb. bomb
BQ-4	INTERSTATE	Twin-engined missile as Navy TDR-1
BQ-5	INTERSTATE	Similar to BQ-4
BQ-6	INTERSTATE	As Navy TD3R-1, changed control system
BQ-7	BOEING	B-17 variant. **Page 103**
BQ-8	CONSOLIDATED	B-24 variant.

BT—BASIC TRAINER, 1930–1947

BT-1	DOUGLAS	O-2K converted. **Page 249**
BT-2	DOUGLAS	O-32 converted. **Page 257**
BT-3	STEARMAN	PT-9 variant. **Page 671**
BT-4	CURTISS	O-1 converted. **Page 219**
BT-5	STEARMAN	PT-9 variant. **Page 671**
BT-6	CONSOLIDATED	PT-11 variant. **Page 172**
BT-7	CONSOLIDATED	Was PT-12. **Page 173**
BT-8	SEVERSKY	**Page 666**
BT-9	NORTH AMERICAN	Model NA-16. **Page 450**
BT-10	NORTH AMERICAN	BT-9 variant. **Page 450**
BT-11	AIRCRAFT RESEARCH	Plywood and plastic project, 1940, R-1340-41. Not built
BT-12	FLEETWINGS	Stainless steel construction, 25 built (39–719, 42–3684/707)
BT-13	VULTEE	Valiant trainer. **Page 589**
BT-14	NORTH AMERICAN	BT-9 variant. **Page 450**
BT-15	VULTEE	BT-13 variant. **Page 589**
BT-16	VIDAL	BT-13 with plastic fuselage. **Page 589**
BT-17	BOEING	Wichita Model X-91 low-wing with R-985-AN-1; 4,150 lb. gross, 42-8726 only
BT-28	NORTH AMERICAN	Numbers 18-27 used in PT series only. 28 followed PT-27 and became T-28. **Page 489**
BT-30	DOUGLAS	Project in competition with BT-28. Became T-30

C—CARGO AND TRANSPORT, 1925–1962

C-1	DOUGLAS	DWC/O-1 development. **Page 634**
C-2	FOKKER	Dutch F. VII design by Atlantic. **Page 323**
C-3	FORD	Stout tri-motor. **Page 647**
C-4	FORD	Stout tri-motor. **Page 647**
C-5	FOKKER	One F. XA tri-motor, 29-405. **Page 323**
C-6	SIKORSKY	Model S-38 amphibian. **Page 667**
C-7	FOKKER	C-2 with engine change. **Page 323**
C-8	FAIRCHILD	Model F-71. **Page 647**
C-9	FORD	C-3 with engine change. **Page 647**
C-10	CURTISS	One commercial Robin-W, 29-452. R-420-1
C-11	CONSOLIDATED	One commercial Fleetster, 31-380. R-1860-1
C-12	DETROIT	One Lockheed DL-1 Vega. **Page 654**
C-13	—	Not used
C-14	FOKKER	Commercial F-XIV by General. **Page 646**
C-15	FOKKER	C-14 variant. **Page 646**
C-16	FOKKER	Commercial F-XI amphibian, tests only
C-17	LOCKHEED	One Speed Vega. **Page 654**
C-18	BOEING	Commercial Model 221 Monomail, tests only
C-19	NORTHROP	Three Alpha 1s, R-1340 engine, 31-516/518
C-20	FOKKER	Commercial F-32 by General. Tests only
C-21	DOUGLAS	Commercial Dolphin, became OA-3. **Page 255**
C-22	CONSOLIDATED	Improved C-11 with R-1820-1. Three only, 31-469/471
C-23	LOCKHEED	Model 8-D Altair commercial. **Page 655**
C-24	FAIRCHILD	Model 100-B Pilgrim by American Airplane. **Page 612**
C-25	LOCKHEED	C-23 with wooden fuselage. **Page 655**
C-26	DOUGLAS	As C-21 with engine change. **Page 255**
C-27	BELLANCA	Commercial P-300 Airbus. **Page 616**
C-28	SIKORSKY	Commercial S--39C with R-985-1. One only 32-411
C-29	DOUGLAS	C-26 variant. **Page 255**
C-30	CURTISS	Commercial T-32 Condor with R-1820-23. Two only 33-320/1
C-31	KREIDER-REISNER	High-wing freighter, R-1820-25 engine, 12,750 lb weight. 34-026 only
C-32	DOUGLAS	Commercial DC-2. **Page 260**
C-33	DOUGLAS	C-32 variant. **Page 260**
C-34	DOUGLAS	C-32 variant. **Page 260**
C-35	LOCKHEED	Commercial Model 10 with pressure cabin. **Page 655**
C-36	LOCKHEED	Commercial Model 10. **Page 656**

C-37	LOCKHEED	C-36 variant. **Page 656**
C-38	DOUGLAS	C-32 variant. **Page 260**
C-39	DOUGLAS	C-32 variant. **Page 260**
C-40	LOCKHEED	Commercial Model 12. **Page 656**
C-41	DOUGLAS	C-39 with engine change. **Page 260**
C-42	DOUGLAS	C-39 variant. **Page 260**
C-43	BEECH	Commercial Model 17. **Page 48**
C-44	MESSERSCHMITT	Bf 108 for Military Attache, Berlin. 39-718 only. **Page 679**
C-45	BEECH	Commercial Model 18, as AT-7 and AT-11. **Page 50**
C-46	CURTISS	Model CW-20 developed. **Page 238**
C-47	DOUGLAS	Military DC-3. Skytrain. **Page 266**
C-48	DOUGLAS	Commercial DC-3. **Page 269**
C-49	DOUGLAS	Commercial DC-3. **Page 270**
C-50	DOUGLAS	Commercial DC-3. **Page 270**
C-51	DOUGLAS	Commercial DC-3. **Page 270**
C-52	DOUGLAS	Commercial DC-3. **Page 273**
C-53	DOUGLAS	Military DC-3. **Page 270**
C-54	DOUGLAS	Commercial DC-4 Skymaster. **Page 289**
C-55	CURTISS	Original Model CW-20, C-46 prototype. **Page 238**
C-56	LOCKHEED	Commercial Model 18. **Page 352**
C-57	LOCKHEED	Commercial Model 18. **Page 352**
C-58	DOUGLAS	B-18 variant for transport. **Page 263**
C-59	LOCKHEED	C-57 variant. **Page 352**
C-60	LOCKHEED	C-56 variant. **Page 352**
C-61	FAIRCHILD	Commercial Model 24. **Page 644**
C-62	WACO	Projected high wing cargo; two R-1830-92; 29,500 lb.; 253 cancelled
C-63	LOCKHEED	Projected A-29 variant as troop transport. Cancelled. **Page 354**
C-64	NOORDUYN	Canadian Norseman. **Page 701**
C-65	STOUT	Commercial Skycar for tests
C-66	LOCKHEED	C-56 variant. **Page 352**
C-67	DOUGLAS	B-23 variant for transport. **Page 636**
C-68	DOUGLAS	C-47 variant. **Page 266**
C-69	LOCKHEED	Commercial L-49 Constellation. **Page 366**
C-70	HOWARD	Commercial DGA-15. **Page 651**
C-71	SPARTAN	Commercial 7-W Executive. **Page 669**
C-72	WACO	Commercial biplane. **Page 675**
C-73	BOEING	Commercial Model 247. **Page 617**
C-74	DOUGLAS	Globemaster I. **Page 636**
C-75	BOEING	Commercial Model 307. **Page 617**
C-76	CURTISS	All-wood Caravan with two R-1830-2. f.f. 1-5-43, 42-86913/28 only
C-77	CESSNA	Commercial Model DC-6. Eleven impressed
C-78	CESSNA	Commercial T-50, as AT-17 and AT-8. **Page 158**
C-79	JUNKERS	One Ju 52/3m, 42-52883
C-80	HARLOW	Four impressed PJC-2, 42-53513, 68692, 97040, 97054
C-81	STINSON	Commercial Reliant. **Page 672**
C-82	FAIRCHILD	Model F-78 Packet. **Page 310**
C-83	PIPER	Commercial Cub, as L-4. **Page 516**
C-84	DOUGLAS	C-47 variant. **Page 266**
C-85	LOCKHEED	One Commercial 9-D2 Orion, 42-62601
C-86	FAIRCHILD	Nine Commercial F24-R-40
C-87	CONVAIR	B-24 transport. **Page 176**
C-88	FAIRCHILD	Two low-wing F-45s, 42-68675, 68677
C-89	HAMILTON	One high-wing H-47, 42-79546
C-90	LUSCOMBE	Two commercial Model 8s, 42-79549/50
C-91	STINSON	One tri-motor SM-6000, 42-79547
C-92	AKRON-FUNK	One commercial B-75-L, 42-79548
C-93	BUDD	All-steel Canestoga project, 600 cancelled
C-94	CESSNA	Three commercial C-165, 42-78018, -78022, -107400
C-95	TAYLORCRAFT	One commercial BL-65, as L-2. **Page 576**

C-96	FAIRCHILD	Model F-71, as C-8. **Page 643**
C-97	BOEING	Model 377 Stratofreighter. **Page 125**
C-98	BOEING	Model 314 flying-boat transferred to Navy. 42-88622, -88630/2
C-99	CONVAIR	B-36 transport derivative. **Page 187**
C-100	NORTHROP	Commercial 2-D Gamma, 42-94140
C-101	LOCKHEED	Commercial Vega. **Page 654**
C-102	REARWIN	Three high-wire Speedsters.
C-103	GRUMMAN	Two G-32 single-seat biplanes, 42-97044/5
C-104	LOCKHEED	Lockheed Model 118 transport derived from civil Lodestar. Became C-60C, then cancelled.
C-105	BOEING	B-15 redesignated. **Page 618**
C-106	CESSNA	High wing; 2xR-1830-11; 92,000 lb. Two for tests
C-107	STOUT	As C-65, Skycar III for tests
C-108	BOEING	B-17 variant. **Page 103**
C-109	CONVAIR	B-24 variant. **Page 176**
C-110	DOUGLAS	Commercial DC-5, three only 44-83230/2 ex-KNILM, impressed 1944 after use by RAAF, for 374th TC Group.
C-111	LOCKHEED	Commercial L-14. **Page 354**
C-112	DOUGLAS	Proposed C-54 variant (XC-112) cancelled. Prototype DC-6 (XC-112A). **Page 637**
C-113	CURTISS	C-46 variant. **Page 238**
C-114	DOUGLAS	C-54 variant. **Page 289**
C-115	DOUGLAS	C-114 variant, cancelled. **Page 289**
C-116	DOUGLAS	C-114 variant. **Page 289**
C-117	DOUGLAS	C-47 variant. **Page 266**
C-118	DOUGLAS	DC-6 for MATS. **Page 637**
C-119	FAIRCHILD	Improved C-82. **Page 310**
C-120	FAIRCHILD	C-119 variant. **Page 310**
C-121	LOCKHEED	Improved C-69. **Page 366**
C-122	CHASE	Powered CG-18. **Page 623**
C-123	FAIRCHILD	Powered CG-20. **Page 310**
C-124	DOUGLAS	Globemaster II. **Page 297**
C-125	NORTHROP	Three-engined N-23. **Page 661**
C-126	CESSNA	Commercial Model 195. **Page 621**
C-127	DE HAVILLAND	Preliminary designation for DHC Beaver, became L-20. **Page 685**
C-128	FAIRCHILD	C-119 variant. **Page 310**
C-129	DOUGLAS	Super DC-3, C-47 variant. **Page 266**
C-130	LOCKHEED	Hercules tactical transport. **Page 383**
C-131	CONVAIR	Model 240/340. **Page 192**
C-132	DOUGLAS	Heavy logistic transport, cancelled
C-133	DOUGLAS	Cargomaster. **Page 299**
C-134	STROUKOFF	C-123 variant. **Page 310**
C-135	BOEING	Tanker-transport. **Page 143**
C-136	—	Reserved for USN. Cancelled
C-137	BOEING	Commercial Model 707 variants. **Pages 129, 149**
C-138	—	Reserved for USN. Cancelled
C-139	—	No information
C-140	LOCKHEED	JetStar utility. **Page 657**
C-141	LOCKHEED	Starlifter strategic jet transport. **Page 399**
C-142	LTV	VTOL tri-service tilt-wing. Four T64-GE-1. f.f. September 29, 1964. 62-5921/5925

C—CARGO/TRANSPORT, 1962–

C-1	GRUMMAN	USN TF-1 Trader redesignated. No USAF use
C-2	GRUMMAN	USN Greyhound. No USAF use
C-3	MARTIN	USN RM redesignated. No USAF use
C-4	GRUMMAN	USN and USCG Academe (Gulfstream I). No USAF use
C-5	LOCKHEED	Model 500 Galaxy. **Page 401**
C-6	BEECH	King Air for VIP squadron. **Page 59**
C-7	DE HAVILLAND	US Army CV-2 redesignated for USAF use. **Page 689**

C-8	DE HAVILLAND	US Army CV-7 Buffalo for USAF use. Four only, 63-13686/13689
C-9	McDONNELL DOUGLAS	DC-9-30 Nightingale for USAF. **Page 660**
C-10	HANDLEY PAGE	Proposed purchase of 11 H.P.137 Jetstream 3 Ms. 68-10378 to 68-10388. Cancelled – see next entry.
C-10	McDONNELL	Reallocation to tanker/transport version of commercial DC-10. **Page 422**
C-11	GRUMMAN	USCG Gulfstream II. No USAF use
C-12	BEECH	Versions of commercial Super King Air 200 for all services. **Page 61**
C-13	—	Not used
C-14	BOEING	USAF Advanced Medium STOL Transport (AMST) two YC-14A, 72-1873/4. Two CF6-50 turbofans and USB system f.f. 6-8-76
C-15	McDONNELL DOUGLAS	USAF Advanced Medium STOL Transport (AMST). Two YC-15A prototypes 72-1875/6. Four JT8D-17 turbofans and EBF systems. f.f. 26-8-75
C-16	—	No information
C-17	McDONNELL DOUGLAS	Outsize cargo STOL transport. **Page 424**
C-18	BOEING	Commercial 707-320 variants. **Page 149**
C-19	BOEING	Commercial 747 personnel/cargo transport for ANG. Not procured
C-20	GULFSTREAM	Commercial Gulfstream III variants. **Page 650**
C-21	GATES LEARJET	Commercial Learjet 35A in OST role. **Page 648**
C-22	BOEING	Commercial 727-100 as staff transport. **Page 619**
C-23	SHORT BROTHERS	Model 330 Sherpa for European Distribution System. **Page 704**
C-24	McDONNELL DOUGLAS	Commercial DC-8 for USN.
C-25	BOEING	Commercial 747 as Air Force One. **Page 153**
C-26	FAIRCHILD	Commercial Metro III for NAG. **Page 644**
C-27	—	Reserved for rapid response light utility transport.
C-28	CESSNA	One commercial Model 404 Titan for USN.
C-29	BRITISH AEROSPACE	Commercial 125 Srs 800 for flight inspection (C-FIN). **Page 681**

CG—CARGO GLIDER, 1941–1947

CG-1	FRANKFORT	Model TCC-41. One ordered, 41-29615, cancelled
CG-2	FRANKFORT	Model TCC-21. One ordered, 41-29616, cancelled
CG-3	WACO	Model NYQ. **Page 676**
CG-4	WACO	Principal USAAF troop carrier. **Page 593**
CG-5	ST LOUIS	One only, 41-29619, same requirement as CG-3
CG-6	ST LOUIS	15-troop carrier. One ordered, 41-29620, cancelled
CG-7	BOWLUS	9-troop carrier, as CG-3. One only, 41-29621
CG-8	BOWLUS	15-troop carrier, as CG-4. One only, 41-29622
CG-9	AGA AVIATION	Model G-5, 30-troop carrier. Two ordered, 42-56697/8, cancelled
CG-10	LAISTER-KAUFFMAN	42-troop carrier, ten delivered, 45-44450/9
CG-11	SNEAD	30-troop carrier. Two ordered, cancelled
CG-12	READ-YORK	As CG-11. Two ordered, cancelled
CG-13	WACO	Enlarged development of CG-4. **Page 676**
CG-14	CHASE	Model MS-1 15-place, 44-90989/90, and 32-seat CG-14B, 46-67
CG-15	WACO	Improved CG-4. **Page 593**
CG-16	GENERAL	Model GATC-MC-2, 42-troops. 44-76193 built, -76194 cancelled
CG-17	DOUGLAS	C-47 variant. **Page 266**
CG-18	CHASE	All-metal development of CG-14. **Page 623**
CG-19	DOUGLAS	30-troop light assault, cancelled
CG-20	CHASE	67-troop heavy glider, became C-123. **Page 317**

CO—CORPS OBSERVATION, 1919-1924

CO-1	ENG. DIVISION	All-metal, high wing. Liberty 12. Two by Eng. Div., one by Gallaudet
CO-2	ENG. DIVISION	Biplane, Liberty 12. One built
CO-3	ENG. DIVISION	As CO-1, fabric covering. Cancelled
CO-4	FOKKER	Dutch D-VII development. **Page 696**
CO-5	ENG. DIVISION	Variant of TP-1, Liberty 12. One only
CO-6	ENG. DIVISION	New design Liberty V-1410. Two built
CO-7	BOEING	Development of DH-4M-1. Three built. **Page 244**
CO-8	ATLANTIC	Development of DH-4M-2. One built. **Page 244**

COA—CORPS OBSERVATION AMPHIBIAN, 1919-1924

COA-1	LOENING	Became OA-1. **Page 405**

CQ—TARGET CONTROL, 1942-1947

CQ-1	FLETCHER	Special design, not built
CQ-2	STINSON	L-1 variant. **Page 572**
CQ-3	BEECH	C-45 variant. **Page 50**

DB—DAY BOMBARDMENT, 1919-1924

DB-1	GALLAUDET	Low wing, Eng. Div. engine, 67 ft. span. One static, one flight test (64238/9)

E—SPECIAL ELECTRONIC INSTALLATION, 1962–

E-1	GRUMMAN	Model G-117 Tracer for USN.
E-2	GRUMMAN	Hawkeye for USN
E-3	BOEING	AEW (AWACS) Sentry based on 707-320. **Page 151**
E-4	BOEING	AABNCP based on commercial 747. **Page 153**
E-5	WINDECKER	One plastics-construction Eagle, 73-1653, for USAF and Army testing of radar detectability
E-6	BOEING	Commercial 707-320 equipped for TACAMO. USN only.
E-7	—	No information
E-8	BOEING	USAF/Army J-STARS based on commercial 707-320. **Page 143**
E-9	DE HAVILLAND CANADA	Commercial Dash 8 as telemetry and data link. **Page 691**

F—RECONNAISSANCE, 1930-1947

F-1	FAIRCHILD	Variant of C-8. **Page 643**
F-2	BEECH	Variant of C-45. **Page 50**
F-3	DOUGLAS	Variant of A-20. **Page 277**
F-4	LOCKHEED	Variant of P-38. **Page 358**
F-5	LOCKHEED	Variant of F-4. **Page 358**
F-6	NORTH AMERICAN	Variant of P-51. **Page 466**
F-7	CONSOLIDATED	Variant of B-24. **Page 176**
F-8	DE HAVILLAND	Canadian-built Mosquito. **Page 684**
F-9	BOEING	Variant of B-17. **Page 103**
F-10	NORTH AMERICAN	Variant of B-25. **Page 458**
F-11	HUGHES	Two prototypes of twin-boom Model D-2; two R-4360-31. f.f. 7-7-46. 44-70155/6
F-12	REPUBLIC	Two prototypes, 44-91002/3 with four R-4360-31 f.f. 7-2-46
F-13	BOEING	Variant of B-29. **Page 113**
F-14	LOCKHEED	Variant of P-80. **Page 370**
F-15	NORTHROP	Variant of P-61. **Page 502**

F—FIGHTER, JUNE, 1948-1962

F-24	DOUGLAS	Redesignated from A-24. **Page 275**
F-38	LOCKHEED	Redesignated from P-38. **Page 358**
F-40	CURTISS	Redesignated from P-40. **Page 231**
F-47	REPUBLIC	Redesignated from P-47. **Page 522**
F-51	NORTH AMERICAN	Redesignated from P-51. **Page 466**

F-59	BELL	Redesignated from P-59. **Page 73**
F-61	NORTHROP	Redesignated from P-61. **Page 502**
F-63	BELL	Redesignated from P-63. **Page 70**
F-80	LOCKHEED	Redesignated from P-80. **Page 370**
F-81	CONVAIR	Combination power, J33-GE-5 and XT31-GE-1. Two only 44-91000/1, f.f. 11-2-45
F-82	NORTH AMERICAN	Redesignated P-82. **Page 476**
F-83	BELL	Developed P-59, two J33-GE-5; wt. 27,500 lb. Two only 44-84990/1. f.f. 27-2-45
F-84	REPUBLIC	Redesignated P-84. **Page 529**
F-85	McDONNELL	Parasite for B-36, J34-WE-22; wt. 4,550 lb. Two only, 46-523/4. f.f. 23-8-48
F-86	NORTH AMERICAN	Redesignated P-86. **Page 481**
F-87	CURTISS	Developed A-43, four J34-WE-7; wt. 49,900 lb. Two only, 45-59600, 46-522. f.f. 5-3-48
F-88	McDONNELL	Penetration fighter, two XJ34-WE-13/15; wt. 23,100 lb. Two only, 46-525/6. f.f. 29-10-48
F-89	NORTHROP	Redesignated P-89. **Page 504**
F-90	LOCKHEED	Penetration fighter, two J34-WE-11/15; wt. 31,060 lb. Two only, 46-687/8. f.f. 6-6-49
F-91	REPUBLIC	Interceptor fighter, J47-GE-33 plus XLR11-RM-9; wt. 27,000 lb. Two only, 46-680/1. f.f. 9-5-49
F-92	CONVAIR	Research delta, forerunner of F-102. **Page 195**
F-93	NORTH AMERICAN	Variant of F-86. **Page 481**
F-94	LOCKHEED	All-weather development of F-80. **Page 376**
F-95	NORTH AMERICAN	Interim designation for F-86D. **Page 481**
F-96	REPUBLIC	Became F-84F. **Page 529**
F-97	LOCKHEED	Became YF-94C. **Page 376**
F-98	HUGHES	Became GAR-1 Falcon AAM
F-99	BOEING	Became IM-99 Bomarc GAM
F-100	NORTH AMERICAN	Super Sabre interceptor. **Page 491**
F-101	McDONNELL	Voodoo penetration fighter. **Page 408**
F-102	CONVAIR	Delta Dagger interceptor. **Page 195**
F-103	REPUBLIC	Delta-wing interceptor project, YJ-67 plus ramjet for M 3. Two prototypes cancelled
F-104	LOCKHEED	Starfighter interceptor. **Page 379**
F-105	REPUBLIC	Thunderchief fighter bomber. **Page 536**
F-106	CONVAIR	Delta Dart all-weather interceptor. **Page 198**
F-107	NORTH AMERICAN	F-100 development. **Page 491**
F-108	NORTH AMERICAN	Rapier Mach 3 delta, two-seat, two J93-GE. Cancelled 23-9-59
F-109	BELL	Design studies based on Model D-188 VTOL project 59-2109 and 60-2715 cancelled
F-110	McDONNELL	Navy F4H-1 for USAF. Because F-4. **Page 412**
F-111	GENERAL DYNAMICS	TFX swing-wing multi-role fighter. **Page 325**

F—FIGHTER, 1962–

F-1	NORTH AMERICAN	USN FJ Fury redesignated. No USAF use
F-2	McDONNELL	USN F2H Banshee redesignated. No USAF use
F-3	McDONNELL	USN F3H Banshee redesignated. No USAF use
F-4	McDONNELL	USN F4H/USAF F-10 redesignated. **Page 412**
F-5	NORTHROP	N-156 Freedom Fighter for USAF and MDAP. **Page 510**
F-6	DOUGLAS	USN F4D Skyray redesignated. No USAF use
F-7	CONVAIR	USN F2Y redesignated. No USAF use
F-8	VOUGHT	USN F8U Crusader redesignated. No USAF use
F-9	GRUMMAN	USN F9F Cougar redesignated. No USAF use
F-10	DOUGLAS	USN F3D redesignated. Few TF-10Bs in Army service.
F-11	GRUMMAN	USN F11F Tiger redesignated. No USAF use
F-12	LOCKHEED	USAF prototypes. **Page 396**
F-13	—	Number not used
F-14	GRUMMAN	New for USN, ordered 1969. No USAF use
F-15	McDONNELL DOUGLAS	Eagle air superiority fighter. **Page 418**
F-16	GENERAL DYNAMICS	Fighting Falcon production. **Page 330**

F-17	NORTHROP	Lightweight fighter (LWF) prototype. Model 600, two YF-17 72-1569/70 with YJ101-GE-100 turbojets. f.f. 9-8-74. No production.
F-18	McDONNELL DOUGLAS	VF-17 development for USN.
F-19	—	No information
F-20	NORTHROP	Redesignation of F-5G. Prototypes only. **Page 510**
F-21	IAI	Leased Kfir fighters for USN/MC
F-22	LOCKHEED/ BOEING/GD	Advanced Tactical Fighter. YF-22A prototypes ordered October 1986 in competition with F-23.
F-23	NORTHROP/ McDONNELL DOUGLAS	Advanced Tactical Fighter. YF-23A prototypes ordered October 1986 in competition with F-22.
F-117	LOCKHEED	Out-of-sequence designation for "stealth" fighter. **Page 404**

FG—FUEL GLIDER, 1944–1947
FG-1	CORNELIUS	Towed, expandable fuel tank with 54 ft. wing. Automatic stability. Two only, 44-28059/60

FM—FIGHTER, MULTIPLACE, 1936–1941
FM-1	BELL	Twin-engined pusher to original XPB-3 requirement **Page 614**
FM-2	LOCKHEED	Model 11 design studies to meet XPB-3 requirement

G—AUTOGIRO, 1935–1939
G-1	KELLET	Model KD-1 for trials. **Page 653**
G-2	PITCAIRN	One Model PA-33 for trials, 35-279, R-975-9; 3,200 lb.;

G—GLIDER, 1948–1955
G-2	WACO	Redesignation of PG-2. **Page 593**
G-3	WACO	Redesignation of PG-3. **Page 593**
G-4	WACO	Redesignation of CG-4. **Page 593**
G-10	LAISTER KAUFFMAN	Redesignation of CG-10. q.v.
G-13	WACO	Redesignation of CG-13. **Page 676**
G-14	CHASE	Redesignation of CG-14. q.v.
G-15	WACO	Redesignation of CG-15. **Page 593**
G-18	CHASE	Redesignation of CG-18. **Page 623**
G-20	CHASE	Redesignation of CG-20. **Page 317**

G—GLIDER, 1962–
G-7	SCHWEIZER	Model SGM2-37 as TG-7A. **Page 666**
G-8	SCHWEIZER	Model SA 2-37A for covert reconnaissance, USAF/Army. Avco Lycoming IO.540 engine. Two procurred, 85-0047/8
G-9	SCHLEICHER	Competition two-seat saikplane, as TG-9A

GA—GROUND ATTACK, 1919–1924
GA-1	BOEING	Engineering Division GAX developed. **Page 642**
GA-2	BOEING	Model 10 with one W-1A-18 engine; 9,150 lb.; 54 ft. span. Two only

H—HELICOPTER, 1948–
H-4	SIKORSKY	Redesignation of R-4. **Page 549**
H-5	SIKORSKY	Redesignation of R-5. **Page 551**
H-6	SIKORSKY	Redesignation of R-6. **Page 668**
H-9	G & A (FIRESTONE)	Redesignation of R-9, one only
H-10	KELLET	Redesignation of R-10. Ten production by Hughes cancelled
H-11	ROTOR-CRAFT	Redesignation of R-11. One only
H-12	BELL	Redesignation of R-12, Bell Model 48. **Page 614**
H-13	BELL	Redesignation of R-13. Bell Model 47. **Page 75**
H-15	BELL	Model 54, four-seat. XO-470-5; 2,800 lb., 37 ft. 4 in. rotor. 46-530/2 only

H-16	PIASECKI	Redesignation of R-16, two only
H-17	KELLET (HUGHES)	42,000 lb. gross crane, two J35-GE, 130 ft. rotor. One only, 50-1842, Hughes-built
H-18	SIKORSKY	Model S-52-2, one O-425-1, 3,000 lb. gross, 33 ft. rotor. 49-2888/91
H-19	SIKORSKY	Model S-55. **Page 553**
H-20	McDONNELL	Model M-38, ramjets at tips of 18 ft. rotor. 46-689/690 only
H-21	PIASECKI	Navy HRP-2 adapted. **Page 514**
H-22	KAMAN	Model K-225 for trials. O-435-C
H-23	HILLER	Model 360 and UH-12. **Page 339**
H-24	SEIBEL	Model S4-A for trials. O--290-11, 1,500 lb. 29 ft. rotor. 51-5112/3 only
H-25	PIASECKI	Navy HUP-2 adapted. **Page 664**
H-26	AMERICAN HELICOPTER	Model XA-8, 1,000 lb. gross; 28 ft. 2 in. rotor; XPJ49-AH-3 pulse jets. 50-1840/1 and 52-7476/8
H-27	PIASECKI	Second H-16 with T38 engines. Became YH-16A
H-28	HUGHES	Projected development of H-17. Cancelled
H-29	McDONNELL	Model M-79, two-seat development of H-20. Cancelled
H-30	McCULLOCH	Model MC-4C tandem rotor, O-335-5; 2,300 lb.; 23 ft. rotors. 52-5837/9 only
H-31	DORMAN	Model LZ-5 for trials. XO-580-1; 4,400 lb.; 48 ft. rotor. 52-5779/80
H-32	HILLER	Model HJ-1 Hornet lightweight. **Page 651**
H-33	BELL	Model 200 tilt wing. Became XV-3
H-34	SIKORSKY	Model S-58. **Page 555**
H-35	McDONNELL	Model M-82. Convertiplane. Became XV-I
H-36	—	No information
H-37	SIKORSKY	Model S-56. **Page 557**
H-38	SIKORSKY	One only, 54-4047, for MAP
H-39	SIKORSKY	Model S-59, H-18 variant with XT51-T-3. 3,560 lb. gross. 49-2888/2891
H-40	BELL	Model 204. Became HU-1. **Page 78**
H-41	CESSNA	CH-1B for Army evaluation; FSO-526-A engine; 3,000 lb. gross. 56-4236/45
H-42	—	No information
H-43	KAMAN	Rescue helicopter. **Page 350**
H-44	—	No information
H-45	—	No information
H-46	BOEING-VERTOL	Army and AF version of Model 107-II. **Page 155**
H-47	BOEING-VERTOL	Redesignation of HC-1 Chinook in 1962. **Page 155**
H-48	BELL	Initial designation for UH-1F missile site support helicopter. **Page 78**
H-49	—	No information
H-50	GYRODYNE	DASH drone. Primarily USN. Army evaluation in 1970–71
H-51	LOCKHEED	Model 186. Two prototypes with T74 turboshaft engines, for joint Army/Navy evaluation. f.f. 2/11/62
H-52	SIKORSKY	Model S-62. USN/USCG use only
H-53	SIKORSKY	Model S-65 Super Jolly. **Page 561**
H-54	SIKORSKY	Model S-64 Tarhe. **Page 668**
H-55	HUGHES	Model 269 Osage. **Page 652**
H-56	LOCKHEED	Cheyenne armed helicopter for Army. T64-GE-16 engine. f.f. September 21, 1967. Ten AH-56A prototypes, 66-8826/8835
H-57	BELL	Model 206A Sea Ranger. Navy use only
H-58	BELL	Model 206A Kiowa. **Page 88**
H-59	SIKORSKY	S.69 high-speed research helicopter for US Army. PT6T-3 Turbo Twin PaC and co-axial ABC rotors. XH-59A 71-1472, f.f. 26-7-73, and two YH-59A, 73-21941/2.
H-60	SIKORSKY	S.70 Black Hawk for Army and AF. **Page 564**

743

H-61	BOEING-VERTOL	UTTAS prototypes in competition with H-60. Three YUH-61A, 73-21656/58, f.f. 29-11-74
H-62	BOEING-VERTOL	Model 301 heavy-lift prototype XCH-62A with three XT701-AD-700 engines and tandom rotors
H-63	BELL	Model 409 Advanced Attack Helicopter (AAH) with two T700-GE-700. Two YAH-63A, 73-22246/7.
H-64	McDONNELL DOUGLAS	Apache. Winning AAH in competition with H-63. **Page 426**
H-65	AEROSPATIALE	SA 365 Dolphin rescue helicopter for USCG

H—HELICOPTER, 1962 –

H-1	BELL	HU-1 Iroquois redesignated. **Page 78**
H-2	KAMAN	USN HU2K redesignated. No USAF use
H-3	SIKORSKY	Model S-61 Jolly Green Giant. **Page 559**
H-4	BELL	Army HO-4 redesignated. **Page 88**
H-5	HILLER	Army HO-5 redesignated. T63 engine. f.f. January 26, 1963. Five OH-5A for Army evaluation, 62-4206/4210
H-6	HUGHES	Army HO-6 redesignated. **Page 347**

HB—HEAVY BOMBARDMENT, 19925–1927

HB-1	HUFF-DALAND	Developed LB-1 with Packard 2A-2540 engine. One only, 26-201
HB-2	ATLANTIC	Projected with two Packard 2A-2540; weight 24,500 lb. Not built
HB-3	HUFF-DALAND	Projected with two Packard 2A-2540. Not built

HC—CARGO HELICOPTER (ARMY AVIATION)

| HC-1 | BOEING VERTOL | Chinook tandem rotor design. Became H-47. **Page 155** |

HO—OBSERVATION HELICOPTER (ARMY AVIATION)

HO-1	SUD	Evaluation of three French Djinns (57-6104/6)
HO-2	HUGHES	Evaluation of five Model 269A (58-1324/8). **Page 652**
HO-3	BRANTLY	Evaluation of five Model B-2 (58-1492/6)
HO-4	BELL	Became H-4 in 1962. **Page 88**
HO-5	HILLER	Five Model 1100 light helicopters ordered 1961. T63-A turboshaft. Became H-5 in 1962
HO-6	HUGHES	T63-A. Became H-6 in 1962. **Page 347**

HU—UTILITY HELICOPTER (ARMY AVIATION)

| HU-1 | BELL | Model 204. H-40 redesignated, became UH-1. **Page 78** |

IL—INFANTRY LIAISON, 1919–1924

| IL-1 | ORENCO | Exp. liaison in 1922. Two only delivered |

L—LIAISON, 1942–1962

L-1	STINSON	Redesignation of O-49. **Page 572**
L-2	TAYLORCRAFT	Redesignation of O-57. **Page 576**
L-3	AERONCA	Redesignation of O-58. **Page 45**
L-4	PIPER	Redesignation of O-59. **Page 516**
L-5	VULTEE-STINSON	Redesignation of O-62. **Page 574**
L-6	INTERSTATE	Redesignation of O-63. **Page 653**
L-7	UNIVERSAL	19 Model 90-AF Monocoupes sent to France. O-200-1 engine
L-8	INTERSTATE	9 commercial S-1A Cadets sent to Bolivia. O-170-3 engine
L-9	STINSON	20 commercial Voyager **Page 574**
L-10	RYAN	One commercial SCW (42-107412); Warner engine
L-11	BELLANCA	One commercial 31-50 (42-107421); R-1340-1
L-12	STINSON	Four commercial Reliants (44-52992, -52994/6)
L-13	CONVAIR	Vultee design developed. **Page 625**
L-14	PIPER	Improved L-4, five built. **Page 516**
L-15	BOEING	Developed for Army Aviation. **Page 618**
L-16	AERONCA	For Air Force, ANG, Army Aviation. **Page 45**

L-17	NORTH AMERICAN	Commercial Navion, later by Ryan. **Page 661**
L-18	PIPER	Improved L-4 for MDAP. **Page 516**
L-19	CESSNA	Model 305 Bird Dog for Army. Become O-1. **Page 161**
L-20	DE HAVILLAND	Canadian-built Beaver. Became U-6. **Page 685**
L-21	PIPER	Model PA-18 for Army. **Page 516**
L-22	RYAN	Three Super Navion with O-435-17 (51-16425/7) became XL-17D. **Page 661**
L-23	BEECH	Twin Bonanza and Queen Air for Army. **Page 56**
L-24	HELIO	Evaluation of one H-391 Courier. **Page 650**
L-25	McDONNELL	Initial designation of XV-1 convertiplane
L-26	AERO COMMANDER	Commercial 520 and 560, became U-4 and U-9. **Page 611**
L-27	CESSNA	Commercial 310, became U-3. **Page 621**
L-28	HELIO	Improved L-24. Became U-10. **Page 650**

LB—LIGHT BOMBARDMENT, 1924–1932

LB-1	HUFF-DALAND	Only single-engined LB. **Page 342**
LB-2	ATLANTIC	Fokker twin engined monoplane bomber, high wing, 12,500 lb. gross. 26-210 only
LB-3	HUFF-DALAND	LB-1 variant completed by Keystone. **Page 342**
LB-4	MARTIN	All-metal project with two R-1690-1. Cancelled
LB-5	HUFF-DALAND	LB-1 variant. **Page 342**
LB-6	KEYSTONE	LB-5 variant. **Page 342**
LB-7	KEYSTONE	LB-6 variant. **Page 342**
LB-8	KEYSTONE	LB-7 variant. **Page 342**
LB-9	KEYSTONE	LB-7 variant. **Page 342**
LB-10	KEYSTONE	LB-6 variant. Became B-3. **Page 342**
LB-11	KEYSTONE	LB-6 variant. **Page 342**
LB-12	KEYSTONE	LB-7 variant. **Page 342**
LB-13	KEYSTONE	Became B-4 and B-6. **Page 342**
LB-14	KEYSTONE	Became B-5. **Page 342**

M—MESSENGER, 1919–1924

| M-1 | ENGINEERING DIV. | Developed by Sperry from E. D. design. **Page 303** |

NBL—NIGHT BOMBARDMENT—LONG DISTANCE, 1919–1924

| NBL-1 | WITTEMAN | Designed by Barling. **Page 641** |
| NBL-2 | MARTIN | Monoplane project, two W-2779 engines, span 98 ft. |

NBS—NIGHT BOMBARDMENT—SHORT DISTANCE, 1919–1924

NBS-1	MARTIN	Developed MB-1. **Page 431**
NBS-2	LWF	Metal structure biplane, two Liberty 12A. Cancelled
NBS-3	ELIAS	Metal and wood biplane, two Liberty; gross 14,343 lb.; span 77·5 ft. 68567 only
NBS-4	CURTISS	Improved NBS-1, two Liberty; gross 13,795 lb.; span 90 ft. 2 in. 68571/2 only

NO—NIGHT OBSERVATION, 1919–1924

| NO-1 | DOUGLAS | Projected pusher with V-1400. Cancelled |
| NO-2 | DOUGLAS | High-wing project, R-790. Cancelled |

O—OBSERVATION, 1924–1942

O-1	CURTISS	First Falcon two-seat biplane. **Page 219**
O-2	DOUGLAS	Two-seat biplane. **Page 249**
O-3	WRIGHT	1924 biplane design, Wright V-1950 engine. Not built
O-4	MARTIN	1924 biplane design, Liberty V-1650-l engine. Not built
O-5	DOUGLAS	Derived from DWC World Cruiser. **Page 634**
O-6	THOMAS-MORSE	Similar to O-2 using metal construction. **Page 672**
O-7	DOUGLAS	O-2 variant. **Page 249**
O-8	DOUGLAS	O-2 variant. **Page 249**
O-9	DOUGLAS	O-2 variant. **Page 249**
O-10	LOENING	Redesignation of XOA-2. **Page 405**
O-11	CURTISS	O-1 variant. **Page 219**

O-12	CURTISS	O-1 variant. **Page 219**
O-13	CURTISS	O-1 variant. **Page 219**
O-14	DOUGLAS	Light biplane; gross 2500 lb. 28-194 only. **Page 249**
O-15	KEYSTONE	Light biplane; R-790-5; span 37 ft. 3 in.; gross 2518 lb. 28-195 only
O-16	CURTISS	O-11 variant. **Page 219**
O-17	CONSOLIDATED	Developed PT-3 for National Guard. **Page 170**
O-18	CURTISS	O-11 variant. **Page 219**
O-19	THOMAS-MORSE	1928 all-metal biplane. **Page 584**
O-20	THOMAS-MORSE	O-19 variant. **Page 584**
O-21	THOMAS-MORSE	O-19 variant. **Page 584**
O-22	DOUGLAS	O-2H variant; R-1340-9; gross 3,800 lb. 29-371/3 only
O-23	THOMAS-MORSE	O-19 variant. **Page 584**
O-24	CURTISS	Biplane project; R-1340-7. Not ordered
O-25	DOUGLAS	O-2 variant. **Page 249**
O-26	CURTISS	O-1 variant. **Page 219**
O-27	FOKKER	First twin-engined 'O'. **Page 646**
O-28	VOUGHT	One Navy O2U-3 (29-323) tested 1929
O-29	DOUGLAS	O-2 variant. **Page 249**
O-30	CURTISS	Twin-engined monoplane project with V-1570-9. Not built
O-31	DOUGLAS	New design, high wing monoplane. **Page 257**
O-32	DOUGLAS	O-2 variant. **Page 249**
O-33	THOMAS-MORSE	O-19 variant. **Page 584**
O-34	DOUGLAS	O-22 with V-1570-11. Span 38 ft. 1 in.; 29-373 only
O-35	DOUGLAS	Twin-engined high wing; provisionally OLR-35. **Page 635**
O-36	DOUGLAS	Version of O-35. **Page 635**
O-37	KEYSTONE	Projected O-10/OA-2 variant with R-1340-9. Not completed
O-38	DOUGLAS	O-25 version. **Page 249**
O-39	CURTISS	O-1 variant. **Page 219**
O-40	CURTISS	Tested as sesqui-plane (32-343) and monoplane (32-415/8). R-1820
O-41	THOMAS-MORSE	Sesquiplane with V-1570-29 tested as XO-932. **Page 585**
O-42	THOMAS-MORSE	1932 monoplane project. Not completed
O-43	DOUGLAS	O-31 variant. **Page 257**
O-44	DOUGLAS	B-11 amphibian redesignated. Became OA-5 (33-017)
O-45	MARTIN	Single YB-10 for tests. **Page 432**
O-46	DOUGLAS	O-43 variant. **Page 257**
O-47	NORTH AMERICAN	1936 three-seat monoplane. **Page 452**
O-48	DOUGLAS	O-46 proposed with R-1670-3. Not built. **Page 257**
O-49	STINSON	High wing light liaison. Became L-1. **Page 572**
O-50	BELLANCA	High wing liaison; V-770-1; span 55 ft. 6 in.; gross 3,887 lb. 40-741/3 only
O-51	RYAN	Dragonfly liaison; R-985-21; span 52 ft. 0 in.; gross 4,206 lb. 40-703/5 only
O-52	CURTISS	Owl high wing monoplane. **Plane 631**
O-53	DOUGLAS	Proposed O variant of A-20. 1,489 cancelled. **Page 277**
O-54	STINSON	Model 105 Voyager; O-170-1. 41-143/148 only. **Page 574**
O-55	ERCO	Ercoupe 415-C on test; YO-170-3. 41-18875 only
O-56	LOCKHEED	B-37 variant. **Page 356**
O-57	TAYLORCRAFT	High wing light liaison. Became L-2. **Page 576**
O-58	AERONCA	High wing light liaison. Became L-3. **Page 45**
O-59	PIPER	High wing light liaison. Became L-4. **Page 516**
O-60	KELLET	Variant of XR-2 autogiro. **Page 653**
O-61	AGA AVIATION	Light autogiro; R-915-3; diameter 48 ft.; gross 3,038 lb. Cancelled
O-62	VULTEE-STINSON	Sentinel high wing light liaison. Became L-5. **Page 574**
O-63	INTERSTATE	Cadet high wing light liaison. Became L-6. **Page 653**

O—OBSERVATION, 1962–

O-1	CESSNA	Redesignation of L-19 Bird Dog. **Page 161**
O-2	CESSNA	Model 337 Skymaster. **Page 168**

| O-3 | LOCKHEED | Q-Star "quiet" aircraft for US Army. **Page 657** |

OA—OBSERVATION AMPHIBIAN, 1925–1947

OA-1	LOENING	Two-seat biplane, originally COA-1. **Page 405**
OA-2	LOENING	Improved OA-1. **Page 405**
OA-3	DOUGLAS	Dolphin. Redesignation of C-21. **Page 255**
OA-4	DOUGLAS	Was C-26. **Page 255**
OA-5	DOUGLAS	B-11 (33-17) redesignated
OA-6	CONSOLIDATED	Flying boat project; two R-1820-45. Cancelled
OA-7	DOUGLAS	OA-4 variant projected with R-1340-33. Cancelled
OA-8	SIKORSKY	S-43 amphibian. **Page 667**
OA-9	GRUMMAN	Commercial G-21A. **Page 649**
OA-10	CONVAIR	Navy PBY-5A Catalina. **Page 624**
OA-11	SIKORSKY	Commercial S-43, as OA-8. **Page 667**
OA-12	GRUMMAN	Navy J2F-5. **Page 648**
OA-13	GRUMMAN	As OA-9 with engine change. **Page 649**
OA-14	GERMAN	Commercial G-44. **Page 649**
OA-15	REPUBLIC	Twelve SeaBee light amphibians ordered 1945; cancelled

P—PURSUIT (FIGHTER), 1945–1947

P-1	CURTISS	Improved PW-8. **Page 211**
P-2	CURTISS	P-1 variant. **Page 211**
P-3	CURTISS	P-1 variant. **Page 211**
P-4	BOEING	Modified PW-9. **Page 91**
P-5	CURTISS	P-1 variant. **Page 211**
P-6	CURTISS	P-1 variant. **Page 211**
P-7	BOEING	PW-9 variant. **Page 91**
P-8	BOEING	Model 66 biplane tested; Packard 2A-1530; gross 3,422 lb. 28-359 only
P-9	BOEING	Model 96 monoplane; V-1570-15; gross 3,604 lb. 28-386 only
P-10	CURTISS	Gull wing biplane; V-1570-15; gross 3,700 lb. 28-387 only
P-11	CURTISS	P-6 variant. **Page 211**
P-12	BOEING	Model 89 developed. **Page 94**
P-13	THOMAS-MORSE	Viper biplane; H-1640-1 or R-1340-9; gross 3,250 lb. 29-453 only
P-14	CURTISS	For competition with P-13. Cancelled
P-15	BOEING	Model 202 for tests; R-1340D; gross 2,790 lb.
P-16	BERLINER-JOYCE	Two-seat biplane became PB-1. **Page 616**
P-17	CURTISS	P-1 variant. **Page 211**
P-18	CURTISS	New biplane design project. Cancelled
P-19	CURTISS	New monoplane design project. Cancelled
P-20	CURTISS	P-11 variant. **Page 211**
P-21	CURTISS	P-3 variant. **Page 211**
P-22	CURTISS	P-6 variant. **Page 211**
P-23	CURTISS	P-22 variant. **Page 211**
P-24	DETROIT	Two-seat monoplane for test as XP-900. 32-320 only. **Page 174**
P-25	CONSOLIDATED	Two-seat monoplane. **Page 174**
P-26	BOEING	Model 248 low-wing. **Page 99**
P-27	CONSOLIDATED	P-25 variant proposed with R-1340-21. Cancelled. **Page 174**
P-28	CONSOLIDATED	P-25 variant proposed with R-1340-19. Cancelled. **Page 174**
P-29	BOEING	Model 264 tested as XP-940; R-1340; span 29 ft. 1 in. 34-023/5 only.
P-30	CONSOLIDATED	Two-seat low wing, became PB-2. **Page 174**
P-31	CURTISS	Low wing design tested as XP-934. V-1570-53. 33-178 only
P-32	BOEING	P-29 variant with R-1535-1. Cancelled
P-33	CONSOLIDATED	Projected improvement of P-30. Cancelled

P-34	WEDELL-WILLIAMS	Light fighter design; R-1535 or R-1830. Gross 4,250 lb. Not built
P-35	SEVERSKY	All-metal low-wing. **Page 547**
P-36	CURTISS	First Hawk monoplane. **Page 227**
P-37	CURTISS	P-36 variant with V-1710. **Page 227**
P-38	LOCKHEED	Twin-boom Lightning. **Page 358**
P-39	BELL	Airacobra with engine amidships. **Page 64**
P-40	CURTISS	Warhawk developed from P-36. **Page 231**
P-41	SEVERSKY	P-35 with turbo-supercharged engine. **Page 547**
P-42	CURTISS	One P-36A with R-1830-31 in streamlined cowl, tested 1939
P-43	REPUBLIC	Developed P-35. **Page 520**
P-44	REPUBLIC	Model AP-4J/L project, R-2180 or R-2800, not built. **Page 520**
P-45	BELL	Initial designation for P-39C. **Page 64**
P-46	CURTISS	Improved P-40; V-1710-39 and ten guns. 40-3053/4 only
P-47	REPUBLIC	Thunderbolt interceptor. **Page 522**
P-48	DOUGLAS	Model 312 project, not built
P-49	LOCKHEED	P-38 variant. **Page 358**
P-50	GRUMMAN	As USN XF5F-1, two R-1820-67, tested March 1941
P-51	NORTH AMERICAN	Mustang interceptor. **Page 466**
P-52	BELL	Model 16 pusher, XIV-1430-5, 8,200 lb. gross. Not built
P-53	CURTISS	P-46 developed with XIV-1430-3, and laminar wing. Not built
P-54	VULTEE	V-70 pusher; XH-2470-1; 19,337 lb. gross; f.f. 15-1-43. 41-1210 and 42-108994 only
P-55	CURTIS	Model 24 Ascender: V-1710-95; 7,930 lb. gross; f.f. 13-7-43, 42-78845/7 only
P-56	NORTHROP	N2M tailless; R-2800-29; 12,145 lb. gross; f.f. 30-9-43; 41-786 and 42-38353 only
P-57	TUCKER	Model AL-5 light fighter; Miller L-510; 3,400 lb. gross, Not built
P-58	LOCKHEED	Developed P-38 escort fighter. **Page 358**
P-59	BELL	Airacomet, first U.S. jet fighter. **Page 73**
P-60	CURTISS	P-53 redesignated with Merlin, V-1710 or R-2800. 42-79423/5, 43-72763, 41-19508
P-61	NORTHROP	Black Widow night fighter. **Page 502**
P-62	CURTISS	High altitude with R-3350-17, 41-35873 only f.f. 21-7-43
P-63	BELL	Kingcobra improved P-39. **Page 70**
P-64	NORTH AMERICAN	Six NA-50 built for Siam. **Page 660**
P-65	GRUMMAN	Improved P-50, two R-2600-10. Not built
P-66	VULTEE	Swedish-ordered Vanguard 48C impressed. **Page 674**
P-67	McDONNELL	High altitude with two XIV-1430-17/19. 42-11677 only, f.f. 6-1-44
P-68	VULTEE	Tornado project, 1941. Not built
P-69	REPUBLIC	AP-18 project with R-2160-3. Cancelled 1943
P-70	DOUGLAS	A-20 as night fighter. **Page 277**
P-71	CURTISS	Two-seat escort, two R-4360-13, 82 ft. span. Cancelled
P-72	REPUBLIC	Developed P-47 with R-4360-13. Two only. f.f. 2-2-44
P-73	—	Designation not used
P-74	—	Designation not used
P-75	GENERAL MOTORS	Fisher Division Eagle with V-3420-19-23. Eight XP-75 (f.f. 30-9-43) and five P-75A built
P-76	BELL	Proposed production of XP-39E. **Page 64**
P-77	BELL	Lightweight, all-wood D-6; XV-770-7; 3,940 lb. gross. 43-34915/6, f.f. 1-4-44
P-78	NORTH AMERICAN	Initial designation of XP-51B. **Page 466**
P-79	NORTHROP	Prone-pilot, all-wing, two Westinghouse 19B, 43-52437, f.f. 12-9-45
P-80	LOCKHEED	Shooting Star. **Page 370**

P-81	CONVAIR	Mixed powerplant, J33-GE-5/XT31. 44-91000/1, f.f. 11.2.45
P-82	NORTH AMERICAN	Twin Mustang. **Page 476**
P-83	BELL	Developed P-59, two J33, GE-5. 44-84990/1, f.f. 27-2-45
P-84	REPUBLIC	Thunderjet/streak/flash series. **Page 529**
P-85	McDONNELL	Became F-85, which see
P-86	NORTH AMERICAN	Sabre. **Page 481**
P-87	CURTISS	Became F-87, which see
P-88	McDONNELL	Became F-88, which see
P-89	NORTHROP	Scorpion. **Page 504**
P-90	LOCKHEED	Became F-90, which see
P-91	REPUBLIC	Became F-91. which see
P-92	CONVAIR	Became F-92. **Page 195**

P—PATROL, 1962–

P-2	LOCKHEED	Neptune, primarily Navy. Some AP-2Es used by Army. **Page 658**
P-3	LOCKHEED	Orion, Navy use only
P-4	CONVAIR	Former P4Y Mercator, Navy use only
P-5	MARTIN	Former P5M Marlin, Navy use only

PA—PURSUIT, AIR COOLED, 1919–1924

PA-1	LOENING	Biplane with R-1454; 2,463 lb. gross. Two built, 1922

PB—PURSUIT, BI-PLACE, 1935–1941

PB-1	BERLINER JOYCE	Redesignation of P-16. **Page 616**
PB-2	CONSOLIDATED	Redesignation of P-30. **Page 174**
PB-3	—	Design competition for new two-seat fighter. Became FM-1/FM-2, q.v.

PG—PURSUIT, GROUND ATTACK, 1919–1924

PG-1	AEROMARINE	1923 biplane design by Eng. Div. with K-2, 37-mm gun. Three built

PG—POWERED GLIDER, 1943–1947

PG-1	WACO	CG-4A conversion by Northwestern. **Page 593**
PG-2	WACO	Assorted CG-4A conversions. **Page 593**
PG-3	WACO	CG-15A conversion. **Page 594**

PN—PURSUIT, NIGHT, 1919–1924

PN-1	CURTISS	1921 biplane with Liberty L-825, 2,780 lb. gross. Two built

PQ—MAN CARRYING TARGET, 1942–1947

PQ-8	CULVER	Redesignation of A-8. **Page 626**
PQ-9	CULVER	As PQ-8 with Franklin O-300-3. Cancelled
PQ-10	CULVER	New design; two O-300. Cancelled
PQ-11	FLETCHER	New design, R-985. Cancelled
PQ-12	FLEETWINGS	Low wing, trike, with O-435. 41-39049/56 only
PQ-13	ENG. RESEARCH	Ercoupe 415-C with O-300. 41-39099
PQ-14	CULVER	Developed PQ-8. **Page 626**
PQ-15	CULVER	PQ-14 with O-405. **Page 626**

PS—ALERT PURSUIT (SPECIAL), 1919–1924

PS-1	DAYTON-WRIGHT	Three parasol monoplanes in 1923; Lawrence J-1 1,715 lb. gross

PT—PRIMARY TRAINER, 1925–1947

PT-1	CONSOLIDATED	Improved TW-3. **Page 170**
PT-2	CONSOLIDATED	PT-1 with R-790. **Page 170**
PT-3	CONSOLIDATED	PT-1 with Clark Y wing areofoil. **Page 170**
PT-4	CONSOLIDATED	PT-3 proposed with Fairchild 447-C engine. Cancelled **Page 170**
PT-5	CONSOLIDATED	XPT-3 re-engined with R-600. **Page 170**

PT-6	FLEET	Model 7 for service trials. **Page 645**
PT-7	MOHAWK	Model M-1C Pinto low wing; YR-370-1; 1,773 lb gross. 30-371 only
PT-8	CONSOLIDATED	One XO-17A, one PT-3A with DR-980 engine. **Page 171**
PT-9	STEARMAN	Commercial Cloudboy for evaluation. **Page 671**
PT-10	VERVILLE	Commercial Sportsman for evaluation, 31-519/52 only
PT-11	CONSOLIDATED	Commercial 21 developed. **Page 171**
PT-12	CONSOLIDATED	Became Y1BT-7. **Page 172**
PT-13	STEARMAN	PT-9 developed. **Page 570**
PT-14	WACO	Commercial UPF-7. **Page 675**
PT-15	ST. LOUIS	Model PT-1W. Last original biplane design submitted to Army. **Page 665**
PT-16	RYAN	Model STA-1 low wing. **Page 544**
PT-17	STEARMAN	PT-13 with engine change. **Page 570**
PT-18	STEARMAN	PT-13 with engine change. **Page 570**
PT-19	FAIRCHILD	Model M-62 low wing. **Page 307**
PT-20	RYAN	PT-16 variant. **Page 544**
PT-21	RYAN	PT-16 variant. **Page 545**
PT-22	RYAN	PT-16 variant. **Page 545**
PT-23	FAIRCHILD	PT-19 variant. **Page 308**
PT-24	DE HAVILAND	Canadian-built Tiger Moth for Lend-Lease to RCAF. 42-964/1163
PT-25	RYAN	Model ST-4, **Page 544**
PT-26	FAIRCHILD	Coupe PT-19. **Page 307**
PT-27	BOEING-STEARMAN	PT-17 variant for Lend-Lease to RCAF. **Page 570**

PW—PURSUIT, WATER COOLED, 1919–1924

PW-1	ENG. DIVISION	VCP-2 redesignated. **Page 642**
PW-2	LOENING	M-8 developed. **Page 659**
PW-3	ORENCO	Model D-2. Three built, never flown
PW-4	GALLAUDET	1922 biplane with Packard 1A-1237. Two built, one flown
PW-5	FOKKER	F-VI (V-40) built in Holland. Ten purchased, 1922 Wright H-2. **Page 695**
PW-6	FOKKER	D-IX purchased in Holland. **Page 695**
PW-7	FOKKER	D-XI purchased in Holland. **Page 695**
PW-8	CURTISS	R-6 developed; Hawk forerunner. **Page 209**
PW-9	BOEING	Model 15 biplane. **Page 91**

Q—AERIAL TARGET, 1948–1962

| Q-8 | CULVER | Redesignation of PQ-8. **Page 626** |
| Q-14 | CULVER | Redesignation of PQ-14. **Page 626** |

R—AIR SERVICE RACER, 1919–1924

R-1	E.D.-VERVILLE	VCP-1 rebuilt as VCP-R and redesignated. **Page 641**
R-2	THOMAS-MORSE	MB-6 for 1921 Pulitzer; Wright 'H'; 2,023 lb. gross. **Page 580**
R-3	VERVILLE-SPERRY	Low-wing design, retractable u/c. **Page 640**
R-4	LOENING	Two monoplanes for 1922 Pulitzer. IA-2025 engine; 3,050 lb. gross
R-5	THOMAS-MORSE	Two for 1922 Pulitzer. 1A-2025 engine; 2,916 lb. gross. **Page 580**
R-6	CURTIS	1922 Pulitzer winners. **Page 629**
R-7	ENG. DIVISION	Not built; no information
R-8	CURTISS	Navy R2C-1, developed into R3C-1. **Page 629**

R—ROTARY WING (HELICOPTER), 1941–1947

R-1	PLATT-LE-PAGE	Side-by-side twin rotors; one R-985. 41-001 and 42-6581
R-2	KELLET	YG-1 variant. **Page 653**
R-3	KELLET	YG-1 variant. **Page 653**
R-4	SIKORSKY	VS-316. **Page 549**
R-5	SIKORSKY	VS-372. Later H-5. **Page 551**

R-6	SIKORSKY	Improved R-4. **Page 668**
R-7	SIKORSKY	XR-6 developed with O-405-9. Not completed
R-8	KELLET	Side-by-side twin rotors; O-405-9. 43-44714 and 44-21908
R-9	G & A (FIRESTONE)	Model 45 lightweight (1,750 lb.) with O-290-7. 46-001 only
R-10	KELLET	Enlarged R-8; two R-985; 13,500 lb. gross. 45-22793 and -22795 only
R-11	ROTOR-CRAFT	Lightweight with Continental A-100. 1,170 lb. gross. One only
R-12	BELL	Model 48, became H-12. **Page 614**
R-13	BELL	Model 47, became H-13. **Page 75**
R-14	G & A (FIRESTONE)	Lightweight with XO-470-1. Not built, three cancelled

R—RECONNAISANCE (1948), 1948–1962
R-11	HUGHES	Redesignation of F-11, q.v.
R-12	REPUBLIC	Redesignation of F-12, q.v.
R-16	BOEING	Initial designation for RB-52. **Page 136**

R—RECONNAISSANCE, 1962–
R-1	LOCKHEED	Developed U-2 for tactical reconnaissance (TR-1). **Page 390**
R-2	LOCKHEED	R-1 variant for NASA (as ER-2) for earth resources reconnaissance
R-71	LOCKHEED	Strategic reconnaissance SR-71 wrongly using "bomber" number. **Page 396**

S—SONIC TEST, 1946–1947
S-1	BELL	Became X-1, q.v.
S-2	BELL	Became X-2, q.v.
S-3	DOUGLAS	Became X-3, q.v.
S-4	NORTHROP	Became X-4, q.v.
S-5	BELL	Became X-5, q.v.

T—TRANSPORT, 1919–1924
T-1	MARTIN	Redesignation of GMP biplane with two Liberty 12A. **Page 429**
T-2	FOKKER	Two F-IV purchased in Holland. **Page 696**
T-3	L.W.F.	Biplane with Liberty 12A; 7,316 lb. gross. One built, nine cancelled

T—TRAINER, 1948
T-6	NORTH AMERICAN	AT-6 redesignated in 1948. **Page 454**
T-7	BEECH	AT-7 redesignated in 1948. **Page 50**
T-11	BEECH	AT-11 redesignated in 1948. **Page 50**
T-17	BOEING	PT-17 redesignated in 1948. **Page 570**
T-19	FAIRCHILD	PT-19 redesignated in 1948. **Page 307**
T-28	NORTH AMERICAN	Continuation from last PT number. **Page 489**
T-29	CONVAIR	Commercial 240. **Page 192**
T-30	DOUGLAS	Competed with T-28. Not built
T-31	FAIRCHILD	One Navy XNQ-1 evaluated; R-680-10. No production
T-32	CONSOLIDATED	Projected bombardier trainer, as T-29. Cancelled. **Page 192**
T-33	LOCKHEED	Two-seat F-80. **Page 370**
T-34	BEECH	Model 45 primary. **Page 54**
T-35	TEMCO	In competition with T-34. 50-738/740 tested and 53-4465/74 for MDAP
T-36	BEECH	Advanced twin; R-2800-52; 25,000 lb. gross. Cancelled
T-37	CESSNA	Model 318 jet basic trainer. **Page 164**
T-38	NORTHROP	Model N-156 advanced jet trainer. **Page 508**
T-39	NORTH AMERICAN	Sabreliner classroom. **Page 496**
T-40	LOCKHEED	Training variant of C-140. **Page 657**
T-41	CESSNA	Model 172 Mescelaro for Air Force and Army. **Page 622**
T-42	BEECH	Baron for Army. **Page 613**
T-43	BOEING	Model 737 for Air Force. **Page 619**

T-44	BEECH	Commercial King Air as navigation trainer for USN.
T-45	McDONNELL DOUGLAS	BAe Hawk modified for USN.
T-46	FAIRCHILD	Winning New Generation Trainer (NGT) in 1982. **Page 644**
T-47	CESSNA	Commercial Citation II radar trainer for USN.
T-48	CESSNA	Proposed T-37 update, as T-46 replacement, with F109-GA-100 turbofan

TA—TRAINER, AIR-COOLED, 1919–1924

TA-1	ELIAS	Three 1921 biplanes; 90 h.p.; 2,235 lb. gross
TA-2	HUFF-DALAND	Three 1921 biplanes; 90 h.p.; 1,764 lb. gross. **Page 652**
TA-3	DAYTON-WRIGHT	Thirteen 1922 biplanes.
TA-4	ENG.DIVISION	1921 project with Lawrence J-1. Gross 1,630 lb. Not built
TA-5	DAYTON-WRIGHT	Improved TA-3. **Page 633**
TA-6	HUFF-DALAND	Improved TA-2; Lawrence J-1; 1,964 lb. gross. **Page 652**

TG—TRAINING GLIDER, 1941–1947

TG-1	FRANKFORT	Two-seat sailplane. **Page 647**
TG-2	SCHWEIZER	Two-seat 1941/42 sailplane. Three XTG-2, 32 TG-2 and 7 TG-2A
TG-3	SCHWEIZER	Model 2-12A. **Page 665**
TG-4	LAISTER-KAUFFMAN	Model LK-1000S. **Page 654**
TG-5	AERONCA	Variant of L-3. **Page 45**
TG-6	TAYLORCRAFT	Variant of L-2. **Page 576**
TG-7	ORLICK	Polish one-seat sailplane purchased 1942. 42-53519 only
TG-8	PIPER	Variant of L-4. **Page 516**
TG-9	BRIEGLEB	Model BG-6 one-seat, delivered 1942. 42-62603/5 only
TG-10	WICHITA ENG.	Two-seat side-by-side, delivered 1943
TG-11	SCHEMP	German one-seat sailplane purchased 1942. 42-53518 only
TG-12	BOWLUS	Two-seat tandem, delivered 1942. 42-57200 plus three commercial
TG-13	BRIEGLEB	Model BG-8 two-seat tandem in 1942. 42-96829,-57158, -57180
TG-14	STEIGLEMAIER	Model S-24 one-seat purchased 1942. 42-57183 only
TG-15	FRANKLIN	Eight commercial PS-2 purchased 1942
TG-16	A.B.C.	One-seat sailplane purchased 1942. 42-57172 and -57202
TG-17	FRANKLIN	Commercial one-seat sailplane purchased 1942. 42-57193 only
TG-18	MID-WEST	Model MU-1 one-seat purchased 1942. 42-57166/7 and -57176
TG-19	SCHWEYER	Rhonsperber purchased 1942. 42-57165 only
TG-20	LAISTER-KAUFFMAN	Four examples of Goeppenden one-seat design delivered 1942
TG-21	NOTRE DAME	Model ND-1 one-seat purchased commercially. 42-57170 only
TG-22	MELHOSE	Single-seat soaring type, purchased 1942, 42-57181 only
TG-23	HARPER-CORCORAN	Single-seat soaring type, purchased 1942. 42-57192 only
TG-24	BOWLUS-DUPONT	Single-seat soaring type, purchased 1942. 42-57185 only
TG-25	PLOVER	Single-seat soaring type, purchased 1942. 42-57182 only
TG-26	UNIVERSAL	Model BT-2 one-seat, purchased 1942. 42-57188 only
TG-27	GRUNAU	Single-seat soaring type, purchased 1942. 42-65552 only
TG-28	HALLER	Hawk Junior one-seat, purchased 1942. 42-65555 only
TG-29	VOLMER-JENSEN	J-10 home-built, purchased 1942. 42-65553 only
TG-30	SMITH	Bluebird two-seat soaring type, purchased 1942. 42-65554 only
TG-31	AERO INDUSTRIES	G-2 built by students; one seat sailplane. 42-57171 only
TG-32	PRATT, READ	Navy LNE-1 side-by-side for Army use. 73 purchased
TG-33	AERONCA	TG-5 converted for prone pilot. **Page 45**

TP—TWO-SEAT PURSUIT, 1919–1924

| TP-1 | ENG. DIVISION | Two tested 1924/5. One to XCO-5 |

TW—TRAINING, WATER-COOLED, 1919–1924

TW-1	ENG. DIVISION	Two tandem-seat biplanes; Liberty 6 or 1A-1237: Gross 3,225 lb.
TW-2	COX-KLEMIN	Three tandem-seat biplanes; Wright E; gross 2,505 lb.
TW-3	D-W/CONSOLIDATED	As TA-5 with Wright I or E. **Page 633**
TW-4	FOKKER	One Dutch-built monoplane, side-by-side; OX-5; gross 1,967 lb
TW-5	HUFF-DALAND	Six tandem-seat biplanes as Navy HN-1. **Page 652**

U—UTILITY, 1952–

U-1	DE HAVILLAND	Canadian-built Otter. **Page 687**
U-2	LOCKHEED	High altitude reconnaissance. **Page 390**
U-3	CESSNA	Redesignation of L-27 light twin. **Page 621**
U-4	AERO COMMANDER	Redesignation of USAF versions of L-26. **Page 611**
U-5	HELIO	Model 500 STOL twin. Two for evaluation, 1962
U-6	DE HAVILLAND	L-20 Beaver redesignated in 1962. **Page 685**
U-7	PIPER	L-21 redesignated in 1962. **Page 516**
U-8	BEECH	L-23 redesignated in 1962. **Page 56**
U-9	AERO COMMANDER	Army versions of L-26 redesignated in 1962. **Page 611**
U-10	HELIO	L-28 redesignated in 1962. **Page 650**
U-11	PIPER	US Navy UO Aztec redesignated. No USAF use
U-12	—	Number not assigned
U-13	—	Number not assigned
U-14	—	Number not assigned
U-15	—	Number not assigned
U-16	GRUMMAN	SA-16 redesignated in 1962. **Page 334**
U-17	CESSNA	Skywagon for MAP. **Page 623**
U-18	NORTH AMERICAN	L-17 redesignated. **Page 661**
U-19	STINSON	Redesignation of L-5G for Air Force Academy. **Page 574**
U-20	CESSNA	Redesignation of LC-126, **Page 621**
U-21	BEECH	King Air variants for US Army. **Page 56**
U-22	BEECH	Bonanza variants as reconnaissance drones. **Page 613**
U-23	FAIRCHILD	Pilatus PC-6 developed, with TPE331-1-101F turboprop for COIN duty. 36 AU-23A built, 72-1304/18; 73-1699; 74-2073/92, of which 33 to Thailand.
U-24	HELIO	H550A Stallion developed, with PT6A-27 turboprop. 15 AU-24A built, 72-1319/33, of which 14 to Cambodia.
U-25	BEECH	Commercial Super King Air 200 for Army. Became C-12. **Page 61**
U-25	DASSAULT-BREGUET	Designation re-used for Falcon 20/Guardian for USCG.
U-26	CESSNA	Commercial 206 Super Skywagon for AFA. One only, 82-667.
U-27	CESSNA	Commercial Caravan I light freighter with PT6A-114 turboprop for Army/FMS programme.

V—CONVERTIPLANE, 1952–1962

V-1	McDONNELL	M-82 with rotor and fixed wing; R-975-19; 53-4016/7, only
V-2	SIKORSKY	S-57 design study, not built
V-3	BELL	Model 200 tilting rotor type; R-985-AN-3. 54-147/8, only

V—VTOL AND STOL, 1954–

V-1	GRUMMAN	Army AO-1 redesignated OV-1. **Page 336**
V-2	DE HAVILLAND	Army AC-1 redesignated CV-2. Became C-7. **Page 689**
V-3	—	Not used, avoiding confusion with Bell XV-3, q.v.
V-4	LOCKHEED	Redesignation of VZ-10, q.v.
V-5	RYAN	Redesignation of VZ-11, q.v.
V-6	HAWKER	Redesignation of VZ-12. Six P.1127 Kestrel for Tri-Service evaluation, 64-18261/18268. Production for USN
V-7	DE HAVILLAND	Army AC-2 turboprop Caribou II redesignated CV-7. **Page 689**
V-8	RYAN	XV-8A Model 164 flexible wing Fleep for Army 63-13003 only
V-9	HUGHES	Model 385 research helicopter for Army. 64-15107 only

753

V-10	NORTH AMERICAN	Model 300 Bronco. **Page 498**
V-11	MARVEL	Boundary layer control research. 65-13070 only
V-12	FAIRCHILD HILLER	Reservation for proposed purchase of 25 OV-12A Turbo-Porter by USN. Cancelled and reallocated
V-12	ROCKWELL	V/STOL fighter prototypes with thrust augmentor wing for USN.
V-13	—	Not used.
V-14	—	No information
V-15	BELL	Model 301 Tilt-wing research aircraft for Army/NASA programme. Two built, f.f. 3-5-77.
V-16	McDONNELL DOUGLAS	Proposed advanced derivative of AV-8 for USN. Not built.
V-17	—	No information
V-18	DE HAVILLAND CANADA	Commercial DHC-6 Twin Otter for Army/USAF. **Page 691**
V-19	—	No information
V-20	PILATUS	PC-6 Turbo Porter for Army in Germany. **Page 702**
V-21	—	No information
V-22	BELL-BOEING	Multi-service, multi-role tilt-wing. **Page 615**

VZ—VERTICAL LIFT RESEARCH, ARMY 1958–1962

VZ-1	HILLER	Ducted propeller "flying platform", 1959. 56-6944/5 originally YHO-1E
VZ-2	VERTOL	Model 76 tilt-wing, April 1957; YT-53-L-1. 56-6943 only
VZ-3	RYAN	Model 72 Vertiplane, deflected slipstream. f.f. 1959 56-6941 only
VZ-4	DOAK	Model 16, tilting ducted fans; YT-53. f.f. 25-2-58. 56-6942 only
VZ-5	FAIRCHILD	Model M-224-1, deflected slipstream. YT58-GE-2. f.f. 18-11-59. 56-6940 only
VZ-6	CHRYSLER	Ducted propellers. Two built. 58-5506/7
VZ-7	CURTISS-WRIGHT	Direct lift, four propellers. Artouste IIB. 58-5508/9
VZ-8	PIASECKI	Model 59K. Direct lift, two ducted rotors. Artouste IIB. 58-5510/1. f.f. 12-10-58
VZ-9	AVRO CANADA	Circular layout with fan lift. Three J69. f.f. 17-5-61 58-7055 only
VZ-10	LOCKHEED	Hummingbird, jet-ejector lift. Two built. f.f. 10.8.62. Two JT12
VZ-11	RYAN	Fan-in-wing direct lift. Two J85-GE-5. f.f. May 25 1964. 62-4505/4506. Became XV-5
VZ-12	HAWKER	Reserved for two P.1127, 62-4507/4508; not delivered Became XV-6, q.v.

X—SPECIAL RESEARCH, 1948–

X-1	BELL	Air-launched SS research. Was XS-1. Six built. f.f. 19-1-46. Rocket
X-2	BELL	Air-launched SS research. Was XS-2. Two built. f.f. 27-6-52. Rocket
X-3	DOUGLAS	SS research. Was XS-3. One built. f.f. 20-10-52. Two J34-WE-17
X-4	NORTHROP	Tailless research. Was XS-4. Two built. f.f. 16-12-48 Two J30-WE-9
X-5	BELL	Variable sweep research. Was XS-5. Two built. f.f. 20-6-51. J35-A-17
X-6	CONVAIR	Projected nuclear-powered research version of B-36 **Page 187**
X-7	LOCKHEED	High altitude ram-jet test vehicle. 28 built. f.f. April 1951
X-8	AEROJET	Aerobee upper atmosphere research vehicle. Over 100 built
X-9	BELL	Shrike rocket test vehicle for GAM-63. 31 built
X-10	NORTH AMERICAN	Tail first test vehicles for SM-64 Navajo. 13 built
X-11	CONVAIR	Test vehicle for SM-65 Atlas. Eight built
X-12	CONVAIR	Test vehicle for SM-65 Atlas. Five built
X-13	RYAN	Vertijet tail-sitting fighter. Two built, 34-1619/20. f.f. 10-12-55. R.R. Avon

X-14	BELL	Vectored jet thrust VTOL research. One built, 56-4022. f.f. 19-2-57. G.E. J85
X-15	NORTH AMERICAN	Air-launched hypersonic research. Three built. 56-6670/2. f.f. 8-6-59. Rocket
X-16	BELL	Model 67 high altitude reconnaissance aircraft with two J57-PW-37A turbojets. 28 ordered, 56-552/579, none built.
X-17	LOCKHEED	Nose-cone entry research vehicle. f.f. 1956. 26 built
X-18	HILLER	Tilt-wing VTOL research. One built, 57-3078. f.f. 24-11-59. Two T40-A-14
X-19	CURTISS-WRIGHT	Model 200 VTOL research with radial lift force propellers. Two T55-L-5 engines. f.f. 26-6-64. Two built, 62-12197/8
X-20	BOEING	Rocket-launched orbital glider Dyna-Soar. Ten ordered, 61-2374/83; none built
X-21	NORTHROP	Two Douglas WB-66D modified for laminar flow control research. Two YJ79-GE-13. f.f. 18-4-63. Two built, 55-408 and 55-410
X-22	BELL	Model D2127 with four titling ducted airscrews; four YT58-GE-8D engines. Two built, Bu Nos 151520/21. f.f. 17-3-66
X-23	MARTIN	Unpiloted lifting-body re-entry test vehicles for USAF. Four built; f.f. 21-12-66.
X-24	MARTIN	SV-5P piloted lifting body prototype, 66-13551. XLR11-RM-13 engine. f.f. 17-4-69.
X-25	BENSEN	Gyro-copter (X-25A, 68-10770), gyro-glider (X-25B, 68-10771) and X-25 discretionary descent vehicle (DDV) for USAF evaluation
X-26	SCHWEIZER	Four Schweizer SGS 2-32 sailplanes (X-26A) for USN, and two powered X-26B (by Lockheed) for "Quiet Thruster" research.
X-27	LOCKHEED	Reserved for proposed USAF evaluation of CL-1200 Lancer
X-28	PEREIRA	Home built seaplane for USN evaluation. Continental C90 flat-four engine. One only, BuNo 158786. f.f. 12-8-70.
X-29	GRUMMAN	Forward-swept wing research aircraft for DARPA programme. F404-GE turbojet. Two built, 82-0003 and 82-0049. f.f. 14-12-84.
X-30	—	Testbed for National Aerospace Plane (NASP). Contractor not chosen up to end-1988
X-31	ROCKWELL-MBB	Two prototypes for Enhanced Fighter Manoeuvrability programme. Delta wing, canard surfaces, F404-GE turbofan.

GENERAL INDEX

THIS volume is largely self-indexing so far as the aircraft descriptions are concerned. The general index below covers all aircraft type names and manufacturers' model numbers or other designations, as well as individuals, organizations and events referred to in the text. All USAF and Army aircraft designations are separately indexed on pp. 731-755.

Bold type is used for the principal manufacturing companies and the first page in the main section or appendices on which their products are described.

A.E.F.—see American Expeditionary Force
Aero Design and Manufacturing Co., 611
  Commander, 611
Aeromarine, 431
Aeronautical Division, U.S. Army, 1
Aeronca Aircraft Corp., The, 45
  Champion, 47
  Defender, 45
  Grasshopper, 45
Aerospace Defense Command—see Air Defense Command
AFRES—see Air Force Reserve
Airacobra—see Bell
Air Corps Act, 2
Air Corps Ferrying Command, 3
Air Corps Maintenance Command, 3
Aircraft colours, 32
Aircraft designations, 10
Aircraft markings, 32
Air Defense Command, 4, 196, 199, 367, 376, 380, 409, 487, 529
Air Force One, 150, 154
Air Forces:
  First, 3
  Second, 3
  Third, 3
  Fourth, 3, 74
  Fifth, 3, 180, 182, 281, 476, 492
  Sixth, 3
  Seventh, 3
  Eighth, 3, 107, 180, 182, 441, 468, 523, 677, 684, 709, 711
  Ninth, 3, 179, 182, 279, 285, 286, 441, 525
  Tenth, 3, 109, 179
  Eleventh, 3, 180
  Twelfth, 3, 286, 681
  Thirteenth, 3, 182
  Fourteenth, 3
  Fifteenth, 3, 279, 525
  Twentieth, 3
Air Force Combat Command, 3
Air Force Reserve, 5, 82, 129, 145, 239, 287, 297, 313, 314, 322, 387, 400, 424, 532, 540, 560
Air Glider Inc., 665

Air Material Command, 297
Air National Guard, 5, 31, 62, 81, 145, 165, 196, 199, 313, 316, 331, 335, 376, 386, 387, 400, 409, 410, 420, 424, 445, 489, 507, 528, 532, 534, 540, 560, 619, 621, 625, 645
Air Rescue Service, 268, 292, 334, 347, 515, 553
Air Service, 2
Airspeed Horsa, 678
Airspeed Oxford, 677
Air Training Command, 5, 54, 239, 489, 496, 507
Air Transport Command, 3, 125, 238, 267, 366, 617
Air University, 4
Airways and Air Communications Service, 252, 292, 667
Air Yacht—see Loening
Alaska, 67, 75, 265, 291, 322, 438, 477, 507, 648, 685, 687, 691
Alaskan Air Command, 4, 5
Albatross—see Grumman
Allen, Edward, 114, 238, 618
All Weather Flying Center, 293
American Pilgrim, 612
American Expeditionary Force, 2, 242, 677, 680, 682, 692, 699, 700, 701, 702, 703, 705, 706, 707, 712
American Volunteer Group, 233
Andrews AFB, 60, 83, 149, 150, 154, 194, 619, 648, 650, 660
A.N.G.—see Air National Guard
Ansaldo SVA-5, 678
Army Air Corps, 2
Army Air Forces, 3
Army Aviation School, 606
Army Mule—see Piasecki
Army National Guard, 62, 349
Army Regulation 95-5, 3
Army Re-organization Act, 2
Army Training School, 598, 609
Arnold, General "Hap", 467
Atlantic Aircraft Corp., 248, 325, 452, 646
Aviation Manufacturing Corp., 572
Avro 504K, 679

756

Avro Anson, 693

Bainbridge AFB, 54
Balfour, Paul, 458
Balikpapan, 182
Barkesdale AFB, 225, 423, 478
Barling, Walter, 641
Barling Bomber, 641
Barnes, Lt.-Col. William F., 485
Bartow AFB, 54
Bataan, Lockheed C-121, 367
Battle of Midway, 438
Beale AFB, 144, 393, 397
Beaufighter—*see* Bristol
Beaver—*see* de Havilland
Beaird, Henry G., 535, 537
Beech Aircraft Corp., 48, 612
  17, 48
  18, 50
  45, 53
  Baron, 613
  Bonanza, 54, 613
  Cochise, 613
  Expediter, 50
  Huron, 61
  Kansan, 51
  King Air, 58
  Mentor, 54
  Navigator, 50
  Queen Air, 57
  Seminole, 56
  Traveler, 48
  Twin Bonanza, 56
Bell Aircraft Corp., 64, 614
  12, 65
  13, 65
  14, 66
  15, 65
  26, 67
  27, 73
  33, 70
  41, 71
  47, 75
  48, 614
  201, 75
  204, 78
  205, 80
  206, 88
  209, 85
  212, 82
  406, 89
  D.250, 88
  P-400, 23, 66
  Airacobra, 23, 64
  Airacomet, 73
  Airacuda, 614
  Cobra, 85
  Iroquois, 78
  Huey, 78
  Huey Cobra, 85
  Kingcobra, 70
  Kiowa, 88
  Osprey, 615
  Ranger, 76
  Rascal GAM-63, 121, 134
  Sioux, 88

Bell Aircraft Corp. *(contd.)*
  Warrior, 89
Bellanca Airbus, 616
Bellinger, Carl, 534
Beltz, Stanley, 383
Berlin, 108, 468
Berlin Air Lift, 126, 268, 291, 311
Berliner-Joyce, 616
Bettis, Lt. Cyrus, 629
BFW Bf 108B, 679
Bikini Atoll, 138, 295
Bird Dog—*see* Cessna
Bird of Paradise, Fokker C-2, 323
Blackbird—*see* Lockheed
Black Widow—*see* Northrop
Bobcat—*see* Cessna
Bock's Car, Boeing B-29, 116
Boeing Airplane Co., 91, 580, 617
  MB-3, 579
  15, 91
  83, 94
  89, 94
  101, 94
  102, 95
  202, 13
  214, 101
  215, 23, 101
  218, 95
  234, 97
  246, 101
  247, 103, 617
  248, 99
  251, 98
  266, 99
  294, 103, 113
  299, 103, 263
  307, 617
  316, 113
  322, 113
  333, 113
  334, 113
  341, 113
  345, 113, 120
  367, 125, 143
  424, 130
  432, 130
  448, 130
  450, 130
  451, 618
  464, 136
  707, 150
  727, 619
  737, 541
  747, 153
  XB-901, 23, 101
  XP-925A, 96
  XP-936, 99
  Flying Fortress, 103
  Stratofortress, 136
  Stratofreighter, 125
  Stratojet, 131
  Stratoliner, 617
  Stratotanker, 143
  Superfortress, 113
Boeing Airplane Co. Stearman Division, 570
Boeing Company Vertol Division, 155
  107, 155

Boeing Company Vertol Division *(contd.)*
114, 155
Chinook, 155
Osprey, 615
Bolling Commission, 301, 628, 707
Bolling Field, 667
Bold Orion, 135
Bong, Capt. Richard I., 361
Boston—*see* Douglas
Boyd, Col. Albert, 372
Brabham, L. L., 522
Breese Penguin, 620
Breguet 14, 680
Bretcher, Fred, 504
Brewster
Buffalo, B-399, 23, 620
Bristol Beaufighter, 681
British Aerospace 125, 681
British Purchasing Commission, 66, 356, 406, 591
Brown, Lt. Russel, 373
Buffalo—*see* Brewster
Bunker Hill AFB, 202
Bureau of Aircraft Production, 2
Burgess, W. Starling, Co., 597
F, 597
H, 598
I, 597
J, 597
Burgess-Dunne, 599
Buzz numbers, 41

Campbell, Douglas, 701
Camel—*see* Sopwith
Camp Wolters, 339
Canadian Aeroplane Corp., 204
Canberra—*see* Martin
Caproni, 669
Cargomaster—*see* Douglas
Caribou—*see* de Havilland
Carlson, Floyd, 78
Carswell AFB, 189, 201, 328
Castle AFB, 138
Caudron G-III, 682
Caudron G-IV, 682
Cavalier Aircraft Corp., 473
Cessna Aircraft Co., 158, 542, 621
T.50, 158
170, 161
172, 622
185, 623, 711
195, 161
206, 711
305A, 161
310, 621
318, 164
Bird Dog, 161
Bobcat, 158
Crane, 158
Dragon fly, 165
Mescelaro, 622
Skymaster, 168
Chandler, Capt. Charles de Forrest, 1
Charleston AFB, 424
Chase Aircraft Co., 317, 623
Avitruc, 317

Chase Aircraft Co. *(contd.)*
MS-1, 623
Chenault, Gen. Clair, 233
Chickasaw—*see* Sikorsky
Chinook—*see* Boeing Vertol
Choctaw—*see* Sikorsky
Civil Air Patrol, 47
Clark Field, 93, 232
Clovis AFB, 487
Cobra—*see* Bell
Cochise—*see* Beech
College Park, Maryland, 1
Collier Trophy (1937), 655
Columbine I, Lockheed C-121, 367
Columbine III, Lockheed C-121, 367
Combat Cargo Command, 221, 269
Commando—*see* Curtiss
Commonwealth Air Training Scheme, 308
Communications Command, 4
Combat Talon, 385, 388
Compass Call, 388
Consolidated Aircraft Corporation, 170
Consolidated Vultee Aircraft Corp., 176, 624
LB-30, 23, 179
31, 176
32, 176
37, 187
Courier, 171
Liberator, 176
Consolidated Vultee Stinson Aircraft Division, 574
Constellation—*see* Lockheed
Convair Division, General Dynamics, 192, 624
4, 201
7, 195
8, 195, 198
240, 192
340, 192
440, 192
Delta Dagger, 195
Delta Dart, 198
Dominator, 624
Hustler, 201
Samaritan, 192
Coronet Solo, 386
Craig AFB, 164
Crane—*see* Cessna
Curtiss Aeroplane & Motor Co., 203, 301, 599, 627
D, 599
E, 599
F, 600
G, 600
J, JN, 15, 203, 206, 601
L, 604
N, 602
O, 602
R, 1, 603
S, 604
18, 627
76, 630
85, 631
CO-X, 209
Baby Scout, 604
Eagle, 629
Falcon, 219
Hawk, 211

Curtiss Aeroplane & Motor Co. *(contd.)*
  Helldiver, 632
  Hornet, 627
  Jenny, 16, 203
  Owl, 631
  SE-5A, 628
  Shrike, 24, 224, 630
  Swift, 24
Curtiss Aeroplane Division, Curtiss-Wright, 227, 571
  CW-20, 238
  25, 631
  81, 231
  87, 233
  Commando, 238
  Hawk, 231, 233
  Kittyhawk, 234
  Tomahawk, 231
  Warhawk, 231
Curtiss, Glenn, 203, 601
Curtiss, Greely S., 597
Culver Cadet, 626
CX-4, *see* Lockheed Galaxy
CX-HLS, *see* Lockheed Galaxy

Darnell, Dan, 484, 492
Day, Charles Healey, 607
Davis-Mouthan AFB, 391
Dayton-Wright Co., 170, 243, 302, 508
Dayton-Wright Chummy, 632
De Havilland, 241
  DH-4, 10, 15, 34, 219, 241
  DH-9, 640
  DH-94, 683
  DH-89B, 683
  Dominie, 683
  Liberty Plane—*see* DH-4
  Mosquito, 684
  Moth Minor, 7, 683
De Havilland Aircraft of Canada, 685
  DHC-2, 685
  DHC-3, 687
  DHC-4, 689
  DHC-6, 691
  DHC-8, 691
  Beaver, 685
  Caribou, 689
  Otter, 687
  Twin Otter, 691
Del Monte Field, 106
Delta Dagger—*see* Convair
Delta Dart—*see* Convair
Der Gabelschwanz Teufel, Lockheed P-38, 361
Designation of aircraft, 10
Destroyer—*see* Douglas
Detroit Aircraft Co., 174, 655
Dewdrop, Lockheed C-121, 367
Disposal of aircraft, 6
Division of Military Aeronautics, 2
Dodd, Major D. O. 274
Dominator—*see* Convair
Doolittle, Lt.-Col. James H., 460, 629
Dorand, Col., 692
Dorand AR.1, 692
Dorand AR.2, 692
Douglas Aircraft Co., 249, 633

Douglas Aircraft Co. *(contd.)*
  8A, 500
  415A, 636
  1129A, 297
  1182, 297
  1317, 297
  1326, 294
  1327A, 295
  1329, 294
  1333, 299
  1430, 299
  DB-1, 263
  DB-2, 264
  DB-7, 22, 277
  DC-2, 260, 266
  DC-3, 266
  DC-4, 289, 636
  DC-6, 637
  DC-9, 660
  DOS, 634
  DST, 266
  DWC, 634
  Bolo, 636
  Cargomaster, 299
  Destroyer, 294
  Dolphin, 255
  Dragon, 636
  Genie MB-1, 409, 507
  Globemaster, 297, 636
  Havoc, 277
  Invader, 284
  Nightingale, 660
  Skybolt GAM-87, 140
  Skymaster, 289
  Skyraider, 638
  Skytrain, 251
  Skytrooper, 251
  World Cruiser, 634
Dover AFB, 299
Dow Field, 530
Dragonfly—*see* Cessna
Driggs Aircraft Corp. 638
Dart, 22, 638
Duck—*see* Grumman
Dunne, 599
Dyess AFB, 542

Eagle—*see* Curtiss
Eagle Squadron, 709
Ebel, William K , 438
Eberhart Steel Products Co., 628
  SE-5E, 16, 628
Eglin AFB, 134, 139, 188, 414, 474
Eisenhower, General Dwight, 367
Electronic Security Command, 4
Ellsworth AFB, 543
Enforcer—*see* Piper
Engineering Division, U.S. Army, 243, 246, 301, 639, 663
  Pomilio FVL-8, 640
  Pomilio BVL-12, 640
  GA-X, 642
  Sperry Messenger, 24, 303
  Sperry MAT, 303
  USA O-1, 301
  US B-1 thru' -4, 301
  XB-1, -2, 301
759

Engineering Division, U.S. Army *(contd.)*
USD-9, 640
VCP-1, 641
VCP-2, 642
VCP-R, 641
Enola Gay, Boeing B-29, 116
Erickson, B. A., 201
Expediter—*see* Beech
External Stores Designating System, 27
Extender—*see* McDonnell Douglas

Fairchild Engine and Airplane Corp., **305**, **643**
24, 644
62, 307
71, 643
78, 310
FC-2W-2, 643
Flying Boxcar, 310
Gunner, 305
Metro III, 645
NGT, 644
Packet, 311
Provider, 317
Thunderbolt II, 321
Falcon—*see* Curtiss
Far East Air Force, 4, 297, 372, 463
Farman F-10, 692
Fat Boy atomic bomb, 116
FEAF—*see* Far East Air Force
Featherweight Convair B-36, 189
Ferrying Command, 179, 184
FICON project, 189, 534
Fieseler Fi 156 Storch, 693
Fighting Falcon—*see* General Dynamics
Fisher Body Works, 669
Fisher Caproni, 669
Fleet Aircraft Corp., **645**
Husky Jr., 645
Flight Refuelling Ltd., 118, 532
Flying Boxcar—*see* Fairchild
Flying Training Command, 3
Flying White House, 150
Fokker Aircraft Corp., **452**
C-IV, 696
D-VIII, 6, 13, 170, 694
D-VIII, 16
D-IX, 695
D-XI, 695
F-IV, 696
F-VII/3m, 323
F-XA, 323
F-XI, 14
F-XIV, 646
F-27, 697
F-32, 14
Folland, H. P., 628
Ford Reliability Tour, 323
Ford Tri-Motor, 647
Ford XB-906, 24
Fort Benning, 555
Fort Bragg, 89, 687
Fort Campbell, 564
Fort Clark, 250
Fort Hood, 427
Fort Monroe, 63
Fort Myer, 1, 608

Fort Rucker, 58, 76, 78, 165, 427, 473, 557
Fort Sill, 56
Fort Wolters, 652
Foster AFB, 492
Frankfort Cinema, 647
Frankfort TCC-21, 55, 593

Gallaudet D-2, D-4, 605
Gates Learjet, 648, 711
Geiger AFB, 199
Gelvin, E. R., 317
General Aeronautical Corp., 610
General Aviation, 452
General Dynamics, 192, **325**,
401, 330
Fighting Falcon, 330
Raven, 329, 388
George AFB, 380, 491
G.H.Q. Air Force, 2
Glenn L. Martin Co.—*see* Martin
Globemaster—*see* Douglas
Gooney Bird—*see* Douglas Skytrain
Graham AFB, 54
Grand Forks AFB, 543
Grasshopper—*see* Aeronca, Interstate, Piper
and Taylorcraft
Grumman Aircraft Engineering Corp., **335**, **649**
G-21, 649
G-44, 649
G-64, 334
G-111, 334
G-134, 336
Albatross, 334
Duck, 648
Mohawk, 336
Raven, 329
Guadalcanal, 66, 361
Guam, 115
Gulfstream Corporation, **650**
Gulfstream I, 711
Gulfstream III, 650
Gunner—*see* Fairchild

Hadrian—*see* Waco
Hahn AFB, 331
Halverson, Col. H. A., 179

Halverson Detachment, 179
Handley Page O-400, 670
Harris, Lt. H. R., 641
Hass, O. P., 532
Havoc—*see* Douglas
Hawaii, 67, 99, 106, 125, 126, 179, 228, 265
Hawk—*see* Curtiss
Hayes Aircraft Corp., 123, 465
Hegenberger, Lt. Albert, 323
Heinkel He-22, 697
Heinrich, Albert S., 673
Heinrich Pursuit, 673
Helio Aircraft Corp., **650**
H-391, 650
H-395, 650
Super Courier, 650
Hercules—*see* Lockheed

Hibbard, H. L., 358
Hickam, Lt. Col. Horace W., 225
Hickam Field, 106, 225, 385
Higgins Aircraft Inc., 238
Hill AFB, 331
Hiller Aircraft Corp., **339, 651**
  12E-4, 339
  360, 339
  UH-12C, 339
  Hornet, 651
  Raven, 339
Hiroshima, 116
Hogan, Robert, 164
Holloman AFB, 509
Honolulu, 299
Horsa—see Airspeed
Howard DGA-15, 651
Hoyt, Capt., 215
Hudson, Lt. William G., 476
Hudson—see Lockheed
Huey—see Bell
HueyCobra—see Bell
Huff-Daland Co. Inc., **342, 652**
  Cyclops, 24
  Panther, 24
Hughes Tool Company, 347, 652
  Apache, 426
  Cayuse, 347, 269, 652 369, 347, 500, 348
  Osage, 652
  Huron—see Beech
  Huskie—see Kaman
  Hustler—see Convair

Iceland, 360
Independence, Douglas VC-118, 637
Interstate Cadet, 653
Interstate Grasshopper, 653
Invader—see Douglas
Iroquois—see Bell
Irwin, Capt. Walter W., 380

Jansen, George R., 294
Java, 91
Jenny—see Curtiss
Johnson, A. M. "Tex", 137
Johnson, Clarence L., 370, 391
Johnson, Major Howard C., 380
Johnson, Richard, 325
Jolly Green Giant—see Sikorsky
Jones, Q. B., 598

Kaiser-Frazer Corp., 317
Kaiser Manufacturing Co., 312
Kaman Aircraft Corp., **350**
  600, 350
  Huskie, 350
Kansan—see Beech
Kartveli, Alexander, 520, 522, 547
Kellet KD-1, 653
Kelly AFB, 192, 368, 580, 625
Kelly Field, 213, 250, 706
Kelsey, Lt. B. S., 358
Keystone Aircraft Corp., **342**
  Cyclops, 24

Keystone Aircraft Corp. *(contd.)*
  Panther, 24
Kingcobra—see Bell
Korat AFB, 368
Korea, 75, 119, 121, 126, 132, 166, 239, 269, 284,
  286, 291, 312, 320, 322, 370, 372, 378, 457,
  472, 476, 480, 483, 530, 533, 574, 686
Krebs, George, 478
Kunming, 233
Kunsan AFB, 331

Laddon, Isaac M. 176, 642
Lancer—see Republic
Langley Aerodrome, 1
Langley Field, 104, 215, 225, 438, 520
Langley—see Handley Page O-400
Laister Kauffman Yankee Doodle, 654
La Vassar, Leonard, 155
Lend-Lease 7, 48, 67, 68, 70, 159, 184, 236, 238,
  260, 278, 309, 354, 357, 442, 455, 459, 462,
  467, 525, 586, 591, 674
Le Pere, Capt., 663
Le Vier, Tony, 370, 379
Lewis and Vought VE-7, VE-9, 673
Liberator—see Consolidated
Liberty Plane—see de Havilland
Lightning—see Lockheed
Little Boy atom bomb, 116
Lippisch, Dr. A., 195
Lockheed Aircraft Corp., **352, 654**
  5, 654
  10, 354, 655, 656
  12, 352, 656
  14, 352, 354
  16, 352
  18, 352, 356
  22, 358
  37, 23, 356
  49, 366
  82, 383
  83, 379
  183, 379
  222, 359
  283, 379
  300, 399
  322, 359
  414, 354
  422, 361
  500, 401
  583, 379
  622, 359
  683, 379
  749, 366
  1049, 367
  1249, 369
  1329, 657
  A-12, 396
  CL-283, 390
  QT-2, 657
  XP-900, 174
  XST, 404
  Altair, 174, 655
  Atlanta, 359
  Blackbird, 397
  Chain Lightning, 364
  Constellation, 366

Lockheed Aircraft Corp. *(contd.)*
  Electra, 318, 655
  Galaxy, 401
  Hercules, 383
  Hudson, 354
  Jet Star, 656
  Lightning, 358
  Lodestar, 352
  Neptune, 658
  Shooting Star, 370
  Starfighter, 379
  Starfire, 376
  Starlifter, 399
  Vega, 654
  Ventura, 23, 356
Loening Aeronautical Engineering Corp., 405, 658
  M-8, 658
  Air Yacht, 659
Loening, Grover C., 405, 598, 607, 659
Logistics Command, 4
Lowe, Willard and Fowler, 247, 431, 605
Luke AFB, 331, 382, 419, 587
Lucky Lady II, Boeing B-50, 117
LUSAC-11, -21, -25, 663
L.W.F. Engineering Co., Inc., 605
  Model F, 605
  Model V, 605
Lynch, Joe, 484

MAC—*see* Military Aircraft Command
MacArthur, Gen. Douglas, 111, 367
MacDill AFB, 331, 413
MacMillan Arctic Expedition, 406
Macon, USS, 712
Magic Dragon—*see* Douglas
Magruder, Peyton M., 437
Maitland, Lt. Lester J., 323, 629
Malden AFB, 54
Marauder—*see* Martin
March Field, 358, 423
Mariana Is., 115
Martin, Glenn L. Co., 429, 606
  GMB, 429
  GMC, 429
  GMT, 429
  GMP, 429
  MB-1, 429
  MB-2, 10, 431, 333, 630
  T, TT, 433, 606
  R, 610
  S, 606
  123, 433
  139, 434, 435
  146, 263, 435
  166, 435
  179, 437
  272, 444
  XB-907, 433
  Bullpup GAM-83, 493
  Canberra, 444
  Marauder, 437
Martin, John F., 289
Martin, J. V., 429
Mather AFB, 619
MATS—*see* Military Air Transport Service

Maughan, Lt. Russell, 209, 629
McArthur-Pratt Agreement, 434
McChord Field, 459
McConnell AFB, 145, 543
McCook Field, 13, 24, 91, 219, 244, 245, 248, 249, 301, 303, 639-642, 673, 680, 696
McDonnell Aircraft Corp., 408
  Phantom II, 412
  Quail GAM-72, 137
  Voodoo, 408
McDonnell Douglas Corporation, 412
  Apache, 426
  DC-10, 422
  Eagle, 418
  Extender, 422
  MD-500, 347
  Phantom II, 412
McEntire AFB, 331
Mentor—*see* Beech
Mescelaro—*see* Cessna
Messenger—*see* Sperry
Messerschmitt Bf 108, 22, 679
Metro III—*see* Fairchild
Miles Master, 677
Military Airlift Command, 5, 135, 148, 400, 648, 660
Military Air Transport Service, 126, 127, 144, 147, 148, 192, 193, 194, 268, 291, 297, 299, 311, 313, 334, 367, 369, 383, 399, 401, 514, 553, 637
Missile designations, 25
Mitchell—*see* North American
Mitchell Field, 322
Mitchell, General "Billy", 431, 458, 629, 696
Mohawk—*see* Grumman
Mojave—*see* Sikorsky
Montieth, C. N., 38
Moody AFB, 164
Moore AFB, 54
Morane Saulnier, 698
  MS-12, 698
  MS-27, 698
  MS-29, 698
  MS-30, 698
  MS-43, 699
  MS-234, 699
  MS-322, 22
Morris, Ray, 488
Morse Chain Company, 608
Mosquito—*see* de Havilland
Moth Minor—*see* de Havilland
Mountain House AFB, 326, 329
Muroc Dry Lake, 370, 484, 529
Mustang—*see* North American
Myrtle Beach AFB, 321, 587

Nagasaki, 116
Nash, Capt. Slade, 485
National Air Races, 211, 214
National Guard, 5, 31, 47, 171, 208, 253, 287
National Security Act, 14
Navigator—*see* Beechcraft
Nellis AFB, 331, 404, 414, 511, 538
Nelson, Lew, 508
Neptune, *see* Lockheed
Netherlands East Indies, 257, 272, 352, 436, 620

762

New Guinea, 67, 283, 438
Nieuport 10, 11 and 12, 699
Nieuport 17, 700
Nieuport 23, 24 and 27, 700
Nieuport 28, 701
Nieuport 80, 81 and 83, 699
Nightingale—*see* Douglas
Noorduyn Aviation Norseman, 41, 701
North American Aviation, 450, 660
NA-16, 450, 454
NA-19, 450
NA-23, 450
NA-25, 452
NA-26, 450, 454
NA-29, 450
NA-36, 454
NA-40, 458
NA-50, 660
NA-54, 454
NA-55, 454
NA-58, 450
NA-59, 454
NA-62, 458
NA-68, 660
NA-73, 466
NA-77, 454
NA-82, 460
NA-83, 467
NA-88, 455
NA-91, 467
NA-96, 461
NA-97, 472
NA-98, 461
NA-99, 467
NA-101, 467
NA-102, 468
NA-103, 468
NA-104, 468
NA-105, 469
NA-106, 468
NA-108, 462
NA-109, 468
NA-110, 468
NA-111, 468
NA-120, 476
NA-122, 468
NA-123, 476
NA-124, 468, 471
NA-126, 471
NA-129, 471
NA-130, 478
NA-140, 481
NA-144, 476
NA-147, 478
NA-149, 476
NA-150, 476
NA-152, 482
NA-153, 478
NA-154, 599
NA-159, 489
NA-168, 455
NA-204, 484
NA-205, 485
NA-214, 492
NA-217, 492
NA-222, 492
NA-223, 492

North American Aviation *(contd.)*
NA-224, 492
NA-234, 493
NA-235, 492
NA-245, 492
NA-246, 496
NA-255, 493
NA-261, 493
NA-262, 493
NA-300, 498
Bronco, 498
Harvard, 454
Hound Dog GAM-77, 139
Mustang, 466
Sabre, 481
Sabreliner, 496
Super Sabre, 491
Texan, 454
Tornado, 480
Trojan, 478
Twin Mustang, 476
North Island, San Diego, 598, 599
Northrop Aircraft Inc., 500, 661
2-C, 500
ATB, 513
N9, 662
N23, 661
N24, 504
N35, 505
N49, 504
N68, 506
N71, 506
N138, 507
N156, 508, 510
N160, 507
MX-324, 24
YA-9, 321
Black Widow, 617
Delta, 500
Flying Wing, 662
Gamma, 247, 500
Pioneer, 661
Raider, 661
Reporter, 503
Scorpion, 504
Talon, 508
Tiger II, 510

Offutt AFB, 153
Okinawa, 299
On Mark Engineering, 287
Operation Oil Burner, 133
Operation Redwing, 295
Ordnance Engineering Co.—*see* Orenco
Orenco D, 663
Osage—*see* Hughes
Osler, Scott, 131
Osprey—*see* Bell
Otter—*see* De Havilland
Overman Act, 2
Owl—*see* L.W.F.
Ozier, Joe, 379

Pacific Air Forces, 4, 5, 148

Packard Motor Car Co., 663
Packet—*see* Fairchild
Panama Canal Zone, 67, 99, 166
Pave Low, 562, 567
Pearl Harbour, 3, 66, 106, 179, 225, 229, 233, 249
Pease AFB, 328
Penguin—*see* Breese
Philippines, 106, 179, 182, 260, 291, 416, 511, 548
Piasecki Helicopter Corp., 514, 664
  22, 514
  42, 514
  43, 514
  71, 514
  Army Mule, 664
  Shawnee, 514
  Workhorse, 514
Pilatus, 702
  Chiricahua, 702
  PC-6, 702
  Turbo Porter, 702
Piper Aircraft Corp., 516
  Cheyenne, 711
  Cub, 516
  Enforcer, 474
  Grasshopper, 516
  PA-48, 474
Plattsburgh AFB, 328
Ploesti attack, 179, 180
Pomilio, 639
Port Moresby, 67
Post Office Dept., 246, 247, 248, 603
Prahl, Val, 326
Procurement of aircraft, 86
Project Castor, 111
Provider—*see* Fairchild
Puff the Magic Dragon—*see* Douglas Skytrain
Pulitzer Race 1920, 641
  1921, 580
  1922, 209, 580, 629
  1923, 629
  1924, 629

Question Mark, Fokker C-2, 323
Quick Fix, 81, 565
Quick Look, 338

RAE BE 2e, 702
RAE FE 2b, 703
Raider—*see* Northrop
Randolph AFB, 445, 496, 509
Ranger—*see* Bell
Raven (H-23)—*see* Hiller
Raven (EF-111A)—*see* Grumman
Reconnaissance Wing 67, 473
Reese AFB, 465
Regensberg raid, 108
Republic Aviation Corp., 520, 664
  2PA, 664
  AP-1, 547
  AP-4, 547
  AP-23, 529
  AP-46, 535
  AP-63, 536

Republic Aviation Corp. *(contd.)*
  Guardsman, 664
  Lancer, 520
  Thunderbolt, 522
  Thunderchief, 536
  Thunderflash, 533
  Thunderjet, 116, 529
  Thunderstreak, 189, 532
Reverse Lend-Lease, 7, 677, 683, 709
Rice, Raymond, 466
Robbins, Bob, 131
Rockwell International, 541
Rogers, Russell R., 625
Roleur, 620, 698
Roma, 712, 713, 723
Romeo-Fokker C-VE, 22
Roosevelt, President Franklin, 291
Roth, Russell, 535, 536
Round-the-World flight, 1924, 634
Ryan Aeronautical Co., 544
  ST, 544
  STA, 544
Ryan, T. Claude, 544

SAC—*see* Strategic Air Command
St. Louis PT-1W, 665
Sabre—*see* North American
SAGE, 198, 367
Salmson 2A-2, 703
Samaritan—*see* Convair
Schilling, Col. David L., 532
Schmued, Edgar, 466
Schneider Contest, 629
Schweizer SGS 2-12, 665
Schweizer SGM 2-37, 666
Schweinfurt raid, 108
Scorpion—*see* Northrop
Selfridge Field, 94, 99, 580
Selfridge, Lt. Thomas B., 608
Seminole—*see* Beech
Sentinel—*see* Stinson
Serial numbers, 28
Seversky Aircraft Corp., 547, 666
  1XP, 547, 666
  2XD, 547
  AP-1, 547
  EP-106, 547
  SEV-7. 547
Seversky, Major Alexander P., 522
Seymour Johnson AFB, 423, 538
"Shadow"—*see* Fairchild Packet
Shaw AFB, 331, 444
Sheppard AFB, 661
Shooting Star—*see* Lockheed
Short Brothers, 704
  Sherpa, 704
  SD-330, 704
Shrike—*see* Curtiss
S.I.A. 7B, 705
Sicily, 268
Signal Corps, Aviation Section, 1
Sikorsky Aircraft Division, United Acft., 549, 667
  S-38, 667
  S-43, 667
  S-55, 553

Sikorsky Aircraft Div. United Acft. *(contd.)*
S-56, 557
S-58, 555
S-61, 559
S-64, 668
S-65, 561
S-70, 564
Black Hawk, 564
Chickasaw, 553
Choctaw, 555
Jolly Green Giant, 559
Mojave, 557
Super Jolly, 561
Tarhe, 558
Sikorsky, Igor I., 549
Simplex Automobile Co., 610
Sioux—*see* Bell
Skyraider—*see* Douglas
Skymaster—*see* Douglas
Skytrain—*see* Douglas
Skytrooper—*see* Douglas
Sloan Aircraft Co., Inc., 607
H-2, 607
H-3, 607
Smith, George, 483
Societe Italiano Aviazione 7B, 705
Sopwith Camel, 705
Sopwith 1½-Strutter, 706
Space Command, 4
Spad VII, 707
Spad 11, 708
Spad 13, 16, 707
Spad 16, 708
Spartan Executive, 669
Spence AFB, 54
Sperry, Lawrence, 303
Sperry Aircraft Co., Messenger, 24, 303
Spitfire—*see* Supermarine
Standard Aircraft Corp., 568, 607, 669
Caproni, 669
E-1, 670
E-4, 568
H, 568
H-2, H-3, 607
H.P. O-400, 670
JR, 568
M-Defense, 670
Pursuit, 568
SJ, 568
Stanley, Max, 662
Stanley, Robert M., 73
Starfighter—*see* Lockheed
Starfire—*see* Lockheed
Starlifter—*see* Lockheed
Stearman Aircraft, 570, 671
XPT-943, 24
Cloudboy, 671
Kaydet, 570
Stevens, Capt. O. A., 245
"Stinger"—*see* Fairchild Packet
Stinson Aircraft Div., Aviation Manufacturing Corp., 572, 672
SR-8, -9, -10, 672
74, 572
105, 574
Reliant, 672
Sentinel, 574

Stinson Aircraft Div. Corp. *(contd.)*
Vigilant, 572
Voyager, 498, 574
Stores Designations, 27
Strategic Air Command, 4, 109, 119, 120, 126, 128, 132, 133, 135, 138, 144, 188, 297, 327, 391, 408, 447, 463, 496, 528, 534
Stratofreighter—*see* Boeing
Stratofortress—*see* Boeing
Stratojet—*see* Boeing
Stratotanker—*see* Boeing
Stroukoff, 317, 318
Sturtevant Aeroplane Co., 607
Superfortress—*see* Boeing
Supermarine Spitfire, 709
Super Sabre—*see* North American
Systems Command, 4

Tactical Air Command, 4, 118, 123, 124, 146, 286, 291, 297, 311, 350, 380, 383, 408, 409, 413, 419, 444, 463, 528, 531, 536
Talon—*see* Northrop
Tarhe—*see* Sikorsky
Taylorcraft Aviation Corp., 576
D. 576
Grasshopper, 576
Taylor, James, 64
Technical Training Command, 3
Texas—*see* North American
TFX, 325
Thomas Brothers Aeroplane Co., 608
D-5, 608
T-2, 608
Thomas, B. Douglas, 203, 580, 601, 608
Thomas-Morse Aircraft Corp., 91, 579, 672
MB-2, 10
MB-3, 91, 579
MB-6, 580
MB-7, 580
MB-9, 580
MB-10, 580
S-4, 582
TM-22, 580
XO-932, 584
Thunderbolt—*see* Republic
Thunderbolt II—*see* Fairchild
Thunderchief—*see* Republic
Thunderflash—*see* Republic
Thunderjet—*see* Republic
Thunderstreak—*see* Republic
Tibbets, Col. Paul W., 116
Tiger II—*see* Northrop
Timm Aircraft Corp., 594
Tinker AFB, 399
Tokyo Raid, 115, 460
Tornado—*see* North American
Tower, Les. R., 101, 104
Traveler—*see* Beech
Travis AFB, 300, 399
Trojan—*see* North American
Troop Carrier Command, 238, 239, 267, 290, 313, 383, 514
T-Stick II—*see* Republic Thunderchief
Turbo-Mustang III, 473
Turner AFB, 532
Twin Mustang—*see* North American

765

Twin Otter—*see* de Havilland Canada
Tyndall, AFB, 691
Tyndall, Frank, 91

Ulmstead, Maj. Stanley M., 635
Upper Heyford, 329
U.S. Air Forces Europe, 4, 196, 286, 326, 383, 414, 416, 419, 478, 511, 531, 538, 704
U.S.S. *Hornet*, 460

Vance AFB, 164
Valiant—*see* Vultee
Valkyrie—*see* North American
Vandenberg, Gen., 367
Vengeance—*see* Vultee
Ventura—*see* Lockheed
Vertol Aircraft Company, *see* Boeing Vertol
Vertol 107—*see* Boeing Vertol
Vertol Chinook—*see* Boeing Vertol
Vertol Workhorse, 514
Verville, Alfred, 303, 640
Verville-Clark Pursuit, 641
Victor Aircraft Corp., 673
Vidal, 589
Vietnam, 59, 81, 82, 85, 86, 88, 92, 93, 140, 141, 157, 163, 165, 168, 240, 270, 288, 316, 319, 326, 336, 368, 384, 392, 400, 414, 445, 490, 493, 498, 510, 536, 559, 561, 587, 613, 638, 650, 657, 668, 689
Vigilant—*see* Stinson
Voisin 8 and 10, 708
Voodoo—*see* McDonnell
Vought Aircraft, 586, 673
VE-7, 673
VE-9, 673
V-143, 24
Vought Sikorsky, 549, 668
VS300, 549
VS316, 549, 668
VS327, 551
Hoverfly, 549, 668
Vultee Aircraft Inc., 589, 674
V-11, 674
V-48, 674
V-54, 589
V-72, 23, 591
Valiant, 589
Vanguard, 674
Vengeance, 23, 591

Waco Aircraft Company, The, 593, 675
9, 22, 40, 41
NEU, 595
NTQ, 593, 676
UPF, 674
Hadrian, 593
Wake Island, 180, 299
Warhawk—*see* Curtiss

Warrior—*see* Bell
Weapon System WS100, 105
WS101, 137
WS102, 201
WS105, 408
WS112, 134
WS119, 143
WS122, 137
WS131, 139
WS199, 135
WS201, 195, 196, 198
WS205, 507
WS214, 367
WS217, 409
WS303, 379
WS306, 536
WS307, 444
WS326, 413
WS327, 412
SS400, 383
SS402, 299
SS420, 508
SS443, 78
SS452, 496
SS471, 155
SS476, 400
SS481, 153
RS638, 140
Webb AFB, 164
Welch, George, 484, 489
Westland Aircraft, 711
Lysander, 711
Wheatley, William, 177
Wheeler Field, 229
Whitcomb, Richard, 195
White, Al, 492
Whiteman AFB, 513
Wiener Neustadt raid, 108
Wild Weasel, 416, 494, 539
Wilhelmshaven raid, 108
Williams AFB, 164, 511
Witteman-Lewis Co., 641
Wood, Robert, 64, 174
Workhorse—*see* Piasecki
Wright Field, 13, 24, 38, 176
Wright Martin Co., 610, 659
Wright Martin Model R, 610
Wright Model A, 608
Wright Model B, 1, 609
Wright Model C, 609
Wright Model F, 609
Wright Model HS, 609
Wright, Orville, 608
Wright-Patterson AFB, 383
Wurtsmith AFB, 140, 507

Yamamoto, Admiral, 361

Zodiac, 730

766